URBAN
LAND DEVELOPMENT

INTRODUCTION

INDUSTRY BACKGROUND

The field of real estate has not generally been noted for its managerial professionalism over the past several decades. Abuses in the industry have been common and have related to overbuilding, overextension of debt as a percentage of the total cost of a project, financing misadventures of syndication, grants of FHA guarantees where demand has not warranted additional building, and many other instances of poor management decisions and misallocation of resources. This is particularly distressing in light of the vast economic importance and social implications of real estate decisions that are cumulative on the economic and social well-being of any area.

The causes of real estate abuses are basically twofold and are closely interrelated:

1. There is a general lack of data and management tools available for real estate decisions. The consequence is a "seat-of-the-pants" type of decision making that characterizes the industry.

2. Real estate decisions encompass types of management needs and financial considerations different from those employed in most traditional industries. Hence, real estate decisions need to be approached in a manner that is not required or readily developed in general management practice.

These factors have kept administrators from properly assessing the economic and social implications of recent forces in our economy that have made the problems of real estate development enormously complex. New trends that must be interpreted and integrated include: (1) the growth of suburbs and changes in home ownership trends; (2) the "exploding metropolis" which promises to create vast stretches of metropolitan area over the United States; (3) the need for "second homes" for retirement and recreational purposes; (4) the proliferation of various urban land development and redevelopment projects ranging from luxury housing through slum clearance; (5) the growth of shopping centers and shifts in location of industrial and office sites; (6) the growth of city and community planned developments; (7) the entry of large non–real estate corporations into real estate, in order to establish the kind of industrialization and integration that has been known to many industries since the last century; (8) government tax law changes and incentives;

and (9) the enormity of government involvement in many phases of finance and construction, which tends to incorporate elements of both public and private administration into the field of land development.

OBJECTIVES AND USE OF THIS BOOK

It is anticipated that this casebook will lead students to a better understanding of real estate and assist them in making improved decisions in complicated real estate problems. Emphasis throughout the book will be on the development of those administrative skills that are unique to land development, and on providing the sense of responsibility and long-range planning that have thus far been lacking in most real estate considerations.

The book should be useful to a variety of people interested in real estate. It was designed initially for students planning a career in one of the many areas of urban land development: residential subdivisions, housing, shopping centers, office buildings, hotels and motels, industrial centers, recreational facilities, new town development, urban renewal and other government-subsidized housing projects. It should, however, also prove useful to students preparing to enter such closely related areas as financial institutions engaged in real estate lending operations; companies whose products are sold to the construction industry; enterprises requiring management of real estate holdings; companies engaged in retail selling, whose administration demands an understanding of store locations and real estate values; and government and the agencies involved in urban planning.

MANAGERIAL VIEWPOINTS AND MAJOR DECISION AREAS IN REAL ESTATE

The text presents a detailed study of urban land development from various managerial viewpoints to give the student a broad appraisal of real estate and its many ramifications. Viewpoints taken include that of the developer; financial institutions as investors and managers of real estate holdings; individuals considering real estate as an appropriate investment medium; and the government promulgating policy.

To meet our objective of improved decisions through a realization and understanding of skills unique to land development, we will place particular emphasis on a developer-investor and his necessary requirements in relation to:

1. Project Development and Management.
2. Financing and Investment Return.
3. Tax Management.
4. Government Relations.

PROJECT DEVELOPMENT AND MANAGEMENT

Inherently, real estate involves a group of factors ond operations that distinguish it sharply from other industries. The development of a $1-billion "New Town" in Columbia, Maryland, the construction of an office building in the One Broadway cases, and the building of the Valley Shopping Center all involve the marshalling of very substantial financial and managerial resources for the creation of new and added real estate values. These types of real estate projects are usually independent of other real estate investments and developments, whether the investor or developer be a large corporation or an individual. To complicate matters, real estate markets could hardly be designed in a manner that would create greater difficulties for the decision maker. They are characterized by a relatively fixed supply, fluctuating demand, and highly localized areas of action. Therefore, they generally involve a need for rapid employment and development by a team of employees and outside experts to create the project from its initial planning stage through critical land location, financing, land aquisition, construction, and marketing. As we can clearly see in the Columbia cases, the assignment of tasks and control of the various phases of any real estate development are critical to the success of a project.

The manager's role in real estate is especially complex because of the long time lag from inception of an idea to completion of a project. This time span generally runs from four to eight years and introduces enormous uncertainties and risks for all parties involved in the project. The developer has a particular problem since he usually advances a substantial part of the equity funds for the land and improvements at the inception of the project, and has minimal flexibility to change plans as the project progresses. The funds he will have to provide will, in most cases, be relatively large sums of money and his liquidity of investment is relatively poor, even when the project is completed. Note that these types of problems are very different from a stock market investment where an investment is extremely liquid in terms of immediate resale to another investor.

THE NATURE OF REAL ESTATE FINANCING AND INVESTMENT RETURN

The problems of real estate development and investment can be exaggerated by the very high debt-to-equity ratios prevalent in the industry. This forces a financial strategy, an attitude toward risk, and an ability to innovate that are not common in other areas of business. For example, many different types of financial markets must usually be tapped for funds. These might include a myriad of mortgage types, equity funding, syndications, investment trusts, government-insured loans, and so on.

The liberal usage of debt financing does, however, create excellent opportunities for earning a high return on investment (ROI) in real estate projects. We can see the fairly dramatic increase in ROI with the financial "leverage" of added debt in the Sutton Town House case, where an additional mortgage raised the investor's present value return substantially.

In order to reap his large returns, the real estate developer-investor must be very careful to manage his risks and make an optimal trade-off between increased return and increased risk. In Sutton Town House, for example, the increased return was effected with an increase in debt (reduction in required equity) which required an increase in annual interest and amortization. Because of this high debt service, which is typical of the industry, poor management of risk-return in the relatively uncertain world of real estate decisions can easily lead to the demise of a real estate project.

TAX IMPLICATIONS OF REAL ESTATE

A real estate investor must also deal with specialized Federal Income Tax and legal considerations. One of the most important aspects related to real estate development and investment concerns income taxes and their actual benefit to real estate projects. These benefits and the concept of depreciation of property—which is an expense deducted from gross income in arriving at taxes to be paid but is a noncash charge—are carefully explained in the Note on Depreciation and Taxes. However, we can see, from many of the cases, the importance of "tax losses" and their relation to such factors as depreciation and self-amortizing mortgages (a mortgage which calls for a constant payment of interest and loan repayment or amortization). The advantage in real estate to a self-amortizing loan, for example, is that in the earlier years of a project's life, when the time value of money is particularly apparent, the bulk of the constant payment is tax deductible interest and only a small portion of the payment is amortization, a nondeductible expense for tax purposes.

The tax implications and their importance to real estate decision making are quite apparent when we see that many real estate projects are engaged in nearly exclusively for the tax benefits available. Projects which would otherwise be rejected are pursued because of the returns provided in the form of tax benefits. We can see the major impact of taxes on ROI in *The Decent Home* material where a legally limited investment return is made attractive as a result of the available tax benefits. The same relationship is also evident in many other cases.

As a packager of financial proposals, a real estate manager must use tax benefits to operate effectively; in many cases, he must use tax benefits if he is to operate at all. Mr. Ravitch could not have even considered a project such as Waterside were he not able to sell his tax-loss benefits to a high-tax-bracket investor who could earn an acceptable return on the losses (tax savings) generated from the project. In somewhat the same manner, our entrepreneur in One Broadway was able to obtain equity funds from high-tax-bracket investors who were looking for book losses to apply against their ordinary income from other sources.

DEALING WITH THE GOVERNMENT

An added skill which a manager of real estate has to develop is the ability to deal with various levels of government, because of the considerable influence these bodies have in virtually every area of operation. In development, we must be concerned with the various and changing government interest and regulations such as zoning, property taxes, real estate tax abatements, building codes, urban renewal, air rights, government mortgage programs, rent supplements, federal government taxes, government loans at below market interest rates, and so forth. Most of these factors have considerable financial implications to real estate decision making.

The problem of controlling and effectively using government intervention is shown in the Columbia cases where such factors as zoning problems were encountered. In Waterside, the developer had to deal with local, state, and federal agencies; he even had to seek a Congressional Act to enable his real estate project to proceed. *The Decent Home* material discusses fixed return government subsidized housing, the financing involved, and the returns to be made with the aid of government supplements and tax incentives.

INSTRUCTION BY THE CASE METHOD

In the case material to follow, each of these broad real estate considerations and other detailed factors of real estate decision making will be presented in the context of business situations. The case method is ideal for discussing the pragmatic area of urban land development because the cases are simulated real life experiences. Despite the unavoidable simplification, the cases in this book parallel very closely actual business problems encountered by real individuals and firms. In the area of real estate, the cases are particularly useful in pointing out such nuances as those which exist in negotiations for property purchase and mortgage financing.

The cases are, in all respects, much more than illustrations. They are very real and important problems which require some type of solution. While no single answer is correct to any of the problems involved, a proper method for dealing with the complex world of real estate can be acquired through analysis and proposals for action in each case situation.

PART I

Investment—Cases

PINCKNEY STREET

In the summer of 1964, Charles Manning began searching for a small income-producing apartment building in which to invest. Mr. Manning had graduated that June from Harvard College, and he was working for a manufacturing firm in Newton, Massachusetts. He had grown up in Boston and was attracted to the investment potential of the Back Bay–Beacon Hill area, which he considered the best residential section of downtown Boston. Many of his contemporaries were renting apartments or had purchased homes there, and he and his wife had attended many of their parties. He considered paying rent to someone else a waste of a capital-building opportunity, since to do so would result in building up someone else's equity.

Mr. Manning wanted to gain experience in the real estate field and build an equity base for future real estate investments. He hoped to increase his return by managing and operating his property on weekends and after normal working hours. Manning had only $10,000 of his own funds to invest, and he wanted to achieve maximum leverage for this equity. Although he had no real estate experience, he had a working knowledge of carpentry gained from three years of designing and building sets for Harvard's Hasty Pudding Show.

BEACON HILL PROPERTIES

Manning began to spend all his free evenings and weekends becoming familiar with the area. He obtained a copy of the U.S. Census Tract, Boston, SMSA, to check the demographic data on age breakdowns, education, employment, marital status, income, length of stay, and ethnic background of present Beacon Hill residents. Most were transient, and either single or young married couples. He checked maps for distances to the city's office, shopping, cultural, and entertainment centers and found that Beacon Hill was close to all these urban amenities.

He studied the real estate sections of newspapers for brokers' names and to get an idea of the types of offerings and range of prices available. He found that the Sunday papers had by far the largest real estate advertising sections. He answered some advertisements, in order to meet real estate brokers and learn about the available properties. He specifically attempted to visit those offices that did the most advertising (or that appeared to do the most business in the area). All were located around Charles Street, the major commercial street of Beacon Hill. He visited William Codman & Co., Wm. F. Otis, Inc., Street & Co., Hunneman & Co., and Chamberlain Real Estate. Normally, the brokers wanted to know the type of property he was interested in, the amount of cash he had to invest, and whether he would live in the building.

Mr. Manning was quite disappointed in the offerings that were shown to him. Although the income and expense statements of one building on Myrtle Street had made it seem quite attractive, the situation was very different when he actually visited the building. It was in a rundown state, and the apartments, occupied by groups of students, were in deplorable condition. The income statement of another property on Myrtle Street showed a 20% return on investment; however, this made no allowance for repairs, vacancies, or management expenses. When considered, these costs reduced the return to 3%. Rentals in another building seemed too high. When Mr. Manning spoke with one of the tenants, he found that the landlord had asked a rental of $180 per month for the apartment, but, when offered $150 per month, accepted on the condition that there be no rent the first two months and then $180 rent per month be paid thereafter. This arrangement would enable the landlord to show a higher monthly income after the initial two months.

Most properties sold for $80,000 and higher, and required an investment of more than $10,000. Mr. Manning expected to obtain a bank loan for part of the purchase price through a mortgage (a legal instrument by which property is hypothecated to secure the payment of a debt or obligation). But institutional lenders were prohibited by law from lending more than 60%–80% of the capitalized value of the property. Additional money might be raised by placing a second or junior mortgage on the property, but interest rates on this type of secondary financing were often 10%–15%, and the personal credit of the borrower was often required as additional collateral. However, sellers were frequently willing to take a purchase money mortgage as part of the purchase consideration of the property to ensure the sale. Nevertheless, having only $10,000 equity proved a major factor in limiting the buildings Mr. Manning might purchase.

Mr. Manning became discouraged. Although the real estate brokers were friendly, they never seemed to show him what he considered to be desirable properties. There rarely appeared to be an opportunity to create value by increasing rents or reducing expenses; if there were, the seller had already taken it into consideration in establishing his price. Mr. Manning soon learned that many of the brokers owned buildings themselves, and were thus, in a sense, competitors of their own customers. Few properties in the area were sold by the owners themselves. Usually they were listed with several brokers, who competed to receive the 5%

sales commission by selling the property to one of their customers. Since there was considerable investor interest in the area, and listings were rarely exclusive with one broker, the brokers had to act quickly on the desirable properties to make their commissions. Therefore, most of the brokers had a few favored customers to whom they gave the chance at purchasing the properties listed. These customers usually had the necessary resources to act quickly to acquire the most desirable situations.

FACTORS AFFECTING VALUE

The same factors which caused Mr. Manning to want to purchase on Beacon Hill had attracted many doctors, engineers, and businessmen also anxious to own real estate. As a result, the market values of most buildings on the Hill had doubled in the past 10 years.

The area's location had considerable natural advantages. To the west was the Charles River; to the south was the Boston Public Gardens, which led to Newbury Street, Boston's best shopping area; and to the east was the State House and Boston's financial district. The West End slums and the undesirable commercial activity of adjacent Scollay Square to the north had restrained values in past years. This had been especially true of the northern slope of the Hill, which had become known as the back slope because of its many lower rent rooming houses. Under Boston's urban redevelopment program, however, the West End slums were torn down and were to be replaced by Charles River Park, a luxury apartment house development. Scollay Square was to be replaced by a new government center. Construction had begun in both areas, and the first buildings were already occupied. As a result of this redevelopment, values all over Beacon Hill had increased, but most drastically on the back or north slope. Rentals there had increased approximately 30% as real estate operators began to buy and improve the properties; they now ranged from $150 to $175 for one-bedroom apartments and $200 to $250 for two-bedroom apartments. In spite of this, because most purchasers in this section were real estate operators who expected a high return on their investment, Mr. Manning felt there would be further growth as investors who were accustomed to lower returns from properties on the lower section of the hill began to buy buildings on the north slope from these real estate operators.

The Massachusetts State Legislature had established the entire Beacon Hill area as an historic district and had set up a commission to preserve the character of the area. The commission had to approve any changes in the exterior of a structure before the building department would issue a building permit. The commission would not permit the erection of any new buildings in the area. While this protected and enhanced the values of existing buildings, it provided a ceiling on land values, since land could not be reused for a different, more valuable purpose.

Mr. Manning knew that this activity and interest in the area, which had driven prices up and was proving a disadvantage in his attempts to buy a property, would turn into an advantage once he owned a building. He could expect a potential buyer of his property to use a conservative capitalization rate to determine value, based upon his net income in appraising or capitalizing its value. Many investors in Beacon Hill appeared to be satisfied with an 8% net return, which meant that for every $1,000 of net income which remained after deducting all charges or costs from gross income, he could expect a buyer to pay $12,500. In an area of higher risk, an investor might look for a 12.5% return; then $1,000 of income would be worth only $8,000.

All these factors led Mr. Manning to believe that there was considerable safety in an investment in the area. There was little chance of depreciation for functional or economic causes. To obtain maximum capital appreciation, however, he would probably have to narrow his investment search to the back slope of Beacon Hill, where values had not risen so much as on the lower slope. He also realized that he would have to purchase a building that would require considerable renovation. Otherwise, once the income had become established the owner would ask a high selling price that would preclude much short-term growth in value. He had learned that he would have to act quickly if he did find an attractive opportunity. He would also have to carefully check all figures given him, since few small buildings had audited financial statements and he could not rely solely on statements made by real estate brokers. Lastly, he knew that his $10,000 equity would limit him to acquiring a relatively small building.

OPERATING EXPENSES

Mr. Manning became familiar with some of the expenses involved in managing property. Real estate taxes and mortgage carrying charges alone take up about two thirds of income.

Real estate taxes are general property taxes based on the assessed valuation of a property. After calculating its expected revenues, a city or locality will set a property tax rate which, when applied to the assessed valuation of the properties within its jurisdiction, will result in the additional revenues it needs for schools, roads, sewers, and police and fire protection. In 1950, property taxes on a national basis accounted for 52.1% of all local revenue. In Boston, the figure was much higher because the city had no other major source of revenue, such as a sales or income tax. To balance the rising costs of providing municipal services, Boston had to increase its assessments on existing properties and raise its overall tax rate. Technically, all properties in Boston were supposed to be assessed at full market value, but this was impractical; with the Boston tax rate in 1963 at $96 per $1,000 of assessment, if a $40,000 house were assessed at full value the tax bill would be $3,840, an amount so large that few individuals would build homes in Boston.

Many cities assess on a percentage-of-value basis rather than on full market price. For example, New York City has a rate of $45.20 per $1,000 of assessed valuation, and the city assesses property at approximately 80% of value. The owner of a $40,000 house would then, according to the New York City formula, pay a tax bill of $1,444.

Boston had no established percent-of-value formula for assessments. Mr. Manning had heard that the lowest percentage assessment-to-value ratios actually occurred in lower- and middle-income areas, where there were a great many registered voters, while in Beacon Hill, with a high number of absentee landlords and nonvoting transient tenants, the assessment-to-value ratio was much higher. This resulted in most landlords paying from 25% to 30% of the rental income in property taxes. Most communities around Boston assess income property so that the tax bill is from 15% to 20% of the property's income. Mr. Manning had also heard that if he purchased a property with a low valuation on which the taxes-to-income ratio was below that of similar properties, the assessors would very likely revalue his property upward based upon purchase price. He had been shown a property on Chestnut Street at a purchase price of $60,000 with a rent roll of $10,000. The return on his $10,000 investment was shown as $2,000, after an estimated real estate tax expense of $1,200, based on the present $12,000 assessment. Mr. Manning thought that with a change of ownership, a revaluation of the building to $24,000 would be likely, which would reduce his return to $800.

The other major operating expense would be mortgage servicing costs. The amount of the mortgage, he had discovered, would determine the amount of equity required. The payment terms determined by the interest rate charged and the length of the mortgage would also affect the net income available for return on this equity. As an example, a $10,000 mortgage with interest charged on the unpaid balance at 6% for a term of 20 years would result in an annual cost of 8.62%, while a mortgage of the same amount at the same interest rate for a term of 15 years would cost 10.16% annually. Thus, the terms of a mortgage, depending on the particular lender's opinion of the property, would considerably affect the owner's cash return on his investment. Because of its stability, Beacon Hill was considered a desirable area by most local mortgage bankers, and there was usually an ample supply of first-mortgage funds available from savings banks all over greater Boston for loans in this area. Mortgage funds for Roxbury, on the other hand, were scarce.

Often a buyer and seller could come to an agreement on a sale by the seller's taking back as secondary financing a purchase money second mortgage at the time of sale, thereby reducing the cash that the buyer would have to pay and increasing, if the interest rate were low, the buyer's return on investment. Therefore, to know the sales price of a property without knowing the terms of the sale could be misleading.

Most of the other operating expense could be estimated with reasonable accuracy based upon comparative local data. Mr. Manning learned that a rule-of-thumb figure of $100 to $125 per room per year was used with a one-bedroom apartment counting as three rooms and a two-bedroom apartment as four rooms. Included in this figure were heat, light, water, insurance, and janitor service expenses. In addition, the management fees charged by real estate firms was usually 5%. Also, an expense figure of 10% was normally carried to allow for repairs and vacancies; this figure could vary considerably, depending on the quality and condition of the building, the rents charged and the services provided for these rents, and the particular market conditions and practices. As an example, in Harvard Square, where rental demand was very high, many landlords did little repair work on older buildings. In new buildings, however, where the rents were higher and the competition more intense, the landlords had to keep the property in better repair. In Beacon Hill, the 10% figure was normally used as an estimate and then adjusted to allow for special circumstances.

19 PINCKNEY STREET

In December of 1964, Mr. Manning learned of a four-unit apartment house on Beacon Hill that was for sale. A local broker with whom he was friendly had called to tell him that 19 Pinckney Street had just come on the market, and that if he acted quickly, he might be able to outbid several real estate brokers who were interested in the property. Mr. Manning knew that brokers always attempted to convey a sense of urgency, but since he was aware that desirable properties did sell quickly, he decided to investigate the property at once.

The property was located on the back slope of the Hill in an improving neighborhood. The removal of the slums that had abutted this section had resulted in some increase in property values. Mr. Manning expected still greater increases when the construction presently in progress on the former slumland was completed. The property was located in the middle of the block, and was set back 100 feet from the road, which would afford an opportunity for creating an attractive entranceway and garden. The property had been built in the mid-1800's, probably as a middle-income town house. After being used as a rooming house for 20 years, it had been gutted by a fire in 1963. Only the structural shell remained. An architect had purchased the shell for $32,000, but the combination of the purchase price and the cost of renovation, already $12,000 with the work only half completed, had proved greater than he had expected, forcing him to discontinue the renovation and place the property on the market. Mr. Manning felt that the architect's plans for renovation were in good taste and that thus far had been done well. Each of the first three floors was to have one two-bedroom apartment, while the fourth floor would have a large one-bedroom apartment. For the first time, Mr. Manning felt that he had seen a property that met his investment criteria. The property had profit potential; it was aesthetically desirable, was in the area he wanted, and, with an asking price of $45,500, was within his price range.

Mr. Manning was told that the $45,500 price was firm because considerable interest had already been shown in the property. A contractor to whom Mr. Manning was referred estimated that it would cost approximately $10,000 to complete the architect's plans, which would result in a total cost of $55,500.

Mr. Manning prepared an income and expense statement to see whether the net income of the property would justify its price (see Exhibit 1).[1] He figured that each of the three two-bedroom apartments could be rented at $225 per month, and the top-floor one-bedroom apartment at $200 per month. This would total $10,500 annually. From this figure, he subtracted a 5% vacancy allowance, which would represent two apartments sitting vacant for slightly more than a month. There was the additional possibility that if he did not rent the apartments himself, he would have to pay a broker's commission, set by the Boston Real Estate Board at 5% of the apartment rental. The broker, licensed by the state, receives this commission for showing the property to prospective tenants, bringing the tenants and landlord together, and helping to negotiate the contract between them.

Mr. Manning estimated real estate taxes at 25% of the net income, or $2,500. This represented a tax rate of $96 per $1,000 of assessment on an assessed value of $26,000, which was approximately 50% of market value, and $11,000 above the present $15,000 assessment. He obtained a quotation of a $250 annual premium from his real estate broker's firm for a package insurance policy providing protection against fire, extended coverage perils, public liability, loss of rents, and boiler explosion. The tenants would pay the electric bills for their own apartments, but the landlord would pay the bill for the public areas. A janitor would keep the public halls clean, change the light bulbs, and take out the trash. There were several services around Beacon Hill that performed this function for an annual fee of $300. Mr. Manning had expected to do some of the repair work and all of the management work himself to

---

[1] Numbered exhibits throughout this book will be found at the ends of the cases.

increase his cash return, but his broker told him that since potential mortgage lenders or future purchasers would include these costs in their "setups," Mr. Manning would have to do so, too. Also, if he should leave the area, he would have to hire outside firms to perform these services.

His projections showed net before financing of $5,350, without any allowance for the work he would do himself. This provided a 9.7% cash return on investment based on a free and clear ownership of the property —that is, with no encumbrances or mortgages on it.

Mr. Manning was very pleased. He told his wife that he had found a building that would be just right. With its skylights, beamed ceiling, and natural brick walls, the top-floor apartment would be just what they wanted to live in. They could live "rent free," while making money by doing their own managing and renting. They could take out the trash and clean the halls themselves. Mr. Manning felt that although outside management would be more experienced, it wouldn't have as much interest as he would in managing the property well. Rent from the other apartments would pay the other expenses, and he would gain real estate experience.

His wife said that while the apartment seemed very nice, she was not sure she liked the idea of living in a building they owned. She would get complaints while he was at work. Also, she thought there might be a problem in doing business with their neighbors if they got friendly with them. She doubted that they would be able to charge maximum rents or raise rents.

The real estate broker questioned his decision to act as his own general contractor because of his lack of experience and time. He said that it was difficult, particularly on a part-time basis, to coordinate several subcontractors who never showed up when they said they would. The work might take longer than Mr. Manning anticipated. Also, the Boston Building Department had a maze of rules and many inspectors; his renovation could be quite costly if he were forced to comply exactly with every regulation. Experienced contractors usually found ways of getting around these requirements. He would have to be careful, however, to minimize changes and avoid extras once the job had been started, since most subcontractors would charge a premium for extras, because it would be too late to get competitive quotes on small amounts of work.

Mr. Manning replied that any remodeling job would involve changes in adapting to field conditions. To avoid the extra charges by subcontractors was one of the reasons he wanted to do the work himself. In giving him a firm bid, an outside contractor would carry a heavy contingency allowance. Certainly the contractor who gave him the $10,000 estimate to complete the renovation must have carried at least $1,000 for profit. Mr. Manning reasoned that he had at least that $1,000 to spend before his lesson in remodeling began to cost him money.

MORTGAGE FINANCING

Mr. Manning then went to see Mr. Smith, the mortgage officer of the savings bank who had recently given the original $40,000 loan on the building. Mr. Smith told him that the existing mortgage was on a constant payment basis, which meant that the payments, including amortization and interest, remained the same throughout the entire term of the loan but that the portion applicable to interest became less as the balance of the mortgage loan decreased. Correspondingly, the portion applicable to amortization increased. This particular loan was for a term of 20 years with 6% interest paid on the outstanding balance, resulting in an annual cost of $3,448 or 8.62%. The mortgage payments with a payment of one twelfth of the estimated real estate taxes were made to the bank monthly. The bank also kept two months' real estate taxes in escrow as additional security. The banker explained that the loan could be paid off at any time but that if it were paid off during the first five years of the loan, the bank would charge a prepayment penalty of 2% of the unpaid balance.

Mr. Manning explained his plans for finishing the work and gave Mr. Smith his projected income and expense statements for the property (see Exhibit 1). He asked whether the bank would increase its mortgage to $46,000. He explained that he might live in the building, manage it, and do some of the work himself, which would create more cash flow to serve the debt. The banker replied that he could not take this extra income into account in making his decision, since the bank always had to consider a loan in light of the costs the bank would incur if it had to foreclose and run the property itself. (A foreclosure occurs when property pledged as security for a loan is sold to pay the debt in the event of default in payment or failure to comply with terms.)

Mr. Smith noticed that Mr. Manning's rental figures were $1,200 higher than those originally submitted by the present owner. At that time, the bank had valued the property at $50,000 and had given an 80% mortgage, the maximum permitted by law. He asked whether Mr. Manning knew his total costs. Mr. Manning told him of the contractor's $10,000 bid. Mr. Smith told him that he should also consider carrying costs while the renovation work was going on. The bank might waive principal payments on the mortgage for six months during construction, but interest of $1,200 on the $40,000 must be paid, as well as real estate taxes of $750, assuming the $15,000 assessment would remain in effect until the renovation was complete. In addition, he still had to pay for six months' insurance at $125 and heat and electricity at $225. These costs totaled $2,300. There was also the two-month real estate tax escrow of $250, which was a cash outlay even though it would eventually be returned to him.

Mr. Manning could assume the architect's existing mortgage, thus eliminating the need for new documents and a new title search by the bank's lawyer. (Assumption of a mortgage occurs when, in purchasing a property, the buyer assumes liability for payment of an existing note secured by a mortgage on the property.) Mr. Smith doubted that the bank would be interested in increasing its loan at this time, since it was not certain that Mr. Manning could get the increased rentals. However, Mr. Smith added that if the income level was increased when the building became rented, the bank might reexamine his request.

Mr. Manning next visited Mr. Harris, the mortgage loan officer at another local savings bank to find out whether his bank would be interested in a $46,000 mortgage. Mr. Manning showed him the income and expense projections, told him his costs, and explained his plans. Mr. Harris said that because of the 80% restriction, his bank would have to appraise the property at $57,500 to justify a $46,000 loan. Appraisals, he told Mr. Manning, could be made on the basis of replacement cost, capitalized income, or market value based on recent comparable sales. He said that his bank preferred the income approach as the most realistic. Taking a capitalization rate of 9% on the $5,350 projected net income, he arrived at an assessed value of $59,450. Mr. Harris considered it likely that based on this appraisal he could justify a $46,000 mortgage at 6% interest for 20 years. He believed that the $5,350 annual net income should be adequate to carry the $3,965 financing charge. He added that he was familiar with the area and considered Mr. Manning's projected figures realistic, although he would have to see the property to be certain of this.

He questioned Mr. Manning about his current personal income. Mr. Manning told him that his present salary was $10,000 per year. Mr. Harris said he would require credit references and certain other information about Mr. Manning, since Mr. Manning would be signing the note personally as additional protection to the bank against loss. Mr. Manning asked why he would have to become personally liable when there was ample value in the property. He knew that his friends who had bought brownstones in New York had not assumed any personal liability. Mr. Smith said that this was the policy of virtually all savings banks in the Boston area for smaller buildings, especially when the loan-to-value ratio was as high as 80%. If Mr. Manning had confidence in the building, he should not worry. Each year the mortgage and his liability declined as a portion of the mortgage loan was amortized.

Mr. Manning asked whether there were other costs, such as closing the mortgage, that he would have to assume. Mr. Harris replied that Mr. Manning would be responsible for legal and title expenses at closing, amounting to about $300, which would cover the cost of the bank's lawyer and his own attorney's fee. (The bank's lawyer is responsible for certifying to the bank that the owner has a valid fee simple ownership in the property, which means that the owner has the right to dispose of it, pledge it, or pass it on to his heirs as he sees fit. Also, he ascertains that there are no liens on the property senior to the bank's interest. The seniority of a lien depends on the date it was recorded at the County Registry of Deeds Office. When a lien is paid off, a discharge is put on record. There are some liens that are a matter of record that a bank will accept as senior to its position. These include zoning or use regulations, building codes, party wall agreements where two buildings share the same wall, or certain easements where one party has specific rights or privileges on the land of the other. The certification of title is often done through the issuance of an insurance policy written by a title insurance company at a one-time cost paid by the borrower or purchaser.)

LEGAL ADVICE

Mr. Manning then consulted Mr. Guber, his family's attorney about the whole transaction. Mr. Manning was very disturbed about the bank's requirement that he personally sign the mortgage note. His attorney told him that he did not want to minimize the risk but that this was a customary bank practice in making small mortgage loans in Massachusetts, where banks were often more conservative than in other areas of the country.

Mr. Manning inquired about alternate methods for raising the extra $6,000. Mr. Guber believed that secondary financing could be obtained, but at an interest rate of 10% and with only a personal endorsement. The seller might take back a purchase money second mortgage, but again Mr. Manning would probably have to sign the note personally and repay the entire loan over a three- to five-year period. In addition, if the demand for the property were as strong as Mr. Manning indicated, an all-cash offer might have a better chance of winning the property than one contingent upon a purchase money second mortgage.

Mr. Manning asked whether he would not be taking a big risk in making an offer for the property without having his financing secured. Mr. Guber explained that while he would have to submit a written offer for the property, together with a deposit to be held by the real estate broker, he could make his offer contingent upon his being permitted to assume the seller's mortgage. This would give him some safety, while still permitting him to attempt to find a higher mortgage. If Mr. Manning's offer were accepted, a purchase and sales contract would be signed, based on a standard Boston Real Estate Board form (see Exhibit 2). Mr. Guber said that in case of forfeiture as a result of the buyer's failure to perform, the sales deposit, normally 5% to 10% of the purchase price, would be kept by the seller as liquidated damages. Therefore, Mr. Manning's risk would be limited to about $2,500.

Also, if the seller could not deliver a quitclaim deed, relinquishing any interest he held in the property and giving a clear title to the buyer, the buyer would be entitled to a refund of his deposit.

Mr. Guber then asked Mr. Manning whether he had adequate funds to complete the project even with a $46,000 mortgage. The asking price for the property was $45,500; the remodeling cost, $10,000; carrying costs during construction, $2,300; closing costs, $400; and escrow funds, $250. These costs totaled $58,450. The $46,000 mortgage or mortgages and his $10,000 equity would still leave him $2,450 short. Mr. Manning replied that he planned to save money by acting as his own general contractor, and he hoped to remodel and rent the property in four rather than six months. A $46,000 first mortgage with an annual carrying charge of $3,965, although requiring a personal guarantee, would give him leverage, increasing his cash return on $10,000 from the 9.7% return based on an all-cash basis to 13.9%. In addition, he would be amortizing a mortgage. The return would be even greater if he lived in the building and managed it himself.

The lawyer said that Mr. Manning's analysis seemed reasonable, but it did not put a dollar value on Mr. Manning's time. He wondered whether this should be considered. Also, he wanted Mr. Manning to realize the seriousness of this time commitment since his full-time job was still his prime responsibility. Finally, he asked him to consider carefully the amount of the offer he was submitting and the risks involved.

EXHIBIT 1
Pinckney Street

Income

1st floor	$225/month	
2d floor	225/month	
3d floor	225/month	
4th floor	200/month	
	$875 × 12 =	$10,500
Allowance for vacancies		500
		$10,000

Operating Expenses

Real estate taxes	$2,500	
Heat	400	
Electricity	100	
Water	100	
Insurance	250	
Janitor	300	
Repairs @ 5%	500	
Management @ 5%	500	
		$4,650
Net before Financing (as if free and clear)		$5,350

EXHIBIT 2 (Concluded)

SCHEDULE

Extension

Date...

The time for the performance of the foregoing agreement is extended until .... o'clock .... M.
on the .... day of .... 19......., time still being of the essence of this agreement
as extended.

This extension, executed in triplicate, ... is intended to take effect as a sealed instrument.

....
Husband or Wife of Seller   *SELLER*

....
Husband or Wife of Buyer   *BUYER*

....
Broker

INSTRUCTIONS IN GENERAL
(These instructions are suggestions only; consult your ATTORNEY for particulars and details.)
1. Prepare agreement in quadruplicate if BUYER intends to apply for VA-guaranteed or FHA-insured loan; otherwise in triplicate.
2. Any lists or schedules to be attached should be properly incorporated by reference and initialed by all parties concerned.
3. This agreement, in its printed form, may not be suitable for use by trustees or other fiduciaries unless amended.
4. Each party should bring his agreement with him when passing title.

INSTRUCTIONS TO SELLER
After this agreement has been executed by all parties, arrange at once for drawing the deed and assigning insurance and obtaining binders if insurance is to be transferred.
Bring at the appointed time to the place designated for completing the transaction:
1. The deed signed by you and your spouse, properly acknowledged before a Notary, and if registered land, the owner's certificate of title.
2. A list of tenants and lessees, with a statement of amount of rents and the dates to which the rents are paid.
3. All leases on the premises and tenancy at will agreements; also all permits you have for the use of the premises.
4. If Buyer has agreed to purchase insurance, all insurance policies (some or all of the policies may be in the custody of the holder of the mortgage on said premises, and if so, obtain certificates of such policies from your insurance agent in advance); receipted insurance bills or a statement from the insurance agent that premiums are paid in full; and assignments of SELLER'S insurance to BUYER and binders from your insurance agent in favor of the BUYER.
5. Receipted bills for taxes for the last two years and all bills for taxes for the current year, whether receipted or not.
6. Water bills for the period of one year next preceding the date of performance.
7. Receipt for your last payment of interest on the mortgage, the mortgage pass book and, if any reduction has been made in the principal of the mortgage, bring a statement from the holder thereof showing how much is due.
8. If an existing mortgage on said premises is to be discharged, be sure to have the mortgage note available for cancellation in addition to the discharge.
9. Guarantees for roof, sidewalks, plumbing, heating or other fixtures.
10. Documentary stamps (Federal and State).

INSTRUCTIONS TO BUYER
If you are giving a mortgage, your spouse must join in signing it and so should be present at time of passing title.
Bring at the appointed time to the place designated for completing the transaction:
1. A certified or Bank's Check (if acceptable to the SELLER) drawn payable to your order and one hundred dollars in cash, the total amount to equal the amount of payment to be made at time of passing title.
2. Sufficient additional cash to pay for apportionment of rents, taxes, water rates, insurance premiums, and other adjustments, attorney's bill, plot plans, and recording fees.
It is customary for the BUYER to pay for drawing any mortgage given by him and fees for recording his deed and purchase money mortgage. He also pays for examination of title and for Tax Collector's report showing whether there are any municipal liens or unpaid taxes.

PURCHASE and SALE AGREEMENT

SELLER
BUYER
Property Address
Date of Agreement
Date for Delivery of Deed

FROM THE OFFICE OF

MEMBER
Greater Boston Real Estate Board

Copyright 1962 Greater Boston Real Estate Board
Revised 1-62

EXHIBIT 2

Purchase and Sale Agreement

This .... day of .... 19.......

1. PARTIES
(fill in)

.... hereinafter called the SELLER, agrees to SELL and

.... hereinafter called the BUYER or PURCHASER, agrees to BUY, upon the terms hereinafter set forth, the following described premises:

2. DESCRIPTION
(fill in and include title reference)

3. BUILDINGS, STRUCTURES, IMPROVEMENTS, FIXTURES

(fill in or delete)

Included in the sale as a part of said premises are the buildings, structures, and improvements now thereon, and the fixtures belonging to the SELLER and used in connection therewith including, if any, all venetian blinds, window shades, screens, screen doors, storm windows and doors, awnings, shutters, furnaces, heaters, heating equipment, stoves, ranges, oil and gas burners and fixtures appurtenant thereto, hot water heaters, plumbing and bathroom fixtures, electric and other lighting fixtures, mantels, outside television antennas, fences, gates, trees, shrubs, plants, and, if built in, air conditioning equipment, ventilators, garbage disposers, dishwashers, washing machines and driers, and but excluding

4. TITLE DEED
(fill in)
* Include here by specific reference any restrictions, easements, rights and obligations in party walls not included in (b), leases, municipal and other liens, other encumbrances, and make provision to protect SELLER against BUYER'S breach of SELLER'S covenants in leases, where necessary.

Said premises are to be conveyed by a good and sufficient .... deed running to the BUYER, or to the nominee designated by the BUYER by written notice to the SELLER at least seven .... days before the deed is to be delivered as herein provided, and said deed shall convey a good and clear record and marketable title thereto, free from encumbrances, except
  (a) Provisions of existing building and zoning laws;
  (b) Existing rights and obligations in party walls which are not the subject of written agreement;
  (c) Such taxes for the then current year as are not due and payable on the date of the delivery of such deed;
  (d) Any liens for municipal betterments assessed after the date of this agreement;
* (e)

5. PLANS

If said deed refers to a plan necessary to be recorded therewith the SELLER shall deliver such plan with the deed in form adequate for recording or registration.

6. REGISTERED TITLE

In addition to the foregoing, if the title to said premises is registered, said deed shall be in form sufficient to entitle the BUYER to a Certificate of Title of said premises, and the SELLER shall deliver with said deed all instruments, if any, necessary to enable the BUYER to obtain such Certificate of Title.

7. PURCHASE PRICE
(fill in); space is allowed to write out the amounts if desired
(provide for payment by certified or Bank's Check acceptable to the SELLER, if required)

The agreed purchase price for said premises is

.... dollars, of which

$....................... have been paid as a deposit this day and

$....................... are to be paid at the time of delivery of the deed in cash

$.......................

$.......................   TOTAL

8. TIME FOR PERFORMANCE; DELIVERY OF DEED *(fill in)*

Such deed is to be delivered at .... o'clock .... M. on the .... day of .... 19......., at the .... Registry of Deeds, unless otherwise agreed upon in writing. It is agreed that time is of the essence of this agreement.

9. POSSESSION and CONDITION of PREMISES. *(attach list of exceptions, if any)*

Full possession of said premises free of all tenants and occupants, except as herein provided, is to be delivered at the time of the delivery of the deed, said premises to be then (a) in the same condition as they now are, reasonable use and wear thereof excepted, and (b) not in violation of said building and zoning laws, and (c) in compliance with the provisions of any instrument referred to in clause 4 hereof.

EXHIBIT 2 (*Continued*)

10. EXTENSION TO PERFECT TITLE OR MAKE PREMISES CONFORM *(Change period of time if desired.)*

If the SELLER shall be unable to give title or to make conveyance, or to deliver possession of the premises, all as herein stipulated, or if at the time of the delivery of the deed the premises do not conform with the provisions hereof, then any payments made under this agreement shall be refunded and all other obligations of the parties hereto shall cease and this agreement shall be void and without recourse to the parties hereto, unless the SELLER elects to use reasonable efforts to remove any defects in title, or to deliver possession as provided herein, or to make the said premises conform to the provisions hereof, as the case may be, in which event the SELLER shall give written notice thereof to the BUYER at or before the time for performance hereunder, and thereupon the time for performance hereof shall be extended for a period of thirty days.

11. FAILURE TO PERFECT TITLE OR MAKE PREMISES CONFORM, etc.

If at the expiration of the extended time the SELLER shall have failed so to remove any defects in title, deliver possession, or make the premises conform, as the case may be, all as herein agreed, or if at any time during the period of this agreement or any extension thereof, the holder of a mortgage on said premises shall refuse to permit the insurance proceeds, if any, to be used for such purposes, then, at the BUYER'S option, any payments made under this agreement shall be forthwith refunded and all other obligations of all parties hereto shall cease and this agreement shall be void without recourse to the parties hereto.

12. BUYER'S ELECTION TO ACCEPT TITLE

The BUYER shall have the election, at either the original or any extended time for performance, to accept such title as the SELLER can deliver to the said premises in their then condition and to pay therefor the purchase price without deduction, in which case the SELLER shall convey such title, except that in the event of such conveyance in accord with the provisions of this clause, if the said premises shall have been damaged by fire or casualty insured against, then the SELLER shall, unless the SELLER has previously restored the premises to their former condition, either

(a) pay over or assign to the BUYER, on delivery of the deed, all amounts recovered or recoverable on account of such insurance, less any amounts reasonably expended by the SELLER for any partial restoration, or

(b) if a holder of a mortgage on said premises shall not permit the insurance proceeds or a part thereof to be used to restore the said premises to their former condition or to be so paid over or assigned, give to the BUYER a credit against the purchase price, on delivery of the deed, equal to said amounts so recovered or recoverable and retained by the holder of the said mortgage less any amounts reasonably expended by the SELLER for any partial restoration.

13. ACCEPTANCE OF DEED

The acceptance of a deed by the BUYER or his nominee as the case may be, shall be deemed to be a full performance and discharge of every agreement and obligation herein contained or expressed, except such as are, by the terms hereof, to be performed after the delivery of said deed.

14. USE OF PURCHASE MONEY TO CLEAR TITLE

To enable the SELLER to make conveyance as herein provided, the SELLER may, at the time of delivery of the deed, use the purchase money or any portion thereof to clear the title of any or all encumbrances or interests, provided that all instruments so procured are recorded simultaneously with the delivery of said deed.

15. INSURANCE ** Insert amount (list additional types of insurance and amounts as agreed)*

Until the delivery of the deed, the SELLER shall maintain insurance on said premises as follows:

Type of Insurance	*Amount of Coverage*
(a) Fire	* $
(b) Extended coverage	*
(c)	

16. ASSIGNMENT OF INSURANCE *(delete entire clause if insurance is not to be assigned)*

Unless otherwise notified in writing by the BUYER at least seven days before the time for delivery of the deed, and unless prevented from doing so by the refusal of the insurance company(s) involved to issue the same, the SELLER shall assign such insurance and deliver binders therefor in proper form to the BUYER at the time for performance of this agreement. In the event of refusal by the insurance company(s) to issue the same, the SELLER shall give notice thereof to the BUYER at least two business days before the time for performance of this agreement.

17. ADJUSTMENTS *(list operating expenses, if any, or attach schedule)*

Collected rents, mortgage interest, prepaid premiums on insurance if assigned as herein provided, water and sewer use charges, operating expenses (if any) according to the schedule attached hereto or set forth below, and taxes for the then current year, shall be apportioned and fuel value shall be adjusted, as of the day of performance of this agreement and the net amount thereof shall be added to or deducted from, as the case may be, the purchase price payable by the BUYER at the time of delivery of the deed. Uncollected rents for the current rental period shall be apportioned if and when collected by either party.

18. ADJUSTMENT OF UNASSESSED AND ABATED TAXES

If the amount of said taxes is not known at the time of the delivery of the deed, they shall be apportioned on the basis of the taxes assessed for the preceding year, with a reapportionment as soon as the new tax rate and valuation can be ascertained; and, if the taxes which are to be apportioned shall thereafter be reduced by abatement, the amount of such abatement, less the reasonable cost of obtaining the same, shall be apportioned between the parties, provided that neither party shall be obligated to institute or prosecute proceedings for an abatement unless herein otherwise agreed.

19. BROKER'S COMMISSION *(fill in space)*

A commission, according to the present schedule of commission rates recommended by the Greater Boston Real Estate Board, is to be paid by the SELLER to .

the Broker(s) herein, but if the SELLER pursuant to the terms of clause 22 hereof retains the deposits made hereunder by the BUYER, said Broker(s) shall be entitled to receive from the SELLER an amount equal to one-half the amount so retained or an amount equal to the commission according to such schedule for this transaction, whichever is the lesser.

20. BROKER(S) WARRANTY *(fill in name)*

The Broker(s) named herein
warrant(s) that he (they) is (are) duly licensed as such by the Commonwealth of Massachusetts.

EXHIBIT 2 (*Continued*)

21. DEPOSIT *(fill in, or delete reference to broker(s) if SELLER holds deposit)*

All deposits made hereunder shall be held by the broker(s)
as agent for the SELLER, subject to the terms of this agreement and shall be duly acc
the time for performance of this agreement.

22. BUYER'S DEFAULT; DAMAGES

If the BUYER shall fail to fulfill the BUYER'S agreements herein, all deposits made here
the BUYER shall be retained by the SELLER as liquidated damages unless within thirty da
the time for performance of this agreement or any extension hereof, the SELLER otherwise
the BUYER in writing.

23. VETERANS FINANCING *(fill in blank spaces or delete entire clause)*

The BUYER, being a Veteran, intends to use his so-called Veterans Administration loan benefits finance the purchase of said premises; it is understood and agreed that if on or before a Certificate of Reasonable Value for not less than the purchase pric shall not be issued by the Veterans Administration Loan Guaranty Division and if an accredited lending institution shall not approve and accept a mortgage loan of $, payable in years at a rate of interest not to exceed % per year, based upon the aforesaid Certificate of Reasonable Value, then all payments hereunder by the BUYER shall be forthwith refunded and all other obligations of all parties hereto shall cease and this agreement shall be void and without recourse to the parties hereto.

24. F.H.A. FINANCING *(fill in blank spaces or delete Clauses 24 & 25)*

The BUYER agrees to apply promptly for a U.S. Government Federal Housing Administration insured loan for not less than $, payable in years at a rate of interest not to exceed % per year, and if he shall not be able to obtain a firm commitment for such loan on or before , then at the BUYER'S option, all payments hereunder by the BUYER shall be forthwith refunded and all other obligations of all parties hereto shall cease and this agreement shall be void and without recourse to the parties hereto.

25. F.H.A. APPRAISAL STATEMENT *(fill in amount or delete Clauses 25 & 24)* *(the wording of this clause is required verbatim by F.H.A. Rules & Regulations)*

It is expressly agreed that, notwithstanding any other provisions of this contract, the PURCHASER shall not be obligated to complete the purchase of the property described herein or to incur any penalty by forfeiture of earnest money deposits or otherwise, unless the SELLER has delivered to the PURCHASER a written statement issued by the Federal Housing Commissioner setting forth the appraised value of the property for mortgage insurance purposes of not less than $, which statement the SELLER hereby agrees to deliver to the PURCHASER promptly after such appraised value statement is made available to the SELLER. The PURCHASER shall, however, have the privilege and option of proceeding with the consummation of this contract without regard to the amount of the appraised valuation made by the Federal Housing Commissioner.

26. SALE OF PERSONAL PROPERTY *(fill in and attach list or delete entire clause)*

The BUYER agrees to buy from the SELLER the articles of personal property enumerated on the attached list for the price of $ and the SELLER agrees to deliver to the BUYER upon delivery of the deed hereunder, a warranty bill of sale therefor on payment of said price. The provisions of this clause shall constitute an agreement separate and apart from the provisions herein contained with respect to the real estate, and any breach of the terms and conditions of this clause shall have no effect on the provisions of this agreement with respect to the real estate.

27. RELEASE BY HUSBAND OR WIFE

The SELLER'S spouse hereby agrees to join in said deed and to release and convey all statutory and other rights and interests in said premises.

28. BROKER AS PARTY

The broker(s) named herein, join(s) in this agreement and become(s) a party hereto, in so far as any provisions of this agreement expressly apply to him (them), and to any amendments or modifications of such provisions to which he (they) agree(s) in writing.

29. LIABILITY OF TRUSTEE, SHAREHOLDER, BENEFICIARY, etc.

If the SELLER or BUYER executes this agreement in a representative or fiduciary capacity, only the principal or the estate represented shall be bound, and neither the SELLER or BUYER so executing, nor any shareholder or beneficiary of any trust, shall be personally liable for any obligation, express or implied, hereunder.

30. CONSTRUCTION OF AGREEMENT ** delete "triplicate" and substitute "quadruplicate" if required. (See "Instructions in General", 1.)*

This instrument, executed in triplicate* is to be construed as a Massachusetts contract, is to take effect as a sealed instrument, sets forth the entire contract between the parties, is binding upon and enures to the benefit of the parties hereto and their respective heirs, devisees, executors, administrators, successors and assigns, and may be cancelled, modified or amended only by a written instrument executed by both the SELLER and the BUYER. If two or more persons are named herein as BUYER their obligations hereunder shall be joint and several. The captions and marginal notes are used only as a matter of convenience and are not to be considered a part of this agreement or to be used in determining the intent of the parties to it.

31. ADDITIONAL PROVISIONS

....	....
Husband or Wife of Seller	*SELLER*
....	....
Husband or Wife of Buyer	*BUYER*

....
Broker

QUESTIONS FOR DISCUSSION

1. What are the elements that affect the demand for a property and its selling price?
2. How did Mr. Manning attempt to find a property? What problems did he face?
3. What were the forms of financing available to him? What are the advantages and disadvantages of each?
4. Should Mr. Manning buy the property? What risks is he taking, personal and financial? How reliable are his income and expense figures?
5. What are the advantages and disadvantages of a real estate investment?

SUTTON TOWN HOUSE
Apartment Building

In June 1965, James Channing was considering the purchase of the Sutton Town House, a 13-story-plus penthouse luxury building on the "fashionable" East Side of Manhattan between 1st Avenue and Sutton Place. The brick-and-concrete structure, completed in October 1961, has 171 centrally air-conditioned rental apartments: 67 2½-room apartments; 27 3-room apartments; 31 3½-room apartments; 20 4-room apartments; 24 4½-room apartments; and 2 5-room apartments, for a total of 555 rooms. The building also has a 56-car garage which is leased to a garage operator for five more years at a net annual rental of $20,000.

The building is situated on an irregular plot of 200 × 102 × 88, or approximately 18,970 square feet of land. Although the assessed value of the land for real estate tax purposes is $488,000, the actual cost of land in this area is over $60 per square foot, or $948,500, almost double the assessed valuation.

This building, with a gross rent roll of $537,960, was being offered for sale at $1.2 million cash above the $2.4 million balance of the first mortgage. The real estate broker assured Mr. Channing that the property could be acquired for $1 million cash (see statement in Exhibit 1). The setup projected a net cash flow of $121,089 before state and federal tax and before vacancies, repairs, and management expense but after repayment or amortization of mortgage debt.

Mr. Channing, who had been offered the property by a broker, felt that the location was excellent and would become even more valuable in the future, since the number of available sites for new apartment buildings in this area was rapidly dwindling while the demand for luxury, "walk-to-work" apartments located in a residential area were becoming increasingly valuable. In addition, the recent change in the New York City zoning laws requiring more costly "setbacks" for new construction was expected to discourage new building in the near future. Any new buildings constructed would require higher rentals to justify the added construction cost.

However, an ironic consequence of the pending zoning regulations was that the impending changes in the law encouraged overbuilding, as landowners rushed to obtain the benefits of the old zoning law. Overbuilding was also encouraged by the availability of substantial amounts of funds raised by syndicates for real estate investments. The fiercely competitive syndicators, since they obtained management fees and sales commissions, did not depend solely on the success of the property for their own profits and consequently tended to enter into the development field in order to generate projects for syndication, regardless of the economic justification and financial soundness of these projects.

Estimating the results of the current overbuilding, Mr. Channing

Sutton Town House Apartments
(photographed July, 1962)

judged that vacancies in these luxury buildings would be about 2% of gross rentals. Upon receiving the rent roll (Exhibit 2), he found that there were two vacancies and four apartments rented on a month-to-month basis in the Sutton Town House. The rented apartments were occupied by tenants whose leases expired and who were planning to move but had stayed on an extra month. The owner of the building, not having found new tenants so far, was not pressuring them to vacate. Mr. Channing was concerned, too, with the high number of leases which were expiring within the next six months (72 out of 171 apartments, or 42%). He did not know how many of the old tenants would enter into a new lease, but he felt that the number would come to at least two thirds of the apartments whose leases expired and that of the remaining 24 apartments becoming vacant, 15 would be leased by a renting broker who would receive one month's rent as a leasing commission. Outside leasing commissions would then average $3,700 a year. The remaining apartments would be leased at a nominal cost, primarily through newspaper advertisements in *The New York Times.*

Although Channing recognized that the building might suffer a 2% vacancy factor, or approximately $10,300, he was more concerned with the high concessions[1] granted to new tenants when those apartments were first leased. Mr. Channing estimated that as an inducement to the tenant to enter into the lease, the owner originally granted one- to three-month concessions, generally averaging a two-month waiver of rent on a three-year lease on apartments receiving such concessions. However, only three quarters of the tenants received any concession. In the future, he felt, probably half of the new tenants would receive concessions, averaging only one month on a three-year lease. This would mean an estimated annual loss of rental of $7,300 because of concessions.

Management fees were another expense item not included in the setup. Usually an outside management firm makes the leases, cares for all details of maintenance, collects rents, attends to insurance, supervises the personnel, makes purchases, pays the bills and furnishes a complete accounting. The management firm Mr. Channing normally employed receives a fee equal to 2% of the actual income or, in this case, about $10,500 per annum.

The one area in which Mr. Channing had difficulty estimating the cash costs was maintenance, repairs, and capital expenditures. Generally, buyers calculated this at 5% of gross rent roll. Painting of apartments

---

[1] Concessions are a waiver of rental for the period of the concession. Property owners grant concessions rather than reduce rentals for various reasons. The owners may be required to evidence a minimum gross rent roll as a condition for obtaining the mortgage financing. Or they may be contemplating a sale of the property and are endeavoring to project the highest possible income. Concessions are not generally shown in a sales setup or in the lease.

alone would cost approximately $7,400, since every apartment was painted on the average of once every three years at an average cost per room of $40. Maintenance on the air conditioners, elevators, dishwashers and other appliances, corridor carpeting, floor scraping, and the purchase of supplies and appliances should cost an additional $17,500 per annum. Mr. Channing therefore felt that 5%, or $25,000, was a conservative estimate for the expenditures on maintenance, repairs, and capital improvements. Though the figure was normally higher on a building like this, the newness of this structure, the excellent state of repair, and the three maintenance men already included in the payroll expense made the 5% estimate a conservative one.

Mr. Channing was not surprised that the seller should be unwilling to corroborate any expense figure other than the rent roll, as supported by the leases furnished; real estate taxes; the outstanding balance of the mortgage, including all terms of the mortgage; the payroll expense; insurance, water, and sewer tax; electricity and gas; and fuel, in this case supplied by New York Steam, both for heating and air conditioning. The seller argued that the expenses for this building were combined with those of other properties and were not separable. They also contended that they included personal expenses in the various expense categories.

Mr. Channing was aware that the use of a broad 10% estimate usually employed for vacancies, repairs, and management expenses could result in overestimating the actual income of the property. There were properties he knew where these factors accounted for 20% of the gross rent roll. But, in this case he felt that the various estimates he had computed were quite conservative.

The price of $3.4 million at which he felt he could acquire this property should result in an increase in the assessed value of the property for real estate tax purposes. Since property in New York City was generally assessed at 80% of actual value, the new assessment should increase to $2,720,000 or $170,000 above the old assessment. At the prevailing tax rate of $4.52 per $100 of assessed value in New York City, the result would probably be a $7,700 increase in the real estate tax.

Mr. Channing provided the following recalculation of the expected cash flow:

Gross rental and income	$538,000
Less: Concessions, vacancies, and renting expenses	21,300
Net rental income	$516,700
Less: Expenses as per setup	416,900
	$ 99,800
Less: Management expense	10,500
Repairs and maintenance	25,000
Additional real estate tax	7,700
Expected cash flow	$ 56,600

While a 5.66% cash flow on his $1 million investment did not seem to justify even considering the property, Channing nevertheless felt that purchasing this high-grade property in a quality location at a yield of approximately 8% on a free and clear basis (before financing) was quite attractive. It was unlikely that he would be permitted to refinance the property before August 1, 1972, under the terms of the mortgage, but he was almost certain, on the basis of his experience, that he could easily recapture the entire amount of the amortization payments made on the mortgage, or about $800,000 (the original $2.6 million balance of the mortgage, less the $1.8 million balance on August 1, 1972), less a $54,000 prepayment penalty.

He also felt that the interest rate of 6%, a high rate during this period, reflected the unknown nature and high risk of the property at the time the mortgage commitment was obtained, which was before construction on the building had begun. If the mortgage were repayable at this time, a mortgage commitment could be obtained at a better than 5.25% interest rate with a maximum level constant payment for interest and amortization of 7%. The annual payment on the present $2.4 million mortgage balance would thus be only $168,000 or $46,500 less than the present cash outflow for interest and amortization. This positive use of leverage would bring the cash yield on investment above 11%, since the property on a free and clear basis was yielding 8%, where the cost of borrowed money would be only 7%.

However, the property was being presently financed at a 9% cost for borrowed funds, a cost higher than the 8% yield on the property before financing charges. In this case, of course, leverage had had a negative effect on the return of equity. Channing thought that when he was permitted to refinance the building, he would be able to arrange mortgage terms at no higher than a constant payment of 7½% with interest at 5½%, or an annual debt servicing cost of $195,000 on a mortgage of $2.6 million. There was also some chance that a higher mortgage could be obtained in 1972, when the mortgage was repayable.

Mr. Channing calculated the taxable income, as defined for federal income tax purposes, by adding back amortization of the mortgage debt to the estimated cash income (since repayment of debt is a nondeductible expense) and deducting depreciation, a noncash expense. The amortization of mortgage debt in the first year would thus be $72,500, and it would increase steadily as a decreasing portion of the constant payment of $214,500 went toward interest payments. As the mortgage was repaid, the interest expense would fall, and a greater portion of the $214,500 would be used to repay the mortgage.

The $3.4 million cost of the property was divided between building— a depreciable asset—and land—a nondepreciable asset. For depreciation purposes, the division used by assessors for real estate tax purposes was normally employed. The $488,000 assessment for the land represented only 19% of the total assessment of $2,550,000 for land and building, allowing Channing to depreciate the 81% or $2,750,000 of his purchase price that had been assigned as the cost of the building. The depreciation was figured over a 36-year remaining life (the original life being 40 years) either on a straight-line basis, taking a deduction of $76,400 per annum for the life of the property; or using the 125% declining balance method,[2] taking a deduction of $95,500.

The statement of income for income tax purposes would be as follows:

Estimated cash income	$ 56,600
Plus: Amortization of mortgage debt	72,500
Total Income	$129,100
Less: Depreciation expense (125%)	95,500
First year's net taxable income	$ 33,600

Of course, as the depreciation deduction declines and amortization payments increase over the years, a greater tax liability will be incurred. During the first year, however, only 59% of the cash flow of $56,600 will be taxable, and the balance can be realized without any income tax liability.

As Exhibit 3 shows, the depreciation expense exceeds the amortization expense through the fourth year and therefore shields part of the cash income from taxes through this period. In the fifth and sixth years, the income tax is payable on not only the cash income estimated at $56,600 but also on the excess of the amortization over depreciation.

One possibility that seemed attractive to Channing in contemplating purchasing the property was its resale after the seventh year, immediately after the $2.6 million refinancing of the property with a constant carrying cost rate of 7.5%, or $195,000. This would result in an additional cash flow of $19,500 ($214,500 − $195,000), increasing the cash income to $76,100 ($19,500 + $56,600).

Mr. Channing also expected the rental income of $77.50 per month per room to go up to $90 per room by 1972, a 16% rise in income, or about $85,000 annually. Although expenses could also be expected to increase by 15%, or $35,000, there was still a difference of $50,000 in increased cash flow that would probably be generated by this property at the end

---

[2] Under the declining-balance method, the greatest amount of depreciation is taken in the first year. Continually decreasing amounts of depreciation are taken in successive years. Under the declining-balance method, a uniform rate is applied to the unrecovered basis for the property. In this case, the straight-line depreciation is 2.778%, and the 125% declining-balance rate is 3.473% of $2,750,000 or $95,500 in the first year. The second year's depreciation is 3.473% of $2,750,000 less $95,500, and so on.

of the seventh year to provide a total expected cash flow of $126,100.[3] Capitalized at an 8% rate, the property should then be salable at $1,575,000, less an estimated brokerage commission of $75,000, leaving the seller with $1.5 million before a capital gains tax.

The depreciated basis of the property at the end of the seventh year would be about $2.8 million ($3.4 million original basis less depreciation of $600,000), while the sales price was expected to be $4,050,000 ($2.6 million—the amount of the new mortgage—less the prepayment penalty of $50,000, plus the $1.5 million realized in cash on the sale of the property). At this time, a capital gains tax at the rate of 35% for the difference between sales price and book value would have to be paid,[4] amounting to a tax liability of $466,000. Channing, at that time, would thus be realizing $750,000 in funds from refinancing and $1.5 million on the sale of the property.

Mr. Channing was interested in receiving an effective return of 12% after all taxes. He estimated his tax bracket at 50% and used this in his own calculations. Exhibit 4 shows his calculation of the annual tax liability on the income for the property for the contemplated seven-year holding period. It uses the $56,600 earnings (cash flow) figure for this period, without adjusting it for the increase in income, on the assumption that the major increase in rentals would come near the end of the period.

As an alternative to purchasing the property for $1 million cash, Mr. Channing had the option of placing a second mortgage of $600,000 on the property at an interest rate of 9%. While the term of the second mortgage would be one year, he was confident he could retain it for the seven-year period without any amortization payments. He did feel that there was, nevertheless, a slight risk that he might be unable to refinance the second mortgage if money became very tight, though he thought the rate would more probably jump to 10% if that occurred. With the second mortgage, he would pay out nearly the entire $56,600 income in interest expenses and so wind up with a taxable loss of $20,400 during the first year. Mr. Channing was certain that he would be able to offset this loss against other income and gain $10,000 in tax savings. Even after all interest payments, he would still have a cash income of $2,600 from this property. But to justify the added risk involved in assuming the second mortgage, Mr. Channing felt that the return in this case should be at least one full percentage point higher than under the nonsecond-mortgage alternative.

In Exhibit 5, the effects of the second mortgage on the after-tax return of the property have been calculated.

---

[3] While the higher income generated by the property would justify a higher mortgage on the property, this has not been used as an assumption in this case.

[4] This does not take into account the new recapture clause on depreciation for tax purposes. For teaching reasons recapture is deliberately disregarded at this point.

EXHIBIT 1

Sutton Town House: Setup

Location:	405 East 56th Street between First Avenue and Sutton Place
Size of plot:	200 × 102 × 89 ft., irregular (approx. 19,000 sq. ft.)
Description:	13-story and penthouse apartment residence. Centrally air conditioned; two high-speed Otis passenger elevators plus separate service elevator; 56-car garage. 1,655,000 cubic feet.
Layout:	67/2½; 27/3; 31/3½; 20/4; 24/4½; and 2/5 Total: 171 apartments, 555 rooms
Assessed value:	Land......................$ 488,000 Land and building.......$2,550,000
1st mortgage:	$2.4 million—Originally $2.6 million. Payable $214,500 per annum constant including 6% interest. Prepayment after 8/1/72 (balance $1.8 million) with 3% penalty on balance. Due 5/1/82. Held by institution.

Estimated income:

Apartments (including free gas)..........$516,160		
Garages................................. 20,000		
Laundry machines........................ 1,800		
Total Estimated Income.............		$537,960

Estimated expenses:

Interest and amortization.................$214,500		
Real estate taxes......................... 115,216		
Water and sewer......................... 3,500		
Payroll and fringe benefits (9 men including elevator operators)..... 45,000		
Insurance................................. 3,500		
Electricity and gas (for cooking)........... 13,655		
New York Steam......................... 21,500		
Total Estimated Expenses...........		$416,871
Estimated net profit before vacancies, repairs, and management.........................		$121,089

Price: $1.2 million over mortgage

Information furnished is subject to errors, omissions, prior sale, or withdrawal without notice.

EXHIBIT 2

Sutton Town House: Rent Roll—6/23/65

Apt. No.	Lease Expiration	Annual Rent	Apt. No.	Lease Expiration	Annual Rent
1A....................		2,460	12A.................	9/30/66	2,040
2A...................	9/30/66	1,980	14A.................	5/31/66	2,304
3A...................	9/30/65	2,220	PHA................	7/31/67	4,740
4A...................	9/30/66	2,040	1B..................	9/30/66	3,510
5A...................	10/31/66	2,052	2B..................	9/30/66	2,940
6A...................	9/30/69	1,800	3B..................	6/30/66	2,964
7A...................	9/30/66	2,057	4B..................	9/30/65	2,940
8A...................	9/30/66	2,112	5B..................	9/30/66	3,053
9A...................	9/30/65	2,304	6B..................	9/30/66	2,783
10A...................	9/30/65	2,280	7B..................	9/30/65	2,796
11A...................	9/30/66	2,112	8B..................	10/31/65	2,988

EXHIBIT 2 (Continued)

Apt. No.	Lease Expiration	Annual Rent	Apt. No.	Lease Expiration	Annual Rent
9B...................	9/30/65	3,048	10F..................	11/30/65	3,012
10B..................	9/30/67	3,048	11F..................	9/30/65	2,783
11B..................	7/15/67	2,520	12F..................	9/30/66	2,808
12B..................	9/30/65	3,060	14F..................	9/30/66	3,240
14B..................	9/30/65	3,060	1G...................	9/30/66	2,040
PHB..................	mo.–mo.	7,020	3G...................	9/30/66	1,992
1C...................	9/30/66	3,720	4G...................	9/30/65	2,184
2C...................	—	2,052	5G...................	9/30/66	2,184
3C...................	7/31/66	2,064	6G...................	3/31/66	2,184
4C...................	9/30/65	1,926	7G...................	9/30/66	2,024
5C...................	9/30/66	1,914	8G...................	7/31/66	2,208
6C...................	9/30/65	2,100	9G...................	6/30/67	2,208
7C...................	9/30/65	1,936	10G..................	9/30/67	2,100
8C...................	5/31/67	2,124	11G..................	9/30/65	2,304
9C...................	9/30/65	2,136	12G..................	9/30/65	2,316
10C..................	9/30/67	1,956	14G..................	9/30/66	2,118
11C..................	9/30/65	4,020	3H...................	9/30/65	2,160
12C..................	9/30/65	3,600	4H...................	9/30/65	2,184
14C..................	9/30/65	3,600	5H...................	9/30/65	2,184
PHC..................	9/30/67	6,780	6H...................	9/30/67	2,220
1D...................	9/30/66	2,160	7H...................	—	2,184
2D...................	9/30/66	2,123	8H...................	9/30/66	2,058
3D...................	9/30/67	3,852	9H...................	9/30/66	2,256
4D...................	9/30/67	3,936	10H..................	9/30/65	2,100
5D...................	9/30/65	3,972	11H..................	9/30/66	2,112
6D...................	9/30/66	3,674	12H..................	9/30/66	2,100
7D...................	9/30/65	4,008	14H..................	9/30/65	2,304
8D...................	9/30/65	4,008	2J...................	9/30/67	2,700
9D...................	9/30/66	4,116	3J...................	10/31/67	2,724
10D..................	9/30/66	4,116	4J...................	mo.–mo.	3,000
PHD..................	9/30/66	5,040	5J...................	9/30/66	2,700
1E...................	9/30/67	3,360	6J...................	9/30/67	3,048
2E...................	9/30/65	4,140	7J...................	9/30/65	2,832
3E...................	9/30/65	4,200	8J...................	11/30/65	3,096
4E...................	9/30/66	4,260	9J...................	9/30/65	3,096
5E...................	9/30/67	3,936	10J..................	9/30/65	3,096
6E...................	9/30/67	4,344	11J..................	9/30/65	3,096
7E...................	9/30/65	4,380	12J..................	10/31/66	2,928
8E...................	9/30/67	4,200	14J..................	9/30/65	3,240
9E...................	9/30/68	4,200	2K...................	9/30/66	4,212
10E..................	mo.–mo.	4,500	3K...................	9/30/67	4,248
11E..................	9/30/65	5,100	4K...................	9/30/65	4,284
12E..................	9/30/65	4,800	5K...................	9/30/66	4,500
14E..................	9/30/65	4,920	6K...................	9/30/66	4,561
1F...................	9/30/65	2,688	7K...................	9/30/67	4,200
2F...................	9/30/66	2,552	8K...................	9/30/65	4,416
3F...................	9/30/66	2,808	9K...................	9/30/65	4,452
4F...................	9/30/65	2,832	10K..................	9/30/65	4,488
5F...................	9/30/66	2,618	11K..................	9/30/67	4,680
6F...................	9/30/66	2,868	12K..................	9/30/68	4,512
7F...................	4/30/66	2,664	14K..................	12/31/65	4,980
8F...................	9/30/65	2,684	2L...................	9/30/67	3,816
9F...................	9/30/66	2,952	3L...................	9/30/66	3,852

EXHIBIT 2 (Continued)

Apt. No.	Lease Expiration	Annual Rent	Apt. No.	Lease Expiration	Annual Rent
4L	9/30/65	3,876	7N	mo.-mo.	3,060
5L	9/30/67	3,600	8N	9/30/66	2,916
6L	9/30/65	3,912	9N	9/30/65	3,132
7L	9/30/65	3,912	10N	9/30/65	3,120
8L	9/30/65	3,936	11N	9/30/66	2,880
9L	9/30/65	3,936	12N	10/31/65	3,060
10L	9/30/66	3,600	14N	9/30/66	3,144
2M	9/30/66	1,881	20	9/30/67	2,088
3M	9/30/65	2,064	30	9/30/66	2,013
4M	9/30/65	1,920	40	10/31/65	2,208
5M	9/30/65	1,914	50	10/31/67	2,220
6M	7/31/67	2,100	60	9/30/66	1,896
7M	9/30/66	1,947	70	9/30/65	2,100
8M	9/30/66	1,947	80	9/30/67	2,256
9M	9/30/66	1,968	90	9/30/65	2,112
10M	9/30/65	1,980	100	9/30/65	2,280
11M	10/31/67	3,600	110	7/14/66	2,200
12M	6/30/65	3,600	120	1/31/68	2,316
14M	9/30/66	3,480	140	6/30/66	2,328
2N	9/30/67	2,940	Subtotal		516,160
3N	9/30/66	2,964	Garages		20,000
4N	9/30/67	2,988	Laundry		1,800
5N	9/30/65	3,012	Total		537,960
6N	9/30/67	3,216			

EXHIBIT 3

Sutton Town House: Mortgage Amortization, Cash Flow after Debt Service, and Depreciation

Year	Annual Mortgage Amortization	Cash Flow	125% Declining Balance Annual Depreciation Expense
1	$ 72,500	$56,600	$95,500
2	76,400		92,000
3	81,000		89,000
4	85,700		85,800
5	91,000		82,900
6	96,300		80,200
7	102,100		77,300
8	108,400		74,500
9	114,800		71,900
10	121,800		69,500

Mortgage balance outstanding at End of Year	Amount
7th year	$1,795,000
10th year	1,450,000

EXHIBIT 4

Sutton Town House: Taxable Income, Taxes Payable, and After-Tax Income

Year	Taxable Income	50% Tax Rate	After-Tax Cash Flow
1........................	$33,600	$16,800	$39,800
2........................	41,000	20,500	36,100
3........................	48,600	24,300	32,300
4........................	56,500	28,250	28,350
5........................	64,700	32,350	24,250
6........................	72,700	36,350	20,250
7........................	81,400	40,700	15,900

EXHIBIT 5

Sutton Town House
Tax Effects of Second Mortgage Loan

Year	Cash Flow	Taxable Income (or Loss)	Tax (Savings) or Tax Payments Due 50% Tax Rate
1	$2,600	$(20,400)	$(10,200)
2		(13,400)	(6,500)
3		(5,400)	(2,700)
4		2,500	1,250
5		10,700	5,350
6		18,700	9,350
7		27,400	13,700

QUESTIONS FOR DISCUSSION

1. If Mr. Channing purchases the property and resells it in 1972, what after-tax return would he receive? How would the assumption of the second mortgage change this?

2. What assumptions were made in arriving at the future purchase price? Are they logical? How much control does the owner have over these factors?

3. Does the size of this building as compared with 19 Pinckney Street alter the investment risk and problems?

NOTE ON
SUTTON TOWN HOUSE

PART I

Exhibit 1 restates the cash flow statement included in the *setup* in the Sutton Town House case on page 27. It reflects the adjustments generated on page 23 (Concessions, vacancies and renting expense—$21,300; Management expense—$10,500; Repairs and maintenance—$25,000; and Additional real estate taxes $7,700).

Inflation

One objective of Exhibit 1 is to illustrate the leverage available from increased rentals. In column (2), we show expenses as a percentage of net rentals. The variable expenses (excluding debt servicing and profit) amounts to 48% of net rents. Thus, better than one half of any increase in rents goes to the equity investor, since debt servicing, a fixed obligation, does not increase as costs rise.

The 16% or $85,000 increase in the rentals projected to occur at the end of 10 years will be offset by an anticipated $35,000 (15%) increase in expenses. This would result in a $50,000 increase in net cash flow to the investor. Thus, a 16% increase in rents would result in a 90% increase in the net cash flow available to the investor. If properties were selling based upon capitalized cash flows, a 90% increase in cash flow also would mean a 90% increase in the sales price of the property.

We can derive other information from Exhibit 1. By dividing the operating expenses ($87,200) by the number of rooms (555), we find that the operating expenses per room is $157 or well in excess of the $100–$125 per room "rule of thumb" recommended in the Pinckney Street case, suggesting that the expenses are not understated in this statement. In fact, if we applied three men's salary to maintenance and reduced operating expenses by $15,000, the operating expenses per room would be $130, more in line with the $125 rule-of-thumb figure.

Exhibit 1 also enables us to calculate the rent per room at $77.50 and to verify whether this is consistent with rents charged for other luxury-type apartments.

31

The 24% of net rents allocated for real estate taxes is consistent with the 20%–30% of rentals payable as real estate taxes discussed in the Pinckney Street case.

Exhibit 2(A) shows that the free and clear (before debt servicing) return would be $271,100, that is, if all the funds were supplied by the equity investor. This would give the investor an 8% cash return on an investment of $3.4 million (the price of the property). However, because he is employing borrowed funds with a higher cost, of 9%,[1] than the free and clear return, the return to the investor is reduced to 5.66%. This is an example of reverse or negative leverage (where the cash cost of borrowed funds is greater than the free and clear return).

Analyzing the free and clear return provides the investor with an opportunity to determine whether, in fact, there is a potential for increasing the leveraged return. If, for example, the investor felt he could refinance the $2.4 million at a 5% interest rate for a 25-year period this would require a level constant payment of 7% and would increase the return on the investor's $1 million to 10.31% (Exhibit 2[B]). (This is a case of positive leverage, where the debt-servicing cost of 7% was below the free and clear return of 8%, thus increasing the return to the equity investor.) Based upon this assumption, he might make an investment that he might have rejected had he only looked at the net cash return of 5.66%.

In determining the amount of the purchase price allocable to the building, we use the percentages for land and building allocated by the real estate tax assessor for real estate tax purposes. We then apply these percentages to the price we paid for the property. (The price we paid includes the cash paid, mortgages assumed, and any other form of consideration given.) In Exhibit 3 (section A), we use the allocation employed by the assessor despite the fact that his estimated value for real estate tax purposes was only $2,550,000, well below the $3.4 million price we paid.

We then apply the percentage of assessed valuation he ascribes to building (81% in this case) to the purchase price, and this gives us the amount of the purchase price that can be depreciated. (Land is not a depreciable asset.)

We then determine the useful life—in this case, 36 years—based upon an original life of 40 years. We employ 125% declining-balance depreciation, which allows us to take 1¼ times the straight-line depreciation in the first year, or at a *rate* 1¼ times that under the straight-line method. However, this rate is constantly applied to the undepreciated part, after deducting all depreciation taken to this point. Thus, each year the

------

[1] $\dfrac{\$214,500 \text{ debt servicing}}{\$2,400,000 \text{ mortgage balance}}$

investor takes the same percentage of a smaller balance (the original building cost less the depreciation taken), and therefore the depreciation expense for tax purposes declines each year from $95,500 in the first year to $89,000 in the third year, and so on. (Exhibit 3 [section B]).

EXHIBIT 1
Income Statement Analysis

	(1) Income and Cash Flow	(2) Expenses as a Percentage of Net Rents
Gross rents.....................................	$516,160	
Garage income..............................	20,000	
Other income...............................	1,800	
Total.......................................	$537,960	
Estimated vacancies, concessions, rental expenditures............................	21,300	4%
Net rental income.........................	$516,700	100%
Expenses:		
Real estate taxes—adjusted...............	$122,900	24%
New York Steam (fuel)....................$ 21,500		
Electricity and gas........................ 13,700		
Insurance................................. 3,500		
Payroll (including some maintenance)..... 45,000		
Water and sewer.......................... 3,500		
	87,200	17%
Management expense.....................	10,500	2%
Repairs and maintenance..................	25,000	5%
Total Expenses........................	$245,600	48%
Net cash flow—if free and clear of debt......	$271,100	52%
Debt servicing annually.....................	214,500	41%
Net cash flow after debt servicing............	$ 56,600	11%

EXHIBIT 2(A)
Analysis of Leverage

				Return as Percentage of Funds Supplied
Total cost	$3,400,000	Free and clear return (net cash flow before debt servicing)	$271,100	8%
Mortgage	2,400,000	Debt servicing—$2,400,000 mortgage balance (This $214,500 payment will give the lender an effective return of 6% and repay the loan over an 18½-year period. The constant payment of $214,500 is approximately 9% of the outstanding mortgage balance.)	214,500	9%
Equity	$1,000,000	Net cash flow available to equity investor after debt servicing	$ 56,600	5.66%

EXHIBIT 2(B)

Total cost	$3,400,000	Free and clear return	$271,100	8%
Mortgage	2,400,000	Debt servicing—5% interest, 25 years, 7% constant payment	168,000	7%
Equity	$1,000,000	Cash flow available to equity investor	$103,100	10.31%

EXHIBIT 3

Analysis of Depreciation

A. Determine the amount allocable to building—depreciable asset
    (1) Assessed valuation for real estate tax purposes—total—$2,550
        Assessed valuation for real estate tax purposes—land only—$488

    (2) $19\% = \dfrac{\$488}{\$2,550}$ = Percentage of assessed valuation allocable to land only

    (3) Therefore, 81%, or balance, allocable to building
    (4) Cost of Sutton Town House—$3,400,000
    (5) $3,400,000 × 81% = $2,750,000, amount of investment allocable to building
B. Assume 36-year remaining useful life
    (1) Straight-line depreciation 1/36 or 2.778% per annum
    (2) 125% declining-balance method 125% × 2.778% per annum or 3.473%
    (3) First-year depreciation 3.473% × $2,750,000 depreciable asset = $95,500
    (4) Second-year depreciation 3.473% × ($2,750,000 − $95,500) $2,654,500 declining
        balance = $92,000
        Third-year depreciation 3.473% × ($2,654,500 − $92,000) declining balance
        $2,562,500 = $89,000

Etc.

EXHIBIT 4
Discounted Cash Flow—Return

A. Refinancing

Original mortgage amount..$2,600,000
Balance owing at end of seven years................................... 1,800,000

Gross proceeds from refinancing.......................................$ 800,000
   Less: Prepayment penalty 3% × $1,800,000............................   54,000

Net proceeds from refinancing at end of seven years...................$ 746,000

B. (1) Sales price

Assume we can sell property to yield an investor a cash return on his equity investment of 8%

(2) Cash flow at end of seven years

Present cash flow..............................		$56,600
Estimated rent increase.........................	$ 85,000	
Estimated expense increase....................	35,000	
Estimated net increase in cash flow............		50,000
Present debt-servicing cost.....................	$214,500	
Estimated debt-servicing cost on refinancing (5½% Interest, 7½% Constant, 24-year Mortgage).................................	195,000	
Net cash flow increase from refinancing........		19,500
Cash flow at end of seven years................		$126,100

(3) Capitalized at $8\% = \dfrac{\$126,100}{8\%} = \$1,575,000$ sales price (equity)

(4) Cash proceeds from sale.......................	$1,575,000
Less: Brokerage commission..................	75,000
Net cash proceeds from sale....................	$1,500,000

C. Capital gains tax payable on sale of property

(1) Original cost....................................	$3,400,000
Depreciation taken over seven years...........	603,000
Tax basis (depreciated basis)..................	$2,797,000
(2) Sales price for tax purposes—net mortgage transferred (after adjustment for prepayment penalty)..............................	$2,546,000
Net cash realized on sale......................	1,500,000
Total Sales Price.........................	$4,046,000
(3) Sales price......................................	$4,046,000
Depreciated basis..............................	2,797,000
Net capital gain...............................	$1,249,000

(4) Capital gains tax at 35% = (35% × $1,249,000) = $437,000*

D. Net proceeds at end of seventh year from refinancing, and sale net of capital gains tax

(1) Refinancing....................................	$ 746,000
(2) Sale of equity.................................	1,500,000
	$2,246,000
(3) Less: Capital gains tax paid..................	437,000
	$1,809,000

E. Annual cash income—after taxes—assuming 50% Tax Rate (see accompanying table)

*This does not take into account the recapture clause on depreciation for tax purposes, and is deliberately disregarded at this point.

EXHIBIT 4 (Continued)

	Year 1	Year 2	Year 3	Year 4	Year 5	Year 6	Year 7
Net rents..........................	$516,700	$516,700	$516,700	$516,700	$516,700	$516,700	$516,700
Less: Expenses.................	245,600	245,600	245,600	245,600	245,600	245,600	245,600
Free and clear return........	$271,100	$271,100	$271,100	$271,100	$271,100	$271,100	$271,100
Interest Expense @ 6%......	142,000	138,100	133,500	128,800	123,500	118,200	112,400
Depreciation expense........	$129,100	$133,000	$137,600	$142,300	$147,600	$152,900	$158,700
	95,500	92,000	89,000	85,800	82,900	80,200	77,300
Taxable income................	$ 33,600	$ 41,000	$ 48,600	$ 56,500	$ 64,700	$ 72,700	$ 81,400
Tax @ 50%.......................	$ 16,800	$ 20,500	$ 24,300	$ 28,250	$ 32,350	$ 36,350	$ 40,700
Cash flow as per Exhibit 1..	$ 56,600	$ 56,600	$ 56,600	$ 56,600	$ 56,600	$ 56,600	$ 56,600
Less: Tax liability.............	16,800	20,500	24,300	28,250	32,350	36,350	40,700
Net cash flow after Taxes...	$ 39,800	$ 36,100	$ 32,300	$ 28,350	$ 24,250	$ 20,250	$ 15,900

EXHIBIT 4 (*Continued*)

F. Present value of cash flows discounted at 11%

Payments Made at End of Year	From E—Cash Flows Less Taxes	Present Value of $1 Discounted at 11%	Present Value of Cash Flow
1.....................	$ 39,800	$0.901	$ 35,900
2.....................	36,100	.812	29,300
3.....................	32,300	.731	23,600
4.....................	28,350	.659	18,600
5.....................	24,250	.593	14,400
6.....................	20,250	.535	10,800
7.....................	15,900	.482	7,700
Net proceeds from sale and refinancing (after taxes) at end of 7th year—from D above.....$1,809,000		$0.482	$ 870,000
Amount that an investor would have to invest today to get the above cash flows, assuming he was satisfied to receive an effective rate of return on his outstanding investment of 11%.............			$1,010,300

Since the investor only has to invest $1 million, this means that he is getting a return slightly in excess of 11%.

PART II

Exhibit 5, page 41, demonstrates the effects of the second mortgage on the return. In this situation, we employ all assumptions used in the earlier exhibits with one addition, that of the second mortgage. As per the Sutton Town House case, it is assumed that we can borrow $600,000 from the seller by having him take back a second mortgage as collateral for his loan. Since the mortgage was taken back by the seller and evolved in the sale of the property as part of the purchase price, it is also called a purchase money mortgage.

The second mortgage in this case requires interest payments at a 9% rate or $54,000 per annum. In Exhibit 5 (section A), we restate the income statement for the first year of ownership, under the second-mortgage assumption. Instead of showing a profit of $33,600, we now reduce this by the interest cost on the second mortgage ($54,000), and show a loss for tax purposes of $20,400. If the investor can offset this loss against other income, it can save him $10,200 in the first year of ownership, assuming that he is in the 50% tax bracket. In fact, the property generated a $2,600 cash profit ($56,600 cash flow before the second mortgage, less second-mortgage interest of $54,000). The loss is an accounting loss resulting from the depreciation deductions allowed, though this is not a cash expense.

The desirability of the use of borrowed funds to increase the tax deductions is demonstrated in this exhibit. The government allows the property owner to depreciate not only the funds provided by him but also to add to the depreciable base the borrowed funds.

While the investor is receiving a deduction for the payments made to this investor-lender in the form of interest, he nevertheless gets full credit for depreciation. In fact, what we are doing here is arbitrarily assigning all the depreciation to the equity investor, though the income is divided up on an entirely different basis. Of course, the equity investor has some offset in the cash amortization payment which he must make for which he receives no tax benefits, since the repayment of debt is not a tax deductible expense. However, this is only a small offset. In this case, depreciation is $95,500, while amortization is $72,500, in the first year.

Students have often been surprised to learn that one investor can take the losses generated by depreciation while the other investor can take all of the income. In fact, this is what happens when we borrow part or all of the cost of a property. One investor-lender gets a substantial part of the cash income. In the case of the second-mortgage assumption, the two mortgage lenders are receiving $268,500 ($214,500 on the first mortgage and $54,000 interest on the second mortgage), while the equity investor is receiving only $2,600. Despite this income distribution and the fact that the two lenders have supplied $3 million of the cost of the property and the equity investor has supplied only $400,000, the equity investor can depreciate $3.4 million of the cost of the property.

In Exhibit 5 (section B) the actual savings in tax that these "losses" would produce for an investor are treated as cash income, since in fact, the investor does save this cash amount in taxes. The amount of savings decline each year as the amount paid out as interest declines. (As the outstanding principal of the loan declines, the interest payments decline.)

The amount of tax savings also declines as the depreciation deduction is reduced. Under the declining-balance method of depreciation, each year a smaller amount of depreciation is deducted. For example, on an asset with a 20-year life, you would be permitted to depreciate 5% of the cost of the depreciable asset each year on a straight-line basis or 10% on the double declining-balance method. Thus, if the cost of the depreciable asset (land excluded) is $1 million, the investor would be allowed to deduct $50,000 on the straight-line method or $100,000 (10% × $1,000,000) on the double declining-balance method in the first year. In the second year, he would be able to deduct 10% of the undepreciated balance or 10% of $900,000 ($1,000,000 − $100,000 depreciation already taken) which is $90,000. As a result, the depreciation deductions decline each year when using one of the forms of accelerated depreciation.

At one point, the investor is paying a tax greater than that based on his pretax cash flow. This occurs when the amount attributable to amortization is greater than the depreciation deduction taken. At that point the noncash income (amortization) is greater than the noncash expense (depreciation). This occurs in the fifth year. Despite the fact that the investor has only $56,600 (assuming no second mortgage) cash flow, he pays taxes on income of $64,700. This requires the investor, under the first-mortgage assumption to pay more than 50% of his cash flow in taxes. For the second-mortgage investor, the tax payments of $5,350, $9,350 and $13,700 required in the fifth, sixth and seventh year are greater than the $2,600 pretax cash flow received from operations, thus producing a net after-tax cash deficit for the investor. This is evident in section C of Exhibit 5, where the operating cash flow is combined with the tax effect.

The net after-tax cash deficits in the fifth, sixth and seventh years are $2,750, $6,750 and $11,100 respectively.

In Exhibit 5 (section C), rather than rework the entire cash statement to arrive at the pretax cash flow, we employ a shortcut. If we were to employ the longer approach we would do the following:

Gross rental income...	$516.7
Less: Operating expenses (including real estate tax).........	245.6
Cash flow before debt servicing................................	$271.1
Debt Servicing—First Mortgage—Interest and Amortization.....	214.5
Net cash flow before second mortgage..........................	$ 56.6
Interest on second mortgage...................................	54.0
Net cash flow—pretax...	$ 2.6

To demonstrate the relationship between taxable income and cash flow, we employed the shortcut in section C. To the net pretax income (or loss), we add back depreciation, a noncash expense, which we already deducted for tax purposes in arriving at the taxable income, (or loss). Since this is not a cash cost, we should not have deducted it to arrive at our cash income, so we add it back. In addition, we subtract amortization, since this is a cash cost even though it has not been deducted for tax purposes. (Repayment of debt is not a deductible expense for tax purposes.) These adjustments to the net taxable income (or loss), produce the pretax cash flow. To this we add the tax savings (or costs), and this gives us our net after tax cash flow.

In Exhibit 5 (section D), we discount these cash receipts. Through trial and error we found that these cash flows give the investor an effective return of over 17% on his investment. This is apparent, since the present value of all the payment discounted at a 17% rate ($416,000) is approximately equal to our investment of $400,000.

The refinancing and sales proceeds at the end of seven years and capital gains tax liability are the same as for the first-mortgage assumption, except for the fact that under the second-mortgage assumption the investor has to repay the second mortgage of $600,000. (We assumed that there would be no principal payments on the second mortgage for seven years.) This reduces the net after-tax proceeds from sale and refinancing from $1,809,000 for the first-mortgage assumption to $1,209,000 for the second-mortgage assumption.

EXHIBIT 5. Second-Mortgage Analysis

A. Income Tax Analysis—First Year

Rental income	$516.7
Operating expenses and real estate taxes	245.6
Net cash flow before debt servicing	$271.1
Interest first year on first mortgage	142.0
Net cash flow after interest on first mortgage	$129.1
Less: Depreciation expenses (first year)	95.5
Net income before second-mortgage financing and income taxes	$ 33.6
Second-mortgage interest—9% of $600,000 loan	54.0
Net loss for income tax purposes	($ 20.4)
Tax savings for an investor in a 50% tax bracket as a result of above loss	$ 10.2

B. Income Tax Analysis—Years 1 to 7

	Year 1	Year 2	Year 3	Year 4	Year 5	Year 6	Year 7
Taxable income before interest on second mortgages*	$33,600	$41,000	$48,600	$56,500	$64,700	$72,700	$81,400
Less: Interest—second mortgage	54,000	54,000	54,000	54,000	54,000	54,000	54,000
Net loss or income for tax purposes	($20,400)	($13,000)	($ 5,400)	$ 2,500	$10,700	$18,700	$ 27,400
Tax savings for investor on a 50% tax bracket who can offset losses against other income	$10,200	$ 6,500	$ 2,700	($ 1,250)	($ 5,350)	($ 9,350)	($ 13,700)

C. Annual Cash Flow Including Tax Savings Resulting from Ownership of Property

	Year 1	Year 2	Year 3	Year 4	Year 5	Year 6	Year 7
Net (loss) or income for income tax purposes as per "B" above	($20,400)	($13,000)	($ 5,400)	$ 2,500	$10,700	$18,700	$ 27,400
Add back depreciation—a noncash cost—deducted in "A" as an expense in arriving at net (loss) above	95,500	92,000	89,000	85,800	82,900	80,200	77,300
Deduct amortization or repayment of mortgage—a cash cost—not deducted in "A" as an expense in arriving at net (loss)	(72,500)	(76,400)	(81,000)	(85,700)	(91,000)	(96,300)	(102,100)
Net cash flow from operations before tax	$ 2,600	$ 2,600	$ 2,600	$ 2,600	$ 2,600	$ 2,600	$ 2,600
Add cash tax savings resulting from ownership of property by being able to offset tax losses generated by the property for tax purposes against investors' other income (from "B" above)	10,200	6,500	2,700	(1,250)	(5,350)	(9,350)	(13,700)
Net cash flow after taxes	$12,800	$ 9,100	$ 5,300	$ 1,350	($ 2,750)	($ 6,750)	($ 11,100)

* From Exhibit 4, column 1 in the Sutton Town House case.

EXHIBIT 5 (*Continued*)

D. Present Value of Cash Receipts (from C) at 17%

	(1)	(2)	(3)
			(3) = (1) × (2)
		Discount	*Present Value*
	Cash Flow†	*Factor*	*of Cash Flow*
Year 1......................$	12,800	0.855	$ 10,900
2.......................	9,100	.731	6,650
3.......................	5,300	.624	3,300
4.......................	1,350	.534	700
5.......................	(2,750)	.456	(1,250)
6.......................	(6,750)	.390	(2,600)
7.......................	(11,100)	.333	(3,700)
7.......................	1,209,000‡	.333	402,000
			$416,000

† Includes tax savings.
‡ (From Exhibit 4 A, B, C & D):
Proceeds from sale.............$1,575,000 − $75,000 brokerage = $1,500,000
Proceeds from refinancing......   800,000 − $54,000 prepayment
                                                penalty   =   746,000

Proceeds from sales and refinancing......................... $2,246,000
Capital gains tax due on sale (see Exhibit 4 C)..............   437,000
                                                              $1,809,000
    Less: Amount due on second-mortgage loan..............   600,000
Net cash proceeds on sale and refinancing.................. $1,209,000

Risks

1. Sale:
    a) Capitalization rates at which properties sell. (What, for example, happens if capitalization rate is 12% rather than 8% employed?)
    b) Rent increases—increased income of $85,000 vs increased expenses of only $35,000. (What happens if real estate taxes increase faster?)
    c) Amount of vacancies and repairs.
    d) Trend of area and growth (affects capitalization rate).
2. Refinancing:
    a) Availability.
    b) Interest rate at which it can be borrowed.
    c) Terms—years.
    d) Amount of loan.
3. Income flow:
    a) Income and expenses (vacancies, rent levels, concessions, real estate taxes, other expenses, repairs and maintenance).
4. Tax losses and benefits.

GRAYBAR
SYNDICATIONS
Office Building Syndicate

In December 1957, Harold Morse was trying to decide whether to recommend a proposed investment in real estate syndications, "Graybar Building Associates" (see Exhibit 1). Mr. Morse was a Long Island attorney whose many clients looked to him for financial advice. Most of these clients lived comfortably and were in tax brackets of about 50%. One of them, Dr. Planter, had sent Mr. Morse the Graybar prospectus, as well as an analysis of "Real Estate Syndicates" (see Exhibit 2). Dr. Planter had recently received both items in the mail from friends who were planning to invest in real estate syndications. He asked Mr. Morse to read the prospectus and the analysis and advise him as to what he should do.

Mr. Morse reviewed the advantages of investing in real estate. He knew that real estate prices were rising sharply. He had read of the "big killings" many had made. The field offered an excellent hedge against inflation, while providing a high annual cash return. Favorable depreciation allowances permitted much of this income to be tax sheltered. Further equity was being built up through mortgage amortization. The New York area, where the two properties being syndicated were located, was supposed to be especially desirable. Since most of his clients' funds were invested in their own businesses, and in the stock market, real estate appeared to provide a sound means of diversification.

Mr. Morse had heard a number of favorable reports in which syndications were recommended as the correct vehicle for owning and investing in real estate. He knew that in the last year or two, many real estate properties had been syndicated, and all of them had furnished the projected or anticipated return. The idea of high guaranteed returns paid out in monthly checks was appealing. Syndications allowed an investor not only to diversify his holdings into another field but to diversify within that field by buying units in several properties of various types.

Syndications appeared to cure the prime drawback to real estate for the small investor, the lack of liquidity. The syndicators were providing markets for the resale of the units they had sold, often at higher than original prices. They appeared to be attempting to institutionalize their operations in the same manner as stock brokerage firms had. The field was taking on a professional character. Mr. Morse knew that during the depression many real estate syndications had failed, but he felt that at the time of the offerings there was much merit in the approach.

The question then revolved around the soundness of these particular offerings. Mr. Morse tried to list the questions he would want answered after he had completed his analysis. He first wanted to examine both the projected cash and after-tax returns offered to the investors, and the opportunities for higher returns through mortgage refinancing, appreciation in value, and increase in rentals and income. How secure were these returns? How was leverage used in each case, and what bearing did it have upon the risks involved? How did the uses to which the properties were being put affect the risk factor?

He was interested in the role of the promoters. What risks were they taking, and what were they getting in return? Was there an equitable relationship between risk and return? Based upon the merchandising techniques used by the promoters in their prospectus, what type of investors would be attracted? Did the promoters appear to be reputable, judged by their background and the way they were presenting the investments? What protection was there from mismanagement by the promoters? Was there any governmental protection, and if not, should there have been?

Lastly, he was concerned about the adequacy and reliability of the information presented. What other information would he want? Could any real estate offering be evaluated solely from the figures?

EXHIBIT 1
Prospectus

$4,180,000 of Participations in Partnership Interests in
GRAYBAR BUILDING ASSOCIATES

PRICE PER PARTICIPATION: $10,000 MINIMUM

THESE SECURITIES HAVE NOT BEEN APPROVED OR DISAPPROVED BY THE SECURITIES AND EXCHANGE COMMISSION NOR HAS THE COMMISSION PASSED UPON THE ACCURACY OR ADEQUACY OF THIS PROSPECTUS. ANY REPRESENTATION TO THE CONTRARY IS A CRIMINAL OFFENSE.

	Price to Public	Underwriting Commissions*	Proceeds to Issuer
Total	$4,180,000	None	$4,180,000
Per unit	10,000	None	10,000

*As to the remuneration and interest of the members of Associates in the transactions described herein, see page 12.

The date of this Prospectus is March 10, 1958

EXHIBIT 1 (Continued)

No person has been authorized to give any information or to make any representations other than those contained in this Prospectus, and, if given or made, such information and representations must not be relied upon as having been authorized by Graybar Building Associates or by any of the members thereof.

A Registration Statement has been filed with the Securities and Exchange Commission, Washington, D.C., by Graybar Building Associates and the individual partners therein, as Co-Registrants, for the Participations offered hereunder.

This Prospectus does not contain all of the information set forth in the Registration Statement, certain items of which are omitted or included in condensed form as permitted by the Rules and Regulations of the Commission. Statements contained herein as to the contents of any contract or other document are not necessarily complete, and in each instance reference is hereby made to the copy of such contract or other document filed as an Exhibit to the Registration Statement, each such statement being qualified in all respects by such reference.

Copies of the Registration Statement may be obtained from the Commission on payment of the prescribed charges.

I. GENERAL NATURE OF THE OFFERING

1. GRAYBAR BUILDING ASSOCIATES ("Associates") is a partnership consisting of Lawrence A. Wien and William F. Purcell. It has contracted to purchase a net lease of the Graybar Building, 420 Lexington Avenue, New York City, for $4,000,000 in cash.

The net lease to be purchased by Associates is referred to as the "Leasehold" in this Prospectus.

2. The Metropolitan Life Insurance Company is the Lessor under the Leasehold, and Associates will be its Lessee. The Metropolitan recently paid $18,000,000 for its position as Lessor.

3. The term of the Leasehold extends to May 30, 1976, but Associates has renewal options to the year 2030. Renewal of the Leasehold is automatic upon the giving of appropriate notice by Associates and does not require the payment of any additional consideration. The Leasehold requires the payment of certain rents, which are described at pages 50–51.

4. Associates will not operate the property. It will purchase the Leasehold subject to an existing Sublease under which Webb & Knapp, Inc., and its wholly-owned subsidiary, Graysler Corporation, operate the premises.

5. The Sublease has a term and renewal options similar to the Leasehold. It provides for the payment by the Sublessees to Associates of an annual net rent in an amount sufficient to enable Associates

EXHIBIT 1 *(Continued)*

(*a*) to pay all rents called for in the Leasehold;

(*b*) to defray administrative costs; and

(*c*) to make a monthly cash distribution to each participant equal to $1,200 per year on each $10,000 Participation during the initial term of the Sublease.

In the event of renewal of the Sublease at the end of the initial term in 1976, the rent payable by the Sublessees is rearranged so that thereafter the cash distribution to participants will be increased to $1,900 per year.

An analysis of such cash distribution and a discussion of the assumptions on which it is calculated appear at pages 56 and 57.

6. The Sublessees pay all expenses connected with the operation of the Graybar Building. The rent payable to Associates will be a net rental, subject only to the expenses listed above. The Sublessees, however, may assign the Sublease under certain conditions, as set forth on page 53, and may then be relieved of further liability. The investment offered hereby should therefore be judged primarily on the basis of the income-producing capacity of the property itself. A summary of operations for the property appears at page 60.

7. Each of the two partners in Associates will himself contribute $10,000 to the partnership capital, and is offering Participations of $2,090,000 in his partnership interest through this Prospectus. The total partnership capital will thus be $4,200,000, which will be used to purchase the Leasehold ($4,000,000), to defray costs incident to the acquisition ($175,000), and to pay the expenses of this offering ($25,000). Purchasers of Participations will share proportionately in the ownership of the partnership interests in Associates, under Participating Agreements with the partners (see pages 54–55).

II. TERMS OF THE OFFERING

1. The offering is being made by the partners in Associates.

2. Offers to purchase Participations will be accepted only from individuals of full age.

3. Each offer to purchase shall be for a minimum of $10,000 or a multiple thereof.

4. A deposit of up to 25 per cent of the price may be required for any Participation. All deposits will be held in Special Account by counsel for Associates, Wien, Lane, Klein & Purcell, 60 East 42d Street, New York, New York.

5. The title closing is scheduled for April 30, 1958, with rights of

EXHIBIT 1 (Continued)

adjournment to May 31 or June 30, 1958. If offers totaling $4,180,000 have not been accepted by June 30, 1958, all deposits will be repaid without interest. This amount, together with the $20,000 contribution of the two partners, is the sum required to make the payment under the purchase contract and defray the costs and expenses noted above.

6. The balance of each Participation will be payable at the office of Wien, Lane, Klein & Purcell, upon demand, at any time after the required amount of offers has been accepted.

III. THE GRAYBAR BUILDING

1. Description

The Graybar Building is one of the largest and best known office buildings in New York City. It occupies the entire city block on the westerly side of Lexington Avenue between 43rd and 44th Streets, in the heart of New York's business center.

The building forms the eastern entrance to the Grand Central Station and provides a broad concourse leading directly to the Main Hall (upper level) of the terminal. It also affords connections to various subway lines and other transit facilities.

Completed in 1927, the Graybar Building is of fireproof, concrete and steel construction and contains 30 stories and penthouse, with ground floor stores and interior shops. It covers a ground area of some 68,400 square feet, has a volume of approximately 16 million cubic feet and a gross floor area of about 1,250,000 square feet. The net rentable area is approximately 971,163 square feet, including store space.

The building is serviced by 32 Otis, signal control, micro-leveling passenger elevators and 2 Otis freight elevators. About 74 per cent of the tenant areas in the building are air-conditioned through 2,060 tons of water-cooled and air-cooled units, of which 315¼ tons are landlord owned. All units utilize permanent electric and water facilities installed by the landlord. Construction of a water cooling system sufficient for the entire building is planned. All requisite piping from the roof down to the second floor has been installed, and one 750-ton cell of the cooling tower has been erected on the roof.

The 406 tenants of the building are of widely diversified types, and include the Great Atlantic and Pacific Tea Company (executive offices), Conde Nast Publications, Inc., the J. Walter Thompson Advertising agency, the Chase Manhattan Bank, the Dictaphone Corporation, American Gas Company and Sun Oil Company.

EXHIBIT 1 *(Continued)*

2. Rental Statistics as of January 1, 1958

Associates is advised that on this date, the building was 99.86 per cent occupied. For the past ten years occupancy percentages were as follows:

1957—99.8%; 1956—99.7%; 1955—99.6%; 1954—99.9%;
1953—99.4%; 1952—99.8%; 1951—99.4%; 1950—98.9%;
1949—98.9%; 1948—98.9%;

On January 1, 1958, the average rate per square foot for the building was $4.61. The total annual rent roll was $4,474,160, exclusive of percentage rentals and tax escalator increases. In addition, leases already executed provide for annual increases amounting to $18,254 beginning in 1958, $5,910 in 1959, and $150,407 in 1960, or a total of $174,571.

On January 1, 1958, the following lease expiration schedule applied:

Year	Square Feet Area	% of Gross Rental Value
1958	102,446	11.06
1959	93,907	11.24
1960	250,447	22.13
1961	153,680	17.88
1962	67,386	6.79
1963	3,539	0.41
1964	8,382	1.17
1965	100,535	11.35
1966	44,174	4.06
1967	29,019	3.66
1970	1,620	0.21
1976	51,082	5.01
Statutory	62,594	4.96
Monthly	1,016	0.07
Total	969,827	100
Vacant	1,336	
	971,163	

The Graybar Building competes with office structures in the Grand Central area and other sections of New York City. In the past five years, new construction has accounted for some 5,800,500 square feet of rentable space in the Grand Central area, which comprises the district between 38th and 50th Street, and Sixth and Second Avenues. Associates is advised that virtually all of this new space is rented, and for the most part is occupied by large tenants under long-term leases. At present, other new buildings under construction are expected to result in approxi-

EXHIBIT 1 (Continued)

mately 3,500,000 square feet of additional space in this area. The greater portion of this space also is reported to be rented at this time.

3. Summary of Operations

A summary, showing the results of operations of the Graybar Building for the five-year period ended December 31, 1957, is set forth at page [60] of this Prospectus.

The total rent payable by the Sublessees to Associates under the Sublease will be $2,540,000 per year during the initial term. As shown in the summary of operations, the net operating revenue from the building in the year 1957 was sufficient to cover this rent, although the net operating revenues for the years prior to 1957 were not. However, neither the 1957 net operating revenues nor those for the previous years are indicative of the present net operating revenue.

For example, the rent roll as of January 1, 1958 was $70,726 more than the total rent collections shown for the year 1957, which in turn were substantially higher than those shown in the summary for prior years. In addition, based upon previous experience, it is expected that approximately $20,000 will be received during the current year for percentage rents and under tax escalator clauses. Also, as indicated above, future rent increases contained in leases already executed, will add approximately $174,571 annually to the rent roll over the next three years.

The present net operating revenues from the building are more than sufficient to cover the rent provided for in the Sublease. Of course, no representation can be made that such net operating revenues necessarily will continue without change in the future since that will depend upon competition and the general state of the economy.

IV. PROPOSED ACQUISITION OF THE LEASEHOLD BY ASSOCIATES

(1) On December 30, 1957, Lawrence A. Wien purchased the Leasehold on the Graybar Building, subject to the Sublease. The purchase was made from Webb & Knapp, Inc., and Graysler Corporation.

(2) The purchase price was $4,000,000, of which Mr. Wien paid $400,000 in cash and the balance by a 6 per cent Mortgage on the Leasehold, maturing July 1, 1958 and prepayable at any time.

(3) On January 22, 1958, Mr. Wien contracted to sell the Leasehold to Associates for $4,000,000 in cash. In addition to the purchase price, Associates will incur expenses of $200,000 in connection with the transactions described in this Prospectus. Thus, its total cost for the Leasehold will be $4,200,000.

EXHIBIT 1 *(Continued)*

(4) The $3,600,000 Leasehold Mortgage will be prepaid and discharged by Mr. Wien on the closing date of the sale to Associates.

(5) The sale is scheduled to close on April 30, 1958, but Associates has the right to adjourn the closing to May 31, 1958, or June 30, 1958.

(6) Until such closing, Mr. Wien will receive on his own behalf the rents paid under the Sublease and will discharge the obligations of the Leasehold and the Leasehold Mortgage. The net return on Mr. Wien's $400,000 investment during the period of his ownership will be $4,167 a month.

V. DESCRIPTION OF THE LEASEHOLD

1. General

(a) The land under the Graybar Building is owned by the New York Central Railroad. Acting through a subsidiary real estate corporation, the railroad created a Ground Lease on the property to May 31, 1976, with renewal options to the year 2030. The original tenant under the Ground Lease built the Graybar Building in 1927.

(b) On December 30, 1957, the then tenant under the Ground Lease created the Leasehold as a net lease of the entire premises for the same term and renewal periods as it had under the Ground Lease, less one day.

(c) Immediately thereafter, Metropolitan Life Insurance Company purchased the position of tenant under the Ground Lease for $18,000,000, and Lawrence A. Wien purchased the position of Lessee of the Leasehold for $4,000,000.

(d) The Leasehold was purchased by Mr. Wien subject to a Sublease, also created on December 30, 1957, under which Webb & Knapp and its wholly-owned subsidiary, Graysler Corporation now operate the Graybar Building as Mr. Wien's Sublessees.

(e) When Associates acquires Mr. Wien's position it will become entitled to receive the rent payable by the Sublessees; the Metropolitan Life Insurance Company will receive the rent called for in the Leasehold; and the New York Central Railroad subsidiary will receive the annual Ground Rent.

2. Important Provisions

The important provisions of the Leasehold are:

(a) The initial term runs to May 30, 1976. By giving written notice,

EXHIBIT 1 *(Continued)*

Associates may renew the Leasehold for three additional terms extending to the year 2030.

(*b*) Upon such notice, renewal of the Leasehold term is automatic. Renewal of the Leasehold also results in a like renewal of the Ground Lease.

(*c*) The Leasehold Rent payable by Associates to Metropolitan Life Insurance Company is $1,620,000 during the initial term. During all renewal periods the Leasehold Rent is $540,000 annually, or a reduction of $1,080,000.

(*d*) Associates, as Lessee, also will be required to pay the Ground Rent to the New York Central Railroad subsidiary. The Ground Rent is $390,000 per year during the initial term of the Leasehold and for each renewal year until 1988. During renewal years from 1988 to 2009, the Ground Rent will be a sum agreed upon by the parties to the Ground Lease or, failing agreement, a sum equal to 5 per cent of the value of the land (considered vacant and unimproved), but not less than $390,000. For the remaining period from 2009 to 2030, the Ground Rent shall be determined by the same formula, but shall not be less than that paid in the prior period.

(*e*) Upon renewal of the Leasehold at the end of the initial term, the total rent payable by Associates (i.e., Leasehold Rent and Ground Rent) will be $930,000 per year.

(*f*) Associates, as Lessee, will be obligated to pay all operating and maintenance expenses, including real estate taxes, make all necessary repairs, maintain insurance coverage of various types and rebuild or replace the building in the event of fire or other casualty.

(*g*) The Lessee also is required to perform all obligations contained in the Ground Lease. Such obligations are the same in all material respects as those contained in the Leasehold itself. The Sublease described below, under which the premises are being operated, imposes upon the Sublessees obligations which are equivalent in all respects to those of Associates under the Leasehold and Ground Lease. The rent payable by the Sublessees includes the funds necessary to meet the Leasehold and Ground Lease rents. The Sublessees also pay all of the operating and maintenance expenses.

(*h*) Associates may assign the Leasehold at any time, without consent of its Lessor, Metropolitan Life Insurance Company, provided the assignment is to a corporation the stock of which is owned equally by its two partners. Consent of the Metropolitan is required for any other type of assignment. In all cases, upon assumption by the assignee of the Leasehold, Associates will be relieved of any further obligaton thereunder.

EXHIBIT 1 *(Continued)*

VI. OPERATION OF THE GRAYBAR BUILDING UNDER THE SUBLEASE

1. Provisions of the Sublease

(*a*) The Sublease is for the same initial term as the Leasehold, less one day and, therefore, extends to May 29, 1976. It has co-extensive renewal privileges.

(*b*) The total annual rent payable to Associates by the Sublessees is $2,540,000 per year to December 31, 1972; $2,530,000 thereafter per year to May 29, 1976; and $1,774,000 per year in the event of renewal at the end of the initial term. This annual rent consists of three parts:

i. a sum sufficient to pay the Leasehold Rent to the Metropolitan Life Insurance Company;
ii. a sum sufficient to pay the Ground Rent to the New York Central subsidiary; and
iii. a basic rent which Associates will use to defray administrative costs and make its cash distributions to participants. This portion of the annual rent payable by the Sublessees will be $530,000 per year to December 31, 1972, $520,000 per year to May 29, 1976, and $844,000 annually during any renewal periods.

(*c*) As previously stated, the annual Leasehold Rent payable to the Metropolitan Life Insurance Company reduces by $1,080,000 at the end of the initial term on May 30, 1976. In the event of a renewal of the Sublease at that time, both Associates and the Sublessees will share in the benefit resulting from this reduction as follows:

Upon any such renewal, the Sublessees will pay an additional $324,000 annually to Associates as basic rent under the Sublease, thus increasing Associates' portion of the total rent from $520,000 to $844,000.

The Sublessees will have the benefit of the remaining $756,000 reduction in the annual Leasehold Rent. Thus, their overall rent obligation, upon a renewal at the end of the initial term, will be reduced from $2,530,000 to $1,774,000.

(*d*) As additional rent, the Sublessees shall pay to Associates one-third of the amount by which the Sublessees' net income derived from the operation of the premises, after payment of operating and maintenance expenses, real estate taxes and all rents, but before amortization of the cost of the Sublease and before income taxes, exceeds $600,000 in any year up to May 31, 1976 and $1,356,000 in any year thereafter.

(*e*) The Sublessees are obligated to pay all operating and maintenance costs and real estate taxes, keep the property in good repair,

EXHIBIT 1 (Continued)

maintain full insurance coverage, rebuild in case of fire or other casualty, and satisfy all other obligations of Associates under the Leasehold.

(*f*) Consent of the Metropolitan Life Insurance Company is required for any assignment of the Sublease, except where the assignment is to a corporation or corporations each stockholder of which owns the same proportionate amount of stock in the Sublessees. Upon compliance with these provisions and the assumption by the assignee of the obligations of the Sublease, the present Sublessees would be relieved of any further obligation thereunder.

2. The Sublessees

In addition to the Graybar Building, Webb & Knapp, Inc., and/or its subsidiary, Graysler Corporation, operate such large New York City office structures, having the following net rentable areas, as: The Equitable Building at 120 Broadway (40 stories—1,215,270 sq. ft.); the Chrysler Building (75 stories—827,724 sq. ft.); Chrysler Building East (32 stories—401,620 sq. ft.); and 1407 Broadway (42 stories—982,000 sq. ft.).

3. Physical Inspections

Helmsley-Spear, Inc., one of New York City's leading real estate management firms, will be retained by Associates to make periodic physical inspections of the building and its equipment, to render reports thereon, and to act as consultant to Associates with respect to any matters arising out of the ownership of the Leasehold. Helmsley-Spear, Inc., will receive $10,000 annually for these services for the period ending December 31, 1972, and $4,000 per annum during the remainder of the initial term and during any renewals of the Leasehold.

VII. FORMATION OF ASSOCIATES

1. Associates was formed in New York, by a written agreement dated January 20, 1958, to purchase the Leasehold on the Graybar Building, subject to the Sublease.

2. Under the partnership agreement, the partners will share equally in all profits and losses of the partnership.

3. The partnership will continue until it shall have disposed of all of its assets. The partnership is not to be interrupted by any other cause, including the death of a partner or assignment of his interest. Provision is made for succession to the interest of a deceased partner by a designee.

EXHIBIT 1 *(Continued)*

4. The consent of both partners is required for any sale, or other transfer of the Leasehold, the modification or renewal of the Leasehold, the making or modification of any mortgage thereon, the making or revision of any lease of the property by the partnership, or the disposal of any partnership asset.

5. Wien, Lane, Klein & Purcell will supervise the operation of the partnership agreement, and will maintain the requisite books and records for the partnership.

VIII. STATUS OF PURCHASERS OF PARTICIPATIONS

1. Participating Agreements

Each of the two partners in Associates will enter into a Participating Agreement with investors contributing $2,090,000 toward the $4,200,000 total required to acquire the property. Each partner also will contribute $10,000 toward the partnership capital.

Each Participating Agreement will create a joint venture among the parties thereto, who will own the particular partner's one-half interest in Associates in proportion to their respective contributions to its total cost. The Agreements will contain the following provisions:

(*a*) The partner will act as "Agent" for the participants in his one-half partnership interest.

(*b*) The participants will share proportionately in all profits or losses realized by the Agent as a partner in Associates. Under New York law, one participant may be liable to a person outside the venture for the full amount of any obligation of the Agent as a partner in Associates or any liability of the partnership. However, in such event he would be entitled to demand and receive pro-rata contributions from his co-participants. As stated previously at page 51, Associates may assign the Leasehold and thereafter be relieved of any further liability thereunder.

(*c*) The Agent may not agree to sell, or transfer the partnership interest or the Leasehold, to make or modify any mortgage thereon, to modify or renew the Leasehold, to make or modify any sublease of the premises, or to dispose of any partnership asset, without the consent of all his participants. However, if participants owning 80 per cent of the Agent's interest consent to any such action, the Agent or his designee shall have the right to purchase the interest of any non-consenting participant at its original cost, less any capital repaid thereon.

(*d*) The Agent will incur no personal liability for any action taken by him, except for wilful misconduct, gross negligence or any liabilities under the Securities Act of 1933.

EXHIBIT 1 (Continued)

(e) Except as above limited, the Agent may bind his participants, and the participants will agree to indemnify him proportionately against any liability arising by reason of his acting as Agent.

(f) The Agent may resign upon accounting to his successor for all funds he has received. He may be removed by the written direction of participants owning at least three-fourths of the Agent's interest.

(g) If the Agent dies, is removed, resigns or is unable to act, he will be succeeded by one of five persons named as successors in each agreement. If no such designee qualifies, the owners of at least three-fourths of the interest shall select the new Agent.

(h) Each joint venture shall continue until it shall have disposed of the entire interest which it owns in Associates. It will not be interrupted by any other cause, including the death of a participant or any transfer of his Participation.

(i) A participant may transfer his Participation in the joint venture to any individual of full age. Any transfer must be of the full Participation owned, unless such Participation exceeds $10,000. In the latter case, the transfer must be in multiples of $5,000, with a minimum transfer of a $10,000 Participation. The transferee must accept the transfer in writing, and duplicate originals of the transfer instruments must be filed with the Agent, before the transfer shall be effective.

(j) Upon the death of a participant, any individual of full age, designated in the decedent's will or by his executor or administrator, may succeed to his Participation. If no such individual qualifies within eight months after date of death, the surviving parties to the joint venture may purchase proportionately the Participation of the decedent, at its original cost, less any capital repaid thereon.

(k) The Agent shall receive no compensation for acting in that capacity.

2. Tax Status of Associates and the Joint Ventures

The status for Federal income tax purposes of Associates and the joint ventures described in this Prospectus has been passed upon by Roswell Magill, Esq., of Cravath, Swaine & Moore, 15 Broad Street, New York City, and by the firm of Stevenson, Paul, Rifkind, Wharton & Garrison, 1614 Eye Street, N.W., Washington, D.C., tax counsel.

Both such counsel have furnished Associates with separate opinions that the members of Associates and of the joint ventures to be formed under the Participating Agreements will qualify as partners for Federal income tax purposes. Therefore, each individual member of Associates and each participant will be taxed on his distributive share of the net

EXHIBIT 1 (*Continued*)

income, but the net incomes of Associates and the joint ventures will not be taxable as such.

Both opinions note that the Treasury Regulations contain provisions under which partnerships or joint ventures may be taxed on their net income in the same manner as corporations and the members thereof may be taxed as shareholders. Each opinion, however, concludes that Associates and the joint ventures involved herein do not fall within the said provisions, and therefore should not be taxable as corporations.

3. Tax Treatment of Cash Distributions to Participants

The following table, which assumes that Associates and the joint ventures will be taxable as partnerships, estimates the aggregate cash income to Associates in each year during the initial term of the Leasehold on the Graybar Building. It also shows the portion of such income distributable to participants under the Participating Agreements.

The rent income shown is based upon the minimum annual net rent provided for in the Sublease to Webb & Knapp, Inc., and Graysler Corporation. The table and the accompanying text below assume that the Sublease will continue in accordance with its terms over all of the years discussed. There is no assurance that the foregoing assumptions necessarily will hold true, but if such rent is paid and Associates and the joint ventures are taxable as partnerships, the following information is applicable:

Rent Income.....................................		$2,540,000.00
Expenses:		
Rent Expense (consisting of $1,620,000 Lease-		
hold Rent and $390,000 Ground Rent).........	$2,010,000.00	
Legal, accounting and consultant's fees........	26,000.00	
		$2,036,000.00
Net Receipts, before Leasehold Amortization....		$ 504,000.00
Leasehold Amortization, write-off over 18 years		
and one month, 5.53% of $4,200,000............		$ 232,258.00
Net Receipts allocable to Participants for Federal		
income tax purposes.........................		$ 271,742.00
Cash Available for Distribution		
Total (Net Receipts, before Leasehold Amortiza-		
tion, as above)...............................		$ 504,000.00
Per $10,000 Participation.........................		1,200.00

The cash available for distribution, shown in the table, will represent both income, and to the extent of annual Leasehold amortization, a return of capital. That portion which represents a return of capital will

EXHIBIT 1 *(Continued)*

not be reportable as income for Federal income tax purposes. On this basis, each $1,200 cash distribution will consist of $647 which constitutes reportable income, and $553 representing a non-taxable return of capital. Although each such return of capital constitutes a partial reduction of the cost of the investment, it does not in any way change the proportionate interest of each participant in Associates.

Deducting the return of capital from the original cost, the rate of income on the remaining invested capital increases each year. The average invested capital over the initial term of the Sublease is $2,100,000, or $5,000 per minimum Participation. The rate of income on the average invested capital over the initial term is 12.94%. Of course, these calculations are based on the assumption that the Sublease will continue and that the rent provided for will be paid throughout the initial term of 18 years and one month.

At the end of the initial term on May 30, 1976, the cost of the Leasehold will have been fully amortized and, thereafter, the entire amount of cash distributed annually in the event of any renewal of the Leasehold will be reportable as income. It should be noted that renewal of the Leasehold by Associates is automatic upon the giving of appropriate notice and does not require the payment of additional consideration.

As heretofore stated, the rent requirements of both the Leasehold and Sublease will change in the event of their renewal at the end of the initial term. In such case, Associates' Rent Income will be $1,774,000 and its Rent Expense will be $930,000. Legal, accounting and consultants' fees will be $46,000 per year during any renewal terms. Thus, upon any such renewal, the cash available for annual distribution to each $10,000 participant will be increased to $1900, all of which will constitute income.

In the above discussion, amortization has been calculated in accordance with present tax law. On January 20, 1958, the House of Representatives passed a bill which would change the law and could require that the cost of a renewable lease be amortized over both the original and renewal terms. This bill has not yet been enacted into law, but is pending before a Senate Committee for its consideration. If enacted, the bill would in no way change the amount of the yearly cash distributions described above. The only effect of the bill could be to decrease the amounts treated as non-taxable return of capital and increase the amounts treated as taxable income during the initial term. However, if this occurred, a portion of the cash distributions received during renewal periods would be treated as a return of capital, which is not the case under the amortization schedule which Associates presently plan to use. Thus, the total amount treated as a return of capital would not be

EXHIBIT 1 (Continued)

affected by the proposed legislation. At this time, no prediction can be made as to whether or when the bill may become law.

IX. INFORMATION AS TO PARTNERS IN ASSOCIATES

1. Biographical

Lawrence A. Wien, Newtown Turnpike, Weston, Connecticut, is a graduate of Columbia College and Columbia Law School, and has been practicing law in New York City since 1928. He is the senior partner in the firm of Wien, Lane, Klein & Purcell. He has specialized in the field of real estate law for over twenty-six years and has been particularly active in creating investments in real property. Such investments include the Hotel Taft at Seventh Avenue and 50th Street, the Equitable Building at 120 Broadway, the Lincoln Building at 60 East 42nd Street, the Garment Center Capitol Buildings at 498, 500 and 512 Seventh Avenue, the Fisk Building at 250 West 57th Street, and the Broad-Exchange Building at 25 Broad Street, all in New York City, and the Warwick Hotel in Philadelphia.

William F. Purcell, 930 Fifth Avenue, New York City, is a graduate of Manhattan College and Fordham Law School, has been a member of the Bar of the State of New York since 1935 and is a partner in the firm of Wien, Lane, Klein & Purcell.

2. Remuneration and Interest in Transactions Described Herein

Wien, Lane, Klein & Purcell, as counsel for Associates, will be paid an annual fee to supervise the operation of the partnership agreement, from which sum they must defray all regular accounting costs and disbursements. Such fee will be $16,000 per year until December 31, 1972, $12,000 per year from January 1, 1973 to May 31, 1976, and $42,000 per year during all renewal periods.

Of the $200,000 to be used by Associates to defray expenses in connection with the transactions described herein, the firm will receive a legal fee now estimated at approximately $125,000.

As more fully set forth at page 50, Associates will purchase the Leasehold from Mr. Wien.

X. LEGAL OPINIONS

The legality of the Participations, and other matters of New York State law relating to this offering, have been passed upon by Wien, Lane,

EXHIBIT 1 *(Continued)*

Klein & Purcell, 60 East 42nd Street, New York, New York. Legal matters in connection with the Securities Act of 1933 have been passed upon by Milton P. Kroll, Esq., Cafritz Building, Washington, D.C. Questions relating to the status for federal income tax purposes of Associates and the joint ventures created under the Participating Agreements have been passed upon by Roswell Magill, Esq., of Cravath, Swaine & Moore, New York, New York, and by the firm of Stevenson, Paul, Rifkind, Wharton & Garrison, Washington, D.C.

CERTIFICATE OF INDEPENDENT PUBLIC ACCOUNTANTS

We have examined the summary of operations of the Graybar Building, New York, New York, for the five years ended December 31, 1957, during which years the property was leased by Eastern Offices, Inc. for the period from January 1, 1953 to October 9, 1953 and thereafter to the extent of an undivided 75% interest by Webb & Knapp, Inc., or its wholly-owned subsidiary, 65039 Corporation, and to the extent of an undivided 25% interest by Graysler Corporation. Our examinations were made in accordance with generally accepted auditing standards, and accordingly included such tests of the accounting records and such other auditing procedures as we considered necessary in the circumstances.

In our opinion, the summary of operations presents fairly the income from property operations of the Graybar Building, New York, New York, for the five years ended December 31, 1957, before deducting mortgage interest, depreciation and amortization, Federal income and State franchise taxes and other expenses, as noted thereon, in conformity with generally accepted accounting principles applied on a consistent basis.

HARRIS, KERR, FORSTER & COMPANY

New York, New York
March 6, 1958

EXHIBIT 1 (*Concluded*)

Graybar Building, New York, N.Y.

(summary of operations)

	Years Ended				
	December 31, 1953	December 31, 1954	December 31, 1955	December 31, 1956	December 31, 1957
Income from Property Operations:					
Rental Income (including Percentage Rents)	$3,326,820.36	$3,479,537.07	$3,725,469.52	$4,087,447.83	$4,403,434.34
Other Charges to Tenants and Other Income (Note B)	438,427.09	471,452.85	407,816.25	775,400.19	1,012,526.39
Total Income	$3,765,247.45	$3,950,989.92	$4,133,285.77	$4,862,848.02	$5,415,960.73
Deduct:					
Operating Expenses Exclusive of Items Below (Note C)	$1,673,346.87	$1,638,861.55	$1,550,019.88	$1,988,192.70	$2,319,425.79
Payroll Taxes	26,885.66	25,718.21	25,845.12	26,766.62	39,415.07
Maintenance and Repairs (Note D)	—	—	—	—	—
Real Estate Taxes	420,323.69	477,603.98	476,591.86	498,124.88	508,438.22
Total	$2,120,556.22	$2,142,183.74	$2,052,456.86	$2,513,084.20	$2,867,279.08
Operating Income before Mortgage Interest, Depreciation and Amortization, Federal Income and State Franchise Taxes, Corporate Expenses and Rental under Basic Ground Lease or Leases Effective December 30, 1957	$1,644,691.23	$1,808,806.18	$2,080,828.91	$2,349,763.82	$2,548,681.65

Notes:

A. The above statement has been prepared from income statements of the present and prior lessees for the applicable periods which have been restated to reflect a net refund of real estate taxes of $12,122.70 applicable to the year 1954 which was received in 1955.

B. Other Charges to Tenants and Other Income include gross billings for electricity, supplies and work orders chargeable to tenants and also commissions on towel service, telephone booths, etc. The fluctuations in "Other Charges to Tenants and Other Income" reflected in the above summary are due primarily to billings on tenant work orders. Prior to 1954 no separate record of such billings or the costs pertaining thereto were maintained, nor are they readily determinable. Gross billings on tenants' work orders amounted to $182,206 in 1954, $74,966 in 1955, $357,350 in 1956 and $597,399 in 1957.

  The costs applicable to such tenants' work orders were in large measure responsible for the fluctuations in "Operating Expenses" shown in the summary. These costs were $106,940 in 1954, $38,087 in 1955, $240,975 in 1956 and $453,733 in 1957. The only other major variation was in salaries and wages which increased $139,104 in 1956 when compared with 1955.

C. Operations for the period from January 1, 1953 to October 9, 1953 include a fee based on collections which covered both management and renting services. Operations after October 9, 1953 include management fees and leasing commissions, computed at standard New York City Real Estate Board rates for commercial properties. The leasing commissions are charged into operations on a pro-rata basis over the term of the individual tenants' leases.

D. Maintenance and repairs are reflected in wages and other building expenses and are not separately classified as such in the accounts or readily determinable.

EXHIBIT 2

Advantages of Real Estate Syndicates*

I. GENERAL INTRODUCTION

Before large-scale real-estate syndication developed, investment in high-priced real estate was confined almost exclusively to the large real estate firms and the well-heeled speculators. During the past decade, however, there has been a rapidly growing tendency for some of these properties to be owned by small investors, who pool their cash in real estate syndicates. It has been estimated that the number of these organizations has more than tripled within the past five years, reaching a total of about $9 billion today. The popularity of such organizations has not been confined to New York alone. Syndicates are being formed in nearly every state in the Union—they control such diverse properties as housing developments, shopping centres, apartment houses, hotels, ship terminals, and even undeveloped land.

The real estate syndicate has many features which are particularly attractive to the investor. As regards the all-important rate of return on investment, 8%–15% is typical, compared to an average yield of 3.2% on Standard & Poor's 500 stock index in a recent typical month. Further, much of the syndicate's return is tax free because of tax shelters offered by high depreciation rates; in reality, it is a return of capital. Other tax savings can be realized by organizing the syndicate in one of the many non-corporate forms outlined in this report. In this way the double tax on dividends is eliminated, i.e., there is no corporate tax.

Aside from tax advantages, a small investor can now put his funds into a real estate venture. Previously, he would have been effectively barred from entry into the field because of his own lack of knowledge regarding real estate transactions and his inability to properly evaluate the earnings capacity of a property. Now his capital can be entrusted to a syndicator, whose previous success in real estate lends confidence to the view that an ample return on investment, as well as protection of capital, will be realized. The investor may feel a further psychological security in the idea that he is investing in something which is tangible and quite durable, quite in contrast to the feelings that many investors have regarding corporate securities, which seem to be quite intangible and subject to the violent and arbitrary actions of the stock market.

Finally, the investor may now diversify his holdings more readily. On one level, he may hold interests in real estate along with his investments in corporate securities, government bonds, and insurance. On a second

---

* This is a description prepared in 1960 by a large New York syndicator for distribution to his clients.

EXHIBIT 2 *(Continued)*

level, his real estate holdings may be diversified by purchasing units in several *different* pieces of syndicate-controlled property. It must be noted, however, that diversification for its own sake is not desirable; *each* part of the portfolio should be purchased with a view to its own protection against capital loss, and an adequate rate of return. With the application of this criteria, a greater source of strength can be found with a diversified portfolio.

II. LEGAL FORMS OF ORGANIZATION

A. Introduction

How are syndicates formed? What are their particular legal forms, and how can they be varied? This section discusses the status of partnerships, limited partnerships, trusts, syndicates, and other unincorporated organizations in relation to their taxability as corporations or "associations taxable as corporations" for Federal income tax purposes.

"Real estate syndicate" generically describes innumerable forms of legal organization. The basic theme of most syndicates is nevertheless strikingly similar. Typically, after acquiring on option or contract on suitable income-producing property (occasionally syndicators are the original owners of the property they syndicate), subject to depreciation allowances, the syndicator pools available funds for combined investment. Individually designed and "tailor-made" to satisfy financial, management, tax, and other considerations, syndicates can take a multitude of forms. The final selection should best fulfill the desires of the interested parties. Generally, the problem for attorneys is developing a form of legal entity containing maximum corporate attributes which is not subject to corporate double taxation. Determination of which of the resembling elements to omit, modify, or temper is crucial.

The ever-present problem is determining whether a particular organization contains *all the salient features of corporateness*. Organizations which do not possess *all the salient features of corporateness* are not subject to double taxation. Therefore, organizations which omit even one salient beneficial feature of corporate entities are not taxed as corporations or as "associations taxable as corporations."

Fortunately, inability to be dogmatic in articulating definite rules, or positively to predict results, does not prevent a critical appraisal of tested plans, nor of those plans currently used by experienced syndicators. It is significant that most syndicators are currently conducting operations, as they have for some time, without being subjected to corporate double taxation.

EXHIBIT 2 (Continued)

B. Limited Partnerships

Limited partnerships are now the most popular form for operations in the real estate syndicate field. This form is ideally adapted for raising venture capital in a noncorporate form while providing the limited partner (as contrasted to the general partner) with immunity from further personal liability. Limited partnership syndicates, which more nearly resemble the salient features of partnerships than corporations, are not taxable as corporations. Under limited partnership agreements, property is generally held in the name of the partnership subject to the control of the several general partners (this latter group usually consists of the syndicator and several heavily invested limited partners). The "conduction of business activities," which is so crucial an issue in the trust field, is not of particular importance in limited partnerships. Limited partnerships are, therefore, not only capable of holding property under long-term and/or net leases, but they may also conduct the business of renting property on its own account. The key issues in this area center on "continuity of operation" and centralization of control by management in a representative capacity, similar to that of a corporation.

C. Joint Ventures

Joint ventures, treated as partnerships for tax purposes, differ somewhat from general partnerships. The duration and scope of activities is more limited in joint ventures. Otherwise, partnership and joint venture law is basically identical.

The following are some key provisions of the participating agreements:

1. Each participating agreement creates a joint venture among the parties for the ownership of the particular senior venturer's interest. Each participant owns an undivided fractional part of this interest based upon the amount that he has contributed to the cost of the property. The joint venture *continues* until the property is disposed of.
2. The participants share proportionately in all profits and losses realized by the senior venturer from whom they purchased their participations. Any one participant may be liable to a person outside the venture for the full amount of any obligation to which his senior venturer may be subject by reason of his ownership in the property. The potential liability assumed by participants is enormous in scope. Certainly the agreement should base liability on a pro rata basis. Limited liability is not, though most people do not realize it, a material characteristic

EXHIBIT 2 (*Continued*)

of "associations taxable as corporations." The personal liability, remote as it may be, is at best undesirable. Here, the agreement creates individual liabilities beyond imagination. With liability of participants being unimportant for favorable tax treatment, should the provision be modified?

3. Record title to the interest in the property remains in the name of the senior venturers. Each senior venturer acts as "agent" for his participants and distributes among them each month the money received from Associates (or collects from them, if there is a loss, as the case may be.)

III. FINANCIAL OPERATIONAL PROBLEMS

A. Depreciation

Depreciation is designed, by accounting principles, to allocate the initial cost disbursement for acquiring depreciable property to an appropriate period. Dollar depreciation (when it includes allowances for absolescence) assumes, for its own purposes, that properties are reduced in dollar value with age. Experience from 1941 to 1958 indicated contrary results. Property values, excluding consideration of bargain purchases, increased substantially. These surplus values were in part created by inflation and increased population pressures. Private realty investors, syndicators included, have capitalized on the favorable conditions existing since 1941. While depreciation dollars, representing partial reduction of investment in property, were nontaxable, the real return values in investment equities (in the form of unrealized appreciation) increased substantially. These tax-sheltered benefits were available for later realization with minimum tax as long-term capital gain. If appreciated property is held by the owner for his life, there is no tax on the unrealized gain. Following death, beneficiaries of appreciated property receive a cost basis freed of decedent's original cost (typically low), and the new basis is the then fair market value (typically high) at the time of the original owner's decease.

The official position of the Revenue Service allows taxpayers to appraise a reasonable allowance representing exhaustion, wear and tear, and obsolescence for depreciable property. Allowances reasonably determined, based on a rational basis, may consider present and anticipated developments (including population and business trends). The useful life inherent in an asset is the period over which the asset may reasonably be expected to be useful to the taxpayer, not the physical life of the property, e.g., an office building with a physical life of 75–100 years can

EXHIBIT 2 (Continued)

be depreciated over its 40 years of useful life. Another official Revenue Service position is to adjust taxpayers' estimated depreciation deductions only where there is a clear and convincing basis for a substantial adjustment, i.e., clearly erroneous.

Allocation of Price between Land and Buildings

Allocating the total purchase price between land and building is the first discretionary process in establishing depreciation schedules. Invariably, syndicators in determining allocations emphasize building and not land values. That is because only portions allocated to the building can produce annual depreciation to offset income (in extraordinary cases taxpayers are allowed obsolescence deductions on land by showing material drops in value and a reduced number of purposes for which the property can be used). Portions allocable to land provide relatively slight tax benefit. The emphasis on building values is therefore obvious.

Once an allocation of cost to building is made, a subsequent alternative in scheduling is permissible. Amounts allocated to buildings can be depreciated at an average rate, or can be broken down to component parts with individual schedules:

1. Air conditioning	5. Plumbing
2. Heating system	6. Roofing
3. Elevators	7. Telephone equipment
4. Lighting systems	8. Etc.

Effects of Alternative Depreciation Methods

Depreciable amounts are analogous to a reserve of expenses which can be used (within certain discretionary limitations) when desired by taxpayers as tax deductions; more now and less later, or less now and more later. The problem is in deciding how much to use now. By proper planning, timing of deductions can significantly minimize taxes.

Straight-line depreciation—is only one basically acceptable method for depreciating real estate. Equal amounts are taken each year for the entire estimated economic life of the property. At the end of the estimated life, depreciation is ended.

Declining balance at 200%—Newly constructed property (after December 31, 1953) held by the original user is allowed more liberal depreciation allowances than under any other depreciating scheme. This method allows depreciation at 200% of the usual straight-line percentage in the first year. This basic percentage remains constant and is afterwards applied to a consistently declining balance. Because of the restrictions to new property, this favorable provision is rarely, if ever, totally and presently available for syndicated properties, i.e., syndicates are

EXHIBIT 2 (Continued)

rarely original users of newly constructed property, except to the extent of new improvements. Syndicate operation is more favorable on properties having substantial unrealized appreciation and established earning power, than on speculative newly constructed property. As indicated below, however, the larger the rate of declining balance taken, the higher the return to the syndicate (other things being equal).

Declining balance at 150%—is another basically accepted method for depreciating real estate. Declining balance at 150% frequently produces more desirable results than straight line. This method requires determination of the straight-line percentage to which 50% additional is added.

The following schedule illustrates an annual depreciation allowance on a $1,000,000 building (excluding land cost) over an estimated 25-year life by straight-line and declining balance at 150%:

Year	Straight Line	Declining Balance—150%*
1.	$40,000	$60,000
2.	"	56,400
3.	"	53,000
4.	"	49,800
5.	"	46,800
6.	"	44,000
7.	" (Turning Point)	41,400
8.	"	38,900
9.	"	36,600
10.	$40,000	34,400

* Adjusted to nearest $100.

As demonstrated by the table, the initial 7½ years are more favorable under the declining-balance method. When syndicators use straight line their justification is usually long-range planning. Their experience indicates the investor's willingness to receive more stable taxable income at the cost of paying more taxes currently than would be required under declining balance.

Constant Payment Mortgages

Depreciation scheduling is substantially affected when mortgage service charges require constant payments. Constant payment mortgages are mortgages which provide for payments for a term of years at constant annual amounts. Of this constant amount, annual mortgage payments

EXHIBIT 2 (Continued)

represent continually decreasing amounts of interest and continually increasing portions of amortization.

Illustration. The following schedule demonstrates basic effects of constant *annual* payments on $1,000,000 mortgage at 5% interest and 5% amortization. With quarterly payments the effect is more dramatic.

Year	Balance at 12/31	Interest	Amortization	Annual Payment
1.................	$950,000	$50,000	$50,000	$100,000
2.................	897,500	47,500	52,500	"
3.................	842,375	44,875	55,125	"
4.................	784,495	42,120	57,880	"
5.................	723,720	39,225	60,775	"
6.................	659,906	36,186	63,814	"
7.................	592,901	32,995	67,005	"
8.................	522,546	29,645	70,355	"
9.................	448,673	26,127	73,873	"
10................	371,106	22,434	77,567	$100,000

B. Leverage

Syndicates can literally create investments to satisfy particular investor groups. Each of the following illustrations necessarily varies in investment leverage and character. Each schedule represents a real syndicate recently organized. In each situation participating interests sold at $10,000 and provided an estimated annual distribution of $1200.

Syndicate	No. 1	No. 2	No. 3
Annual cash receipts................	$1,200	$1,200	$1,200
Taxable income.....................	835	312	None
Tax-free return.....................	365	888	1,200*
Total........................	$1,200	$1,200	$1,200

* Plus some slight additional tax loss to offset other ordinary income.

Syndicate No. 1 has 33⅓% debt (thereby providing relative stability), No. 2 has 46% debt. Figures on percentage of debt on No. 3 were unavailable, but is probably 60% or more of the total investment. On the assumption of all things being otherwise equal (which is never the case), interest of high-bracket taxpayers will naturally tend more towards the tax-free return of No. 3, rather than No. 1 or No. 2. Security prone investors, requiring less investment leverage and greater security will be

EXHIBIT 2 (Continued)

more interested in No. 1. Syndicate No. 1 is also suitable for high-income earners seeking stable investments to be held in trust for dependents. Syndicate No. 2 could well be characterized as the businessman's investment. The degree of leverage and risk are the essential factors in determining to which group an investor is attracted.

Listed below are a number of reasons why values are stabilized on the downside:

1. Syndicated properties frequently involve long-term leases which provide stable long-term rental income.
2. Syndicators are fairly astute analysts; values frequently exceed original cost.
3. Syndicators must maintain prices to protect reputation and future offerings.
4. Unless older participations returning $1,200 distributions annually are worth $10,000, new offerings returning $1,200 are difficult to sell at $10,000.

The pressure to maintain prices forces syndicators to discourage trading of interest at less than original price. Investors are discouraged by syndicators refusing disclosure of potential buyers listed with them unless the buyer offers original cost. This somewhat artificial pressure even extends to independent brokers interested in completing sales.

Conclusion

Existing conditions are such that most participants are long-term investors. Unless extreme pressure is placed on rapid liquidation, participants may continue to enjoy relatively high yields, security, marketability, and liquidity of real estate syndication.

Restrictions and limitations of sale in syndicate agreements (which increase internal control) limit the free transferability of interests. Unless a broker is aware of these intricate provisions and niceties contained in a syndicate agreement, he is seriously handicapped. For example,

Substituted Limited Partner—18 (a) No assignee of the whole or any portion of a Limited Partner's interest in the Partnership shall have the right to become a Substituted Limited partner in place of his assignor, unless (i) his assignor shall designate such intention in the instrument of assignment, and (ii) the written consent of the General Partner to such substitution shall be obtained, the granting or denial of which shall be the sole and absolute discretion of such a General Partner.

Additional restrictions take the form of first options to buy, option of first refusal, etc. As a general matter, these provisions are seldom relied upon and participations are freely transferable. Syndicates avoid representing interests with negotiable certificates for a very practical reason. Under current law, whether interests are represented by negotiable certificate is probably of no effect in determining taxability of syndicates as partnerships rather than as "associations taxable as corporations." The reason for avoiding this feature, therefore, is self-restraint in avoiding corporate similarity. The balancing benefit of free transferability of interests is not particularly significant to long-term investors. Another consideration for syndication may be to avoid loss of control.

IV. PROBLEMS OF DISCLOSURE

Syndicators are gradually being conditioned to regulation either by state authorities or by the S.E.C. Whether "interests of participation in a Limited Partnership" are "securities" controllable by the S.E.C. under current law is an interesting question. Suffice it to say, as of this time the S.E.C. is not exerting direct effects on syndicates. Realtors generally rely on restricting sales to "Single States" to avoid regulation. The only sign indicating possible exercise of regulation is a statement by Paul Windels, Jr., head of the S.E.C.'s New York office. Mr. Windels claims, "syndicates are subject to regulation if the syndicated property lies outside the state of organization, if a major tenant or leaseholder lies outside the state, or even if any investors live outside the state."

NORTH DAKOTA
HOTEL PLAN
Syndications—Public
Investment—Motel

PRELIMINARY STATEMENT

North Dakota Hotel Plan, Inc. (hereinafter interchangeably referred to as "the company" or by the pronouns "we," "us," and "our") is making this offering only to legal residents of the state of North Dakota under the exemption from registration permitted by Section 3(a) (11) of the Federal Securities Act of 1933.

Statements contained in this Offering Circular as to the contents of any contract or other documents referred to are not necessarily complete and whenever, in connection with any such statement, reference is made to such contract or other document, each such reference is deemed to be qualified and amplified in all respects by the contract or other document referred to. Such contract or document is on file in our office where it may be examined by appointment.

HISTORY AND PURPOSE OF OFFERING

On March 1st, 1957, our affiliate, Portfolio Management, Inc., acquired title to the North Dakota Hotel with some additional vacant land, pursuant to a written contract of purchase dated September 19th, 1956, entered into with the then owner. The purchase price under said contract by Portfolio Management, Inc., was $760,000.

Such purchase was an "arm's-length" transaction. None of the stockholders, directors or officers of the then owner-seller was or is affiliated in any way with any Portfolio Management, Inc.

By deed dated and acknowledged October 10th, 1957, Portfolio Management, Inc., conveyed title to the property to North Dakota Hotel Plan, Inc., the Issuer of this offering. The purchase price was $820,800, which gave the seller, The Portfolio Management, Inc., a profit of $60,800, equal to 8% on the original purchase price of $760,000 out of which the seller is paying to its affiliate, the Portfolio Real Estate Plan, Inc., a real estate brokerage commission of $15,200, which is equal to 2% on said original purchase price.

Acquisition of title to said property by this company is not an "arm's-length" transaction is that it involved "self-dealing" between affiliates.

The terms of the contract under which this company acquired title to the property, and the arrangements for payment to Portfolio Management, Inc., as seller, of the purchase price, involved, are described elsewhere in this circular [page 84].

The purpose of this offering is to finance our acquisition of title to this property, subject to a first mortgage, held by the Dollar Savings Bank of North Dakota, in the original amount of $250,000 and reduced, as of October 10th, 1957, to $228,307.15.

Details as to the manner in which the gross proceeds of this offering amounting to $700,000 is to be disbursed are furnished under the caption of this circular "Application of Proceeds" [pages 83–84].

DESCRIPTION OF UNITS

7,000 8% Escalator Interest Rate Debentures at $50 face amount, to provide a total of $350,000. Secured by pledge of all of the Common Stock of the company under a Trust Indenture:

1. Debentures mature 10 years from date.
2. Constant quarterly interest distributions totaling $4 a year on each debenture. Equivalent to 8% on $50 face amount the first year and rising in subsequent years to 10% in 10th year.
3. Constant quarterly principal payments totaling $1 a year. This is equivalent to a 2% return of principal the first year and rises to 2½% in the 10th year.
4. $40 lump-sum principal payment at end of 10th year.

7,000 6% Cumulative Participating Preferred Stock at $50 Par Value each, to provide a total of $350,000:

1. Quarterly preferred dividends totaling $3 a year on each share. Equivalent to 6% on $50 par value.
2. Dividends of 6% a year are cumulative.
3. Preference in dividends over common stock up to the first $8 a year on each share (equivalent to 16% on $50 par value) when, as and if declared.
4. Participation with common stock to the extent of 50% of any dividends in excess of $8 a share on each share of preferred stock, when, as and if declared.
5. Preference to the extent of $50 per share on liquidation or dissolution and participation with common stock to the extent of 75% of any surplus above $50 per share and unpaid cumulative dividends on preferred stock.

In addition to the securities described hereinabove, the authorized capital stock of the company includes 200 shares of common stock without par value, owned by its affiliate, The Portfolio Management, Inc., which shares of stock were issued to Portfolio Management, Inc., for the cash consideration of $1,000 and as part consideration for its transfer of title to the company of the North Dakota Hotel properties described below.

The common stock is the voting stock of the company. However, it has been pledged as security for the payment of the debentures under a legal instrument designed as a "Trust Indenture," under which the Trustee will hold the common stock as collateral with the power to sell or acquire such common stock for the benefit of the debenture holders upon the occurrence of certain contingencies provided for in the Trust Indenture, including any default with reference to the payment of principal or interest on the debentures.

The voting rights are vested in the owners of the common stock until and unless the corporation shall have failed to pay dividends of at least 6% to the holders of the preferred stock for any period of two consecutive years. In such event, all voting rights are transferred to the preferred stockholders where they remain until dividend arrears have been fully paid, at which time voting rights revert to the common stockholders.

At this point, we consider that it might be helpful if we acquaint you with the meaning of the terms "debentures," "cumulative preferred stock" and "capital stock."

In its essence, a debenture evidences a loan to a corporation, which is usually unsecured.

Debenture holders have an advantage over stockholders because interest on the debentures is an obligation of the corporation which legally takes preference over dividends on capital stock and must be paid before net income allocable to dividends is determined.

The capital stock of a corporation represents the ownership of that corporation.

As the owner of a share of stock you own a part of the corporation, which entitles you to share in its profits, through dividends, and in its growth if the value of your stock should increase.

There are two types of capital stock—"preferred" stock and "common" stock.

As a holder of 6% "preferred" stock, the dividends due you must be paid before any dividends can be declared on "common" stock.

The fact that, under the Plan, such dividends are payable to you on a "cumulative" basis means that if the earnings of the corporation are insufficient in any one year to provide for a declaration of 6% dividends to preferred stockholders, the difference is added to the preferred dividends payable the next year.

You will please bear in mind that dividends can be declared only out of corporate surplus or net earnings legally available for the payment thereof.

An examination of our 10-Year Projection [page 82] establishes, on the basis of the continuance of assumptions underlying such projection, that there should be corporate net earnings available to meet interest (8%) and principal (2%) payments required on your debenture and the minimum dividends (6%) called for by your preferred stock.

While repayment of the debenture loan that you are making to this corporation under this offering is not secured, in view of the fact, however, that the sole business of the corporation involves the ownership of this hotel, operated by a tenant under a net lease, and in view of the further fact that no part of the corporation's income is used to pay officers or employees' salaries (except those expenses indicated on the said 10-year Projection), we think that your position as a debenture-creditor of this corporation, of which you are a part owner, furnishes you with reasonable protection.

As we have previously emphasized, an affiliate, Portfolio Management, Inc., is the owner of the outstanding 200 shares of common stock, which has been pledged and is being held by the Trustee as security for the payment of the debentures.

Dividends payable to the common stockholders, when, as, and if declared, some out of the excess in net income above $8 per share of preferred stock to the extent of 50%. In other words, you receive the first $8 on each share of your preferred stock out of the net earnings of the corporation available for dividend distribution. Should net earnings exceed $8 a share on each outstanding share of preferred stock, then and only in such event do the common stockholders participate in such excess net earnings of the corporation and only to the extent of 50% thereof, the other 50% being payable to the preferred stockholders on a pro rata basis as additional "participating" preferred dividends.

When, as, and if this property should be resold, then the corporation would be dissolved and liquidated, and you would, in the normal course of events, receive the balance due you on your debenture plus 8% interest, together with any unpaid cumulative dividends, plus your original preferred stock investment of $50 per share, and, in addition, 75% of any remaining surplus, the balance of 25% of such remaining surplus going to the holders of the common stock.

HOW THIS NORTH DAKOTA HOTEL PLAN OPERATES

This is how your investment will work if you invest $1,000 for the purchase of 10 units in this Plan offering.

Five hundred dollars of your purchase price will buy 10 shares of preferred stock and the remaining $500 will purchase a $500 debenture.

You will then receive:

Quarterly distributions totaling $40 per year (8%)
as interest on your debenture;
Quarterly distributions totaling $10 per year (2%)

as reduction of your debenture; and
Quarterly distributions totaling $30 per year (6%)
on your preferred stock.

Thus, you will receive a total of $80.

Although your debenture yield starts out at the rate of 8% a year, it escalates up to 10% a year during the 10th year because notwithstanding the reduction of $10 a year on your debenture, the amount of interest that you receive remains the same ($40 per year), and consequently your yield escalates upward. Thus, in 10 years the balance on your debenture is $400 on which you are receiving $40 interest, which is a 10% yield.

The value of your preferred stock should increase in proportion to payments made in reduction of your debenture plus payments made in reduction of the first mortgage, on the assumption, however, as to which no guarantees can be made that the market value of the property will be the same as its original acquisition cost.

The 10-year chart below illustrates the amount of reduction of the principal amount of the debentures and the mortgage, together with a projection estimating the capital growth of your preferred stock.

Year	Debenture	Debenture Reduction	Mortgage Reduction	Estimated Value of Preferred Stock
Start	$500			$500
1	490	$10	$20	531
2	480	10	21	561
3	470	10	22	593
4	460	10	23	626
5	450	10	24	660
6	440	10	25	695
7	430	10	27	732
8	420	10	28	770
9	410	10	29	809
10	400	10	31	850

Our projection estimating the value of your 10 shares of preferred stock at $850 after 10 years would indicate a capital growth of $350, which is reduced to $262.50 because of the 25% participation therein by the common stockholders. Let it be again repeated, however, that said growth projection is based on the assumption, as to which no assurances can be given, that the market value of this property after 10 years will be at least the amount of its acquisition cost.

Now, let us look at your investment picture 10 years hence.

You have received a total of $800 in cash ($80 a year), and there remains a balance due you on your debenture of $400, payable to you in one lump sum, and you still have your preferred stock, which originally cost you $500.

At the end of the 10th year you will become entitled to a lump sum of $400 in payment of the balance due on your debenture, and, in addition, you will still be the owner of 10 shares of preferred stock.

Dividends on your 10 shares of preferred stock would be paid to you to the extent of all of the first $80 of net earnings, if available for dividend declaration, which would be the equivalent of a 16% yield on your original $500 preferred stock cost.

And, in addition, you will have a pro rata interest in 50% of excess net earnings, if any, above $80.

With reference to the source from which the company will be able to pay you the balance of $400 due you on your debenture at maturity, it will be necessary for the company to either (*a*) raise such amount via the mortgage route (please bear in mind that at the end of 10 years there will be a balance of only $55,000 outstanding on the original $250,000 first mortgage and the balance due on the entire debenture loan issue will then be $280,000), or (*b*) if a large enough mortgage cannot be obtained, it will be necessary for the company to make a refunding offering to you of new debentures in full or partial payment of the balance of the debenture that you hold.

10-Year Recapitulation Chart

| | Cash Distributions | | | | | Projection of Estimated Capital Growth of Unit | | |
Year	Interest Received on Debenture Each year	Principal Payments on Debenture Each year	Dividend on Preferred Stock Each year	Total Yearly Distribution	Total Distribution for all Years	Unpaid Principal Amount of Debenture	Growth Projection of Preferred Stock (Includes Mortgage Reduction)	Totals*
Start						$500	$500	$1,000
1	$40	$10	$30	$80	$ 80	490	530	1,020
2	40	10	30	80	160	480	561	1,041
3	40	10	30	80	240	470	593	1,063
4	40	10	30	80	320	460	626	1,086
5	40	10	30	80	400	450	660	1,110
6	40	10	30	80	480	440	695	1,135
7	40	10	30	80	560	430	732	1,162
8	40	10	30	80	640	420	770	1,190
9	40	10	30	80	720	410	809	1,219
10	40	10	30	80	800	400	850	1,250

* It is emphasized that this recapitulation is entirely a projection of future events and circumstances, and no assurances or guarantees are or can be given that the assumptions underlying such projection will be achieved or attained.

Note: At the end of the 10th year you also become entitled to payment of the $400 balance due on your debenture, making total cash receipts over the 10-year period of $1,200. Assuming that the net earnings of the corporation remain the same, as to which no guarantees are made, you would then receive $80 per year as dividends on your preferred stock, when, as, and if declared, plus your pro rata share of 50% of excess earnings, if any, above $80.

RENTAL INCOME

This hotel is under lease to a North Dakota corporation, Gold Corporation, a Portfolio Management, Inc. operating affiliate, under which lease said company is in possession of the property and engaged in its management and in the operation of the hotel and restaurant and bar business conducted therein.

The legal relationship of this operating company to North Dakota Hotel Plan is that of landlord and tenant. In other words, we are not concerned, to any extent whatsoever, with the day-to-day operation of this property, nor are we obligated with reference to any repairs or replacements.

Gold Corporation, as tenant, is required, under its lease, to pay us a net annual rental of $90,000 in monthly installments of $7,500 each.

The term "net" rental means that all operational expenses, including the cost of insurance, the obligation to make repairs and to replace capital fixtures and pay real estate taxes, water charges, and all utility and any and all maintenance expenses and disbursements must be borne by the tenant, in addition to its obligation to pay the said annual rental of $90,000.

The lease also provides that if the gross income received by the tenant from room rentals exceeds $225,000 a year, we, as landlord, are entitled to additional rent equivalent to 25% of the income from rooms above such base figure of $225,000. Reference is made to the topic of this circular "Summary of Net Lease" for more details concerning the provisions of said lease [page 77].

Reference is made to "Summary Statement of Income and Expenses of North Dakota Hotel for the 6-Month Period from March 1, 1957 to August 31, 1957," during which period the property was owned by our affiliate, Portfolio Management, Inc., and operated by the Lessee, Gold Corporation [page 85].

It will be noted from such operational statement that the net profit from the operation during the six-month period involved was $51,312.31.

If the earnings continue on said basis, as to which no assurances can be given, the net income of the hotel will be a little over $102,000 a year, out of which the company will receive its net rental of $90,000 a year and the balance of approximately $12,000 will constitute the leasehold profit to the Portfolio Management, Inc. affiliate, Gold Corporation, which is in possession under a net lease, subject, however, to the obligation to pay, as additional rent, 25% of the gross income above $225,000. It thus appears that on said basis, the profit of the Lessee on its lease will be approximately 3% of the total gross income from all sources.

You will note that the operational statement does not furnish a "breakdown" of income and expenses. These are matters which are deemed confidential and, in the best interest of the hotel, should not be furnished to the public. However, detailed operational statements, certified to by a certified public accountant, will be furnished, upon request, to subscribers to this offering.

The 10 Year Projection of Income and Disbursements set forth in this circular [page 82], will furnish you with detailed information as to the manner in which the net rental of $90,000 will be paid out.

OPERATION OF THE HOTEL UNDER NET LEASE

As has previously been indicated, the day-to-day operation of the hotel and the payment of all expenses in connection therewith will be the responsibility of the Portfolio Management, Inc. operating affiliate, Gold Corporation, as tenant under the net lease.

This lease instrument contains clauses and provisions customary in documents of this type. Included in the important provisions are the following:

a) The term of the lease will be for 15 years from October 1st, 1957.

b) The annual net rental is $90,000, payable in monthly instalments of $7,500 each.

c) The lessee will pay all operating and maintenance expenses, all real estate taxes, will make necessary repairs and replacements, and will keep the property adequately insured against fire and accident.

d) The lessee cannot assign the lease without the consent of the Landlord.

e) If the Lessee's gross income from room rentals exceeds $225,000 a year (its income for the last 6 months from this source has been at the rate of approximately $240,000 a year), then and in such event we would be entitled, as additional rent, to an amount equivalent to 25% of the excess above $225,000.

The Lessee, Gold Corporation, is a Portfolio Management, Inc. operating affiliate and will, in effect, function as the managing agent of this property. This lessee company has been capitalized at $2,500, so that its financial responsibility is not extensive enough to enable damages to be collected if, at any time in the future, the income from this hotel property should prove insufficient to pay its operating expenses and the net rental above referred to. The lease does, however, require the lessee to maintain, for our benefit, all types of fire, casualty and liability insurance, including rent insurance.

DESCRIPTION OF THE PROPERTY

North Dakota Hotel is an ultramodern, highly attractive hotel-motel building. The hotel is almost three years old, having opened for business on December 15, 1954. The physical structure consists of two buildings, the main building being two stories in height and containing the hotel lobby; 22 guest rooms, each with bath; and a restaurant and lounge. Detached from the main building and in an ell-shape is a one-story cottage building containing 18 additional guest rooms, each with bath. These two buildings are grouped around an interior landscaped plot around which circles a driveway leading from the lobby entrance of the main building around and past the cottages.

Both buildings are constructed wholly of red clay faced brick with a wide overhang covered with stainless steel facia. At the rear of the main building and facing toward the parkway is a two-story glass tower that encloses a rear fire exit. This glass tower is entirely lit up at night and is a striking landmark as seen from the parkway.

Recently a new beautifully landscaped "Flight Deck," with an area of about 1,500 square feet, was added for summertime outdoor dining. The "Flight Deck" adjoins the rear of the hotel and overlooks the airport and the parkway.

The lounge and restaurant face on the boulevard, while the hotel entrance is on the side of the interior driveway. Both the lobby and the lounge are framed entirely in sectional thermopane glass with glass Herculite doors. The lobby is two stories in height and is furnished in modern decor and all wall decorations have modes of air travel as the central motif. Part of the second floor extends over the lobby and forms into a public sitting room.

The North Dakota Hotel buildings are unique in that they were the first hotel buildings in the United States to be wholly soundproof. A special constuction method was devised and the roof and walls were so hung and insulated as to absorb and deflect the drone of the constant air traffic of the North Dakota Airport. About the only sound heard in the guest rooms of airplane motors is the equivalent of a quiet conversational voice.

All rooms and hallways are completely carpeted; the furniture in the guest rooms is by Drexel. Free television is furnished to each guest room. Each bathroom is in ceramic colored tile with set-in tubs and shower-heads.

All buildings are centrally air-conditioned, and heating is by gas.

The restaurant and lounge is known as the "Sky Room," and here again the motif of air travel is carried through. The Sky Room is appealing to the patron in its charm, and the soft browns of its walls are conducive to a feeling of quietude. The restaurant has earned a deserved reputation for the fine quality of its American cuisine. The restaurant has a daily menu for breakfast, lunch and dinner and serves a la carte after 9 P.M.

Immediately adjoining the hotel proper and to the east and as a part of this Portfolio Management, Inc. acquisition, is an extensive parcel of vacant land comprising about 60,000 square feet in area. This parcel slopes gently to the level of the parkway and approximately two thirds thereof is at such level. Because of the exceptionally high occupancy rate at the North Dakota Hotel, additional hotel facilities are sorely needed and it is anticipated that additional rooms will be built on this vacant land and incorporated as an integral part of the present hotel. This vacant land is large enough to permit the building of a minimum of 60 additional guest rooms with ample parking thereon for at least 100 cars. Between the hotel and this plot of land is a strip of land owned by the city for the use of which, as additional parking space, a rental of $50 a month is paid by the tenant Gold Corporation.

The North Dakota Hotel is universally impressive, and it has a quality of charm that is appealing to all. It is unique to hotel operation in this area, permitting the guest the freedom of a motel and an overabundance of car parking facilities. It has also fitted a definite need for hotel accommodations for over 5 million air travelers who annually come in and out of North Dakota Airport.

The hotel rates start from $12 per day single occupancy.

COMPETITION

In addition to the North Dakota Hotel, there is one other hotel now in existence within a radius of a half mile from this property. This hotel was constructed after the North Dakota Hotel and has a capacity of approximately 70 rooms. Plans have been filed for the construction of a third hotel within 10 blocks of the property, involving approximately 50 rooms.

The North Dakota Hotel is the only one that is visible from and adjacent to the parkway, and we think it occupies a most desirable location.

It will be noted that our property includes an unimproved tract of land with an area of approximately 60,000 square feet. We expect, in the not too distant future, to construct an addition or extension to the North Dakota Hotel, for which public funds may be sought.

MORTGAGE INDEBTEDNESS

This property has been acquired by the company subject to a first mortgage on the parcel on which the hotel is situated only, held by the Dollar Savings Bank of North Dakota, originally in the sum of $250,000, which, as of October 10th, 1957, had been reduced to $228,307.15.

The mortgage payments that the company will be required to make will be $2,084 a month, which is at the rate of $25,008 a year. Out of each monthly installment, interest will first be deducted at the rate of 5% a year, and the balance will be applied to the reduction of principal.

The mortgage matures on February 5th, 1966, at which time the entire unpaid balance becomes due and payable. Between October 15th, 1957 and February 5th, 1966, the mortgage will be reduced by approximately $143,000 (equivalent to about $20 on each share of preferred stock), so that the balance due on its maturity date February 5, 1966 will be approximately $85,000.

None of the unit purchasers are assuming any personal liability with reference to this mortgage, nor is any liability imposed on the company for the payment thereof, because title to the property is being acquired by the company subject to the first mortgage and without obligation to assume the payment thereof.

At the present time there are three other mortgages affecting the property, as follows, which are also liens on this property: (*a*) a second mortgage originally in the sum of $200,000 but reduced to $150,000, covering the hotel (Parcel A); (*b*) a first mortgage of $38,333.34 on the parcel of vacant land adjoining the hotel (Parcel B); and (*c*) a blanket mortgage on all three parcels in the amount of $56,250.00. In line with the policy of Portfolio Management, Inc. not to sponsor acquisition of properties subject to more than a first mortgage, these three mortgages will be paid off in cash from the proceeds of this offering, so that the only mortgage that will remain a lien on this property will be the first mortgage described hereinabove.

MANAGEMENT AND "OVERHEAD"

North Dakota Hotel Plan, Inc., the Issuer of this offering is a North Dakota corporation organized on March 25, 1957, and maintains its offices in North Dakota.

The officers and directors of the company are as follows: *President and Director,* Robert Gold, North Dakota; *Vice President and Director,* Edward Davis, North Dakota; *Secretary-Treasurer and Director,* Elliot Ryan, North Dakota.

Robert Gold is a lawyer, admitted to practice in the state of North Dakota on June 10th, 1938. Mr. Gold's specialty is real estate investments and real estate law. During the past years, his real estate investment activities have involved properties situated in North Dakota, Illinois, Tennessee, Pennsylvania, and Georgia.

Edward Davis, the vice president and a director of this company, is also an employee of the Portfolio Management, Inc., group of affiliates and has had extensive experience in the securities business, being registered as a broker-dealer with the Securities and Exchange Commission.

Elliot Ryan has a diversified background in construction and maintenance of rental income of real estate extending over a period of approximately 15 years. He is at present maintenance supervisor for Maintenance Systems, Inc., an affiliate of this company.

Our fiscal operations contemplate that rents collected from the tenant will be accumulated and, from time to time, remittances will be made to the Trustee for the purpose of making distributions to service the debentures and for the payment of dividends.

The officers and directors of the company are also employees of other Portfolio Management, Inc. operating affiliates.

This company will be under no obligation whatsoever for the payment of salaries to any of its officers or directors, who will function in such capacity for the company without compensation.

The company will be obligated to pay the fees of the Trustee, which will amount to $900 a year. The budget of the company for rent, telephones, stationery, postage, etc., should not exceed $600 a year. An additional $1,000 will be allocated for the payment of any miscellaneous items of expense that may be incurred, including the services of a part-time bookkeeper. The only other expense that the company will have will be the fees of its auditor, which should not exceed $1,000 a year. These items, collectively, aggregate $3,500.

THE TRUSTEE

The debentures will be issued under a Trust Indenture between this company, as obligor, George Ferrell as Trustee, and Portfolio Management, Inc., as and pledgor to the Trustee of the common stock.

This Trust Agreement consists of 24 pages and 8 Articles.

The statements in this Offering Circular do not purport to include or summarize all the provisions of the Trust Agreement and are subject to the detailed provisions thereof, to which reference is hereby made, and all such statements are qualified in their entirety by such reference.

Mr. Ferrell also functions as a co-trustee for the owners and tenants in common of various properties acquired by the public under the Portfolio Management, Inc.

In addition to his functions as Trustee, Mr. Ferrell also performs services on a contractual basis as public relations consultant for various Portfolio Management, Inc. affiliates.

TAX MATTERS

On the matter of corporate taxes, the company has been advised as follows:

1. By James Jones, Esq., Attorney-at-law and an independent certified public accountant of New York City, that (a) interest payable on the debentures should be allowed as a corporate tax deduction; (b) that payments in reduction of principal on the debentures constitute a return of capital to the debenture holders and, therefore, are not taxable; and (c) that the aggregate debenture discount of $38,500

10-Year Projection of Estimated Corporate Taxable Income, Cash Income, and Disbursements

	1st Yr.	2nd Yr.	3rd Yr.	4th Yr.	5th Yr.	6th Yr.	7th Yr.	8th Yr.	9th Yr.	10th Yr.
1 Net rent income after mortgage payments	$65,000	$65,000	$65,000	$65,000	$65,000	$65,000	$65,000	$65,000	$65,000	$65,000
2 Add: Mortgage amortization payments	13,900	14,620	15,360	16,150	16,970	17,840	18,750	19,700	20,710	21,770
	$78,900	$79,620	$80,360	$81,150	$81,970	$82,840	$83,750	$84,700	$85,710	$86,770
Less:										
3 Debenture interest	$28,000	$28,000	$28,000	$28,000	$28,000	$28,000	$28,000	$28,000	$28,000	$28,000
4 Amortization of debenture discount	3,850	3,850	3,850	3,850	3,850	3,850	3,850	3,850	3,850	3,850
5 Estimated depreciation	39,430	39,430	39,430	39,430	39,430	39,430	39,430	39,430	39,430	39,430
6 Trustee's fees	900	900	900	900	900	900	900	900	900	900
7 Miscellaneous (bookkeeping and audit charges, office expenses, etc.)	2,600	2,600	2,600	2,600	2,600	2,600	2,600	2,600	2,600	2,600
8 North Dakota franchise tax	1,200	1,200	1,200	1,200	1,200	1,200	1,200	1,200	1,200	1,200
9 Total Deductions	$75,980	$75,980	$75,980	$75,980	$75,980	$75,980	$75,980	$75,980	$75,980	$75,980
10 Taxable income for federal income tax purposes	$ 2,920	$ 3,640	$ 4,380	$ 5,170	$ 5,990	$ 6,860	$ 7,770	$ 8,720	$ 9,730	$10,790
11 Cash receipts—net rent income after mortgage payments	$65,000	$65,000	$65,000	$65,000	$65,000	$65,000	$65,000	$65,000	$65,000	$65,000
Cash Disbursements:										
12 Debenture interest	$28,000	$28,000	$28,000	$28,000	$28,000	$28,000	$28,000	$28,000	$28,000	$28,000
13 Debenture principal	7,000	7,000	7,000	7,000	7,000	7,000	7,000	7,000	7,000	7,000
14 6% preferred stock dividend	21,000	21,000	21,000	21,000	21,000	21,000	21,000	21,000	21,000	21,000
15 Trustee's fees	900	900	900	900	900	900	900	900	900	900
16 Miscellaneous (bookkeeping and audit charges, office expenses, etc.)	2,600	2,600	2,600	2,600	2,600	2,600	2,600	2,600	2,600	2,600
17 North Dakota franchise tax	1,200	1,200	1,200	1,200	1,200	1,200	1,200	1,200	1,200	1,200
18 Federal income taxes	981	1,197	1,419	1,656	1,902	2,163	2,436	2,721	3,024	3,342
	$61,681	$61,897	$62,119	$62,356	$62,602	$62,863	$63,136	$63,421	$63,724	$64,042
19 Annual excess of cash receipts over cash disbursements	$ 3,319	$ 3,103	$ 2,881	$ 2,644	$ 2,398	$ 2,137	$ 1,864	$ 1,579	$ 1,276	$ 958
20 Accumulated excess of cash receipts over cash disbursements	$ 3,319	$ 6,422	$ 9,303	$11,947	$14,345	$16,482	$18,346	$19,925	$21,201	$22,159

may be taken as a corporate tax deduction, at the rate of $3,850 for each year during the 10-year term of the debentures.

2. By Sid Kaplan, a consulting engineer of New York City, that the depreciation, on a "straight-line" basis, should be $39,430 a year for 14 years, which is the amount taken as a corporate tax deduction in the projection set forth below.

Attention is directed to the fact that the 10-year projection which follows is entirely a projection of future events and circumstances, and that no assurances or guarantees are or can be made that the assumptions underlying such projection will be achieved or realized. These assumptions and contingencies include but are not limited to:

a) that the net cash income of the corporation after the payment of mortgage requirements, will continue to be $65,000 during each year of such 10-year period; and

b) that the provisions of existing tax laws will continue in force with respect to basis for and computation of depreciation, and that the allocations and estimates underlying the depreciation accounting reflected in the projection are reasonable and will be acceptable for federal tax purposes.

APPLICATION OF PROCEEDS

The proceeds of this offering will be disposed of as follows:

$339,767.73	will be paid to our affiliate, Portfolio Management, Inc., as and in full payment of the cash consideration to which it is entitled as the seller of this property [page 70]; this payment will be made on the basis of $50 per unit when sold;
250,000.00	(approximate) will be used to pay off existing junior mortgage indebtedness aggregating $244,583.34, plus interest thereon;
77,000.00	will be paid as underwriting discount. Pursuant to written agreement entered into by this company with its affiliate, Portfolio Management, Inc., said latter company is to receive underwriting discounts of $11 per unit;
17,500.00	on the basis of $2.50 per unit when sold, will be paid to the underwriter as and for reimbursement of any and all expenses incurred and advanced by it in connection with this offering and for legal fees; any excess remaining after the payment of all such offering expenses and fees will be retained by the underwriter as additional compensation; and
15,732.27	(balance) is to be retained by the company as working capital, out of which it will pay title insurance and title acquisition costs and disbursements, together with the cost of affixing federal and/or state documentary stamps in connection with the issuance of the units involved in this offering. This fund includes an adjustment of $5,000 rental income for the period October 10th to October 31st, 1957.
$700,000.00	

TERMS OF ACQUISITION

This company acquired title to this property on October 10th, 1957, at a purchase price of $820,800, which does not include the underwriting discounts, offering expenses and working capital previously referred to.

Out of said purchase price of........................		$820,800.00
this company received the following credits:		
First mortgage...	$228,307.15	
Interest—10/5/57 to 10/10/57 @ 5%.................	156.37	
Second mortgage......................................	150,000.00	
Interest—8/10/57 to 10/10/57 @ 7%.................	1,754.79	
Blanket junior mortgage..............................	56,250.00	
Interest—6/3/57 to 10/10/57 @ 6%.................	1,192.81	
Land mortgage..	38,333.34	
Interest—10/7/57 to 10/10/57 @ 12%................	37.81	
Net lease rent adjustment for period from 10/10/57 to		
10/31/57, at the rate of $7,500.00 a month..........	5,000.00	
Total Credits....................................		$481,032.27
Balance due Seller.................................		$339,767.73

The sum of $339,767.73, which is the amount due the seller, is to be paid to the seller on a deferred basis, out of the proceeds of the sale of the offering, with the option on the part of said seller to take down units, in lieu of cash, in such amount and to such extent as it may elect to do.

The purchase agreement under which this company acquired title to this property gives it the option to postpone the payment of the monies due Portfolio Management, Inc., so as to enable the company to "use and apply so much" thereof "as may be necessary to pay and discharge of record" the above-mentioned junior mortgage indebtedness as quickly as possible so that the ownership of the property will be subject to only the balance due on the existing first mortgage held by the Dollar Savings Bank of North Dakota.

In order to furnish you with maximum protection for your investment, it is the fixed policy of the Portfolio Management, Inc., to sponsor offerings either on a free-and-clear basis, without any mortgage, or subject only to a first mortgage.

While we estimate that this property should yield a cash return to the company of 8% a year after mortgage reduction but before depreciation, such estimate is based on our projection of anticipated rental income from the tenant, Gold Corporation.

The carrying charges of interest and amortization on the first mortgage on this property amount to $25,000.

The maturity date of this mortgage is February 5th, 1966, at which date the balance of principal due thereon will be approximately $85,000.

If the mortgage is then renewed at a constant interest and amortization rate of 8% on its then balance, which renewal we think should be accomplished with ease, such renewal would then reduce the carrying charges of the first mortgage from $25,000 to about $6,800 a year thereby creating an additional safety "cushion" of about $18,200.

It is the long-range objective of Portfolio Management, Inc., ownership to pay off mortgage indebtedness and retain ownership on a free-and-clear basis. By eventually owning this property on a free-and-clear basis, without any mortgage, your investment should be able to survive any downward economic fluctuation.

Here, again, let it be borne in mind that paying off the first mortgage cannot be accomplished, unless the rental income of the property continues to be sufficient to meet all fixed charges and operating expenses. Assuming an uninterrupted continuance of payments called for under the net lease, the company will still owe you $40 on each debenture at the end of 10 years. We anticipate that this balance will be paid out of a refinancing of the first mortgage or, if this cannot produce sufficient funds for such purpose, by an offering to make payment thereof in the form of a new refunding debenture in the amount of the balance due you.

SUMMARY

Statement of Income and Expenses
Re: North Dakota Hotel*

(for six-month period from March 1st, 1957 to August 31st, 1957)

Gross income from room rentals, bar, restaurant, and other service charges...............................		$200,800.04
Less: Expenses:		
Operating and administrative expenses including cost of food and liquor............................	$75,893.37	
Payroll, payroll taxes, and Employee Benefits.......	63,554.56	
Fixed charges—real estate taxes and insurance......	10,039.80	
Total Expenses..................................		$149,487.73
Excess of income over expenses.....................		$ 51,312.31

*This summary is based on actual operations for said six-month period adjusted so as to eliminate all mortgage indebtedness payments. The information upon which this statement is based was taken from the books and records of the tenant, Gold Corporation.

PART II

Investment—Tax Effect

DEPRECIATION
AND TAX NOTE

INTRODUCTION

The Nature of Depreciation

The Internal Revenue Tax Code permits an expense deduction for the exhaustion of property utilized in a trade or a business or for property held in the production of income. This expense deduction is termed *depreciation*, and it is confined to property that has a limited useful life. Thus, land is considered not to depreciate, and an expense allowance is not permitted for the cost basis of land. The actual amount of the annual depreciation deduction may be calculated in any way consistent with the tax bill of 1969, recently enacted into law. The straight-line method and various accelerated approaches, such as 150% declining balance, are specifically enumerated in the 1969 code.

Tax Implications of Depreciation

An expense, just as the expiration of prepaid insurance is an expense, depreciation is a deduction taken along with other expenses in arriving at taxable income. Depreciation has another very important characteristic. Unlike most expenses, it does not cause cash to flow out of a business operation, because it is a noncash expense allocation. In addition, the amount charged as depreciation for tax purposes shields the same amount of revenue from income taxes. It is thus an important element in determining annual cash flows. We shall, at a later point in this note, discuss the detailed factors of importance which make depreciation and its tax consequences so crucial to real estate investments.

BASIS FOR DEPRECIATION

Determination and Characteristics

The basis for the depreciation of a property is usually the actual construction cost of property improvement (the building) or the cost of the improvement in the acquisition of a property. In almost all cases, the depreciation basis will be greater than the equity funds provided by the purchaser, since mortgage funds usually supply a substantial part of the cost of a property.

As an example of basis determination, assume that Mr. Gold buys a property consisting of land and a building for $100,000. He puts up $20,000 in cash and assumes a mortgage of $80,000. Assume that for depreciation and tax purposes the value of the land is $30,000 and, therefore, that the buiding is valued at 70% of the total purchase price. In this case, the depreciation basis is $70,000. Note that the land cannot be depreciated and that the depreciable basis is much higher than Mr. Gold's $20,000 equity.

Purchase Price Allocation

The allocations of a lump-sum purchase price between improvements (building or structure) and land for a determination of the depreciable base is normally determined by the relative market value for the land and building prevailing at the time of sale. The allocation of assessed value between land and buildings for real estate purposes is the most extensively employed basis for determining the allocation of a reasonable percentage of the cost between the land and the improvements. While, in certain cases, a sales contract may be established which sets forth separately the cost of land and buildings, the use of this allocation of purchase price between land and building is not normally accepted by the tax authorities.

Depreciation Basis Other than Cost

Depreciation is always based upon the actual cost basis of the property and not its value, or the basis in the hands of the seller. In certain situations, however, the basis for depreciation might not be the original construction cost or purchase price, but the original cost less the amount of depreciation already taken. In these cases, the basis is the same as the adjusted basis which would be used in determining gain on a sale. For example, assume that Mr. Jones constructed a building with a 10-year useful life estimation at a cost of $20,000. Mr. Jones chooses to deduct straight-line depreciation of $2,000 per year on his building. At the end of year five, he discovers that the building will have a useful life of 30 years instead of 10 years. The adjusted basis for the building is now the $20,000 original cost less the $10,000 depreciation already taken or $10,000. The depreciation allowance on a straight-line rate for the additional 25 years of useful life will be $400 per year. Note that the original cost basis, or book value, of $20,000 is not relevant in this situation.

USEFUL LIFE OF DEPRECIABLE PROPERTY

Determination and Factors of Useful Life

The estimated useful life of a property is another input necessary to determine the annual allowable depreciation deduction for tax purposes. The useful life is the period in which a property will be useful for income production. This life has no relation to the physical life of a property.

Actual useful life is dependent upon such factors as (1) obsolescence, (2) wear and tear, (3) inadequacy, (4) economic changes, (5) climatic conditions, (6) technological change, (7) repair and maintenance policies, and (8) acts of God.

The influence of these factors upon the depreciable life is mainly a function of experience with a specific property, a general group of properties, or a particular area. Each useful-life consideration is really different, although there are broad guidelines provided by the government.

Useful-Life Guidelines

The 1962 "Depreciation Guidelines and Rules" provide periods of useful lives for approximately 75 broad classes of assets. Taxpayers may choose to depreciate business properties over the periods indicated by the guidelines provided that these parameters reasonably apply to a particular group of assets. However, taxpayers may depreciate the property over any period that can be justified to the Internal Revenue Service. An illustration of the government guidelines is shown in Table A.

TABLE A
Useful Life

Type of Building	Depreciation Guideline (Years)
Apartments	40
Banks	50
Factories	45
Farm buildings	25
Grain elevators	60
Hotels	40
Loft buildings	50
Office buildings	45
Stores	50
Theaters	40
Warehouses	60

DEPRECIATION METHODS

Residential Rental Properties

The 1969 tax law provides that an investor in residential rental properties may use the following methods of depreciation for new real estate properties:

1. Straight-line method
2. Declining-balance methods up to double the straight-line depreciation allowed in the first year.
3. Sum-of-the-years'-digits method
4. Any other method consistent with trade practice which provides a reasonable depreciation allowance.

For used residential rental properties, with a useful life of 20 or more years, an investor may use the straight-line, 125% declining-balance, or any consistent method that does not provide an allowance greater than 125% of the straight-line rate in the first year of depreciation. In order to qualify for the depreciation methods applicable to a residential rental property, at least 80% of the gross rental income from a property must be rental income from dwelling units.

Commercial Properties

All other new properties, specifically commercial properties, are limited to a maximum of 150% declining-balance depreciation. Sum-of-the-years'-digits, or other accelerated methods of depreciation, cannot be employed. Used property in the commercial category must be depreciated by the straight-line method or at a rate comparable to the straight-line rate.

Rehabilitated Housing

Rehabilitated housing receives a special depreciation method allowance. The rehabilitated portion of a building may be depreciated on a straight-line rate using a short useful life of only five years. The shell or purchase price of the building must, however, be depreciated on a method comparable to any allowable on residential rental housing.

Additional Taxpayer Elections

It is not necessary for a property owner to depreciate all of his residential holdings, or all of his commercial holdings, by the same depreciation method. A straight-line method may be used on some properties and a declining balance method may be used on other improvements. This election is up to the investor.

It is also possible for a taxpayer to change methods of depreciation. A change from declining balance or sum-of-the-years'-digits methods to a straight-line rate may be made at any time. Any other depreciation method change—such as straight-line to declining balance—must be accompanied by permission from the IRS.

Straight-Line Method

The straight-line method provides for equal yearly depreciation expense charges over the life of a property. If a property has an estimated useful life of 40 years, the taxpayer can depreciate 1/40th of the cost of the building each year over the life of the property. The cost of the property is the depreciable basis. However, if there is any estimated salvage value, this must be deducted in arriving at a basis for straight-line depreciation. For example, Mr. Hillary constructs a building on his own land for $200,000. The building is expected to last 40 years and have a salvage value of $40,000 at the end of that time. The depreciation expense in each year is:

```
Cost................................$200,000
    Less: Salvage......................  40,000
Depreciable Basis....................$160,000
    $160,000/40 years equals $4,000 per year
```

If the building had no estimated salvage value, the depreciation allowance would be $200,000/40 years, or $5,000 per year.

Declining-Balance Method of Depreciation

Various declining-balance methods of depreciation may be used by an investor in real estate. The maximum declining-balance rate of depreciation allowed for any property is 200% of, or double, the straight-line rate exclusive of salvage value.

The declining-balance method provides that the greatest expense allowance is taken in the first year. The depreciation expense in subsequent years decreases, as a constant percentage is applied to the declining balance or undepreciated basis of the property.

By way of example, Mr. White has a $200,000 building with a 40-year life that is eligible, as a new residential rental property, for double the straight-line rate in the first year. The depreciation allowance, in the first year, using the straight-line method would be 2.5% of $200,000, or $5,000 (an asset with a 40-year life that is depreciated on a straight-line rate would be depreciated at 2.5% per year). Using the double declining-balance method, the rate would be 5% (200% × 2.5%) of $200,000 or $10,000. The allowance in the second year would be $200,000 less $10,000, or $190,000 (the undepreciated balance) × 5% to equal $9,500. In each year, the 5% rate is applied to the undepreciated balance or remaining basis of the property.

The same method of calculation applies regardless of the declining-balance rate employed. For example, the $200,000 building with a 40-year life at 150% declining-balance depreciation would yield an expense allocation of 3.75% (150% × 2.5%) × $200,000 or $7,500 in the first year. Subsequent yearly depreciation allowances would equal 3.75% of the book value or undepreciated balance.

Sum-of-the-Years'-Digits Method

In addition to declining-balance methods, the other accelerated form of depreciation which yields greater expense charges than straight line is sum of the years' digits. The appropriate basis for this method is the cost less estimated salvage value, if any. The sum-of-the-years'-digits method provides that a changing fraction be applied to the depreciable base, which remains constant. Under this reducing-fraction method, the years of a property's useful life are summed, and their total becomes the denominator of a series of fractions used in allocating depreciation expenses in each year. The numerators of the fractions are the remaining years in the property's life.

For example, let us assume we have an asset with a five-year estimated useful life. The fraction we would use in the first year of depreciation would be $5/15$, where the numerator 5 is the number of years of useful life remaining and the denominator 15 is the sum of the years of property life, $1 + 2 + 3 + 4 + 5 = 15$. In the second year, the applicable fraction would be $4/15$, and so forth.

The annual depreciation charges on a five-year property costing $12,000, with no salvage value, would be as shown in the accompanying table.

Year	Calculation	Depreciation Expense
1	5/15 × $12,000	$ 4,000
2	4/15 × "	3,200
3	3/15 × "	2,400
4	2/15 × "	1,600
5	1/15 × "	800
Total		$12,000

It is obviously tedious to figure out the sum-of-the-years'-digits denominator if the useful life is for a long period, such as 40 years. The following formula yields this denominator:

$$D = N \left(\frac{N + 1}{2} \right)$$

Where:

D = Sum-of-the-digits' denominator.
N = Estimated useful life.

In the above example: $N = 5$ years as the useful life gives us D, the denominator of $5(5 + 1)/2 = 15$.

Change to Straight-Line Method

If an investor decides to change depreciation from the declining-balance or sum-of-the-years'-digits to the straight-line method, the remaining balance is merely recovered equally over the remaining useful life of the property. In the case of declining balance, if there is any estimated salvage value, this value must be subtracted from the basis before the straight-line calculation can be performed.

For example, assume that Mr. Davis purchased a property for $20,000. This particular property has a five-year estimated useful life, and Mr. Davis chooses to depreciate the $20,000 basis at 125% declining balance. At the end of the first year, he wishes to switch to straight-line depreciation. At this time, there is a basis of $15,000 ($20,000 cost less $5,000 depreciation already taken). There are four years remaining in the useful life of the property, and there is no salvage value. Therefore, the annual depreciation deduction will be $3,750 in each of the next four years. The $15,000 is divided equally by four years to arrive at this depreciation expense.

COMPARISON OF DEPRECIATION METHODS

Declining-balance depreciation methods and the sum-of-the-years'-digits method are accelerated forms of depreciation which offer larger deductions than straight-line depreciation in earlier years and smaller deductions in later years.

As an example of the difference among these methods, assume that Mr. Ryan purchases a property (a leasehold with no land) for $100,000 with a cash investment of $20,000 and the assumption of a mortgage for $80,000. The building is estimated to have a five-year useful life and no salvage value. The yearly and cumulative depreciation totals for each method are as shown in the accompanying table.

Year	Straight-Line		D.B. 200%		D.B. 150%		S.Y.D.	
	Depre-ciation Expense	Cumu-lative Depre-ciation	Depre-ciation Expense	Cumu-lative Depre-ciation	Depre-ciation Expense	Cumu-lative Depre-ciation	Depre-ciation Expense	Cumu-lative Depre-ciation
1.........$	20,000	$ 20,000	$40,000	$40,000	$30,000	$30,000	$33,000	$ 33,000
2.........	20,000	40,000	30,000	70,000	26,250	56,000	27,000	60,000
3.........	20,000	60,000	15,000	85,000	16,500	72,750	20,000	80,000
4.........	20,000	80,000	7,500	92,500	10,750	83,500	13,000	93,000
5.........	20,000	100,000	3,750	96,250	6,225	89,725	7,000	100,000

IMPORTANCE OF DEPRECIATION

The foregoing table, while showing differences among depreciation methods, also gives an indication of the effects of depreciation for the real estate investor.

First of all, the investor receives a depreciation deduction on the total value of the property and not just the 20% actual equity invested; that is, he can depreciate the portion of the cost financed with mortgage funds.

Second, the accelerated methods provide for increased working capital in the early years of a property's life by reducing tax payments, since depreciation is a tax deductible expense which, when increased, reduces taxable income without reducing cash income.

To better illustrate these factors, assume that Mr. Ferrell purchased a property for $800,000 with $200,000 in cash and a first mortgage of $600,000. The property consists of land valued at $100,000 and an apartment building valued at $700,000.

Declining-balance depreciation of 200% is used with a useful life of 40 years. The income and cash flow are as follows in the first year.

Income Statement

Income before interest, depreciation, taxes.................		$84,000
Less:		
Interest..	$54,000	
Depreciation (5% × $700,000)..........................	35,000	89,000
Taxable loss...		$(5,000)

Cash Flow Statement

Cash flow from operations..................................	$84,000
Less: Loan service (principal, interest)....................	62,000
Net cash flow to investor..................................	$22,000

Although there is no taxable income from the project, cash flow is sufficient to cover debt service and generate a $22,000 cash flow to the investor. Note that in addition there is an increase in the owner's equity of $8,000 by virtue of the principal payment on the mortgage. This, of course, assumes that the property has not, in fact, depreciated in value.

Capital Gains and Depreciation

Depreciation expense deductions shelter ordinary income from taxes and reduce the taxable basis of a property each year. However, real estate property values are such that the worth of a property will probably increase or, at least, depreciate more slowly than allowable depreciation expense over time. This relationship frequently results in a real estate investor being able to sell his property for a taxable gain. To the extent that the owner has been building up his equity through a tax-free cash flow, he will have converted ordinary income into capital gains income. Thus, depreciation deductions shield income which is taxed at ordinary income rates, while the gain resulting from the sale of the property at its original (undepreciated) cost may be taxed at the lower capital gains rates.

As an example, assume that Mr. Kelly builds an apartment house for $100,000. The building has a 20-year estimated remaining life and can be depreciated on the straight-line method. At the end of five years, Mr. Kelly sells the building for $100,000. His depreciation schedule on the structure is as follows:

Year	Depreciation
1	$ 5,000
2	5,000
3	5,000
4	5,000
5	5,000
Total	$25,000

Since Mr. Kelly is in a 70% tax bracket, depreciation charges enabled him to save $17,500 ($25,000 × 70%) in ordinary income taxes over five years. His gain on the sale is $25,000 ($100,000 sales price less $75,000 undepreciated basis or book value), which is the amount of depreciation taken, although the building did not depreciate in terms of sales value.

Mr. Kelly must pay a capital gains tax on the $25,000. We will assume he pays a 35% capital gains tax rate of $8,750 in taxes in year 5. He has been able to save $17,500 in ordinary income taxes while paying only $8,750 in capital gains taxes.

He has thus built up an equity by the use of tax-free cash flow and saved $8,750 in taxes.

Under the 1969 tax code, capital gains tax rates are set at a maximum of 29½% in 1970 and 32½% in 1971, and 35% in 1972 and thereafter.

Corporate capital gains rates will be 28% in 1970 and level off at 30% in 1971 and future years. Since the ordinary income tax rates for a real estate investor will be higher than these capital gains provisions, depreciation reduction of taxable income in any year provides some permanent deferral of taxes, and when payable they will be taxed at an advantageous (lower) rate. This can clearly be seen in the above example of Mr. Kelly's apartment building.

DEPRECIATION RECAPTURE

Introduction

The tax advantages of depreciation are somewhat reduced by recapture provisions. Depreciation recapture is such that a certain amount of capital gains will be treated as ordinary income.

The 1969 tax law—which applies to all depreciation taken after December 31, 1969—maintains the recapture of all depreciation, including straight-line, on all property held for 12 months or less. In other words, any gain is taxed at ordinary income rates to the extent of any depreciation taken in the 12-month period.

For example, Mr. Fowler purchased a rooming house on January 1, 1970, for $50,000, which he sells on October 1, 1970, for $50,000, after having taken $5,000 in depreciation deductions. He will have realized $5,000 in ordinary income, not capital gains ($50,000 sales price less $5,000 depreciation taken equals $45,000 taxable basis, which produces a gain of $5,000).

Residential Rental Property Recapture

For a period up to 100 months, assuming that a taxable profit is realized on the sale of a residential property held for income purposes, the gain is subject to the recapture (taxable at ordinary rather than capital gains rate) of all depreciation taken in excess of that which would have been taken had the straight-line method been employed. At the end of 100 months, depreciation recapture is subject to an "applicable percentage" of the depreciation taken in excess of that which would have been taken under a straight-line rate—but only to the extent that a gain is realized on the property disposition. The applicable percentage is 100% less 1% per month for each month the property is held over 100 months. Thus, there will be no recapture if a property is held for 200 months or 16 years and 8 months and, at that point, all income will be taxed at a capital gains rate. In any event, the amount of gain subject to recapture (taxed at ordinary income rates) is equal to the lesser of the gain realized on the sale of the property or the amount of "additional depreciation" taken.

As an example, Mr. Royce sells an apartment building with an adjusted basis of $200,000 for $400,000. He therefore has a gain of $200,000 on the property.

Of this gain, $100,000 consists of excess depreciation above that which he would have been allowed had he used the straight-line method. Mr. Royce has held the property for 10 years or 120 months. His applicable percentage is, therefore, 80% because he receives a 1% credit or recapture reduction for each of the 20 months over 100 months he has held the property.

In paying taxes on the sale, Smith will pay ordinary tax rates on 80% of $100,000 or $80,000. The remaining $120,000 portion of the gain will be taxed at the more favorable capital gains rate.

If Smith had received a gain of only $90,000 for the building, the ordinary income would be 80% of $90,000 or $72,000, since the gain of $90,000 is less than the excess depreciation.

Rehabilitation Recapture

Residential rehabilitation projects subject to the special five-year write-off fall under the same recapture provisions as any other residential rental property. In this case, excess depreciation means the special write-off in excess of what would have resulted by a straight-line rate applied to the basis of the useful life of improvements instead of the special 60-month life permitted for tax purposes.

By way of illustration, assume that Mr. Thomas made a $30,000 rehabilitation improvement which qualifies for the special five-year write-off. The rehabilitation improvement has a useful life of 15 years. The property is sold in the 10th year after Mr. Thomas has already deducted the entire $30,000. In this case, Mr. Thomas would have had $20,000 depreciation under a straight-line method using a useful life of 15 years. Therefore the depreciation subject to recapture (taxed at ordinary rates) is $10,000.

RESIDENTIAL GOVERNMENT-SUBSIDIZED PROPERTY RECAPTURE

If residential rental property is subsidized by the federal government, such as those financed under the 221(d)(3) or 236 programs, then the recapture rules are more favorable. As before, all depreciation is recaptured if the property is sold within the first 12 months. All additional depreciation is recaptured up to 20 months. However, the applicable percentage is 100% at 20 months and is reduced 1% per month for each month the property is held over 20 months. In the previous example of Mr. Royce—who sold his building at the end of 10 years or 120 months —there would not have been any gain subject to recapture if the building owned had been included in a project subsidized by the federal government.

Projects subsidized by the federal government receive additional advantages under the present tax laws. If the proceeds from a project sold at a profit to a tenant cooperative or nonprofit organization are reinvested one year before or one year after in a like property, then there is no tax liability on the gain.

Commercial Property Recapture

Under the 1969 tax law, all commercial properties are subject to the recapture (treatment of all gains, equal to or less than the excess depreciation taken, as ordinary income) of all excess depreciation regardless of the holding period involved. This means that there is effectively no applicable percentage other than 100% to apply to the excess depreciation portion of any gain.

Although there legally appears to be full recapture of depreciation excess on commercial properties, such is not technically true if a property is held long enough. At some point in the life of a property, straight-line depreciation will exceed declining-balance depreciation. For example, as shown in the accompanying table, a $100,000 property with a 25-year useful life is depreciated on a straight-line rate and 150% declining balance.

Year	Straight Line	150% Declining Balance
1	$4,000	$6,000
2	4,000	5,650
3	4,000	5,300
4	4,000	5,000
5	4,000	4,700
6	4,000	4,400
7	4,000	4,120
8	4,000	3,890

In the eighth year the point is reached where straight line exceeds declining balance. From this time on, the excess depreciation to be recaptured is reduced. The excess depreciation on this particular property is completely erased should an investor hold his property through the 16th year. The same basic result holds true if a switch is made in the eighth year to straight-line depreciation on the remining basis. In this case, however, the practical holding period becomes several years longer for the complete avoidance of recapture.

CALCULATION OF RECAPTURE INVOLVING POST-1969 AND PRE-1970 DEPRECIATION

The new recapture rules of the 1969 tax act apply regardless of the age of a real estate property. However, only depreciation taken after December 31, 1969, is subject to the new rules. Depreciation taken before this date is subject to the old tax law provisions, which apply equally to all classes of properties.

Under past tax laws, if a property was held 12 months or less, all depreciation was recaptured. If the property was sold between one year and 20 months, all excess depreciation would be taxed at ordinary income tax rates. At the end of 20 months, depreciation recapture was subject to an applicable percentage of the excess depreciation over straight line. This percentage was 100% less 1% per month for each month the property was held over 20 months. Any property held for 120 months or 10 years was free from depreciation recapture.

In order to calculate the depreciation recapture of a property that has been held for more than 20 months or less than 10 years and is disposed of after December 31, 1969, two calculations are necessary:

1. Determine excess post-1969 depreciation (a percentage will need to be applied if the property is residential and has been held over 100 months). If this result is greater than the gain on sale, the recapture will be limited to the gain.
2. Providing that the excess post-1969 depreciation is less than the gain, the following must be done: Calculate excess pre-1970 depreciation and multiply by the applicable recapture percentage. The total of this figure and the excess post-1969 depreciation will be subject to ordinary income taxes unless the amount is greater than the sale gain. Should this result, the gain on sale provides the recapture limit.

To illustrate the preceding: On January 1, 1966, Mr. Grimm developed a new apartment building on his own land at a cost of $500,000. The useful life of the building was 40 years, and Mr. Grimm chose the double declining-balance method of depreciation. He sold the building in January 1972 for $600,000, realizing a $232,430 gain ($600,000 less the depreciated book value of $367,670). The depreciation recapture would be calculated as shown in the accompanying table.

Year	D.B. 200%	Straight-Line	Difference
1966	$25,000	$12,500	$12,500
1967	23,750	12,500	11,250
1968	22,565	12,500	10,065
1969	21,400	12,500	8,900
Total	$92,715	$50,000	$42,715
1970	$20,365	$12,500	$ 7,865
1971	19,350	12,500	6,850
Total	$39,715	$25,000	$14,715

Post-1969 excess depreciation.....................................$14,715
Pre-1970 excess depreciation....................................... 42,715
Recapture percentage (100% − 52% for 72 months holding).........   48%
Pre-1970 recapture (48% × $42,715)................................$20,903
Total Amount Subject to Ordinary Income Tax as Recaptured..$14,715
                                                                     20,903
                                                                    $35,618

MINIMUM TAX

Tax laws now impose a 10% tax (in addition to other taxes) on certain tax preference items of an individual or corporation. Included in these preference items are:

1. Capital gains.
2. Accelerated depreciation on real property above the straight-line rate.
3. Excess investment interest until 1972 (individuals only).

The 10% minimum tax is imposed on each person's total of tax preference items in excess of $30,000 plus the regular tax imposed upon the person. As an illustration, Mr. Simmons has tax preferences of $150,000, which include $75,000 of excess investment interest and $75,000 in accelerated depreciation on a net lease he holds. Mr. Brown paid $95,000 in income taxes, and his tax preference deduction is $30,000. He therefore has $150,000 less $125,000, or $25,000 subject to the minimum 10% tax and will have to pay $2,500 in additional taxes.

Capital Gains as a Preference Item

The untaxed portion of long-term capital gains is a tax preference item. This amounts to 50% of the excess of net long-term capital gains over net short-term capital losses.

In the case of corporations, a theoretical untaxed portion of the long-term capital gain is the tax preference. This preference is calculated by multiplying the excess capital gains by a fraction whose numerator is the regular tax rate less the capital gains rate and whose denominator is the regular corporate rate.

For example, in 1971 the Deuce Trucking Company had net long-term capital gains which exceeded its net short-term capital losses by $250,000. This amount would include $100,000 as a tax preference item:

$$\$250,000 \quad \frac{0.50 - 0.30}{0.50} \quad = \$100,000$$

It is important to note that the tax on capital gains adds to the total exemptions for tax preference items, since it is part of the regular tax. This allows for a large amount of capital gains realization before any minimum tax is applicable.

Accelerated Depreciation on Real Property as a Preference Item

A 10% tax is assessed—subject to the $30,000 deduction and regular tax payments—on all excess depreciation over that which would have been taken with a straight-line method in any one year.

Excess Investment Interest as a Preference Item

The investment interest expense which exceeds net investment income for the taxable year involved is excess interest for minimum tax purposes. The preference provision does not apply to corporations and individuals for the year beginning in 1972. At that time, the excess investment interest will not be treated as a tax preference item, but one half will be disallowed as a deduction.

Investment interest is the charge incurred for purchasing and/or holding property for investment. For purposes of definition, net investment income is the excess of investment income over investment expenses. The income portion is made up of such factors as interest, dividends, rents, royalties, and net short-term capital gains on property held for investment purposes.

For purposes of determining investment interest, property subject to a net lease entered into after October 9, 1969, is specifically treated as held for investment purposes and is therefore included as investment interest expense.

Beginning in 1972, not all excess investment interest will be allowed as a deductible item for tax purposes. It is quite prevalent in real estate to incur large interest expenses as a by-product of holding investment property which produces little current income but is expected to yield capital gains at a future date. The present tax laws penalize this practice.

Under the 1969 act, investment interest can be used only to offset specified income after a $25,000 exemption:

1. Net investment income.
2. Excess of net long-term capital gain over net short-term capital losses.
3. Fifty percent of the excess of investment interest over the total of the $25,000 plus the other items mentioned.

The law does allow a carry-over of disallowed interest (post-1972), and it can be used to offset investment income and capital gains in future years. Interest on income-producing properties may not be subject to the provisions of this section. If the interest expense is related to a property used in a trade or a business, the interest expense is fully deductible and is not a preference tax item.

Excess Investment Interest and Net Leases

Property which is on a net lease is treated as held for investment if:

1. The lessor is guaranteed a specific return or protected against income loss.
2. The business expense deductions total less than 15% of rental income.

The law makes no distinction between real and personal property; it covers all property subject to a net lease.

From a tax standpoint, the inclusion of net leases as investment income could have very negative effects with regard to the deductibility of investment interest paid to carry a net lease property. If the property generates a taxable loss—which is often the case in real estate—there will be no investment income from the project to offset the interest expense, which is classified as investment interest because the income from a net lease is considered investment income.

Excess Investment Interest and Construction Interest

Construction interest paid while a property is being built for a trade or business is not investment interest. Therefore, the interest will be deductible even if there is no income generated. This, of course, would be the case during property construction, where taxable losses generated from interest expense and real estate taxes paid during the construction period can be deducted for tax purposes or capitalized.

INCREASING REAL INCOME THROUGH REAL ESTATE TAX PLANNING

Expenses Used to Build Up Capital Values

A method an investor could use to build up capital values with dollars that are rightfully the government's is for him to improve his property and deduct, within limits, the cost of the improvement as "maintenance and repair" expense in calculating his tax liability. As an example of this technique, assume that an individual in a 50% tax bracket spends $30,000 for "repairs and maintenance" that result in an increase in the value of the property by that amount. He has reduced his taxable income by $30,000, since this amount will probably be treated as a tax deductible expense. Though his actual cash expenditure was $30,000, the reduction in taxes cut his net outlay to $15,000, while at the same time it increased the value of the property by $30,000. Should he sell the property and realize $30,000 more on the sale price because of this improvement, he would have a maximum tax liability on the capital gain of 25%, or $7,500.[1] The investor would realize $22,500 after taxes as a result of this expenditure as against the $15,000 he would have retained had he not improved the property. As a result of this $15,000 after-tax expenditure, the investor retains an additional $7,500 for a 50% return.

Another method of avoiding taxes through property improvements can be practiced by a property owner who takes rental income in a nontaxable form by having the tenant erect an improvement in lieu of the rent. An example is cited of a man who owned vacant land and had several offers from companies that wanted to buy or lease the land and build on it. After sifting out various offers to purchase or lease the property, he accepted an offer to lease at a rental well below the highest offer. He was influenced by the relatively short period of the lease and the fact that the type of improvement that the prospective lessee would build was a general-purpose building of high marketability. In short, he was more influenced by the prospect of getting an improvement on his property tax free to him than he was by the amount of taxable cash rental he would receive.[2] The lessee can either depreciate the improvement over the life of the lease or expense the improvement as a "repair."

Another advantage offered by the operation of a property stems from the fact that real estate, unlike stock and bond investments, has been

---

[1] Should the investor die, the property's basis would increase by this $30,000, and no capital gains tax would be incurred when the sales value of this improvement was realized.

[2] William J. Casey, *Tax Shelter in Real Estate* (New York: Institute for Business Planning, 1957), p. 9

used by high-income individuals to deduct from income certain personal expenses connected with the operation and management of property. Entertainment, an automobile, traveling expenses, and the portion of an individual's house being used as his office may be deducted from taxes as business expenses. In a recent interview, a high-income investor disclosed his plans to acquire several small pieces of real estate that required management. He felt that this policy would allow him to deduct substantial personal expenses from his taxable income.

Taxes on the Sale of Property

A method of increasing real income through "tax planning" in real estate involves the avoidance or deferral of the extremely liberal capital gains tax through several alternative methods. The most obvious method of avoiding taxation on a real estate investment that has increased in value is to hold it until death. At that time, the asset, with an enhanced value, is passed on to the heirs without the incurrence of any capital gains tax, despite the fact that the heirs receive a stepped-up tax basis for the property equal to the market value at time of death. If, at time of death, the decedent's property has been fully depreciated and its tax basis is zero while it has a market value of $1 million, the heir's tax basis becomes $1 million without either party paying a capital gains tax. And if sale were to then take place for $1 million for a profit of $1 million, no income tax liability would be incurred.[3] Thus, the capital gains tax on the realized gain on the property would be avoided permanently.

Mortgaging—an Alternative to Selling

A second, and less painful, method of achieving liquidity on an asset with an unrealized profit without incurring a tax liability is to borrow against the enhanced value of the property. No personal liability need be assumed in arranging a mortgage against the property, since the mortgage can be taken in the name of a nominee.[4] Even though the tax basis in the hands of the investor is zero, a mortgage loan providing $1 million would not be taxable.[5]

A variation on the same theme would be for the investor to mortgage the property and then donate it as a gift. As an example of this, consider the case of a donor in a 75% bracket who owns income-producing

---

[3] The only tax that may be payable is the estate tax. However, the heirs of the investor who avoided the capital gains tax would remain with more money even after the estate tax than the heirs of the investor who realized the gain while he was alive and had to pay the tax.

[4] The mortgage lender is looking only to the property for repayment of the loan.

[5] Funds received as a loan are nontaxable.

property worth $50,000 with a tax basis of $20,000, on which a $30,000 mortgage is available. The owner has two children who are in the 25% tax bracket to whom he wishes to make gifts of $10,000 each. If the owner encumbers the property for $30,000 and then makes a gift of the property to the children, he has acquired $30,000 cash tax free for himself from the mortgage; he has arranged to have the mortgage paid off with 25% taxed income rather than 75% taxed income by shifting the income to the children and has effectively reduced the combined tax load payable by all parties compared to what would have been paid had he retained the property; and he has made a $20,000 gift with monies that would have been reduced to $12,500 had he sold the property to obtain the cash to make the gift and paid the $7,500 capital gains tax on the sale.[6]

Another method for avoiding a taxable gain on a property that has appreciated in value, and where it is difficult to obtain an adequate mortgage, is to lease the property to a financially strong tenant on a long-term net lease, even at a somewhat reduced rental. This would make it possible for him to borrow against the discounted value of the stream of net rentals to be received from the financially strong tenant, who is obligated under the lease to make these payments. The funds received from this loan should be nontaxable to the property owner.

Tax-Free Exchange

We have thus far been discussing situations where the investor retains ownership of the property. However, where the individual actually wants to dispose of the property, perhaps because of the substantial tax liabilities that would be incurred by retaining ownership (depreciation has been exhausted), or because he feels that this property will decline in value, there are several ways for him to avoid or defer the capital gains tax liability. One method under the present tax law involves the exchange of his property for other property. No tax liability would be incurred on this exchange regardless of the basis of the exchanged property. His tax basis of the received property is the basis of the old property plus any cash paid or mortgage assumed in excess of the mortgage transferred on his old property. Thus, if the investor assumed a substantial mortgage on the new property, though the tax basis for the old property is zero, he would be entitled to a depreciation allowance equal to the amount that the mortgage assumed was above the mortgage transferred, though no cash was involved in the exchange.

As an example of a tax-free exchange, a case is cited of a doctor who

---

[6] Melvin A. Spears, "Disposing of Property Mortgaged Above Basis; Opportunities and Hazards," *Journal of Taxation*, February 1960.

had a substantial personal income and who had inherited a plot of vacant ground some 30 years ago and had a basis for it of only $6,000. The property had been leased to a major oil company which had erected a building on it; the lease period had elapsed, the improvement went to the doctor, and the property had been devoted to other retail purposes. The doctor had no need for immediate taxable income, as his practice was substantial. The realizable cash value of the property was now $150,000, but his basis was the $6,000 basis for his land plus some additional capital improvements he had made but which had been depreciated down to $10,000. His income from the property was completely taxable, and inasmuch as he was in a 50% bracket, the property was a poor investment for him. The tenant of the property was anxious to buy it but the doctor was reluctant to sell; he wanted a retirement income and the possibility of a secure income if his medical practice should diminish.

However, after discussion with the owner, the doctor's tax lawyer arranged a trade with a builder for an apartment house. The doctor got credit for his full equity and was able to buy the apartment house for $450,000 subject to a first mortgage of $300,000. The cost allocable to depreciable assets was $306,520. Inasmuch as the building was new and had not been fully completed, his tax advisor recommended the use of double declining-balance method which gave him an original annual depreciation of over $15,000. This resulted in a $9,000 net after-tax cash flow to the doctor currently, and the prospect that, if value remained constant, he would have a substantially greater income 15 to 20 years hence, when the mortgage was fully paid. The builder, incidentally, sold the doctor's original property to its tenant and retrieved his cash investment.[7] In effect, the original landowner sold the land to the interested buyer, through the use of the contractor as an intermediary and purchased an apartment house without realizing any taxable gain.

Installment Sale

As a means of deferring taxes on a property that has appreciated in value, the investor could sell his property on the installment method.[8] The seller only pays a tax on the pro rata share of the capital gains he realizes in the year payment is received.[9] Meanwhile, the seller could

---

[7] Herbert Bernfeld, "How Taxfree Exchanges Freed Some Investors Locked into Real Estate," *Journal of Taxation*, October 1959, pp. 220–21.

[8] To qualify, not more than 30% of the gross sales price can be received in the year of the sale.

[9] If he sells a property with a $100,000 basis for $1 million with a $300,000 payment in the first year and the other $700,000 to be paid over the next seven years, he would only pay a capital gains tax on $270,000 income in the first year. He would only pay tax on the other payments as he receives them, regardless of the financial strength of the purchaser and the firmness of the obligation.

borrow $700,000 against the future payments receivable under the installment contract and would have no tax liability until he actually received the funds from the purchaser. He is thus able to defer payment of the capital gains tax though he has received a substantial part of the purchase price.

PART III

Development and Investment Cases

WHITE CORPORATION—
BUY OR LEASE

On June 25, 1966, Harold Robins of White Corporation visited the office of James Hahn, a real estate consultant. At the meeting, Mr. Robins pointed out that he was new in his position with White Corporation and wanted some general information about the real estate business. After a brief discussion, Mr. Robins gave Mr. Hahn an example of the kind of problems and decisions with which he was concerned at White Corporation.

White Corporation was planning to lease a proposed new warehouse to be built in Paramus, N.J., specifically for the corporation and had taken bids from developers and/or investors located in the area. The corporation wanted the developers to lease the space to it on a *net net rental* basis,[1] that is, it would pay all expenses, including real estate taxes, insurance, fuel costs, electricity, maintenance, and structural repairs. In addition, it would pay a fixed rental to the developer-investor. The bid terms included the annual net net rental, the term of the lease, the terms of any renewal options, and the terms of a proposed purchase option, if any. The lowest bid received, which also offered the most desirable terms, was proposed by a landowner-investor in the area. He was prepared to build for White a fully air-conditioned, sprinklered, 100,000-square-foot warehouse, having a floor load capacity of 200 pounds per square foot, with 10,000 of the 100,000 square feet designed for offices, plus a paved parking lot with 65 spaces adjacent to the building. The total land area was 5 acres.

All of these met White Corporation's specifications. The low bidder wanted a net net rental of $147,000 per annum for an initial lease period of 10 years, the lease term proposed by White. The short lease term, White felt, provided the corporation with maximum flexibility. Under this lease proposal, White would also have an option to purchase the property at the end of 10 years for $1 million, or alternatively, White would have four renewal options of 5 years each, for a total additional lease term of 20 years, assuming all options were exercised. The annual net net rental during the first five-year option period was to decline to

---
[1] It is assumed that the investor finds this arrangement satisfactory despite some negative aspects of net net leases which have resulted with the 1969 tax law. This case does not specifically deal with the new tax considerations which might make net leases less attractive for investment purposes.

$110,000; it was to fall to $88,000 during the second lease period, to $77,000 during the third lease period, and to $68,000 during the last five-year option period. White would have an option to purchase the property for $1 million during the second option period, for $850,000 during the third option period, and for $800,000 during the fourth option period beginning 25 years from the date of initial occupancy.

Mr. Robins thought this to be a fair offer and expected White Corporation to enter into the lease arrangement. Mr. Hahn asked Mr. Robins if the land owned by this bidder was the only plot available and was told that an equally attractive five-acre plot was available in the area at $22,000 per acre for a total land cost of $110,000. Mr. Robins added that the low bidder was planning to have a general contractor construct the proposed warehouse-office and had obtained construction cost estimates which, together with other costs to be incurred during construction (including interest on an interim loan to finance the construction, costs of landscaping the property and paving the parking area, architectural and legal fees, insurance, and real estate taxes) totaled approximately $970,000.

Mr. Hahn asked Mr. Robins why the company did not buy the land and have the warehouse built for White with White retaining ownership. Mr. Hahn knew that White was a large, rapidly growing manufacturer of electronic equipment. Mr. Robins gave Mr. Hahn a copy of White's financial statement, which showed a net worth of approximately $125 million, net current assets of $90 million, and total assets of $170 million, with sales of $250 million and net after-tax profits of $25 million.

Mr. Hahn asked why White didn't purchase the available 5-acre plot and have the warehouse constructed on this plot. He was certain the total cost for the warehouse-office building, including land, would not be in excess of $1.1 million. The $147,000 rental proposed by the low bidder would be sufficient to provide a 6% yield to a mortgage lender on the outstanding balance of the mortgage loan of $1 million and repay the full amount of the loan over a 10-year period—the proposed term of the lease (see Exhibit 1).

With this approach, White would own the building outright at the end of 10 years and would not have to pay $1.2 million to purchase it at that time. Nor would White have any rental obligations of $110,000 per annum if it did not wish to buy the property but preferred to lease it.

Mr. Hahn was certain that White could borrow enough to cover the full cost of the warehouse. After all, the proposed investor-lessor was panning to borrow the total cost of the land and building of $1.1 million from a life insurance lender on the basis of the security of the rental payment set forth in the lease, even though the lender did take a first mortgage on the property.[2] The lender was not really interested in the

_____

[2] Capitalizing this annual rental income at a rate as high as 9% would put the value of the property at $1,630,000. The $1.1 million mortgage loan would represent

value of the land and building and was not holding the mortgager-lessor personally liable, but was looking to the financial ability of White to meet its rental commitments. This was the primary security of the lender.

Mr. Robins stated that this ownership approach could not be pursued since White was reluctant to show any long-term debt on its balance sheet. Although he was aware that some very sophisticated lenders suggested capitalizing the value of a lease as an asset and showing the discounted rental payments due, as a contraliability, few lenders, in fact, followed this approach. In addition, Mr. Robins observed, White would only make investments offering a 25% rate of return. This investment provided a return of only 6%.

As a way of dealing with the objective of not showing debt on White Corporation's balance sheet, Mr. Hahn suggested that a subsidiary be formed of which only 50% would be owned by White, since a company does not consolidate any subsidiary in its balance sheet in which it does not own a majority of the stock. Thus, bringing in someone else to hold a one-half interest in the property in the subsidiary corporation would avoid the problem of having to show the mortgage liability for the building on the balance sheet. Since the owner of the other 50% of the stock will be investing only a negligible amount in the building, he will not be very much concerned with the repurchase terms of the lease terms, after the first 10 years; $250,000 would be a generous price for a one-half interest.

Mr. Hahn then pointed out that if White had outright ownership of the warehouse or owned 50% of a subsidiary owning the warehouse, there would be an important tax disadvantage. The real estate would show a taxable profit for income tax purpose even though it had no positive cash flow. He did the calculation shown in the accompanying tables (page 116).

Thus, during the first 10 years, the annual cash cost to White or to the proposed lessor would be greater under the ownership assumption than under the rental assumption by the amount of the annual tax liability. The tax liability would become even more substantial in the later years, since the depreciation deductions decline annually, while a greater part of the annual payment to the mortgage goes toward the repayment of debt—a nontax deductible payment—as a lesser part is used for the interest payments—a tax deductible expense. However, Mr. Hahn wondered whether even with the higher tax payments it would be preferable for White to own rather than lease. He computed the annual tax liability in Exhibit 3. If, in fact, the income tax liability did make the lease alternative more attractive, Mr. Hahn suggested that a charity or nontax-

---

two thirds of the capitalized value of the property. The legal maximum loan-to-value ratio is 75% for life insurance companies in most states. Of course, with the use of a lower capitalization rate, the property would have a higher value.

Income Statement for Income Tax Purposes

Gross rental income...		$147,000
Less: Interest expense.................................	$64,200	
Depreciation (150% declining-balance method)*....	36,750	
Total...		100,950
Net profit (before taxes).................................		$ 46,050
Income tax payable (50% rate)...........................		$ 23,025

Cash Flow Statement

Gross rental...	$147,000
Interest and amortization payments......................	(147,000)
Net cash flow..	0
Less: Income tax payable...............................	(23,025)
Net cash flow after taxes................................	$(23,025)

* Assumes a 40-year life. Depreciation under the straight-line method is 2.5% of the depreciable asset. Under the 150% declining-balance method, it is 3.75% of the undepreciated book value of the property. Only $990,000 of the property is a depreciable asset. The land cannot be depreciated for tax purposes.

able pension fund construct the building and lease it to White for $147,000 per annum for 10 years, giving White an option to either buy it for $500,000 at the end of the 10-year period, or lease it then at a substantially reduced rental.[3] This approach, Mr. Hahn thought, would obviously be more attractive than the present lease arrangement.

Mr. Hahn suggested another alternative as a means of avoiding this tax problem, that regardless of the rental or ownership approach, White should pay $85,200 per annum for a 25-year period rather than pay $147,000 per annum for a 10-year period. This would assume a 25-year lease period and make possible a mortgage loan repayable over the longer period. The $85,200 payment would provide a 6% return to the mortgage lender and repay him over a 25-year period (see Exhibit 2). By extending the mortgage to a 25-year term, he thought there might even be a positive tax benefit to the 50% owned corporation. For this alternative, he did the following computation:

Tax Computation

Gross rental......................................		$ 85,200
Less: Interest expense..........................	$(65,000)	
Depreciation expense....................	(36,750)	
Total expenses.............................		101,750
Taxable gain or (loss).............................		$(16,550)
Tax liability..		0

Cash Flow

Gross rental......................................	$ 85,200
Interest and amortization payment...............	(85,200)
Net cash flow.....................................	0

---

[3] The reason White could not enter into a more attractive repurchase option—at $20,000, for example—is that the government might then treat the property as owned by White during the entire period and forbid the deductions for rent during the period.

Under this assumption, there would be no tax liability to the proposed real estate company until year 8 (see Exhibit 4). As a matter of fact, it would have a loss against which it could offset other income. At one point, the real estate company might decide to sell the property to avoid the tax liability, that is, when the declining depreciation charges fell below the rising mortgage amortization payments. At that time, if the property was sold, a capital gains tax would have to be paid. Nevertheless, under the complete ownership or 50% ownership alternatives, White would be in a position to own the property at the lowest cost.

In addition, under the complete ownership alternative, as a result of the reduced rental, White would have the advantage of the tax losses generated during the first 10 years.

Mr. Robins said that White preferred the shorter 10-year lease term to the 25-year term, since it wanted the flexibility to move, though he did agree that in the history of the corporation, it had seldom vacated a property. Furthermore, why should White make total payments of $2,130,000 ($85,200 × 25 years) rather than $1,470,000 ($147,000 × 10 years)? Mr. Hahn explained that the additional payments were being made because the funds were outstanding for a longer period. In effect, the average borrowing was larger. In one case, $852,000 would be paid, while in the other, $1,470,000 would be paid, both during the same 10-year period. Thus, the company would have had the use of an additional $618,000 by the end of 10 years under the longer lease term. To illustrate his point, Mr. Hahn said that under the assumption that the alternative involving the lowest total payments was the optimum approach, the corporation should make only one payment of $1.1 million in advance for the entire cost of the property.

Mr. Hahn offered one last alternative to Mr. Robins. He suggested that White acquire the 5-acre plot and have the warehouse built according to its specifications. Mr. Hahn was confident that White would certainly be able to have the warehouse built for $970,000, including all costs. Generally, Mr. Hahn estimated the construction and other costs for general warehouse space, which also included 10% for offices, at $8 per square foot. Nevertheless, for the sake of conservatism, Mr. Hahn used the cost figure of $9.70 per square foot, which White had received from the low bidder. Upon completion of construction, White would obtain a permanent mortgage on the property in the amount of $1.1 million taxable over a 25-year period with interest at 6% on the outstanding balance of the mortgage. A constant payment of 7.75% of the $1.1 million mortgage loan, or $85,200 per annum, would repay the lender the $1.1 million over a 25-year period and provide the lender with an effective return of 6% (see Exhibit 2).

Mr. Hahn proposed that White should then sell the property to an investor in a high tax bracket seeking a tax shelter for his income for $1,120,000 of which $20,000 would be payable in cash. The balance of the purchase price would be paid by assuming the mortgage liability in the amount of $1.1 million.[4] An investor in a 50% tax bracket would obtain tax benefits yielding him an effective rate of return of approximately 20% on his investment over the first 10 years, assuming he were able to offset against his other income the tax losses generated by this property. Mr. Hahn knew of numerous investors interested in this type of transaction.

White Corporation would agree to pay a rental of $85,200 to the investor for the first 25 years, an amount sufficient to amortize the mortgage over the life of the lease. White would also have a right to purchase the property at the end of various periods at various purchase prices. The purchase price at the end of the 25th year, for example, would be the undepreciated book value of the property at that time, or approximately $381,000. White would also have the option of leasing the property for additional five-year terms at 7% of the undepreciated book value of the property at that time. At the beginning of the 25th year, the lease rental would be $26,700 for each of the next five years.

Mr. Hahn said that while the $20,000 excess cash received upon the sale of this property appeared insignificant in this case, it could be material if White adopted this policy with some of its larger properties. Mr. Robins agreed that he was concerned with the approach, regardless of the amounts invested. Even a sum as insignificant as $20,000 at the 25% projected rate of return for White would grow to $190,000 over a 10-year period.

Mr. Robins wanted to reflect on the various alternatives before submitting his recommendation to the head of the real estate at White Corporation.

---

[4] This does not mean that the purchaser would assume personal liability on the mortgage. The borrower on a mortgage on income-producing property does not usually assume personal liability for the mortgage debt.

EXHIBIT 1

Schedule of Quarterly Payments per $1000 at 6% Interest for 10 Years
(quarterly payment per $1,000 is $33.43; exact figure, $33.427102)

| Time | | | Payment on | | Balance |
Yrs.	Mos.	Periods	Interest	Principal	of Loan
0	3	1	15.00	18.43	981.57
0	6	2	14.72	18.71	962.86
0	9	3	14.44	18.99	943.87
1	0	4	14.16	19.27	924.60
1	3	5	13.87	19.56	905.04
1	6	6	13.58	19.85	885.19
1	9	7	13.28	20.15	865.04
2	0	8	12.98	20.45	844.59
2	3	9	12.67	20.76	823.83
2	6	10	12.36	21.07	802.76
2	9	11	12.04	21.39	781.37
3	0	12	11.72	21.71	759.66
3	3	13	11.39	22.04	737.62
3	6	14	11.06	22.37	715.25
3	9	15	10.73	22.70	692.55
4	0	16	10.39	23.04	669.51
4	3	17	10.04	23.39	646.12
4	6	18	9.69	23.74	622.38
4	9	19	9.34	24.09	598.29
5	0	20	8.97	24.46	573.83
5	3	21	8.61	24.82	549.01
5	6	22	8.24	25.19	523.82
5	9	23	7.86	25.57	498.25
6	0	24	7.47	25.96	472.29
6	3	25	7.08	26.35	445.94
6	6	26	6.69	26.74	419.20
6	9	27	6.29	27.14	392.06
7	0	28	5.88	27.55	364.51
7	3	29	5.47	27.96	336.55
7	6	30	5.05	28.38	308.17
7	9	31	4.62	28.81	279.36
8	0	32	4.19	29.24	250.12
8	3	33	3.75	29.68	220.44
8	6	34	3.31	30.12	190.32
8	9	35	2.85	30.58	159.74
9	0	36	2.40	31.03	128.71
9	3	37	1.93	31.50	97.21
9	6	38	1.46	31.97	65.24
9	9	39	0.98	32.45	32.79
10	0	40	0.49	32.79	0.00
			Final Payment		33.28

Note: Qu–6%–4.

EXHIBIT 2

Schedule of Quarterly Payments per $1000 at 6% Interest for 25 Years
(quarterly payment per $1,000 is $19.38; exact figure, $19.370571)

Yrs.	Mos.	Periods	Interest	Principal	Balance of Loan
0	3	1	15.00	4.38	995.62
0	6	2	14.93	4.45	991.17
0	9	3	14.87	4.51	986.66
1	0	4	14.80	4.58	982.08
1	3	5	14.73	4.65	977.43
1	6	6	14.66	4.72	972.71
1	9	7	14.59	4.79	967.92
2	0	8	14.52	4.86	963.06
2	3	9	14.45	4.93	958.13
2	6	10	14.37	5.01	953.12
2	9	11	14.30	5.08	948.04
3	0	12	14.22	5.16	942.88
3	3	13	14.14	5.24	937.64
3	6	14	14.06	5.32	932.32
3	9	15	13.98	5.40	926.92
4	0	16	13.90	5.48	921.44
4	3	17	13.82	5.56	915.88
4	6	18	13.74	5.64	910.24
4	9	19	13.65	5.73	904.51
5	0	20	13.57	5.81	898.70
5	3	21	13.48	5.90	892.80
5	6	22	13.39	5.99	886.81
5	9	23	13.30	6.08	880.73
6	0	24	13.21	6.17	874.56
6	3	25	13.12	6.26	868.30
6	6	26	13.02	6.36	861.94
6	9	27	12.93	6.45	855.49
7	0	28	12.83	6.55	848.94
7	3	29	12.73	6.65	842.29
7	6	30	12.63	6.75	835.54
7	9	31	12.53	6.85	828.69
8	0	32	12.43	6.95	821.74
8	3	33	12.33	7.05	814.69
8	6	34	12.22	7.16	807.53
8	9	35	12.11	7.27	800.26
9	0	36	12.00	7.38	792.88
9	3	37	11.89	7.49	785.39
9	6	38	11.78	7.60	777.79
9	9	39	11.67	7.71	770.08
10	0	40	11.55	7.83	762.25
10	3	41	11.43	7.95	754.30
10	6	42	11.31	8.07	746.23
10	9	43	11.19	8.19	738.04
11	0	44	11.07	8.31	729.73
11	3	45	10.95	8.43	721.30
11	6	46	10.82	8.56	712.74
11	9	47	10.69	8.69	704.05
12	0	48	10.56	8.82	695.23

Note: Qu–6%–21.

EXHIBIT 2 (Continued)

| Time | | | Payment on | | Balance |
Yrs.	Mos.	Periods	Interest	Principal	of Loan
12	3	49	10.43	8.95	686.28
12	6	50	10.29	9.09	677.19
12	9	51	10.16	9.22	667.97
13	0	52	10.02	9.36	658.61
13	3	53	9.88	9.50	649.11
13	6	54	9.74	9.64	639.47
13	9	55	9.59	9.79	629.68
14	0	56	9.45	9.93	619.75
14	3	57	9.30	10.08	609.67
14	6	58	9.15	10.23	599.44
14	9	59	8.99	10.39	589.05
15	0	60	8.84	10.54	578.51
15	3	61	8.68	10.70	567.81
15	6	62	8.52	10.86	556.95
15	9	63	8.35	11.03	545.92
16	0	64	8.19	11.19	534.73
16	3	65	8.02	11.36	523.37
16	6	66	7.85	11.53	511.84
16	9	67	7.68	11.70	500.14
17	0	68	7.50	11.88	488.26
17	3	69	7.32	12.06	476.20
17	6	70	7.14	12.24	463.96
17	9	71	6.96	12.42	451.54
18	0	72	6.77	12.61	438.93
18	3	73	6.58	12.80	426.13
18	6	74	6.39	12.99	413.14
18	9	75	6.20	13.18	399.96
19	0	76	6.00	13.38	386.58
19	3	77	5.80	13.58	373.00
19	6	78	5.60	13.78	359.22
19	9	79	5.39	13.99	345.23
20	0	80	5.18	14.20	331.03

EXHIBIT 3

Tax Effects to Property Owner under 10-Year Mortgage Assumption

	Year 1	Year 2	Year 3	Year 4	Year 5	Year 6	Year 7	Year 8	Year 9	Year 10
Rent	$147,000	$147,000	$147,000	$147,000	$147,000	$147,000	$147,000	$147,000	$147,000	$147,000
Interest expenses	64,200	59,100	53,700	49,900	41,800	35,400	28,500	21,300	13,500	5,300
Depreciation	36,750	35,700	34,400	33,100	31,900	30,600	29,500	28,400	27,200	26,300
	$100,950	$ 94,800	$ 88,100	$ 83,000	$ 73,700	$ 66,000	$ 58,000	$ 49,700	$ 40,700	$ 31,600
Net income or (loss)	$ 46,050	$ 52,200	$ 58,900	$ 64,000	$ 73,300	$ 81,000	$ 89,000	$ 97,300	$106,300	$115,400
Tax	$ 23,025	$ 26,100	$ 29,450	$ 32,000	$ 36,650	$ 40,500	$ 44,500	$ 48,650	$ 53,150	$ 57,700

EXHIBIT 4

Tax Effects to Property Owner under 25-Year Mortgage Assumption

	Year 1	Year 2	Year 3	Year 4	Year 5	Year 6	Year 7	Year 8	Year 9	Year 10
Rent	$ 85,200	$ 85,200	$ 85,200	$ 85,200	$ 85,200	$ 85,200	$ 85,200	$ 85,200	$ 85,200	$ 85,200
Interest expenses	(65,600)	(64,500)	(63,100)	(61,700)	(60,300)	(58,700)	(57,100)	(55,300)	(53,500)	(51,600)
Depreciation	(36,750)	(35,700)	(34,400)	(33,100)	(31,900)	(30,600)	(29,500)	(28,400)	(27,200)	(26,300)
	$(102,350)	$(100,200)	$(97,500)	$(94,800)	$(92,200)	$(89,300)	$(86,600)	$(83,700)	$(80,700)	$(77,900)
Net income or (loss)	$ (17,150)	$ (15,000)	$(12,300)	$ (9,600)	$ (7,000)	$ (4,100)	$ (1,400)	$ 1,500	$ 4,500	$ 7,300
Tax								$ 750	$ 2,250	$ 3,650

GOLF ACRES
SHOPPING CENTER

MEMORANDUM   May 1, 1963
RE: Golf Acres Shopping Center, Flat Hills, Michigan

Great Eastern Life Insurance Company is one of America's 15 largest life companies with total assets of $2.5 billion. Its policy has been to keep approximately 40% of its money in mortgages and real estate, and its present portfolio is approximately $1 billion. Each year the mortgage department has about $80 million for new investment, of which about $35 million represents the mortgage department's share of net asset growth and the remainder consists of repayments of principal. The amount available fluctuates some, both because of wide fluctuations in rate of principal repayment and because it is the company's policy to shift a portion of its growth in assets from the mortgage department to the securities department or vice versa, dependent on the relative attractiveness of interest rates in the two fields.

At present, about 65% of Great Eastern's mortgage portfolio is in one- to four-family residential loans, and the remainder is in commercial property. The company has had an increasing tendency to make larger commercial loans, however, and its present program is to put 65% of its new funds into conventional and insured and guaranteed residential loans, with the remaining 35% put into income property.

With approximately $54 million a year for investment in income properties, Great Eastern has decided that as a practical measure, it should not consider an individual transaction of more than $4 million, and it should go that high only rarely. On two or three occasions, however, it has worked out arrangements to divide a particularly attractive, very large loan with one of four other large life companies under which a single mortgage secured two notes, one held by each company. In these instances, the borrower made his payments direct to each of the two companies involved.

The company has tried to follow a "rolling" commitment policy under which its backlog of committed but undisbursed commercial loans would average out at two thirds of its anticipated 18 months' disbursements in the field. Thus, for the $54 million amount available annually, its backlog of committed cases would also run to about $54 million. In recent months, the company, in anticipation of a possible slight decline in yields, has permitted its backlog of committed business to build up to $60 million, which leaves less room for future deals but does not preclude them.

Great Eastern is thoroughly committed to the correspondent system. It is represented in Flat Hills, Michigan, by Flat Hills Realty Mortgage, Inc. Flat Hills Realty Mortgage was formed in 1925 and has represented Great Eastern since 1927. It also represents one of the larger East Coast companies with assets of approximately $5 billion and an active interest in both residential and commercial loans; it represents, too, several smaller eastern and midwestern life companies largely interested in residential loans and services for a number of New York savings banks.

Flat Hills Realty Mortgage is headed by A. T. Donn, 62 years old, who was primarily a residential mortgage man when he first joined the business in 1930. His principal capacity now is in the executive direction of the business, and he rarely gets involved in specific transactions. His chief commercial production man, with the misleading title of executive vice president, is 44-year-old Al Robie, who had seven years in the mortgage department of the Equitable Life's Cleveland office and two years in the home office before joining Flat Hills Realty Mortgage in 1950.

Flat Hills has done a good job of developing its business and is presently servicing a portfolio of about $110 million. Al Robie, assisted by Mr. Donn, has proved adept at brokering several rather attractive loans, which for one reason or another his companies were unable to handle.

There is only one other full-fledged mortgage correspondent in Flat Hills, that being the Michifirst Mortgage Company, which also represents two large eastern companies and a number of smaller ones. There are a number of other MBA members in Flat Hills, but they represent small companies and are interested purely in the residential business.

Besides finding Michifirst strong competition, Flat Hills Realty has been annoyed on several occasions to lose choice loans to Detroit and Chicago mortgage bankers. The most attractive recent piece of business, financing of the new Michigan Utility Bank Building downtown, was placed by a New York brokerage firm, which really hurt.

Exhibit 1 is an outline map of the city of Flat Hills. The city, located about 80 miles outside Detroit, is largely supported by the manufacturing industries. It has no automobile assembly plants, but there are seven major plants manufacturing parts for the various auto companies. There are also two furniture factories, a cannery for the vegetable crops, a tire factory, a paper manufacturer, and miscellaneous smaller industries. The town also boasts a State Teachers College whose football team was undefeated in 1962.

Agriculture is also important to the area, flat, rich soils surrounding the city being well suited for the truck vegetable crops, for dairy farming, the raising of beans, corn, and some wheat.

The population statistics for the last four censuses are as shown in the accompanying table.

Census Year	City	Metropolitan Area
1962*.....................196,000		285,000
1950.....................181,000		228,000
1940.....................170,000		205,000
1930.....................165,000		190,000

* Estimated.

Sales Management[1] figures show estimated effective buying income per capita of $1,820, estimated per household effective buying income of $6,512. Comparative figures for Detroit Metropolitan area are $2,175 and $7,593; for the Lansing area, $2,028 and $6,889; for the Saginaw area, $1,851 and $6,413; and for all of the areas of the state an average of $2,089 and $7,215. Retail sales per household are $3,937 divided as follows:

	%		%
Food	21	Automobiles	27
Bar-restaurant	5	Gas stations	7
General merchandise	14	Lumber-building materials	7
Apparel	9	Drugs	5
Furniture-appliances	5	Total	100%

In terms of quality index and sales activity index, the figures for Flat Hills County are 99% and 104% respectively, as compared with Wayne County (Detroit), 111% and 103%; Ingham County (Lansing), 115% and 121%; and Saginaw County, 100% and 101%.

In the department store field, Sears, Roebuck has a 150,000-square-foot store on the edge of downtown, which was opened in 1938. Sales are estimated to exceed $15 million. Sears reportedly wants to enlarge the store.

There are three locally owned stores in town. The Green Company founded in 1901 by A. T. Green is the old-line quality goods store. The store was solely owned by A. T. Green, Jr., from 1914 until he died in 1957 at the age of 83. Green's has always prided itself on the quality of its merchandise and the excellence of its service. While the store was relatively profitable in its earlier years, its volume has declined consider-

---

[1] "Survey of Buying Power," in *Sales Management: The Marketing Magazine*, 630 Third Avenue, New York 10017, New York.

ably in the past five years and is now below 1950 levels. Decreasing volume and increases in operating costs have put it into the red for the past three years. Summary balance sheets and sales and earnings records from 1952 to date are shown in Exhibit 2.

Green's has a downtown store only, occupying about 120,000 square feet in a building it rents in a good location. Green's is still probably the number one prestige store in town, despite the fact that from a volume and earnings standpoint it has been falling steadily behind.

There has been a recent change of management in Green's. In January 1962, the executors of the A. T. Green estate sold the store to 45-year-old Fred Wish. Wish was graduated in retailing from Northwestern University, went with the J. L. Hudson Company in Detroit, and left them after the war to start building a fortune via the capital gains route as applied to retailing. He has done well by buying older, distressed retail properties, revitalizing them, cutting expenses while building up sales, putting them on a profitable operating basis, and then selling out. He has been three times through the cycle since 1948, with an average duration of ownership in any one store of five years. Each time he has sold a store, he has bought a larger operation in a larger city. This purchase in Flat Hills is his largest undertaking to date. Mr. Wish claims that he has made enough money via the capital gains route; that he wants to stay and operate the Green store; that it is a marvelous potential retail property. He claims he has no desire to move his family again. In the period since he took over active management in March of 1962, he has dressed up the store with considerable paint, started an installation of new escalators, drastically reduced the number of employees without too seriously affecting service, and improved the store's inventory situation. In August 1962, the store showed black operating figures for the first time in 42 months, excluding the annual Christmas and Easter peak seasons.

Part of Wish's program for Green's is to open a suburban branch. He will be the key tenant in the Golf Acres shopping Center. Green's has agreed to take 100,000 square feet on a 20-year lease at $1.40 a square foot versus 2½% of gross sales, breaking to 2% on sales above $5 million. Wish is requiring, however, a turn key job, as he claims that the cost of fixturing and of stocking the new branch, together with work that had to be done downtown, strains his financial capacity just a bit.

The leading volume store in the city, aside from Sears, is the White Company. Traditionally, White's has been the number two store in town, and in prestige perhaps still is. It is generally considered by the business people and bankers in town that it has moved ahead while Green's stagnated. No figures are available, but fairly reliable estimates are that sales currently exceed $12 million annually, of which about $8 million is done downtown and $4 million done in the 35,000-square-foot branch store at Ford Square, the only major shopping center in Flat Hills, which was opened in 1958. Ford Square has just completed a 30,000-square-foot addition for White's, bringing its total area to 65,000 square feet. Local guesses are that volume will run above $6 million in this branch, which opened for the Easter trade in 1963.

The only other department store close to being a full-line store in Flat Hills is Reddy & Company, which has been a low price line, high-volume, promotional operation. It has only 30,000 square feet of off-location space downtown, spread over seven stories, but opened a 15,000-square-foot branch at Norside Center in 1957, and a 20,000-square-foot branch at Eastway in 1959. The latest Dun & Bradstreet report rates Reddy & Company at A plus 1, with sales for the year ending January 13, 1963 of $5,125,000. The company's net worth is $900,000, and its current ratio is 1.90. According to the Dun & Bradstreet report, sales and profits have been increasing rather steadily at a rate of about 8% per year for the past five years, due to the dynamic merchandising of Barney Solomon, who really runs the store, though J. P. Reddy retains the title of president and chairman.

Geographically, as can be seen from Exhibit 1, Flat Hills is rather typical of many midwestern metropolitan areas of a quarter of a million. The Flat River curves through the city, with the central business area being laid out in the bend on the east bank, where the town originally started. Downtown is considered to be neither better nor worse than downtown in most cities of similar size. The main access roads to downtown are Mackinaw Avenue, U.S. 92, running north and south, and Huron Avenue, U.S. 103, running east and west. These are wide, straight, four-lane highways. A problem is created by the rather antiquated bridges where the highways cross the Flat River. Downtown is adversely affected by a curved, irregular street pattern following the lines of the original town, which causes considerable traffic congestion, particularly at rush hours. There is also a railroad grade-level intersection, just north of the downtown district. The adjacent freight yards, however, are being taken over by the city and will be put into multistory municipal parking, which should help alleviate the parking shortage. There is also hot discussion running between the Town Council and the downtown merchants concerning the merits and demerits of a permanent mall installation a la Kalamazoo. Volume has suffered downtown during the past few years, and there are several retail vacancies.

The northeast quadrant of the city is largely industrial and older residential, now about 80% occupied by blacks. The southeast quadrant, divided by the river, is largely older housing occupied by skilled industrial workers and the lower white-collar echelons, with some FHA development south of the river and south of Allegan Avenue. The northwest quadrant is somewhat similar, though more sparsely developed and with a heavier concentration of industry along the railroad.

For the last 40 years, the so-called "best" residential area has been the southwest quadrant, which, developed rather recently in the history of the city. For a number of years, the city limits on the west side were along Flint Road, with Saginaw Street limiting the town on the south. During the 1920's, the limits were extended westward to Woodward Avenue; east of Flint Road, they were moved south to the Lansing Turnpike.

During the early 1930's, the diagonal bypass highway connecting U.S. 103 with U.S. 92, and missing the center of the city, was built. At the time, this was a four-lane nondivided highway through open country, and despite a couple of bad traffic hazards at diagonal intersections, it was considered the ultimate in highway development.

By now, the better residential area has expanded into the township, going first west of Woodward Avenue, out beyond the bypass; more recently it has filled in east of Woodward and south of the Lansing Turnpike around the country club. Houses in this area range in price from $20,000 to $50,000, with the bulk of the more expensive homes being in the country club area. The bypass is no longer regarded as adequate. It is, in fact, a slow, dangerous road with a lot of truck traffic on it. About all that can be said in its favor is that it is to be preferred to taking 103 and 92 across the bridges and through the center of town. There is considerable talk of a circumferential highway running around the city, 8 to 10 miles out. So far no rights-of-way have been acquired.

The Golf Acres Shopping Center site was originally a semiprivate, 18-hole golf course, put in as a profit-making development and opened to the public in the mid-1920's. It went broke in 1932, and its 120 acres grew up largely in weeds during the latter part of the 1930's. Being in the township, it lacks sanitary sewerage, though city water is available to it, and by contract between the township and the city, it has fire protection. The County Sheriff's Department is relied on for policing the area.

The township adopted a zoning ordinance in 1946, and the old Golf Acres site was Zone AA residential. As the area was flat, and had no particularly attractive features, there was little tendency for it to develop during the immediate postwar period. At this time, most of the development was north of Saginaw Street. Max Reinhart, a builder, bought the area for $60,000 in 1946, expecting to hold it for several years, then subdivide it. He felt this could be done more profitably after the area to the east of the country club began to develop.

By 1956, Reinhart considered the land right for development, but about that time he became intrigued by the planned J. L. Hudson Northland development in Detroit and decided that the Golf Acres site should also be developed as a regional shopping center. He ran into a really stiff fight on zoning, however, and it took two trips to court, four years, and $40,000 to get the zoning accomplished. By late 1960, when the battle was finally won, acreage for residential development in the general vicinity was bringing from $1,500 to $2,000 an acre. Reinhart considers his land to be worth $10,000 an acre, though he carries the 120 acres on his statement at $1.5 million.

Also in 1956, about simultaneously with Reinhart, a local commercial real estate developer named Mahoney conceived the idea of developing Ford Square as a shopping center. This being located just within the city limits, zoning proved to be no particular problem, and the development went forward quite rapidly. Ford Square opened with 130,000 square feet of stores, including the 35,000-square-foot White unit, in 1958, and the development has been outstandingly successful. Mahoney and his architect had a flair for attractive design, and Mahoney balanced a good assortment of local merchants with White's, Woolworth's, his two supermarkets, and a Cunningham drugstore. Additions to the center have been made almost annually to the point where it now exceeds 280,000 square feet in area on 65 acres, with the White addition opened. Mahoney has never released any figures as to the exact performance of his center. A number of the local merchants have increased their space, however; turnover is low and despite a by-now shortage of parking and a somewhat helter-skelter arrangement, the center is obviously doing well.

At the time the two centers were conceived in 1956, both Reinhart and Mahoney had wanted White as the key tenant. White took the first deal to develop and is now well anchored at Ford Square. Reinhart, however, feels that with Green's in new hands, occupying 100,000 square feet of space, and with Reddy's taking 62,000 square feet, also for 20 years, Golf Acres will have the best of the department store picture.

Reinhart and his 10% partner and lease broker Joe Flinch have completed most of the leasing of 400,000 square feet of gross leasable area. Part of Exhibit 7 is a tabulation of the leasing done to date.

Plans for the center call for an open mall development with the two department stores at either end and the other stores facing each other across 35 feet of landscaped mall. Plans show a truck tunnel running the full length of the mall with landing platforms serving each store. Of the total of 400,000 square feet of gross leasable area, approximately 120,000 is in private basements and landing platforms. Exhibit 3 is the basic plot plan.

Reinhart's architect estimates that the center will cost about $6,650,000 to build. Reinhart values his land at $1.5 million and feels that with a total security value of $8,150,000, he should be able to get a loan of $5.5 million to $6 million.

Reinhart, who is single, 65, and has no dependents, makes a statement showing a net worth of $4.5 million. The bulk of this, however, is in real estate equities and land held for development. A copy of this statement submitted by a CPA is shown in Exhibit 4. This is Reinhart's first real experience in the shopping center business, although, as the statement shows, he owns a number of pieces of downtown real estate. His partner, Flinch, both owned and developed the much smaller Norside and Eastway Centers and has participated in some way in the leasing or developing of approximately a dozen centers, largely neighborhood size, in various central Michigan towns. Flinch shows a net worth of approximately $300,000, of which $7,000 is in cash and $11,000 in marketable securities. The balance is in his residence and real estate equities.

Tom Raft, Great Eastern's mortgage analyst working out of the home office, but covering the central Midwest, has had an eye on the Reinhart land for several years, and he and Al Robie have talked with Reinhart about financing the development on it on several occasions. Raft was last in Flat Hills in October 1962, at which time Reinhart indicated that he would like to borrow $5.5 million to $6 million on the development. Raft and Robie did some pencil work with Reinhart at the time, and indicated a possible interest on Great Eastern's part, but in the $4 million to $4.5 million range.

In March 1963, Reinhart came to Al Robie and stated that he wanted to submit an application to Great Eastern for a loan of $5.5 million at 5¾% on a 25-year fully amortized basis. Robie, knowing that Great Eastern considered 6% to be its prime rate, and knowing also the company's feelings as to possible loan amount and probable amortization term, negotiated for several days with Reinhart, at the conclusion of which he took a firm application for a loan of $5 million for 20 years at 6%. He appraised the property on a reproduction basis for $7.7 million, on an economic basis for $7 million, and submitted the loan application, recommending its approval at $4.5 million. A summary of his appraisal is shown in Exhibit 5.

Robie submitted with it a market study done by Walter Blue Associates in 1958, analyzing current population and spendable income and establishing as a primary market area a rectangle whose sides are parallel to Golf Acres lot lines and roughly three miles distant in each direction. The secondary market area extended another mile beyond the limits of the primary area. The complete report is appended as Exhibit 6.

Great Eastern's analytical processors had briefed the loan, including a summary of leasing to date. A copy of the brief is shown in as Exhibit 7. They turned the submission over to Tom Raft without comment or recommendation, which was somewhat unusual.

Also submitted, but not reproduced here, were:

Complete Audits of the Green Company, 1952 to Date
Dun & Bradstreet Reports on All Major Tenants
Numerous Aerial Views
Architect's Preliminary Plans and Outline Specifications
Current Retail Credit Report on Fred Wish
Cost Estimate Prepared by Architect
Preliminary Draft of Green Lease
Detailed Appraisal on Great Eastern's Form

As Tom Raft studied the case and reviewed it with the officers of Great Eastern, a great many questions arose. What questions would occur to you as a loan officer for Great Eastern, and what would be your recommended course of action?

EXHIBIT 1

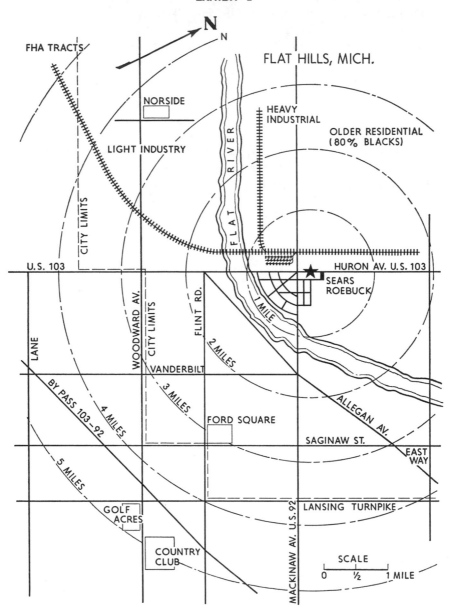

FLAT HILLS, MICH.

EXHIBIT 2

Green Company: Summary of Balance Sheets and Operating Results, Years Ending January 31
(000 omitted)

	1952	1953	1954	1955	1956	1957	1958	1959	1960	1961	1962
Sales	7,983	8,601	8,209	9,485	9,306	9,158	8,991	8,909	8,756	8,321	7,887
Cost of sales	5,422	5,548	5,380	6,363	6,279	6,156	6,208	6,318	6,371	6,325	6,116
Gross profit, owned depts.	2,561	3,053	2,829	3,122	3,027	3,002	2,783	2,591	2,385	1,996	1,771
Income from leased departments	128	131	142	146	151	149	152	156	146	149	138
Total Gross Profit	2,689	3,184	2,971	3,268	3,178	3,151	2,935	2,747	2,531	2,145	1,909
Expenses	2,584	2,929	2,932	3,199	3,126	3,102	2,902	2,730	2,971	2,566	2,518
Operating profit	105	255	39	69	52	49	33	17	(440)	(421)	(609)
Income tax	47	116	10	18	16	15	10	9	—	—	—
To surplus	58	139	29	51	36	34	23	8	(440)	(421)	(609)
Assets											
Current assets	2,409	2,715	2,961	2,916	3,270	3,683	3,643	3,886	3,114	2,792	2,348
Prepaid items, etc.	106	142	320	397	455	505	490	452	452	450	418
Fixed assets	181	193	193	200	200	200	212	412	396	370	340
Total Assets	2,696	3,050	3,474	3,513	3,935	4,389	4,345	4,750	3,962	3,612	3,106
Liabilities											
Current liabilities	591	865	1,279	1,232	1,673	1,593	1,526	1,570	1,252	1,353	1,486
Funded debt	—	—	—	—	—	500	500	900	870	840	810
Capital stock	750	750	750	800	800	800	800	800	800	800	800
Earned surplus	1,355	1,435	1,445	1,481	1,462	1,496	1,519	1,480	1,040	619	10
Total Liabilities	2,696	3,050	3,474	3,513	3,935	4,389	4,345	4,750	3,962	3,612	3,106
Current ratio	4.04	3.14	2.26	2.28	1.96	2.32	2.38	2.47	2.48	2.06	1.58

EXHIBIT 3

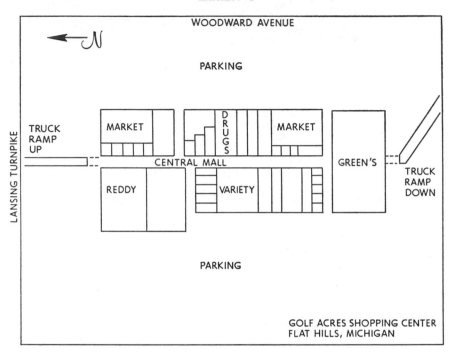

GOLF ACRES SHOPPING CENTER
FLAT HILLS, MICHIGAN

EXHIBIT 4

Max W. Reinhart, Builder: Statement of Net Worth as of December 31, 1962

Assets

Current assets

Cash.....................................$	34,193		
Accounts receivable......................	28,465		
Notes receivable, unsecured.............	131,000		$ 193,658

Investments

200 shares General Motors...............	8,400		
100 shares Detroit Edison.................	4,400	$ 12,800	
Golf Acres land...........................	1,500,000		
Francis Building, one-half interest........	175,000		
208 S. Mackinaw..........................	650,000		
360 acres Jackson County................	360,000		
200 acres for subdivision.................	2,000,000	4,685,000	4,697,800

Other

Home...................................	42,000		
Car, 1962 Cadillac........................	6,250		48,250
			$4,939,708

Liabilities

Current liabilities

Accounts payable........................$	16,128		
Notes payable, bank.....................	135,000		$ 151,128

Mortgages Payable

208 S. Mackinaw.........................	330,000		330,000

Max Reinhart, Net Worth...$4,939,708

EXHIBIT 5

Golf Acres Shopping Center, Inc.: Appraisal

Physical

Land: 120 acres at $11,650/acre or 27 cents/sq. ft..................		$1,400,000
Buildings: 420,000 sq. ft. gross at $13.57/sq. ft......................		5,700,000
Mall, truck tunnel, paving, etc....................................		650,000
Total Physical Valuation.....................................		$7,750,000

Economic

Major tenant minimums...............................	$486,609	
Minor tenant minimums..............................	230,689	
One-half estimated overages..........................	30,000	
Total Gross Income..		747,298
Less: 20% vacancy on minors................................		45,900
Effective gross income.......................................		$ 701,398
Taxes..	$ 75,000	
Operating Expenses....................................	66,000	141,000
Net Income before Depreciation...............................		$ 560,398
Less: 2% Depreciation on $5,600,000............................		114,000
Net Income..		$ 446,398

Net before depreciation capitalized at 8%	= $7,000,000
Net capitalized at 6.5%	= $7,000,000
Final Valuation for mortgage loan purposes	= $7,000,000

April 15, 1963

Al Robie
Appraiser

EXHIBIT 6(A)

Market Area

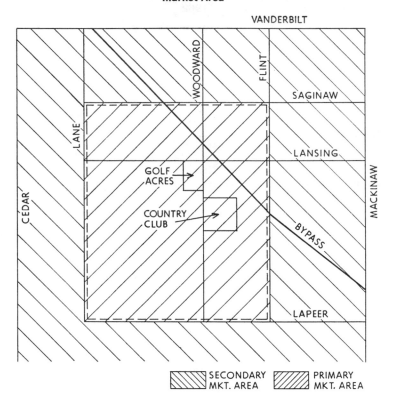

EXHIBIT 6(B)

Golf Acres Shopping Center, Inc.: Market Survey
(prepared by Walter Blue Associates, June, 1958)

Golf Acres Shopping Center, Inc., proposes to develop approximately 60 acres of the 120-acre site at the southwest corner of Lansing Turnpike and Woodward Avenue, just beyond the Flat Hills city limits, with approximately 400,000 square feet of retail stores.

On a separate exhibit we have outlined the approximate limits of this regional shopping center's primary and secondary market areas. These market areas were selected by our personnel after an exhaustive analysis of potentially competitive retail locations and after extensive research on driving times and shopping habits in this general area southwest of downtown Flat Hills.

The site of Golf Acres Shopping Center lies at the edge of the presently built-up residential area and directly within the path of Metropolitan Flat Hills' strongest residential growth.

The primary market area:

a) The area approximately 1 mile square to the northeast of the site.

This is a fully developed residential area with some homes up to 20 years old, most homes in the $20,000–$25,000 bracket.

b) The rectangular area of approximately 2¾ square miles to the northwest of the site. This is a residential area, approximately 75% developed with homes up to 15 years old, most homes in the $25,000–$35,000 bracket.

c) The large rectangular area of approximately 4 square miles to the southwest of the site. This area will grow rapidly in the next several years. At present there are a scattered number of homes in the $20,000–$25,000 bracket here.

d) The rectangular area of approximately 2¼ square miles to the southeast of the site. This attractive residential area is about 50% developed with most homes in the $30,000–$50,000 bracket.

The secondary market area:

a) The entire secondary market area to the north of the site, approximately 10 square miles, is 85% to 90% developed with homes 10 to 25 years old. It is a stable, lower-middle-income area.

b) The entire secondary market area to the east of the site is similar to "a."

c) The remaining secondary market areas to the south and west of the site show only scattered residential development in the $14,000–$20,000 bracket. These are strong growth areas, however, and should move rapidly in the next five to seven years.

EXHIBIT 6(C)
Golf Acres Shopping Center, Inc.: 1958

Primary Market Area			
Region	No. Persons	Effective per Capita Buying Income	Total Buying Income
a).	4,000	$1,900	$ 7,600,000
b).	8,000	2,300	18,400,000
c).	1,100	2,300	2,500,000
d).	2,400	4,000	9,600,000
Total Buying Income			$ 38,100,000

Secondary Market Area			
Region	No. Persons	Effective per Capita Buying Income	Total Buying Income
a).	35,000	$1,700	$ 59,500,000
b).	25,000	1,700	42,500,000
c).	3,000	1,900	5,700,000
Total Buying Income			$107,700,000

Total income available to Golf Acres Shopping Center:
Total income (primary area)..$ 38,100,000
One-half total income (secondary area)............................. 54,000,000
    Total Available..$ 92,100,000

If Golf Acres Shopping Center can, on the whole, capture $20 million of this income (or slightly over 20% of the total, it will be doing an over-all volume of approximately $50 per square foot of rentable area, which would be entirely satisfactory. This goal should not be difficult to achieve. The success of Golf Acres is further assured when one considers the established residential growth trend to the south, southwest, and west of the site. This should bring a minimum 25% increase in total income into Golf Acres trading area within the next five to seven years.

All significant facts and trends in this area, when considered in the light of the diversified array of tenants proposed for Golf Acres, point clearly to this shopping center's inevitable success.

Attached you will find projection of primary and secondary market area population to 1973.

Walter Blue Associates

Att.

EXHIBIT 6(D)

Golf Acres Shopping Center, Inc.: Market Area Population Projections

Primary Market Area			
	1958	1963	1968	1973
a)	4,000	4,200	4,300	4,300
b)	8,000	8,400	8,900	9,400
c)	1,100	1,600	2,600	3,600
d)	2,400	2,500	2,700	2,900
Total	15,500	16,700	18,500	20,200

Secondary Market Area			
	1958	1963	1968	1973
a)	35,000	36,000	37,000	37,000
b)	25,000	26,000	26,000	27,000
c)	3,000	3,800	6,000	9,000
Total	63,000	65,800	69,000	73,000

Total Market Area			
	1958	1963	1968	1973
	78,500	82,500	87,500	93,200

EXHIBIT 7

Loan Amount **$4,500,000**	_____Golf Acres_____ SHOPPING CENTER Note: All sq.ft. units shown hereon are gross leasable area.	City	Flat Hills	
		State	Michigan	
Loan Terms 20 yrs. - 6% - $32,265 mo. Int. & Prin. to fully amortize. Bal. end of 5 yrs. - $3,818,700 " " " 10 yrs. - 2,899,300 " " " 15 yrs. - 1,659,600 Annual Debt Service - $387,180	Location S. W. Corner of Lansing Turnpike and Woodward Avenue, Flat Hills, about 5 miles SW of the center of the city and directly in the path of the area's strongest residential growth.	Approx. Land Dim.	5,227,200 sq. ft.	
		No. Acres Land	120	
		No. Auto Pkg. spaces #	4,300	
		Parking Index	10.7	
		Year Bldg. Erected	To be 1963	
Option 10% in any one year; in full at 105 in the 6th year, declining ½ of 1% to 101 where it remains until maturity.	Improvements 5 buildings, 1 story, built around an open landscaped mall, with a truck tunnel running the full length of mall with underground loading platform ser- vicing each store. Construction in reinforced concrete frame, roof over steel joists. Interior partitions are masonry, exterior walls masonry; interior attrac- tive and well decorated; fully air conditioned.	No. Stores	1A	
		No.		
		Sq.ft. Finished Base		
		Sq.ft. Other Base	120,000	
		Sq.ft. Ground Floor	280,000	
Purpose To provide approximately 70% of total cost.		Sq.ft. Upper Floors		
		Total Leasable Area	405,670	
		Total Gross Area	420,000	
		% Coverage Land	9%	
		%G.L.A. to Tot. Gr. Area		

Economic Valuation (By: Al Robie, F.H. Realty & Mortgage)			Physical Valuation		HO Est. of Value	
Min. Inc. Major Tenants	$ 486,609	$ 1.61 /sq.ft.	Land @ $ ___ /ft.ft. or $ .27 /sq.ft.	$ 1,400,000	$	
Min. Inc. Minor Tenants	$ 230,689	$ 2.22 /sq.ft.	*Bldg. @ $ ___ /ft.ft. or $ 13.57 /sq.ft.	$ 5,700,000	$	
Total Minimum Income	$ 717,298	$ 1.77 /sq.ft.	Paving @ $ ___ /sq.ft. Mall, Tunnel	$ 650,000	$	
0% Overage Income	$ 30,000	$ .08 /sq.ft.		$	$	
Total Gross Income	$ 747,298	$ 1.85 /sq.ft.		$	$	
Less Vacancy Allowance	$ 45,900	$ .15 /sq.ft.	Total Physical Valuation	$ 7,750,000	$	
Stabilized Income	$ 701,398	$ 1.73 /sq.ft.	Net Income before Depr. Capitalized @ 8 %	$ 7,000,000	$ @ %	
Taxes .. $75,000		$ .19 /sq.ft.	Net Income before Depr. Capitalized @ %		$ @ %	
Op. Exp. .. 66,000		$ .16 /sq.ft.		Total HO Val./Sq.ft.	$	
Less Ten. Cont.	$ 141,000	$ /sq.ft.	Mortgagors Investment $1,910,000 or	Loan to Gross	6.2	
Net Income before Depr.	$ 560,398	$ 1.32 /sq.ft.	Est. Cost of Land $ 60,000 %	Loan to Net	10.5	
Depreciation % 2 %	$ 114,000	$ .28 /sq.ft.	Est. Cost of Imp. $6,350,000 Equity above	Loan per sq.ft.GLA	11.25	
Net Income	$ 446,398	$ 1.06 /sq.ft.	Total $6,410,000 Mortgage	Loan to App. Val.	64.2 %	

Debt Service $387,180	Mortgagor Golf Acres Shopping Center, Inc. Principal is M. Reinhart, age 65, net worth $4,500,000. Rein-		
D.S./sq.ft. .97	hart has been active in real estate and the bulk of his worth is in real estate. This is his		
Carrying Chgs. $528,180	first venture in the shopping center business. Flinch, Reinhart's partner, has owned and developed small		
C. Chgs./sq.ft. $ 1.32	centers, as Norside and Eastway, also has had experience in leasing and developing other centers.		
C. Chgs. to Gross 73.6%	Flinch's net worth $300,000.		
C. Chgs. to Maj. Ten Min. %			

Comments: *Based on Cost New Today of $ 15.00 /sq.ft. 1st floor
                                                    10.00   basement

*60 acres of 120 being developed for buildings, mall, and parking facilities.

Date___5-1-63___   Prepared by___GWT___   Reviewed by_____

EXHIBIT 8

Golf Acres Shopping Center, Inc.: Record of Leases

Area	Tenant	Term	Min. Rental	Per Sq. Ft.	% Rental	Est. Overage	Sales to Produce Overage	Options and Comments	Sales Sq. Ft. to Produce Overage
	Major Tenants								
1,400	Savings & Loan	5	4,200	3.00	5%	1,000	$ 212,000		$60
3,500	American Shoe	15	9,625	2.65	5%	2,000	371,000		60
6,300	MacCann Shoe	15	16,590	2.65	5%	2,000	371,000		55
6,750	Rinney Shoe	20	16,538	2.45	5%	2,500	540,000		51
10,500	Grand Auto	15	13,650	1.30	3%				
10,500	Lerbels (ladies RTW)	20	24,500	2.33	4%	3,000	636,000		65
11,400	Rex Drug	20	23,445	2.05	3%	5,000	950,000		84
19,800	FNS Market	20	36,357	1.83	1¼%				
22,100	Penniwise Market	20	43,257	1.94	1¼%				
47,000	H. L. Kreske (variety)	20	71,647	1.53	5%	5,000	1,530,000		33
62,000	Reddys Dept.	20	86,800	1.40	2½%	14,000	4,025,000		65
100,000	Greens	20	140,000	1.40	2½%	14,000	6,150,000		62
301,250	Total Majors		486,609	1.61					
	Minor Tenants								
8,500	Meadows	15	21,225	2.50	4%				
1,400	Retail Liquor	5	4,200	3.00	5%	2,800	56,000		40
1,400	Barber	10	4,200	3.00	5%				
1,600	Bill's Records	5	5,400	3.38	5%				
2,100	Ben's Jewelry	10	7,350	3.50	4%				
2,100	Mahel Beauty	10	6,300	3.00	6%				
2,100	Flower Shop	5	6,300	3.00	6%				
3,700	Dress Shop	10	12,100	3.27	5%				
11,000	Roger's Cafeteria	5	23,539	2.15	5%	10,000	670,000		60
7,750	Ben Best	15	14,850	1.92	5%				
29,000	Clarkes	20	40,900	1.41	5%				
70,650	Total Minor		146,364	2.04					
33,770	To be leased		84,325	2.50					
405,670	Grand Total		$717,298	$1.77		$61,300			

VALLEY SHOPPING CENTER

Investment Bankers in Real Estate

W. Hillary had been asked by a senior partner of Eastman Dillon to evaluate Valley Shopping Center, a syndication that the company was proposing to issue in September 1965 to a select group of its wealthy clientele (see Exhibit 1). Part I of the report deals with the company's application for $5.5 million of first-mortgage financing. Part II describes the proposed equity arrangement to raise $1 million. Mr. Hillary also received a market analysis of the site's potential done by Larry Smith, one of the foremost shopping center location authorities (see Exhibit 2). Eastman Dillon had received indications from a large insurance company that it would quite likely take the first mortgage on the terms outlined in the first part of the memorandum. The partners of Eastman Dillon would acquire the Class B interests. Mr. Hillary was asked what he thought the value of the Class B interests would be upon completion of the project.

Eastman Dillon had become involved in real estate through the development of "off balance sheet financing" for certain major corporations, such as oil firms, who did not want to show large amounts of fixed assets and long-term mortgage debt on their statements. Long-term leases were only footnoted in the statements. The credit of these firms was excellent, and Eastman Dillon was able on the basis of these long-term leases to sell the properties at rates only one fourth of 1% above corporate bond rates. Purchasers were either pension funds which were not so concerned with liquidity and liked the higher return, or wealthy individuals who were attracted by the depreciation which provided a tax shelter to their return. Eastman Dillon placed over $1 billion of funds in this manner.

However, as other investment banking firms became interested in the approach, competition became much greater for this type of business. Many of the partners of Eastman Dillon were anxious to find other areas of real estate in which to invest not only their clients' but their own funds. The next step for the firm was to become involved in equity financing. A slightly higher risk could result in higher return. Shopping centers appeared to the partners to be the most logical area of real estate. The tremendous increase in shopping centers in recent years had resulted from population growth, especially in suburban areas, higher incomes, better parking facilities, easier access, and changed merchandising techniques. Long-term leases from Triple A tenants could provide a secure return, with possibilities for growth through percentage rents tied to sales volume in the leases. If financed properly, the major portion of the income from the shopping centers could be covered by depreciation. Most of the Eastman Dillon partners were at least in a 50% tax bracket. Shopping centers also involved little management activity and involvement in operations on the part of the investors.

Mr. Hillary considered the Valley Shopping Center in the light of the above history. He knew that Eastman Dillon was very much concerned with its reputation as an investment banker. He wondered whether the firm was acting in this case as a banker or developer. The circumstances might be different in that the customers for these investments were private investors rather than the general public.

Mr. Hillary tried to consider the Valley Shopping Center from the viewpoint of security of income and predictability of expense. The return in a shopping center depended upon not only the after-tax cash return but on assumptions about future income from percentage rents and refinancing or sales opportunities.

Mr. Hillary felt it was very important to assess the possibility of the Center's rentals reaching the stabilized rent level which included percentage rents, as opposed to the guaranteed rents. The valuation of the location is the most critical factor in predicting the future of a center, but he also wanted to consider the market characteristics and merchandising ability of the stores. Then, he could arrive at a minimum value for the Class B interests and a projected value based upon his estimate of future income.

EXHIBIT 1

EASTMAN DILLON, UNION SECURITIES & Co.
MEMBERS NEW YORK STOCK EXCHANGE
One Chase Manhattan Plaza
New York, N.Y. 10005

PART I

September 20, 1965

Confidential Memorandum

Mortgage Placement

VALLEY SHOPPING CENTER
Denver, Colorado
$5,500,000, 5½% Mortgage
Due March 31, 1997

Eastman Dillon, Union Securities & Co. ("EDUS"), and Winmar Realty Development Company, Inc. ("Winmar") are presently developing a new regional shopping center, Valley Shopping Center (the "Center"), to be located in the suburban area 7 miles north of the central business district of Denver, Colorado. The total value of the improvements on the property, based upon estimated net income of about $559,000 capitalized at 7½% will be about $7,450,000.

General

Winmar, an affiliate of Larry Smith & Co., is developing and will operate the Center for EDUS partners and certain of their business associates (the "owners"). Construction is scheduled to begin in March 1966, and completion is expected by the spring of 1967. The Center will be located in the Westminister-Thornton area of Denver, at the intersection of West 48th Avenue and the Valley Freeway (Interstate 25) on approximately 36.5 acres of leasehold land. The land is held under a 99-year lease (the "ground lease"). The Center will contain approximately 545,000 square feet of enclosed building floor area, 50,000 of which will comprise an enclosed mall, air-conditioned in the summer and heated in the winter. The May Department Stores Company ("May") and Montgomery Ward & Co., Inc. ("Ward") will be the major tenants of the Center. Since Ward will build and finance its own store, the Ward store is not a part of the mortgage financing.

EXHIBIT 1 *(Continued)*

Mortgage Financing

Valley Shopping Center Realty Corporation (the "company"), a Colorado corporation, will borrow the funds necessary to finance the Center and will give a first leasehold mortgage to secure the loan. The proceeds from the mortgage financing will be applied to the repayment of construction loans incurred during the building of the Center. The amount of mortgage financing requested for the Center is $5.5 million, to bear interest at 5½%. The requested term is 30 years. Interest and principal should be payable quarterly in arrears in a constant amount sufficient to retire 100% of the mortgage by March 31, 1997. The maturity of the mortgage will coincide with or be prior to the expiration of the initial terms of the May and Ward lease agreements, and such mortgage will be secured in the manner set forth under the heading "Mortgage Security."

Development

In order to implement the development and financing of the Center, the following steps have been or will be taken.

The owners have made their equity investment in, and will develop, the Center through a limited partnership formed under the laws of the state of Colorado. EDUS, acting as agent for the owners, has formed the company to act as the owner's nominee for the purpose of financing construction of the Center for the benefit of the limited partnership. The development arrangements made with May and Winmar require the owners to make a minimum cash equity investment of $1 million in the Center.

The company is the assignee of the May Stores Shopping Centers, Inc.'s interest as tenant under a ground lease from certain fee owners to the 36.5-acre site. The term of the ground lease is 99 years, terminable after 40 years and every 5 years thereafter. The ground lease rental is $30,000 annually until July 1966, and $40,000 annually until July 1974. Thereafter, rent is subject to adjustment in accordance with changes in the Consumer Price Index but shall in no event exceed $50,000 per year or be less than $40,000 per year. The company is required to pay May $10,000 per annum as consideration for the assignment of the ground lease.

The company entered into a store lease with May simultaneously with the assignment of the ground lease by May to the company. During the initial lease term (which will not expire prior to the maturity of the mortgage), the guaranteed annual rent payable by May for its 138,345-square-foot store will be $184,545. May will be obligated to pay percentage rentals equal to 2% of gross receipts against the guaranteed mini-

EXHIBIT I (Continued)

mum of $184,545. The lease also includes the normal tax and other escalation clauses found in standard department store gross leases.

The company has entered into a ground lease with Ward covering an 11.3-acre portion of the 36.5-acre site. Under this ground lease, Ward will be required to construct its own store, subject to the approval of the company. It is anticipated that Ward will utilize Winmar's services in the construction of the store. The ground rent payable to the company by Ward under the Ward ground lease will be approximately $21,000 per annum. Ward will also be required to maintain its 11.3 acres, contribute to the expenses of maintaining the common area of the Center, pay taxes on its proportionate share of the leasehold, and pay all other expenses relating to its store.

The company has entered into a contract with Winmar for construction of the Center. The company has also entered into a development management services agreement with Winmar, as the agent of the company, covering (i) general development management, (ii) design and construction management, (iii) leasing services, and (iv) legal services related to leasing in connection with development of the Center.

The company will sublease the entire Center under a net master sublease (the "master lease") to 84th Leasing Corporation ("84th Leasing"), a wholly owned subsidiary of Winmar, and it will assign the May store lease and the Ward ground lease to 84th Leasing. Pursuant to the master lease, 84th Leasing will operate the Center on a net basis, assuming all obligations of the company under the ground lease and assignment from May, the May store lease and the Ward ground lease. The master lease will expire at the same time as the ground lease, and the basic rent commencing upon the opening of the Center will be equal to 8% of the total original development cost of the Center. As additional rental, 84th Leasing is obligated to pay 50% of the net income from the Center in excess of the sum of operating expenses (including the ground lease rentals and the $10,000 payable to May), the 8% rental, and $17,000 per annum for 10 years payable to Winmar for services rendered in the initial operating phases of the Center.

The interest of the company in the Center, as well as in the ground lease and in the master lease, will be transferred to the limited partnership as soon as no longer required by the company to effect any of the transactions described above.

Mortgage Security

The mortgage will be secured by (a) a first lien on the leasehold estate of the tenant (but not on the fee title) under the ground lease, (b) an assignment of the landlord's interest in the May store lease, the

EXHIBIT 1 *(Continued)*

Ward ground lease and the master lease and (*c*) a pledge and assignment of all rentals payable pursuant to such leases.

Economic Value Based on Cash Flow

Gross receipts from the Center's operations at the guaranteed rent levels will amount to about $812,000 per annum, based on 97% occupancy. Net operating expenses will total about $253,000 annually, leaving $559,000 available for debt service and the return on equity investment. Capitalizing this net income at 7½% indicates a value of about $7,450,000.

Description of the Center

The interior and exterior architecture of the Center will be of modern design. All of the various buildings will be one story in height, with the exception of the two department stores, which will be constructed on two levels. The Center will be constructed principally of reinforced concrete for the foundations, frames, and floors. The roof slabs will be of precast concrete, and the floors in the covered mall will be of polished terrazzo on a reinforced concrete base. Exterior walls will be made of decorative precast concrete panels, brick, stone, and an assortment of other materials. The parking lot will provide spaces for more than 2,700 cars. Raymond Loewy/William Snaith of New York and Robert Ewing Associates of Los Angeles, California, are architects for the Center.

Firm leases, agreements to lease, and ground leases are being negotiated for 367,000 (or 74.1%) of the 495,000 square feet of rentable floor area. (Refer to the Table 1–3, Preliminary Rent Schedule, on page 149.) Negotiations are presently being conducted for the rental of the balance of space. It is expected that the Center will be fully leased by the end of 1966 but that the Center will not open until early 1967.

The Site

The Center is well located to serve the Thornton-Westminster area. Its location is excellent from the point of view of immediate access to major thoroughfares, and it should benefit considerably from the favorable growth potential anticipated in the area directly north of the site. The population of Adams County is currently growing at the compound rate of 5½% per annum, compared to a growth rate of 3% in the Denver area as a whole.

The only significant competition presently operating in the area of the subject site is the Westminster Plaza Shopping Center, which has a 47,000-square-foot J. C. Penney Store as its major tenant. In addition, Woolco has recently opened a major store within 1 mile of the shopping

EXHIBIT 1 *(Continued)*

center. Westminster Plaza and the Woolco store, with their emphasis on the lower price lines, will be likely to absorb some of the sales potential from lower-income families, but the Center should nonetheless derive considerable sales volume from the Westminster area.

It has recently been announced that a home developer is planning to construct a competing center, to be located 3 miles to the north of the company's site. It is our understanding that this center will not open for at least three years. It may include stores operated by Denver Dry Goods, J. C. Penney, and Sears, Roebuck & Co. While it is impossible at this time to forecast the impact of this competition upon the operations of the Center, it should be noted that (1) this Center is expected to open considerably before the other, giving it time to establish a good market position, (2) the projected site of the competing center is substantially beyond current population concentrations in north Denver, and (3) May and Ward historically have been the stronger retailers in Denver. We understand that Ward's per-square-foot sales are higher in Denver than in any comparable Ward city.

Tenant Leases

The total building floor area of the Center is divided as follows:

Tenant	Gross Building Floor Area
May	133,345
May—TBA (tires, batteries and accessories)	5,000
Specialty shops	195,289
Montgomery Ward*	130,000
Montgomery Ward—TBA*	21,000
Theater	10,000
Enclosed Mall	50,000
Total Area	544,634

* Ground lease.

All of the tenant leases will be gross leases with respect to fire and casualty insurance, general maintenance, and so on, but most will contain provisions for the tenants to pay a proportionate share of common area maintenance and of any increase in real estate taxes. The leases provide that the lessees will make stipulated contributions to mall upkeep and parking area expenses.

Following are tables which indicate actual and projected lease terms, a pro forma income and expense summary, and calculations to indicate monies available for debt service (all relating to Valley Shopping Center).

EXHIBIT 1 (Continued)

TABLE 1–1

Junior Tenants-in-Common (Class B)
Income and Loss Schedule
(years ended March 31)

		Mortgage		150%	Total	Income or (Loss)		Net Cash
	Rent	Interest	Amortization	Depreciation	Deductions	Taxable	Cumulative	Flow
1966–67.......	66	..		67	133	(133)	(133)	..
1968.......239	239	152	36	183	335	(96)	(229)	51
1969.......239	239	150	38	171	321	(82)	(311)	51
1970.......239	239	147	41	162	309	(70)	(381)	51
1971.......239	239	145	43	152	297	(58)	(439)	51
1972.......239	239	142	46	143	285	(46)	(485)	51
1973.......239	239	140	48	135	275	(36)	(521)	51
1974.......239	239	137	51	127	264	(25)	(546)	51
1975.......239	239	134	54	120	254	(15)	(551)	51
1976.......239	239	131	57	113	244	(5)	(556)	51
1977.......239	239	128	60	107	235	(4)	(552)	51

TABLE 1–2

Cash Flow

At Guaranteed
Rent Level

I. Revenue
  A. Rent—per schedule......................................$763,000
      Less: Vacancy and bad-debt allowance @ 8% ×
          30% (non-AAA credit) guaranteed rent
          income.................................... 16,000
              Adjusted rent....................................$747,000
  B. Net income from mall HVAC and central systems*........ 65,000
          Gross Income.......................................$812,000
II. Expenditures
    Per schedule of operating expenses........................ 203,000
III. Net operating income..$609,000
IV. Less: Land rent†.. 50,000
V. Net cash before debt servicing.............................$559,000
VI. Debt service.. 376,000
VII. Cash return on equity......................................$183,000

  * Based on income of 10 cents per square foot from HVAC and 40 cents per square foot from sale of hot and cold air to mall tenants plus $12,000 HVAC income from department stores. Operating expense estimated at $30,000. This leaves $75,000 net; however, a $10,000 contingency factor is introduced here.
  † Payments to the ground lessors and May will be $50,000 per year through July 1974. After that date, there will be a cost-of-living index adjustment; but in no case will the land rental and payment to May exceed $60,000 per year.

EXHIBIT 1 (Continued)

TABLE 1-3
Preliminary Rent Schedule

Tenant Type	Rentable Area (sq. ft.)	Guaranteed Rent (in dollars) Per sq. ft.	Total	Stabilized Sales (in dollars) Per sq. ft.	Total	Stabilized Rent %	Total (in dollars)
Food..............	29,600		72,800				75,200
Supermarket.....	24,000	2.00	48,000	125	3,000,000	1½% over minimum	48,000
Barricini—							
Candy.........	800	7.00	5,600	75	60,000	8%	5,600
Other Food.......	4,800	4.00	19,200	75	360,000	6%	21,600
Department stores...	136,700		205,545				231,500
May Co...........	136,700	1.35	184,545	75	10,525,000	2%	210,500
Montgomery-Ward ground lease..........			21,000				21,000
Variety.............	15,000	2.00	30,000	40	600,000	4%	30,000
Apparel.............	75,000		193,701				235,106
Baker—women's shoes..........	4,200	3.50	14,700	70	294,000	5%	14,700
Kinney—family shoes..........	4,600	3.06	14,076	60	276,000	5%	14,076
Fashion Bar—women's wear..	14,200	2.30	32,660	70	994,000	3% over $664,000	32,660
Bond's—family wear...........	11,900	2.15	25,585	70	833,000	4%	33,320
Other.............	40,100	2.66	106,680	70	2,807,000	5%	140,350
Furniture and appliances........	10,000	1.75	17,500	40	400,000	4%	17,500
Drugs..............	10,000	2.25	22,500	75	750,000	3%	22,500
Eating and drinking..........	17,000	3.70	62,950	70	1,190,000	5%	62,950
Other retail.........	17,000		68,390				74,925
Jupiter—Hallmark cards.....	1,200	6.00	7,200	75	90,000	6%	7,200
Zale's—jewelry....	3,000	3.33	9,990	75	225,000	4½%	10,125
Miscellaneous....	12,800	4.00	51,200	75	960,000	6%	57,600
Services............	6,000	3.50	21,000	40	240,000	8%	21,000
Recreation—Theater...........	10,000	3.10	31,000	30	300,000	12½%	37,500
Finance—office......	10,000	3.75	37,500				37,500
Total (excluding department stores)......	200,000	2.80 av.	557,341				614,181
Total (including department stores)......	336,300		762,886				845,681

EXHIBIT 1 (Continued)

TABLE 1–4

Operating Expenses

Administration	$ 45,000
Promotion	15,000
Insurance	15,000
Common area—net	8,000
Real estate taxes	120,000
Total	$203,000

EASTMAN DILLON, UNION SECURITIES & CO.
MEMBERS NEW YORK STOCK EXCHANGE
One Chase Manhattan Plaza
New York, N.Y. 10005

PART II

Confidential Memorandum

Equity Financing

VALLEY SHOPPING CENTER
Denver, Colorado

The total equity cash investment in this Center will be $1 million (except in the case of certain overcalls described under "Equity Participants" below) in excess of $5.5 million of mortgage financing on terms which are more fully described below. The equity will be divided into two levels of participation: senior and junior. The senior level will have a minimum priority return of 8½% on cash invested plus tax deductions available against other income and preference on liquidation or distribution. Junior equity participants will share the remaining net income and tax deductions. The owners will share all percentage rents on an equal (50/50) basis with the developer. Tax deductions will be available during the period of construction.

Equity Participants

Concurrently with the assignment of the ground lease and execution of the May store lease described more fully in "Development" (pages 144 and 145), EDUS will cause the owners to contribute the equity investment of $1 million to a limited partnership formed under the laws of Colorado. The partnership will have three general partners, each of

EXHIBIT 1 (Continued)

whom will be a partner of EDUS. The general partners will have control over operations of the Center. Class A limited partners will comprise the senior level of equity, and Class B limited partners, all of whom will be partners of EDUS, will comprise the junior level of equity. In all matters relating to income and cash distribution and losses, the general partners will be treated as Class B limited partners.

Class A limited partners will contribute $600,000 to acquire a 50% interest in the profits and related tax deductions. Class B limited partners will contribute $400,000 to acquire a 50% interest in the profits and related tax deductions. In the event that additional equity is necessary, Class B participants will be required to contribute up to an additional $200,000. If such amount is still insufficient, the senior and junior participants will have the right to provide funds (in the capacity of Class A limited partners) on a pro rata basis in an amount not in excess of $200,000.

Class A limited partners shall first receive an annual cash distribution equal to 8½% of the amount of their respective initial capital contribution. The general partners and Class B limited partners shall then receive the balance, if any, of the annual net cash receipts from the guaranteed rents, with each such partner sharing therein in that proportion which his respective capital contribution bears to the aggregate capital contribution of all Class B limited partners and general partners. All cash receipts from percentage rents will be shared by the Class A and Class B partners on an equal (50/50) basis.

The total cost of the investment for a 1% participation in the senior equity position (one half of 1% participation in the entire equity) will be $33,500 and will be funded as follows:

Cash	$ 6,000
Share of mortgage	27,500
Total	$33,500

The figures indicated above, while based on information which we believe to be accurate, are naturally subject to revision in the event that certain unforeseen events, such as strikes or natural disasters, should occur. Should revision occur, increased equity may be necessary and will be computed as described above. Since the income received by the partnership will be equal to 8% of the cost of the Center, additional equity requirements should have a minor effect on the cash return to the participants.

Breed, Abbott & Morgan is representing the leasehold principals in this transaction. Eastman Dillon, Union Securities & Co. will act as

EXHIBIT 1 *(Concluded)*

administrative and fiscal agent for the owners and will be paid $5,000 annually for this service. Messrs. Breed, Abbott & Morgan has given the firm an opinion relating to the federal taxation aspects of this transaction, and this will be made available to all of the individual leasehold principals.

All estimates and assumptions as to federal tax treatment of this transaction including the depreciable life of improvements and methods of depreciation allowable have been made for the convenience of the purchaser and the purchaser must rely upon their own calculations and independent business judgment of its worth, and upon their own accountants and tax counsel and be responsible for their fees. The effect of the depreciation depends upon the income bracket of the investor. In the event that the purchaser uses a different method of depreciation or depreciable life, said calculations and their results will vary accordingly. It should also be understood that the present tax law may be changed adversely in the future. We are not lawyers or accountants, and any communication from us is not to be construed as legal or tax advice. Under no circumstances is any communication from us to be considered an offering prospectus or as a representation by EDUS.

EXHIBIT 2

SHOPPING CENTER ANALYSIS
West 84th and Valley Highway
Denver, Colorado

Prepared for WINMAR REALTY DEVELOPMENT COMPANY
Seattle, Washington

June 28, 1965 (Final Copy—July 20, 1965)

By LARRY SMITH & COMPANY
333 Montgomery Street
San Francisco, California

Introduction

Purpose

The primary purpose of this study has been to determine the feasibility of establishing a regional shopping center on a 36½-acre site at the intersection of West 84th Avenue and the Valley Highway (Interstate

EXHIBIT 2 *(Continued)*

25) In Denver, Colorado. This report presents the results of our analyses, evaluations, and consideration of various factors influencing the feasibility of a shopping center at the site.

Method

Conclusions regarding the feasibility of a shopping center at this site have been drawn in part from findings concerning the location of the proposed center in relation to present and planned future access routes to the site and considerations of population, income, and expenditure characteristics of the trade area which could be served from this site. These considerations have led to an estimate of the trade area market potential for the various retail outlets, such as general merchandise (including department stores), apparel stores, furniture stores, and so on. This total market potential has been compared to "normal" capacities of existing competitive retail facilities in order to arrive at estimates of sales potential which may be available to facilities at the proposed site.

Another method, the "market-share" approach, has been used to supplement the preceding method in analyzing the opportunity for department store facilities at the site. The market-share method gives consideration to the anticipated competitive impact of the subject facility, recognizing that aggressively merchandised stores entering an area acquire a certain share of the total available volume related to their historical acceptance in the market and their specific merchandising in the new store.

Organization of Report

Section I discusses the physical character of the site and its relationship to the various proposed access changes in road patterns serving the Denver Metropolitan area.

In Section II, an estimate is made of the opportunity for DSTM (department store type merchandise) facilities at the site. The population, income, and expenditure patterns of the DSTM trade area are discussed, and a determination is made of the market potential at the site for general merchandise, apparel, furniture-appliance, and other retail outlets.

The analysis in Section III concerns the opportunity for department store facilities at the site, based on the market-share method of determining future potential.

Section IV analyzes the development opportunity for convenience facilities at the site, assuming a department store traffic generator.

In Section V, we have provided in summary form our findings and conclusions with respect to this site, as well as a recommended develop-

EXHIBIT 2 *(Continued)*

ment schedule based upon the retail sales potential derived previously.

The appendices contain additional data on trade area comparison and convenience goods competition and include a summary of the existing Denver Standard Metropolitan Statistical Area (SMSA) department store competition.

Assumptions

In any report of this nature, certain assumptions and qualifications must be made at given points in the analysis. These have been discussed at various points in the report; however, it has also been necessary to establish the following basic assumptions and qualifications which underlie the entire report:

1. The Denver Metropolitan area, the state of Colorado, and the nation as a whole will not suffer any major economic decline during the period covered by this report, so that income levels and purchasing power will remain steady or rise to some extent.
2. Population will increase at the rate predicted or at an even higher rate during the period covered by this report.
3. The actual development of the recommended facilities of the site will be so planned and designed as to create a reasonably substantial impact on the local market.
4. Every effort will be made on the part of the developer to attract only the strongest available tenants for all store types within the project.
5. No other major competitive facilities will be developed to serve the estimated demand until the proposed facilities are in full operation.
6. The project will be developed within a reasonable time to preclude future changes in conditions assumed in this report.
7. All dollar figures (and corresponding sales volume estimates) are based upon the current level of purchasing power and value of the dollar. Projections (unless otherwise indicated), therefore, have been made on this basis and are not adjusted for any expected change in these values.

Section I: Site and Access

The site analyzed consists of some 36½ acres of land located at the intersection of West 84th Avenue and the Valley Highway (Interstate 25) in the Westminster-Thornton area of Adams County, Colorado, approximately 7 miles north of the Denver Central Business District (CBD). The map on page 157 shows the location of the site in relation to the Denver Metropolitan area.

The rapidly growing Westminster and Thornton communities sur-

EXHIBIT 2 (Continued)

round the site in the westerly and easterly directions, respectively. The North Glenn area, which is 2 to 3 miles north of the site has been developed since 1960 and currently has a population of some 16,500 persons.

There is ample space with few physical barriers to impede continued growth in the northeasterly and northwesterly directions from the site. However, the South Platte River, with its flood plain to the east and southeast, will tend to limit growth in these directions.

Regionally, direct access is excellent from the west, north, and south via the Valley Highway (Interstate 25) and the Denver-Boulder Turnpike. Regional access from the east will be improved to some extent once the connection between Interstate 80/U.S. 6 and the Valley Highway at 70th Avenue has been completed. This extension is programmed for construction prior to 1970. The northern portion of the outer belt freeway, scheduled for construction by 1980, would improve access to the site from the northeasterly direction. The routing of this system has not been firmly established, although a right-of-way has been donated at 104th Avenue, 2½ miles north of the site.

Ingress to and egress from the site from the local arterials are potentially good from all directions off bordering 84th Avenue and Washington Boulevard. Huron and Pecos Streets to the west and East 78th and East 88th to the east provide easy access to the site via the bordering streets.

Section II: Development Opportunity for a Regional Shopping Center

DSTM[1] Trade Area

The drawing power of a retail store, or group of retail stores, is generally limited to areas which are rather well defined by consideration of distance, driving time, topography, and the availability of alternative shopping facilities. The first step in the analysis of market potential is to determine the "trade area"—the area whose residents could be expected to be tributary to the proposed retail facilities at the site under study.

The concept of a trade area calls for clarification and emphasis, since a given business district will normally derive *some* support from residents living beyond almost any reasonable trade area boundary that

---

[1] The DSTM market includes merchandise lines which are found in most department stores and which are referred to in the U.S. census categories of general merchandise (excluding variety), apparel, furniture/appliances, and "other" lines, such as jewelry, sporting goods, cameras, books, and stationery. The term *DSTM* is used in the subsequent portions of the report.

EXHIBIT 2 (Continued)

could be drawn. Experience indicates, however, that for purposes of making reliable estimates of the sales potential for any group of commercial facilities, attention should be concentrated upon a rather well-defined area, acknowledging that some 10% to 20% of the facilities' sales will originate from beyond this area. By focusing the analysis upon a limited area, specific population, income, and competition influences can be studied. Trends and characteristics within such areas will have generally predictable influences and, therefore, warrant the most intensive analysis.

The site is large enough for a center of regional draw in this area. We have been instructed to assume that the center would be developed with two major department store tenants, a May–D&F unit of 137,000 square feet and a Montgomery Ward unit of 151,600 square feet.[2] Therefore, the trade area for a regional center at the site with these two stores as major tenants has been indicated on the map shown in Figure 1. Its limits are determined primarily by distance from the site, driving time, and competitive facilities.

The DSTM trade area has been divided into a convenience zone and a comparison zone. Residents of the convenience zone would be expected to provide most of the day-to-day support for the convenience items such as food, drug, variety, and hardware. The comparison zone is much larger than the convenience zone, as it represents the base of support for department stores, apparel shops, furniture and appliance stores, and other specialized retail outlets. Residents of the comparison zone are not expected to provide strong support for convenience facilities located at the site.

The *convenience* zone extends from Federal Boulevard on the west to the eastern edge of Thornton on the east and from the vicinity of 120th Avenue (northernmost portion of the North Glenn area) on the north to the intersection of the Valley Highway and the Denver-Boulder Turnpike on the south. It is not expected that persons residing on the far side of these arterials will cross them to use the proposed shopping center for convenience shopping on a regular basis, due to the availability of competing facilities.

The *comparison* zone extends to the north for a distance of nearly 9 miles. It has been limited in this direction by factors of distance and absence of population. The comparison zone extends to the east and west for a distance of from 4 to 5 miles from the site. The area beyond the trade area in these directions is rural, with a very small population; access to the site is more difficult, and alternative shopping facilities can be reached more easily.

---

[2] The Montgomery Ward store includes approximately 21,600 square feet of TBA space. The May–D&F unit includes approximately 6,000 square feet of TBA.

FIGURE 1
DSTM Trade Area

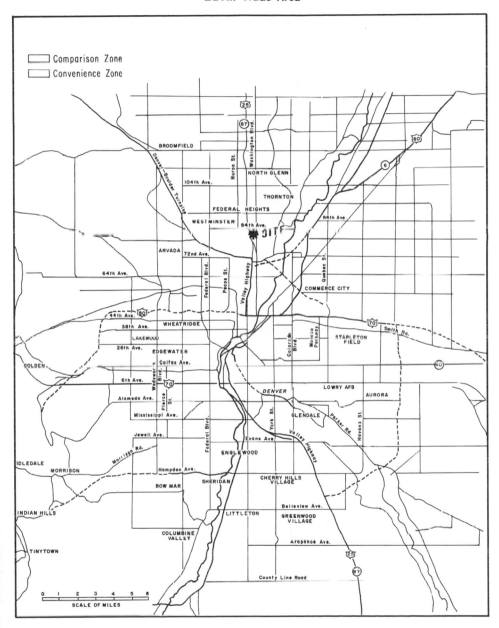

EXHIBIT 2 *(Continued)*

The comparison zone extends to the south for a distance of from 3 to 4 miles, being restricted in this direction by access considerations but primarily by the competitive influence of shopping facilities in shopping centers to the southwest and in the Denver CBD to the south.

In this section, only the DSTM potential will be analyzed, since it is the DSTM facilities which are critical in the justification of the total size of the shopping center. The convenience goods (food, variety, drug, hardware, and so on) potential will be examined in Section IV.

Trade Area Population

Trade area population statistics are based on data contained in the 1950 and 1960 *Census of Population* for the areas involved and upon projections of population made by the Inter-County Regional Planning Commission in 1965. Adams County had grown from a population of approximately 22,500 persons in 1940 to roughly 40,200 persons in 1950 and 120,300 persons in 1960. The population for the five-county Denver SMSA (Adams, Arapahoe, Boulder, Denver, and Jefferson Counties) has grown from 445,200 in 1940 to 929,400 persons in 1960. Past, present, and projected future population levels in the Denver SMSA and its individual counties are shown in Table 2–1.

TABLE 2–1
Denver SMSA: Past and Projected Population Levels

	1940*	1950*	1960*	1965†	1970†	1980†
Denver SMSA						
Adams County	22,481	40,234	120,296	156,000	195,000	270,000
Arapahoe County	32,150	52,125	113,426	138,000	160,000	225,000
Boulder County	37,438	48,296	74,254	95,000	120,000	200,000
Denver County	322,412	415,786	493,887	505,000	532,000	570,000
Jefferson County	30,725	55,687	127,520	180,000	225,000	325,000
Total SMSA	445,206	612,128	929,383	1,074,000	1,232,000	1,590,000

* U.S. census.
† Inter-County Regional Planning Commission.

Estimated past, present, and projected future population levels in the DSTM trade area are set forth in Table 2–2. It is estimated that the total trade area contained approximately 14,200 persons in 1950 (that area was not tracted in 1950). The 1960 census tract data indicate that the total trade area grew to a level of approximately 73,000 by 1960. Based on Inter-County Regional Planning Commission data, it is estimated that in mid-1965, the total trade area had a population of approximately 104,000 persons. Based on past trends, total trade area population

EXHIBIT 2 (Continued)

is expected to reach levels of 122,000 by 1968, 135,000 by 1970, and 198,000 by 1980.

TABLE 2–2
Trade Area Population
Estimates and Projections

	DSTM Trade Area		
Year	Convenience Zone	Comparison Zone	Combined Zones
1950	5,100	9,100	14,200
1960	26,300	47,100	73,400
1965	39,500	64,500	104,000
1968	47,000	75,000	122,000
1970	52,000	83,000	135,000
1975	63,000	103,000	166,000
1980	73,000	126,000	190,000

The basic projections of population have been made on a "straight-line basis" related to the past 15 years' experience, as indicated in the *Census of Population* and were compared to the current (1965) projections developed by the Inter-County Regional Planning Commission for Adams County and for the Denver SMSA. On this basis, total trade area population growth represents nearly 20% of the total projected population for the Denver SMSA. If population levels in the western portion of Adams County or the southern portion of Boulder County grow at faster rates than presently anticipated by the Planning Commission, these projections would be revised upwards.

The industrial and service base in the area, although not analyzed in depth, appears to be sufficiently strong and growing to support further population growth of the type indicated by the projections.

Per Capita and Per Family Incomes

Per capita and per family personal income estimates have been derived from the most recent census information (1960). These income levels have been updated based on current information published by the U.S. Department of Commerce. In Table 2–3 an estimate is made of the current income of residents in the trade area, and this estimate is compared with estimates for the state of Colorado and for the Denver SMSA. The table shows that per capita incomes in the Denver SMSA are significantly higher than those for the individual zones with the DSTM trade area as well as the state as a whole. Both the convenience zone and

EXHIBIT 2 (Continued)

comparison zone per family incomes, however, are substantially higher than those of the state and somewhat above those of the SMSA. The higher per family incomes but lower per capita incomes in the trade area reflect the larger number of persons per family found in new residential developments.

TABLE 2–3

Area	Per Capita Incomes	Per Family Incomes
State of Colorado...................$2,410		$ 7,190
Denver (SMSA)..................... 2,770		9,595
DSTM trade area		
Convenience zone................ 2,420		10,200
Comparison zone................ 2,520		10,035

Per Capita Expenditures

Normally, in the case where an area has undergone substantial residential development, no attempt is made to adjust the present expenditure pattern for future changes in income levels in the trade area when projecting total retail potential levels. This is true in part because of the general unreliability of methods attempting to forecast changes in income levels, but it is primarily due to the fact that any changes are not likely to be significant in terms of the total analysis. However, in the present case, an upward adjustment in the present local expenditure pattern has been made to reflect the probable increase in the average trade area income level resulting as the area undergoes continued residential development. It has been assumed that the trade area will tend to assume more closely the per capita income level characteristics of the presently urbanized metropolitan and suburban areas. Allowance has been made for the fact that lower per capita incomes can be expected to remain characteristic of some segments of the population, recognizing that this segment can be expected to become an increasingly smaller portion of the total trade area population. The adjusted retail expenditure pattern utilized in subsequent projections of retail potential is shown in Table 2–4.

The per capita expenditures shown in Table 2–5 represent spending by trade area residents in all facilities of the selected types, including facilities in both the immediate vicinity of the site and beyond. It should be emphasized that the pattern as indicated pertains to the probable situation which will prevail in the trade area, assuming adequate facilities and a normally competitive retail situation.

EXHIBIT 2 (Continued)

TABLE 2-4
Per Capita Expenditures

Convenience Goods

Food......................$320
Drug........................ 65
Variety..................... 25
Hardware................... 20
Liquor...................... 35
Total................$465

* Excluding variety.

Comparison Goods

General merchandise*......$195
(Department store).......(180)
Apparel..................... 70
Furniture and appliance.... 75
Other....................... 45
Total................$385

TABLE 2-5
West 84th and Valley Highway Shopping Center: Total DSTM—Sales Potential

	Per Capita Expenditure	Total Sales Potential (000's)				
		1965	1968	1970	1975	1980
Convenience zone (population).		(39,500)	(47,000)	(52,000)	(63,000)	(73,000)
General merchandise*........	$195	$ 7,703	$ 9,165	$10,140	$12,285	$14,235
Apparel......................	70	2,765	3,290	3,640	4,410	5,110
Furniture/appliances.........	75	2,962	3,525	3,900	4,725	5,475
Other........................	45	1,778	2,115	2,340	2,835	3,285
Total....................	$385	$15,208	$18,095	$20,020	$24,255	$28,105
Comparison zone (population)..		(64,500)	(75,000)	(83,000)	(103,000)	(125,000)
General merchandise	$195	$12,578	$14,625	$16,185	$20,085	$24,375
Apparel......................	70	4,515	5,250	5,810	7,210	8,750
Furniture/appliances.........	75	4,838	5,625	6,225	7,725	9,375
Other........................	45	2,902	3,375	3,735	4,635	5,625
Total....................	$385	$24,833	$28,875	$31,955	$39,655	$48,125
Total DSTM Trade Area						
General merchandise*........		$20,281	$23,790	$26,325	$32,370	$38,610
Apparel......................		7,280	8,540	9,450	11,620	13,860
Furniture/appliances.........		7,800	9,150	10,125	12,450	14,850
Other........................		4,680	5,490	6,075	7,470	8,910
Total....................		$40,041	$46,970	$51,975	$63,910	$76,230

* Excludes variety.
Note: Figures in ( ) are population estimates.

Methods of Determining Retail Potential

Two analytical methods have been used in deriving estimates of the anticipated market support available to DSTM facilities in a regional shopping center at the proposed site. First, the available support has been tested by the method of "residual analysis." Another method, the

EXHIBIT 2 (*Continued*)

"market-share" approach, has been used to supplement the preceding method in analyzing the opportunity for department store facilities at the site in Section III.

The residual-analysis method gives a measure of the ease of entry of future facilities into a trade area market by measuring the degree to which trade area retail expenditures can be expected to exceed the normal sales capacity of existing retail outlets serving the trade area. The market-share method, on the other hand, unlike the "residual analysis," gives consideration to the anticipated competitive impact of the subject facility, recognizing that aggressively merchandised stores can enter an area and acquire a certain share of the available volume regardless of the competitive situation. The market-share approach, and its implications, will be explained further at the appropriate point in the analysis.

Total DSTM Sales Potential

The projected trade area population levels and retail expenditure pattern of trade area residents, discussed previously, form the basis for estimating the total sales potential which may be anticipated from trade area residents in the various DSTM categories. The results of these calculations are shown in Table 2–6. Estimates of potential are shown for the DSTM categories only, since the estimated support available to convenience goods facilities at the site is discussed separately in Section IV. It is estimated that residents of the combined zones will generate a total potential in the selected categories of about $40 million in 1965, increasing to nearly $52 million by 1970 and to approximately $76 million by 1980.

Trade Area Suburban Shares

The potential figures in Table 2–6 represent the total retail spending of trade area residents in all stores regardless of their location. Not all of the expenditures generated by trade area residents will be available to retail facilities located within the trade area. Some portion of this spending will be made in facilities located at suburban locations outside of the trade area, and a substantial portion will be made in facilities located in the Denver central business district. The CBD will remain the strongest single focus of retail shopping in the Denver Metropolitan area during the foreseeable future and can be expected to continue to retain a significant proportion of the comparison merchandise expenditures made by trade area residents. An assessment of the relative strength of CBD and suburban facilities, at present and during the period under consideration, has been made and an estimate has been developed of the percent-

EXHIBIT 2 (Continued)

TABLE 2–6

West 84th and Valley Highway Shopping Center: Suburban DSTM Sales Potential

DSTM Trade Area	Suburban Share (%)	Suburban Sales Potential (000's)				
		1965	1968	1970	1975	1980
Convenience zone						
General merchandise*............80%		$ 6,162	$ 7,332	$ 8,112	$ 9,828	$11,388
Apparel............................65		1,797	2,138	2,366	2,866	3,322
Furniture/appliance..............80		2,370	2,820	3,120	3,780	4,380
Other............................75		1,334	1,586	1,755	2,126	2,464
Total........................		$11,663	$13,876	$15,353	$18,600	$21,554
Comparison zone						
General merchandise*............75%		$ 9,434	$10,969	$12,139	$15,064	$18,281
Apparel............................60		2,709	3,150	3,486	4,326	5,250
Furniture/appliance..............75		3,629	4,219	4,669	5,794	7,031
Other............................70		2,031	2,362	2,614	3,244	3,938
Total....................		$17,803	$20,700	$22,908	$28,428	$34,500
Total DSTM Trade Area						
General merchandise*............		$15,596	$18,301	$20,251	$24,892	$29,669
Apparel...........................		4,506	5,288	5,852	7,192	8,572
Furniture/appliance..............		5,999	7,039	7,789	9,574	11,411
Other............................		3,365	3,948	4,369	5,370	6,402
Total..................		$29,466	$34,576	$38,261	$47,028	$56,054

* Excludes variety.

age of total trade area expenditures which can be expected to be made in suburban versus CBD facilities.

The percentage of total sales which can be expected to be made in suburban facilities will vary between the various store categories. The suburban share for convenience goods spending, which is discussed in Section IV, can be expected to be quite high, since convenience goods shoppers are typically unwilling to travel more than a few miles from their place of residence to do this kind of shopping. On the other hand, since comparison goods shoppers are usually willing to travel considerable distance to find a greater depth and breadth of merchandise selection than commonly found in suburban areas, it may be expected that comparison facilities in the CBD will have a considerable drawing power, even in the distant outlying suburban areas, and consequently, the suburban share for comparison stores is considerably lower than for convenience stores.

These shares are based on our knowledge and studies of the retail strength of the Denver CBD and our general knowledge of the pattern of retail spending in other suburban areas with characteristics similar to those of the subject trade area. While it may be possible to exceed these

EXHIBIT 2 *(Continued)*

shares, given a situation of uniquely aggressive merchandising by retail facilities within the trade area, the shares indicated are believed to be the most realistic for planning purposes.

Suburban DSTM Sales Potential

Application of the suburban shares, by store category at the various stated time periods, results in the total suburban sales potential estimates shown in Table 2–6. It is estimated that the total suburban sales potential generated by trade area residents will approximate $30 million by 1965, increasing to about $38 million by 1970, and $56 million by 1980.

Competitive Retail Facilities

In determining the retail sales potential for a proposed shopping center development, full consideration must be given to the existing retail facilities now serving the trade area. Competing retail facilities may be defined as those which derive all or part of their volumes from trade area residents. They represent the competition with which the proposed shopping center must contend. In order to determine the nature and amount of competing retail facilities, a field survey was undertaken by our field representatives. The primary emphasis in this survey was on determination of the size, location, and type of the major retail units serving the trade area. On the basis of this investigation, compared with data obtained from the Inter-County Regional Planning Commission, estimates were made of the capacity of these retail facilities.

The word *capacity,* as used throughout this report, refers to the estimated amount of sales volume that existing facilities are capable of obtaining and holding under normal competitive conditions, assuming adequate and competent management. In no way does the use of this term connote the maximum physical capacity of a given store to obtain volumes, nor is it used to refer to the actual sales volumes of those stores at the present time.

The location of those facilities which were surveyed are indicated in the table in Appendix A. In surveying the existing retail facilities, it was determined that the two major competing locations for DSTM facilities at this location would be the Westminster Plaza Shopping Center with the nearby Woolco unit between 72nd and 74th Avenues on Federal Boulevard and the Lakeside Shopping Center near 44th and Sheridan.

However, we understand that a major regional shopping center, with the Denver Dry Goods Company, Sears, and J. C. Penney has been proposed in North Glenn at a site 3 miles north of the subject site. The

EXHIBIT 2 *(Continued)*

effective capacity volumes indicated in this report do not reflect this proposed facility. This would appear to be a fair assumption when the sparseness of the tributary population to the North Glenn site is considered. In planning the center at the subject site, it should be assumed that the North Glenn location will ultimately be developed. This development will more than likely be timed to take place at a time when the population in the vicinity of the site has increased to a greater degree than at the present. This is only an assumption on our part and should be periodically checked.

Effective Competition

The competitive retail facilities for the trade area have been discussed previously. Estimates have also been made of the "effectiveness" of these competitive facilities in merchandising to residents of the trade area. Again, the term *effectiveness* is an analytical concept which refers to that portion of the total capacity of a competitive retail facility which could be expected to be obtained from within the trade area tributary to the site. The relative effectiveness of each of the facilities, as tabulated, has been totaled for each of the trade areas as shown in Table 2–7.

The total "effective competition" in the DSTM categories, as shown in the table, is estimated at approximately $8.9 million in the total DSTM trade area.

TABLE 2–7

West 84th and Valley Highway Shopping Center: DSTM Unsatisfied Sales Potential and Additional Space Warranted

	Effective Competition (000's)	Unsatisfied Sales Potential (000's)				
		1965	1968	1970	1975	1980
General merchandise*	$7,183	$ 8,413	$11,118	$13,068	$17,709	$22,486
Apparel	1,115	3,391	4,173	4,737	6,077	7,457
Furniture/appliance	164	5,835	6,875	7,625	9,410	11,247
Other	477	2,888	3,471	3,892	4,893	5,925
Total	$8,939	$20,527	$25,637	$29,322	$38,089	$47,115

	Normal Sales Per Sq. Ft.	Additional Space Warranted (Sq. Ft.)				
		1965	1968	1970	1975	1980
General merchandise*	$55	153,000	202,000	238,000	322,000	409,000
Apparel	60	57,000	70,000	79,000	101,000	124,000
Furniture/appliance	45	130,000	153,000	169,000	209,000	250,000
Other	50	58,000	69,000	78,000	98,000	119,000
Total		398,000	494,000	564,000	730,000	902,000

* Excludes variety.

EXHIBIT 2 *(Continued)*

Unsatisfied Sales Potential

The "unsatisfied sales potential" in each of the DSTM categories at the various population levels has been estimated by deducting the estimated effective competition by store type from the total sales potential in each of the appropriate store categories. These unsatisfied sales-potential estimates represent the volume opportunity available to additional retail facilities after allowing for the full effective competitive capacity of existing facilities.

As noted at the beginning of this section, the unsatisfied sales-potential levels are not meant to indicate an absolute limit on the retail opportunities within a trade area. It may be expected that aggressively merchandised facilities could enter the trade area and acquire a portion of the total sales volume available, regardless of the competitive situation. The unsatisfied trade area potential is, however, a valuable measure of the net need for future facilities in an area and of the ease with which new facilities can expect to enter the market. The results of these calculations (presented in the table on page 165) indicate that in 1965 the unsatisfied sales potential in the selected categories in the DSTM trade area is expected to approximate $21 million and that this level should rise to some $29 million by 1970 and to some $47 million by 1980.

ADDITIONAL SPACE WARRANTED. Sales volumes per square foot normally considered adequate for the introduction of retail stores have been applied to the sales potential in order to project the amount of additional DSTM facilities warranted in future years, based on the level of unsatisfied sales potential. These estimates indicate that about 398,000 square feet of DSTM space at the subject site would be supported by the unsatisfied sales potential in 1965. This demand is expected to increase to 564,000 square feet by 1970 and to 902,000 square feet by 1980.

Again, it should be noted that these space demands are only those resulting from the unsatisfied potential after giving full credit to the stores existing in the area at the present time and without consideration of replacement needs or locational obsolescence. They are a measure of minimum needs, therefore, rather than a recommendation of the size of facilities that should be constructed at the subject site, which recommendations are presented subsequently. The foregoing residual analysis, as applied to department store potential, has been supplemented by the market share analysis in the following section.

EXHIBIT 2 *(Continued)*

Section III: Department Store Opportunity—Market Share Analysis

The "residual" or "unsatisfied" sales-potential analysis, as discussed in the previous section, is a measure of the volume potential available after giving full sales volume to the existing stores and thus assumes that no new units will be introduced into the area which are "competitive" in the full sense.

New, aggressively merchandised stores entering an area actually compete for, and derive their volume from, a share of the *total* volume available in the trade area rather than only the "unsatisfied" volume potential. Obviously, the number, size, and aggressiveness of competing facilities will affect the share of the market which each can achieve, and individual merchandising skill can cause substantial variations in each store's ability to attract its share of the market. Therefore, the level of volumes which these facilities can achieve will depend in large part upon the individual abilities of the merchants involved—not only the merchants of the new facilities but also those operating the old facilities which are now serving the trade area.

In order to estimate the share of the market which may be available to a department store, or stores, an assumption must be made of the merchandising ability of possible future tenants of the proposed regional shopping center.

For purposes of this analysis, we have been instructed to assume that the center will be developed with two full-line department stores, a May–D&F unit of 137,000 square feet (including 6,000 square feet of TBA space) and a Montgomery Ward unit of 151,600 square feet (including 21,600 square feet of TBA space). The table in Appendix B of this report illustrates the current department store situation in the Denver SMSA. Table 2–8 indicates our estimate of the current market position of the individual department store organizations in the Denver department store market.

TABLE 2–8

Store	Market Share (%)
May–D&F	25%
Denver Dry Goods	20
Sears, Roebuck	25*
J. C. Penney	
Montgomery Ward	10
Joslin's	5
Others	15
Total	100%

* Approximately equal.

EXHIBIT 2 (Continued)

Certain types of institutionalized stores with accepted customer appeal can expect to enter a new section of a metropolitan market, or a nearby new suburban area, and develop a measure of support related to their normal customer acceptance. This is particularly true of certain department stores which have achieved an image and a consumer acceptance based on their established name, merchandising pattern, and resultant position in a regional market. Because of shoppers' allegiance to a particular store, a branch unit will usually have local acceptance equal to the parent firm's metropolitan share, and often more than its average share, depending upon the competitive situation.

Strong department stores such as the May–D&F and Montgomery Ward, with presently developed acceptance in the Denver market and a significant regional acceptance on an institutional basis could, in our opinion, achieve market shares in the upper range indicated in Table 2–9, particularly in the earlier years. As the trade area becomes more densely developed and new competition (such as the proposed regional center in North Glenn) develops to serve the larger population base, it is expected that the May–D&F and Montgomery Ward department stores would tend to achieve volumes in the lower range shown in Table 2–9, which are more in line with their present market share in the total metropolitan market.

Based on these considerations, an estimate of the general merchandise volume potential which would be available to support the indicated department store tenants is presented in the table. The top line of the table indicates the total suburban sales potential for department stores, as developed in the previous section. The range of market shares, together with the resulting volume potentials, are shown in Table 2–9.

In addition, it is normal for a department store to realize approximately 15% of its volume from outside the normally defined trade area. This amount, therefore, has been added to the estimated sales potential available to support new department store facilities at the shopping center. These sales-potential estimates have subsequently been converted to estimates of space potential, or space justified, by the assumption of productivity levels of $50 per square foot and $60 per square foot. A $50-per-square-foot productivity level, or under, is often acceptable for new store planning purposes, depending upon the department store organization involved. "Mature" productivity levels at, or above, $60 per square foot are usually desirable for long-run operations, however.

An examination of the space-potential estimates indicates that, on a combined 50% to 60% market-share basis in the early years, there is sufficient market potential, excluding TBA potential, to support a May–D&F unit and a Montgomery Ward unit operating from a com-

EXHIBIT 2 (Continued)

bined total space of some 261,000 square feet (excluding TBA) by 1970 (based on third-year operating volume following an assumed opening year of 1967), provided that a productivity level of approximately $50 per square foot were acceptable in the early years. In the later years, as the market share declines, sufficient support is still available to warrant the development of the two department stores planned for this site.

TABLE 2–9
West 84th and Valley Highway Shopping Center: Market-Share Analysis
(department store sales and space potential)

	Total Suburban Sales Potential Department Store (000's)				
	1965	1968	1970	1975	1980
Total Department Store Potential*.........	$15,596	$18,301	$20,251	$24,892	$29,669

	Department Store Sales Potential (000's)				
	1965	1968	1970	1975	1980
Market share					
@ 40%.................................	$ 6,238	$ 7,320	$ 8,100	$ 9,957	$11,868
@ 50%.................................	7,798	9,161	10,126	12,446	14,835
@ 60%.................................	9,357	10,981	12,151	14,935	17,801

	Total Department Store Sales Potential (000's)†				
	1965	1968	1970	1975	1980
Market share (including trade from beyond):					
@ 40%.................................	$ 7,300	$ 8,600	$ 9,500	$11,700	$14,000
@ 50%.................................	9,200	10,800	11,900	14,600	17,400
@ 60%.................................	11,000	12,900	14,300	17,600	20,900

	Total Department Store Space Potential (Sq. Ft.)†				
	1965	1968	1970	1975	1980
Space justified					
40% Market share @ $50 sq. ft...........	146,000	172,000	190,000	234,000	280,000
@ $60 sq. ft...........	122,000	143,000	158,000	195,000	233,000
50% Market share @ $50 sq. ft...........	184,000	216,000	238,000	292,000	348,000
@ $60 sq. ft...........	153,000	180,000	198,000	243,000	290,000
60% Market share @ $50 sq. ft...........	220,000	258,000	286,000	352,000	418,000
@ $60 sq. ft...........	183,000	215,000	238,000	293,000	348,000

* Department store potential has been defined to include all general merchandise potential. This has been done since it may be expected that a strong department store could compete for a share of general merchandise expenditures now being made at nondepartment store facilities.
† Figures rounded; excludes TBA space.

EXHIBIT 2 (Continued)

Section IV: Development Opportunity for Convenience Facilities with a Department Store Traffic Generator

Trade Area

The convenience facilities, such as food, drug, variety, hardware, and liquor stores, serve the daily shopping needs of local residents and are the major components of a neighborhood center. These facilities tend to locate at rather frequent intervals in well-established suburban areas. Therefore, the shoppers in convenience (neighborhood) facilities usually would not travel more than 2 miles in order to reach such facilities *unless* a major traffic generator, such as a department store, were also located at the site to attract shoppers from greater distances. However, some support for convenience facilities in a regional center at the site with department store traffic generators might normally be expected to be derived from the population located within 3 to 4½ miles of the site.

Based on this assumption, the trade area that would be tributary to convenience goods facilities at the site is indicated on the map in Figure 1 (page 157) as the convenience zone of the DSTM trade area. This trade area is generally limited in the east and south by other competitive facilities, and on the north and west by distance as well as competitive facilities, as discussed previously.

Trade Area Population

The 1960 population of the convenience zone of the trade area was thus estimated from census tract data to have been approximately 26,300 persons, as compared to an estimate of about 5,100 persons residing there in 1950. A projection of population to 1980 has been made, taking into account past growth, relationship to the SMSA, and further expected suburbanization of the area as shown in the following table.

Estimated and Projected Trade Area Population

1950	1960	1965	1968	1970	1975	1980
5,100	26,300	39,500	47,000	52,000	63,000	73,000

Per Capita Incomes

Income levels have been estimated on the same basis and from the same sources as were used in the previous analysis and are indicated on the following table.

EXHIBIT 2 (Continued)

Per Capita Incomes

State of Colorado..............$2,410
Denver SMSA................... 2,770
DSTM trade area:
    Convenience zone........... 2,420

Per Capita Expenditures

For purposes of this report, the current expenditure pattern is used in projecting the future convenience goods sales potential. No adjustments have been made for any potential rise in the over-all general level of prices due to further inflationary trends, since it is assumed that the current relationships between store size and physical volume of sales will remain constant. Per capita convenience expenditures have been estimated as in Table 2–10.

TABLE 2–10

**Trade Area per Capita Expenditures
for Convenience Goods**

Type of Store	Per Capita Expenditures
Food........................	$320
Drug........................	65
Variety.....................	25
Hardware...................	20
Liquor......................	35
Total.................	$465

Convenience Sales Potential

A residual approach to market potential, previously explained, is summarized in Table 2–11. By applying the present and projected convenience zone population levels to the estimated per capita expenditures in the selected retail categories, the total potential is estimated at about $18.4 million in 1965, rising to about $24.2 million by 1970, and to nearly $34 million by 1980.

The proportion of the total sales potential which we would expect to be available to trade area retail outlets has been indicated in Table 2–11 by both percentage and dollar figures. Because of the attraction of retail concentration in nearby Westminster, as well as in North Glenn, it can be expected that not all of the total sales potential generated by trade area residents will be spent in trade area retail locations. Assuming that adequate retail facilities are available within the trade area, the percentage share of total expenditures by trade area residents at convenience

EXHIBIT 2 (*Continued*)

zone facilities has been estimated for each of the various convenience facilities.

Convenience zone shares differ by type of retail category. However, in the convenience-oriented food, drug, variety, hardware, and liquor store

TABLE 2–11

West 84th and Valley Highway Trade Area: Convenience Goods Potential

DSTM Trade Area	Per Capita Expenditure	Total Sales Potential (000's) 1965	1968	1970	1975	1980
Convenience zone						
(population)..............		(39,500)	(47,000)	(52,000)	(63,000)	(73,000)
Food........................$320		$12,640	$15,040	$16,640	$20,160	$23,360
Drug........................	65	2,568	3,055	3,380	4,095	4,745
Variety......................	25	988	1,175	1,300	1,575	1,825
Hardware...................	20	790	940	1,040	1,260	1,460
Liquor......................	35	1,382	1,645	1,820	2,205	2,555
Total...................$465		$18,368	$21,855	$24,180	$29,295	$33,945

	Suburban Share (%)	Suburban Sales Potential (000's) 1965	1968	1970	1975	1980
Food.........................95		$12,008	$14,288	$15,808	$19,152	$22,192
Drug.........................90		2,311	2,750	3,042	3,686	4,270
Variety......................75		741	881	975	1,181	1,369
Hardware...................95		750	893	988	1,197	1,387
Liquor.......................90		1,244	1,480	1,638	1,984	2,300
Total.....................		$17,054	$20,292	$22,451	$27,200	$31,518

	Effective Competition (000's)	Unsatisfied Sales Potential (000's) 1965	1968	1970	1975	1980
Food........................$15,886		...	...	...	$3,266	$ 6,306
Drug........................	1,980	$ 331	$ 770	$1,062	1,706	2,290
Variety......................	1,139	...	...	...	42	230
Hardware...................	632	118	261	356	565	755
Liquor......................	424	820	1,056	1,214	1,560	1,876
Total...................$20,061		$1,269	$2,087	$2,632	$7,139	$11,457

	Normal Sales Per Sq. Ft.	Additional Space Warranted (Sq. Ft.) 1965	1968	1970	1975	1980
Food.........................$125		...	...	...	26,000	50,000
Drug........................	65	5,000	12,000	16,000	26,000	35,000
Variety......................	35	...	...	...	1,000	7,000
Hardware...................	45	3,000	6,000	8,000	13,000	17,000
Liquor......................	55	15,000	19,000	22,000	28,000	34,000
Total......................		23,000	37,000	46,000	96,000	143,000

EXHIBIT 2 (Continued)

categories, all but a very small percentage of business will be done at convenience zone locations. By applying these shares to the estimates of total sales potential, a measure of the sales potential has been derived. On this basis, the sales potential which could be available to retail facilities located to serve residents of the site's convenience zone trade area is expected to increase from about $17 million in 1965 to about $22.5 million in 1970 and $31.5 million in 1980 (see Table 2–11).

Competition

This trade area sales potential, indicated in Table 2–11 presently supports a number of retail facilities which would be competitive with facilities located at the site. The size and character of all such competing facilities has been determined by a field survey made by this company. The effective competitive volume capacity of these facilities has been estimated by assigning square-foot volume levels which would be expected of such facilities under normally good management and average competitive conditions. These dollar amounts do not, therefore, necessarily reflect the maximum dollar volume levels possible by such facilities, nor do they represent estimates of the actual volume levels of these facilities in any given year. However, they are useful in assessing the longer-term volume capacity of these facilities as measured against our concepts of normal competition.

By subtracting the estimates of effective competition from the convenience zone sales potential, an unsatisfied sales potential has been determined for each of the selected retail categories. This unsatisfied sales potential rises from approximately $1.3 million in 1965 to about $2.6 million in 1970 and $11.5 million in 1980.

Convenience Goods Facilities Justified

At volumes per square foot which are considered to be adequate for new retail development standards, an estimate of the space requirements for new facilities to serve the site's convenience zone residents has been shown in Table 2–11. The amount of unsatisfied space potential ranges from 23,000 square feet in 1965 to 46,000 square feet in 1970 and 148,000 square feet in 1980.

Obviously, individually strong retail units might exceed the residual volumes indicated, depending on their merchandising effectiveness, size, advertising policies, and so on. Additionally, as discussed previously in the report, convenience retail facilities would also have market share volumes of a larger trade area if included in a center with a department

EXHIBIT 2 (Continued)

store as a major traffic generator. Therefore, a representation of these types of stores should be present in a center which includes a department store traffic generator for completeness of service, and so on, as indicated in the conclusions and recommendations. However, it is apparent that the demand is *not* strong enough to warrant the development of a *neighborhood shopping center* at the proposed site in the *absence* of a major department store tenant, or other comparable traffic-generating complex of comparison shopping stores.

Section V: Conclusions and Recommendations

The analysis undertaken by this office of the shopping center development opportunities at the West 84th and Valley Highway site in Denver, Colorado, as presented in the preceding sections, indicates that, in our opinion, there is an opportunity for the construction of a regional shopping center at this site at the present time keyed to a May–D&F unit of 137,000 square feet and a Montgomery Ward unit of 151,600 square feet (including TBA) as the major tenants. Our analyses further indicated that:

1. The population in the trade area for a regional shopping center at the proposed site is expected to increase from approximately 104,000 at the present time to 198,000 by 1980.
2. The trade area for the proposed center is one of the fastest growing areas of the Denver Metropolitan area. Regional access to the site is excellent from the north, south, and west via the Valley Highway (Interstate 25) and the Denver-Boulder Turnpike. Improvements in the Interstate system to the east prior to 1970 will improve access to the site from that direction. Local arterials provide good access to the site from all directions.
3. The total unsatisfied DSTM sales potential available to facilities located in the trade area is expected to increase from approximately $20.5 million at the present time (1965) to approximately $47.1 million by 1980.
4. As indicated in the analysis, the market share available to the May–D&F and Montgomery Ward department stores in the regional shopping center would vary over time, depending upon the competive situation. However, if these department stores could achieve market shares in this trade area somewhat in excess of their total metropolitan area market shares, at least in the early years, approximately $14 million (including TBA volume) should be available to the two stores by 1970 (or third-year operating volume following an assumed opening year of 1967), increasing to $17–20 million (including TBA) in

EXHIBIT 2 *(Continued)*

the 1975–80 period, depending in part of course, upon further moves by competitors.

5. As demonstrated in Section IV, it is our opinion that the demand is *not* strong enough to warrant the development of a neighborhood shopping center (depending entirely upon such convenience facilities as supermarkets, drug, variety, and hardware stores) at the proposed site at the present time in the absence of department store tenants as major traffic generators. However, in order to provide a well-balanced retail concentration, a representative of these types of stores should be present in a center which includes a department store traffic generator.

An illustrative area development schedule has been prepared (and presented in Table 2–12) to indicate the range of representative store types and sizes which could be planned for the site. It may be noted that with department store branches totaling 265,000 square feet, a recommended balanced center development would consist of 400,000 to 425,000 square feet of gross rentable area. A shopping center of the size range indicated in Table 2–12 would normally require from 36 to 39 acres of land at a 3:1 ratio for parking space, walks, malls, and other such areas of common usage. However, careful architectural planning would cut down on this requirement to some extent, assuming that no additional property adjoining the site is available.

The recommended floor areas have been derived by an analysis of the total potential which will be available as modified to conform to the standards of balanced shopping center developments. The recommended floor areas are, therefore, basic guides which should be used in planning the center but which might be modified to conform to the desires of particular tenants, the availability of other tenants, site problems which might affect architectural design, and so on.

In planning the subject center, consideration must be given to the proposed center at 104th and Valley Highway known as North Glenn. On preliminary view, the North Glenn site is approximately 3 miles farther north and outboard of the subject site and has a rather sparse population immediately tributary to it. Thus, supporting tenants would be more likely to be inclined to locate at the West 84th and Valley site rather than locate at the 104th site and have to endure the "pioneering." It has been our experience that the population lying outboard of a site is at least substantially more effective than that lying to the inboard. For this reason, we believe that the subject site is much more logical for immediate development than is the North Glenn location. It would be prudent, however, for the timing of the North Glenn site to be taken into consideration in the planning of the development at the subject site.

EXHIBIT 2 (Continued)

In undertaking the development of a regional center at the proposed site, we would suggest the following work be undertaken:

1. Review and evaluate this report.
2. If the conclusions appear satisfactory to you, proceed with the preparation of a financial analysis of the expected development.
3. If, on the basis of the above, a decision is made to proceed with the development, authorize the preparation of a preliminary site plan, architectural renderings, and preliminary leasing documents.
4. Based on our understanding that principal tenant interest has already been established, have full-leasing documents and sales brochures prepared and commence a full-leasing program and development.

TABLE 2–12

West 84th and Valley Highway Shopping Center
Illustrative Development Schedules
(rentable area in square feet)

Tenant	Illustrative Development Schedule (Sq. Ft.)
Department store............................	265,000*
Variety......................................	18,000– 20,000
Apparel.....................................	45,000– 50,000
Furniture/appliances.........................	8,000– 10,000
Other specialty..............................	10,000– 15,000
Food..	18,000– 20,000
Drug..	12,000– 15,000
Eating and drinking..........................	8,000– 9,000
Services.....................................	6,000– 8,000
Institutions..................................	10,000– 13,000
Total Building Area.....................	400,000–425,000
Total Site Area (Acres)†.................	36.7 39.0

* Excluding TBA Space.
† At 3:1 ratio for parking space, walks, malls, and other areas of joint usage.

EXHIBIT 2 (Concluded)

TABLE 2–13

North Valley Shopping Center: Total Capital Development Cost Budget

	Development Cost Budget
Construction costs	
May–D&F store and TBA	$1,923,500.00
Specialty shops buildings including Mall HVAC	1,542,850.00
Tenant finish work including Central HVAC	1,392,000.00
On-site and off-site work	640,000.00
Total Construction Costs	$5,498,350.00
Design costs	
Design services	
May–D&F and TBA	94,000.00
Specialty shops building shell	100,000.00
Tenant finish work including Central HVAC	(included in TFW Construction)
On-site and off-site work	30,000.00
Montgomery Ward	1,500.00
Landscaping	11,000.00
Other design services and reimbursables	25,500.00
Design and construction management	158,400.00
Total Design Costs	$ 420,400.00
Other development expenses	
Leasing fees	270,900.00
General development management	105,300.00
Leasing reimbursables	2,000.00
Construction financing fee and legal costs	46,650.00
Permanent mortgage good-faith deposit (to be reimbursed by lender)	–0–
Interest on construction financing	150,000.00
Appraisal costs	7,550.00
Title Insurance, revenue stamps, etc.	14,000.00
Real estate taxes	8,000.00
Pre-opening publicity and leasing aids	47,500.00
Ground rent to completion	108,600.00
Consulting fees	11,500.00
Insurance bonds, etc.	17,000.00
Organization and origination fee	50,000.00
EDUS accounting and administration	10,000.00
Mellon bank fee	4,100.00
Legal fees	100,000.00
EDUS travel and reimbursables	4,000.00
Total Other Development Expenses	$ 957,100.00
Total Development Cost Budget	$6,875,850.00
Minus: Cost reimbursed from tenants	
Wards Site Work	216,400.00
May D&F Extras	172,500.00
Adjusted Total Development Cost Budget	$6,486,950.00

PRESCRIPTION FOR
A SUCCESSFUL
SHOPPING CENTER

Paul E. Smith

A phenomenally successful post–World War II retail institution is the shopping center. The reasons for this success have been well documented by various writers. A product of entrepreneurs in retailing and in land and real estate development, it was greeted with enthusiasm by the middle-class market that had moved to the suburbs from the large cities and small country towns.

The shopping center concept is not new; the idea of one-stop shopping began with the village and country fairs in the Middle Ages. The first department store comprised many individual shops, which were leased to merchants who operated them as specialty shops within the walls of the huge building. This is not unlike the enclosed mall shopping centers that have been developed since 1960.

The chief difference between the original concept of the department store and the modern shopping center lies in the use of space. The original department stores had fewer leased departments, had little or no off-street parking, and made more use of the vertical dimension of space than the shopping center does.

The concept of a specific shopping center begins in the mind of one or more entrepreneurs; they are often building contractors, real estate developers, or successful operators of retail stores. Sometimes the developers, especially those who generate regional centers, are familiar with retailing, but some of them know little or nothing about the fundamentals involved in developing a successful shopping center.

A shopping center is more than a dream in the mind of the entrepreneur. It is a complex of retail institutions created in a relatively short period of time, and located where none existed heretofore. Its concept must be based on a realistic appraisal of certain facts and observed trends in the economic life of the community.

In considering this subject, certain assumptions regarding the eco-

* Reprinted from *Business Topics*, Autumn, 1966. Used by permission.

nomics of retailing are required to lay the groundwork for a discussion of the fundamentals.

FUNDAMENTALS

Retailing does not create wealth. It does add value to the worth of a product, and in this context it will add value to an inventory. However, if a store exists in a given market, the addition of another store will not expand that market unless it expands the size of the trading area. It is true that a retail store does add to the economic base of the community in the form of wages to employees, taxes on inventory and real estate, and the value of the services it requires from supporting institutions. But sales of stores in a shopping center must be primarily obtained through competition with other stores in the trading area. Thus the size of the pie must be increased. It is not realistic to expect that the size of the piece in the existing pie will be enlarged.

Counter actions will be taken by existing retail enterprises to meet the threat of a new retail enterprise. These measures will often receive the support of government and local merchant associations. The threat of new competitors disturbs the equilibrium of the community, and established retailers bring countervailing power to bear on the situation.

A shopping center is in its entirety a retail institution. Although composed of stores with different corporate identities, it is in concept no different from individual department stores, supermarkets, or low-margin retailers. The concept of a shopping center begins with the market. A shopping center exists in a given place in space. Abstractly, space has many shapes of height, breadth, and depth, but its value to a developer lies in its ability to produce a profit. In its concrete form, space is land—a tangible piece of property that exists in a specific market area.

THE MARKET STUDY

The first stage, therefore, in the development of a shopping center (always undertaken before land is purchased) is a study of the market. A well-designed market study must define the geographic trading area and the present population in that area. It must determine the market in terms of income, occupation, age, marital status, wage earners in the family, car ownership, education, leisure-time interests, and shopping attitudes and behavior toward specific retail stores. The study must also delineate road patterns, traffic, and public transportation facilities. Plans for the future are projected from these facts.

Two cases may serve to illustrate the importance of a market study prior to the purchase of land. In one instance, an owner of a building supply company and a commercial builder purchased sixty acres of land, which fronted on a four-lane expressway, on the edge of a city. They paid more than double the value of the land had it been used for farming. They were ignorant of laws pertaining to expressway entrances and exits, which prohibit exits except at interchanges. In another city, two owners of retail stores paid $1,300 an acre for ten acres of land in a location that did not have a market large enough to support even a supermarket. In both of these cases, failure was inherent because the first stage in development had been neglected.

One regional shopping center, although now a profitable concern, went through bankruptcy proceedings several years ago. Regarding the reasons for the failure of the center, the present manager stated in a recent letter:

Both developers and lenders lacked experience with shopping centers at the time the center was being planned. . . . The market area population was at that time insufficient to support the center.

A primary cause of shopping center failure lies in looking at a specific location with too much optimism. Projections of shopping sales involve estimates of incomes and spending for specific merchandise lines. It also allows for competitive store volume, taking into consideration road patterns and shopping habits of the potential customers. Accurate estimates of the ability of merchants to attract customers from existing stores in established retail shopping areas are difficult to make and at best are subject to error.

TOTAL SYSTEM CONCEPT

The second stage in the development of a shopping center is a preliminary concept of its entirety. A shopping center is more than a collection of miscellaneous stores. In its ideal form, it is an institution that meets the requirements of its market upon completion, and has in addition an expansion program to meet the requirements of a projected market. For a regional shopping center, this may mean one-stop shopping. For the neighborhood center, it may mean something different. In any event, the total system concept must be based on the market study. One market will require a developing center size, perhaps to be built in stages over several years, whereas another may have a retail spatial vacuum, dictating a complete development over a one- or two-year period.

The inherent characteristics of certain kinds of merchandise dictate their ability to pay the costs of occupying space in a store. A diamond occupies small space compared to its value, whereas a mattress is exactly the reverse. Some merchandise has high turnover; other merchandise, such as diamond rings, has lower turnover. Thus the type of store, the merchandise it sells, the price lines it carries, and the sales per square foot affect the development of the aggregate shopping center as well as each store within the center.

FINANCIAL ANALYSIS

The third stage in the development of a shopping center involves a financial analysis. Shopping centers must provide the developer with an opportunity to make a profit. An individual store's ability to pay rent in turn largely depends on its management skills, the characteristics of the merchandise it sells, the image it projects in its trading area, and the effectiveness of its sales promotion efforts.

Financial problems center around specific problem areas. Sometimes low construction costs hide defects that later require heavy capital expenditures. These unforeseen expenditures sap money from maintenance, sales promotion expenditures, and contingency funds for other unexpected expenses such as an increase in taxes.

Three of the centers studied in some detail went through bankruptcy proceedings because they spent too little for maintenance. In one case the operating expenses were as follows:

	Bankruptcy Case (Percent)	Average for the Industry (Percent)
Maintenance	3.3	17.0
Promotion	2.9	4.6
Administration	7.4	2.0

Another center, which suffered through two bankruptcies, had four years of management neglect. The buildings and parking areas needed considerable repair; there were faded lines, chuck holes in the parking area, masonry deterioration, and peeling paint on the buildings. One can imagine customers' reactions to the neglect of the center. In addition, the center had been built for a specific purpose with small shops, none large enough for even a medium-size supermarket. This layout had proved to be unprofitable. Unfortunately, the architectural and structural problems involved in changing the layout preclude anything but total destruction of the center.

A shopping center is composed of successful individual stores. However, it is more than that; it is an entity in itself. The concept of shopping centers as a total system recognizes that to be successful, it must have a balanced financial system. Most lenders require that taxes, fixed operating costs, and mortgage payments be covered by lease commitments of triple A tenants. Some lenders specify that triple A tenants occupy two-thirds of the space and pay two-thirds of the guaranteed rent. The dollar value of a shopping center is calculated by capitalizing the net income at an 8–12 percent rate.

Lease Terms

Leases are the legal ties between the developer and the store owners. They extend from five to twenty-five years with further options, and bind both parties to perform certain legal obligations. The terms of a lease should be based on a firm theoretical foundation. A magnet store deserves a lower percentage lease than a non-magnet store because of its size, image, the type of merchandise it sells, and its acceptance in a community. However, chain stores vary in their acceptance in various communities, as do independent specialty stores within various sections of a city. Generalizations as to specific stores are dangerous and may create a financial imbalance in a shopping center. Because financial institutions require it, developers are forced to give better lease terms to some tenants who really should not be in the center because they may have little local acceptance, pay too low rent, or create an imbalance of merchandise lines.

Lease terms should not be based on the financial position of the developer and his power position with the lessee, but rather on the ability of the specific store to attract traffic, the capacity of the store to pay a specified rent, the building and equipping costs, and the location of the store in the center in relation to magnet stores.

The capacity of a store to pay rent depends largely on the kinds of merchandise it sells, price lines, brands, and sales per square foot. *Dollars and Cents of Shopping Centers,* published by the Urban Land Institute, has provided vital financial data for centers that are being planned. It should be noted, however, that many figures on lease terms come from leases signed before industry-wide figures were available. Percentage lease terms, for example, for various kinds of stores may not represent an "economic" rent; the percentage terms should be used only as guides. The International Council of Shopping Centers and *The Chain Store Age* have recently published a new study, "Percentage Lease Summary," which contains some valuable information.

Adequate Financing

The financial problems of shopping centers appear to begin with inadequate financing. Every shopping center that has gone through bankruptcy has suffered from this. They lacked sufficient capital to provide for expenses incurred during the initial opening period. A community center, for example, failed in its second effort, in part because it had no money left for promotion expenses. Many shopping centers are paying a heavy penalty for failing to include a provision for increased taxes in their leases.

In one case, a bankrupt center is attempting to become profitable under the following lease terms: guaranteed rent with two-thirds discount the first year, one-third discount the second year, and full rent the third year. Another bankrupt center had average annual rental from triple A tenants of $1.29 per square foot with one lessee paying $0.79 per square foot. Independent and service stores paid $2.65 per square foot. The average annual rental from all tenants was $1.36, whereas the industry-wide average for this section of the country was $1.57 at the time of the bankruptcy. Net operating profit after loan service produced a net loss of $1,500.

Critical Operating Ratios

Dollars and Cents of Shopping Centers (*1966*) lists certain ratios as being critical in the financial health of a shopping center. Data were collected from shopping centers and grouped according to their size and geographical location. The data relate various centers in terms of gross leasable area, gross receipts (largely rent), operating expenses, and net profits. Certain parts of the study are used here to indicate the tremendous variations in shopping centers in those ratios that are critical in sustaining the financial health of the enterprise. All the figures are based on a calculation of the operating results per square foot of gross leasable area (see Tables 1, 2, and 3). Attention should be called to the fact that not all centers are comparable even though they are the same size. For example, the type of stores will affect the guaranteed rent because the kind of merchandise sold determines to a large extent the ability of a store to pay a specific guaranteed rent.

LAYOUT

The fourth stage in the development of a shopping center involves several theoretical concepts about layout. A shopping center is a retail institution. The planning of the layout of the center, the location of stores, the distribution of pedestrian traffic, the distribution and location of parking, and the provision for service functions must be based on sound retailing theory and practice. The first fundamental might be stated as follows: stores should be located in relation to each other so that each store can take advantage of the principle of traffic generator versus traffic user. Certain kinds of stores attract traffic to the center and to certain locations therein. In a small center of ten stores or less, the application of this principle is less important within the center since pedestrian traffic is easily distributed. In a shopping center with 100 stores and a mall extending 1,500 feet, it is critical. Some stores do not have the ability to attract people. A nut shop or a laundromat are examples. I have seen many shopping centers that have ignored the principle of traffic generator and traffic user in the layout of the center.

TABLE 1

	Average Sales Per Sq. Ft.	Range of Rent Per Sq. Ft.	Average Gross Receipts	Average Operating Expenses	Average Operating Balance
Neighborhood shopping centers........................$54		$0.87–$3.07	$1.94	$0.63	$1.31
Community shopping centers........................$50		$0.96–$2.83	$1.85	$0.61	$1.24
Regional shopping centers........................$50		$1.11–$3.30	$1.99	$0.66	$1.33

TABLE 2

Average Gross Leasable Area
Sales and Total Rent of Selected Tenants

Tenant Classification	G.L.A. Sq. Ft.	Sales Sq. Ft.	Total Rent Per Sq. Ft. of G.L.A.
Supermarkets.............................. 21,000		$96.	$1.49
Department stores.........................164,000		52.	1.31
Junior department stores................... 35,800		43.	1.47
Variety stores............................. 19,900		27.	1.43
Drugstores................................. 8,700		57.	2.21

TABLE 3

Regional Centers
Operating Results per Square Foot
Gross Leasable Area, 1966

	Range	Average
Building...$0.005–0.195		$0.035
Parking lot and public areas................... .026– .460		.142
Maintenance expenses........................ .035– .655		.186
Advertising and promotion.................... .009– .194		.044
Real estate taxes............................. .085– .679		.287
Insurance.................................... .005– .068		.027
General and administrative.................... .024– .345		.118
Total Operating Expenses...............$0.245–1.452		$0.658

The manager of a center that went bankrupt several years ago reported in a recent letter:

The original tenant mix was incorrect. The original layout included another department store which did not lease space. . . . Construction will start in 1966 on a new major store which will anchor the mall on the end that lacked the department store. . . . Over the years tenancies have been upgraded and weaker tenants screened out. This year the parking area was expanded 58% and a modern lighting system installed. . . . To sum it all up, we are very optimistic on the center's future. . . . 99% of the center is leased and we look forward to expanding further as the needs of the market area warrant.

Affinity

A second important concept that must be considered in planning the layout of a center might be called the principle of affinity. Certain merchandise must be located in close proximity because of customer shopping behavior. The characteristics and uses determine the affinity of one kind of merchandise to another. Characteristics associated with ultimate use and price dictate the location of items within a store and also dictate the location of a store in a shopping center. Examples of merchandise requiring close proximity are women's ready-to-wear and women's accessories. The pattern of distribution of pedestrian traffic throughout the center is critical to its success. It makes little difference whether the center is a strip, mall, cluster, or a modified version of each. Certain locations in the center will be dead if the principles of "traffic generator—traffic user" and "merchandise affinity" are ignored.

Exposure

The principle of visual exposure to pedestrian and automobile traffic is the next important concept to consider. Drug stores, restaurants, and the like are frequently open longer hours than other retail establishments in the center. They also attract a different segment of the market. That is, their customers patronize them for specific reasons, one of which is convenience. It is therefore critical to their success that they be located where people can see them from the street. They must be well lighted and marked with identifying signs.

Parking and Circulation

An elaborate research project by the Urban Land Institute and the International Council of Shopping centers has helped to resolve the issue of the size of the parking area. The study indicates that 5.5 car parking spaces are needed for each 1,000 square feet of gross leasable area:

This standard accommodates the need for parking spaces for all but the ten highest hours of demand during an entire year. The ten highest hours occur during the three peak days of the year. It is uneconomic to provide parking space for such limited peak periods. . . . Office space up to 20% of the gross leasable area can be added without a noticeable increase in the peak parking demand. . . . Significant value of walking customers or arrivals by means of public transit reduce needs proportionately.

However, a large number of car spaces does not necessarily contribute to the success of the center. More important is where they are in the center, their location in relation to specific types of stores, and the entrances and exits to the center. Planning the layout of the parking area involves such difficult problems as: Who will require the most parking, and for how long? Department store customers shop longer than supermarket customers. Service store customers prefer parking nearby, especially for dry cleaning and laundry. Parking areas must be designed that will encourage a minimum amount of in-center movement of cars and trucks with a minimum amount of danger to pedestrians.

Shopping centers, particularly the enclosed mall type, should consider opening up the side walls in stores to permit circulation of customer traffic. Old ideas of circulation of traffic from front to rear should be replaced with a total shopping center concept. With modern construction techniques, there is no reason to prevent customers from going to another store through a door in a side wall rather than forcing them to go out through front or rear doors. This would reinforce the feeling of a complete one-stop shopping center.

Services

The last important concept to consider in layout concerns a provision for the efficient and economical performance of the service functions. Provision for delivery and removal of merchandise and supplies, removal of rubbish from stores and common property, and mechanical snow and dirt removal are critical. All of the four bankrupt centers studied had not provided for adequate maintenance.

CONSTRUCTION

The fifth stage concerns the actual construction. The developer is quickly faced with an economic law that governs his building costs. A store cannot pay more rent than its sales will justify. Land costs are related to location and, theoretically, the better the location in relation to the market, the more sales a given square foot of land will produce. However, the cost and quality of construction of the building are determined by the projected sales. There is also the sticky question of quality construction and low maintenance costs versus low construction standards and high maintenance cost. In any event, construction costs are a factor in rent charges, which in turn affect the ability of the developer to obtain adequate financing.

Imagination in design, interesting architectural features, creative use of materials and colors on exterior and interior walls, and on the mall and sidewalks, contribute toward a total shopping center concept.

Every shopping center must be built with a view to the future. The original market study projects the character of the market. It has been pointed out that a shopping center is planned to develop in stages over several years. Equally important is the concept of allowance for future building changes and modifications in the parking area. If possible, side walls should not be load-bearing, since it may be desirable to increase or decrease the size of a store. Quite often a store will want to expand to add greater variety of merchandise; in many cases this is impossible due to load-bearing walls. One of the bankrupt centers, and others I have visited, failed to provide for changes in the layout of the center. Failure to plan for future development frequently results in improvisation or complete inability to make changes when modification is needed.

IDENTIFICATION

The sixth stage involves the whole concept of communication and shopping center identification to its market. A shopping center is more than a collection of stores; it is an institution. Each store contributes to the total shopping center image in the mind of the customer, but no single store is more important than the center in its entirety. It competes with established business districts, with other shopping centers, and with free-standing stores. The ability of a shopping center to establish a distinct identity by using well-conceived and well-planned sales promotion devices may well be the factor that provides its greatest competitive advantage. Merchandise is becoming similar, stores are beginning to look alike. Differences between variety stores, drug stores, and promotional department stores are becoming blurred. This reasoning points up the importance of the vision, imagination, and skills of the center manager.

Publicity

The management of the center has many aspects; not the least important is the publicity effort of the total center. Shopping center identification results from having adequate signs, centerwide sales, promotion efforts, special-purpose promotion and publicity, and provision in the original layout for community events.

Early shopping centers usually lacked a provision in the lease that required financial contribution by individual merchants for centerwide promotion. Many chain store organizations failed to realize the importance of coordinated promotion efforts.

The total shopping center image is not limited to the external face it presents to its customers. The internal face, the quality of the maintenance of buildings and parking area, safety and police protection during and after store hours, and the removal of snow and debris promptly, all affect customers' attitudes toward the center and its stores.

It is interesting that all four of the centers that went bankrupt reported inadequate financing to cover maintenance and sales promotion. Three of them indicated that unforeseen capital expenditures reduced the amount available for these expenses.

Environment

The shopping center as an open system can best be shown by means of a chart that delineates the center in terms of its internal and external environments (see Chart 1). The management of the center can best be judged by its ability to modify both of these environments to meet the objectives of the company.

It should be noted that the chart indicates the need for a viable, progressive, and interested group of merchants who band together with the manager to form a merchant association. Often retailers are reluctant to join together in common efforts, yet the degree of cooperation through the merchant association may well affect the present and future health of the center.

Few shopping centers have gone bankrupt—apparently only 5 centers out of perhaps 7,000 that have been built during the past fifteen years. This is not to say, however, that all centers are perfectly planned and operated. Some succeed in spite of a poor location, opportunistic selection of stores, inadequate parking, little sales promotion effort, and neglect of maintenance.

Actually, it is almost impossible for a center that is built in 1966 to fail. The combined knowledge of the developer, the financing agent, and the real estate departments of chain stores assures a high degree of success but, nevertheless, does not guarantee 100 percent functioning of all of the parts of the enterprise. The skillful and intelligent manipulation of the parts of the system is the job of the shopping center manager; this is a highly demanding position well described in *Shopping Center Management and Operation*, published by the National Retail Merchants Association in 1956:

Wanted! Man to manage a Shopping Center. Must have had executive experience in a retail store. Sales Promotion and Public Relations experience essential. Legal and some engineering training highly desirable. Personal

CHART 1

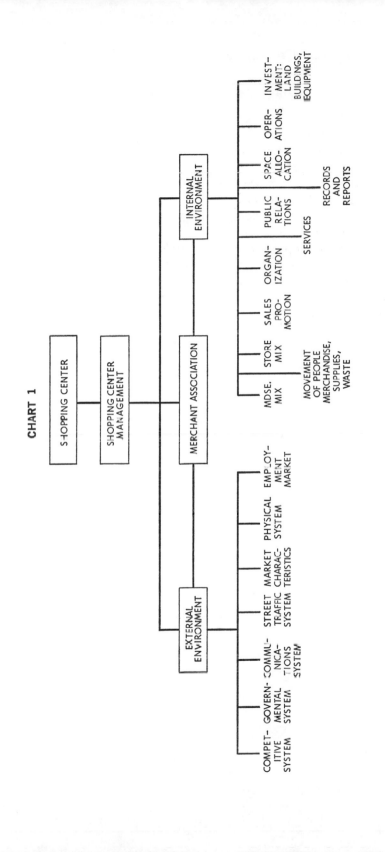

characteristics should include a high degree of tact and diplomacy. Must be able to weld . . . forty or more merchants into a harmonious group.

When I visit a new shopping center such as Summit Mall, near Akron, Ohio, I reflect on a similar trip to the Northgate Center in Seattle, Washington eleven years ago. At that period of time I could only find 25 regional shopping centers in all of the United States; there are possibly 250 of these in existence at the present time. Since then, experiments in layout, construction, internal store location, maintenance, and leasing terms and conditions of rental have been adding to the fund of knowledge about shopping centers.

Large retail shopping complexes such as Cross Country in the Bronx, formerly a swamp, and Northland in Detroit, at one time a farm and now surrounded by expressways and thousands of cars each day, prove that entrepreneurs with dreams, ambition, and capital can bring together the merchant and the market to serve both in equal measure.

UNITED SHOE
BUILDINGS
Office Building

In March 1964, Maurice Gordon was trying to decide how much to offer
for the properties owned and 50% occupied by the United Shoe Machinery Corporation in downtown Boston. United Shoe had issued an invitation on February 21, 1964, for sealed bids for the four parcels
comprising:

1. 140 Federal Street, a 24-story tower with 300,000 total square feet of
   space.
2. 136 Federal Street, a six-story office building, with 50,000 square feet
   of space.
3. 80 High Street, a garage with parking space for 355 vehicles.
4. 39–49 High Street, a vacant parcel of approximately 8,400 square feet,
   used as a parking lot for approximately 40 vehicles.

The minimum acceptable bid price was announced by United Shoe to
be $6,150,000, and because of the size and prominence of the properties
and its prime location in the city's financial district there was considerable interest in the bidding on the part of local and out-of-town realtors.

DESCRIPTION OF PROPERTY

The property was located only a few blocks from the city's major
department stores and was easily accessible to the Southeast Expressway,
the Massachusetts Turnpike, and to the South Station. The main building, located at 140 Federal Street, was known as the United Shoe
Machinery Building, and its tower had served as one of the city's
landmarks. Views from its upper floors looked out on the Boston Harbor
on one side and the Boston Common on the other. Built 34 years ago of
first-class construction, the structure was well maintained, serviced by 10
recently installed Otis automatic passenger elevators replacing the man-
ually operated ones. The building was air conditioned with ceiling
suspended units, also a recent improvement. Very little of the office space

had been modernized; nevertheless, 97% of the space was leased primarily to financially strong old-line Boston firms. Rentals including electricity averaged \$5.50–\$5.75 per rentable square foot. Approximately 80% of the building's 300,000 gross footage was usable. The remainder was public space such as stairways, elevators, and public corridors and toilets used by more than one tenant.

The adjoining six-story building at 136 Federal Street, of brick and wood construction, was less desirable because of its smaller lobby and elevators and the deteriorated condition of its office space. Nevertheless, because of its favorable location and lower rents at \$4.50–\$4.75 per net square foot including electricity, the building had few vacancies. Approximately 40,000 of the 50,000 gross square feet was usable. The parking garage constructed in 1957 was within 100 yards of the main entrance to 140 Federal Street, and preference in monthly parking was given to tenants of United Shoe. The small lot of 8,400 square feet was located diagonally across from the parking garage and used for additional parking. The present zoning laws made it possible to build a small office building on the site, though none was contemplated at this time.

COMPANY HISTORY

Maurice Gordon & Sons, a real estate investment company, solely owned by Mr. Gordon, his son, and his son-in-law, was the largest private property owner in the Boston area, if not New England. Since shortly after World War II, Mr. Gordon had accumulated approximately 10,000 apartment units throughout Massachusetts and over 1.2 million square feet of office space in approximately 12 downtown Boston office buildings. He specialized in modernizing older apartment houses and office buildings and followed a policy of investing exclusively in this area of real estate as opposed to constructing new buildings in which he had no experience. According to Mr. Gordon, each area of real estate required its own special talents, and his talents were in this area.

Mr. Gordon was aware that the risks of developing new properties were considerable because of the uncertainties of predicting five to seven years ahead the costs of construction, financing charges, tenant rentals, and completion dates. He felt that he was making a positive contribution to society and the preservation of urban values by rehabilitating areas that had not yet become slums, but were deteriorating rapidly. He was able to do this without government subsidies or without destroying or demolishing neighborhoods. Also, his rental levels enabled the middle-class residents to live and work in the city. He did not drive them to the suburbs with the high rents common in new construction. In answer to critics who claimed that his rehabilitation resulted only in a cheap stopgap measure that merely perpetuated slums, he pointed out that the federal government was now emphasizing rehabilitation as the remedy for curing slums. Yet, he could see that the government was not always realistic in attempting to rehabilitate what was often beyond repair. One had to know what was worth rehabilitating. The costs of rehabilitation varied considerably.

The federal government also was considering the spending of millions of dollars in experimental grants to reduce rehabilitation costs to levels he had already achieved. A continuous and large volume of work was one factor that enabled him to achieve this efficiency. He was able to develop a full-time, year-round, experienced staff of construction and maintenance personnel. He attained economies through large-scale purchasing, often of manufacturer's closeouts. He closely supervised all phases of his operation, from maintenance to the negotiation of most office leases. His imagination was important in solving many difficult problems. Because of his personal attention to detail, he considered it desirable to concentrate his real estate investments in the Greater Boston area.

Mr. Gordon managed his real estate operations from his office, consisting of four rooms and a small secretarial area in an older office building he had renovated on Milk Street. This office handled the bookkeeping for all his properties and the rental and management for the office buildings. The apartments were managed from local offices, and maintenance was handled by full-time maintenance personnel operating from company-owned, radio-controlled trucks dispatched from a central supply warehouse in the low-rent area of Roxbury.

Mr. Gordon began after World War II to acquire apartment buildings, in the Brighton-Brookline area, close to Boston and accessible to public transportation. Rents for older one-bedroom apartments ran from $75 to $100 per month. He characterized this area as stable and middle class, with many long-term residents capable of paying higher rents but expecting greater value in the form of modernized lobbies and kitchen and bathroom facilities. Yet, when modernized, apartments still rented for $100 to $125 per month. This was much less than the rental for new apartments, and as a result, Gordon's units served a larger rental market.

As an example of the economies of his operation, Mr. Gordon would spend $1,500 to modernize the kitchen and bathroom and to redecorate a one-bedroom apartment. By increasing the rents by $25 a month or $300 per year, he could recapture his investment in five years. Immediately, his $1,500 investment was worth from $1,800 to $2,000, since apartment buildings in the area were being valued at 6 to 6½ times their annual rental income. The value of his investment was increased still further because the modernization program resulted in the reduction of maintenance costs and in the elimination of the substantial vacancies in the buildings he bought. The relatively low price paid by Mr. Gordon for the properties he acquired reflected the high vacancy rate and the poor physical condition of the buildings. Because approximately 60% of the operating costs of a property are fixed, a difference of 5% in vacancies can have a major impact on the owner's return on investment. That is, a $1,200 increase in rentals could increase the owner's return by $720.

In 1959, Mr. Gordon started to acquire office buildings in downtown Boston. He felt that market conditions at that time were ideal. While the high Boston tax rates were discouraging new construction, tenants were demanding more modern air-conditioned space. Most Boston property owners at that time were conservative and had done little to upgrade their property. If a tenant wanted to have his space modernized, he would often have to have the work done at his own expense. Mr. Gordon's first major office building purchase in 1959 was 141 Milk Street, a 100-year old structure with 50% of the building's 200,000 square feet of floor space vacant. Shortly thereafter he purchased 147 Milk Street, a building that had prior to his acquisition been vacated by the Traveler's Life Insurance Company. He renovated both buildings and as a result increased occupancy to 98%. He then purchased 33 Broad Street, where he added 9% to the building's rentable floor area by building an extra floor between the old first and second floors, exploiting a ceiling height of 20 feet on the first floor. At 89 State Street, his next acquisition, he enclosed an interior court and added 10% to the rentable floor area. This additional space was quickly rented, since Mr. Gordon's modernization of the building made the interior space, now air conditioned and properly lit, desirable.

PROPOSED SALE OF PROPERTY

Mr. Gordon first heard of the proposed sale of the United Shoe Building in February 1964. The thought of owning this building was very appealing to him. He had always regarded the building as one of the most outstanding landmarks in Boston. He doubted whether he would again have an opportunity to purchase this building. United Shoe had owned and had been the major tenant of the building since its completion in 1930. It had fully depreciated the property on its balance sheet and as a result decided that its investment in the building could better be used in other areas of its business. An earlier purchase offer was almost accepted, but United Shoe was uncertain about the optimum price available. As a result, the company decided to have a sealed-bid auction for the property with the prospective bidders prescreened as to their financial responsibility. Bids had to be received by March 30, 1964, and would be opened on April 15. To insure that any bids submitted would be serious, a $400,000 deposit was required with each submission.

An offering circular was printed describing the terms and conditions of the proposed sale with the current income and expense figures.

United Shoe decided to utilize the services of six local established real estate brokerage firms to offer the property. The broker of the successful bidder was to receive a commission of $135,000 plus 2% of the amount that the successful bid exceeded the minimum price of $6,150,000.

EVALUATION OF PROPERTY

Based upon the income and expense figures supplied to him by the United Shoe Machinery Corporation (see Exhibit 1), Mr. Gordon attempted to evaluate the property. He saw that the gross income figure of $1,659,000 was based on a new lease entered into by the United Shoe Machinery Corporation for 12 years. United Shoe had also retained rights to extend the lease for two five-year periods at an annual rent of $664,000 including electricity. The space covered by the lease was 139,000 gross square feet or 46% of the gross rentable area at 140 Federal Street. Although the rental averaging $4.77 per square foot at first seemed low, Mr. Gordon was satisfied when he saw that the area rented included a considerable amount of basement space and was calculated on a gross square footage basis and included public areas. This made the effective office rent on a net usable basis about $6 per square foot. Also, United Shoe was taking the space in its present condition. There also was a tax clause covering 46% of any property tax increase over the 1963 level, and an operations clause covering a similar portion of increased cleaning expenses. The operating expenses for the building were based on the actual experience of the United Shoe Machinery Corporation with the building and totaled $1,093,000. This left a net before financing of $566,000. Mr. Gordon then took an allowance for vacancies of 3% of income and a management expense figure of 2%, which reduced this net figure to $485,000.

Mr. Gordon estimated that he would probably be able to get an institutional first mortgage equal to 75% of the price paid for the property. The mortgage term would be for 20 years with interest at 5½%, requiring a constant annual payment of 8.2%. He had recently placed another mortgage at this level. On this basis, if he made the minimum bid of $6,150,000, he could obtain a $4,612,500 first mortgage costing $378,000 per year. This left $107,000 as the return on his investment of $1,538,000 or approximately 7%. Mr. Gordon was not satisfied with so low a return on his investment. In addition, he felt that competitive bids would be in excess of the minimum, as indicated by the high level of public interest.

INCOME

Mr. Gordon began to analyze those factors that affected the income of the property. He first considered the general market area. Federal Street was in the center of Boston's financial district. The First National Bank, the city's largest bank, was at one end. At the other was the central business artery, South Station, and the Massachusetts Turnpike, making accessibility to the area excellent for both automobiles and public transportation. The State Street Bank had begun construction of a major office tower three blocks away, and the Traveler's Insurance Company and Blue Cross–Blue Shield had completed major new buildings nearby. In another area of the city, the Prudential Center with a large 52-story office tower was under construction. Also, work had commenced on the Government Center project, which would contain office buildings for city, state, and federal agencies. The aggressive Boston Redevelopment Authority under a new mayor had announced plans to begin studies for revitalization of both Boston's waterfront, only four blocks away, and the adjacent downtown retail center, which included all the city's major department stores.

On the one hand, Mr. Gordon was pleased to see all this activity going on in Boston. On the other hand, he was concerned with the vacancies which might be generated in existing buildings once the new space came on the market. Government agencies alone occupied 838,044 square feet or about 5% of all available office space in the existing buildings, space that would be entirely vacated when the Government Center was finished in the next two years. New incomplete buildings totaled another 958,000 square feet. The annual survey vacancy report of the Boston Building Owners' and Managers' Association had just been published, and the results showed an overall 9.2% vacancy figure for the downtown area, with little hope for improvement (see Exhibit 2). Mr. Gordon knew that he would have competition for several years and knew that the United Shoe properties would be hard put to maintain their present 97% occupancy rate. Although Mr. Gordon knew that the age of 140 Federal Street and 130 Federal Street precluded the $7 per foot rents charged by the new buildings, he felt that the existing rents of $5.50 to $6 per square foot were reasonable.

Along with location and competition, another factor affecting income was the character of the existing tenancy. He reviewed the list of the present tenants, and he recognized most of the names as financially responsible old-line Boston firms, which had helped give the building its prestige. He wondered whether a change of ownership from United Shoe, even though United Shoe itself was staying, would affect the tenancies of this type of firm. Also, few leases in the building other than United Shoe had more than three years to run, and tenants might wish to upgrade their space by moving to one of the new buildings owned by one of the large financial institutions.

Mr. Gordon next considered the amount of space available for rent. He knew from his past experience that although a building was fixed in size, there were several approaches to measuring rentable square footage. He saw that there was about 25,000 square feet of nonincome-producing yet potentially rentable space. He took a plan of a typical floor at 140 Federal Street (see Exhibit 3). Of the 19,662 feet on the floor, approximately 2,200 square feet was used for elevators, the elevator lobby, and stairs and would always be public and unrentable. But 3,480 square feet of corridor space and 2,300 square feet of toilet and storage space might be rentable if used by a single tenant. By rearranging certain areas and by attempting to lease individual floors to only one or two tenants, he thought it was reasonable to expect that he could increase his rented space by at least 10,000 square feet, which at $6 per square foot could increase his income by $60,000. Another 5,000 square feet with income potential of $30,000 per year could be "created" by adopting the New York approach to measuring space rather than the Boston standard still used in some of the older buildings in town. The basic difference between the two approaches was that in the New York standards, measurements were taken from the window or glass line of the building to the glass line of the entrance door. In Boston, the measurements were taken from the inside walls of the space. In an older building with 18-inch masonry walls, the 9 additional inches included in rentable area because of the New York approach could add materially to the number of square feet included in rentable space. The periphery of many of the floors was as much as 750 feet.

Mr. Gordon also had an idea which he thought could add to the total "fixed" space of the property. Between 130 and 140 Federal Street was an open area of approximately 600 square feet. By filling this area with a new structure, he could not only create 500 square feet of rentable space at each level but make it possible for the floors at 130 Federal Street to be entered off the elevator lobby at 140 Federal Street, the building with the greater prestige and the higher rental levels. The 3,000 rentable square feet created could be rented at $6 per square foot or $18,000 per year. In addition, the 40,000 square feet at 130 Federal Street now renting at a lower level than 140 Federal Street could then be worth almost automatically as much as $0.50 per square foot more or $20,000 per year merely because of the change in address and entrance.

Another means of increasing income was to increase the quality of the space offered through modernization. He estimated that he could increase rentals by $110,000 by improving 110,000 square feet of space for both existing tenants and new tenants coming into the building.

He analyzed whether rental income could be increased by offering additional services to the tenants. Although Mr. Gordon intended to clean, operate, and maintain the building in a first-rate manner, he knew that United Shoe had also done so. Therefore, he concluded that he would probably not be able to increase income in this manner. Mr. Gordon felt, though, that his active promotional efforts, his encouragement of local rental brokers, and his existing institutional advertising might give him a broader choice of tenants; but essentially since the building was already well known he did not feel that this advantage was substantial. Nevertheless, the more property he owned, the more likely it was that tenants would come to him for space and that he would have some place to accommodate them, either in this property or other buildings he owned.

In summary, through renovation, the building of new space, and the remeasuring of old, Mr. Gordon expected to increase rents by $238,000. He knew that this increase would not be achieved immediately but would probably take about three years. A reasonable estimate would be that income would increase over the $1,659,000 level by $30,000 in year 1, $100,000 in year 2, $170,000 in year 3, and $238,000 in year 4.

EXPENSES

To remodel space and to build the new addition involved substantial capital expenses. Also, additional vacancy must be expected, since a tenant could not occupy space until the work was complete. In addition to the $50,000 for vacancy already included in his expense statement, Mr. Gordon allowed for an additional $50,000 in vacancy the first year, $100,000 the second year, and $50,000 the third year. Then the present overall allowance of 3% should again be adequate. The major capital expense would come from the renovation of 40,000 square feet at 130 Federal Street, 70,000 square feet at 140 Federal Street, and approximately 15,000 square feet of public space to permit its inclusion as rentable area. Mr. Gordon felt that this renovation would cost the normal property owner $10 per square foot or $1.1 million but that because of his expertise he could probably do the work for $6.50 per square foot, or $715,000.

For this $6.50 per square foot he could remodel a typical office to include: a new vinyl-asbestos floor; dropped acoustic ceiling; recessed fluorescent lighting; air conditioning; the enclosure of all pipes and radiators; partitioning finished at the tenant's option with prefinished wood paneling, paint, or vinyl wall covering; overhead storage cabinets, shelving, new entrance doors; counters; and closets. The layout was designed to the tenant's particular specifications, prepared by an architect selected and paid for by Mr. Gordon. Yet, Mr. Gordon chose materials, such as paneling, that he expected would reduce the landlord's future maintenance responsibilities.

There were many reasons why Mr. Gordon's costs were lower than average, none of which he felt affected the quality of his finished product. First of all, because of the amount of work he was doing he could effect large economies through mass purchasing. As an example, he bought his own lumber direct from Oregon with carload deliveries twice a month at $54 per 1,000 board feet as opposed to the normal builder price of $110. Walnut paneling bought in quantity cost $0.18 per square foot rather than $0.48. Vinyl asbestos flooring installed cost him only $0.22 per square foot rather than $0.30 to $0.35. The vinyl wall covering was bought direct from the manufacturers as closeouts at 60% off. Rather than buy 8-foot-long, four-tube lighting fixtures from a manufacturer for $30 each, he bent and painted the metal troffers himself, and then separately purchased and added the ballast, socket, tube, and plastic cover, all for a cost of only $10 per fixture. In renovating one major building, he took out the old-fashioned marble dividing partitions in the toilet areas and replaced them with new metal partitions. Then he had the marble repolished and reused to create an elegant marble entrance lobby. Imagination was an important factor in remodeling.

Besides his savings on material, Mr. Gordon's labor costs were well below average. In an industry noted for its cyclical employment practices, he had experienced, nonunion work crews whom he employed on a year-round basis. He was able to take nonskilled workers at $2–$3 per hour and teach them to do tasks that normally were done by employees receiving $5 per hour. Each individual was expected to do work in more than one trade. By subcontracting only ceiling, floor tile, and air-conditioning installation, he was able to reduce the number of outside trades involved, saving both time and money.

The six-story addition of 600 square feet per floor would cost $75,000 to complete. The cost of this was high because of the difficulty of installing steel and materials in such a small enclosed space. Few outside contractors would even attempt the job. Mr. Gordon expected to install a new boiler costing $35,000. At the present, the heat was purchased from Edison Steam, a method Mr. Gordon, from his experience in other buildings, knew to be very expensive. He also put in an allowance for $25,000 to cover contingencies.

These capital costs totaled $850,000, and the increased vacancies over the three-year period $200,000. Mr. Gordon expected to finance this $1,050,000 partially through reinvesting any money received from operating the property over the three-year period and the remainder through a second mortgage from a private source. Until he knew his actual mortgage cost based on the amount of his bid to United Shoe, he could not estimate exactly how much would be available from operations. Based on existing figures and the minimum bid price after payments on a $4,612,500 mortgage of $378,000, $107,000 per year was available.

OPERATING EXPENSES

Mr. Gordon then examined the various operating expense figures submitted to him by United Shoe to see whether or not, through more efficient operation, he could increase his return. He knew that in any building that had been owned by the same owner for a long period of time, inefficiencies in operation would be bound to occur. This was especially apt to be true in a company such as United Shoe where the property was being operated not for its real estate return but for the service of the office and executive employees of the company. The building payroll figure of $344,000 Mr. Gordon expected to be reduced to $200,000. Since the buildings had been recently converted to automatic elevators, 15 operators could be released immediately, saving $60,000. The other major cost of building payroll was office cleaning. His cost in other buildings was $0.50 per square foot, and he expected his cost to be the same here, resulting in another saving of $60,000. The permanent maintenance staff of the building payroll would consist of an engineer and three helpers at a cost of $30,000 per year as compared with United Shoe's cost of $54,000. He realized that his costs were below that of published national average figures (see Exhibit 4). Yet, because of his efficiencies and because the building would be easier to maintain and clean as it was modernized, he felt the $200,000 figure was adequate. Also, he knew that in the early years of owning a property the owner normally pays more attention to details and is more efficient. It was natural even in his own properties for a certain degree of inefficiency to creep in in later years.

Mr. Gordon knew that he was not expected to retain any of the present building employees or be responsible for their severance, vacation, or unemployment pay if they were discharged. United Shoe was prepared to assume these costs. As payroll costs were reduced, there would be a corresponding percentage decrease in unemployment compensation taxes which were based on payroll cost.

Heating costs could be expected to drop from $37,000 to $25,000 for two reasons. He was installing his own boiler system, probably in the summer of the third year when the present Edison contract expired. In addition, as the ceilings in the offices were dropped, less area was required to be heated.

He checked with his insurance agent, who told him that because of a special package policy written by the Factory Mutual Insurance Company for all his properties, his insurance costs would be reduced almost 50% from $17,400 to $9,300.

Electricity, which cost $80,000 per year, was a large expense and was a service included in the basic rent. Normally, each tenant had his own meter and paid the utility company directly. On a rent-inclusion basis the landlord often made money, since he purchased electricity with one meter at a bulk rate.[1] A disadvantage was that a tenant, even though it was more expensive, might be inclined to rent space at $6 per foot without electricity than at $6.25 with electricity. In any case, Mr. Gordon knew that it would be a very expensive electrical job to change over the system to individual meters, and United Shoe had recently put in a new modern electric service to the building capable of handling all the foreseeable needs of the tenants based upon the rent-inclusion principle. The electricity charge also included the usage for air conditioning. He would have to wait for more experience before deciding if there were any savings in electricity.

Mr. Gordon next analyzed the alterations, repairs, and decorating figure. Historically, in 1963 the repair figure was $102,700. This seemed high to him. He thought it might represent some unusual expenditures because of the impending sale of the property. Furthermore, as the building was modernized, repairs should decrease. He calculated that $73,700, approximately 4% of gross income, was reasonable, especially since his own staff was accustomed to doing most of the repair work themselves.

Real estate taxes were his major operating expense item, and it was in this area that he was especially sensitive. The tax rate in Boston had gone down in the last three years from $100.60 per $1,000 of assessed valuation in 1961 to $99.80 in 1962, to $96.00 in 1963. Still, the history of Boston before this time was for rising expenditures, especially since Massachusetts did not have a sales tax as an alternative source of revenue. Also, he had a special problem with the Boston assessors. Since his business was modernizing and increasing the rent rolls of older buildings, the assessors kept careful watch of his operations and continually tried to raise his assessments, so that taxes represented 28% of income. This level was normal for downtown office buildings. Mr. Gordon knew that new construction was being taxed at a 20%-of-income basis but had been unable to convince the assessors that his work was entitled to the same tax benefit. He felt it should be so valued, both because his renovation of the property was so complete and because his work also benefited the city by upgrading an area. Instead, the assessors valued his property at an amount that resulted in his income being taxed at a 28% rate, a rate that was high but fairly standard for existing downtown office properties in Boston.

---

[1] The landlord had to be very careful, though, in estimating his costs, since Massachusetts' law permitted an arrangement where the landlord had one meter and included electricity in the rent, but it did not permit an arrangement where the landlord put in his own submeter for each tenant and billed electricity separately to each tenant based upon usage.

Mr. Gordon adjusted his expenses so that his tax figure was in line with the 28% rate throughout the period that his income increased. He knew, though, that 140 Federal Street, which represented 80% of the assessment for all three parcels, was occupied primarily by United Shoe, which had a tax clause in its lease to pay 46% of any increase in taxes for that building. Since the leases of the other tenants were expiring, the tax clauses in the new leases would most likely be based on the year after the construction was completed. Based upon the present income figures alone, an increase in taxes of $42,000 could be expected immediately. Then, assuming a $240,000 further increase in income, taxes would increase over the period by another $67,000. Reducing this $109,000 figure by the amount to be paid by United Shoe left a projected increase of $70,000 to a total of $479,000.

A management figure of 2% seemed fair to him for this property, even though this percentage was higher than his cost in other areas. He knew that this high-grade property would require special attention. The $37,000 figure would include the salary of a manager and secretary plus office expenses and professional fees.

In any case, he knew that a potential mortgagor always put a figure for management in his expense setup to determine the net income of the property for appraisal purposes. The reason for this is that a potential mortgagor must consider that if he comes into ownership of the property through foreclosure he will have to hire an outside management firm.

Mr. Gordon now made a new income and expense statement based upon his adjustments of the figures submitted to him (see Exhibit 5). His income after vacancy on a stabilized basis was increased to $1,840,000 and his expenses on an adjusted basis were reduced to $999,000. This left a figure of $841,000 before financing, rather than the $485,000 originally calculated. His net return was increased by $356,000, with a capital outlay of only $1,050,000, including the $200,000 allowance for extra vacancies during construction.

BIDDING STRATEGY

The question now became how much to bid for the property. He wanted to win the auction. The prestige of owning the property was worth $250,000 to $500,000 to him both in pride and in that this building would upgrade his whole portfolio of properties. The more property he owned, the more flexibility he would have in satisfying space needs of new or existing tenants. Mr. Gordon, however, did not want to pay any more for the property than he had to. He knew that all the bidders, including himself, would use the income method for determining value. Replacement cost produced a value far higher than the actual market value of the property. The 67,771 square feet of land for all the parcels was worth at least $20 per square foot as raw land. This is the figure he would use for depreciation purposes. The 350,000 square feet of building would cost $30 per square foot, and the garage for 355 cars would cost $2,500 per space, for a total of $12,750,000 to build new. Taking an allowance for depreciation of 1% per year of age for the building reduced the figure to $9.2 million. On the older building he could take depreciation on a 33-year basis and on the improvements on a 15-year basis, both using a straight-line depreciation rate. The $9.2 million price appeared out of line for the United Shoe property.[2] On the other hand, $6,150,000 seemed too low.

Other bidders might be satisfied with an 8% return on their investment. Normally, Mr. Gordon expected a cash return after federal income taxes of 12% on his invested capital, plus amortization of mortgages. He rarely sold any of his properties. Yet, he doubted whether other bidders would see as many areas to increase net income as he did, especially with regard to the connection between 130 and 140 Federal Street. This $75,000 expenditure increased income by $38,000. Another bidder might be willing to modernize 110,000 square feet to obtain the extra $110,000 income, but it might cost him almost $400,000 more. This would be uneconomical unless the new tenant would pay more than the $1 per square foot extra for the improvements. Other bidders, if experienced in the area, would also plan on converting from Edison Steam and would know of the elimination of the elevator operators. They would also make an effort to reduce public areas and would try to use the New York measurements standard. Whether they could be as persuasive as Mr. Gordon in obtaining tenants, he did not know.

His prospective mortgage lender had informed him that as long as his purchase price was within reason he could still expect a 75% mortgage at 5½% interest for 20 years. Based upon his personal reputation and the prestige of the property, he was able to secure the pledge of a three-year, $1 million second mortgage at 12% annual interest with only interest payments during the period. At that time, he felt he could increase his first mortgage, which already had three years of amortization, by an amount adequate to repay the second, on the same terms as his present mortgage.

The number of competitors he would have in this bidding was another question. He knew that virtually all the outstanding real estate firms in the area and a few from New York City were analyzing the property, but

---

[2] A new building in Boston can afford these costs because rentals of $1 per square foot more are obtainable; for new space, real estate taxes are 20% of income rather than 28%; and operating costs are about $1.40 per square foot rather than $1.65. This meant that a new building renting at $7 per square foot after taxes and operating costs would have $4.20 to cover financing, while an older building renting at $6 would have $2.67. Although the risks of development of a new property could be much higher, a potential mortgagee might capitalize for appraisal purposes the income from the new building at 8½% and the old building at 9%.

he expected only five or six to put up the $400,000 deposit and actually make a bid.

Another question in his mind was whether these other bidders would visualize the approach he was taking to upgrade the value of 130 Federal Street through installation of the connection. If they did not, it was unlikely that their potential rental increase would be as great as his. On the other hand, the high vacancy predictions for older buildings made by the real estate association, the existing 9.2% vacancy rate, and the competition of the new buildings gave him cause for concern. Mr. Gordon sat down to weigh all the factors and to prepare his final bid.

EXHIBIT 1
United Shoe Machinery Properties 1963 Annual Income and Expenses

	130–136 Federal St.	140–156 Federal St.	80 High St.	39–49 High St.	Total
Income					
United Shoe.............. $ —	$ 664,000	$ —	$ —	$ 664,000
Other tenants............. 153,000	721,000	100,000	8,000	982,000
Miscellaneous............. —	13,000	—	—	13,000
Gross Income......... $153,000	$1,398,000	$100,000	$8,000	$1,659,000
Expenses					
Building payroll............ $ 29,000	$ 315,000	$ —	$ —	$ 344,000
Window cleaning.......... 3,000	13,000	—	—	16,000
Elevator inspection........ 3,000	20,000	—	—	23,000
Unemployment compensation................ 2,000	19,000	—	—	21,000
Insurance................. 3,000	14,000	300	—	17,300
Water..................... 1,000	7,000	—	—	8,000
Heat...................... 5,000	32,000	—	—	37,000
Electricity.................. 7,000	73,000	—	—	80,000
Decorating and repairs...... 7,000	95,000	700	—	102,700
Real estate taxes.......... 28,000	336,000	40,000	5,000	409,000
Miscellaneous............. 3,000	32,000	—	—	35,000
Gross Expenses........ $ 91,000	$ 956,000	$ 41,000	$5,000	$1,093,000
Net before Financing........ $ 62,000	$ 442,000	$ 59,000	$3,000	$ 566,000

EXHIBIT 2

BOMA Reports . . .
Latest Vacancy Survey Shows:
—*119 buildings reported*
—*9.2% Vacancy*
—*70.1% Air Conditioning*

Nearly 11.5 million square feet of office space, a record amount, was accounted for in the latest vacancy survey completed by the Boston Building Owners and Managers Association.

EXHIBIT 2 (Continued)

Robert A. Pihlcrantz, Association president, said reports were received from 119 buildings in downtown Boston and the Back Bay, the city's major office rental area.

The composite results show slightly more than one million square feet of space vacant. That represents 9.2 percent of the total, no significant change from the 10.9 percent reported in the previous survey taken January 1.

In a letter to the owners and managers who took part in the semi-annual survey, Pihlcrantz cautioned against placing too much emphasis on the vacancy percentage figure itself. The letter said:

"We should concentrate on these facts.

"The report shows 1,060,123 square feet of vacant space.

"A major part (if not all) of the 838,044 square feet of government occupancy will move from these 119 buildings into the Government Center whose buildings are not reflected in the report.

"The vacancy figure is lower than it should be because in some areas we are reporting tenants in their present quarters and also in the new, incompleted buildings to which they will eventually move."

Pihlcrantz, who is a partner in the C. W. Whittier & Bro. firm, stressed that there are a number of different approaches to interpretation of vacancy figures and that a precisely accurate percentage figure will not be achieved for another year or year and a half when the current construction is completed and occupied.

"We are now establishing a base of information," he said, "and from the information we now have, we can predict that there will be a marked increase in vacancy in Boston office buildings within 12 to 18 months."

With the building of the "New Boston," there is increased significance in the office space information compiled by the Association, a division of the Greater Boston Real Estate Board.

Builders, developers, realtors, planners and all involved in office building construction and renovation, base their future plans on known facts. Such data as revealed in the BOMA surveys has important meaning in the real estate industry.

The concern is made clear in the number of buildings now being reported. Before Pihlcrantz improved the survey form and method, only about 40 buildings submitted their vacancy figures. It is now nearly triple that amount.

Seventy-six of the buildings reported are located in downtown Boston with the bulk of them in the $3–$4 rental class. In this rent category it is noted with interest that some 22 percent of the space is now occupied by government agencies.

Also noted was the high vacancy rate in the lower rent office space in both downtown and the Back Bay; Commercial and Specialty buildings in the downtown business district also report high vacancies.

In an effort to help build the data file, Pihlcrantz invited non-members of his association to submit information. Many did so. There has been a lag in this type of statistic and it has been sought eagerly here since urban renewal has become an important factor in the city's real estate industry.

EXHIBIT 2 (Continued)
Office Vacancy Survey—as of October 1, 1964

Classification	No. of Bldgs.	Total Sq. Ft. Rentable Area	Total Sq. Ft. Vacant Area	% of Vacancy	Federal Tenancy	State & Local Tenancy	Total Government Occupancy	% Government Occupancy
Downtown								
New—Complete	2	264,180	—	—	—	—	—	—
New—Incomplete	2	958,900	385,400	40.1	—	—	—	—
Over $4	27	2,528,422	112,641	4.5	64,180	13,136	77,316	3.1
$3–$4	31	2,665,218	80,612	3.0	397,789	194,978	592,767	22.2
$2–$3	4	121,922	17,409	14.2	—	—	—	—
Comm. and Spec.	10	573,738	104,146	18.1	25,000	67,961	92,961	16.2
Total	76	7,112,380	700,208	9.8%	486,969	276,075	760,344	10.6%
Back Bay								
New—Complete	4	209,000	13,700	6.5	—	—	—	—
New—Incomplete	3	1,025,000	265,000	25.8	—	—	—	—
Over $4	7	2,237,806	15,556	.7	—	—	—	—
$3–$4	19	524,733	35,027	6.6	19,000	700	19,700	3.0
$2–$3	5	177,610	21,607	12.2	—	22,000	22,000	12.3
Comm. and Spec.	5	211,050	9,025	4.2	36,000	—	36,000	17.0
Total	43	4,385,199	359,915	8.2%	55,000	22,700	77,700	1.7%
Grand Totals	119	11,497,579	1,060,123	9.2%	541,969	298,775	838,044	7.0%

EXHIBIT 2 (Continued). Office Vacancy Survey—Supplemental Data

Classification	Air Conditioned in Square Feet	% of Total Space Air Conditioned	Store Occupancy Total	Vacant	%
Downtown					
New—Complete	264,180	100%	—	—	—
New—Incomplete	958,900	100%	54,000	31,000	57.4%
Over $4	1,647,211	65.1%	199,887	44,400	22.2%
$3–$4	1,226,341	46.0%	191,791	4,550	2.4%
$2–$3	26,750	21.9%	18,226	6,373	34.9%
Comm. & Spec.	69,400	12.1%	45,128	9,505	21.0%
Total	4,192,782	58.9%	509,032	95,828	2.2%
Back Bay					
New—Complete	209,000	100%	15,600	—	—
New—Incomplete	1,025,000	100%	12,000	—	—
Over $4	2,070,268	92.5%	29,905	1,784	5.9%
$3–$4	414,275	78.9%	88,497	3,328	3.7%
$2–$3	32,148	18.1%	47,380	—	—
Comm. & Spec.	101,000	47.9%	46,200	800	1.7%
Total	3,851,691	85.8%	239,582	5,912	.1%
Grand Totals	8,044,473	70.1%	748,614	101,740	.8%

EXHIBIT 3

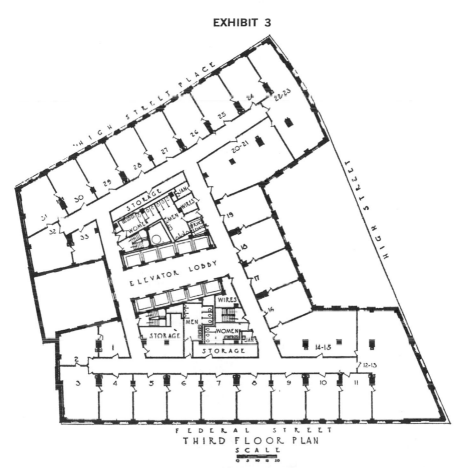

THIRD FLOOR PLAN
SCALE

ONE-FORTY FEDERAL STREET

EXHIBIT 4
1965 General Averages
(cents per square foot)

Population (All Cities)	300,000 to 500,000 Population			500,000 to 750,000 Population			750,000 and Over Population		
Number of buildings......	166	166	166	57	57	57	255	255	255
Building rentable area.....	19,259,864			11,545,983			51,146,276		
Office rentable area........	15,644,239			9,245,486			42,900,304		
Office rented area.........	14,738,155			8,600,833			41,476,058		

Account	Building Total	Office Total	Office Rented	Building Total	Office Total	Office Rented	Building Total	Office Total	Office Rented
A1 Cleaning.............	44.2 (166)	48.9 (166)	51.9 (166)	53.8 (57)	63.9 (57)	68.7 (57)	60.2 (255)	65.9 (255)	68.2 (255)
A2 Electric system........	15.3 (166)	17.1 (166)	18.1 (166)	18.1 (57)	22.2 (57)	23.8 (57)	15.4 (255)	17.1 (255)	17.7 (255)
A3a Heating..............	13.1 (166)	13.1 (166)	13.9 (166)	11.8 (57)	12.4 (57)	13.3 (57)	14.6 (255)	15.2 (255)	15.8 (255)
A3b Air cond.–ventilating...	17.2 (95)	19.4 (95)	20.4 (95)	16.3 (31)	19.6 (31)	20.5 (31)	19.2 (101)	21.1 (101)	21.7 (101)
A4 Plumbing system......	3.9 (166)	4.3 (166)	4.6 (166)	3.9 (57)	4.4 (57)	4.8 (57)	3.9 (255)	4.1 (255)	4.3 (255)
A5 Elevators.............	14.1 (166)	17.3 (166)	18.4 (166)	15.8 (57)	19.7 (57)	21.2 (57)	19.0 (255)	22.7 (255)	23.5 (255)
A6 Genl. expense—office..	19.1 (166)	19.3 (166)	20.5 (166)	19.6 (57)	20.2 (57)	21.7 (57)	18.5 (255)	18.9 (255)	19.6 (255)
Genl. expense—bldg...	17.1 (166)	17.5 (166)	18.5 (166)	20.0 (57)	21.3 (57)	22.9 (57)	19.4 (255)	19.6 (255)	20.3 (255)
Total Operating........	139.5 (166)	151.9 (166)	161.2 (166)	154.6 (57)	178.0 (57)	191.3 (57)	163.3 (255)	177.3 (255)	183.4 (255)
B1 Tenant alterations......	11.2 (123)	12.9 (123)	13.7 (123)	8.7 (35)	10.7 (35)	11.8 (35)	16.4 (143)	16.9 (143)	17.6 (143)
B2 Repairs–maintenance ...	9.7 (158)	10.5 (158)	11.2 (158)	11.7 (54)	14.2 (54)	15.3 (54)	11.1 (242)	12.4 (242)	12.9 (242)
B3 Tenant decorating......	5.5 (117)	6.3 (117)	6.7 (117)	5.5 (44)	6.8 (44)	7.4 (44)	7.0 (156)	7.8 (156)	8.1 (156)
Total Construction......	22.0 (165)	24.7 (165)	26.3 (165)	20.6 (55)	24.7 (55)	26.5 (55)	27.6 (252)	29.5 (252)	30.5 (252)
Total A and B..........	161.4 (166)	176.4 (166)	187.2 (166)	175.0 (57)	202.3 (57)	217.5 (57)	189.8 (255)	205.6 (255)	212.7 (255)
C1a Fire insurance.........	2.0 (103)	1.9 (103)	2.1 (103)	1.4 (47)	1.4 (47)	1.5 (47)	1.8 (137)	1.8 (137)	1.8 (137)
C1b Insurance (other).......	2.7 (154)	2.7 (154)	2.9 (154)	2.2 (51)	2.4 (51)	2.6 (51)	2.8 (206)	2.8 (206)	2.9 (206)

C2a Prop. taxes—land	12.3 (156)	6.1 (156)	6.5 (156)	13.4 (53)	8.3 (53)	9.0 (53)	18.6 (222)	10.9 (222)	11.3 (222)
Prop. taxes—bldg.	43.6 (156)	41.9 (156)	44.5 (156)	58.3 (53)	55.5 (53)	60.8 (53)	55.2 (222)	54.7 (222)	56.3 (222)
C2b Pers. prop. assessment	1.1 (57)	1.1 (57)	1.1 (57)	1.2 (23)	1.3 (23)	1.5 (23)	2.5 (76)	2.8 (76)	2.3 (76)
C3 Depreciation	69.2 (150)	68.5 (150)	72.7 (150)	72.2 (51)	71.9 (51)	77.0 (51)	66.3 (193)	65.9 (193)	68.3 (193)
Total Fixed Charges	131.1 (150)	121.6 (150)	129.1 (150)	148.0 (51)	141.4 (51)	151.3 (51)	144.5 (193)	136.3 (193)	141.5 (193)
Total Expense (A, B and C)	293.4 (150)	299.6 (150)	318.1 (150)	324.8 (51)	345.9 (51)	370.0 (51)	335.8 (193)	343.3 (193)	356.3 (193)
Net (before Cap Charges)	86.5 (131)	84.8 (122)	90.5 (122)	99.9 (44)	88.1 (44)	95.9 (44)	108.0 (168)	118.4 (146)	124.0 (146)
Office rental income		377.7 (131)	403.0 (131)		421.1 (46)	461.2 (46)		448.3 (161)	469.5 (161)
Store rent (store area)	455.1 (92)			493.4 (41)			473.8 (138)		
Total Rental Income	371.3 (140)			407.7 (46)			416.9 (195)		
Miscellaneous income	5.6 (75)			12.2 (33)			15.8 (112)		
Total Income	374.8 (140)			417.8 (46)			427.2 (195)		
Store area—M sq. ft	1487 (166)			747 (57)			2938 (255)		
Lot area—M sq. ft	2807 (123)			1197 (49)			4490 (198)		
Operating ratio—%	77.2 (131)			76.3 (44)			74.5 (168)		
Management ratio—%	43.7 (140)			42.4 (46)			43.8 (195)		
Fire ins. rate—$100—¢	7.8 (90)			5.3 (41)			7.1 (102)		
Bad debt loss	0.2 (165)			0.2 (57)			0.1 (255)		
Avg. sq. ft. per person	154.3 (77)	141.3 (80)	134.3 (30)	159.9 (47)	133.9 (45)	124.9 (45)	136.7 (195)	120.5 (141)	115.0 (141)
Avg. office vacancy %			5.8 (156)			7.0 (57)			3.3 (255)

( ) Indicates Number of Buildings Giving this Information.
* Includes Alterations and Decorating in Non-Rentable Areas.

EXHIBIT 4 (Continued)
1965 Regional Averages
(cents per square foot)

Region	Canadian†			Middle Atlantic‡		
Number of buildings	22	22	22	89	89	89
Building rentable area	3,109,073			20,485,157		
Office rentable area		2,609,481			18,235,456	
Office rented area			2,588,473			17,926,033

Account	Building Total	Office Total	Office Rented	Building Total	Office Total	Office Rented
A1 Cleaning	53.1 (22)	55.5 (22)	56.0 (22)	59.1 (89)	61.4 (89)	62.4 (89)
A2 Electric system	14.4 (22)	16.0 (22)	16.3 (22)	21.2 (89)	22.3 (89)	22.7 (89)
A3a Heating	16.5 (22)	16.0 (22)	16.1 (22)	15.2 (89)	14.9 (89)	15.1 (89)
A3b Air cond.–ventilating	15.4 (9)	17.7 (9)	17.8 (9)	21.4 (53)	22.9 (53)	23.1 (53)
A4 Plumbing system	2.9 (22)	3.0 (22)	3.0 (22)	4.2 (89)	4.4 (89)	4.4 (89)
A5 Elevators	19.3 (22)	23.0 (22)	23.2 (22)	17.8 (89)	20.0 (89)	20.3 (89)
A6 Genl. expense—office	15.1 (22)	15.0 (22)	15.1 (22)	16.7 (89)	16.9 (89)	17.1 (89)
Genl. expense—bldg.	14.5 (22)	14.4 (22)	14.5 (22)	22.2 (89)	22.4 (89)	22.8 (89)
Total operating	147.3 (22)	156.3 (22)	157.5 (22)	172.1 (89)	179.2 (89)	182.3 (89)
B1 Tenant alterations	10.2 (11)	11.7 (11)	11.8 (11)	11.6 (41)	12.3 (41)	12.7 (41)
B2 Repairs–maintenance*	9.6 (21)	10.5 (21)	10.6 (21)	10.4 (81)	10.9 (81)	11.1 (81)
B3 Tenant decorating	6.5 (15)	6.7 (15)	6.8 (15)	5.6 (43)	5.7 (43)	5.8 (43)
Total Construction	21.7 (22)	24.0 (22)	24.2 (22)	19.3 (86)	19.9 (86)	20.2 (86)
Total A and B	169.0 (22)	180.2 (22)	181.7 (22)	189.6 (89)	197.3 (89)	200.7 (89)
C1a Fire insurance	1.9 (14)	1.7 (14)	1.7 (14)	1.2 (41)	1.2 (41)	1.2 (41)
C1b Insurance (other)	1.4 (19)	1.4 (19)	1.4 (19)	2.6 (68)	2.7 (68)	2.7 (68)

	Col 1	Col 2	Col 3	Col 4	Col 5	Col 6
C2a Prop. taxes—land	20.8 (21)	11.0 (21)	11.0 (21)	18.4 (73)	12.4 (73)	12.6 (73)
Prop. taxes—bldg.	91.3 (21)	85.5 (21)	3€.1 (21)	55.6 (73)	54.3 (73)	55.4 (73)
C2b Pers. prop. assessment	0.13 (3)	0.14 (3)	C.14 (3)	5.0 (24)	5.3 (24)	5.3 (24)
C3 Depreciation	62.5 (20)	57.8 (20)	5€.2 (20)	76.2 (64)	74.2 (64)	75.1 (64)
Total Fixed Charges	177.1 (20)	156.7 (20)	15?.8 (20)	156.7 (64)	147.2 (64)	149.0 (64)
Total Expense (A, B, and C)	346.0 (20)	337.2 (20)	38C.5 (20)	344.2 (64)	342.3 (64)	346.4 (64)
Net (Before Cap Charges)	100.6 (18)	129.3 (16)	13C.2 (16)	168.9 (53)	193.7 (52)	196.8 (52)
Office rental income		458.4 (18)	45?.5 (18)		501.6 (57)	515.3 (57)
Store rent (store area)	796.9 (11)			429.8 (44)		
Total rental income	436.4 (20)			479.8 (59)		
Miscellaneous income	7.4 (9)			12.2 (43)		
Total Income.	441.1 (20)			488.5 (59)		
Store area—M sq. ft.	127 (22)			713 (89)		
Lot area—M sq. ft.	527 (22)			1363 (57)		
Operating ratio—%	77.4 (18)			66.1 (53)		
Management ratio—%	36.9 (20)			38.1 (59)		
Fire ins. rate—$100—¢	6.3 (14)			3.8 (25)		
Bad debt loss.	0.3 (22)			0.02 (89)		
Avg. sq. ft. per person	153.4 (22)	140.0 (22)	13€.9 (22)	133.1 (48)	113.8 (44)	110.2 (44)
Avg. office vacancy %			C.8 (22)			1.7 (89)

( ) Indicates number of buildings giving this information.
*Includes alterations and decorating in nonrentable areas.
†Montreal, Regina, Toronto, Vancouver, Victoria, Winnipeg.
‡Baltimore, Camden, Newark, (Del.); New York, Philadelphia, Pittsburgh, Providence, Washington, D.C., Wilkes-Barre, Wilmington (Del.).

EXHIBIT 4 (Continued)
1965 Breakdown of Operating Costs Total Building Rentable Area
(cents per square foot)

A. Canadian

Item	Cleaning A1	Electric System A2	Heating A3a	Air Cond. & Vent. A3b	Plumbing System A4	Elevators A5	Alterations B1	Repairs & Maintenance B2	Tenants Decorating B3
Wages	47.2 (13)	4.4 (8)	5.9 (15)	6.7 (7)	1.8 (8)	12.8 (12)	2.7 (1)	6.5 (7)	6.4 (5)
Supplies	3.1 (14)	3.0 (13)	1.3 (14)	1.5 (8)	0.6 (7)	0.2 (4)	3.9 (5)	5.4 (6)	2.0 (6)
Fuel			8.7 (16)	1.9 (2)	0.7 (6)	1.8 (9)			
Electricity	0.4 (2)	7.6 (18)	0.8 (7)	6.9 (8)	0.3 (4)				
Refrigeration									
Water				1.1 (4)	1.5 (14)				
Outside services	6.6 (11)	1.2 (6)	0.6 (6)	0.5 (6)	1.3 (6)	5.5 (18)	2.1 (3)	4.0 (10)	1.8 (8)
Unclassified	0.8 (9)	0.2 (4)	0.4 (5)	0.2 (1)	0.02 (4)	1.0 (6)		0.5 (3)	0.1 (1)
Total	52.7 (17)	14.1 (18)	15.3 (18)	16.2 (8)	2.9 (18)	19.1 (18)	3.3 (8)	10.6 (14)	6.5 (13)

B. Middle Atlantic

Item	Cleaning A1	Electric System A2	Heating A3a	Air Cond. & Vent. A3b	Plumbing System A4	Elevators A5	Alterations B1	Repairs & Maintenance B2	Tenants Decorating B3
Wages	54.5 (61)	4.8 (49)	6.4 (54)	6.8 (40)	2.3 (48)	11.0 (58)	6.3 (18)	5.2 (33)	3.7 (23)
Supplies	3.0 (60)	2.0 (56)	1.0 (44)	1.1 (38)	0.6 (47)	0.4 (33)	2.2 (22)	2.5 (40)	1.1 (25)
Fuel			9.0 (58)	4.8 (14)	1.3 (14)				
Electricity	0.7 (9)	17.5 (58)	0.8 (16)	7.9 (34)	1.3 (7)	2.6 (44)			
Refrigeration					2.7 (1)				
Water				0.5 (9)	1.8 (46)				
Outside services	3.4 (43)	1.1 (12)	1.2 (23)	2.0 (20)	0.8 (21)	9.8 (35)	11.5 (18)	7.0 (34)	2.2 (18)
Unclassified	2.6 (26)	0.7 (29)	0.3 (20)	3.7 (20)	0.1 (20)	1.2 (32)	2.6 (4)	1.5 (15)	1.5 (7)
Total	61.0 (63)	21.7 (63)	15.5 (63)	20.7 (40)	4.8 (63)	19.2 (63)	12.0 (33)	12.3 (47)	5.5 (33)

	1	2	3	4	5	6	7	8	9
Wages	52.2 (107)	3.9 (76)	6.5 (82)	5.9 (42)	2.5 (62)	13.3 (93)	6.5 (47)	6.7 (65)	6.5 (57)
Supplies	3.0 (105)	1.9 (100)	1.1 (89)	1.5 (47)	0.9 (84)	1.3 (64)	5.0 (48)	4.7 (67)	1.3 (59)
Fuel		7.3 (92)	9.3 (105)	5.5 (1-)	1.0 (39)				
Electricity	0.3 (3)		2.0 (41)	8.8 (46)	1.1 (20)	2.2 (70)			
Refrigeration				1.0 (3-)	0.3 (3)				
Water				2.8 (3-)	1.5 (91)				
Outside services	6.6 (81)	1.0 (37)	1.8 (47)	0.7 (17)	1.6 (43)	6.7 (78)	13.3 (43)	4.3 (62)	4.1 (48)
Unclassified	2.4 (52)	0.6 (34)	0.6 (48)		0.5 (29)	0.9 (56)	6.9 (33)	4.2 (40)	2.4 (29)
Total	60.9 (108)	11.6 (108)	18.2 (108)	18.6 (52)	4.9 (107)	20.6 (106)	18.8 (76)	14.3 (91)	8.5 (91)

D. Midwest Northern

	1	2	3	4	5	6	7	8	9
Wages	37.2 (87)	2.3 (65)	4.7 (76)	4.3 (55)	1.9 (56)	9.6 (62)	2.7 (33)	4.5 (48)	4.8 (47)
Supplies	2.2 (83)	1.4 (82)	0.7 (62)	1.9 (48)	0.6 (59)	0.7 (43)	3.2 (37)	1.9 (45)	0.8 (54)
Fuel		11.9 (79)	9.6 (92)	4.8 (1-)	1.0 (29)				
Electricity	2.9 (16)		2.6 (31)	7.4 (5-)	0.5 (20)	2.4 (70)			
Refrigeration					0.3 (10)				
Water				1.4 (29)	1.4 (84)				
Outside services	10.7 (68)	1.8 (46)	1.4 (35)	1.6 (26)	1.0 (44)	5.0 (70)	6.1 (44)	4.3 (60)	3.5 (44)
Unclassified	2.0 (43)	0.8 (23)	0.7 (23)	1.2 (14)	0.4 (18)	1.0 (39)	7.8 (16)	4.8 (30)	0.5 (3)
Total	44.6 (94)	13.8 (94)	15.4 (94)	16.2 (59)	3.8 (95)	13.6 (94)	9.1 (69)	9.5 (83)	6.1 (77)

E. Pacific Northwest

	1	2	3	4	5	6	7	8	9
Wages	38.8 (20)	2.3 (14)	2.5 (15)	3.2 (4)	1.7 (13)	14.1 (17)	3.2 (10)	2.4 (10)	6.5 (10)
Supplies	2.0 (18)	1.7 (18)	0.8 (10)	0.5 (3)	0.8 (14)	1.0 (13)	3.2 (10)	8.3 (9)	3.3 (10)
Fuel		8.9 (21)	7.5 (19)		2.9 (4)				
Electricity	0.1 (2)		4.4 (6)	3.1 (4)	0.6 (2)	1.3 (11)			
Refrigeration									
Water				1.5 (2)	1.7 (20)				
Outside services	22.6 (12)	6.8 (4)	2.7 (7)	1.5 (3)	1.1 (8)	7.7 (12)	13.4 (12)	4.0 (10)	4.5 (9)
Unclassified	1.7 (3)	0.4 (5)	0.4 (4)	0.2 (-)	1.2 (7)	3.8 (15)	11.9 (9)	4.2 (9)	2.5 (7)
Total	50.1 (22)	12.5 (22)	10.4 (22)	8.1 (4)	4.5 (22)	20.4 (22)	18.5 (20)	9.0 (20)	8.4 (19)

EXHIBIT 4 *(Continued)*

Air-Conditioned Buildings

Year 1965 Account	Building Total	Office Total	Office Rented
A1 Cleaning.....................................	56.4	61.3	63.5
A2 Electric system.............................	16.7	18.6	19.3
A3a Heating......................................	14.1	14.3	14.8
A3b Air conditioning–ventilating.................	18.2	20.4	21.1
A4 Plumbing system..........................	4.1	4.4	4.5
A5 Elevators...................................	16.4	19.7	20.4
A6 Genl. expense—office......................	18.3	18.6	19.3
Genl. expense—building....................	19.9	20.3	21.1
Total Operating...........................	164.2	177.5	183.9
B1 Tenant alterations.........................	14.4	15.3	15.9
B2 Repairs—maintenance.....................	10.8	12.0	12.5
B3 Tenant decorating.........................	6.1	6.8	7.1
Total Construction........................	24.7	26.6	27.5
Total A and B.............................	188.8	203.9	211.3
C1a Fire insurance.............................	1.7	1.7	1.8
C1b Insurance (other).........................	2.5	2.5	2.6
C2a Prop taxes—land..........................	15.7	9.7	10.1
Prop taxes—building.....................	56.6	55.3	57.5
C2b Pers. prop assessment....................	2.0	2.0	2.1
C3 Depreciation...............................	77.6	76.1	79.1
Total Fixed Charges.......................	153.5	144.7	150.5
Total Expense (A, B, and C)..............	341.5	348.5	362.5
Net (before cap charges).................	105.7	115.3	121.0
Office Rental Income..........................		454.8	476.5

Note: Store rent 484.8; total rental income 429.3; miscellaneous income 15.1; total income 439.9; operating ratio 75.9%; average office rental rate $4.77; office occupancy 96.5%.

Operatorless Operation

The 1965 study of self service elevator operation of the fully automatic type is based on 298 returns.

The increase in the number of buildings included in the table lends more weight to the favorable results. Average rental rate for this office space is $4.765 per square foot.

The indicated costs breakdown as follows in terms of cents per square foot.

	Buildings Total	Office Total
Wages..............................	6.2	7.7
Supplies............................	.9	1.1
Power...............................	2.5	3.0
Outside service.....................	7.3	9.2
Unclassified........................	.8	1.0
Total........................	13.6	16.7

EXHIBIT 4 (Continued)

The building area involved is 52,707,854 square feet, of which 42,760,719 is office area. The wages naturally include starters as well as mechanical help; there may even be some instance where elevators are manned, despite the character of controls.

Breakdown of 1965 Air-Conditioning Costs

The current analysis of air conditioning costs in buildings with central plant installations, cover 229 properties and 47,541,942 square feet of office area.

Costs itemized below are again calculated on area serviced. The unit cost reported (19.3¢ square foot) compares with 19.6¢ a year earlier.

Air-Conditioning Analysis, 1965

Item	Buildings	Building Total	Office Total	AC Area	AC Cost	Sq. Ft.
Wages........................205	205	49,144,213	40,721,398	45,285,570	2,785,722	8.1
Supplies....................202	202	47,591,328	39,475,432	44,131,436	701,680	1.6
Fuel............................ 50	50	13,783,048	11,926,890	12,810,901	650,519	5.1
Electricity..................213	213	48,742,110	40,673,614	45,109,729	3,823,415	8.5
Water........................105	105	22,039,927	17,951,466	20,377,879	216,136	1.1
Outside......................122	122	27,440,253	22,595,669	25,285,874	569,955	2.3
Unclassified.............. 76	76	23,253,976	19,087,964	21,766,413	445,551	2.1
Total.................229	229	51,671,375	42,789,444	47,541,912	9,168,679	19.3

Note: All figures used are for operating only. On ownership costs, as reflected in depreciation, this additional information is supplied. Seventy (70) buildings with 14,942,601 sq. ft. of air conditioned space, take $2,781,853 depreciation, an average of 18.6 cents per square foot. Total tonnage is 159,404, an average of 225 square feet per ton. Depreciation was taken on an average life expectancy of 17.9 years on compressors, 17.1 years on fans and 23.9 years on ducts.

EXHIBIT 4 (Continued)

Nonair-Conditioned Buildings with Manually Operated Elevators

	Year 1965 Account	Building Total	Office Total	Office Rented
A1	Cleaning	51.7	59.9	65.9
A2	Electric system	13.6	15.8	17.4
A3a	Heating	14.0	14.9	16.3
A3b	Air conditioning-ventilating			
A4	Plumbing system	3.9	4.3	4.7
A5	Elevators	27.7	34.9	38.4
A6	Genl. expense—office	20.2	21.1	23.2
	Genl. expense—buildings	17.1	17.7	19.5
	Total Operating	148.3	168.7	185.5
B1	Tenant alterations	12.2	14.1	15.8
B2	Repairs—maintenance	10.9	12.6	13.8
B3	Tenant decorating	7.4	8.7	9.7
	Total Construction	24.7	28.7	31.6
	Total A and B	172.9	197.3	217.0
C1a	Fire insurance	1.8	1.7	1.9
C1b	Insurance (other)	3.2	3.3	3.6
C2a	Prop. taxes—land	14.2	7.0	7.7
	Prop. Taxes—buildings	35.9	35.5	39.1
C2b	Pers. Prop. assessment	3.8	4.4	4.9
C3	Depreciation	47.9	47.1	51.6
	Total Fixed Charges	104.6	96.9	106.2
	Total Expense (A, B and C)	279.4	297.6	326.3
	Net (before cap charges)	53.7	35.9	40.1
	Office Rental Income		316.6	356.3

Note: Store rent 421.8; total rental income 312.3; miscellaneous income 5.5; total income 316.2; operating ratio 83.3%; average office rental rate $3.56; office occupancy 90.9%.

Air-Conditioned Buildings with Manually Operated Elevators

	Year 1965 Account	Building Total	Office Total	Office Rented
A1	Cleaning	57.3	61.9	65.5
A2	Electric system	14.7	15.7	16.6
A3a	Heating	13.3	13.3	14.1
A3b	Air conditioning-ventilating	16.5	18.2	19.3
A4	Plumbing system	4.0	4.2	4.4
A5	Elevators	26.1	30.8	32.6
A6	Genl. expense—office	18.6	18.9	20.0
	Genl. expense—buildings	19.5	19.4	20.5
	Total Operating	170.0	182.4	193.0
B1	Tenant alterations	12.1	13.6	14.3
B2	Repairs—maintenance	12.1	13.1	13.9
B3	Tenant decorating	5.8	6.1	6.5
	Total Construction	25.9	28.4	30.0
	Total A and B	195.9	210.7	223.0
C1a	Fire insurance	1.8	1.7	1.8
C1b	Insurance (other)	3.0	3.0	3.1
C2a	Prop. Taxes—land	14.5	7.9	8.4
	Prop. Taxes—building	52.8	51.0	54.7
C2b	Pers. prop. assessment	1.3	1.3	1.4
C3	Depreciation	61.7	59.7	64.0
	Total Fixed Charges	133.5	122.6	131.5
	Total Expense (A, B and C)	324.6	327.7	351.6
	Net (before cap charges)	61.0	65.9	72.0
	Office Rental Income		422.6	456.7

Note: Store rent 408.7; total rental income 408.1; miscellaneous income 3.9; total income 411.1; operating ratio 84.3%; average office rental rate $4.57; office occupancy 94.5%.

EXHIBIT 4 (Continued)

Nonair-Conditioned and Operatorless Elevator Buildings

	Year 1965 Account	Building Total	Office Total	Office Rented
A1	Cleaning	53.2	61.9	65.2
A2	Electric system	14.3	16.5	17.4
A3a	Heating	13.1	13.7	14.4
A3b	Air conditioning-ventilating			
A4	Plumbing system	3.8	4.2	4.4
A5	Elevators	12.8	16.0	16.9
A6	Genl. expense—office	19.5	16.9	21.0
A6	Genl. expense—buildings	18.4	18.8	19.8
	Total Operating	135.1	151.1	159.2
B1	Tenant alterations	12.2	14.3	15.2
B2	Repairs—maintenance	10.9	12.6	13.3
B3	Tenant decorating	7.5	8.8	9.3
	Total Construction	24.9	29.2	30.8
	Total A and B	157.2	176.9	186.4
C1a	Fire Insurance	2.2	2.1	2.3
C1b	Insurance (other)	3.0	3.0	3.1
C2a	Prop. taxes—land	15.0	6.7	7.1
C2a	Prop. taxes—buildings	42.0	40.4	42.5
C2b	Pers. Prop. assessment	0.8	0.8	0.9
C3	Depreciation	46.5	45.0	47.4
	Total Fixed Charges	107.5	97.3	102.5
	Total Expense (A, B and C)	266.6	275.3	290.2
	Net (before cap charges)	109.6	116.4	123.2
	Office Rental Income		382.1	405.7

Note: Store rent 436.9; total rental income 365.4; miscellaneous income 5.7; total income 368.5; operating ratio 70.9%; average office rental rate $4.06; office occupancy 94.9%.

Operatorless—Elevator Buildings Air Conditioned

	Year 1965 Account	Building Total	Office Total	Office Rented
A1	Cleaning	56.0	61.0	62.8
A2	Electric system	17.4	19.6	20.1
A3a	Heating	14.4	14.6	15.0
A3b	Air conditioning-ventilating	18.8	21.2	21.2
A4	Plumbing system	4.2	4.5	4.6
A5	Elevators	13.1	15.7	16.2
A6	Genl. expense—office	18.2	18.6	19.1
A6	Genl. expense—buildings	20.0	20.7	21.3
	Total Operating	162.2	175.8	180.8
B1	Tenant alterations	15.4	16.0	16.7
B2	Repairs—maintenance	10.4	11.6	12.0
B3	Tenant decorating	6.2	7.1	7.4
	Total Construction	24.3	25.9	26.7
	Total A and B	186.4	201.5	207.3
C1a	Fire Insurance	1.7	1.7	1.8
C1b	Insurance (other)	2.3	2.3	2.4
C2a	Prop. taxes—land	16.0	10.3	10.6
C2a	Prop. taxes—buildings	57.8	56.7	58.4
C2b	Pers. prop. assessment	2.1	2.2	2.3
C3	Depreciation	82.2	81.1	83.5
	Total Fixed Charges	159.4	151.4	156.0
	Total Expense (A, B and C)	346.5	354.8	365.7
	Net (before cap charges)	118.8	93.9	136.2
	Office Rental Income		465.7	483.6

Note: Store rent 525.6; total rental income 436.3; miscellaneous income 19.3; total income 449.3; operating ratio 73.8%; average office rental rate $4.84; office occupancy 97.2%.

EXHIBIT 4 (Continued)

Chart of General Ledger Accounts for Office Buildings

ASSETS

†*Current Assets*
100 Cash
   101 Cash Fund (petty cash)
110 Bank Accounts
   111 General Account Bank "A"
   112 Pay-Roll Account Bank "A"
   113 Savings Account Bank "A"
120 Marketable Securities
   121 Securities
      (If a variety of securities are owned, individual accounts may be kept for each kind of security.)
130 Accounts and Notes Receivable
   131 Accounts Receivable—Rents and Services
   132 Accounts Receivable—Alterations
   133 Notes Receivable
   134 Accrued Receivables
   139 Reserve for Doubtful Receivables (credit)
140 Inventory
   141 Inventories—Materials
      (There may be items, such as removable partition stock, which should be carried in Inventory Accounts; however, miscellaneous supplies which will be consumed within a short time should not be included in these accounts. See also Account 281.)
Investments
150 Investments
   151 Investment in Subsidiary Companies
   152 Sinking Fund Investments
†*Fixed Assets*
200 Land
210 Leasehold
   210R Reserve for Amortization of Leasehold
220 Building
   220R Reserve for Depreciation of Building
230 Equipment—Building
   230R Reserve for Depreciation of Building Equipment
      (If desirable, separate accounts can be used for the various kinds of equipment numbering the accounts from 231 to 239 inclusive.)
240 Office Furniture and Fixtures
   240R Reserve for Depreciation of Furniture and Fixtures
      (If more than one building is operated, separate accounts should be kept for each building. Use a capital letter prefix with the account number to distinguish the separate properties, as: A220, A230, A240.)
Deferred Charges
280 Deferred Charges
   281 Supplies
   282 Unexpired Insurance Premiums
   283 Prepaid Taxes
   284 Organization Expense
   285 Unamortized Bond Discounts
   286 Unamortized Capital Stock Discount
   289 Other Deferred Charges
Other Assets
290 Other Assets
   291 Utility Deposits
   292 Deposit on Workmen's Compensation Insurance

LIABILITIES

†*Current Liabilities*
300 Notes and Accounts Payable
   301 Notes Payable (short term)
   302 Accounts or Vouchers Payable
   305 Dividends Payable
310 Accrued Liabilities
   311 Accrued Pay Roll
   312 Employee Pay-Roll Contributions
      312a Federal Old-Age Benefit Tax
      312b State Unemployment Insurance Tax
   313 Employer Pay-Roll Taxes Payable
      313a Federal Old-Age Benefit Tax
      313b Federal Unemployment Insurance Tax
      313c State Unemployment Insurance Tax
   314 Accrued Property Taxes
   315 Provision for Federal and State Taxes
   316 Accrued Interest Payable
320 Other Current Liabilities
†*Fixed Liabilities*
330 Bonds Payable
340 Mortgages Payable
350 Long-Term Notes Payable
Deferred Income
360 Deferred Income
   361 Advance Rentals
   362 Deferred Interest Income
   363 Deposits Held
Reserves
370 Reserve for Contingencies

CAPITAL

Corporation
400 Preferred Stock
   401 Authorized
   402 Unissued
410 Common Stock
   411 Authorized
   412 Unissued
420 Surplus—Capital
430 Surplus—Earned
440 Surplus—Appropriated
490 Profit and Loss—Current Year
Sole Proprietorship or Partnership
(The following accounts should be used only in the event ownership of the building is in a partnership or sole proprietorship)
400 Capital (An account is provided for each partner)
450 Drawings (An account is provided for each partner)
490 Profit and Loss—Current Year

INCOME

Rental Income
500 Rental Income
   501 Office Rent
   502 Ground Floor Rent
   503 Basement Rent
   504 Rent of Special Areas
Service Income
510 Service Income
   511 Electric Light
   512 Steam
   513 Ice and Water
   514 Towels
   515 Clock Service
   517 Alterations for Tenants

EXHIBIT 4 (Continued)

518 Jobbing
519 Other Services
Miscellaneous Income
530 Miscellaneous Income
531 Interest Earned
532 Cash Discounts Received
533 Recovery of Accounts Receivable Previously Charged Off as Uncollectible
539 Miscellaneous

EXPENSES

Operations
600 Cleaning
601 Wages
602 *Social Security Taxes
603 †Compensation Insurance
604 Supplies
606 Electricity
609 Unclassified
610 Electrical
611 Wages
612 *Social Security
613 †Compensation Insurance
614 Supplies (include electric lamps)
616 Electricity
619 Unclassified
620 Heating
621 Wages
622 *Social Security Taxes
623 †Compensation Insurance
624 Supplies
625 Fuel and/or Steam Purchases
626 Electricity
629 Unclassified
630 Air Conditioning and Ventilating
631 Wages
632 *Social Security Taxes
633 †Compensation Insurance
634 Supplies
635 Fuel and/or Steam Purchased
636 Power
637 Water
639 Unclassified
650 Plumbing
651 Wages
652 *Social Security Taxes
653 †Compensation Insurance
654 Supplies
655 Fuel and/or Steam Purchased
656 Electricity
657 Refrigeration
658 Water
659 Unclassified
660 Elevators
661 Wages
662 *Social Security Taxes
663 †Compensation Insurance
664 Supplies
666 Electricity
669 Unclassified
670 General Expenses—Building
671 Wages (watchman, matron, storekeepers, etc.)
672 *Social Security Taxes
(If social security taxes are not charged to each expense group on the basis of the wages charged to each, charge the entire social security tax to this account and prorate to expense groups at the end of the year.)
673 †Compensation Insurance
(If compensation insurance is not charged to each expense group on the basis of the wages charged to each, charge all compensation insurance expense to this account and prorate to expense groups at the end of the year.)
674 Supplies (include toilet supplies)
675 Services Furnished Tenants Without Charge
(compressed air, gas, towels, keys, lettering on doors and windows, etc.)
676 Electric Power—Miscellaneous Motors
(Use this account only if it is impossible to charge electric power to the expense group of the specific operating division in which the power was used.)
677 Cleaning—Special
(Charge this account with the cost of cleaning the building exterior, roof, sidewalks, basement, workshops, etc.)
679 Unclassified
679a Employee Expense (retirement or pension system, group insurance, etc.)
679b Lounge and/or Lunch Room Maintained for Tenants and/or Employees
679c Scavenger Service (rubbish removal)
679d Fire and/or Crime Prevention
679e Hand Tools and Small Equipment
679f Directory of Building Tenants
679g Miscellaneous
(Include such expense as damage to tenants' equipment by company employees, rodent extermination, etc.)
680 Administrative Expense
681 Salaries
681a Management
681b Clerical
682 *Social Security Taxes
683 †Compensation Insurance
684 Building Office Expense
684a Supplies and Stationery
684b Other
685 Management or Agency Fee
686 Leasing Expense
686a Commissions
686b Advertising
686c Other Leasing Expense
687 Professional Fees
(legal, auditing, appraisal, consulting engineer, etc.)
689 Unclassified
689a Business Association Memberships and Dues
689b Donations, Subscriptions, and Gifts
689c Other
Alterations, Decorating, and Repairs
Alterations and Decorating in Tenants' Premises
700 Alterations—Tenants' Premises (not charged to tenants)
701 Wages
702 *Social Security Taxes
703 †Compensation Insurance
704 Materials
705 Outside Services
709 Unclassified

EXHIBIT 4 (Continued)

710 Painting or Decorating—Tenants' Premises
711 Wages
712 *Social Security Taxes
713 †Compensation Insurance
714 Materials
715 Outside Services
719 Unclassified
(It may be desirable to segregate Accounts 700 and 710 between (a) Ground Floor Tenants (b) Office Tenants, in which case sub-accounts can be created.)

Repairs
720 Alterations—Non-Rentable Areas
721 Wages
722 *Social Security Taxes
723 †Compensation Insurance
724 Materials
725 Outside Services
729 Unclassified
730 Painting or Decorating—Non-Rentable Areas
731 Wages
732 *Social Security Taxes
733 †Compensation Insurance
734 Materials
735 Outside Services
739 Unclassified
740 Repairs
(Accounts 741 to 747 inclusive may be consolidated into one account. If this is done, name the account General Repairs, Account 740.)
741 Repairs—Cleaning Department
741a Wages
741b *Social Security Taxes
741c †Compensation Insurance
741d Materials
741e Outside Service
741f Unclassified
742 Repairs—Electric System
742a Wages
742b *Social Security Taxes
742c †Compensation Insurance
742d Materials
742e Outside Services
742f Unclassified
743 Repairs—Heating
743a Wages
743b *Social Security Taxes
743c †Compensation Insurance
743d Materials
743e Outside Services
743f Unclassified
744 Repairs—Air Conditioning and Ventilating
744a Wages
744b *Social Security Taxes
744c †Compensation Insurance
744d Materials
744e Outside Services
744f Unclassified
745 Repairs—Plumbing System
745a Wages

745b *Social Security Taxes
745c †Compensation Insurance
745d Materials
745e Outside Services
745f Unclassified
746 Repairs—Elevators
746a Wages
746b *Social Security Taxes
746c †Compensation Insurance
746d Materials
746e Outside Services
746f Unclassified
747 Repairs—General—Building
747a Wages
747b *Social Security Taxes
747c †Compensation Insurance
747d Materials
747e Outside Services
747f Unclassified

Fixed Charges
800 Insurance
801 Fire Insurance
802 Earthquake Insurance
803 Liability Insurance
804 Other Insurance
810 Operating Taxes
811 Real Estate Taxes
812 Personal Property Taxes
813 Licenses
820 Depreciation
821 Building
822 Building Equipment
829 Office Furniture and Fixtures

Financial Expenses
910 Ground Rent
911 Ground Rent
912 Amortization of Leasehold
920 Organization Expense
921 Amortization of Organization Expense
923 Amortization of Capital Stock Discount
930 Interest Expense
931 Interest on Notes and Mortgages
932 Bond Interest Paid
933 Amortization of Bond Discount
950 Corporate Taxes (see also Accounts 811 to 813)
951 State and Federal Taxes (except income taxes)
952 Income Taxes
960 Loss on Uncollectible Accounts
970 Other Financial Expense

Service Costs
1000 Service Expense (cost of producing service income)
1001 Electric Light
1002 Steam
1003 Ice and Water
1004 Towels
1005 Clock Service
1007 Alterations for Tenants (billed)
1008 Jobbing Expense
1009 Other Services

Note: The suggested outline, above, is primarily intended as a guide for individual property accounting, and is in no sense mandatory. So long as recognized accounting practices and procedures are followed, the asset, liability, and capital accounts may be modified to meet requirements which necessarily vary, depending upon type of organization. In cases of ownership of several buildings, the classification of assets and liabilities between current and non-current may not be applicable to the type of operation involved.

* Social Security Taxes should be charged to each expense group. Accounts 600 to 740 inclusive on the basis of the wages charged to each group. If Social Security Taxes cannot conveniently be segregated in this manner each month, charge all such taxes to Account 672, Social Security Taxes, in the General Expense—Building group of expenses and prorate to the proper expense group at the end of the year.

† Compensation Insurance should be charged to each expense group on the basis of the wages charged to each. If compensation insurance cannot conveniently be segregated in this manner each month, charge all such insurance to Account 673, Compensation Insurance, in the General Expense—Building group of expenses and prorate the proper expense group at the end of the year.

EXHIBIT 4 *(Continued)*
OFFICE BUILDING COMPANY
Profit and Loss Statement
Six Months Ending June 30, 19—

Rental Income
501 Office Rent.......................................xxxx.xx
502 Ground Floor Rent................................xxxx.xx
503 Basement Rent................................. xxx.xx
504 Rent of Special Areas...........................xxxx.xx

     Total Rental Income.......................   xxxxx.xx
Miscellaneous Income
531 Interest Earned................................. xx.xx
532 Cash Discounts Received........................ xx.xx
539 Miscellaneous................................... xx.xx

     Total Miscellaneous Income...............   xxx.xx

     Total rental and misc. income (Groups
        A and C).............................   xxxxx.xx
Operating Expenses
600 Cleaning Expense (see schedule)................ xxx.xx
610 Electrical Expense (see schedule)................ xxx.xx
620 Heating Expense (see schedule)................ xxx.xx
630 Air Conditioning and Ventilating Expense (see
        schedule).................................... xxx.xx
650 Plumbing Expense (see schedule)............... xx.xx
660 Elevator Expense (see schedule)................. xx.xx
670 General Expense—Building (see schedule)....... xxx.xx
680 Administrative Expense (see schedule).......... xxx.xx

     Total Operating Expense...................   xxxx.xx
Alterations, Decorating, and Repair Expenses
700 Alterations—Tenants' Premises (see schedule)... xxx.xx
710 Painting or Decorating—Tenants' Premises (see
        schedule).................................... xxx.xx
720 Alterations—Non-Rentable Areas (see schedule). xx.xx
730 Painting or Decorating—Non-Rentable Areas
        (see schedule)............................. xx.xx
740 Repairs (see schedule)........................... xx.xx

     Total Alterations, Decorating, and Repairs
        Expense.............................   xxxx.xx
Fixed Charges
800 Insurance Expense (see schedule)............... xxx.xx
810 Operating Taxes Expense (see schedule)........ xxx.xx
820 Depreciation (see schedule)..................... xxx.xx

     Total Fixed Charges Expense..............   xxxx.xx

        Total Expenses.........................   xxxx.xx
        Net operating profit....................   xxxx.xx
Service Income
511 Electric Light..................................... xxx.xx
513 Ice and Water.................................... xxx.xx
514 Towels.. xx.xx
517 Alterations for Tenants.......................... xx.xx
518 Jobbing... xxx.xx
519 Other Services................................... xx.xx

     Total Service Income......................   xxxx.xx
Service Costs
1001 Electric Light.................................... xxx.xx

EXHIBIT 4 (*Concluded*)

1003	Ice and Water.....................................	xx.xx		
1004	Towels...	xx.xx		
1007	Alterations for Tenants (billed)...................	xx.xx		
1008	Jobbing..	xxx.xx		
1009	Other Services...................................	xx.xx		
	Total Service Costs........................		xxx.xx	
	Net service profit........................			xxxx.xx
	Total net operating and service profit...			xxxx.xx
910	Ground Rent (see schedule).....................xxxx.xx			
920	Organization Expense (see schedule)............ xxx.xx			
930	Interest Expense (see schedule)................. xx.xx			
950	Corporate Taxes (see schedule).................. xx.xx			
960	Loss on Uncollectible Accounts.................. xx.xx			
970	Other Financial Expense......................... xx.xx			
	Total financial expense...................			xxxx.xx
	Final Net Profit.........................			xxxx.xx

Note: Subsidiary schedules must be prepared for each expense group indicated in this condensed statement.

Use of Operating Statement

The Profit and Loss Statement, as it appears above, is practically the same as the Operating and Service sections of the Experience Exchange report form. By adopting this standard breakdown for your monthly and annual statements, the extra effort involved in making out your Experience Exchange return will be eliminated and the procedure simplified throughout.

The reference, "see schedule," appearing in several places, calls for a supporting memorandum which will correspond with the Analysis of Operating Costs on the reverse side of the Experience Exchange form.

The great advantage of adopting this standard operating statement is that its use enables you to make accurate comparisons with local, regional and national unit cost figures, as compiled from industry experience, thus deriving practical benefit from the authoritative information contained in the Office Building Experience Exchange Report.

EXHIBIT 5

United Shoe Machinery Properties
Projected Income and Expenses

Income
United Shoe.................................$ 664,000		
Other tenants............................. 1,220,000		
Miscellaneous.............................. 13,000		
Gross Income.............................	$1,897,000	
Allowance for vacancies....................	57,000	
Net Income.............................	$1,840,000	

Expenses
Building payroll..............................$ 200,000		
Window cleaning............................ 16,000		
Elevator inspection.......................... 23,000		
Unemployment compensation................ 13,000		
Insurance.................................... 9,300		
Water.. 8,000		
Heat... 25,000		
Electricity................................... 80,000		
Decorating and repairs...................... 73,700		
Real estate taxes............................ 479,000		
Miscellaneous............................... 35,000		
Management................................ 37,000		
Gross Expenses...........................	$ 999,000	
Net before Financing......................	$ 841,000	

QUESTIONS FOR DISCUSSION

1. What price should Mr. Gordon bid for the property? List the assumptions made in arriving at this price.

2. Assume that Mr. Gordon were to sell the property at the end of the third year to another investor, who could also obtain a 75% mortgage on the same terms and who also wanted a 12% after-tax return on his investment. What would Mr. Gordon's after-tax return, based on your bid price in Question 1, be at that time? Do the same calculation based on a sale at the end of the 10th year.

3. What are some of the advantages and disadvantages of rehabilitation versus new construction?

4. What are some of the factors that affect value? How many are within the developer's control?

5. What is the difference between estimating the return on equity investment and valuing a property on a free and clear basis? Who would use each approach?

6. What are the risks inherent in this investment?

7. What are the considerations one must take into account in preparing a bid of this sort?

ONE BROADWAY—
PART I
Office Building

In August 1964, Robert Douglas had acquired 30-day options on two parcels of land in downtown Los Angeles. The two parcels were equal in size, each about 43,000 square feet. Each option entailed a cash outlay of $10,000 plus the agreement to turn over all plans developed for each site if he did not exercise the options. If the options were exercised, the $10,000 would be credited toward the purchase price.

Mr. Douglas was interested in the land as a possible site for an office building which he planned to construct to serve as the major location for the State National Bank, a small bank in which he had a major stock interest, and of which he was the board chairman.

PERSONAL HISTORY

In 1946, at the age of 22, Mr. Douglas had come to Los Angeles from Detroit, where his father had been a small home builder. In Los Angeles, Mr. Douglas started as a carpenter, quickly became a general superintendent, and then began to build expensive homes for resale. In 1948, his business failed, and he had to start again.

He became a general contractor specializing in small office buildings. After several years of building for others, he developed, for his own account, a building in Beverly Hills with a bank as the major tenant. Then, in 1960, as his reputation grew, choice properties which had not been placed on the market were increasingly offered to him for development. Directly across from the bank building, a choice site became available. He studied the site for maximum utilization, which he felt was the key to urban development, and then purchased the property. This was to become the site of the largest office building in Beverly Hills, being twice the size of the next largest office building.

Maximum utilization of space was particularly important in this office-building development due to restrictive Beverly Hills "ground rules," coupled with high land prices. The city code had a density requirement of four times the area of the site. But, through a technicality in the code, Mr. Douglas was able to develop a utilization of 5.3. On this

60,000-square-foot site, he was able to develop a building with a gross area of 320,000 square feet and a rentable area of 262,000 feet. The land was purchased at one of the highest prices per square foot for Beverly Hills land, but because of the ultimate design of the building, the high cost was amortized so as to be comparable to a lower-priced property not utilized to its maximum.

Mr. Douglas named this building the Los Angeles National Bank Building after its major tenant. Originally, he had projected a need for a $7 million loan during the early stages of planning. As both the size and cost of the building grew, projections changed from $9 million to $10 million, and finally, a $10 million figure was submitted to the lender, the Chase Life Insurance Company. To bind this loan, he had posted a deposit of $440,000, but prior to closing, a commitment was received from another source for $12 million. Chase could not increase its loan commitment, but created an unusual method of financing a multiple-occupancy building.

Mr. Douglas sold the building to Chase for $14.6 million with a proviso for a 50-year leaseback at an annual payment of 7½%, or $1,050,000. A further proviso gave him the right to repurchase the building at the end of 20 years, for $10 million, or, after 30 years, at $7.5 million. If he did not repurchase the building, the annual payment would be reduced by 50% after 30 years. The profit immediately was several million dollars. For having arranged the venture, Mr. Douglas had personally retained a majority of the equity, though he had furnished a very small portion of the equity funds. He had acquired the land, arranged the financing, developed the plans with the architects, negotiated prices for and supervised the construction, and leased the space. His investors realized a 22% return on their investment. Mr. Douglas personally realized a profit of over $1 million on the sale to Chase. He also was entitled to all income generated by the property in excess of the lease rental payment he had to make to Chase (see Exhibit 1).

Mr. Douglas felt that the key to profit for himself was the leasability of the building that made it appealing to tenants and desirable to the lending agency. As a speculative developer, Mr. Douglas felt he had to be acutely aware of the environmental needs of his prospective tenants. Low rent was not the paramount appeal of his office space. The top-notch concern seeks a total business environment and is conscious of the impact of surroundings on efficiency of operations. Executives and employees are becoming highly sophisticated on the subject of their home-away-from-home working life. Office appointments and services were designed to keep the tenants happy. The absolute rule of his management operations was, "Pamper the tenant." Maintenance and cleaning services were of the highest quality. In addition, with parking a severe problem in Beverly Hills, he offered tenants a 1,000-car underground garage with gas station service, permitting four cars for each 1,000 square feet of leased space.

The building's luxurious offices, prime location, on-site parking, elevators, and air conditioning created the totality of an ideal business environment and culminated in this unique and favorable financing. These same factors also enabled Mr. Douglas to charge an average $6.45 per square foot for office space in the building, which was a higher rate than other competitors charged. He still maintained 100% occupancy with long-term leases to important institutional tenants. Among ground floor tenants were: United California Bank; Goodbody & Co.; Shearson, Hammill & Co.; McDonald & Co.; and Tiffany & Co.

Mr. Douglas considered the ground floor tenants a key to establishing the image of the building. Obviously, if a delicatessen or women's ready-to-wear were on the ground floor, he would have difficulty in acquiring the major law firms, accounting firms, or other institutional tenants for the upper floors. He could not then ask or receive what was the highest rate per square foot in any Beverly Hills office building. Therefore, he reduced his rent to Tiffany, because of the prestige in adding its name to the building marquee.

SITE ANALYSIS

Subsequently, Douglas organized a commercial bank, the State National Bank, with a capitalization of $2 million. He owned 35% of the stock himself, and spent a great deal of time in furthering the bank's growth and development. He felt that its home office location would be an important element in its future success. A commercial bank conveniently located in a prestigious building in a major downtown site close to the heavily populated business area and financial center would automatically attract depositors. It would, however, be difficult for a bank as small as the State National to compete with the major commercial banks in the area in obtaining a favored location.

Therefore, Mr. Douglas decided to look for a site for a new office building in which to locate his bank. Both land parcels on which he had obtained options were close to each other, but Douglas preferred the property at the terminus of Broadway Boulevard, located near such buildings as the Biltmore Hotel, the head offices of various financial institutions, the County Court House, City Hall, the Statler Hilton, and the Transportation Center. This land, located on the east side of Atlantic Avenue, had 258 feet of frontage on Atlantic Avenue and a depth of about 168 feet along Broadway. He felt that this parcel was more advantageous because of the greater concentration of potential bank customers, both corporate and individuals, in this location. As a result, he exercised his purchase option on the Broadway parcel, which involved a purchase price of $2,450,000 including a six month nonrecourse deed of trust of $2,150,000.

Mr. Douglas then initiated an in-depth survey of office building tenants in downtown Los Angeles. This was a door-to-door canvass of hundreds of company owners and employees conducted by his own staff. Some questions asked were: If a new office building were to be constructed, would you consider leasing in that building? What location in the downtown area would you prefer? Would you be willing to pay $1 more than your present rate per square foot? $2 more? $3 more?

The survey also questioned future space needs versus present occupancy, parking requirements, present type of lighting, air conditioning, and elevator service.

From this survey, Mr. Douglas drew the following conclusions, which he felt validated his move into the downtown area:

1. Cheap rent was not of paramount consideration in selecting office space. (This finding confirmed his Beverly Hills studies.) Those surveyed indicated complete willingness to pay higher rates for better services.
2. Older office buildings provided inefficient space with proper utilization impossible due to column-interrupted footage and smaller floor areas.
3. Company growth had forced tenants to expand into other floors of older buildings, or even into other buildings. This caused great corporate discomfort and inefficiency.
4. Lighting, air conditioning, and elevator service were sorely deficient, by modern standards, in the older buildings. The tenants spoke out for a better business environment.
5. Parking was found to be crucial in all instances. Need for on-premises parking was documented again and again. This was especially a factor because of the lack of rapid transit facilities in Los Angeles.
6. The western part of the downtown area, a section removed from the old financial district, was noted as the most desirable location for construction of a new high-rise office building. The older financial section was across from what had become the Skid Row area. Tenants were afraid to leave their offices after dark.

SITE PLANNING

Although it was not the actual address of the building, Mr. Douglas intended to call the building One Broadway, or the "West's First Address." As the landmark of the city's major street, the name had to connote prestige and exclusiveness. The actual address was on Atlantic Avenue, and the frontage on Broadway Boulevard was at 600 not One. Still, Mr. Douglas made his presentation to the mayor and then the City Council. He showed a model of the building and told how it would not only help revitalize the area but contribute $400,000 in real estate taxes to the city, as contrasted with the present tax bill of $50,000. As a result, his petition was granted.

Then, the Post Office Department said that they would not deliver mail to the building. All buildings must have a number of at least three digits. Finally, Mr. Douglas agreed to give the Post Office Department a free office in the building, and the Post Office Department then agreed to deliver the mail. Mr. Douglas felt that without the address One Broadway, it would be like building an office building in New York on Second Avenue rather than Park Avenue.

The next step was to select an architect who would do justice to the site. Prior to selection, he toured the United States for weeks, studying new high-rise office buildings in 25 cities. Innovations for efficiency, new materials, space utilization, and tenant comforts were his points of research. He sought the marks of creative architecture, backed by practical tenancy.

The Chase Manhattan Building in New York, First National Bank in Houston, and the Crown Zellerbach high-rise in San Francisco topped his list of the largest and best in office building planning and design. All were by the noted architectural firm of Walters, John, and Stevens. He asked this firm to prepare preliminary sketches and plans for a proposed office building. The firm was interested in working with Mr. Douglas, since they had never done a building for a speculative developer or a building in Los Angeles. Because of the $56-per-square-foot cost of land, the highest per-square-foot cost ever paid in Los Angeles, the architect was instructed to use the site to its maximum. The result was a design for a building containing 700,000 square feet, plus a five-level subterranean parking facility, able to accommodate 545 cars. The local zoning law called for a minimum of one parking space for each rentable 1,000 square feet. Mr. Douglas would have preferred even more parking if feasible. Of the 700,000 square feet, 525,000 was rentable for offices with the remainder required for elevators, stairways, hallways, bathrooms, lobbies, corridors, and other services. These were placed in a central core to provide greater flexibility in subdividing the individual floors.

After reviewing the proposed designs of Walters, John, and Stevens, Mr. Douglas commented, "Never before in the history of Los Angeles has an office building with such rare architectural imagination illuminated that great city's skyline." Douglas agreed with the architects in their design of a building of the maximum square feet allowable. While a taller structure entailed additional costs, this increment was not at all comparable to the benefits obtained from the more effective use made of the land. When land was as costly as it was in this case, it should be exploited to its fullest extent. In addition, a tall building was far more prestigious and attracted more tenants than did a smaller one. Dominating the surrounding area, it would serve as an advertisement for itself. He also spent $300,000 extra for steel to provide 30-foot column spacing for more flexible floors. Having a floor area of 23,104 net rentable feet, which was approximately 50% bigger than his competitors' buildings, gave him a greater opportunity to attract firms with large per-floor space requirements.

Mr. Douglas then took the preliminary design to William Phillips & Co., builders and general contractors, to determine the cost of construction. The proposed building was to be completely Class "A" construction, consisting of structural steel frame, concrete floors, marble and glass exterior walls, marble lobby walls on the main floor, zoned refrigerated air conditioning, acoustical tile ceilings, and 15 high-speed passenger elevators. Phillips estimated the construction cost to be approximately $20 per square foot, or $14 million for the 700,000 square foot building, and $2 million for the 545-space parking area. The parking cost seemed a little high, but Mr. Douglas realized that the ramps for a five-level garage occupied considerable space, creating a fairly inefficient use. He thought that Phillips' estimate was fair. He summarized the cost of the proposed project as follows:

Land—43,000 square feet @ $56/sq. ft.	$ 2,400,000
Land carrying costs until construction	300,000
Building cost @ $20/sq. ft. × 700,000	14,000,000
Parking—$3,500/space × 545 spaces	2,000,000
Architects' fee	700,000
Interim construction loan @ 6% interest ($16,000,000 × 2 years × average balance of ½ plus a servicing fee (2¾%)	1,400,000
Rental, legal, other financing, administrative, insurance, miscellaneous	1,650,000
Total	$22,450,000

PROJECT FINANCING

Mr. Douglas approached the Chase Life Insurance Company to arrange for his permanent mortgage financing. Chase requested a summary of costs. He added about 10% as a safety factor to his previous figures and provided Chase with an estimated value or cost for the land and construction of $24,750,000, including financing costs, interim loan fees, mortgage commitment fees, and title and escrow charges in connection with the interim loan. He requested a loan for 80% of this amount or $19,750,000. Chase was very pleased with the results of the Los Angeles National Bank Building which he had sold to them and leased back, and they were very interested in continuing the profitable relationship with Mr. Douglas. They asked Mr. Douglas for an earnings estimate of the building. He prepared the following rough estimate for them, based upon his experience with the Los Angeles National Bank Building:

Income Projection*

Projected gross income
  Net rentable area—524,000 sq. ft. @ $6.35/sq. ft....................$ 3,324,000
  Parking income—545 cars/$250 per year (net) per space..........   136,000
                                               $ 3,460,000
    Less: 5% vacancy factor (excluding ground floor)..............   160,000
                                                $ 3,300,000
Projected operating expense
  524,000 sq. ft... 1,200,000
Projected annual income..$ 2,100,000
Capitalized value of building
  $2,100,000 income capitalized @ 8%............................$26,250,000

    * See Exhibit 3.

After a thorough review of his proposal and estimates, Chase proposed a mortgage loan in the maximum amount of $19,750,000. However, Chase would make this commitment subject to certain leasing requirements. Approximately 40%, or 200,000 square feet of space, would have to be leased to tenants approved by Chase, for rental periods of not less than five years at an average rate of not less than $6.35 per square foot before the initial portion of the commitment, or $15,750,000, was to become effective. The additional $4 million loan would become available when total annual rental reached $3 million. This would occur when approximately 90% of the space was leased. The loan would be at an interest rate of 6%, repayable over approximately 26 years. The constant payment on the $15,750,000 loan would be $1,182,000 annually, payable in equal monthly installments. At the $19,750,000 level, the requisite mortgage payments would be $123,437.50, payable monthly, or $1,481,125 annually.

Chase also insisted that as consideration for granting this commitment they be given an option to purchase the entire project at $22,750,000 within one year from the date the building was complete and had achieved a $3.1 million rent roll. Chase would then lease the building back to Mr. Douglas, who would pay a rental equal to 7¾% of the sale price for a 30-year period. After the 30th year, the rent payable to Chase would become 25% of the gross rent roll. Douglas was not happy with the proposed purchase price. He, therefore, proposed a $26,250,000 price to Chase, based upon his capitalized value. They finally agreed on a purchase price of $24,750,000, with an annual rental charge of 7¾% or $1,918,000. He also received from Chase the right to repurchase the building for $17,350,000 at the end of the 20th year, and for $13,350,000 at the end of the 30th year.

Of course, if Chase were to exercise their purchase option, they would not have to advance the final portion of the mortgage financing. Or if they had already advanced it, the amount advanced under the mortgage would be deductible from the purchase price. The mortgage funds were to be advanced only upon completion of construction.

Mr. Douglas then called upon the First National Bank for an interim construction loan in the amount of $15,750,000, or the minimum amount of the permanent loan. Mr. Douglas showed First National that he would soon have an automatic "takeout" from the Chase upon completion of the building, since the building was already 30% rented. That is, once the building was completed, First National would have a commitment from Chase to repay this loan. The interest rate was to be 6%, plus a one-time 2¾% financing fee. The bank insisted on this 2¾% financing fee because of the risk involved to them, since the building was not yet 40% leased. Mr. Douglas assented to this on condition that the loan be for three years. This was most important to him, since he would have a year after his two-year construction period to provide a period for rent-up and move-ins. Another large bank agreed to participate with the First National Bank in the construction loan.

Mr. Douglas approached the architects to determine their fee for their work on this building. While a fee of $700,000 was normal, Mr. Douglas, after long and arduous negotiations, and as a result of the architect's desire to do this particular job, was able to have the fee set at $350,000. He knew that it was very important that he use both Walters, John, and Stevens as architects and William Phillips Corporation as the general contractor, since the Chase Life Insurance Company held the proposed architect and builder in high respect.

Mr. Douglas was next interested in determining the portion of construction costs that the general contractor would be willing to advance. In effect, he wanted Phillips, the general contractor, and several of the subcontractors (subs) to defer $1,440,000 of the total construction cost for a period of three years after completion of the basic structure. He would be willing to give them a third deed of trust on the project equivalent to a third mortgage, for the security of the "deferment holders." He was also prepared to pledge a portion of his interest in the building. In negotiations with the general contractor and after their consultation with the subs, Phillips agreed to defer only $1.3 million of the construction costs for a period of three years on the terms Mr. Douglas outlined to them. A major portion of this amount came from aluminum, marble, and elevator suppliers, who were eager to have their products used in this prestigious building (see Exhibit 2). Also, this deferment served as a final negotiating point with the plumbing and air-conditioning companies. Since in each case Mr. Douglas had competitive bidders who would meet the others' bids in all other respects, he used this as the lever for final selection. However, these subs insisted that he be personally liable for these payments and that interest after completion of construction be at the rate of 10% per annum.

Mr. Douglas also arranged to borrow $1 million by placing a second deed of trust (see Exhibit 4), the approximate equivalent of a second mortgage, against the property if and when he were to acquire the land. The "second-mortgage" lender expected a 10% rate of return and agreed to keep the proposed loan out for a three-year period. Douglas was also to assume personal liability for this $1 million loan.

He also obtained a pledge from the same second-mortgage lender who was loaning him $1 million on this property to furnish him with $800,000 against a first deed of trust against his lease position on the Los Angeles National Bank Building, which was generating income (in excess of the lease rental payment) of approximately $237,000 per annum. The prospective lender was confident that his position was worth substantially in excess of $800,000, the amount of the proposed loan.

Mr. Douglas estimated that he needed $400,000 of this proposed $800,000 loan for other purposes and that only $400,000 would be available for this proposed office building project.

He recapitulated his available sources of funds:

Interim bank construction loan	$15,750,000
Deferrals on part of general contractor and subcontractors secured by third deed of trust (personal guarantee)	1,300,000
Loan secured by second deed of trust (personal guarantee)	1,000,000
Loan secured by first deed of trust against his leasehold on Los Angeles National Bank Building (partial)	400,000
Total	$18,450,000
Uses of Funds (after savings in architect's fee)	22,100,000
Net funds deficit	($ 3,650,000)

Mr. Douglas felt that he could probably raise additional equity funds from among the individuals who had invested in the Los Angeles National Bank Building and who had realized a substantial profit on their investment. However, he was reluctant to give up an equity interest in this building. The investors in the Los Angeles National Bank Building were Hollywood actors and movie producers, all in tax brackets of 60% and over.

Mr. Douglas developed the following proposal for these investors. They would invest $2.5 million in a partnership to be capitalized at $4 million and for which they would receive a 62½% interest in the property. Mr. Douglas would be the general partner. The partnership would be formed for the purpose of acquiring, developing, operating, leasing, and otherwise dealing with the 1 acre of undeveloped land called One Broadway.

Mr. Douglas would receive a 32½% interest for the personal liability he was assuming on the $1.3 million that would be due the contractors. He agreed to pledge this 32½% equity interest to the contractors to secure this deferral.

Mr. Douglas was also to receive a 5% general-partnership interest for turning over to the partnership the land, proposed plans, all financial arrangements, and a lease for a small amount of space with the State National Bank.

Mr. Douglas knew that "tax losses" of $2 million would be sustained during the estimated two-year construction period. Those losses would be the sum of interest payments due on the interim loan, insurance and real estate taxes payable during construction, and other cash outlays which could be expensed for tax purposes. The investors would therefore receive 62.5% of these $2 million "losses" having a value of $750,000 to an individual in a 60% tax bracket. Calculated over a three-year period, these construction losses alone would furnish the investor with an effective annual return of slightly over 10% per annum.

In addition, the general partner agreed to pay to the investors a tax-free (see Exhibit 5) 8% annual cash return on their capital investment, and for this payment the general partner (Douglas) would have the right for 10 years to purchase all or any part of the interest of the limited partners by returning an amount equal to their original capital investment plus an additional 4% per annum on the capital investment. Any cash which the proposed limited partners were to receive in excess of 8% would be deducted from the 4% option price. The cash return to the investors would be 12% per annum if the option were exercised, at which point Mr. Douglas would own 100% of the equity in the One Broadway Building. The investors would not pay any tax until the option was exercised and then at the capital gains rate. If not exercised, an ordinary income tax would be due.

Mr. Douglas called many of the prospective investors and found them to be enthusiastic about the proposed investment. From the investor response, he was certain that he could raise $2.5 million by selling these limited partnership interests. However, even with these funds he would still be $1,150,000 short of the required funds ($22,100,000 required funds less $18,450,000 + $2,500,000 available funds). In addition, Douglas knew that he would need funds to pay interest on the personal loans, including the interest on the $1 million second deed of trust on One

Broadway (10% per annum) and the 8% payments due on the $2.5 million limited partnership interests. He estimated that all of these loans would be outstanding for a two-year period.

PROFIT POTENTIAL AND RISKS

Mr. Douglas was concerned with the personal liability he would be compelled to assume were he to proceed with the acquisition of the land and construction of the building. He knew that he would normally need at least $5 million to $6 million in equity funds to finance a project of this size and scope (approximately 25% of actual cost). Under his proposal he would be advancing very little of his own funds, with $2.5 million available from limited partners, $1.3 million from the general contractor, $1 million from a second-mortgage lender, and only $400,000 to be furnished by him. He would be personally liable for $2.3 million of this debt on the property. Furthermore, he did not know whether he would be able to obtain the additional $1,150,000 which appeared to be the estimated deficiency in the cash required to complete the project. He felt confident that once the building was underway he would be able to arrange additional financing in some form. This would certainly be true if he was close to 90% rented at that time. For in that case, he would be able to arrange additional bank borrowing of $4 million—the incremental amount which Chase would be obliged to provide when he reached that rental level. However, additional financing at this point would create a potential total liability for the project of more than the $24,750,000, which was the purchase option figure of the Chase.

Mr. Douglas reviewed the leasing and rental situation in downtown Los Angeles. He knew that from an ideal point of view he would like all prime credit tenants. Also, it would be best for lease expiration dates to be staggered so that all the space would not come on the market at once if the tenants did not renew. As a practical matter, he had to consider transportation patterns, existing vacancy rates, expansion and demolition projected for other buildings, competitive renting practices both as to rates and services offered, and local and regional economic characteristics. Unlike New York City and other big cities where people located their offices in the downtown area, in Los Angeles only the governmental offices and service companies, such as large accounting firms, law firms, banks, insurance companies, and brokerage firms were located in the downtown area. There were few comparables available for determining demand. While he felt that One Broadway was situated at the "core of the Southwest's business activity," conveniently accessible via freeway, surface transportation, or the heliports located nearby, he still did not know whether, despite the excellent location, there was sufficient demand for new space. He was troubled by a large office building being constructed nearby and the question of the adequacy of the demand to fill both of these large buildings. In addition, the other office building was being constructed by institutional investors taking the major portion of space for themselves. The major tenant also could attract others, which was unlikely to be the case in One Broadway, with the small State National as major tenant. He already had to turn down one major bank for 60,000 square feet because of his commitment to State National.

Mr. Douglas was, however, encouraged by the $6.25 to $6.50 rental that was presently being obtained for first-class office space in the downtown Los Angeles area. He also knew that vacancies were at a minimum. Yet, developers did not usually build office buildings on speculation without having a substantial part of the space leased before commencing construction.

After two months of an active leasing campaign, Mr. Douglas only had proposed leases for 152,000 square feet of space, of which 35,000 square feet was to be leased to the State National Bank for a period of 20 years, and the remainder to substantial accounting and law firms. The annual rental from these prospective tenants would be $950,000. However, he was not too concerned about reaching the 40% minimum rental level required before the permanent takeout became effective. He felt that State National might lease additional space, and this, along with a few other prospective tenants, would put him at the 40% level of occupancy.

He did not feel that there would be a substantial increase in rentals once construction had begun. Unlike those in New York City, tenants in Los Angeles tended not to rent from plans but only upon seeing a completed building. He thought that it could take up to two years after completion to reach the 90% occupancy level. He hoped to be 60% leased upon completion, and 75% after one year. He assumed various occupancy levels to determine the minimum rental levels at which he would break even (see Exhibit 3). He knew he did not have to repay the bank for three years, which meant that he would not have to commence mortgage amortization payments until then.

Of course, he felt that were the building to be 95% rented he would realize a profit of over $2,750,000 on the sale of the building to the Chase after payment of all his loans and repurchase of all partnership interests. In addition, he would still have a residual interest in the profits of over $1,918,000 generated by the building and would hold a favorable repurchase option. He would also have a prestigious location for his bank.

His purchase money mortgage of $2,150,000 on the land was going to be due soon, and he knew that he would have to act quickly to formalize all the verbal arrangements that he had discussed over the past six months. He did not want to lose his deposit, but on the other hand, he did not want to enter into a transaction involving all this potential risk without feeling quite sure he would succeed.

EXHIBIT 1

**Los Angeles National Bank Building, Los Angeles, California
Pro Forma Income Statement—1965 and Subsequent Years
Based on Executed Leases and Historical Operating Expenses**

	Monthly	Annual
Rental income*	$132,000	$1,584,000
Parking income (net)	15,000	180,000
Total Income	$147,000	$1,764,000
Operating expenses—including real estate taxes†	36,000	432,000
Net operating income	$111,000	$1,332,000
Chase Lease Rental	91,250	1,095,000
Net building income	$ 19,750	$ 237,000

* Chase entitled to 20% over $1.9 million gross.
† Includes $36,000 annually for decorating, improvements, and lease commissions. Increases in operating expense and taxes covered by escalation clauses.

EXHIBIT 2

**One Broadway Building
Deferments**

	Contract Price	Deferment
Setone Marble	$ 660,000	$ 200,000
Town Plumbing	413,000	50,000
Alltone Aluminum	549,600	150,000
Southern Air and Refrigeration	1,750,000	200,000
Rotco Corporation (electrical)	1,098,726	250,000
William Phillips Corporation		200,000
Easy Ride Elevator	1,100,000	250,000
Total		$1,300,000

Note: Deferments become due and payable September 30, 1969, or at a date three years and 90 days after the completion of the basic structure, as defined in the deferment agreement, whichever is the later.

EXHIBIT 3

One Broadway Building
3 Pro Forma Income Statements—One Year after Completion
(000 omitted)

	(1)	(2)	(3)
Rental income (100% occupied)	$3,324	$3,300	$3,475
Parking income (Net)	136	165	165
Total Income	$3,460	$3,465	$3,640
Allowance for vacancy	160	1,715	175
Net income	$3,300	$1,750	$3,465
Operating expenses:			
Real estate taxes	$ 440	$ 250	$ 440
Cleaning	195	100	195
Electricity	125	65	125
Heat	25	15	25
Elevator repairs	45	30	45
General maintenance (10 men)	60	40	60
Supplies	20	15	20
Insurance	20	20	20
Water treatment	5	5	5
Repairs, alterations, decorating	120	40	120
Management @ 3%	95	50	100
Miscellaneous	50	20	50
Total Operating Expenses	$1,200	$ 650	$1,205
Net cash income before financing	$2,100	$1,100	$2,260

(1)—Average rent—$6.35/square foot at 95% occupancy.
(2)—Average rent—$6.35/square foot at 50% occupancy.
(3)—Average rent—$6.50/square foot at 95% occupancy.

EXHIBIT 4

One Broadway

Deeds of Trust Increasing in U.S.*

Mortgages Can Be Replaced in Lending Procedure
Washington, February 4 (A.P.)

Mortgage officials say the use of the deed of trust, which facilitates and sometimes reduces the cost of real estate foreclosures, is spreading.

Nineteen states give the mortgage industry a choice between the deed of trust and the straight mortgage form of lending. In recent years one or two more states have turned each year to the deed-of-trust procedure.

Thousands of buyers have purchased homes under one or the other of these forms without knowing the difference between them or even that both types exist.

Suppose that a home buyer finds himself in financial straits. He has defaulted payments and faces the possibility of losing his property.

---

* From *New York Times*, February 5, 1967.

EXHIBIT 4 (*Continued*)

Trustees Have Authority

If he has purchased the property on a deed of trust he likely would find that:

The authority to sell the property was vested in a trustee or trustees.

The trustees could post notice that the borrower has defaulted and the property was for sale.

In some cases the property could be sold and the money turned over to the lender within a few months.

The owner would likely find that his right to redeem the property has been extinguished. He could not obtain a new loan, pay off the original lender and regain the property unless the lender agreed.

Different Factors

If, however, the house was bought with a straight mortgage, and the owner defaulted and the lender was demanding his money, the circumstances would be different:

The lender would have to advertise that the owner has defaulted.

The certain period of time would have to elapse before the lender could take possession.

The case would have to go through court if the owner chose to contest the foreclosure. If the docket was crowded there would be a waiting period.

If the lender won the right to sell the property and did sell it, the borrower would have a certain period in which to redeem it by making back payments plus other costs.

The whole process, mortgage lawyers say, might take a couple of years or even longer but under a deed of trust the owner might lose his right to the recovery of his property in as short a time as two months.

So far as is known, lenders offer no financial inducements to borrowers to use the deed of trust. Some lenders may prefer a straight mortgage because it has one advantage to them: Generally it gives the lender the opportunity to obtain a default judgment against the borrower, requiring the borrower to make up the difference between the amount of the loan and the price at which a property is sold.

For example, if the mortgage was for $20,000 and the house sold for $19,000 the borrower would be required to pay the difference. Usually the borrower escapes this possibility under a deed-of-trust settlement.

Because of the advantages of a deed of trust in favor of the lender, some mortgage officials say the use of these deeds may attract more mortgage money to states that recognize this form. But they have not statistics to bear this out.

Neither are there statistics to indicate whether there are more foreclosures under a deed of trust, since usually it is easier for the lender to take possession.

The deed of trust was created years ago because in some states mortgage laws had become encumbered with clauses sought by both borrower and

EXHIBIT 4 (Concluded)

lender. This complicated the administrative rights for trustees to bypass court action.

Efforts to standardize lending procedures in all states have met with little success through the years, mortgage officials say.

EXHIBIT 5
One Broadway
¶4892

Option Payments.—The amount paid for an option to purchase property is not includible in the seller's income until the option is exercised or is forfeited or allowed to expire unexercised (.05).

If an option expires unexercised or is forfeited, so that the amount paid for the option is income to the person who granted the option (seller), the gain is in all cases ordinary income. The optionee has a loss, the character of which is governed by the property covered by the option. If the option covers property which would have been a capital asset if acquired by the optionee, such as vacant land purchased as an investment, then the law provides that the loss is a capital loss. For this purpose, the privilege or option is deemed to have been sold or exchanged on the day it expired.

If the option is sold or exchanged, the gain or loss is capital gain or loss only if the property covered by the option would have been a capital asset if it had been acquired by the optionee. The holding period of an option must exceed six months, measured from the date it was acquired to the date it is disposed of, is forfeited, or expires. A loss is deductible only if incurred in a trade or business or in a transaction entered into for profit. Loss of an amount paid for an option to buy a personal residence is not deductible.

These provisions do not apply to privileges or options which are stock in trade of a tax payer (such as a dealer in securities), or to losses attributable to failure to exercise an option to sell property at a fixed price, which option is acquired on the same day on which the property covered by the option is acquired. In such case, the cost of the option is added to the basis of the property with which it is identified.

Neither do these provisions apply to gain attributable to sale or exchange of an option if it would not be capital gain without regard to this provision (for example, if an option were given as compensation for services), nor to gain attributable to sale or exchange of an option acquired by the taxpayer before March 1, 1954, if in the hands of the taxpayer such option is a capital asset. (Options acquired before March 1, 1954, were capital assets except in the hands of a person who dealt in them in his trade of business.)

01. Code Sec. 1234: Reg. 1.1234–1.

.05 Virginia Iron, Coal & Coke Co., (CA-438–2 USTC ¶ 9572, 99 F. 2nd 919, cert. denied, 307 U.S. 630.

QUESTIONS FOR DISCUSSION

1. Do you recommend that Mr. Douglas acquire the land and proceed with the development of the building? Why?
2. What are the profit potentials for this project? (What is Mr. Douglas' investment and return on investment?)
3. What risk would he have to assume if he undertakes the development? How could he control and limit these risks?
4. If you were an investment advisor to a group of clients in a 50% tax bracket, looking for a minimum after tax return of 12%; and at this time they had an opportunity of acquiring the entire equity of the proposed building for $6,750,000 when completed, subject only to the $15,750,000 first mortgage and no other debt, would you recommend that they buy it? What return would you get? Assume the first owner of an office building can depreciate it over a 40-year life and can use the double declining balance method of depreciation (old tax law).
5. If Chase Life Insurance Company were to exercise its purchase option:
   a) What incremental return would Chase realize on the incremental investment? ($24,750,000 purchase price less $19,750,000 first mortgage —$5 million incremental investment.)
   b) What additional risk would Chase be assuming?
6. As a prospective investor what is your appraisal of the proposed limited partnership investment?

ONE BROADWAY—
PART II
Office Building

In November 1965, Robert Douglas was trying to decide whether or not to accept a $1.1 million loan from the Lamb Corporation to complete his project at One Broadway.

Mr. Douglas had decided to complete the land transaction and construct the 30-story office building the previous spring, after a study of the site's potential. He was able, in a series of virtually simultaneous closings, to pull together into legally binding form all the verbal commitments that he had received from banks, insurance companies, architects, contractors, second mortgagees, and investors. The cost of the legal fees alone amounted to $156,000.

At the last minute, one of his largest investors, who had agreed to purchase $400,000 of limited-partnership interests, backed out, but Mr. Douglas, nevertheless, proceeded, feeling confident that he would soon find another investor. The other investors were a little dismayed at first, but Mr. Douglas guaranteed personally either to find a substitute investor or to buy this interest himself. The other investors also insisted on a guarantee from him that he would furnish any additional moneys needed if the total project costs exceeded $20,750,000. In other words, liens against the property could not exceed $20,750,000, plus the $4 million limited-partnership capitalization. Mr. Douglas was not disturbed by this provision, knowing he had the option to repurchase their interest.

In any case, Mr. Douglas felt he should go ahead. The potential of the $2 million profit plus a leasehold and repurchase interest if the Chase Life Insurance Company exercised its purchase option, or the value of the $600,000 to $700,000 annual income on an investment of less than $3 million at such time as his rentals reached $3 million annually outweighed, in his mind, the risks he assumed by undertaking the project.

Within a few weeks after closing, he qualified for the Chase permanent loan by reaching the 40% rental level. He did so by taking 25,000 additional square feet for future expansion of the State National Bank. As the bank's deposits were then only $20 million, the bank felt it did not immediately need the space, but Mr. Douglas gave the bank's board of directors his personal assurance that he would make every effort to sublease the space for a short period. He also found a substitute to replace the investor of $400,000 who had withdrawn.

Then, in April 1965, he started construction with completion estimated in under two years. He prepared a "critical dollar path schedule" showing the expected stage of construction for each week for each subcontractor, and the dollar outlay. Unfortunately, 60 days after work started, a 32-day strike delayed construction. Mr. Douglas carried strike insurance, which covered most of this loss, but the insurance company canceled his strike insurance for the future.

Rentals at One Broadway proceeded a little more slowly than Mr. Douglas would have wanted. He had to reach at least 60% to break even. The rentals on the lower floors averaged $5.80 per square foot, but on the upper floors, he was obtaining $7 per square foot. He was optimistic that his eventual average would be $6.50 per square foot. He continued his newspaper advertising, selected mailings, and contacts with outside rental brokers, but very few leases were being generated by this activity. Most of the potential tenants were service industries, and they placed a great emphasis upon the prestigious aspect of the building. As a result, they appeared to want to see the building completed before they committed themselves.

Recently, three other institutional tenants had announced plans to build new buildings in the area, occupying part for themselves, and part for others. This additional competition was hurting Mr. Douglas considerably. He was considering offering a bonus or concession to new tenants of an allowance of $3 per square foot toward the purchase of new furniture. This was the equivalent of about six months' free rent. He felt the extra cost would attract tenants in a way that would provide additional short-term depreciation for his company as owner of the furniture. He also was being forced to assume the remaining portion of existing leases in other buildings being vacated by his tenants. These leases ran from six months to three years beyond his scheduled completion date, and if not sublet by him could cost $300,000 over the three-year period. The negotiations with tenants seemed interminable. There always appeared to be more sets of people who had to approve the space. Management groups changed, as well as company needs.

Still, he had received a definite interest from an excellent company that was planning to build its own building in the area. The tenant needed 100,000 square feet for 3 years with a one-year option until its building was supposed to be ready. The company was willing to make its own improvements. Mr. Douglas was supposed to quote it a fair rent. He weighed the advantage of the quick occupancy to the wear and tear on his space, the future vacancy, and the problem of how to structure the lease so that Chase, with its clause requiring minimum five-year leases, would approve it. If Chase did not count this space as rented, he would not qualify for a $4 million increase in the loan or for the purchase option. He tried to decide what to do.

In October 1965, Mr. Douglas knew that he must begin to raise additional funds. He was aware that he was beginning to run short of funds, and after updating a cash flow analysis (see Exhibit 1) that he had constructed earlier, he set the ultimate size of his deficiency at $1,750,000. Originally, he had hoped to meet this deficit by increasing his rentals during the first year to the $3 million level so that he could qualify for the additional $4 million loan from Chase. However, by this time it was apparent that he would probably not reach the rental levels required to take down these funds.

He also knew it would be difficult to reduce construction costs. However, there was one area where some savings were probable. He had assumed that all of the space would be leased by outside brokers, who would be entitled on an average 10-year lease to 30% of one year's rent, as their commissions. This would result in a leasing cost of $930,000. One third of the space, he felt, could be leased without commissions, saving $310,000. He also assumed that he would be able to negotiate arrangements with a few of the brokers to pay them their commissions over the first five years of the lease and defer approximately $140,000. Real estate commissions are normally paid at the time the lease is signed or upon occupancy of the space.

He then made arrangements with a nationally known firm of parking garage operators, Alan Associates, to manage his parking. They agreed to pay him a minimum rental of $160,000 per year for 15 years, or 50% of gross income, whichever figure was higher. They also gave him $50,000 as a security deposit for the term of their lease. The funds for this not only guaranteed their performance but were available to One Broadway Associates to help pay for construction costs. Because of the national credit reputation of Alan Associates, Mr. Douglas was certain that Chase would allow him to include the minimum rental income from Alan Associates in the $3 million rentals he needed to qualify for the additional $4 million in mortgage funds.

In November 1965, the construction was well under way, and the building was almost 50% completed. The final architectural plans consisted of 200 sheets of drawings. An average of 250 workers reported each day to build this high-rise structure. The air-conditioning system was large enough to climatize 2,000 single-family homes. A quarter of a million square feet of solar glass had been installed. One thousand tons of white Carrara marble; more than 10,000 tons of steel; and 16 high-speed elevators were being installed. Eventually, there would be 5,000 employed by firms. But right at that moment, the elevator specialist went out on strike. The elevators were not being programmed on dry runs as the schedule called for. This strike would cost $5,000 a day if the completion date were not met.

Mr. Douglas, though, still had $1,250,000 to raise. He did not think he could obtain financing under a fourth deed of trust on One Broadway at that time. He did feel that he had a considerable equity left in his leasehold interest in the Los Angeles National Bank Building. His return on the building was $237,000, less $80,000 interest on an $800,000 first mortgage of his leasehold. This left him with an income of $157,000, which he felt he could value at a 10% capitalization rate or $1,570,000.

In early November, he received a call from his attorney who said he had been contacted by Mr. Henry, executive vice president of the Lamb Corporation. Mr. Henry, who had met his attorney before, had told him that he understood Mr. Douglas needed cash and said that the Lamb Corporation was looking for real estate investments.

Mr. Douglas met with Mr. Henry in Los Angeles and proposed to Mr. Henry that the Lamb Corporation lend him $1.5 million at 10% interest for five years, with Mr. Douglas' personal endorsement.

Mr. Henry explained that his company did not go into a situation unless the loan were secured. They also expected a 10% cash return on equity, the benefit of 1.5% more in amortization payments, and a chance for a capital gain at some point. He suggested a $1 million loan at 10% on the Los Angeles National leasehold, but with a right to convert his loan into a 25% interest in One Broadway.

Mr. Douglas refused this, saying that he felt that the cash amount was too low and that considering the security he was giving up, the conversion price was too low. Finally, at a meeting in New York a few weeks later, the attorney suggested a compromise. Lamb Corporation would advance $1.1 million at 6% interest, the bank rate, with an option to buy a 50% interest for $3.7 million over the $19,750,000 mortgage, if Chase did not exercise its purchase option. If Chase did exercise its option and paid $24,750,000 for One Broadway, Lamb could convert his $1.1 million into a 50% interest in the leasehold from Chase. Mr. Henry said that he felt that if Chase exercised its option, Mr. Douglas would do so well that he could afford to reduce the option price to $950,000, and repay the balance. The Lamb Corporation would also want a six-year option. If Lamb failed to exercise its option, it would want Mr. Douglas to make a final payment to it, sufficient to provide an effective 10% return on its $1.1 million loan. This was the absolute minimum Mr. Henry was willing to accept. He also insisted upon a very strict management contract if Douglas managed the property, if they ever became partners.

Both Mr. Douglas and Mr. Henry wanted a few days to think over the situation. Mr. Henry wanted to analyze his return on investment considering the various alternatives, and present the situation to his board of directors with his recommendation. Mr. Douglas wanted to think over whether this seemed to be the best offer he could reasonably expect. They agreed to meet again in a few days, after Mr. Henry's board of directors had met and given him their decision.

Before sitting down to write a report to his board, Mr. Henry attempted to organize his thoughts. He felt that One Broadway would rent slowly but would eventually achieve 95% occupancy and, most likely, at a $6.50-per-square-foot average rent level. In addition, he thought Mr. Douglas' operating expense estimates were a little high. He calculated that if Chase exercised its purchase during the six-year period at $3.7 million, he would get an 11% return on a prestigious building that his company would be happy to own (see Exhibit 2).

On the other hand, he had never gone into a situation as a lender, even though here he had an opportunity to convert to an equity position. He felt that the partnership was still undercapitalized, and if costs came in higher, construction took longer than anticipated, or operating losses were sustained in the early years, Mr. Douglas might have trouble. Mr. Henry thought the situation resembled too much an "SBIC-type second-mortgage loan with a kicker" where he might have to sell the collateral to protect himself. Representing a public company, he knew his board would not want to be in this position. Analyzing the collateral, he capitalized the $150,000 return at 12% for a value of $1,275,000, which would be enough to protect him. Still, he felt reluctant to go into the transaction unless he felt that Mr. Douglas and One Broadway had a good chance to succeed.

EXHIBIT 1
One Broadway Building
(000 omitted)

	Total	1st Quarter	2nd Quarter	3rd Quarter	4th Quarter	5th Quarter	6th Quarter	7th Quarter	8th Quarter
Source									
Construction loan	15,750	1,800	1,800	2,000	1,800	1,800	1,800	1,800	2,950
2nd deed of trust	1,000	1,000	—	—	—	—	—	—	—
Contractor's deferrals	1,300	120	130	130	130	130	130	130	400
Limited partners	2,500	2,500	—	—	—	—	—	—	—
Owner's equity	400	400	—	—	—	—	—	—	—
	20,950	5,820	1,930	2,130	1,930	1,930	1,930	1,930	3,350
Use									
Land (including carrying)	2,700	2,700	—	—	—	—	—	—	—
Building	14,000	1,000	1,500	2,000	2,000	2,000	2,000	1,500	2,000
Garage	2,000	300	300	300	300	300	200	200	100
Architect	350	210	15	15	15	15	15	15	50
Engineering	25	15	—	—	—	10	—	—	—
Insurance	55	25	—	—	—	30	—	—	—
Taxes during construction	90	—	15	—	15	—	30	—	30
Interest during construction plus fee	1,400	430	55	85	110	135	160	185	210
1st mortgage brokerage fee	150	—	50	—	—	—	—	—	100
Administration	100	25	15	15	15	15	15	15	15
Rental and promotion	100	20	20	10	10	10	10	10	10
Outside rental commissions	930	30	50	50	50	50	50	50	600
Title, escrow, legal	200	150	5	5	5	5	5	5	20
Net	22,100	4,905	2,025	2,480	2,520	2,570	2,485	1,980	3,135
Available cash	(1,150)	915	(95)	(350)	(590)	(640)	(555)	(50)	215
Other Uses of Funds									
Interest—2nd deed of trust	200	25	25	25	25	25	25	25	25
Return limited partners	400	50	50	50	50	50	50	50	50
	(600)	(75)	(75)	(75)	(75)	(75)	(75)	(75)	(75)
Total cash available	—	840	(170)	(425)	(665)	(715)	(630)	(125)	140
Cumulative cash available	(1,750)	840	670	245	(420)	(1,135)	(1,765)	(1,890)	(1,750)

EXHIBIT 2

One Broadway Building
3 Pro Forma Income Statements—One Year after Completion
(000 omitted)

	(1)	(2)	(3)
Rental income (100% occupied).................	3,300	3,300	3,475
Parking income (Net)...........................	165	165	165
Total Income.............................	3,465	3,465	3,640
Allowance for vacancy..........................	165	1,715	175
Net income.............................	3,300	1,750	3,465
Operating Expenses			
Real estate taxes.............................	440	250	440
Cleaning......................................	195	100	195
Electricity....................................	125	65	125
Heat..	25	15	25
Elevator repairs...............................	45	30	45
General maintenance (10 men).................	60	40	60
Supplies......................................	20	15	20
Insurance.....................................	20	20	20
Water treatment..............................	5	5	5
Repairs, alterations, decorating................	120	40	120
Management @ 3%...........................	95	50	100
Miscellaneous................................	50	20	50
Total Operating Expenses..................	1,200	650	1,205
Net cash income before financing...............	2,100	1,100	2,260

(1) Average rent—$6.35/square foot at 95% occupancy.
(2) Average rent—$6.35/square foot at 50% occupancy.
(3) Average rent—$6.50/square foot at 95% occupancy.

QUESTIONS

1. As Mr. Henry, what would you recommend to the board of directors of the Lamb Corporation? Why?
2. As Mr. Douglas, should you accept the offer? What could this additional money be costing you?
3. What rent and what terms should Mr. Douglas quote to the potential 100,000-square-foot tenant? Do you think that Chase will approve them?

FRANCIS LEE TOWERS OFFICE BUILDING

In April 1967, Mr. Potter was considering investing in Francis Lee Towers, a 45-story, 95% completed building in Nottingham. The property had been developed by Mr. Hood. Having experienced serious financial problems, Mr. Hood was frantically searching for a partner with the capital to enable him to complete the building. Mr. Potter was attempting to analyze the building's history and potential profitability. He wondered whether it would be advisable to have Mr. Hood as a partner, and what terms and controls he would need before investing in Francis Lee Towers. He knew that Mr. Hood was having serious problems with his other properties, but Mr. Hood had told him that other local people were willing to finance those. Francis Lee Towers, his largest and most expensive property, required funds beyond their capacity.

Mr. Hood had approached Mr. Potter because Mr. Potter had substantial funds and had been involved in many successful speculative real estate and other business ventures in the United States and Europe.

HISTORY

Mr. Hood's background had been a flamboyant one. By the age of 37 he had made two fortunes, lost one, and appeared about to lose the second. He had started his career at 15, selling watermelons in the Nottingham area. A year later he had expanded his activities into trucking and operated a chain of watermelon stands in the area. Optimistic and visionary, Hood was able to convince potential lenders and investors of his ability. The post–World War II expansion, together with the low interest rates then available, encouraged him to go into real estate. By age 19 he had completed his first building, a two-story office structure in downtown Nottingham.

He then went into land speculation and began trading oil leases in the South. He was successful and soon began drilling operations on his own. By 1955, at the age of 25, he was reported to have a net worth of over $2.5 million; he was the director and manager of a number of successful corporations. However, he soon suffered some major reversals. In 1956, he hit several dry holes in succession and lost over $1.5 million. Although he still had some income from producing properties, he had incurred additional debts of $1 million, partially as a result of his lavish standard of living. Therefore, Hood turned over his financial affairs to trustees, who administered them until late 1957, when he arranged for adequate capital to satisfy his creditors.

During the next few years, he concentrated his activities in the real estate field. He became interested in the Old Quarter of Nottingham. Although slightly run down, the area was close to downtown and had a number of charming older buildings that could be quite attractive if restored. The Old Quarter with its excellent restaurants and nightclubs had always been a major tourist attraction. Mr. Hood felt that the charm of the area could attract a better class of single and young married professional people to live and shop there. They would contribute to both the excitement and the stability of the area. Mr. Hood began to purchase these run-down buildings, and convert them into apartments and commercial space. These activities were financially successful, and the general restoration and improvement of the area gained considerable civic recognition for Hood. He was able to expand the size of his projects and began the restoration of two buildings in the area with the idea of converting them into hotels.

He also bought a 13,500-acre undeveloped tract in the central part of the state for $760,000. Shortly thereafter, he sold off half of this land for $1.5 million, and got an appraised value for the remaining acreage of $4 million. This transaction gave him working capital and increased his borrowing power with the local banks.

Hood began to expand his operations. This time, however, he attempted to attract associates to assist him. While he felt confident of his own abilities, he realized that he needed assistance. Therefore, he brought in a well-known and respected attorney, a former president of the local bar association with wide connections in Nottingham, as a partner. He also retained a bright young architect, who had formerly worked with an award-winning firm. He developed a close relationship with a major principal of the National Bank of Nottingham, established in 1920, with deposits in early 1964 of about $300 million. The 1960–64 period had been one of relatively easy money, and the bank had been glad to loan Mr. Hood money for his various projects.

Mr. Hood's successes of the past few years had restored both his financial and personal reputation. He felt it was now an appropriate time to become involved in the development of new office buildings in Nottingham. Prior to the early 1960's, Nottingham had suffered a decline in building when compared with other major U.S. cities. The local realtors were conservative and did not believe there was a sufficient number of potential tenants willing to pay the higher rentals required to justify new buildings. Then, too, since the city is below sea level, the soft surface land creates extra construction expense. Also, there had been little road-building, and Nottingham did not have good access to either the rest of the Bay area or its own suburbs.

SEARCH FOR LAND

Mr. Hood felt that Nottingham's position had changed drastically with the completion of Interstate Highways 7 and 14 in early 1964. He believed that with a catalyst to start the trend going, the city would expand once again to serve as a business and distribution center for the whole area. There was already talk of a new trade center, a new stadium, and a new convention hall.

Mr. Hood began to search for a site for his building. He wanted it to be the tallest building in the city to give it prestige. He also wanted it to have considerable parking space available, since the new roads would obviously bring more cars into the city. However, since a 500-car ground-level lot would require at least 175,000 square feet of land, and since he doubted whether he could find enough land for both the building and adjacent ground-level parking, he decided to have a multi-level parking garage within the building itself. Because of the high cost of land and the poor condition of the soil, this approach would also be more economical than having a separate parking facility. After talking with his architect, he felt that the minimum site with which he could work would be about 40,000 square feet.

It proved very difficult to locate a site of this size in the existing office area of downtown Nottingham. Most buildings were close together on 5,000- or 10,000-square-foot lots. Even if a site could be assembled, the acquisition costs, including demolition, would amount to over $60 per square foot because of the existing income-producing properties. Mr. Hood thought that at this point of the city's growth such a price would be excessive.

Mr. Hood began to look at less developed areas of the city that might have potential. He examined the new road patterns and selected a fairly blighted block close to downtown in a light industrial zone, which, because of its location adjacent both to the main exit from Interstate Highway 7 and the Railroad Terminal, was in the path of the city's new growth.

The triangular 40,000-square-foot site consisted of eight properties for which he began negotiations simultaneously. Because the existing buildings were only one and two stories, and the area was still considered run down, he was able to acquire all but one of these properties at an average land price of $25 per square foot. He even purchased some of the properties on surrounding blocks in anticipation of a rise in prices once his plans were announced. The lone problem site in the block was a city-owned fire station.

Mr. Hood tried to discover a means of coercing the city to sell him this last piece. Hearing that the city was about to purchase a parcel to establish a new cemetery, Mr. Hood quickly acquired this site and offered to trade it to the city for the fire station site. The city told him that it could not eliminate a fire station because there would be too much local criticism. Mr. Hood remembered that in New York City, William Zeckendorf had once solved a similar problem by buying another site and building the city a new fire station. The cost of the new fire station, exclusive of land, would be over $300,000, adding over $7.50 per square foot to his average land price. However, Mr. Hood felt he had no choice, and therefore he proposed to the city that he buy a nearby parcel and build a new fire station within 120 days. In addition, he would resell the cemetery land to the city at his cost. The city acquiesced, and the transaction was completed in April 1964.

Mr. Hood had now completed his land acquisition at a total cost (including the new fire station) of $1,376,000 or $34.40 per square foot. Although the mayor was much criticized for allowing himself to be "outmaneuvered," Mr. Hood felt that the city had benefited from the transaction, since it had received not only the land for a cemetery and a new fire station but also the potential for additional tax revenue from his new building.

BUILDING DESIGN

Mr. Hood next considered the design of the building. He wanted the building to be architecturally outstanding so that it would become a landmark in the city. The triangular nature of the site made it difficult to construct a building on much more than half the area. With the present zoning ordinances restricting height to 175 feet, he would not be able to construct a building of more than 350,000 square feet. This would cause his land cost per rentable foot to be high and would prevent his building from being tall enough to achieve the prominence he desired. Despite the restrictions, he and his architect worked out a design for a 40-story, 420-foot-high building of white marble and bronze-tinted glass, to be the tallest structure in the region.

The plan called for a 14-story base structure with 18,250 square feet per floor. Rising from this would be a 26-story tower with 8,000 square feet per floor on the first floors and 11,600 on the top four floors. The structure contained a total of 477,900 square feet, of which 413,000 were rentable: 175,000 for a garage use; 30,000 for retail use; 168,000 for office space; and 40,000 for apartments.

Mr. Hood then announced his plans to the public and applied for a

zoning change from the city to permit the additional height. His announcement created considerable commotion in the city, with many of
the established realtors in the city opposing the plan as unnecessary and
too visionary. Mr. Hood countered this by announcing that he had
received such an enthusiastic reception that he would amend his application to request permission to add five more stories in the tower portion
for offices. In addition, he would build a five-story, 60,000-square-foot
annex to include a ground floor restaurant, a health club, barbershop,
and other retail uses. He would create a "city within a city." The total
usable space now planned, including the annex, was 577,500 square feet,
of which 505,000 was rentable. This would reduce his land cost per
rentable foot to $2.72. In June 1964, after considerable discussion, the
city officials, who were favorably disposed to Mr. Hood because of his
close political connections, decided that the climate in Nottingham for
change and innovation was strong enough to permit their approval of the
lifting of the height restrictions.

INITIAL FINANCING INVESTIGATION

Mr. Hood then turned to the financing of the building. He had
acquired the land with only $250,000 cash plus an $826,000 purchase
money mortgage due in one year. In addition, he had to construct the
$300,000 fire station for the city within 120 days. The National Bank
agreed to lend him the money for the fire station, but, because of the
large amount of money required for the proposed tower construction, it
referred Mr. Hood to its correspondent in New York, the Commercial
Trust, for further financial assistance.

Mr. Hood's gross estimate cost for the new building was $15 million
(see Exhibit 1). His estimates of construction costs were based on
industry averages for the different uses contemplated, adjusted for Nottingham wage and price scales. He included a heavy allowance for extra
foundation costs because of the large plaza he was planning and the
poor soil condition. He calculated interest during construction at $6\frac{1}{2}\%$
plus a 1% processing fee on a two-year $12 million loan. He also was told
to allow for a standby fee for the permanent lender. He included
generous allowances for legal expenses and administration plus travel,
advertising, and promotional expenses. He knew that his figures seemed
high, but his standard of living and operations were such that he
normally spent sums of this magnitude. Leasing commissions were calculated on the basis of outside brokers doing all the renting. In actuality,
he hoped he could reduce his costs by having his own staff do much of
the leasing, thus saving $350,000, and by finishing the building ahead of
schedule, in 18 rather than 24 months, which would enable him to earn

operating revenues of $400,000 after expenses during that six-month period.

He also prepared an income and expense estimate showing income before financing of $1.2 million, which he capitalized at 8%, showing a value of $15 million. He requested a $12 million loan from the Commercial Trust.

Income
Retail.................................. 90,000 sq. ft. @ $6.50 = $ 585,000
Office.................................200,000 "   " @ 5.00 =   1,000,000
Garage................................175,000 "   " @   .70 =   122,000
Apartments (25 units @ $400 mo.)........ 40,000 "   " @ 2.95 =   118,000
                                        505,000 $1,825,000
Less 5% vacancy allowance.......................................   91,000
Net rental income..$1,734,000
Estimated operating expense
Office @ $1.70 sq. ft.*..$ 340,000
Retail @ $0.10 sq. ft..   9,000
Apartments @ $800/unit..   20,000
Real estate taxes...   165,000
    Total Operating Expenses....................................$ 534,000
Net before financing..$1,200,000

* Including electricity

The Commercial Trust looked at Mr. Hood's figures and said that it would be interested in the construction loan only if there were a guaranteed permanent mortgage "takeout," since its business was not to provide long-term mortgage funds. The bank referred him to the Pilgrim Life Insurance Company for permanent financing.

Pilgrim looked at the situation, and told Mr. Hood that it would not consider the loan until the building became 60% leased. Since it was the first major new office building in the area, the life insurance company wanted a firm assurance that there would be demand for this space. Mr. Hood consulted his friends at the National Bank. They told him that Pilgrim's reaction was typical of what he could expect at this time; they advised him to concentrate on rentals. They believed there would be ample mortgage funds available once he had secured firm leases.

LEASING

Mr. Hood then began to search for tenants. He wanted to lease the property quickly in order to obtain his financing and proceed with the construction. First, he attempted to find national companies whose credit standing would assist him in getting his financing. The Jones Company, a major industrial firm, agreed to lease 47,049 square feet of office space at a rental rate of $4.50 per square foot for a term of 20 years, under the condition that it would have the option of canceling the lease after 10 years. As an additional condition, the company required that Mr. Hood's company assume three of its existing leases, which would expire at various dates through January 31, 1970. The aggregate rentals on these leases would be approximately $155,000 starting from October 1, 1966, the Jones Company's expected occupancy date. Mr. Hood believed he would be able to sublet the space fairly easily. Although he considered the $4.50 per square foot rental rate low, and did not like the tenant's cancellation privilege, he accepted Jones' conditions. Jones' international division then agreed to take an additional 8,000 square feet at the same $4.50 rental.

The Manufacturer's Finance Corporation took two floors of the tower section for 20 years at a rental of $4.75 per square foot. Each floor of the tower included 6,700 square feet of rentable space. It too insisted on having the option of canceling after 10 years. The Able Insurance Corporation, Ltd., signed a 20-year lease for 29,222 square feet at a rental of $4.50. It insisted on having a right to cancel the lease if the space were not ready for occupancy by July 1, 1966. Mr. Hood knew that he would not have much time to prepare the space, but since he did expect to be ready by that date, and, in any event, did not think the tenant would cancel if there were a one- or two-month delay, he accepted Able's conditions.

Mr. Hood was also able to talk some of his associates into making space commitments. He told them that his activities were expanding at a rate such that each of them would probably need more space soon. If not, they would be able to sublet easily any space they did not need. Meanwhile, he needed their help to get his space leased quickly. His architect, one of his major construction subcontractors, and the management firm for his Old Quarter properties each signed a 20-year lease at $5.50 per square foot for a full floor in the tower section. Twelve other tenants signed leases for 20-year periods for a total of about 37,000 square feet at $5.50-per-square-foot rentals. By September 1964, Mr. Hood had rented 154,726 square feet, a little less than 75% of the available office space, at an annual rental, including electricity, of $759,000.

He had little trouble renting his retail space. A local clothing store took two floors of the annex, totaling 21,300 square feet, for 20 years at a rental of $5 per square foot plus $0.50 for electricity. An experienced restauranteur formed a new corporation to handle the food operations for the complex. He signed a 20-year lease for 9,815 square feet for a first-floor cafeteria in the annex at a rental of $7 per square foot plus $0.75 for all utilities. He took 20,000 square feet in the top section of the tower for a first-class restaurant with private dining rooms overlooking the city. The basic rental rate here was also $7 per square foot for 20 years, although in this case a percentage of the income was to be paid as additional rent. The charge for utilities was $0.50 per square foot. The tenant insisted that the space be ready by mid 1966, saying that since he was a relatively small entrepreneur he could not afford to have his capital unused for any longer time period. Mr. Hood knew that this restauranteur's credit was not "Triple A," but he felt that his food operations would be a considerable attraction for the building.

A small instrument company approached him with a novel approach for using the 45th floor. It would use 1,325 square feet for its own offices and operate the remaining 9,670 as an observation tower, charging admission, as was done at the Empire State Building. Although the company's credit was minimal, it would pay a share of the profits if the business were successful. Mr. Hood was impressed with the idea, and agreed to a formula whereby if the business were unsuccessful, rent could be accumulated for three years, after which it did not have to be paid at all. On the other hand, if it were successful, he would receive 50% of the profits plus the fixed rent of $5 per square foot for the office section and $9 for the observation area.

These leases, plus a few other minor ones, gave him a total signed gross annual rental of $493,000 for 69,000 square feet of retail space. The garage space was his next rental concern. Occupying over 175,000 square feet, it was most important that he have a lease for the area. He found that it was usual in the industry for the rental to be tied to some extent to the success of the building, since the garage operator had no control over the amount of space leased in the building, which was the most important determinant of parking demand. Mr. Hood knew that he had already signed leases for most of his space; therefore, he did not regard this as a major problem. He agreed to rent the entire garage area to Urban Parking, Inc., a substantial firm, on the following terms: (1) prior to 70% occupancy of the building, the tenant would pay 25% of his gross income with no minimum; (2) over 70% occupancy the tenant would pay $30,000 per year minimum plus 33⅓% of gross income over $130,000; and (3) the landlord would have the right to reduce the monthly minimum by $750 per month in exchange for free parking rights on 2 of the 11 floors. The entire lease was subject to renegotiation at the end of the 10th and 15th years, or if the landlord were to build another garage within three blocks, or if the top floor were not used continuously as a restaurant or cocktail lounge. Mr. Hood believed that he would easily receive the minimum rental of $30,000 per year and most likely another $90,000. He formed this assumption on the basis of talks with many potential operators who had estimated that the 500-car location should gross at least $800 per space per year. At this level, the tenant would be paying 30% of his income as rent.

FINAL FINANCING ARRANGEMENTS

Mr. Hood then summarized his projections and prepared a new income and expense statement to present to Pilgrim (see Exhibit 2). He showed a gross rental income including utility income of $1,841,000, of which 75% was based on signed leases, and a net income after operating expenses and before financing of $1,216,000. He capitalized this at an 8% rate, which resulted in a value of $15.2 million. He then requested a mortgage of approximately 80% of value, or $12 million.

After receiving this information, Pilgrim told Mr. Hood that it would do its own investigation. The company recommended that an outside firm of real estate consultants, Jonathan Associates, be hired by Mr. Hood to do an independent evaluation of the project. This report would assist Pilgrim considerably in making a decision. In the meanwhile, the staff of Pilgrim would examine the building plans, projected income and expense statements, and existing leases, as well as investigate the personal reputations and financial conditions of Mr. Hood and his associates. The insurance company wanted to make sure that the project would not falter for lack of equity capital.

Mr. Hood hired Jonathan Associates to do the suggested project evaluation. Their report came back confirming Mr. Hood's estimates. They believed that the project was economically sound, that the schedule of rents was reasonable, and that the future of the area was good. The personal reports on Mr. Hood were contradictory. His past financial problems were brought out, as well as a history of a number of claims against him. On the positive side was Mr. Hood's personal but unaudited balance sheet which showed assets of $3.6 million, liabilities of $700,000 and a personal net worth of $2.9 million. The major portion of his assets were in real estate, listed at appraised market value rather than cost. His bank reference, the National Bank, could not have been more positive in its recommendation of him and his associates. In answer to the question of the claims against Mr. Hood, his friends said that they guessed he was just too busy to pay his bills.

Lastly, the insurance company's own staff submitted its report, which endorsed the project with two reservations. First, the rental level of $4 per square foot without utilities appeared low in comparison with other new multistory buildings in other cities. Second, because of the conditional nature of many of the clauses in some of the leases, and the free parking provisions in the garage lease, it was difficult to assess the percentage of rental income that could be considered as definite.

Pilgrim's officials reviewed this report and decided to approve the loan, but only in the amount of $10.5 million. They valued the property at $15 million, but decided to loan only 70% rather than 80% of the value. They told Mr. Hood that when the project was completed, and if the new rents were at a higher rate, and the contingent conditions were met, they might be willing to discuss a higher amount. In the meantime, the $10.5 million loan was the largest they had ever made. Most of their commitments were in the $1 million to $2 million range, and Francis Lee Towers was a notable undertaking for them. The commitment was conditional upon the building's being completed by October 1, 1966, and provided for a 25-year mortgage at 6% interest with a 7½% constant payment. The agreement had a clause permitting repayment after five years with a 3% penalty payment. Pilgrim also would collect immediately a nonrefundable commitment fee of $105,000 or 1% of the commitment amount.

Mr. Hood returned to Commercial Trust to discuss interim financing. Commercial felt that the $10.5 million commitment was too low to guarantee completion of the project but would not loan beyond the amount of the permanent mortgage takeout. Mr. Hood explained that he and his associates had a combined net worth of from $3 to $5 million. He also expected to reduce the $15 million projected cost by doing much of the renting through his own staff without outside brokerage commissions, which should produce savings of $350,000. By finishing the building ahead of schedule, he should realize extra rental income of $400,000. Commercial still felt that additional permanent takeout financing was required. If it were obtained, Commercial would increase its construction loan accordingly. It would not, however, grant a loan at the $10.5 million level.

Commercial introduced Mr. Hood to James & Co., a New York factoring company which also makes real estate loans. James in turn contacted Michaels Company, a New York investment group, to act as its consultant. Based on Michaels' appraisal that the deal would be sufficiently sound to attract additional financing of at least $1.5 million upon completion, James issued a standby commitment for that amount. The $1.5 million commitment was conditional upon Mr. Hood's obtaining the Pilgrim mortgage. The term was to be five years, with amortization based on a 10-year payout with interest at 8%. James would receive a commitment fee of $150,000, which represented extra interest of 5% per year for two years. Actually, the company anticipated that it would have to fund this commitment only as a last resort. Either Pilgrim would increase its mortgage or another source of second-mortgage funds would be found at the time of closing.

The commitment with James & Co. proved satisfactory to Commercial Trust, which then increased its commitment to $12 million, with interest at 6½% for a term of two years. Commercial was also to receive a processing fee of 1%.

CONSTRUCTION

Meanwhile, Mr. Hood had been receiving construction bids from various contractors. He had settled on the Western Construction Company because of its reputation and experience and the confidence that the lenders to whom he had talked had in the company. The company's bid of $10.5 million, including a fee of $404,000, was in line with Mr. Hood's estimate. Western's preliminary schedule called for completion of the tower building by December 31, 1965, and the annex three months later. The $10.5 million was guaranteed as an upset price, with Mr. Hood to receive 50% of any savings beyond $25,000. This contract price was geared to a specific set of architect's plans and specifications, and any changes would be accepted only at the cost of the owner and only after consent of the lending institution had been obtained. Also, the contractor would not be responsible for delays incurred because of changes made by the owner, or by the owner's inability to pay him. Construction advances would be made directly to the contractor by the bank upon receipt of approval of the expenditure by the architect. Ten percent of each advance would be withheld by the bank as security for Western's performance. In addition, Western would be required to take out a performance bond insuring the bank and the owner of its satisfactory performance of the contract.

Mr. Hood was not overjoyed with his financing arrangements. He did not like the cost of the James arrangement, whereby he was, in effect, paying a $150,000 standby fee for the additional $1.5 million. However, he had great confidence in the future of the project. He anticipated a considerable increase in rents over the years through percentage clauses in some leases and higher rates for unrented areas. Also, he felt that he was too committed to this project in the public's eye to back down at this point. Since further delays might jeopardize his completion date, he decided to arrange the higher mortgage later, after the building was in process.

Thus, in October of 1964, as was reported in a local newspaper, "After a helicopter soared into the air to hover at the building's proposed height, the Secretary of Commerce, the Mayor of Nottingham, and Mr. Hood threw a switch setting a pile driver in motion to start the ceremonial pile." Francis Lee Towers was under way with considerable fanfare.

OTHER VENTURES

Shortly after construction began, Mr. Hood was presented with the opportunity to purchase the Frank Building, the second largest office building in Nottingham. Built recently by a wealthy investor from Detroit, the building was 60% vacant as the result of a decision by the major tenant to move out at the expiration of its lease. The owner had tried to re-lease the space through a large national rental broker, but in spite of the building's location in the heart of Nottingham, he had been unsuccessful.

Mr. Hood was offered the building at $12 million, only $1.1 million above a $10.9 million first mortgage. He knew that the purchase was a gamble. The building was losing money at the rate of $500,000 a year. However he was impressed by the rapidity with which he had rented 75% of Francis Lee Towers. He believed that the Frank Building would be worth $15 million if fully rented. He knew he could borrow the necessary $1.1 million of equity funds from the National Bank.

His associates advised him against the transaction, saying that the renting of the Frank Building would be much more difficult than that of Francis Lee Towers, where he had had the advantages of extensive publicity, good parking, and a number of captive tenants. He would also be jeopardizing the Towers by reducing his borrowing power and would be overextending himself.

Nevertheless, Mr. Hood decided to ignore their advice and buy the building. He canceled the exclusive rental agreement, employed multiple brokers, paid extra commissions, and offered to take over tenants' existing leases in other buildings to facilitate their moving to the Frank Building. His heavy promotional efforts proved successful, and within a few months the building's occupancy rate had increased to 90%. Mr. Hood estimated that the value of his equity was now $4 million over the first mortgage.

He then decided that Nottingham was on the threshold of a hotel construction boom. Nottingham's limited hotel, exhibition, and arena facilities had thus far reduced its appeal as a convention center. Nottingham was presently applying for franchises for various professional sports teams. In connection with this application, a 60,000-seat domed stadium had been proposed. A 110,000-square-foot exhibition and convention facility, with a 16,000-person capacity, was being planned. An International Trade Mart was to be built within walking distance of the Old Quarter. Mr. Hood felt that the only factor missing in order for Nottingham to become a major convention center was an adequate supply of hotel rooms.

He had already started the $1 million hotel renovation in the Old Quarter and had purchased other land in the area. Against the advice of many of his associates, he bought another large parcel in Nottingham for the construction of a new hotel. Since the land price was high, Mr. Hood decided that the right approach would be again to build as high as possible. He announced plans for a 72-story convention hotel, which would be 700 feet high, making it the largest hotel in the world. He had developed his plans and he had received a construction bid from Western Company for $23.6 million. Since he planned to turn the operation of the hotel over to a national chain, he had hired an outside group as financial consultants to assist him in negotiating a management contract and arranging the financing.

INTERNATIONAL OIL

Mr. Hood had not forgotten the need to increase the number of rentals at Francis Lee Towers. He had sought out several national companies, and finally, in the summer of 1965, International Oil became interested in leasing 48,000 square feet. Since this was approximately the amount of office space still to be rented, Mr. Hood attempted to reassign the locations of some of the previously committed tenants in order to provide International with space on consecutive floors. However, he was unable to get a sufficient number of tenants to agree to this to satisfy International. Since Hood thought he could get additional financing if he could get International, a well-rated tenant, on a 10-year lease, to move to the Towers, he did not want to lose the company. Therefore he thought of converting three of the garage floors into offices.

International agreed to lease this space if Mr. Hood could make the necessary arrangements. The extra construction costs for this were estimated to run about $750,000, in addition to $50,000 for new architectural and engineering drawings. The rental income from international, at $4.75 per square foot, would be $228,000. The garage income would probably be reduced by about $40,000, and operating expenses increased by about $70,000, leaving a net increase of $118,000. Capitalized at 8%, the increased value would be $1,475,000, well above the $800,000 cost figure. He also believed that he could use this new lease as the lever to increase his mortgage. He talked with the Western Construction Company about the changes; Western agreed to go ahead with the changes, since it appeared likely that the mortgage would be increased. In any case, Western insisted on and received Mr. Hood's personal guarantee that he would pay for the change orders. Mr. Hood did not consider it necessary to obtain approval from Commercial Trust at this time, since he was only spending more money improving the property, without any additional cost to the bank.

He convinced Urban Parking to give up the top three floors of the garage, although this would reduce the number of car spaces from 500 to 350. He told Urban Parking that with this arrangement there would be an increased demand for spaces, which would increase its income. Mr. Hood agreed to give up his rights to free parking on 2 of the 11 floors as part of this space reduction. The base rent was reduced to $26,000 and the percentage to 33⅓% over $100,000.

Some of Mr. Hood's associates disagreed sharply with this new plan. They argued that any changes would be costly and create delays, and from now on, if Western were late, the delays would be blamed on the change orders. In addition, even after the lease with International Oil was signed, the design of the plans, involving architects and structural, mechanical, and electrical engineers, would take a minimum of two months. By then the time clauses in some tenants' leases would begin to be pressing. Delays would cause Hood to lose some or all of the $400,000 income he expected to receive from running the property during the final 6 months of the 24-month construction period. However, Mr. Hood wanted something new to take to the Pilgrim to persuade the insurance company to increase its loan. Therefore, he decided to go ahead with the plan.

ADDITIONAL FINANCING

Mr. Hood decided to reduce some of his short-term loans in order to increase his working capital. He placed a $3.6 million second mortage on the Frank Building, with James & Co. The original $1.1 million National Bank loan was subordinated and given the security of a third mortgage. The funds from this loan should have provided all the equity needed for the Towers, including the change orders. However, Mr. Hood had to use some of these funds for other projects and to repay other loans. In any case, he was able to tell his associates that if he had listened to their advice and not gambled on purchasing the Frank Building, he would have been in an impossible cash position.

Meanwhile, Western was proceeding with the construction, although now, because of the changes, the completion schedule was at least four months later than the first estimate. In the spring of 1966, Mr. Hood decided to return to Pilgrim Life Insurance for an increase in his mortgage. He presented a new profit and loss statement showing $1.44 million as the net before financing (see Exhibit 3). The projected $224,000 net increase over the original statement came from the International rental and from estimated percentage rents from the retail facilities. He requested a 70%, $12.6 million mortgage based on a capitalization rate of 8%, which valued the property at $18 million.

Pilgrim turned down this request, saying that it was not interested in any increase at this time. Several reasons were given. First, as a lender it could not consider percentage rents as firm income. It could give some weight to it, if earned, but certainly not on a projected basis. Second, there was no provision in the new statement for increased real estate taxes, although projected income had been increased. Third, in view of the delays that had been incurred, the conditional occupancy clauses in the leases made the company anxious about its present loan. Lastly, they were reluctant to increase the present loan because money was getting tighter and this was already the company's largest commitment. The 6% interest rate was beginning to look like a favorable rate for borrowers, not lenders.

As he began to investigate other mortgage sources in the late spring of 1966, Mr. Hood found this to be true. He was especially interested in finding financing to replace the James & Co. loan. It was not the 8% interest rate that bothered him so much as the rapid amortization, which made the annual carrying cost for the $1.5 million loan almost $250,000. Most lenders did not want to consider a loan in the $12 million range; if they did consider it, they insisted that it be fully secured by long-term net leases from "Triple A" tenants. Even then, they were talking about a 6½%–7% interest rate. At the time he was searching for a new loan for the Towers, Mr. Hood was also seeking financing for his hotels. The hotel industry was even more restricted than new office construction by the tight money market, since lenders regarded hotels as among the most marginal of investments, and such loans were, therefore, the first to be restricted. This proved especially true in the case of something as visionary as his projected 72-story hotel.

FORECLOSURE

As his personal cash position worsened, Mr. Hood began to get behind in his payments to Western. When Mr. Hood failed to meet his August interest payments to Commercial Trust, the bank refused to advance further funds. Since Mr. Hood already owed Western $750,000 on an unsecured basis for the change orders, Western walked off the job, leaving it 95% completed.

When this occurred, Mr. Hood's remaining creditors began to take action. The holders of the third mortgage on the Frank Building purchased it from Mr. Hood for $15.5 million to protect their position. The Long Island Bank began foreclosure proceedings as first mortgagee of the recently completed hotel. On October 1, 1966, the Pilgrim announced that it was allowing its commitment to expire since the completion date had not been met, some of the leases were now questionable, and the owner's financial condition had weakened substantially.

Commercial Trust then began its own foreclosure proceedings, and a date for the foreclosure sale was set by the state courts for December 1, 1966. During this two-month period, the bank and the Western Company worked together in establishing a strategy to save their positions. No work was being done on the Towers, since there was no one to pay for it, and the bank did not want to make the necessary expenditures until it had received title. However, all parties were afraid that the building might be damaged if it stayed vacant. Windows had not yet been installed.

The Commercial Trust and Western began to approach the lessees to renegotiate occupancy dates and establish higher rentals to finish the building and justify a higher appraisal. The prospective tenants were in an unusual position. On the one hand, they had made plans to vacate their existing locations to move to the Towers; it would be almost impossible for the larger tenants to secure substitute space quickly. On the other hand, the tenants recognized that they too had considerable bargaining power with whomever became the ultimate owner of the building, since a new owner taking over through foreclosure would not want leases canceled when the space was already 95% ready for occupancy.

The bank assumed that at the time of the foreclosure sale it would be the only bidder. Because of the clarity of its agreement with Mr. Hood, it anticipated no legal difficulty with the acquisition. Commercial Trust knew that even at its $12 million mortgage level it faced the possibility of considerable loss because of the increased construction costs. It now estimated the gross project cost at $16 million. The reasons for this cost increase were the changes for International, the extra legal expenses, and the added interest for the period from October until completion.

On November 30, the day before the expected public sale of the Towers, Mr. Hood filed a petition in the federal district court for voluntary bankruptcy. The federal laws would permit him to reorganize if he could prove sufficient assets to pay off his debts to the satisfaction of his creditors and the court. Mr. Hood claimed that Francis Lee Towers would, at a later date, be worth $20 million, and this, with his other properties, would place him in a solvent position. He argued that the Towers was already worth $18 million. If his petition were granted, the foreclosure sale would be postponed in spite of the clause in the Commercial Trust's note, by which Mr. Hood waived bankruptcy rights. In opposition to the petition, Commercial claimed that Mr. Hood had waived bankruptcy rights, that Mr. Hood's appraisal of the property was inflated, that further delays endangered its security, and that Mr. Hood was only attempting to stall, since the bankruptcy hearing could last several months.

The federal judge hearing the evidence felt that Mr. Hood should be given the opportunity of presenting a plan to the courts. He granted Mr. Hood's petition and canceled the foreclosure sale.

EXHIBIT 1

Francis Lee Towers
Total Project Cost
(July 1964)

Building (nongarage) @ $20 sq. ft.	$ 8,000,000	
Garage @ $10	1,750,000	
Extra foundation	750,000	
	$10,500,000	
Plaza work	200,000	
Relocating of utilities	200,000	
Permits, tests	18,000	
Demolition	50,000	
		$10,968,000
Architectural and engineering		540,000
Insurance and real estate taxes		167,000
Interest during construction (6½% × 2 years × ½ $12,000,000)		780,000
Interim finance fees		
Bank attorney	$ 25,000	
Appraisals	12,000	
Bank fee @ 1%	120,000	
Other fees	—	
		$ 157,000
Standby fee		105,000
Legal and administrative		182,000
Travel, advertising, and promotion		200,000
Leasing commissions		525,000
		$13,624,000
Land (including fire station)		1,376,000
Gross Project Cost		$15,000,000

EXHIBIT 2

Francis Lee Towers
Income and Expense Statement
(June 1964)

	Square Feet	Gross Rental (in 000's)	
Income (including utilities)			
Retail			
Rented................................	68,665	$ 492	
Vacant................................	21,322	117	
Total...............................	89,987		$ 609
Office			
Rented................................	154,726	$ 759	
Vacant................................	46,055	230	
Total.............................	200,781		989
Garage			
Rented................................	175,601	$ 35	
Plus percentage rents..................		90	
Total.............................	175,681		125
Apartments			
Vacant................................	38,661	$ 118	
Total.............................	38,661		118
Total Income.....................	505,110		$1,841

Summary

	Square Feet	Gross Rental (in 000's)	
Income			
Rented................................	399,072	$1,286	
Vacant................................	106,038	465	
Percentage rentals......................	—	90	
Gross Income.......................	505,110	$1,841	
5% vacancy allowance.....................		$ 91	
Net rental income........................			$1,750
Estimated operating expense			
Office @ $1.75/sq. ft. rented..............		$ 340	
Retail....................................		9	
Apartments @ $800 unit..................		20	$ 369
Real estate tax...........................			165
Total Operating Expenses............			$ 534
Net before financing......................			$1,216

EXHIBIT 3

Francis Lee Towers
Income and Expense Statement
(April, 1966)

	Square Feet	Total (In 000's)
Income (including utilities)		
Retail		
Rented................................	68,665	$ 492
Vacant................................	21,322	117
Plus percentage rents..................	—	111
Total................................	89,987	$ 720
Office		
Rented.............................203,193		$ 987
Vacant................................	46,055	253
Total................................	248,781	1,240
Garage		
Rented.............................127,681		$ 26
Plus percentage rents..................	—	60*
Total................................	127,681	86
Apartments		
Vacant................................	38,661	$ 118
Total................................	38,661	118
Base rent.............................	—	—
Total Income.......................	505,110	$2,164

Summary

	Square Feet	Total (In 000's)
Income		
Rented................................	399,072	$1,505
Vacant................................	106,038	488
Percentage rentals.......................	—	171
Gross Income........................	505,110	$2,164
5% vacancy allowance......................		108
Net rental income..........................		$2,056
Estimated operating expense		
Office @ $1.70/sq. ft. rented..............		$ 422
Retail.....................................		9
Apartments @ $800/unit..................		20
		$ 451
Real estate tax...........................		165
Total Operating Expense.............		$ 616
Net before financing..		$1,440

*Assumes 350 cars at $800 = $280,000 − $100,000 = $180,000 × ⅓ = $60,000.

PART IV

Development—
Government Programs

FEDERAL HOUSING ADMINISTRATION MULTIFAMILY DEVELOPMENT PROGRAMS

The Federal Housing Administration (FHA) has written, since its creation in 1934 under the National Housing Act, mortgage and loan insurance aggregating over $100 billion, covering over 7.5 million single family homes, 1.2 million multifamily units, and over 27.5 million individual properties improved through home-improvement loans. Over 35 million families have been affected by this program. Currently, over $40 billion of mortgages are insured.

This program revolutionized the housing industry through the device of providing mortgage insurance against losses on money advanced by approved lenders. Because of this reduction in risk, lenders were able to make loans with a higher loan-to-value ratio, longer maturities, lower interest rates, and with less emphasis upon the personal credit of the borrower. If a loss occurred, the lender would be reimbursed at the option of the Federal National Mortgage Association through either cash or government bonds. A mortgage instrument that could be traded nationally developed. As a result, the commitment of institutional funds to this type of loan increased sharply. Control over the borrower was kept by requiring level monthly payments which included principal, interest, FHA mortgage insurance premium of one half of 1% of the outstanding balance of the loan, and accruals for local real estate taxes.

Another major purpose of the FHA was to encourage improvements in housing standards and conditions. To implement this, minimum property requirements for construction, design, and maintenance were established, with regular procedures for inspection.

The success of the program in stimulating new housing starts was especially apparent after World War II, when the need for more housing and for the funds to finance this housing was acute. In 1950, almost half of the new housing starts carried mortgages insured by the federal government. By 1965, the government's share of housing starts was down to 17%. This reflected the increased prosperity of the economy. Buyers wanted more expensive homes subject to loans with larger down payments and shorter maturities, while the lenders were willing to assume more risk themselves without the government guarantee. The FHA changed its regulations to some extent to meet this change in demand through legislation permitting insurance of more expensive homes with loans of longer maturities. Interest rates varied in accordance with general market rates, up to a maximum of 7½%.

However, in recent years, Congress has increasingly used the FHA programs to promote the construction of houses which Congress felt would not otherwise be built for particular groups who would not qualify under usual lending standards. Racial discrimination clauses have been omitted from the administrative guidelines. Special programs, mostly involving multifamily construction, for the elderly and lower-income families were developed. Loans have been made in "blighted areas" where a general neighborhood could not be improved by private enterprise alone, and interest rate and other subsidies have been given to marginal groups who could not afford the rental levels prevalent in standard housing. Therefore, whereas FHA's influence on the total housing picture has declined, its specialized effects are still quite important.

The 0.5% mortgage insurance premium charged together with initial fees totaling 1.3% of the original mortgage amount has proved ample to finance the agency and set up reserves that have been in excess of losses by $1.2 billion since the agency's inception. Losses since the beginning of the agency in 1934 through June 1964 amounted to only $280.3 million and represented 0.37% of the total amount of insurance written.

Established with the FHA in 1934 under the National Housing Act were the Federal National Mortgage Association (FNMA) and the Federal Savings and Loan Insurance Corporation (FSLIC). Then, in 1942, the National Housing Agency (NHA) was created by Executive order to include the FHA and the Public Housing Administration (PHA). In 1947, the Housing and Home Finance Agency (HHFA) became the successor to the NHA. In 1949, HHFA was given control of the new Slum Clearance Program, and in the 1954 Housing Act, the scope of this program was increased to include rehabilitation and conservation. At that time, the Urban Renewal Administration (URA) and the Community Facilities Agency were added to HHFA. In 1964, the Mass Transportation Act extended the powers of the HHFA into this field.

Lastly, in 1965, the Housing and Urban Development Act changed the name of the HHFA to the Housing and Urban Development Department, and elevated the Department to Cabinet status. As of January 31, 1966, HUD had 13,554 employees and controlled outlays for 1966 of $4.357 billion. Under this reorganization plan, the FHA became part of the Office of Mortgage Credit headed by an assistant secretary known as the Federal Housing Commissioner. There were also four other assistant secretaries for Renewal and Housing Assistance, Metropolitan Development, Demonstration and Inter-Governmental Relations, and Administration.

The FHA itself, through its 76 field offices, still has the responsibility for insuring mortgages on land development; rental and private housing for families of low, moderate, and upper incomes; housing for the elderly or handicapped; group practice facilities for doctors and dentists; nursing homes; cooperative housing and condominiums; experimental housing, mobile home parks; housing at military installations; and long-term rehabilitation for major home and apartment improvements.

The greatest portion of FHA loans have been made in the private single-family new-home field, although in recent years with the growing scarcity of urban land; the population increase, especially among the young-married and over-65 age groups; the expansion of federal urban renewal programs; and the liberalization of the FHA laws, the amount of multifamily rental housing starts under the FHA program has greatly increased both numerically and in relation to the total program. In the past six years, the gross number of units has increased from 890,589 to 1,196,180 and the dollar amount insured from approximately $8 billion to $13 billion. This parallels the national trend whereby in 1960, 23% of the private nonfarm residential construction was for multifamily units and in 1964, almost 40%.

There are six basic sections to the private multifamily program (see Exhibit 1 for summary of FHA statistics). Section 207, the oldest one, is intended to facilitate the production of rental accommodations at middle-to upper-middle-income rent levels. Section 220 is designed for the same market but must be within urban renewal areas.[1] As such, the mortgage terms and allowances under 220 are more favorable to the developer, since it is assumed that a private developer needs special incentives to invest his capital in an area requiring slum clearance and rehabilitation.

Section 213 deals with cooperative housing. Three types are permitted under this section. The "sales-type" covers the situation where a nonprofit group builds a development and then sells the individual units to its own members; the "management-type" where a nonprofit group builds and owns a development and then leases the units on a nonprofit basis to its members; and the "investor-type" where a private developer builds and then sells a project in its entirety to a cooperative, which would then lease the individual units to its members. Section 213 offers the least

---

[1] An urban renewal area is in a community which has a "workable program" and an approved Urban Renewal Plan as certified by HUD. The plan for a particular area is instigated and operated by the local government, but the federal government provides two thirds of the cost, establishes standards of operation, and offers technical assistance. The state may also agree to share some of the costs of the city's one third.

incentives to private developers, since the profit goes to the builder as a fixed fee which is treated as normal income for tax purposes.

Section 221(d)(3) is designed to assist private interests and nonprofit organizations in providing multifamily housing for low- and moderate-income families in communities that have a "workable program."[2] Since there is a limitation on the maximum annual income of tenants eligible for these housing units, the maximum monthly rent they may pay, and the sponsor's profit, the permanent mortgage bears a "below market" interest rate, currently 3%. (Exhibit 2 shows a current sample rent ceiling and tenant income limitation form for Boston.) Other provisions, such as the waiving of the one half of 1% mortgage insurance premium also help to keep rental levels approximately 25% below other sections. Since a private lender will not take a mortgage at a 3% interest rate, the mortgage is taken by FNMA from funds appropriated to it by Congress.

Section 236, added in 1968, has objectives similar to 221(d)(3), but incorporates several changes. Unlike 221(d)(3), in which a 3% mortgage is funded by FNMA, a 236 project is financed through a conventional mortgage at the market rate; the FHA then subsidizes all but 1% to 3% of the interest payments. In addition, Section 236 has lower ceilings on tenants' incomes—about 80% of the income levels shown in Exhibit 1. (This is still 135% of the Public Housing maximums.) Also, a 236 project does not have to be in an area with a "workable program." Eventually, the FHA plans to phase 221(d)(3) into 236.

The various groups eligible to build under this program are: nonprofit organizations; builders who will sell at a fixed 7% profit to a nonprofit group, nonprofit cooperatives; investor/sponsor who will sell to the cooperative at a fixed profit of 7%; and limited-distribution sponsors whose profit is limited to a cumulative return of 6% on 11.11% of the initially endorsed mortgage amount.

Section 221(d)(4) is in its operation more similar to Section 220 than Section 221(d)(3). The differences are that the project does not have to be built in an urban renewal area or in a community with a "workable program," although priority of occupancy must be given to families displaced by urban renewal. Also, the per-unit construction allowances are at least 10% less than under the Section 220 program. As a result, units built under the program are normally garden apartments or lower-cost high-rise built in lower-cost land areas.

There are many features common to the operation of all of these programs. The projects financed must be economically sound; be built on

---

[2] A "workable program" is an official plan subject to approval by HUD showing how a local community is utilizing all its appropriate private and public resources to eliminate and prevent the development and spread of blight. Such elements as up-to-date building codes and enforcement procedures, master plans, and citizen participation are part of such a program.

owned or leased land; owned by trusts, partnerships, corporations, associations, or individuals; secured by first mortgages on an FHA prescribed form; without second mortgages; and in new or rehabilitated, detached, semidetached, row, or high-rise buildings. Currently, Sections 207, 213, 220, and 221(d)(4) bear a 7½% interest rate. The interest rate in past years has normally been 5¼%. Amortization schedules may extend to 40 years, except that there is a limitation on Sections 207, 213, 221(d)(4) that the mortgage be for no more than 75% of the remaining economic life of the building. Commercial facilities may be included to serve the project, although Section 220 permits any commercial facility to be included in a residential project if it is consistent with the overall urban renewal plan for the area. Each single mortgage insured for a private lender cannot exceed $12.5 million under Section (d)(3) or (d)(4); $20 million under Sections 207 and 213; or $30 million under Section 220. The minimum number of units per project to be insured is two for Section 220, five for Sections 213, 221(d)(3) or (d)(4); or eight for Section 207. Except for 221(d)(3), there is a one half of 1% mortgage insurance premium.

Insured in these mortgages are all projects costs, including: land, exterior land improvements; construction of dwellings, garages, and stores; architectural fees; interest, taxes, and insurance during construction; FHA premiums of 1.3%; title and recording, including title insurance; financing of 1.5%; and legal and organizational expenses, usually 0.5%. A builders and sponsors risk fee is permitted, the amount dependent upon the program. Section 207 permits a builder's fee of from 5%–10%, depending upon the size of the project, taken as a percentage of construction costs only. Section 213, 220, and 221(d)(4) have an allowance of 10% figured as a percentage of total cost less land. A limited-distribution sponsor under 221(d)(3) is permitted 10% of total cost less land, but a nonprofit sponsor only 7%. In addition, the builder in all sections is permitted an off-site overhead allowance averaging about 2% of construction costs. The builders or builders and sponsors allowance is the only cost that does not have to be certified as actually paid, but may be considered as a part of the owner's equity. That is, if the mortgage is for 90% of total cost, the owner can use this fee as part of his required cash investment. Since he does not receive the fee in cash, he is not subject to a tax at that time.

All other costs must be certified as actually paid. The penalties under these programs for borrowing more FHA-insured money than is actually spent are quite severe and subject the offender to criminal prosecution. This concern for formal cost certification came to a head because of several scandals soon after World War II under Sections 608 and 908, when many builders were able to obtain mortgage funds well in excess of 100% of cost. During the period 1942–52, after which time these sections were repealed, Section 608 was by far the most popular program, resulting in construction of 465,474 units.

An FHA-insured mortgage requires that existing labor standards and prevailing wages be paid for all construction workers. In effect, this limits construction to union employees.

FHA uses several methods for determining the maximum amount of the mortgage that can be given under any section. It is always the test that provides the lowest mortgage that is applicable. The first is the per-unit allowance, depending upon the size of the unit. In the past, projects were determined by per-room allowances, but it was felt that per-unit allowances permitted greater flexibility of design. The current per-unit schedule is as shown in the accompanying table. These figures

	Walk-Up or Garden Structure	
	Secs. 207, 213, 220	Secs. 221(d)(3) and (d)(4)
Without a bedroom	$ 9,000	$ 8,000
One bedroom	12,500	11,250
Two bedroom	15,000	13,500
Three bedroom	18,500	17,000
Four bedroom	21,000	19,250
	Elevator-Type Structures	
Without a bedroom	$10,500	$ 9,500
One bedroom	15,000	13,500
Two bedroom	18,000	16,000
Three bedroom	22,500	20,000
Four bedroom	25,500	22,750

may be increased up to 45% at the discretion of the FHA administrator where local cost levels require. Allowances in Boston, as an example, qualify for a 45% increase.

In addition, no mortgage can exceed 90% of FHA's estimated property replacement cost, except a nonprofit 213 project, which may receive 97%, and a nonprofit 221(d)(3), which may receive 100%. Section 207 and Section 221(d)(3) restrict the debt service to 90% of net income in the case of 207 and 95% in the case of 221(d)(3). Net income is defined as gross income less operating expenses, but before financing charges.

To apply for a mortgage, several steps must be followed. The first is the preapplication procedure for the purpose of determining basic site and market feasibility. It consists of a preliminary meeting between the local FHA and the proposed sponsor. If the FHA feels the project is feasible, it will then send a letter to the proposed sponsor inviting the submission of a more detailed application on Form 2013 (see Exhibit 3). In the case of a 221(d)(3) application, the sponsor must also apply for and receive a reservation of mortgage funds from FNMA.

The 2013 form must be accompanied by an examination fee of 0.15% of the mortgage amount. It provides for a more detailed project analysis, including preliminary architectural drawings and rough construction estimates. If this form is accepted, the sponsor develops his architectural drawings to a more complete stage, the working drawing stage, and hires an FHA-approved professional estimator to do a detailed construction estimate. Also at this stage, land value is determined by FHA. This evaluation is most important to the sponsor. If he has held the land for a long time or if he has changed the use of the land through rezoning, there is a chance for a markup in the value of the land over what the developer has paid for it. On the opposite side, the FHA has certain maximum values it will pay for land under different sections. Under a low-rent section, such as 221(d)(3), a value of up to $1,200 per dwelling unit may be permitted, but in Section 220, $2,500 per unit may be allowed. The value is also affected by the cost of site improvements, which are part of the cost to prepare the land for building. As an example, unfavorable soil conditions resulting in extra foundation costs will lower land value. Lastly, because of much recent criticism, the FHA is quite reluctant, without special cause, to allow a land value that is very different from any recent arm's-length sales price for the parcel.

After this stage is completed, the sponsor goes to final or commitment drawings, which are submitted with the remainder of the 0.3% examination fee, and upon approval, the mortgage is ready for initial closing.

Certain offices of the FHA, including the Boston office, have been selected to participate on an experimental basis in a special program to reduce the processing time for 221(d)(3) application.

During this entire period, the proposed sponsor is expected to make arrangements for private lenders to provide him with permanent mortgage money, except in the case of Section 221(d)(3) and with interim or construction financing in all cases. Although the interest rate of the mortgage may be fixed at 7½%, if money-market conditions are such that a private lender demands either a higher or lower interest rate than 7½%, the lender may either require a discount to be paid to him to increase his yield, or the borrower may negotiate a bonus to decrease the yield. FHA recognizes this problem and, partially to assist the owner, allows as a mortgage expense up to a 1½% financing fee. On a mortgage taken by FNMA, there is an additional fee of 1%. FNMA stabilizes the market somewhat through purchase or sales of mortgages, but the effect of this is limited by the amount of funds Congress has appropriated to it, and even more so by the rates of return private lenders can receive in other investments. Therefore, by maintaining the 5¼% interest rate on Section 207 housing during the tight-money period of 1966, the FHA in effect stopped housing from being built under this program, since the lenders were demanding a discount far in excess of the FHA allowance.

At the initial closing, the sponsor is entitled to draw the mortgage funds for many of the expenses which he incurred prior to closing, such as 75% of the total architectural and engineering fees, all legal and organizational fees, and financing expenses. These payments often enable the sponsor to recoup most of the out-of-pocket expenses he has already incurred. Under Section 207, he must wait until the end of the project for compensation for his land, but under the others he is entitled to be paid for his land at initial closing.

At initial closing, the sponsor must also put up a 2% working capital deposit, in cash, government bonds, or other acceptable security. This deposit is not, except in a nonprofit 221(d)(3), included as a part of the mortgage. This money may be drawn upon for renting expenses, or for operating losses after the project has been initially opened. The FHA is also starting in some cases to require additional escrow funds in cases where it believes that the property may take longer to rent and will suffer greater losses in the start-up period. The FHA understands, especially in urban renewal areas, that this may be the case and oftentimes permits a mortgagee, if he so desires, to defer mortgage amortization and interest charges until the property is able to pay these expenses.

Before the permanent mortgage is finally closed, the sponsor must prove that, excluding his builder's-sponsor's allowance, he has invested in the project at least 3% of the mortgage amount in cash, aside from the 2% working capital reserve. If he does not, he must place this money in escrow for a period of at least three years to provide funds for possible operating losses. If not used at the end of this time, the money is then returned to the sponsor. Since the three years starts upon final closing of the mortgage, which could take place a year after the project is initially open for occupancy, the investment period could actually run four years.

When the project is complete, the FHA still maintains several operating controls over the project. Rents cannot be increased over the originally authorized maximum gross level without FHA approval, which is granted if operating costs increase and if the FHA feels that the rental increase can be absorbed by the market. Management fees are subject to FHA control. A 7% vacancy allowance is permitted irrespective of the actual experience. There are semiannual physical inspection reports of the property, and the property owner must comply with the recommendations made in this report. Replacement reserve funds are deposited monthly with the FHA and may be used for capital improvements only if the particular expenditure is approved by the FHA. If the project is sold, the remaining amount in the fund must be transferred to the new owner. The mortgage itself can be paid off in full in the first five years with a maximum 2% prepayment penalty and thereafter with a 1% penalty, except in a 221(d)(3) loan, which cannot be repaid for 20 years to insure that the housing at these low rentals is actually made available.

Distributions to the owner may be made no more frequently than quarterly and only out of surplus cash which is defined as after-tax income plus depreciation less mortgage amortization and replacement reserve payments.

Annual reports are also made to the FHA, based on a standard bookkeeping system of FHA accounts. The owner must also agree not to rent space in the property for shorter than monthly periods, so that the premises may not be used for transient purposes. There can be no discrimination of tenancy based upon race, color, creed, or national origin. FHA also must approve all transfers of the property or changes of control of the owning entity. This approval, although normally not difficult to obtain, will delay a sale for from six weeks to four months, while the FHA investigates the new sponsor and approves all the papers of the new entity.

SUMMARY

The utilization of FHA-insured financing involves a considerable amount of delays, red tape, and additional operational controls. Although part of HUD, the FHA has been criticized for acting independently, often more like a conservative banker than an agency designed to encourage housing development. This stems largely from its reluctance to change its approach from that prevailing when its only responsibility was middle-income housing. Officials of the FHA have been very proud of making a financial profit each year. Some disadvantages are additional costs, including FHA fees of 1.3%, the necessity of using union construction, an annual mortgage insurance fee of 0.5%, the necessity of establishing a cost replacement reserve, the difficulty of raising rents and increasing profits, the relative difficulty of transfer of property, and the necessity of conforming construction design to existing FHA standards and loan limits. FHA itself is aware of these limitations and is investigating means of streamlining its procedures.

On the other hand, there are many advantages arising out of the FHA process. There is the high leverage achieved by the high ratio of mortgage to cost, normally at least 90%. The owner's equity can be reduced even below 10% through utilization of the noncash allowance, such as the builder's-sponsor's fee or a markup in land valuation. Because of this leverage, the return on investment is often quite high. The length of the mortgage, up to 40 years, permits, compared to most conventional mortgages, lower debt service requirements, lower rents to the tenant, and higher cash returns to the sponsor, even with the higher project costs involved and the one half of 1% annual mortgage insurance premium. Also, the long amortization period with lower annual amortization payments results in a larger cash tax shelter, given the sure depreciation allowances. In fact, the prime stimulus at this time to the construction of many large urban renewal projects is the large noncash operating losses being sustained because of the accelerated depreciation permitted by Internal Revenue. The government agency guarantee of the loan has broadened the mortgage market both from the number of lenders and the area in which they are willing to operate. This leads to a lower interest rate to the borrower and in the approval of many projects that might otherwise be rejected. FNMA's operations both exercise a stabilizing effect in the existing market and provide below market rate funds for projects built under Section 221(d)(3), and subsidize interest rates under Section 236. There is also no personal liability under the mortgage for the borrower.

The desirability of the program is evident, since about 1.2 million multifamily units have been constructed under the various sections of this program, almost 15% of all multifamily units constructed since the war. What is most important to the potential developer is that the FHA has given an institutional quality to what must be considered speculative building. From the public policy standpoint, even if the individual developer, because of his low equity, should fail, more housing will have been added to the national supply.

What the individual developer must not forget, however, is that FHA-insured or not, the value of the property as an investment will eventually be determined by its cash flow. Merely because FHA permits a certain level of rents does not mean that tenants will lease the apartments at that rental level. If a project is not well conceived or well timed, the leverage that can work to an investor's advantage can work equally to his disadvantage. FHA requires a certain specialized expertise but still requires the same skills in site evaluation, good project planning and designing, construction, and rental and management that maximize profits in any real estate project.

EXHIBIT 1. Federal Housing Administration Statistics

	Sec. 207 Middle- and Upper-Income Housing	Sec. 213 Lower- and Middle-Income Cooperative Housing	Sec. 220 Middle- and Upper-Middle-Income Housing in Urban Renewal Area	Sec. 221(d)(3) Lower-Middle-Income Subsidized Housing (Note 1)	Sec. 221(c)(4) Middle-Income Housing	Sec. 236 Low-Income Housing (Note 1)
Minimum number units (note 2)	8	5	2	5	5	5
Maximum private mortgage	$20,000,000	$20,000,000	$20,000,000	$12,500,000	$12,500,000	$12,500,000
Maximum mortgage allowance, Lowest of:						
(1) Replacement cost (note 3)	90%	Profit, 90% Nonprofit, 97%	90%	Limited dividend, 90% Nonprofit, 100%	90%	Limited Dividend, 90% Nonprofit, 100%
(2) Annual mortgage cost as % of net income	90%					
(3) per unit allowance	(note 4)	(note 4)	(note 4)	(note 4)	90% (note 4)	(note 4)
Maximum mortgage maturity (note 5)	40 yrs.	40 yrs.	40 yrs.	40 yrs.	40 yrs.	40 yrs.
Current maximum interest rate (note 6)	6%	6%	6%	3%	6%	1% to 3%
FHA mortgage insurance premium	0.5%	0.5%	0.5%	—	0.5%	—
Builders and Sponsors risk allowance						
As % of construction cost	.5% to 10%					
As % of total cost—less land (private)	—	10%	10%	10%	10%	10%
As % of total cost—less land (nonprofit)	—	—	—	7%	—	—
Total Insured Units to January 31, 1967	230,567	113,281	—	52,698	17,488	—

Note 1. There are maximum limits on the income of tenants eligible for this program.
Note 2. Detached, semidetached, row, or multifamily high-rise structures permitted.
Note 3. Exterior land improvements, construction costs for buildings, garages, and accessory commercial space, architectural and engineering fees. Two percent builder's general overhead interest during construction, real estate taxes, insurance, FHA fees of 1.3% financing allowance of 1.5% title and recording, legal and organization of 0.5% builder's and sponsor's fee, and land cost are included in computing replacement cost. Section 220 may also include nonaccessory commercial space if part of urban renewal plan.
Note 4. All per-unit allowances subject to 45% increase if in high-cost area.

	Sections 207, 213, 220		Sections 221(d)(3) or (d)(4)	
	Walk-Up	Elevator	Walk-Up	Elevator
Without a bedroom	$ 9,000	$10,500	$ 8,000	$ 9,500
One bedroom	12,500	15,000	11,250	13,500
Two bedroom	15,000	15,000	13,500	16,000
Three bedroom	18,500	22,500	17,000	20,000
Four bedroom	21,000	25,500	19,250	22,750

Note 5. In all new construction, except under Section 220, and in all cases of rehabilitation, the mortgage may not exceed 75% of the remaining economic life of the property.
Note 6. Except in the case of the FHA 221(d)(3) and 236 mortgages, a higher allowable interest rate may be an advantage to the developer, because the actual interest rate is determined by the money market, and a mortgage with a 5½% rate will require the borrower to pay a large discount, only 1½% of which is financed under the insured mortgage. If the rate is below 5½%, the borrower may receive a bonus from the lender.

EXHIBIT 2

Federal Housing Administration

No. in Family	No. of Bedrooms	Maximum Monthly Housing Expense	Maximum Annual Income
1................Efficiency		$ 95.84	$ 5,750
2................	1	115.83	6,950
3 and 4..........	2	136.67	8,200
5 and 6..........	3	157.50	9,450
7 or more........	4	177.50	10,650

Note: Maximum housing expense represents monthly rental with all utilities provided. Single-person occupancy permitted only for elderly (i.e., over 62 years old) and for physically handicapped.

EXHIBIT 3
Federal Housing Administration

FHA FORM NO. 2013 Rev. 10/68	U. S. DEPARTMENT OF HOUSING AND URBAN DEVELOPMENT FEDERAL HOUSING ADMINISTRATION **APPLICATION - PROJECT MORTGAGE INSURANCE**	Form Approved Budget Bureau No. 63-R0676

Project Name _____ Project No. _____

TO: _____ and the FEDERAL HOUSING COMMISSIONER.

The undersigned hereby requests a loan in the principal amount of $_____ to be insured under the provisions of Section _____ of the National Housing Act, said loan to be secured by a first mortgage on the property hereinafter described.

Insurance of advances during construction ☐ is, ☐ is not desired. ☐ Feasibility ☐ Conditional ☐ Firm
Type of Mortgagor: ☐ PM ☐ LD ☐ B-S ☐ NP ☐ COOP. Permanent Mortgage Interest Rate _____ %.

A. LOCATION AND DESCRIPTION OF PROPERTY:

1. Street Nos.	2. Street	3. Municipality	4. County	5. State

6. Type of Project ☐ Elevator ☐ Walkup	7. No. Stories	8. Check Applicable Box(es) ☐ Row ☐ Detached ☐ Semi-detached	9. Est. Ave. Monthly Rental per Unit $_____ Mo.

10. ☐ Proposed ☐ Existing	11. No. Units	12. No. Bldgs.	13. List Accessory Buildings or Space:

SITE INFORMATION		BUILDING INFORMATION	
14. Dimensions _____ ft. by _____ ft., or _____ sq. ft.		16. Structural System	16a. Yr. Built
15. Zoning (If recently changed, submit evidence)		17. Exterior Finish	18. Heating & AC System

B. INFORMATION CONCERNING LAND OR PROPERTY:

19. Date Acquired	20. Purchase Price	21. Additional Costs Paid or Accrued	22. If Leasehold Annual Ground Rent	23. TOTAL COST	24. Relationship-Business, Personal or Other Between Seller & Sponsor
	$	$	$	$	

25. Utilities—	Public	Community	26. Unusual Site Features—		
Water	☐	☐	☐ Cuts ☐ Fills	☐ Rock Formations	☐ Erosion
Sewers	☐	☐	☐ Poor Drainage	☐ High Water Table	☐ Retaining Walls
			☐ Other (Specify) _____		☐ None

C. ESTIMATE OF INCOME:

27. No. of Each Family Type Unit	Living Area (Sq. Ft.)	Composition of Units	Unit Rent Per Month	Total Monthly Rent For Unit Type
			$	$

28. TOTAL ESTIMATED RENTALS FOR ALL FAMILY UNITS $_____

29. No. Parking Spaces—	
☐ Attended	Open Spaces _____ @ $_____ per month
☐ Self Park	Covered Spaces _____ @ $_____ per month

30. Commercial
Area-Ground Level _____ Sq. Ft. @ $_____ per sq. ft./mo.
Other Levels _____ Sq. Ft. @ $_____ per sq. ft./mo.

31. TOTAL ESTIMATED GROSS PROJECT INCOME AT 100% OCCUPANCY $_____

32. TOTAL ANNUAL RENT (Item 31 x 12 months) $_____

33. Gross Floor Area— _____ Sq. Ft.	34. Net Rentable Residential Area— _____ Sq. Ft.	35. Net Rentable Commercial Area— _____ Sq. Ft.

36. NON-REVENUE PRODUCING SPACE

Type of Employee	No. Rms.	Composition of Unit	Location of Unit in Project

D. EQUIPMENT AND SERVICES INCLUDED IN RENT: (Check appropriate items)

37. EQUIPMENT—		38. SERVICES—	FOR FHA USE ONLY
☐ Ranges (Gas or Elec.)	☐ Kitchen Exhaust Fan ☐ Laundry Facilities	☐ Gas ☐ Electricity	Date Rec.
☐ Refrigerators (Gas or Elec.)	☐ Disposal ☐ Dishwasher	☐ Heat ☐ Air Conditioning	Amount / Code
☐ Other (Specify)	☐ Drapes ☐ Carpet	☐ Other (Specify)	Schedule / Rec. By

EXHIBIT 3 (Continued)

- 2 -

E. ESTIMATE OF ANNUAL EXPENSE:	G. ESTIMATED REPLACEMENT COST:

E. ESTIMATE OF ANNUAL EXPENSE:

ADMINISTRATIVE—
▲ 1. Advertising - - - - - - - - - - - - $ _____
▲ 2. Management - - - - - - - - - - - - _____
▲ 3. Other - - - - - - - - - - - - - - - _____
▲ 4.   TOTAL ADMINISTRATIVE - - $ _____
OPERATING—
▲ 5. Elevator Main. Exp. - - - - - - $ _____
▲ 6. Fuel (Heating and
        Domestic Hot Water)- - - - _____
▲ 7. Lighting & Misc. Power - - - - _____
▲ 8. Water - - - - - - - - - - - - - - - _____
▲ 9. Gas - - - - - - - - - - - - - - - - _____
▲10. Garb. & Trash Removal - - - - - _____
▲11. Payroll - - - - - - - - - - - - - - - _____
▲12. Other - - - - - - - - - - - - - - - _____
▲13.   TOTAL OPERATING - - - - - - $ _____
MAINTENANCE—
▲14. Decorating - - - - - - - - - - - - $ _____
▲15. Repairs - - - - - - - - - - - - - - _____
▲16. Exterminating - - - - - - - - - - - _____
▲17. Insurance - - - - - - - - - - - - - _____
▲18. Ground Expense - - - - - - - - - _____
▲19. Other - - - - - - - - - - - - - - - _____
▲20   TOTAL MAINTENANCE - - - - $ _____
▲21. Replacement Reserve (.0050 x total for all
        improvements Line 50) - - - - - - - - - - - - - $ _____
22.   TOTAL EXPENSE - - - - - $ _____
TAXES—
▲23. Real Estate: Est. Assessed
        Val. $ _____ @
        $ _____ per $1000— $ _____
▲24. Personal Prop. Est. Assessed
        Val. $ _____ @
        $ _____ per $1000— _____
▲25. Empl. Payroll Tax - - - - - - - - _____
▲26. Empl. Social Security - - - - - - _____
▲27. Other - - - - - - - - - - - - - - - _____
28.   TOTAL TAXES - - - - - - - - - $ _____
29. TOTAL EXPENSE & TAXES - - - - - - - - - - - $ _____

F. INCOME COMPUTATIONS:

30. Estimated Project
        Gross Income (Line C32 Page 1) - - - - - - - $ _____
31. Occupancy (Entire Project)
        Percentage - _____ %
32. Effective Gross Income (Line 30 x 31) - - - - - - $ _____
33. Total Project Expenses (Line 29) - - - - - - - - - $ _____
34. Net Income to Project (Line 32 – Line 33) - - - $ _____
35. Expense Ratio (Line 29 ÷ Line 32) - - - - - - - - _____ %

G. ESTIMATED REPLACEMENT COST:

▲ 36a. Unusual Land Improvements - - - $ _____
▲ 36b. Other Land Improvements - - - - $ _____
▲ 36c. Total Land Improvements - - - - - - - - - - $ _____
        STRUCTURES—
▲ 37. Main Buildings - - - - - - - - - - $ _____
▲ 38. Accessory Buildings _____
▲ 39. Garage - - - - - - - - - - - - - - - _____
▲ 40. All other Buildings - - - - - - - - _____
▲ 41.   TOTAL STRUCTURES - - - - - - - - $ _____
▲ 42. General Requirements - - - - - - - - - - - - - - $ _____
        FEES—
▲ 43. Builder's Gen. Overhead
        _____ % - - - - - - - - - - - - - $ _____
▲ 44. Builder's Profit
        _____ % - - - - - - - - - - - - - _____
▲ 45. Arch. Fee-Design
        _____ % _____
▲ 46. Arch. Fee-Supvr.
        _____ % _____
▲ 47. Bond Premium - - - - - - - - - - - _____
▲ 48. Other Fees - - - - - - - - - - - - - _____
▲ 49.   TOTAL FEES - - - - - - - - - - - $ _____
50. TOT. for all Imprmts. (Lines 36c, 41, 42 & 49) $ _____
51. Cost Per Gross Sq. Ft. - - - - - - - - - - - - - - $ _____
52. Estimated Construction Time - - - - - - - - - - - _____ Months
        CARRYING CHARGES & FINANCING—
▲ 53. Int. _____ Mos. $ _____ %
        on $ _____ - - $ _____
▲ 54. Taxes - - - - - - - - - - - - - - - _____
▲ 55. Insurance - - - - - - - - - - - - - _____
▲ 56. FHA Mtg. Ins. Pre. (0.5%) _____
▲ 57. FHA Exam. Fee (0.3%) _____
▲ 58. FHA Inspec. Fee (0.5%) _____
▲ 59. Financing Fee (%) _____
▲ 60. AMPO (%) _____
▲ 61. FNMA Fee (%) _____
▲ 62. Title & Recording - - - - - - - _____
63. TOTAL CARRYING CHGS. & FINANCING - - $ _____
        LEGAL AND ORGANIZATION—
▲ 64. Legal - - - - - - - - - - - - - $ _____
▲ 65. Organization - - - - - - - - - - _____
66.   TOTAL LEGAL AND ORGANIZATION - - - - - $ _____
▲ 67. Consultant Fee - - - - - - - - - - - - - - - - - - $ _____
68. Builder and Sponsor Profit & Risk - - - - - - - - $ _____
69.   TOTAL EST. DEVELOPMENT COST (Excl. of
        Land or Off-site Cost)(Line 50+63+66+67+68) $ _____
70. LAND (Est. Market Price of Site)
        _____ sq. ft. ÷ $ _____ per sq. ft. $ _____
71. TOTAL ESTIMATED REPLACEMENT
        COST OF PROJECT (Add 69 + 70) - - - - - $ _____

H. TOTAL REQUIREMENTS FOR SETTLEMENT:

72. DEVELOPMENT COSTS (Line 69) - - - - - - - - - $ _____
73. LAND INDEBTEDNESS (or Cash required
        for land acquisition) - - - - - - - - - - - - - - - - $ _____
74. SUBTOTAL (Line 72 + 73) - - - - - - - - - - - - - $ _____
75. Mortgage Amount - - - - - - - - - - $ _____
76. Fees Paid by Other Than Cash - $ _____
77. Line 75 + Line 76 - - - - - - - - - - - - - - - - - - $ _____
78. CASH INVESTMENT REQUIRED (Line 74 – 77)- $ _____
79. INITIAL OPERATING DEFICIT - - - - - - - - - - - $ _____
80. ANTICIPATED DISCOUNT - - - - - - - - - - - - - $ _____
81. Working Cap. (2% of Mtge. Amount) - - - - - - - $ _____
82. ADD Off-site Construction Costs - - - - - - - - $ _____
83. TOTAL ESTIMATED CASH REQUIREMENT
        (Lines 78 + 79 + 80 + 81 + 82) - - - - - - - - - $ _____

Source of Cash to meet Requirements:	Amount
	$
	$
	$
	$
	$
TOTAL	$

I. ATTACHMENTS: (Required Exhibits)

1.	Location Map	7.	Personal Financial & Credit Statement of Sponsors
2.	Evidence of Site Control (Option or Purchase) and Legal Description of Property	8.	Form 2530 Previous Participation Certification
		9. ▲	Architectural Exhibits - Preliminary
3.	Form 2010 Equal Employment Opportunity Certification	10. ▲	Architectural Exhibits - Final
4.	Form 3433 Eligibility as Non-Profit Corporation	11. ▲	Survey
5.	Evidence of Last Arms-Length Transaction Price	12. ▲	Evidence of Architect E & O Insurance Coverage
6.	Sketch Plan of Site	13. ▲	Copy of Owner Architect Agreement

EXHIBIT 3 *(Continued)*

- 3 -

J. NAMES, ADDRESSES AND TELEPHONE NUMBERS OF THE FOLLOWING:

1. Sponsor(s)

2. General Contractor

3. Architect

4. Sponsor's Attorney

K. CERTIFICATION:

The undersigned, as the principal sponsor of the proposed mortgagor, certifies that he is familiar with the provisions of the Regulations of the Federal Housing Commissioner under the above identified Section of the National Housing Act and that to the best of his knowledge and belief the mortgagor has complied, or will be able to comply, with all of the requirements thereof which are prerequisite to insurance of the mortgage under such Section.

The undersigned further certifies that to the best of his knowledge and belief no information or data contained herein or in the exhibits or attachments listed herein are in any way false or incorrect and that they are truly descriptive of the project or property which is intended as the security for the proposed mortgage and that the proposed construction will not violate zoning ordinances or restrictions of record.

The undersigned agrees with the Federal Housing Administration that pursuant to the requirements of the FHA Regulations, (a) neither he nor anyone authorized to act for him will decline to sell, rent or otherwise make available any of the property or housing in the multifamily project to a prospective purchaser or tenant because of his race, color, religion or national origin; (b) he will comply with state and local laws and ordinances prohibiting discrimination; and (c) his failure or refusal to comply with the requirements of either (a) or (b) shall be a proper basis for the Commissioner to reject requests for future business with which the sponsor is identified or to take any other corrective action he may deem necessary.

Signed _____

(Sponsor)

Date _____

REQUEST FOR CONDITIONAL COMMITMENT

TO: FEDERAL HOUSING COMMISSIONER:

Pursuant to the provisions of the Section of the National Housing Act identified in the foregoing application and FHA Regulations applicable thereto, request is hereby made for the issuance of a conditional commitment to insure a mortgage covering the property described above.

After examination of the application and the proposed security, the undersigned considers the project to be desirable and is interested, subject to the issuance of a firm commitment by FHA, in making a loan in the principal amount of $_____, which will bear interest at _____%, will require repayment of principal over a period of _____ months according to an amortization plan to be agreed upon.

Insurance of advances during construction ☐ is, ☐ is not desired.

It is understood that the financing expense in the amount of $_____ is subject to adjustment so that the total will not exceed ____ % of the amount of your commitment.

Herewith is check for $_____, which is in payment of the application fee required by said FHA Regulations.

Signed _____

(Proposed Mortgagee)

_____

(Address of Mortgagee)

REQUEST FOR FIRM COMMITMENT

TO: FEDERAL HOUSING COMMISSIONER:

Pursuant to the provisions of the Section of the National Housing Act identified in the foregoing application and FHA Regulations applicable thereto, request is hereby made for the issuance of a firm commitment to insure a mortgage covering the property described above.

After examination of the application and the proposed security, the undersigned considers the project to be desirable and is interested in making a loan in the principal amount of $_____, which will bear interest at _____%, will require repayment of principal over a period of _____ months according to amortization plan to be agreed upon.

Insurance of advances during construction ☐ is, ☐ is not desired.

It is understood that the financing expense in the amount of $_____ is subject to adjustment so that the total will not exceed _____ % of the amount of your commitment.

Herewith is check for $_____, which is in payment of the application and/or commitment fee required by said FHA Regulations.

Signed _____

(Proposed Mortgagee)

_____

(Address of Mortgagee)

EXHIBIT 3 (*Concluded*)

U. S. DEPARTMENT OF HOUSING AND URBAN DEVELOPMENT
FEDERAL HOUSING ADMINISTRATION

INSTRUCTIONS FOR COMPLETION OF FHA FORM NO. 2013-APPLICATION - PROJECT MORTGAGE INSURANCE

FORWORD TO INSTRUCTIONS- FHA procedures divide the process of filing an application for project insurance into a maximum of three stages, the first being a request for feasibility analysis, the second being a request through an approved mortgagee for a conditional commitment, and the third being a formal application through an approved mortgagee for a firm commitment.

Processing flexibility is emphasized under the accelerated multifamily procedures. This will enable a sponsor to by-pass feasibility stage or conditional commitment stage, or both, provided he has plans and exhibits in a sufficient detail to permit processing for a firm commitment.

FHA field office personnel will provide advice and assistance to sponsors and potential sponsors at all stages in connection with the submission of applications.

INSTRUCTIONS

A request for feasibility analysis may be submitted directly to the FHA insuring office by letter or in person. All items except those identified by ▲ on Form 2013 must be completed.

A request for a conditional commitment must be submitted by an approved mortgagee on Form 2013 with all items except those identified by ▲ completed and with the sponsor's certification and mortgagee's request executed. All information must be submitted in triplicate. Preliminary architectural exhibits must accompany this application, and architect must be identified.

A request for a Firm Commitment must be submitted by an approved mortgagee on Form 2013 complete in its entirety. All information must be submitted in triplicate.

Section A. Self-explanatory.

Section B. In line 21 insert any cost paid, or contracted, in addition to the stipulated purchase price.

If the site will require demolition expense, or other preparatory expense, this should be indicated and explained on an attached sheet If the proposed site is leased, indicate the annual dollar amount of the ground rental. All other items in this section are self-explanatory.

Section C. Item 27-Area Sq. Ft. is within interior walls of unit.

Feasibility:
Line 33: Insert the estimated gross floor area which is the sum of all floor areas of headroom height within the exterior walls.

Request for Conditional or Firm Commitment:
Line 33: Insert the gross floor area, computed from the plans.

At Feasibility:
Line 34&35: Insert the estimated net rentable area. Existing comparable structures should be used as a guide in making this estimate.

Request for Conditional or Firm Commitment:
Line 34&35: Compute the net rentable area from the plans. Net rentable area is the area within the inside finish of permanent outer walls of the structure measured to the apartment side of corridors or other permanent partitions or both, and to the center of partitions separating the premises from adjoining rentable areas.

Section D. Self-explanatory.

Section E. Self-explanatory.

Section F. Line 31 - Occupancy percentage is estimated from market experience if data are available;otherwise sponsor's best estimate.

Section G. Line 36a - Enter cost for unusual site preparation such as piling, retaining walls, fill, etc.

Line 36b: Enter cost of other land improvements such as on-site utilities, landscape work, walks and drives.

Line 42: See Uniform System for Construction Specifications, Data Filing and Cost Accounting Pages 1.3 and 1.4.

Line 51 - Enter the estimated cost per gross square foot of building area. (Line 50 ÷ Line C33 Page 1).

Carrying Charges and Financing:
Line 53: Interest is the amount estimated to accrue during the anticipated period of construction. It is computed on one-half of the loan amount.

Line 54: Taxes which accrue during the construction period are estimated on a pro rata basis for the construction period. Special assessments, if any, should be estimated on a similar basis and included in the tax amount.

Line 55: Insurance includes fire, windstorm, extended coverage, liability, and other risks customarily insured against in the community. It does not include workman's compensation, public liability insurance, and architects E&O insurance, which are included in the cost estimate.

Line 56: FHA mortgage insurance premium is the amount to be earned during the estimated construction period. The amount should be computed on the requested loan amount on a yearly basis. If the estimated construction period exceeds one year, the premium will be based on a two-year period. (Fee waived for 221(d)(3) below market interest rate projects).

Line 57: FHA examination fee is computed on the requested loan amount.

Line 58: FHA inspection fee is computed on the requested loan amount when the project involves new construction, and on the estimated cost of rehabilitation when the project involves the rehabilitation of an existing structure.

Line 59: Financing fee is computed at 2% on the loan amount. It is an initial service-charge. This is not to be confused with discounts.

Line 60: A.M.P.O. is an allowance to make the project operational, computed at 2% of the maximum insurable mortgage amount. This is allowable in cases involving non-profit mortgagors, (this does not include cooperative mortgagors).

Line 61: FNMA Fee: The local insuring office personnel will advise interested sponsors of the current maximum rate for, and applicablity of, this expense.

Line 62: Title and Recording Expense: This is the cost typically incurred by a mortgagor, in connection with a mortgage transaction. This cost generally includes such items as recording fees, mortgage and stamp taxes, cost of survey and title insurance including all title work involved between initial and final endorsement.

Line 64 & 65: Legal and Organizational Expense: Estimate will be based upon the typical cost usually incurred for these services in the area where the project is to be located. These items should be recorded separately.

Line 67: Consultant fee, if any, enter amount to be charged the non-profit sponsor by qualified consultant.

Line 68: Builder's and sponsor's profit and risk allowance: This is based on total estimated cost of on-site utilities, landscape work, structures, general overhead expense, architect's fees, carrying charges, financing, and legal and organization expense. It is allowable only in 220, 221(d)(3) Limited Dividend, 221(d)(4) and 231 Profit Motivated projects and in these projects it is in lieu of, and not in addition to, builder's profit.

Line 70: Land: Enter purchase price if purchased from local public authority; otherwise, sponsor's estimate of value in.finished condition (including off-sites, cuts, fills, drainage, etc.).

Section H. Requirements for Settlement:
Line 72 - Self-explanatory.

Line 73 - Reflect amount required to clear title to site. If land is to be acquired, the unpaid balance of the purchase price shall be entered. If leasehold or if land is owned free and clear of encumbrances, enter "None." Indebtedness against land should be supported by options, purchase agreements, etc.

Line 74 - Enter the sum of "Development Cost" and "Land Indebtedness."

Line 75 - Enter principal amount of mortgage requested.

Line 76 - Enter any portion of the Builder's Profit, Builder's and Sponsor's Profit and Risk Allowance or that portion of the Design Architect's Fee to be paid by means other than cash, or waived.

Line 77 - Self-explanatory.

Line 78 - Self-explanatory.

Line 79 - Insert the amount required to meet operating and debt service expense from project completion, until such time as income is adequate to provide a self-sustaining operation.

Line 80 - Enter discount to be paid for placement of the permanent mortgage as well as any discount required by the construction lender.

Line 81 - Enter 2% of mortgage requested.

Line 82 - The cost of improvements outside property lines such as streets and utilities, which will not be installed at public or utility company expense should be entered here.

Section I. (Required Exhibits) All exhibits necessary for a particular stage of processing must accompany the application, see first three paragraphs under "INSTRUCTIONS" above.

Section J. Self-explanatory.

Section K. Self-explanatory.

FHA FORM NO. 2013
Rev. 10/68

A DECENT HOME*
SECTION II; FEDERAL
HOUSING PROGRAMS

PART TWO: HISTORY, DESCRIPTION, AND COMPARISON

Since 1934 the United States has established an array of housing programs of bewildering complexity. Some of these have been successful in meeting the problems they were supposed to solve. Others have had mixed success, have generated undesirable side effects, or have simply failed. Still others are very new and have yet to prove what they will do. One advantage of the multiplicity of housing programs is that a variety of approaches have been tried, providing a body of experience with different techniques.

Housing programs have been enacted for a variety of purposes—to create jobs, to clear slums, to improve the tax base of central cities, and to help the poor. Some of these purposes, if pursued too single-mindedly, are contradictory. For instance, indiscriminate slum clearance may severely hurt poor families by restricting the supply of low-cost housing. In addition, housing programs may not be a particularly effective means for achieving some of the goals at which they have been aimed. During the 1930's, most housing programs were passed in large part to create jobs. Today, with our greatly increased understanding of economic problems, job creation is handled primarily through national policy.

Just as the purposes of housing programs have changed in the last one-third of the century, so have there been enormous changes in urban conditions. Our perceptions both of acceptable housing and of poverty are now very different from what they were; expectations have risen. The characteristics of the urban poor have changed and the absolute gap between the hard-core poor and the great majority increases steadily.

We believe that the primary purpose of housing programs should be to meet the housing needs of today's urban poor. By this standard, the existing arsenal of Federal housing programs, while greatly improved during the last decade, still shows serious deficiencies.

---

* Excerpt from A Decent Home (Report of the President's Committee on Urban Housing [Washington, D.C., U.S. Government Printing Office, 1968]).

Inadequate Volume.   First, the programs have simply not produced an adequate number of dwellings. There are approximately 7.8 million households unable "to afford" decent housing, even after giving account to existing subsidized units. About 800,000 such units have been built in the entire history of Federal activity in the field. In other words, after more than one-third of a century, Federal efforts have met only one-tenth of the nation's subsidized housing need.

Not Primarily for the Poor.   Furthermore, as previously mentioned, the basic purpose of many existing housing programs has not been to provide housing for the poor. In the 1930's, construction of public housing was proposed largely to create jobs. FHA was established in part to start money moving again during the Depression years, and again largely to create jobs. In their earlier years, slum clearance was the stated goal of the Public Housing and Urban Renewal programs, even though this may sometimes have resulted in an overall reduction in the supply of low-cost housing. The most successful housing programs were not aimed at the poor at all, but rather were designed to help the middle class obtain mortgage financing. The nation has been slow to recognize unequivocally the necessity for subsidy if the poor are to be adequately housed.

Even programs whose announced purpose is to provide housing for the poor do not reach as far down as their originators intended. The subsidies provided under even the Public Housing and Rent Supplement programs are not sufficient to allow the very poorest families to live in such housing. Housing subsidy programs have tended (at least until recently) to be narrow and particularized, thus segregating different population groups. Many of the earlier programs have had adverse social consequences not anticipated by their founders.

Belated Recognition of the Role for Business.   The nation has been slow to realize that private industry in many cases is an efficient vehicle for achieving social goals. The Federal housing subsidy programs of the 1930's assumed that the initiation and ownership of subsidized housing were the direct and full responsibilities of government. In 1959 Federally subsidized housing programs first provided a small role to the private sector, but then only to nonprofit groups. Not until 1961 did subsidy programs permit participation by profit-motivated entrepreneurs. Since then reliance on the private sector has expanded rapidly. More opportunities have been provided for private ownership of subsidized units, private development or management of publicly owned housing projects, and private financing of mortgages. Nevertheless, some programs still make too little use of the talents of private entrepreneurs. Others are shackled with restrictions and administrative hurdles that tend to discourage private interest.

One of the basic lessons of the history of Federal housing programs sccms to be that the programs which work best—such as the FHA mortgage insurance programs—are those that channel the forces of existing economic institutions into productive areas. This approach has proved to be better than wholly ignoring existing institutions and starting afresh outside the prevailing market system. Reliance on market forces should be increased in the future.

The history of Federal housing activity dates primarily from the 1930's; but there were forerunners during and after World War I and even as early as the 1890's. This history is briefly traced in Part I. The major housing subsidy programs—such as Public Housing, 221(d)(3), and others—are discussed only briefly. These programs are analyzed in detail after the historical overview.

I. A Brief History of Federal Housing Programs

Initial Efforts.   Congress directed its attention to housing problems as early as the 1890's when it held the first hearings on slums and blight. These hearings, and the writings of reformers like Jacob Riis, helped to create a national awareness of housing problems although no governmental programs resulted.

The Federal Government became active in the housing field during World War I for more immediate and practical reasons. The demands of war production created new concentrations of workers near major shipyards and munitions plants. In response, the Federal Government built close to 30,000 units, about half of them as dormitories. Most were completed after the armistice and all were eventually sold.

Considerable Congressional interest in housing sprang up following World War I. Bills were submitted, without success, to create a system of banks oriented to residential finance and to give special consideration to veterans. During the 1920's the Departments of Labor and Commerce both looked into housing questions. The U.S. Bureau of Standards produced a series of uniform codes dealing with building standards and zoning which became the foundation for much of the legislation enacted later at state and local levels. However, substantial Federal efforts to influence the production and financing of housing did not occur until the 1930's.

Home Finance.   In the early thirties, Congress and the Executive Branch found themselves faced with two overwhelming problems: (1) the collapse of mortgage credit and the system of home finance which had been in use; and (2) the need to generate jobs. The collapse of the savings and loan industry was dealt with first.

In 1931 the White House Conference on Home Building and Home-ownership convened by President Hoover directed its attention to the growing crisis in mortgage lending. Informed opinion was divided over whether Government action was necessary and, if it were, what form it should take. By the time the Home Loan Bank System was created in 1932, symptoms of financial collapse had spread from savings and loan associations to other lenders in the real estate credit market. The new Home Loan Bank Board was authorized to extend loans to its member savings and loan institutions through regional Federal Home Loan Banks. In effect, the savings and loan associations were required to invest primarily in real estate mortgages and, consequently, became major factors in residential finance. The Board faced a financial crisis with limited jurisdiction and found itself plagued with opposition from other banking sources of mortgage funds that had hoped for the creation of a central mortgage bank of broader jurisdiction.

After the inauguration of President Franklin Roosevelt and the bank holiday which followed, a system of deposit insurance was set up to guarantee deposits in commercial and savings banks. A separate insurance system was eventually created for savings and loan associations. Public confidence in the banking system was greatly enhanced.

Another effective measure to support the mortgage market was the establishment in 1933 of the Home Owners Loan Corporation (HOLC) which had the power to buy mortgages threatened with foreclosure. The Corporation was able to rescue families for whom loss of home was imminent and also to provide an opportunity for mortgage lenders to convert "frozen" assets to cash, thereby shoring up the banking system and protecting depositors from the loss of their savings. Although established amid dire predictions of its financial future, the Home Owners Loan Corporation at its peak held over 15 percent of the mortgage debt of the entire country and proved extremely effective in its role. By the time of its end some years after World War II, it had fully repaid the Treasury and its books showed a small profit.

Mortgage Insurance.   A second major effort, this time in the area of mortgage instruments, was also highly successful. This was the National Housing Act of 1934, which established a system of mortgage insurance to be administered by the newly created Federal Housing Administration (FHA). The motivation was primarily that of creating jobs by improving the flow of mortgage credit, but FHA eventually brought about major changes in the practices used in financing housing.

Prior to the creation of HOLC and FHA, most mortgages had short terms with a large lump sum payment due at the end of the term, when the homebuyer had to refinance. In addition, mortgages rarely covered more than 50 percent of the value of the structure, so that down payments were usually more than one-half of the purchase price. Second and third mortgages were common, adding to both interest costs and legal and recording costs.

The FHA mortgage insurance programs begun in 1934 were designed to reduce the risks of mortgage lenders in order to induce them to make credit available on more liberal terms. In return for a premium paid by the borrower, FHA insures the lender against the risk that the borrower will default. (The lender does absorb some of the foreclosure costs.) In case of default, FHA pays the lender the amount due on the mortgage from a fund in which the premiums are deposited. Because of this protection, lenders were willing to lengthen the term of the mortgage and to make it "fully amortized," so that no large lump sum had to be paid at the end of the term. In addition, lenders were willing to increase their loan-to-value ratios so that homes could be purchased with smaller down payments. Thus, by making mortgage financing more readily available, the FHA programs brought the possibility of homeownership within the reach of millions of additional American families, all at no cost to the taxpayer. In no other country in the world is private home financing generally available at such generous terms. In addition, FHA mortgage insurance with its long-term loans, high loan-to-value ratios, and level of payment amortization has become a major tool for meeting the credit needs of the subsidized housing market.

Another development which also helped primarily the middle-class market was the creation of secondary market facilities in which government insured mortgages could be bought and sold. As will be noted in our description of major events of the fifties, the Federal National Mortgage Association (FNMA, commonly known as Fannie May), originally incorporated in 1938, is chartered to perform this function.

Public Housing.   The effort to create jobs took other forms besides the new mortgage insurance technique. In 1933 the Public Works Administration had offered loans to nonprofit and limited dividend housing corporations for the construction of inexpensive apartments. So little interest developed that a program of direct Federal construction of low-rent housing projects, primarily in slum areas, was initiated in 1934. Some 60 projects were built, but the program ran into local opposition and eventually into legal obstacles. A change in technique became politically imperative, and the Public Housing program was born with the passage of the United States Housing Act of 1937.

The salient feature of the Public Housing program is that the development, ownership, and management of projects are the responsibilities of local governmental bodies. Rents in Public Housing projects are lowered significantly by a combination of Federal and local subsidies. Thus, 1937 was a major watershed in Federal housing policy: in that year the first significant subsidy program to lower rents was established. (Other countries acted earlier; housing subsidy programs had been established in England and Sweden by 1919.) Admission to, and continued occupancy of, Public Housing was restricted to families of relatively low income. The families of fully employed blue-collar and semiskilled workers were intended to be eligible. The Housing Assistance Administration, which presently is responsible for handling Federal relations with local housing authorities, is the successor to the Public Housing Administration, which itself succeeded the original United States Housing Authority.

The War and After.   With the revival of the economy that preceded U.S. entry into World War II the home building industry experienced a brief spurt of activity. This was very shortly curtailed by growing shortages of materials and labor and the limited priority given to housing during the war. As might be expected, the housing tools developed during the thirties were now directed to the immediate development of dwellings, by construction or conversion, for warworkers and their families.

World War II also brought with it the creation of the National Housing Agency. For the first time many of the numerous activities of the Federal Government having a direct concern with housing were pulled together under one roof. A second major development of the war years was the creation in 1944 of the veterans' mortgage guarantee program administered by the Veterans Administration (VA). This was part of the package of veterans' benefits known as the G.I. Bill of Rights. The G.I. Loan, as it became known, is in effect an extension of the FHA system. Instead of insuring mortgages, however, the Veterans Administration guarantees the top portion of a mortgage loan without fee, enabling qualifying veterans to borrow 100 percent of the cost of the house.

By the end of World War II residential construction had been at a relatively low level for 15 years. The collapse of the housing credit system during the Depression, and the restrictions of the war period contributed to tremendous pent-up demand for housing which exploded after the war. Housing production leaped from 140,000 units in 1944 to one million in 1946 to close to two million in 1950. The growing pace of post-war housing activity brought pressure on interest rates and Congressional efforts to maintain these rates at a low level. At the same time Congress liberalized the basic FHA mortgage terms by authorizing a longer mortgage life and higher loan-to-value ratios. Mortgage loans based on estimated replacement costs were allowed under the 608 Multifamily program; and because of the severe housing shortage, builders were encouraged by FHA to take advantage of the profit potential under this program. The industry responded and production reached required levels. Construction of 608 projects often cost less than had been estimated, however, leading to the later "windfall profit" scandals and the requirement that builders certify their actual costs.

In response to the need for greater Federal support if relatively low interest rates were to be maintained, Congress restructured the Federal National Mortgage Association in 1948 and expressly prohibited creation of the other Federally-chartered, privately funded National Mortgage Associations that had been authorized through the 1930's. FNMA was authorized to make commitments to purchase in advance and by such commitments began to support the low interest rates of VA loans.

The period immediately following World War II was a time of heated controversy over the policies of the Federal Government toward housing. Was Public Housing to be the only vehicle for slum clearance? Or was the need for Federal support to local governments in the latter's efforts to eliminate slum conditions to be met in another way? This issue was settled in the landmark Housing Act of 1949. Although it authorized a Public Housing program of 135,000 units annually for six years, the '49 Act established a separate slum clearance and urban redevelopment program, which has since evolved into Urban Renewal. It was to be the responsibility of this program to clear slums and blighted areas and (later in its growth) to provide sites for private enterprise to build new moderate-cost housing as well as for such residential, commercial, industrial, and public facilities as were most appropriate for the sites.

The best known provision of the Act of 1949 was its statement of a National Housing Policy. The most frequently quoted extract of this policy statement is that which establishes the goal of "a decent home and a suitable living environment for every American family." Other portions of this declaration of National Policy are equally important but less well known. They include the statement that "private enterprise shall be encouraged to serve as large a part of the total market as it can," and that "Governmental assistance shall be utilized where feasible to enable private enterprise to serve more of the total need."

The 1950's.   Although Congress had authorized large appropriations for Public Housing in the Housing Act of 1949, the program was curtailed in the early 1950's. This cutback was a result both of Korean conflict budget stringencies and successful efforts of the Appropriations Committee to reduce the number of new units as well as their design amenities. The housing shortage faced by the voting majority received top priority. Congress spent much time designing stop-gap schemes for holding the lid on interest rates. For example, FNMA's financial authority was increased whenever the statutory limits on its secondary mortgage portfolio were approached. In 1950 FNMA became part of the Housing and Home Finance Agency (successor to the National Housing Agency in 1947).

The major housing legislation of the fifties was the Housing Act of 1954. It represented the first opportunity since the early 1930's for a Republican administration to have a major impact on national housing policy. Because the Act of 1954 made few major changes in the programs which had been established in the two preceding decades, it was looked upon as a confirmation of the bipartisan nature of housing policy. The

Act grew out of a report by the President's Advisory Committee on Government Housing Policy and Programs established by President Eisenhower in 1953. In addition to the Charter Act which created the framework of FNMA as it operated until 1968, the bill added conservation and rehabilitation programs to broaden the 1949 slum clearance and urban redevelopment program into a more comprehensive tool.

The Housing Act of 1954 also initiated the requirement that a local government develop a "workable program" for community improvement before it could be eligible for assistance under the Public Housing, Urban Renewal and, later, the 221(d)(3) programs. To be certified as having a workable program, a locality was required to develop a master plan, to adopt or to update various codes governing building, zoning, and fire standards, and to muster relocation and financial resources. Although they were not required to be in effect at once, a community had to show significant progress toward enacting the necessary local legislation and carrying it out.

Public Housing was continued at its reduced Korean conflict appropriation levels. The high-density, minimum-amenity projects which the Act promoted are now looked upon by many as "horror" cases demonstrating a lack of understanding that adequate housing means more than four walls, a roof, and a door. During the post-war years, Public Housing slowly lost many of its working class residents and came to house large concentrations of poor families, many with serious social problems.

FNMA's responsibilities were divided in 1954 into three functions, all separately funded. These were its secondary market operations, its special assistance functions, and its management and liquidation operations. The secondary market function involves the trading of FHA and VA supported mortgages originated by private institutions. "Special assistance" involves the purchase of mortgages which cannot be marketed to private lenders because of noncompetitive interest or because of lack of market experience with the program or instrument. This function became important in later subsidy programs like 221(d)(3). The special assistance purchases are entirely funded by Government borrowing, whereas the secondary market operations use federal borrowing to support private borrowing, and for that reason can be used as an instrument of monetary policy.

The 1954 Act modified Urban Renewal to enable production of housing at reduced cost. The more liberal multi-family and single-family terms offered under the new Section 220 FHA mortgage insurance program for Urban Renewal areas were designed, in combination with provision for a land cost write-down, to attract the private sector into building middle-income housing in Urban Renewal areas. FNMA special assistance was made available for these insured loans. Remembering the difficulties under the 608 program, Congress required cost certification to prevent windfall profits. It was still generally assumed that existing techniques would be adequate to serve those families above Public Housing levels. Later in the fifties it was found that even with urban renewal write-downs and more liberal mortgage terms, housing cost levels within the reach of moderate-income families could not be achieved.

Evolution of Subsidies in Privately Owned Buildings. The Housing Act of 1959 contained the first break in the pattern that restricted development and operation of subsidized projects to public owners. The Section 202 program begun in that year authorized direct loans from the Federal Government, originally at a rate based on interest rates on outstanding Federal debt (amended in 1965 to be no higher than 3 percent per year), to nonprofit sponsors of rental projects for the elderly and handicapped. The major significance of the 202 program is that, by its adoption, Congress authorized direct loans at less than market rates to *nonprofit private corporations*, although only nonprofit ones. In addition, this was the first statutory expression of the need for subsidy if the cost of shelter for those marginally above Public Housing levels was to be met.

The 221(d)(3) Below Market Interest Rate (BMIR) program, established by the Housing Act of 1961, expanded opportunities for private development of subsidized housing. The program authorized FNMA to purchase mortgage loans made to limited dividend and cooperative, as well as nonprofit, entities at low interest rates based on the average interest paid on the outstanding Federal debt. For the first time in the history of American housing, *profit-motivated private organizations* could develop subsidized housing. The subsidy was rather modest and indirect, being in effect a tender of the Federal borrowing power through FNMA's special assistance functions.

More important steps toward the use of subsidies in privately owned buildings were taken in the Housing Act of 1965. By the spring of 1965 the average interest on the Federal debt had risen above 4 percent. The 1965 Act acknowledged the decreasing utility of the borrowing power technique used in the 221(d)(3) and 202 programs and pegged the below market interest rate at no higher than 3 percent. Both programs now enjoyed direct subsidies since FNMA and ultimately the Treasury would have to make up the difference between the Federal borrowing rate and 3 percent.

The 1965 Act also created two new subsidy techniques, one of which, Rent Supplements, became the subject of heated political controversy. The Rent Supplement program, unlike 202 and 221(d)(3), attempted to adjust housing subsidies to the needs of individual families, rather than simply to provide financial support of total project costs. Tenants were required to pay at least 25 percent of their income toward rent, and the Federal Government would make up the difference between that payment and the rental value of the units they occupied. As with the earlier private programs, rent levels were to be controlled to prevent private owners from making undue profits. The second new technique introduced in 1965 was the Section 23 leasing program which enabled local public housing authorities to subsidize rents in existing rental units.

The year 1965 also saw the creation of the Cabinet-level Department of Housing and Urban Development to succeed the Housing and Home Finance Agency.

Other Federal efforts in the 1960's attacked the non-physical aspects of slum problems. The Model Cities program, which attempts to coordinate Government policies, both physical and social within a defined neighborhood, was established in 1966. The various manpower programs, poverty programs, and changes in welfare policy had their own effects on housing conditions.

The Housing Act of 1968 culminated the strong movement toward use of housing subsidies in private dwellings. Its most important new feature was the Homeownership program in Section 235. This program provided modest subsidies to enable lower-income families to purchase new and, in some cases, existing homes. The Act also initiated a new rental program, Section 236, for families above the Public Housing income levels. This program is intended ultimately to replace both the 202 and 221(d)(3) programs since it provides a larger interest subsidy equal to the excess over an interest rate of 1 percent instead of 3 percent and since it has the advantage of correlating the amount of subsidy with the tenant's need. Both of these new programs rely almost exclusively on private developers—profit-motivated, nonprofit, and cooperative. Both programs also rely totally on private mortgage financing supported by subsidies payable directly to the mortgage lender in contrast to the Government's purchase of the mortgage in addition to the interest subsidy.

The Act of 1968 contained many other important innovations. It made FHA mortgage insurance more easily available in declining urban areas and for families with imperfect (but defensible) credit histories. FNMA's secondary market operations were transferred to a new privately owned corporation, and a new Government National Mortgage Association was established within HUD to handle the special assistance management and liquidating functions. The National Housing Partnership proposal, which was developed by this Committee, was enacted. Urban Renewal was given a new slant by the introduction of the "neighborhood development program" which provides greater program flexibility and encourages and rewards steady annual performance.

Most important of all, the Act of 1968 authorized large appropriations for the new homeownership and rental programs, as well as Rent Supplements and Public Housing, thereby making possible the President's goal of the construction and rehabilitation of six million housing units over a 10-year period for low- and moderate-income families. An annual report to establish targets and report progress was also required. In addition, the Act extended and expanded the funding of the Model Cities, Urban Renewal, Code Enforcement, and Community Facilities programs to permit a comprehensive attack on central city programs.

In the discussion which follows we leave the historical thread to take a closer look at the major subsidy techniques—how they work, their successes and failures—as a background for our program proposals.

II. Principal Federal Housing Subsidy Programs

There are a great many Federal housing programs. Most are administered by HUD, but the Veterans Administration, the Farmers Home Administration, and the Department of Defense all have significant housing programs of their own. Many of the HUD programs, like the traditional mortgage insurance programs of FHA, do not involve the subsidization of housing costs. The major HUD housing subsidy programs are outlined below. . . . Other Federal activities such as favorable income tax treatment for home-owners, and the write-down of land costs available under urban renewal, have also served to lower housing costs paid by consumers.

Public Housing. Although the layman may refer to all Government-assisted housing as "public housing," the term is used by housing professionals only to denote the specific program begun in 1937. The Public Housing program, as it has traditionally operated, places responsibility for development, ownership, and management of subsidized rental projects in the hands of independent local government agencies called housing authorities. A local housing authority cannot receive Federal assistance without the approval of both its local government and the Housing Assistance Administration, a subdivision of the Department of Housing and Urban Development. Some state laws go further and require local government approval of specific sites. Some jurisdictions, like the entire states of California and Texas, require that the Federal contract to support Public Housing projects be approved by local voters in referenda. Although practically all large cities have established housing authorities, many small jurisdictions, particularly suburban ones, do not participate in the program. For example, in 1967 less than half of the localities with populations between 25,000 and 50,000 had housing authorities.

A housing authority generally can only build within the boundaries of the local jurisdiction which established it. In addition, since 1954 Public Housing projects cannot be built in areas which do not have HUD-certified Workable Programs for community improvement. Thus, local governments which do not wish to have more subsidized projects located within their boundaries can "veto" them by simply letting their Workable Programs lapse. The result of all these forces is that most urban Public Housing projects have been located in decaying areas of central cities.

Rents in Public Housing are lowered through a number of subsidies, both Federal and local. The cost of project development is financed with long-term tax-exempt local bonds. This tax exemption lowers direct debt retirement costs. The Federal Government makes annual contributions to the local housing authority which *cover all costs* of retiring the bonds. The Federal Government is also authorized to pay a local authority an additional $120 per year for the benefit of each family which is elderly, displaced, extremely poor, or contains four or more children. Lastly, public housing projects do not pay normal local real estate taxes but instead pay lower amounts in-lieu-of-taxes.

Because of these substantial subsidies, admission to public housing projects is restricted to families whose incomes are below limits established by the local housing authority under statutory Federal guidelines. At the end of 1964 the median income limit for admission for a family of two adults and two children, in localities within urbanized areas, was $4,000. The highest limit ($5,760) was in New York City. The median income of all families admitted to Public Housing in recent years has been roughly $2,500. The median rent for all public housing units is approximately $45. Roughly one-half of all public housing units are occupied by Negro tenants and one-third by elderly persons. Given the inadequate coverage and size of welfare payments, there are still millions of families who are too poor to live in public housing projects. Even those who live there may have to commit a disproportionate share of their incomes to pay the low rents.

Local housing authorities also set income limits for continued occupancy of public housing, normally at 125 percent of the limits for admission. Until a few years ago, tenants who earned more than the limits for continued occupancy were evicted—a practice widely believed to be damaging to incentives and to add to the instability within public housing. Recently, this practice has been softened somewhat.

The Public Housing program has been exclusively a rental program. Some recent efforts have been made to encourage ownership by tenants. For most of its history, Congressional pressure has required that projects have few amenities. This has proved to be short-sighted since many projects have been so distinctive in appearance that they have tended to stigmatize the neighborhoods in which they are located and the tenants themselves. Fortunately, in recent years there has been some change in attitude, and HUD has attempted, with some notable results, to encourage good design.

In 1967 the Public Housing program included some 650,000 units which housed almost 2.4 million persons. This figure dwarfs production totals under the other programs described below, principally because Public Housing was the only housing subsidy program in the United States until the last decade. Table 2–1 presents production figures for all Public Housing programs between 1939 and 1967. Production has been rather erratic, at least until recent years; the highest production peaks were reached in 1941 and 1952–53.

Some housing experts believe that the conventional Public Housing program as presently structured has proved to be an awkward method of producing housing. The requirement of local government approval of

TABLE 2–1

Low-Rent Public Housing Units Completed, Acquired,
or Leased for Calendar Years 1939–67

Year	Units	Year	Units
1939	4,960	1954	44,293
1940	34,308	1955	20,899
1941	61,065	1956	11,993
1942	36,172	1957	10,513
1943	24,296	1958	15,472
1944	3,269	1959	21,939
1945	2,080	1960	16,401
1946	1,925	1961	20,965
1947	466	1962	28,682
1948	1,348	1963	27,327
1949	547	1964	24,488
1950	1,255	1965	30,769
1951	10,246	1966	31,483
1952	58,258	1967	38,756
1953	58,214		

Source: Housing Assistance Administration

sites (not to mention problems raised by local referenda and the Workable Program requirement) has restricted the expansion of the program since Public Housing has rarely proved to be a popular neighbor. In addition, housing authorities have been criticized for using authoritarian management policies typified by complex tenant regulations. Surveys indicate that many poor families believe that public housing will not offer them an attractive living environment. Many even prefer to live in unsubsidized, substandard private buildings. HUD has recently begun to place careful controls on project size, on use of high-rise structures, on design, and has encouraged more flexible management, all in an effort to make future public housing projects more attractive.

A number of new developments have been introduced by HUD to involve the private sector in the production and management of public housing. These are discussed in another section.

202 and 221(d)(3) Below Market Interest Rate Programs. These two low-interest loan programs, although differing in details, use the same subsidy technique and are best analyzed together. The 202 program begun in 1959 is administered by the Housing Assistance Administration which is also responsible for Public Housing. The subsidy used is a direct loan from HUD to sponsoring nonprofit corporations, originally at an interest rate based on the outstanding Federal debt and since 1965 at a flat 3 percent interest rate. Profit-motivated sponsors are not permitted to own these projects; only elderly or handicapped persons may live in 202 projects. Current income limits for tenant eligiblity are the lesser of: (1) $4,500 per year for single persons, and $5,400 per year for two-person families; or (2) 80 percent of the appropriate 221(d)(3) BMIR limits. Under this program, HUD also provides the interim financing needed for construction, again at a 3 percent rate of interest. The permanent loans may have a term of up to 50 years and can cover up to 100 percent of the costs of a project. Projects built under 202 are *not* restricted to jurisdictions which have HUD-approved Workable Programs.

The 221(d)(3) Below Market Interest Rate program (221(d)(3) BMIR), a considerably broader program than 202 in terms of eligible sponsors and eligible tenants, was begun in 1961. FNMA is now authorized to purchase 221(d)(3) mortgages bearing interest rates of 3 percent. Unlike 202, profit-seeking corporations as well as nonprofit ones can own 221(d)(3) projects. FHA, which administers 221(d)(3), prevents undue profits by requiring cost certification and by controlling rent levels and the distribution of profits. Interim financing must be arranged with conventional private lenders at market interest rates. The maximum term for the low-interest permanent mortgages has been established by HUD regulation at 40 years. The mortgage can cover up to 100 percent of replacement costs for nonprofit and cooperative sponsors and 90 percent for profit-oriented sponsors.

The majority of 221(d)(3) projects consist of newly constructed row houses and walkup apartments. They are either rental projects or cooperatives. They must be located in communities which have Workable Programs, a requirement which has restricted use of 221(d)(3).

The availability of a 3 percent loan permits a reduction of monthly rents in 221(d)(3) and 202 units of roughly $30 to $40 below the rents which would be charged if they were financed with market-rate mortgages. The income limits for admission to 221(d)(3) BMIR projects are usually several thousand dollars higher than the limit for admission to public housing in the same area. Income limits are established by HUD and depend upon family size and geographic area. In each area, they are set at the lower of: (1) the median income for families of that size in that area, or (2) the carrying costs of a unit with design characteristics which strike a balance between limited amenities and avoidance of market unacceptability. Most limits are based on the latter factor, and consequently, rising construction costs require increases in income limits within the overall limit of median income. In the relatively few cases where the median income figure is controlling, increases in construction costs may make the program economically infeasible. An extreme example of this problem has arisen in the Upper Peninsula of Michigan where construction costs, because of unusual transportation charges and temperature problems, tend to be high, while the typical median income is relatively low. In a few instances like these, HUD has permitted higher income limits than it otherwise permits. In April 1968 the maximum income limit for admission to a 221(d)(3) project for a family of four was $9,050 in New York City; $7,500 in Denver, Colorado; and $5,950 in Montgomery, Alabama. Unlike 202, admission is not restricted to the elderly and handicapped. However, families displaced by Government action are given priority.

Table 2-2 presents projections of the rent levels achievable in Detroit with the 221(d)(3) BMIR, Public Housing and Rent Supplement programs and compares them with those achievable in nonsubsidized housing represented by the Section 207 program. It also indicates the incomes needed to support the required rents for 20 and 25 percent rent-income ratios. While this table is based only on Detroit cost data and contains some assumptions which may not be generally applicable, it does serve to illustrate that housing cannot be generally built for rents which low-income groups can be expected to pay without subsidies at least as great as those provided by the Rent Supplement program.

Both the 202 and 221(d)(3) programs have certain disadvantages inherent in any below-market interest rate programs. Federal accounting techniques require that a Government purchase of a mortgage be treated as an expenditure in the year of purchase, but no credit is given to the fact that a mortgage is an asset. The result is a substantial increase in the apparent Government deficit for the year in question. In addition, it is difficult to adjust the amount of subsidy provided to a project through a low-interest loan to the varying needs of individual families living in that project. As a result of these budgetary and flexibility problems, the more recent housing subsidy programs—Rent Supplements and the new Home-ownership and Rental programs—rely not on low-interest loans but on annual Federal payments to reduce housing costs. This approach spreads out the budgetary impact over several decades and permits better correlation of the amount of subsidy with the needs of the recipient.

As of June 1967, 62,000 units of 221(d)(3) BMIR housing had been completed or were under construction. Roughly one-half of these units had been built by profit-motivated developers and about one-half by nonprofit and cooperative sponsors. The recent annual production rate under the 221(d)(3) BMIR program—roughly 13,000 units per year—is about one-half the recent annual production rate under the conventional Public Housing program. Production under the Section 202 program has

TABLE 2-2

Average or Minimum Required Rentals on Newly Constructed One- and Two-Bedroom Apartments under Different Federal Housing Programs and the Required Family Income Implied at Specified Rent-Income Ratios*

Program	Required Annual (Monthly) Rentals on Units with—		Required Income at Rent-Income Ratios of 20 or 25 Percent for Families Occupying—			
			One Bedroom		Two Bedrooms	
	One Bedroom	Two Bedrooms	20 Percent	25 Percent	20 Percent	25 Percent
207 average (no subsidy)............	$2,270 ($189)	$2,719 ($227)	$11,350	$9,080	$13,595	$10,876
Public Housing average...........	905 (75)	1,161 (97)	4,525	3,620	5,805	4,644
Rent Supplement minimum...........	472 (39)	540 (45)	2,360	1,888	2,700	2,160
236 minimum...........	1,472 (123)	1,763 (147)	7,360	5,888	8,815	7,052
221(d)(3) BMIR average...........	1,664 (139)	1,993 (166)	8,320	6,656	9,965	7,972

* The calculations apply to Detroit in 1967 and cities with similar cost levels. Within the group of cities with more than 2 million inhabitants, Detroit had the lowest dwelling construction cost limits for Public Housing in 1966. They were at the same level as those in Dallas (population 1.1 million in 1960). Development cost limits in all other cases except the Rent Supplement program (RS) were assumed to be equal to those specified for 221(d)(3) BMIR. These were $14,150 for one-bedroom and $16,950 for a two-bedroom dwelling unit. No rent supplement projects have been completed in Detroit by 1967.

Source: Von Furstenberg and Moskof: *Federally Assisted Rental Housing Programs: Which Income Groups Have They Served or Whom Can They Be Expected To Serve?*

been somewhat less than under 221(d)(3), with 23,000 units in all having been started by June 1967. Although the 202 program is restricted to nonprofit owners, and projects can only be occupied by elderly or handicapped tenants, it has proved to be relatively popular compared to some of the more broadly applicable programs.

Rent Supplement. The Rent Supplement program was offered by the Administration in 1965 as a substitute for 221(d)(3) BMIR. Under the rent supplement technique, the tenant family pays 25 percent of its income toward rent, while the Federal Government pays directly to the landlord the difference between economic rent levels and the tenant's contribution. This approach has the advantages of keying the amount of subsidy to the tenant's need and of spreading the cost to the Federal Government over a long period. In its deliberations on the Housing Act of 1965, Congress did not accept the Administration's recommendation that the Rent Supplement program be aimed at moderate-income families as well as low-income families. Instead, it adopted the Rent Supplement program only after restricting eligibility for supplements to families whose incomes on admission are below the eligibility limits for Public Housing in the same locality. In addition, Congress continued the 221(d)(3) program instead of substituting the Rent Supplement program for it as the Administration had recommended.

In essence, the Rent Supplement program attempts to shift the responsibility for building and operating low-rent housing projects from the local housing authorities (relied on in the Public Housing program) to private groups, both profit-motivated and nonprofit. After receiving approval of a proposed project from FHA (which administers the program), the private housing owner finances his project with a private mortgage at the market interest rate. On completion of construction, the housing owner rents units in the project to any family he chooses. However, not all tenants in a project are eligible for supplements. To be eligible, a family must have a low income (one below limits established by the Secretary of HUD which themselves must be below the limit for admission to Public Housing in that area), have few assets, and be a member of one of the following deserving groups: elderly, handicapped, displaced by Government action or natural disaster, or now living in substandard housing. As mentioned, these eligible tenants pay 25 percent of their income toward rent, and the Federal Government pays any remainder directly to the landlord. Tenants who are not eligible for supplements pay the entire rent themselves. As a tenant's income rises, his supplement is reduced. For this reason, a family whose income rises substantially after admission to a Rent Supplement project is not required to leave it.

Congress passed the Rent Supplement program by the smallest of margins in 1965 and has since limited its implementation in a number of ways. The program has received few appropriations; in fact it has barely survived attacks during the appropriations stage. To mollify Congressional pressures, HUD has been forced to impose regulations on the program which have made it increasingly unworkable. One regulation requires that in no instance may a tenant receive a supplement which exceeds 70 percent of the fair market rental of the unit. Other regulations which have proved to be very damaging to the program establish specific dollar limits on construction costs and on maximum fair market rentals. These low maximums inhibit production and force those who do build to produce rather austere projects. Still other regulations flatly prohibit even some of the limited amenities allowed in 221(d)(3) BMIR projects.

The limits on maximum rents and construction costs have made the Rent Supplement program generally unworkable for new construction in major central cities outside the South and Southwest. In addition, the limitations on amenities have made the program much less attractive to builders since they now fear they will be unable to produce a project which will appeal to those ineligible for supplements. At present, both builders and FHA generally assume that at least 90 percent of the tenants in Rent Supplement projects will in fact receive supplements. Thus, these regulations, which have been forced on HUD by Congressional pressure, defeat the Administration's goal of economically integrated tenancies within projects and scare away builders who are reluctant to own projects housing mostly low-income families.

The Appropriations Committees have also restricted the program through riders on appropriations bills. The Rent Supplement program as enacted is largely free of the Workable Program requirement. One rider has restricted location of Rent Supplement projects to localities which either have Workable Programs or whose governments approve the projects. Another rider has increased the equity requirements for nonprofit sponsors who receive special assistance from GNMA. Congress's hostility to the Rent Supplement program has severely restricted production under it. Twelve hundred units were started under the program in fiscal year 1967 and about 12,000 in fiscal year 1968.

The basic rent supplement approach, emphasizing flexible subsidies as well as private ownership, private financing, and private management, has many advantages. As Table 2–2 illustrates, this program can reach rather low income levels. If Congressional limits were removed, this program could serve the full range of families in need and could be used effectively by private business.

Section 236 Rental Housing Program.   The new 236 program, part of the Housing Act of 1968, is designed to replace eventually both the 202 and 221(d)(3) programs. Like the Rent Supplement program, it relies on private developers—both nonprofit and profit-oriented—of rental or cooperative housing. The subsidy technique is similar to that used in the

Rent Supplement program: tenants pay 25 percent of their income toward rent, and the Federal Government pays a supplement which makes up the difference between a tenant's payment and market rents. There is, however, a crucial difference. The maximum Federal payment on a unit lowers the rent to the level which would be achieved had the project been financed with a 1 percent mortgage. Thus, the primary difference between 236 and the Rent Supplement program is that the subsidy under 236 is not as deep.

The maximum Federal subsidy to a tenant per month will be about $50 to $60. This is not enough to reach the poorest families. To be eligible, a family's income (less $300 per child) must not exceed 135 percent of the limits for admission to Public Housing projects. Thus, 236 will serve primarily families whose incomes range between $4,000 and $6,500 per year. Table 2–2 indicates that in high-cost areas, such as Detroit, tenant incomes must be higher unless families chose to allocate more than 25 percent of gross income to housing. To alleviate this problem partially, 20 percent of the units of a 236 project can be occupied by tenants receiving Rent Supplement payments and who thus might have lower incomes.

In some communities the basic income limits for the 236 program may be too low to make the program economically feasible. Not only would the very poor not be able to afford these projects, but moderate-income families may be excluded because they exceed the rather low income limits. In many communities, particularly higher-cost urban centers, the income spectrum the 236 program can serve may have been narrowed so much that some builders will be reluctant to participate in the program for fear they will be unable to find enough eligible tenants willing to occupy the units. However, some relief is provided by a provision permitting 20 percent of the appropriations to be used for families whose incomes exceed the limits for admission, but whose incomes are still below 90 percent of the 221(d)(3) BMIR limits in that area (with $300 deductions for each minor child).

Despite this feasibility issue and the inability of the 236 program to reach very poor families, it has several advantages over the earlier moderate-income programs. It offers deeper subsidies than those available under 202 and 221(d)(3) BMIR by providing the equivalent of 1 percent loans instead of 3 percent loans. In addition, it avoids the budgetary impact problems raised by direct loan programs and provides a technique for adjusting the amount of subsidy to a tenant's income. Lastly, the program is not subject to the Workable Program requirement, which does apply to 221(d)(3).

The authorization for appropriations for Section 236 in the Housing Act of 1968 should be sufficient to enable the construction of 700,000 housing units over a three year period.

Homeownership Program—Section 235.   The Homeownership program contained in the Housing Act of 1968 is a major landmark in the history of Federal housing legislation. Prior to its enactment, all major housing subsidy programs were limited to rental units, with cooperative housing units permitted in a few instances.

Assistance under the new Homeownership program generally will be restricted to new or substantially rehabilitated units. Private homebuilders will plan the housing and have it approved by FHA for inclusion in the program prior to the beginning of construction. When built, the houses will be sold to eligible buyers who will finance their purchases with FHA-insured market rate mortgages from private lenders. The subsidy technique used is similar to that in the Section 236 rental program. The Federal Government contracts to pay part of the homebuyer's mortgage payments. The maximum Government subsidy reduces the homebuyer's payment to that which he would owe if his purchase had been financed with a mortgage bearing an interest rate of 1 percent. Translated into dollars, the maximum subsidy will be about $40 to $70 a month, depending on the value of the house and the market interest rate. The actual amount of the subsidy may be somewhat less, depending on the income of the family buying the house. All families must devote at least 20 percent of their income to paying off the mortgage. (This figure of 20 percent is lower than the 25 percent used under the rental programs because the homebuyer must bear all utility charges, maintenance, and repair expenses himself.) As family income rises, the Federal payments due to the lender consequently will be gradually reduced and eventually eliminated. Because the maximum Federal subsidy is limited, the program will not be of much help to families with very low incomes. However, it will provide assistance to those in the broad range of incomes between $3,000 and $7,000 a year.

Some examples might help explain how the program works. Assuming a $15,000, 35-year mortgage at 6¾ percent, the required monthly payment due the lender (counting principal and interest due on the mortgage, mortgage insurance premium, hazard insurance, and taxes) would be $125. A family with an annual income of $6,000 would pay $100 of this, while the Government would pay the remaining $25. A family with an annual income of $4,000 or less would, pay $68 a month, and the Government would pay the remaining $57.

Houses built under the program will be of modest but adequate quality. In general, the mortgage on a house cannot exceed $15,000. A mortgage of up to $17,500 is allowed in high-cost areas and of up to $20,000 for large families in high-cost areas. Down payments would be low, as little as $200 for some families, and in no case greater than 3 percent of the value of the house.

During the debate in Congress, the hottest issue was whether the eligibility for assistance under the Homeownership program should be restricted to persons below certain income levels. Such limits, of course, were not strictly necessary since the amount of subsidy is automatically keyed to the homebuyer's income and thus the well to do could not have received any benefits even if there were no income limits. Congress eventually adopted income limits like those used in the Section 236 program. Assistance payments are restricted to homebuyers who, when they buy the houses, have incomes (less $300 per child) which do not exceed 135 percent of the income limits for admission to Public Housing projects in that locality. These limits are roughly $5,000–$6,000 per year for four-person families in major metropolitan areas.

Although the program is restricted primarily to new construction and substantial rehabilitation, a limited number of families, such as those displaced by Government action, can qualify for assistance in the purchase of an existing house. Public or private agencies will be hired to counsel families who need help in assuming the responsibilities of homeownership. Families which have imperfect but acceptable credit histories or irregular income patterns which would normally disqualify them from mortgage insurance under FHA programs, but who still make reasonably satisfactory risks, may participate in the program.

The Housing Act of 1968 authorizes large appropriations for the Homeownership program. Assuming that the average subsidy per house is $50 a month, the Act could enable nearly 500,000 families to become homeowners over the next three years.

Subsidies for Rehabilitation.   All programs discussed above can be used to subsidize housing costs in rehabilitated dwellings. In addition to these programs, there are a number of relatively minor ones which can be used only for rehabilitation. Two of these, the Section 312 loan program and Section 115 rehabilitation grant program, can only be used within limited Urban Renewal or Concentrated Code Enforcement areas. In fact, they are administered by the Renewal Assistance Administration in HUD which is generally responsible for the Urban Renewal programs. The Section 312 program, enacted in 1964, provides direct 3 percent loans to homeowners, the proceeds of which can be used for rehabilitation and, if necessary, also for refinancing existing mortgages. The 312 program was the first to authorize Federal housing loans at less than the average cost of Federal borrowing.

The Section 115 rehabilitation grant program, also designed to support the Urban Renewal process, was begun in 1965. Only families who own and occupy their own homes and who have very low incomes are eligible for these grants. The maximum grant now available is $3,000.

A third rehabilitation subsidy program, Section 221(h), was enacted in 1966. This program is extremely limited in scope. Its main significance is that it provided a historical precedent for the Homeownership program of 1968 into which it has been merged. Sponsors of 221(h) projects must be nonprofit organizations. These nonprofit sponsors acquire and rehabilitate single-family units and then sell them to families whose incomes are below Public Housing income limits. The subsidy provided is a 3 percent 25-year mortgage purchased by FNMA. This subsidy is often inadequate to enable these families to participate in the program.

This brief description of the major Federal housing programs reveals that a striking acceleration in the innovation of new programs has occurred in the last decade and particularly in the last five years. Even the conventional Public Housing program, the only Federal housing subsidy program in existence between 1937 and 1959, has been rejuvenated with recent innovations. The basic trends in policy development are:

1. Increased reliance on private development, private financing, private ownership, and private management of subsidized housing;
2. Greater subsidization of homeownership (and membership in cooperatives or condominiums) and less exclusive emphasis on rental buildings;
3. Less reliance on low interest loans and greater reliance on periodic Federal subsidies;
4. Less emphasis on particularized programs—such as 202 and 221(h) —in favor of broadly applicable programs; and
5. More emphasis on subsidy programs for families somewhat above the very lowest income levels.

III. Proposals on Basic Issues

The above review of existing housing programs serves as a backdrop to our basic proposals for the future. The following are some of the fundamental issues involved in national housing policy:

Who Shall Receive Government Housing Assistance? The basic conclusion in this study is that Government assistance be provided to all persons—regardless of family size, age, marital status, or health—who need help to afford the cost of modest, decent, safe, and sanitary housing. Despite great improvements in the last decade, existing government housing programs do not yet completely meet this basic goal. Most of the programs serve rather narrow populations within the income spectrum. Prior to passage of the Housing Act of 1968, there was a considerable gap between the income groups served by the Public Housing and 221(d)(3) BMIR programs. This is shown graphically in Figure 2–1.

The Rent Supplement program did little to fill this gap because to be eligible initially for subsidies, families had to be below Public Housing income limits. However, the new 236 program will help fill it.

FIGURE 2-1

Estimated Total Annual Family Income in 1968

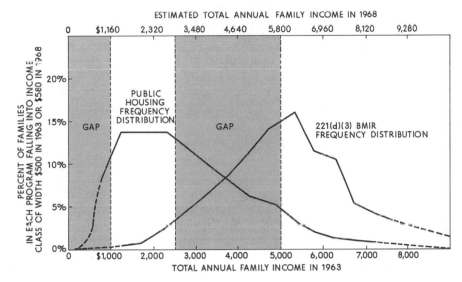

Figure 2–1 also shows that existing programs are of little help to the very poorest families, especially those earning less than $1,200 per year. Many of these families, without some form of welfare assistance, cannot afford even the low rents in Public Housing or Rent Supplement projects.

Figure 2–1 suggests that of the families presently served by Public Housing, a large percentage are earning between $1,200 and $2,900. This may be somewhat misleading because while the lower end of the income scale is being served in the aggregate, this chart hides locational variations. A disproportionate number of families in the lowest income classes live primarily in low-cost areas, such as the South, or in small towns. Many poor families living in higher-cost areas like Detroit (see Table 2–2) cannot afford to live in Public Housing projects.

. . . a family earning $2,000 could not afford to live in a two-bedroom unit in even a new Rent Supplement project without paying more than 25 percent of income toward rent. As suggested earlier, this may not be applicable to all communities and is based on some assumptions which may have to be modified by actual experience. But it does indicate the inability of existing subsidy programs to serve the very poor.

The implications of this finding are clear. Larger subsidies are needed.

How Much Assistance Should a Family Receive? The amount of assistance a family receives should be determined by a flexible formula based on need. Existing programs in general use a formula based on a flat percentage of family income, with some allowing deductions for children. For example, the Rent Supplement program and Section 236 program require recipients to devote at least 25 percent of their income for rent; the Public Housing program (in general) and the Section 235 Homeownership program require 20 percent. As observed previously, there is little foundation for the use of these percentages. Von Furstenberg's paper in the volume of technical reports on "The Impact of Rent Formulas" shows how flat formulas work to the disadvantage of large families. It is questionable whether the same flat percentage should be required of all families regardless of their individual characteristics. It is suggested that the Departments of HUD and HEW undertake a comprehensive study of the patterns of family expenses and develop better formulas for Federal housing subsidies. Such a study would explore the effect on housing expenses of such variables as age of family, size of family, and location of the household to reflect the variations in the cost of living. In addition, the income concept as a determinant of social need and Federal subsidies may have to be amended or supplemented. Some families, particularly the elderly, may be expected to engage, without hardship, in planned dissaving out of previously accumulated net worth.

The amount of subsidy available to a family under the various programs must be continuously reassessed. All existing programs establish certain maximum limits on the amount of subsidy, and all of these maxima are entirely arbitrary. For example, under Public Housing the basic subsidy covers all of development costs, but project income must cover most occupancy costs. Under the Rent Supplement program, the subsidy cannot exceed 70 percent of the unsubsidized cost of the unit. The technique used under the new Section 235 and 236 programs sets the maximum subsidy at the amount by which housing costs would be lowered if development were financed with 1 percent loans. This latter approach has the advantage of seeming to use low-interest loans, a politically familiar technique; but otherwise it is arbitrary. The keying of subsidies to interest rates tends to make people believe that the maximum subsidy is available when the interest rate is reduced to zero. This, of course, is not true. Additional subsidies can be made available to retire the principal of a loan or to cover the operating costs of housing. If the amount of subsidy is keyed to a recipient's income, limits on maximum subsidies are theoretically unneeded.

Congress has often unwittingly undermined the feasibility of these programs by imposing income limits for eligibility which are too low *given the maximum subsidy provided*. If only a small subsidy is provided, but eligibility is restricted to poor families, the program will not work and private sponsors will refuse to use it. The Congressional motivation for imposing low limits for eligibility is apparently to make sure that the most needy families receive priority. This is indeed a worthy goal. But lowering eligibility limits without at the same time increasing the depth of the subsidy, in effect, squeezes the lift out of the programs by narrowing the effective target population. It is possible, for example, that Congress has seriously damaged the 235 Homeownership program and 236 Rental program by imposing income limits too low for the subsidy available.

Who Shall Develop, Own, and Manage the Housing?   The basic trend toward increased involvement of the private sector in housing programs is laudable. In view of the large volume of production required in the next few years, it is clear that private entrepreneurs, public agencies, and nonprofit developers must all be encouraged to take part in the production effort. Even where public developers are used, opportunities are still available for private contractors and subsequent private ownership and management of the subsidized units.

Full opportunities should be provided under the various programs for the subsidy recipients to own their units, either outright or through cooperatives or condominiums. Many studies have found that ownership is highly correlated with good maintenance and neighborhood stability. The Housing Act of 1968 made great strides in its direction in its Homeownership program (235) and in provisions for the acquisition of public housing units by tenants and of 221(d)(3) projects by cooperatives. After these programs have been digested, additional opportunities no doubt can be provided.

In What Kind of Neighborhood Should the Housing Be Located?   Housing should be built where people want to live. The location of assisted housing should be decided primarily by the play of market forces, which take into account both the desires of consumers and the costs of production to the builders. Different families may have strongly divergent tastes about the location of housing: some will want to remain in the central city near the excitement of downtown; others may prefer the relative peace of suburban life; still others may enjoy the adventure of living in a new community built far from existing metropolitan centers. In any case, the household will have to live near the location of the breadwinner's job.

It must be emphasized that the removal of existing constraints on freedom of location—such as racial discrimination and zoning abuses—is essential to the achievement of decent housing for all. Strong measures should be taken to remove barriers which prevent ghetto dwellers from leaving the ghetto.

In approving the location of proposed subsidized housing projects, HUD must be mindful of the community facilities and transportation resources already available, or which can be expected to become available as the market responds to the development of the project. Experience under the Public Housing program has indicated that the availability of housing subsidies will sometimes cause families to move into areas even though they are seriously deficient in community facilities. In such cases,

HUD should permit needed commercial, job-producing, and community facilities to be included in the mortgage.

What Quality of Housing Should Be Built under Subsidy Programs?
Housing built under Federal subsidy programs should avoid two extremes. Its quality should not exceed that of the housing of moderate-income families who do not need subsidies. On the other hand, the housing should be of high enough quality, in both design and construction, to avoid the dangers of early economic obsolescence and tenant stigmatization. The austere character of many of the Public Housing projects built during the 1950's is a somber reminder of the false economy of building at low quality levels. We urge expenditure of the modest amount of money necessary to make housing developments attractive enough to be positive additions to their environments.

At present, many different sets of quality standards apply to the various housing subsidy programs. Administration of these programs would be considerably simplified if the various statutes and HUD regulations were unified into a single consistent set of housing standards for the entire range of subsidy programs. Such standards should be flexible enough to reflect changes in popular perceptions of what is "modest housing." In addition, standards should vary according to location. Finally, standards should be flexible enough to allow design and market preferences to be tested.

Recognizing the need for a dynamic standard for housing quality, we recommend that housing developed under Federal subsidy programs should roughly correspond to the quality of new low-cost unsubsidized housing being built in the locality. Such housing can be made reasonably attractive and should avoid early economic obsolescence. For purposes of efficient administration, development cost limits in dollars based on this test should periodically be established by HUD for each locality. Development cost limits now in existence which are too low to permit economically feasible development of attractive projects should be raised. The practice of establishing maximum monthly rentals, which has limited the effectiveness of the Rent Supplement program, should be discontinued.

Builders should be given maximum flexibility within these development cost dollar limits. Flat prohibitions against specific amenities in subsidized housing make little sense.

To What Extent Should Subsidies Be Restricted to New Construction?
With some exceptions, notably the "leased housing" variation of Public Housing, all major housing subsidy programs have been used primarily to promote new construction and, to a lesser extent, substantial rehabilitation. The basic rationale for this emphasis on new construction is that new projects on vacant sites increase the total housing stock. So long as there is some interplay between different sectors of the housing market,

an addition to the stock of housing tends to relieve prices for everyone. Thus, the construction of moderate-income projects in the suburbs may indirectly help to lessen housing shortages in central city slums. The extent to which this actually happens depends on the little-understood workings of the housing market. In areas where the supply of housing is tight (as indicated by low vacancy rates), there can be little doubt that the emphasis on new construction is proper.

Where vacancy rates are high, however, more use can be made of existing stock. In such cases, rehabilitation, where economically feasible, is equally as appropriate as new construction. In addition, it may occasionally be appropriate to permit the conversion of existing housing into subsidized housing under one of the programs. Policy-makers have long been reluctant to do this for fear they would merely inflate rents and bring about no betterment in the housing stock. The workings of the housing market may be such, however, that a shift upward of the demand curve brought about through the subsidization of existing housing will eventually result in increased production by housing suppliers, either through additional new construction or through higher expenditures for the maintenance and improvement of existing structures. The full potential of using housing subsidies with the existing stock has yet to be tapped.

Should Another Approach—Involving Housing Allowances—Also Be Tried?   There are three basic techniques used to assist lower-income families in improvement of their housing conditions:

1. *Project subsidies* tied to specific dwellings. If the recipient leaves the subsidized dwelling, he loses the subsidy.
2. *Housing allowances* made available to families according to their needs. These cash allowances could be spent for housing only. Housing allowances are tied to recipient families, not to specific dwellings. Thus, a family could take the subsidy with them when they move.
3. *Income maintenance* involving some sort of unrestricted cash payments to needy families. Here again the subsidy is tied to the family; but unlike the housing allowance approach, the recipient would himself decide whether to spend the funds on housing or other items.

All current American housing programs rely on project subsidies. Assistance under the programs is tied to specific dwellings, not to specific families. Different families benefit as they move in and out of the subsidized units. Although there are still some program gaps to be filled, the present range of project subsidy programs is actually rather comprehensive.

The principal advantage of project subsidies is that they are the most direct tool for rapidly increasing new housing production. In the long run, however, we believe that the housing allowance subsidy technique may possibly prove to be the most efficient technique for adjusting the supply of housing to the needs of both subsidized and nonsubsidized users. Housing allowances provide purchasing power directly to the housing consumer, who decides where in the total housing market, of both new and existing units, to apply it. A housing allowance system thus offers the opportunity for the free market to operate in its traditional fashion. Widespread distribution of housing allowances to poor families should reduce the economic dependence on slum housing and shift the demand upward for standard units. In response to this shift in demand, suppliers of housing would be induced to produce more standard housing, either by upgrading slum properties or through new construction. Thus, a housing allowance program should bring about, albeit indirectly, the gradual elimination of slums and a general increase in the quality of the housing stock. In order to accelerate the effects of housing allowances on the removal of slums, it is imperative that their use be restricted to units of standard quality. Owners of slums would then have to upgrade or find it difficult to rent their apartments.

A housing allowance system appears to have several potential advantages. It would permit the consumer to make his own choices in the market place, a freedom which tends to enhance personal dignity. By relying on market forces, it should bring about a better matching of consumer demands and housing supply. Low-income consumers would make their own decisions on location and housing style rather than having others make these decisions for them. The project subsidy programs are now largely insulated from the healthy influences of market forces. In addition, by allowing recipients of housing assistance to make their own decisions on location, public controversy over the location of subsidized projects would be avoided. Distribution of the benefits of housing allowances could be made more equitably than is possible under project subsidy programs. Lastly, it is possible, though not certain, that a housing allowance approach would eliminate administrative processing of projects and would involve lower administrative expenses for government than do the present project subsidy programs.

Several factors militate against a full-scale housing allowance program and have led to a conclusion that such a subsidy system initially be attempted on an experimental basis only. There is a strong need to stimulate new construction as quickly as possible and the project subsidy approach best lends itself to this purpose. In addition, the immediate adoption of a massive housing allowance system would be likely to inflate the cost of existing housing considerably, at least in the short run. The large infusion of new purchasing power would result in a bidding up of housing prices for the existing standard inventory. Consequently, any large-scale housing allowance system would have to be introduced gradually. Such a system might also require strong programs of consumer education and vigorous attacks on racial discrimination in order to work effectively. Despite these possible shortcomings, the potential merits of the housing allowance approach are such that it should be tried promptly on the experimental basis suggested.

The broader issues involved in income maintenance fall beyond the scope of our assignment. Major changes in the present welfare system would obviously affect the ability of poor families to participate in the market for standard housing, and thus would warrant the reconsideration of the structure of housing subsidy programs. We look forward to the findings of other commissions which have been charged with investigating these critical issues.

Can Housing Programs Be Simplified?   With the passage of the Housing Act of 1968, the Federal Government has available to it a wide variety of housing subsidy tools. There are two major programs for low-income families—Public Housing and Rent Supplements—and two for families with low to moderate incomes—the Section 235 Homeownership program and Section 236 (eventually to replace 221(d)(3) and 202). Some program gaps still exist. There is as yet, for example, no significant homeownership program for low-income families or any program which can by itself reach the very poor.

It is theoretically possible that the Federal Government could develop a single housing subsidy technique, involving periodic payments, which could be used for all income groups and for both rental and owner-occupied housing. The use of fewer approaches would reduce administrative costs to the Government and reduce confusion among private sponsors. Most of the programs are but a few years old, and thus a complete assessment of their merits cannot yet be made. Even the old Public Housing program has been transformed by so many new variations that it is no longer clear whether the old criticisms of it are still valid.

There must be continued reliance, at least for the next few years, on a variety of project subsidy techniques capable of integrated use. Given the great variety of urban housing problems, a comprehensive housing policy may well require a number of different programs. At present, the availability of a multiplicity of tools is desirable. However, programs extremely narrow in terms of sponsors or eligible beneficiaries should be avoided and all subsidy techniques should be capable of integrated use.

How Shall the Federal Government Administer These Programs?   Federal housing programs are now the responsibility of two separate divisions of HUD, headed by two different Assistant Secretaries. This administrative structure is an anachronism reflecting a time when the Public Housing Administration and the Federal Houseing Administration were separate agencies. It is proposed that all housing programs be placed under one Assistant Secretary or other appropriate official. We believe this would eliminate public confusion caused by unnecessary dissimilari-

ties in the processing of applications and the separate standards which
now apply to each program. The development of one housing division
would maximize the use of available Government expertise by reducing
the duplication of effort. Finally, simplification of program administration could lead to uniform standards, forms, and processing techniques
which would ultimately accelerate production.

In reviewing this difficult administrative problem, we considered and
rejected recommendations to create a new authority outside HUD to
administer subsidized housing programs or to create a new division within
HUD for the same purpose. It was determined that HUD has the
necessary expertise and experience to administer the programs. Furthermore, HUD has demonstrated a real interest and ability to reform
present procedures to improve upon its past record. It is noted that
HUD's past performance was in part due to legislative requirements
under which the agency was required to operate and in part a response
to Congressional pressures to eliminate mortgage defaults. The Housing
and Urban Development Act of 1968 contains directives which will free
HUD from these constraints. HUD's efforts in the past year indicate that
a major transformation is under way. There is a danger that the establishment of a new bureaucracy would bring few benefits and would
delay progress at a time when we can least afford such a delay.

How Can State Governments Assume Greater Responsibility?   It is
surprising how little most state governments have participated in efforts
to solve housing and urban development problems. Although most states
have metropolitan areas of some size, only sixteen have created departments oriented to urban problems. States are eligible to participate in the
Federal Public Housing program, but only one or two presently do so. A
state agency is potentially a particularly effective sponsor since it can
condemn land without regard to local boundaries and preempt local
building codes and zoning ordinances. The State of New York has
recently approved legislation creating a state corporation to sponsor
urban development programs.

Virtually all states would be well advised to reexamine their potential
for bettering housing conditions. For example, a state government could
enact legislation to supplement subsidies provided under Federal programs. Some states already reimburse localities which abate real estate
taxes on structures housing low- and moderate-income families, and
some have decided to supplement Urban Renewal funding.

The Housing Act of 1968 permits use of Rent Supplements and
Section 236 subsidies in state-assisted projects. This provides a sound
opportunity for cooperative Federalism, and we urge the states to pick
up the challenge.

How Can the Poor Be Involved in Housing Programs?   Federal
strategies for meeting the problems of the poor in the cities have recently

undergone a transformation. The goal of maximum involvement of the poor in efforts to remedy their condition, which began with the Economic Opportunity Act of 1964, is becoming a watchword. This notion has become an important part of the Model Cities and Urban Renewal programs. Effective citizen participation can lead to more responsive public decisions and to enhance dignity and responsibility. Of course, it is difficult to involve all the people in a neighborhood in any project and naive to think that they will always concur in their views. Efforts to involve the poor have of necessity been tentative and experimental. In many instances prompt consultation has allayed fears and misunderstanding.

The sponsors and owners of housing projects should be encouraged to consult with area residents in planning and policy making. Resident participation in the management of projects (tenant services, policing, etc.) is often essential for harmonious relations. It is proposed that a $10 million fund administered by HUD be established to underwrite promising public and private ventures in this field—training programs for resident real estate managers, programs to develop tenant management councils, efforts to create tenant maintenance contractors, and the like.

Housing programs also offer good opportunities for job training and employment of poor persons and members of minority groups. Section 3 of the Housing Act of 1968 directs HUD in its administration of the major housing subsidy programs to provide, to the greatest extent feasible, training and employment opportunities arising in connection with subsidized projects to lower-income persons residing in the area of such housing.

Lastly, housing programs should be used to encourage development of minority group entrepreneurs whose emergence would promote neighborhood stability and provide jobs for area residents. Negroes and other recent migrants to the cities are only beginning to form webs of small and medium-sized businesses. Negroes, for example, account for 11 percent of the national population but only 3.2 percent of self-employed persons. Housing programs can be especially useful in developing new entrepreneurial opportunities for minority group contractors and subcontractors. These entrepreneurs often have not been accepted in contactors' associations, are not used to bidding on large-scale jobs, and may not have the necessary capabilities in contract estimation, manpower scheduling, and job supervision. Many have encountered problems in obtaining credit and in posting required surety and performance bonds. Recent pilot projects, such as the one sponsored by the Ford Foundation in Oakland, California, have begun attacking these problems. Minority groups can also be assisted in developing other businesses related to housing—lending institutions, real estate agencies, architecture and engineering firms, and the like. Minority groups outside the mainstream of our free enterprise system should be brought into it. Self-reliance and self-help are surer roads to progress than continued dependency.

PART THREE: PRIVATE DEVELOPERS AND PUBLIC PROGRAMS

This section reviews Federal housing programs and considers whether they offer ample opportunities for business to participate in the development of housing for the poor. The profitability of these programs is examined in detail because literature explaining their profit potential is not readily available. It is our hope that the materials presented here will stimulate wider program interest on the part of business.

The staff concentrated on the private sector in accordance with the Committee's charge, recognizing that this country will not reach the required level of production without the full involvement of American business.

Housing of the poor, however, cannot be considered the province of any single element of society; it requires all. Proposals are offered to improve the capabilities of local public agencies and nonprofit organizations.

In addition to determining what may be required to attract *existing* development talent to Federal housing programs for the poor, this paper considers ways to develop new instruments and to attract talent presently inactive in the field. One result of these studies is the National Housing Partnership, which was introduced as part of the President's 1968 Housing Program and has now been enacted into law. A portion of this discussion will explain the purposes and organization of the National Housing Partnership.

I. The Private Sector's Role in Federal Programs

A. Public Housing.   At its inception Public Housing offered the private sector few opportunities to participate. The "conventional" system of developing public housing followed the usual public works format, limiting the role of the private entrepreneur to that of contractor. The private sector was afforded no opportunity to be a developer of housing (purchasing land, supervising the design, constructing the building, selling or leasing all or a portion of the completed project) or to be a builder (supervising the design and constructing the building) or even to be a manager of a completed project. However, in recent years opportunities for private participation in the development and management of public housing have been greatly expanded.

1. TURNKEY I (DEVELOPMENT).   The Turnkey process, started by the Department of Housing and Urban Development on an experimental basis in January of 1966, permits a local Public Housing authority to

enter into a commitment to eventually purchase a housing project (land and building) from a private developer who has built the project in accordance with plans approved by the authority. The purchase price is established under a procedure set forth in the contract between the parties and contains ample protection for both. Joseph Burstein, Associate General Counsel for Legal Services of HUD, summarized the significance of this program in an article appearing in the Summer, 1967 issue of "Law and Contemporary Problems" as follows:

Although simple in concept, the Turnkey system completely reverses the traditional method of producing public housing—site acquisition by purchase or condemnation, preparation of competitive-bidding type plans and specifications by an architect retained by the Local Housing Authority, competitive bidding and award, and construction by the low bidder. This "conventional" system followed the pattern of public construction with its built-in safeguards and its comcomitant built-in delays and expenses. More important from the standpoint of residential construction the system excluded the great bulk of private entrepreneurs engaged in private construction and thereby lost the potential benefit of their expertise and efficiency, developed in the residential field through competition for public acceptability. The purpose of Turnkey was to permit more adequate utilization of the means and knowledge of private enterprise in producing the finished public housing.

This Turnkey I program is very much like the turnkey process often employed by the private sector for the development of new plants. In this system the purchaser contracts with a builder to design and build a plant to certain specifications; a predetermined price is paid when the keys to the completed building are delivered.

The details of the Turnkey process in public housing are as follows:

(a) *Selection of Developer.* The local housing authority can accept solicited or unsolicited proposals for development of a project. The proposal should contain a preliminary price for land and building; a description of the site, including a citywide map showing the relationship of the site to schools, shopping centers and transportation; a rough sketch of a feasible site plan with a rough sketch of the building and typical units, and description of the type of construction and heating system to be used.

(b) *Letter Designating Turnkey Developer.* The local authority selects a developer on the basis of the suitability and feasibility of the proposal. No further selection or bidding process is required. Once selected, the authority will send a letter to the developer notifying him that his proposal has been approved and requesting him to prepare and submit preliminary plans, specifications, and a proposed sales price subdivided into land cost, construction cost, and architectural and engineering cost services.

(*c*) *Negotiation and Execution of Letter of Intent.* Upon receiving the "Letter Designating Turnkey Developer," the developer submits preliminary plans, outline specifications, evidence of ownership of the site (or that the developer will own the site prior to the start of construction), and a sales price. This submission must be complete enough to permit the local authority to obtain two independent land appraisals and construction cost estimates. On the basis of these independent estimates, the local authority negotiates a purchase price which is inserted in a Letter of Intent and executed by the developer and the authority and then approved by HUD.

The "Letter of Intent to Enter into Contract of Sale of Low-Rent Housing Project to Local Authority" obligates the parties to enter into a contract to sell the finished project when completed in accordance with plans prepared by the developer and approved by the local authority. The parties agree that the sale price shall be the lesser of (1) the price stated in the Letter of Intent or (2) the sum of (*a*) the negotiated land price, (*b*) architectural and engineering fees, and (*c*) the midpoint between two independent cost estimates based upon the final working drawings and detailed construction specifications. To protect the developer, the Letter provides that if the final cost estimate is less than 95 percent of the price stated in the Letter of Intent, and if the parties cannot negotiate an acceptable purchase price, then the developer may sell the site together with the plans, and the local authority must purchase the land and plans for a price equal to the stated value of the site and the stated cost of preparing plans and performing architectural and engineering services. If the parties agree not to sell the site, the developer must absorb the cost of the plans.

The Letter of Intent also contains a timetable for submission and approval of plans and execution of the Contract of Sale. In the event that there is a delay in the submission or approval of plans, the construction cost estimate is adjusted in accordance with the percentage change in the Department of Commerce composite cost index.

(*d*) *Executive of Contract of Sale.* After execution of the Letter of Intent the developer prepares and submits working drawings and detailed specifications. The local authority obtains a cost estimate based upon these final plans. Once the final cost estimates are available, the parties execute the Contract of Sale. The price is determined in accordance with the pricing procedure set out in the Letter of Intent.

(*e*) *Construction and Purchase.* After execution of the Contract of Sale, work on the site proceeds. If required, Federal guarantees of interim financing can be arranged. Upon completion of the project, title is transferred to the local authority.

The program is based on the belief that involving the private sector in acquisition of sites and preparation of plans will produce public housing

more quickly and at less cost. While precise results must await comple
tion of a study now underway within the HAA, preliminary indications
suggest that these objectives are being attained.

In addition to being beneficial to the public, the Turnkey procedure
has proved attractive to the businessman. A price based on cost estimates
provides the private developer with an adequate profit, but is subject to
reasonable safeguards. The negotiation system does present some risk of
excessive profit taking, but the risks are no different from those of
business elsewhere and professional cost estimators can reduce substantially the possibility of excessive profits.

The Federal Government should encourage the use of Turnkey I by
urging local housing authorities to solicit Turnkey proposals before
proceeding with conventional methods.

2. TURNKEY II MANAGEMENT.   The Department of Housing and
Urban Development has recently tried on an experimental basis the
private *management* of housing projects owned by public authorities.
This new practice, called Turnkey II, is a logical extension of the
Turnkey I program. The new program was referred to the Committee for
comment prior to its announcement and its response was favorable. It
was felt that business can develop the management teams skilled in the
special problems of managing low-income housing developments. The
introduction of competent private management will provide a competitive element that will encourage flexibility in the traditional attitudes
reflected in present practices. The feasibility of such a program depends,
of course, upon adequate compensation to the private management.

At the present time management contracts are negotiated on the basis
of an agreed budget plus a fixed fee. The local authority pays the direct
expenses or reimburses the management firm for them. The management
firm receives a fee based on that customarily paid for comparable services in the locality. The firm is required to manage the project within the
annual budget. The budget may be revised for good cause with approval
by the local authority and HUD.

While almost any type of fee arrangement is legally possible, HUD's
budget plus fixed fee contract protects both the public interest and the
owner from excessive risks. The parties can negotiate a budget containing a maximum figure which affords the manager a reasonable operating
margin. Since the public agency pays only actual costs, in the event the
manager is able to operate economically, the savings are passed along to
the public.

Turnkey II can also add variety to the type and character of the
housing to be provided. The proposed Lavanburg Foundation development in New York City, one of the pilot projects announced by HUD, is
an illustration. The Lavanburg Foundation, a nonprofit organization,
proposes to develop and sell to the New York City Housing Authority on

a Turnkey basis an undivided interest in the residential portion of a project which includes moderate-income housing and accompanying commercial, recreational, medical, and community facilities. In addition, the Foundation will retain complete management responsibility by negotiating a Turnkey II management contract for the Housing Authority's project activities. In this manner, public housing tenants will be provided with a conventional housing setting. Any Public Housing tenant whose income exceeds Public Housing levels will be permitted to remain in the development and will receive the benefits of the moderate-income assistance. The transfer of a tenant from one program to another would appear only as a book entry.

3. LEASING PROGRAM. The new Section 23 leasing program authorizes local Public Housing authorities to lease privately owned real estate for occupancy by families eligible for Public Housing. The difference between the rental received by the landlord and that part paid by the tenant—the subsidy—is contributed, subject to limitations as to amount, by the Federal Government.

HUD anticipates that in fiscal year 1969 the leasing techniques will account for approximately 16 percent of the total number of subsidized units to be provided under all Federal subsidy programs. Although only three years old, this program has proved the feasibility of subsidizing existing standard housing.

The leasing technique allows the private housing market to make existing standard housing units available to Public Housing authorities at market rentals. The private property owner executes a lease with the local housing authority. Selection of tenants is usually the function of the local authority. Rentals to be charged are decided by negotiation. The power to give notice to vacate is reserved to the local authority. The lease provisions fixing responsibility for maintenance and replacement (including redecoration) are required to conform to standard practice for the rental of other units in the building.

Section 23 of the U.S. Housing Act restricts the lease term to one to five years. However, with the approval of HUD, the lease may contain renewal options to be exercised at the discretion of the parties or automatically, which could extend the term to 10 years, or longer in rare instances. The Section 10(c) leasing program permits leasing up to 40 years. This program, however, requires:

1. The existence of an approved "Workable Program," and
2. Partial tax exemption or tax remission by the local community.

From a private investment standpoint, the leasing program can be economically attractive. In addition to earning a fair return on the lease, the developer retains the benefits of the tax savings available to owners of real estate. Given such a broadened profit opportunity, the negotiating position of Public Housing authorities should be substantially improved. The authority should be able to negotiate favorable lease terms, including the option to acquire the development, on attractive terms, at termination of the lease.

Both the Section 10(c) and Section 23 programs limit the use of Federal subsidies to existing structures. While this will not prohibit local authorities from executing leases with developers prior to the construction of a property, it does expose the local authority and the developer of a new project to unnecessary risks since there is no absolute assurance that the Federal subsidies will be available. It increases the difficulties of financing low-income housing development. The restriction of the leasing program to existing structures and the limitations placed on the Section 23 lease term unnecessarily complicate a program which offers substantial opportunity for the private sector to develop public housing.

For these reasons, a modification of the leasing program is proposed: HUD should permit lease renewal options to extend for that period of time that will best facilitate project financing, and Congress should remove the restriction to existing structures.

B. FHA Programs. The Federal Housing Administration administers the new Section 235 Homeownership program and the major rental programs involving private ownership. A homebuilder earns profits under Section 235 in essentially the same way that he earns them when he builds and sells conventional houses. The builder prepares plans and has them approved by FHA prior to the beginning of construction. On completion, the units are sold to qualifying purchasers who will receive a mortgage in an amount established by FHA. If the builder is efficient, this price should include a fair profit.

Substantial opportunities for profit are also available under the rental programs—221(d)(3) Below Market Interest Rate (BMIR), Rent Supplements and 236—but the situation is considerably more complex. We shall discuss at some length the prospects for profit under the 221(d)(3) BMIR program. Except for minor variations, this analysis is equally applicable to Rent Supplement projects and those developed under Section 236.

The 221(d)(3) BMIR projects can be developed in a variety of ways. They may be sponsored on behalf of a cooperative, a nonprofit corporation, or by an entity (which can be an individual, partnership, or trust) which contracts to accept a limited return on its equity (as calculated by FHA), thus referred to as a "limited dividend entity." If the ultimate owner is to be a cooperative or nonprofit corporation, profit opportunities —except for management services—are limited to the project development stage. However, if the sponsor is a limited dividend entity, profits may be achieved in both the development phase and during the life of the project. The discussion which follows will use the terms "sponsor" and "builder" as they are used in the FHA regulations governing the program. In general, the "sponsor" is what is usually called a developer, and the "builder" corresponds to a general contractor. The profit opportunities in the development process and during ownership (the investment stage) are analyzed separately.

1. PRIVATE BUSINESS OPPORTUNITIES IN THE DEVELOPMENT PROCESS. The development process of a 221(d)(3) BMIR project can offer reasonable fees to general contractors, architectural and engineering firms, mortgage servicers, lawyers, consultants for nonprofit sponsors, and in some cases land owners. FHA permits mortgage proceeds to be spent as follows:

Builder's profit and overhead. For almost all 221(d)(3) BMIR projects,[1] FHA regulations require a cost plus fixed fee contract with a maximum upset price. Under the terms of this contract, the builder is required to complete the project for no more than the predetermined maximum. However, in no case can he receive mortgage proceeds in excess of certified costs plus his fee allowance. Local FHA offices prepare percentage fee schedules for the builder's general overhead and profit. These fees will depend on the nature of the project and on the local experience. Total fees may vary from 10 percent on a $100,000 project to 4.25 percent on a $12,000,000 project. Where an "identity of interest" is established between the builder and the sponsor of a limited divided entity, a flat 10 percent (exclusive of land) "builders and sponsors profit and risk allowance" is allowed in place of the profit fee schedule. This allowance is discussed more fully below.

Architectural and engineering fees. The architect's fee allowed by FHA depends upon services rendered, professional fees prevailing in the locality, the complexity of the work, and the degree of repetition in planning. Local FHA offices prepare a schedule of allowable fees.

Mortgage loan placement and servicing. A fee of up to 2 percent is currently recognized in calculating the mortgage to meet the costs of construction loan placement and its servicing. The amount of the fee is adjusted according to market conditions as reflected by prevailing interest rates for conventional and insured loans.

Legal and organizational fees. FHA allows a fee which covers both legal and organizational services. Amounts approved for such expenses are those established by local practice. FHA has established a guideline which varies from 0.75 percent to 0.5 percent of the mortgage amount, depending on the size of the mortgage.

Organizational consultant to nonprofit sponsors. A fee for consulting services needed by a nonprofessional sponsor is allowed in the case of a

---

[1] A lump sum contract can be used only where a cooperative housing project is being built, and there is no identity of interest between the cooperative (or its agent) and the builder.

nonprofit sponsor. This fee reflects recognition of the difficulties that otherwise capable nonprofit sponsors have encountered because of their lack of expertise in the fundamentals of real estate development.

Sale of land. Profits on land are possible because the present market value of land rather than its cost is included in calculating the mortgage. But the economics of the program rarely permit land costs which are excessive. If land cost is too high, it would be impossible to complete the project and rent the units at a profit within the FHA-established rental ceilings. Thus, in many areas of the South, raw land value per unit is rarely permitted to exceed $850. In metropolitan markets in the East, this figure has reached $1,400 per unit.

2. PROFIT OPPORTUNITY FOR THE INVESTOR. The investor's profits are generated by project operation and the structure of the Federal tax system. There are three possible sources of profit: management fees, cash distributions from gross receipts which are allowed for limited dividend entities, and savings resulting from income tax deductions allowed both during and after construction.

Since the amount of tax savings (offsets against income subject to tax) depends on a taxpayer's "bracket," profits vary with the scale of an investor's taxable income from other sources. To illustrate the yield which may be achieved in a 221(d)(3) BMIR project, an illustrative case is considered based on a project developed by a limited dividend entity. An identity of interest is assumed between the builder and sponsor, thus permitting the use of the 10 percent "Builders and Sponsors Profit and Risk Allowance" in computing the mortgage. This is the sort of organizational approach many private builders could be expected to use.

To measure profit potential, the first tasks are to calculate the equity and the out-of-pocket cash investment required. The 221(d)(3) program provides for a mortgage loan to a limited dividend entity in an amount equal to 90 percent of a project's "actual" cost as defined by FHA. Table 2–3 illustrates the items included in the initial computation of "estimated replacement cost" and shows how the mortgage amount and equity requirements are computed.

Table 2–3 indicates that actual costs as defined by FHA include all development costs with the exception of a 2 percent working capital requirement to be deposited at the time the mortgage is signed and a 1 percent commitment fee payable to the Federal National Mortgage Association (FNMA). Since the mortgage amount equals 90 percent of approved actual costs, cash requirements would presumably be the remaining 10 percent balance (in our typical case, $408,000) plus working capital and the FNMA fee.

Actual cash requirements are shown in Table 2–4. In calculating the mortgage, a 10 percent builder's and sponsor's profit and risk allowance was credited to the sponsor. This is not an out-of-pocket cost. The

TABLE 2–3

221(d)(3) Below Market Interest Rate Project (Identity of Interest Between Builder and Sponsor)[1]

Construction cost (272 garden apartment units) excluding builder's overhead and profit		$3,000,000
Construction fees:		
Architect and engineers (4.5 percent)	$135,000	
Builder's general overhead[2]	60,000	
Quantity survey	4,000	199,000
Carrying charges and financing:		
Interest during construction	146,000	
Financing	73,000	
Taxes during construction	32,000	
Title and recording	20,000	
FHA examination fee	11,000	
FHA inspection fee	18,000	300,000
Legal and organizational expenses		$ 28,000
Builders and sponsors profit and risk allowance[3]		353,000
Land		200,000
Total Estimated Replacement Cost		$4,080,000
Maximum FHA-insurable mortage (90 percent)		3,672,000
Equity[4]		$ 408,000

[1] An identity of interest exists when the builder has a proprietary interest in the project or when the sponsor has a proprietary interest in the builder.

[2] The builder's overhead allowance is calculated pursuant to informal FHA guidelines. In addition to overhead, the builder receives a profit fee. In this example, the profit fee is $90,000. Payments to the builder thus total $150,000—5 percent of construction costs.

[3] When there is an "identity of interest" between the builder and the sponsor, FHA regulations allow a "builders and sponsors profit and risk allowance" of 10 percent of all costs other than land. The builder's profit must be paid from this allowance.

[4] The equity of $408,000 usually does not represent an actual cash requirement of the builder-sponsor.

TABLE 2–4

Analysis of Sponsor's Potential Cash Requirements

Equity needs	$408,000
Less:	
Builder's and Sponsor's Profit and Risk Allowance	353,000
Cash needed to meet closing requirements	$ 55,000
Cash needs:	
To meet closing requirements	55,000
2 percent working capital[1]	73,000
1 percent FNMA commitment fee[2]	37,000
Builder's profit[3]	90,000
Sponsor's overhead costs[3]	153,000[4]
Total	$408,000

[1] Any unexpended funds returned at final closing.

[2] Recoverable from mortgage proceeds to the extent that savings are achieved in items for which use of mortgage proceeds is authorized.

[3] If the builder and sponsor are wholly identical, no cash payment is necessary.

[4] Experience suggests that the sponsor's overhead may be less than noted. "Cash needs" are correspondingly reduced. Sponsors may provide a portion of these needs in the form of services.

balance of potential cash expenditures is shown in the table. It should be emphasized that it is a rare situation in which the sponsor's cash requirements equal the stated equity. Since stated equity is based in part on estimated costs, the cash required will vary, thereby penalizing or rewarding entrepreneurial skill as the case may be. For example, if the sponsor has to spend an inordinate amount of time in developing the project, or if he has to pay his architect, builder, or construction money lender more than FHA estimates, the cash requirements could increase above the stated 10 percent figure. An efficient operator can obviously reduce his cash requirements. Even if the cash requirements are below the stated equity figure, this is not unreasonable considering the other real estate and business opportunities foregone and the risks involved.

With equity and cash requirements defined, the next question is the return to the owner-investor. As previously mentioned, profits may be realized from management, the limited dividend payment, and tax deductions.

Management Fees. FHA allowances for management expense vary with the size and type of project and location. However, they usually run from 3 to 6 percent of gross rents. For Rent Supplement projects, allowances for management expense may be as high as 8 percent.

If outside professional management is hired, it can receive the prevailing percentage (plus a fee) of gross rental income. If owner-management is chosen, FHA allows expenses (for salaries, overhead, and the like) equal to those typically found in similar projects. A paid employee-manager is customary in larger projects. His compensation often includes a project living unit.

Management profits have proven to be varied and hard to calculate in advance. Profits from management have not been included in computing yields for the illustrative case.

Cash Return—The Limited Dividend Payment. In a subsidized project insured by FHA, statutes and regulations control the amount of the mortgage, the rents which can be charged, and the amount of the net income which may be distributed to the owner. The regulations are embodied in the Regulatory Agreement executed by the project owner and FHA. The effect of FHA regulations is to place a ceiling on cash profits, regardless of actual earnings. Table 2–5 illustrates a typical *pro forma* operating statement.

As shown in Table 2–5, the impact of the Regulatory Agreement is to restrict cash distribution to 6 percent of one-ninth of the mortgage. In the illustrative case, this is equal to 6 percent of the equity as shown in Table 2–3. While there is no guarantee that the project will have high occupancy and produce income, should some of the estimates in the *pro forma* operating statement prove unduly conservative (i.e., if the project has less than 7 percent vacancy or operating expenses are less than

TABLE 2–5

Pro Forma Annual Operating Statement
(after construction and start-up)

	221(d)(3) BMIR Program: 40-Year, 3 Percent Mortgage
Number of units..	272
Monthly rent per unit.....................................	$ 120
Gross rental income.......................................	$392,000
Vacancy factor[1]...	$ 28,000
Net rental income...	$364,000
Operating expenses and property taxes[2]....................	$172,000
Replacement reserve......................................	$ 10,000
Debt service[3]...	$157,500
Cash flow to investors[4]..................................	$ 24,500

[1] Assumed 7 percent of gross rents.
[2] Includes a management fee of 5 percent of gross rents or $20,000. Operating expenses, property taxes, and replacement reserve assumed to total $56 per unit per month (Replacement reserve is noted separately.) This figure is based on FHA experience related to a $1,500,000 project. Larger projects such as this should have lower per unit operating expenses, and rents would be reduced accordingly.
[3] Based on mortgage of $3,672,000 (see Table 2–3), at 3 percent for 40 years.
[4] Limited to 6 percent of 11.11 percent of the mortgage. In this case annual cash flow is equal to 6 percent of the equity of $408,000. (See Table 2–3.)

anticipated), the investors would still not be permitted to receive more than 6 percent. Any profits in excess of this amount are used to prepay the mortgage, to increase operating reserves, to finance project improvements, or to reduce rents.

It is submitted that such a cash return is unrealistic when compared to current rates of cash return for alternative investments. Because there is a risk inherent in any such investment, it is proper that its rate of return exceed that being paid for bonds, mortgages, and other debt paper of less risk. For these reasons it is suggested that *FHA increase the rate of return to 8 percent or some other figure which is more realistic than 6 percent.* If the rate were increased to 8 percent, the annual cash income in the illustrative case would increase from $24,500 to $32,600 per year. The increase to 8 percent would increase rents slightly—by about $2.50 per unit per month in the illustrative case. However, this is justified by the need to provide a more realistic return, particularly to sponsors who are not in high tax brackets and who cannot enjoy the benefits of tax savings generated by the project.

Tax Savings. While Federal regulations limit cash returns, the owner of a subsidized housing project is entitled to take normal depreciation deductions on project development cost (excluding land) in calculating his Federal income taxes. Moreover, under existing tax law, depreciation may be taken in various accelerated forms so that deductions are greater during the early years of project life. (A 1964 amendment of the Internal Revenue Code provided that some or all of the benefits of accelerated depreciation are recaptured.) Other tax deductions are also available in early years. If a project is owned by a partnership, individual and corporate partners can obtain the benefit of the partnership's tax losses. Each investor may use these book losses to offset other income in computing annual taxes. Thus, while the cash yield by itself may not be impressive, a Federally subsidized project may be sufficiently "profitable" to an investor who can offset other income with substantial book losses, thus reducing the amount of tax currently payable.

Total Yields. Ignoring for the moment the tax consequences of sale, the total annual return—net cash income plus tax savings—available to taxpayers in various tax brackets is shown in Table 2–6. The table shows both the cumulative average return on equity ("average") and the discounted return ("dis"). The discounted yield takes into account the time when the return is received. Since income is higher in the early years and available for reinvestment, it is more valuable, and, therefore, the discounted yield computation would exceed average yield.

While the yields shown in Table 2–6 appear to be reasonably attractive, at least in the earlier years when tax savings are highest, the table does not reflect the serious impact upon those returns of the tax consequences of the sale of a project. In the year of sale the seller is required to pay taxes on the difference between the sales price and the depreciated basis of the project. Furthermore, depending on the length of time the property was held by the seller, some portion of this amount may be taxable as ordinary income.

The taxes on sale diminish the established yields substantially. Appendix H–3 shows the amount of tax payable on the sale of a project after various holding periods; the sale price is assumed equivalent to the unamortized mortgage amount which would be outstanding if the project had originally had a 100 percent mortgage (3 percent interest rate for 40 years). The effect on yields of the tax payable on sale is presented in Table 2–7 for taxpayers in the 50 percent bracket.

The tax consequences of the sale of the project seriously diminish the attractiveness of the investment since many investors seek a discounted after-tax return of at least 15 percent. It is apparent that the tax on sale may reduce reasonable returns in the early years to unrealistic levels and also reduce the previously marginal long-term yields.

Because of rising real estate values, the tax consequences of sale are minimized in the conventional housing market. Profits from the sale are available to pay the taxes. However, under past FHA procedures this

TABLE 2-6

Cumulative Average After-Tax Yield—(Including 6 Percent Cash Return and Tax Saving) on Investment of $408,000[1] (221(d)(3) Below Market Interest Rate Project) for Investors in 30, 50, and 70 Percent Bracket Ignoring Tax Consequences on Sale

Years before Sale[2]	Yield for Taxpayer 30 Percent Bracket			Yield for Taxpayer 50 Percent Bracket			Yield for Taxpayer 70 Percent Bracket		
	Annual Return[3]	Dis[4] Percent	Average[5] Percent	Annual return[3]	Dis[4] Percent	Average[5] Percent	Annual return[3]	Dis[4] Percent	Average[5] Percent
1	$77,000	14.5	18.9	$128,300	24.4	31.4	$179,600	37.7	44.0
2	38,600		14.2	64,000		23.6	90,100		33.1
3	49,800		13.5	66,600		21.1	83,400		28.8
4	46,900		13.0	61,800		19.7	76,700		26.3
5	44,100	12.9	12.6	57,200	19.9	18.5	70,200	27.4	24.5
6	39,700		12.1	49,900		17.5	60,000		22.8
7	37,100		11.7	45,500		16.6	54,000		21.5
8	34,600		11.3	41,400		15.8	48,200		20.3
9	32,200		10.9	37,400		15.0	42,500		19.2
10	29,900	11.3	10.5	33,500	16.8	14.4	37,000	23.2	18.2
11	27,600		10.2	29,700		13.7	31,700		17.2
12	25,400		9.9	26,000		13.1	26,600		16.3
13	23,300		9.5	22,400		12.5	21,600		15.5
14	21,200		9.2	19,000		12.0	16,800		14.7
15	19,200	10.2	8.9	15,600	15.0	11.4	12,100	21.2	13.9
16	17,200		8.6	12,300		10.9	7,500		13.1
17	15,300		8.3	9,100		10.4	3,000		12.4
18	13,500		8.1	6,000		9.9	(1,400)		11.7
19	11,600		7.8	2,900		9.4	(5,700)		11.0
20	9,800	9.4	7.5	(100)	13.8	8.9	(9,900)	20.0	10.3

[1] If real equity is less than $408,000, yields would increase proportionately. Assumes that return is received annually, and that entire equity investment must be made at the beginning of construction.

[2] Assumes one-year construction period and one-year break even period.

[3] "Annual return" is the sum of Columns A (net cash income) plus applicable Column B, C, or D (tax savings) in the table in Appendix H-2.

[4] "Dis" represents the average cumulative rate of return on the $408,000 equity, discounted in accordance with accepted financial practice.

[5] "Average" represents the average cumulative rate of return on the $408,000 equity, not discounted.

TABLE 2–7

**Effect of Tax on Sale[1] of 221(d)(3)BMIR Project on Yield[2]
Taxpayer in 50 Percent Tax Bracket**

	After Tax Rate of Return Before Sale[3] in Percent		After Tax Rate of Return After Sale[4] in Percent	
	Discount	Average	Discount	Average
Sale after 2 years..................24.4	23.6	3.3	3.3	
Sale after 5 years..................19.9	18.5	5.8	4.5	
Sale after 10 years................16.8	14.4	9.7	5.6	
Sale after 15 years................15.0	11.4	10.7	4.7	
Sale after 20 years................13.8	8.9	11.0	3.5	

[1] The sale price is assumed equivalent to the unamortized mortgage amount which would be outstanding had the project initially received 100 percent mortgage financing.
[2] If real equity is less than $408,000, yields would increase proportionately.
[3] See Table 3–4.
[4] Table 3–4 yields reduced by tax consequences of sale. See Appendix H-3.

solution is not available to owners of subsidized projects. Regulations have prohibited refinancing for 20 years, and sale has rarely been permitted to a subsequent owner without loss of subsidies on the project.

In light of the magnitude of the goal of six to eight million subsidized units in the next decade, it appears necessary to assure the satisfactory yield pictured in Table 2–6. This will require a solution of the tax-on-sale problem which reduces yields to the unsatisfactory levels shown in Table 2–7. We propose the following to maintain yields at adequate levels:

1. Table 2–6 shows that apart from tax consequences of the sale, profits can be maximized by a sale in the early years. The first step, therefore, is to make use of the new authority added by Section 105(a) of the 1968 Act which permits sale of 221(d)(3) BMIR projects in their early years to similarly financed cooperatives and condominiums and the comparable provisions in new Section 236(j)(3).

2. The second step is to reduce the impact of the tax on the sale of the project. This critical problem can be approached in several ways.

Recognize tax in sale price. In the case of the sale of a project to a cooperative, condominium, or nonprofit organization, FHA should be authorized to recognize a sale price which will permit the owner-investor to recover his equity investment and sufficient cash to pay the tax due on the sale. This would maintain yields at the levels shown in Table 2–6. This is the approach adopted with regard to Section 236 of the National Housing Act incorporated in the 1968 Housing Act. As the House Committee on Banking and Currency reported:

Mortgage insurance would also be available under this section [236] to enable a cooperative or private nonprofit organization to purchase a project from a limited-dividend mortgagor. In such a case, the Secretary would be authorized to insure the purchaser's mortgage in an amount not exceeding the appraised value of the property at the time of purchase, *thereby making it possible for the cooperative or nonprofit organization to borrow, under a single mortgage, the funds needed to obtain ownership, while enabling the limited-dividend seller to realize a net amount out of the sales proceeds in many cases sufficient to recover its cash, land, and other investment and to retire the outstanding mortgage.* This will be especially useful in connection with the goal of attracting large amounts of private-equity money into the provision of low and moderate income housing through the establishment of national partnerships (proposed by title VIII of the bill). It will give the limited-dividend mortgagor a ready means of disposing of his project, thereby making his investment more liquid and attractive. [Emphasis added.]

Meeting tax requirements from sale proceeds would require, however, an increase in the mortgage, which could affect monthly rents. To avoid any increase in rents, we propose that FHA be authorized to extend the term of the mortgage. For example, if the project with an original cost of $4,080,000 were sold after 10 years, the sale price would be at least $4,012,000 computed as follows: $3,181,000 unamortized mortgage outstanding which has to be refinanced, plus $408,000 equity plus $423,000 to cover the tax liability on the sale. In order to maintain the same rent payments, the term of the new mortgage would have to be at least 36.1 years. (See Appendix H–4 for further details.)

Tax credit. While the approach discussed above is simple to administer and requires no modification of the tax law, it does extend the term or increase the amount of the mortgage. This is not burdensome, but would be better avoided. Instead, the sponsor might be allowed, upon completion of development, a tax credit equal to 3 percent of the total replacement cost of the project. This would be similar to the existing 7 percent investment tax credit available to those who place new machinery and equipment into service but not to those developing real property. It would be identical to the 3 percent investment tax credit available for placing into service qualified public utility property.

The advantage of the tax credit approach is that it allows tenants to assume ownership or control (through a nonprofit, cooperative or condominium) without an increase in monthly payment or without extending the mortgage term. Moreover, it removes the problems the Secretary might face in trying to appraise value fairly while cognizant of the economic constraints imposed on a seller facing a heavy tax burden. Finally, it is a widely accepted, well-understood mechanism available to the vast majority of industrial firms. Appendix H–5 indicates the effect on yields of the combination of a 3 percent tax credit and the recommendation to increase annual cash return to 8 percent.

Tax forgiveness. As a third alternative, it is proposed that the tax laws be amended to limit the taxable gain on sale to the amount by which the sale price exceeds the original value of the project (equity plus original mortgage). This approach would also maintain the yields shown in Table 2–6. In order to assure that this tax benefit encourages the development of subsidized housing, the tax forgiveness might be conditioned on the investment of proceeds of sale in similar projects within a reasonable period of time.

II. A New Private Instrument—The National Housing Partnerships

How many private firms are ready and willing to join in the development of housing for low- and moderate-income families?

The Committee commissioned Walter Gerson and Associates, Inc. to survey business attitudes toward sponsoring housing projects. While hardly definitive, the survey did indicate that given the opportunities available last year when the survey was taken, big business as a whole was not likely to be much involved in the development of subsidized housing. Lack of technical knowledge and reluctance to become the owner of individual projects were the principal explanations for this inactivity.

The Committee, therefore, recommended to the President the creation of a new private instrument—The National Housing Partnerships—to permit firms not now engaged in the subsidized housing field to come into it on a sound business basis. This recommendation was later enacted into law as Title IX of the Housing and Urban Development Act of 1968. In acting on the Committee's recommendation in his message on "The Crisis of the Cities" of February 1968, the President said this:

I propose that the Congress authorize the formation of privately funded partnerships that will join private capital with business skills to help close the low-income housing gap.

The Kaiser Committee identified three principal reasons why American industry has not yet been attracted to the field of low and moderate-income housing. The problems and the steps proposed to meet them are:

1. Concentration of Risk

The profitability of individual housing projects varies widely and the risk of loss on any one project is high. The proposed national partnerships would permit industrial and financing firms to pool their investments and spread their risks over a large number of projects.

2. Rate of Return

Substantial operating losses are usually incurred in the first 10 years of a housing project's life as the result of operating and interest expenses and depreciation.

Under existing law the partnership form of organization, now used by some building owners permits these operating losses to be "passed through" to each investor, and used by him as an offset against his other taxable income. This reduces current income taxes otherwise payable, and makes possible an annual cash return on investment comparable to the average earnings of American business in other manufacturing enterprises.

3. Management

The management personnel of major corporations are inexperienced in the field of low income housing. They cannot afford to devote substantial time to occasional housing ventures.

The proposed national partnerships would be strongly financed organizations fully committed to long-term activity in the single field of housing for the poor. As such, the proposed partnerships should be able to attract top flight management and technical experts on a competitive career basis.

The objective of these partnerships will be to attract capital from American industry and to put that capital to work. Their exclusive purpose will be to generate a substantial additional volume of low and moderate income housing. They will use the best private management talent, planning techniques, and advanced methods of construction. They will probe for savings inherent in the latest technology and in economies of scale. They will:

—participate in joint ventures throughout the country in partnership with local builders, developers, and investors;

—join with American labor to open new job opportunities for the very people their projects will house;

—participate in our existing and proposed federal programs for assisting low and moderate income projects on the same basis as other project sponsors.

This new undertaking will begin with one national partnership. We expect that others will follow as the approach proves itself.

As the President noted, the partnership form was chosen to permit the passing through of book losses (resulting from depreciation and other deductions) to each investor. Title IX of the Housing and Urban Development Act of 1968 governs the organization of the partnerships. The President has appointed the incorporators of a profit-motivated corporate General Partner. The incorporators will establish the General Partner and provide the framework for the partnership itself. They will raise capital from American business and financial institutions by sale of shares in the Corporation and interests in the Partnership.

The Partnership has the special purpose of engaging in activities related to providing housing for low- or moderate-income persons, relying primarily on the Federal housing subsidy programs. Local builder and investor participation is contemplated in all developments. The law assures that the Partnership will include local investors by limiting nonlocal investment to 25 percent of the equity of any specific project, except where additional funds cannot be raised from local sources.

Although neither the General Partner nor the Partnership has been given any special powers, it was deemed advisable to establish them by Act of Congress for the following reasons:

1. The existence of the legislation serves as a national invitation to industry to participate—to join in the development of housing for low- and moderate-income families on a profit-making basis;
2. The legislative history secures the feasibility of the pass-through of tax savings to individual partners; and
3. Provisions of the Act specifically settle questions of local law which might be thought unresolved, such as the power of the Corporation to operate as the General Partner of the Partnership.

In addition to helping to produce housing for low- and moderate-income families, the National Housing Partnership was conceived of as a laboratory for the development of practical solutions to the problems of reducing construction costs and production time, improving landlord-tenant relationships, and promoting and assuring successful homeownership for low- and moderate-income families.

No single private organization presently develops and only a few operate any large volume of housing for low- and moderate-income families. Accordingly, no single producer has the occasion or the incentive to develop solutions to problems inherent in the production of such housing. Those who have the incentive in management often do not have the capital. Reduced costs, timely construction, and good landlord-tenant relationships can lower rents and increase profits. For that reason, the profit-motivated Partnership will be stimulated to develop creative and effective solutions. Furthermore, given a sufficient volume of units, the Partnership can support meaningful research efforts. Finally, by devices such as incentives for sale to nonprofit or cooperative tenant groups, the Partnership will be motivated to seek citizen participation in its projects.

III. Ensuring Participation of the Private Sector

The availability of reasonable profits may not alone ensure the volume of private participation required to produce the needed housing. Other potential problems which may deter developers or investors must be attacked.

A. Accelerating Processing of Federal Programs. Developers frequently state that the time required to process mortgage applications has dampened their interest. Rapid processing is required to achieve the production of six to eight million subsidized units in the next decade.

1. FHA PROGRAMS. FHA has recently instituted an Accelerated Multi-family Processing (AMP) system for multi-family programs like 221(d)(3) BMIR, Rent Supplements, and 236. Because of the importance of prompt processing, the Committee requested a panel of mortgage experts to review the new AMP procedures in detail. The panel received the cooperation of FHA officials. It was clear from the outset

that the simplification of forms, the elimination of seriatim reviews, and the emphasis on the early determination of market feasibility could dramatically reduce processing time. In a report submitted to the Committee, the review panel stated:

The Panel unanimously agreed that the concepts underlined in the AMP proposal represent a very significant improvement in the FHA processing of multifamily projects. Panel members who have already had experience with AMP processing have been most favorably impressed.

It appears that with the proper training of local office personnel, the AMP program can effectively shorten processing time. From all reports available to the Committee, processing delays are not nearly as serious as they once were. The record of average processing time from initial application to occupancy has been:

221(d)(3) BMIR; before AMP; *32 months.*

221(d)(3) BMIR; processed under AMP; *19 months.*

Clearly the AMP program has brought about a substantial improvement.

In implementing AMP, FHA should dispatch a small team to review all applications pending in the local offices, with authority to expedite the processing of projects which are lagging. Early in 1967, FHA circulated such a team with great effectiveness.

2. PUBLIC HOUSING PROGRAMS. While FHA has made a vast improvement in the processing of its multi-family housing programs, improvement in the development time for public housing has not been as impressive. Table 2–8 indicates the average time it has taken to complete a public housing development in the various regions of the country.

Responsibility for the long development periods cannot be charged to HUD alone. Table 2–9, discussed later in this section, clearly indicates that projects are often delayed at the local level. Our concern, however, is not to pinpoint blame for past delays but to accelerate the process for the future. The Turnkey procedures introduced by the Housing Assistance Administration (HAA), discussed earlier, have dramatically reduced the development time ordinarily required for public housing. Furthermore, HAA has recently delegated responsibilities to local HAA offices, which should reduce excessive review and accelerate processing. One reform which is particularly noteworthy is the delegation to the local HAA office of the responsibility of developing reasonable cost limitations for each locality.

There is room for more improvement. We propose that a review team similar to that suggested for FHA programs be formed to review and expedite all public housing projects pending in the local offices. Second, and equally important, we propose that if a project has been pending for more than two years, and if development is not imminent, the reservation

TABLE 2–8

Median Time for Development of Public Housing[1]

	Months
The approximate median "pipeline" time taken by a project from start to finish	44
The median time by stage is:	
Program reservation to preliminary loan (estimated)	2
Preliminary loan contract to annual contributions contract	10
Annual contributions contract to construction start	20
Construction start to date of full availability	12
The median time by region is:	
Region I (Maine, New Hampshire, Vermont, New York, Massachusetts, Connecticut, Rhode Island, New Jersey)	57
Region II (Pennsylvania, Maryland, Delaware, West Virginia, Virginia, District of Columbia)	122
Region III (Kentucky, Tennessee, Mississippi, Alabama, Florida, Georgia, South Carolina, North Carolina)	40
Region IV (Ohio, Indiana, Illinois, Wisconsin, Michigan, Iowa, Minnesota, Nebraska, North Dakota, South Dakota)	106
Region V (Texas, Louisiana, Arkansas, Missouri, Oklahoma, Kansas, New Mexico, Colorado)	37
Region VI (Alabama, Hawaii, Guam, Washington, Oregon, California, Nevada, Arizona, Utah, Idaho, Montana, Wyoming)	46
Region VII (Puerto Rico, Virgin Islands)	Not available

[1] The times are based in part on a survey of 745 projects between 1962–64. Only the 20 months median period for Annual Contributions Contract to Construction is based on 1967 figures.
Source: Housing Assistance Administration.

of funds should be taken away from the locality and reallocated to communities better able to use them. Finally, the fund reservation system should be reviewed and revised to assure that communities promptly use funds allocated to them. One reform to be considered is a delay of formal reservation of funds until local site approvals have been secured.

B. Reducing the Risks.   Private development of housing for low-income families is still a relatively new approach. Private firms with little experience in the management of housing for the poor may be hesitant to undertake rental projects. Even more important, recent FHA administrative actions have made those interested in sponsoring subsidized projects particularly fearful of possible problems in making mortgage payments, since any record of a request for mortgage forebearance, let alone one of delinquency or default, may jeopardize a firm's future opportunities to produce housing under FHA multi-family programs.

Subsidized housing programs should be administered with sufficient sensitivity to such concerns of the private developer. Specifically, in the event a project has a high vacancy rate or high management costs and there is no evidence of mismanagement, it should be HUD's stated policy that with the consent of the lender, interest and amortization payments may be deferred and the mortgage term adjusted to reflect the change in the payment schedule but, if possible, without requiring a change in rents. Further, where a default is likely, it is recommended that in the absence of mismanagement the sponsor should have the option of tendering the project to FHA for the unamortized value of the mortgage. In that case he would not recover his equity or his operating losses, but he would not lose the privilege of sponsoring other FHA projects. It should be clear, however, that the tender should not result in, in the absence of any wrongdoing, the risk of such a loss. This is an excessive consequence to add to the financial losses; and as already noted, it could well discourage sponsorship of subsidized projects.

An additional approach to the risk problem is the development of a Federal insurance or reinsurance program which would cover operating losses for a specified period. It is recommended that HUD be directed to develop such a program and that the cost of premiums be allowed as an operating expense.

C. Providing Additional Incentives. 1. DEVELOPMENT FUND. The development of housing projects requires the sponsor to advance about 2½ percent of total development costs before receiving any assurance that the project will be approved for mortgage insurance. These "front money" costs of Public Housing and FHA projects are described in detail in Appendix H–6.

Because of the risks involved, it is generally difficult to finance "front money" except at inordinately high interest rates. In order to encourage the widest possible participation of developers, a revolving Development Fund similar to that provided for nonprofit sponsors should be established to make money available at a reasonable rate of interest to finance the purchase of land and to underwrite the initial planning of low-income housing developments where such funds are not otherwise available at a reasonable cost. To create the Development Fund, the Federal Government should either: (1) modify the provisions of the nonprofit revolving fund for nonprofit corporations to include limited distribution entities; (2) establish a program to guarantee such loans; or (3) make direct interest bearing loans from a special revolving fund. All loans or guarantees should be interest bearing and should be with recourse against the individual sponsor in the event of default. The cost of such loans should not be included as an eligible mortgage cost since in this case the purpose of the program is to make funds available, not to reduce the developer's equity.

2. DEPRECIATION OF SUBSIDIZED PROJECTS. Efforts should be made to encourage the Internal Revenue Service to recognize administratively a shorter "useful life" for all Federally subsidized housing developments. Under present procedures, the IRS generally requires that a taxpayer depreciate all housing properties over a 40-year period ("useful life") regardless of location or type of occupancy. It is submitted that a project

occupied by low- and moderate-income families is likely to depreciate more rapidly than a conventionally financed project. For this reason the "useful life" for Federally subsidized housing should be reduced. This would increase the tax write-offs generated by such projects, increase yields, and thereby make such projects more attractive investments.

IV. Improving the Capabilities of Public and Nonprofit Developers

This report should make it clear that the development of housing for the poor is indeed a complex undertaking. The successful developer must have professional experience and competence, an understanding of market requirements, and adequate funds to support initial planning. Nonprofit organizations and local public housing authorities may lack these, but their deficiencies are amenable to solution.

A. Nonprofit Organizations. Nonprofit organizations were first thrust into the development of subsidized housing by Section 202 of the Housing Act of 1959 and have been heavily involved in the Section 221(d)(3)BMIR and Rent Supplement programs. Experience has been mixed. Well-intentioned but inexperienced and underfunded charitable organizations have sometimes been over-ambitious and have become disillusioned. This is unfortunate and unnecessary.

FHA's recent action allowing the cost to nonprofit organizations of hiring competent advisors knowledgeable in real estate and FHA programs to be met from mortgage proceeds is admirable.

Many charitable organizations do not have the necessary "front money" required to begin a project. We urge that HUD bring into operation immediately the revolving fund authorized by the 1968 Act to provide this front money to nonprofit sponsors.

B. Public Agencies. 1. FEDERAL ASSISTANCE TO LOCAL HOUSING AUTHORITIES. We have already noted the problems of local processing delays in the development of public housing. Table 2–9, derived from a recent report by a task force of the Housing Assistance Administration, indicates the number of units under Annual Contributions Contract on which construction has yet to begin.

Since Table 2–9 is based on elapsed time since the last Federal action for which records are kept, it does not show the total time that has elapsed from either the date of the original reservation of funds or execution of the Annual Contributions Contract. For example, a project which received an Annual Contributions Contract 10 years ago but for which land was purchased five months ago would not appear in the tabulation. Thus, the full dimensions of the iceberg are not presently known.

To some extent these delays are reported to reflect the fact that local housing authorities lack the technical staff to prepare plans and specifi-

TABLE 2–9

Public Housing: Time Elapsed Since Last Federal Action[1]

Time since Last Action	Number of Units (Cumulative)
3 years or more	15,931
2 years or more	22,933
18 months or more	27,947
1 year or more	44,959
6 months or more	62,330

[1] As of June 30, 1967, for projects at the stage between Annual Contributions Contract and construction start.

Source: Housing Assistance Administration.

cations and to supervise bidding and the construction of a project. To help meet this problem, it is recommended that HUD be granted the necessary authority to assume full responsibility for the preparation of plans and supervision of bidding and construction when requested to do so by a local housing authority. This approach offers substantial potential for speeding up production. It might also enable HUD to operate on a scale sufficient to encourage private development of cost saving techniques and to support experimentation in new methods.

2. FUNDING COMMUNITY HOUSING PLANS. Perhaps even more important than strengthening the capability of the local housing authority is the need to strengthen the ability of the entire local government structure to deal with housing problems. It is becoming increasingly apparent that most local communities have neither made adequate assessments of their housing needs nor developed a program to assure that these needs are met. Responsibilities are often diffused among several uncoordinated agencies. Code enforcement, Urban Renewal, and Public Housing are often separately administered with no one public official being responsible for total housing requirements.

The Federal Government should provide funds to local governments to finance the preparation of plans to meet the housing needs of all their citizens. With appropriate modification of regulations governing existing programs, these needed planning efforts could be funded under existing authority. Public Housing, Urban Renewal, Model Cities, and the Community Renewal programs all offer possible funding sources.

APPENDIX H–1

Analysis of Annual Tax Loss[1] [221(d)(3) Below Market Interest Rate Project]

Year[2]	A	B	C	D	E
1................$	0	$ 0	[3]$251,000	$5,600	$256,600
2................	0	48,300	171,400	5,600	128,700
3................	34,500	49,700	162,800	5,600	84,200
4................	34,500	51,200	154,700	5,600	74,600
5................	34,500	52,800	147,000	5,600	65,300
6................	34,500	54,400	139,600	0	50,700
7................	34,500	56,000	132,600	0	42,100
8................	34,500	57,700	126,000	0	33,800
9................	34,500	59,500	119,700	0	25,700
10...............	34,500	61,300	113,700	0	17,900
11...............	34,500	63,200	108,000	0	10,300
12...............	34,500	65,100	102,600	0	3,000
13...............	34,500	67,100	97,500	0	(4,100)
14...............	34,500	69,100	92,600	0	(11,000)
15...............	34,500	71,200	88,000	0	(17,700)
16...............	34,500	73,400	83,600	0	(24,300)
17...............	34,500	75,600	79,400	0	(30,700)
18...............	34,500	77,900	75,400	0	(37,000)
19...............	34,500	80,300	71,700	0	(43,100)
20...............	34,500	82,700	68,100	0	(49,100)

Explanation of column headings: A—Cash flow plus nondeductible payments to Reserve for Replacements;[4] B—Mortgage amortization payments[4] which are nondeductible; C—Depreciation deduction (double declining balance); D—Legal and organization fee deduction; E—Tax loss, C plus D less A less B.

[1] The total figure (Column E) represents the net tax losses which are available to compute tax savings (Appendix H–2). The tax savings = tax upon the marginal income tax rate, or "tax bracket" (tax savings = tax loss × tax bracket). Figures in Column E in parentheses represent additional taxable income.

[2] Assuming 12 months construction period, and "break even" in first year of operations.

[3] This figure represents the sum of interest payments, financing premium, and state and local taxes. There is no depreciation deduction during the year of construction.

[4] Column A plus Column B equals gross income less tax, interest, and operating expense deductions.

APPENDIX H–2

Annual Cash Income and Tax Savings[1] [221(d)(3) Below Market Interest Rate Project] for Taxpayers in 30, 50, and 70 Percent Tax Brackets

Year[2]	A. Net Cash Return from Operations	B. Additional Tax Saving 30 Percent Bracket[3]	C. Additional Tax Saving 50 Percent Bracket[3]	D. Additional Tax Saving 70 Percent Bracket[3]
1.....................	$ 0	$77,000	$128,300	$179,600
2....................	0	38,600	64,000	90,100
3....................	24,500	25,300	42,100	58,900
4....................	24,500	22,400	37,300	52,200
5....................	24,500	19,600	32,700	45,700
6....................	24,500	15,200	25,400	35,500
7....................	24,500	12,600	21,000	29,500
8....................	24,500	10,100	16,900	23,700
9....................	24,500	7,700	12,900	18,000
10...................	24,500	5,400	9,000	12,500
11...................	24,500	3,100	5,200	7,200
12...................	24,500	900	1,500	2,100
13...................	24,500	(1,200)	(2,100)	(2,900)
14...................	24,500	(3,300)	(5,500)	(7,700)
15...................	24,500	(5,300)	(8,900)	(12,400)
16...................	24,500	(7,300)	(12,200)	(17,000)
17...................	24,500	(9,200)	(15,400)	(21,500)
18...................	24,500	(11,100)	(18,500)	(25,900)
19...................	24,500	(12,900)	(21,600)	(30,200)
20...................	24,500	(14,700)	(24,600)	(34,400)

[1] Exclusive of the effects of project sale. Total annual return is computed by adding Column A to Columns B, C, or D as applicable.

[2] Assumes 12-month construction period and "break even" in the first full year of operations.

[3] Data derived from Appendix H–1 showing actual taxes saved as compared with tax loss. Depreciation based upon "double declining balance" method. Parentheses indicate tax payments required.

APPENDIX H–3

Tax Consequences of Sale of 221(d)(3) BMIR Projects
(sponsor: limited distribution entity)
(total "replacement cost" = $4,080,000; 90 percent mortgage = $3,672,000)
(taxpayer in 50 percent tax bracket)

	Sale after—				
	2 Years	5 Years	10 Years	15 Years	20 Years
1. Sale price.........	$4,026,000	$3,856,000	$3,535,000	$3,161,000	$2,728,000
2. Unamortized mortgage.........	3,624,000	3,470,000	3,181,000	2,845,000	2,455,000
3. Cash realized (1–2).............	402,000	386,000	354,000	316,000	273,000
4. Adjusted basis[2]....	3,477,000	3,012,000	2,381,000	1,891,000	1,514,000
5. Taxable gain (1–4).............	549,000	844,000	1,154,000	1,270,000	1,214,000
6. Tax..............	159,000[3]	264,000[3]	303,000[3]	317,000	304,000
7. Net cash gain after tax (line 3 less line 6)........	243,000	122,000	51,000	(1,000)[4]	(31,000)[4]

[1] The sale price is assumed equivalent to the unamortized mortgage had the project been initiated by a nonprofit sponsor (100 percent mortgage as compared to the 90 percent mortgage available to limited dividend sponsors). The $153,000 of sponsor's operating cost is excluded from the yield computations; the additional tax loss from expensing or depreciation would increase yields accordingly.

[2] Reflects cost basis as reduced by accelerated depreciation.

[3] The effective tax rate exceeds the 25 percent capital gain rate as a result of Internal Revenue Code Section 1250.

[4] Figures In parentheses indicate cash loss.

APPENDIX H–4

Effect of 100 percent BMIR Financing on the Sale of a 221(d)(3) Project
at a Price Sufficient to Recover $408,000 Equity After Taxes
(original project "replacement cost" = $4,080,000)
(original project BMIR mortgage = $3,672,000)
(original loan terms = 40 years, 3 percent)

	Sale after—				
	2 Years	5 Years	10 Years	15 Years	20 Years
1. Sale price.........	$4,245,000	$4,237,000	$4,012,000	$3,707,000	$3,313,000
2. Adjusted basis....	3,477,000	3,012,000	2,381,000	1,891,000	1,514,000
3. Tax..............	213,000[1]	359,000[1]	423,000[1]	454,000	450,000
4. Unamortized mortgage.........	3,624,000	3,470,000	3,181,000	2,845,000	2,455,000
5. Net cash return (line 1 less 3 less 4)............	408,000	408,000	408,000	408,000	408,000
6. Term (years) of refinanced mortgage[2]........	40.1	40.0	36.1	31.5	26.3

[1] The effective tax rate exceeds the 25 percent capital gain rate as a result of Internal Revenue Code Sec. 1250. The $153,000 of sponsor's operating cost is excluded from the yield computations the additional tax loss from expensing or depreciation would increase yields accordingly.

[2] Maturity required when 6 percent cash distribution is no longer a factor, interest rate remains at 3 percent level, and rents are not increased. If interest rate is lowered below original BMIR level, maturity or rents could be reduced.

APPENDIX H–5

Cumulative Average After-Tax Yield on Investment of $408,000 Assuming Investor Is in 50 Percent Tax Bracket, 8 Percent Annual Operating Cash Flow, and Sale Price Equivalent to Unamortized 100 Percent Mortgage Loan Balance
(221(d)(3) below market interest rate project)
(assumes identity of interest between sponsor and contractor)
(assuming 3 percent tax credit on completion of development)

	Yield with 3 Percent Tax Credit	
Sale after—	Dis Percent	Nondis Percent
2 years	22.8	18.3
5 years	18.9	11.1
10 years	20.8	9.4
15 years	21.2	7.6
20 years	21.4	5.9

APPENDIX H–6

"Front Money" Requirements for Typical Project Processed under Turnkey Public Housing Procedures and FHA Conventional and Accelerated Multifamily Processing Procedures
Typical Project, 272 units at an average construction cost of $11,000 per unit and an average development cost of $14,500

Construction cost	$3,000,000
Architects and engineering (4.5 percent)	135,000[1]
Overhead and profit	300,000
Carrying charges and financing	300,000
Legal and organizational	28,000
Land	250,000
Total	4,013,000

Note: This is an effort to indicate the typical cash expenditures which may be anticipated in the development of the several Federally subsidized housing programs. For purposes of this discussion, we have prepared a typical development containing 272 units with a construction cost of $11,000 per unit. The total development costs for the typical unit are set forth below.

[1] Includes allowance for inspection of construction.

A. PUBLIC HOUSING—TURNKEY

Phase I—Housing Authority Issues "Letter Designating Turnkey Developer"

The Public Housing authority will invite private developers to submit proposals for the development of public housing units, or proposals may be submitted on the developer's own initiative. The proposal will include preliminary sketches of the proposed site plan and typical units. If the proposal is accepted, the authority will issue a Letter Designating Turnkey Developer. The costs involved in securing this Letter are as follows:

Land—No purchase expense if use of urban renewal land is contemplated.[1] If use of private land is intended an option is required........$5,000*
Architect—Preliminary sketches to estimate the number and type of
units may be appropriate to secure an expression of interest on the
part of the housing authority. This is very preliminary site planning
which will not require a large expenditure—if any...................$1,000*
Legal—Except for the option to purchase, no legal work is required at
this point...$ 200

* Indicates the amount will vary and is subject to negotiation.
[1] Should a presentation be required to be selected as developer—$1,000 to $5,000.

Phase II—Letter of Interest to Letter of Intent

The objective in this phase is to secure a formal letter of intent wherein the local Public Housing authority indicates that they will enter into a contract to buy the units shown in preliminary plans on the site described in the proposal for a price between $X and $Y with the final purchase price to be based on completed plans. Further, the local Housing Authority agrees in the letter of intent that, in the event the price established by appraisal (plus architectural costs and land value) is less than 95 percent of the seller's offered price and an agreement cannot be negotiated, the LHA will buy the land and reimburse the developer for the cost of preparing plans. The expenditures required to secure a formal letter of intent are as follows:

Land—If urban renewal land, no expense. If private land
an option to purchase of sufficient length to cover
processing ti me will be necessary. Cost will be a matter of negotiation between the developer and the land
owner... $250,000 if cannot ne-
                                                    gotiate option.
Architect—The local housing authority will require the
developer to prepare plans in sufficient detail to permit the authority to estimate the value of the construction. Detailed preliminary drawings will involve
about two-fifths of the total architectural fee less
funds already expended. Of course, the precise fee
schedule will be subject to negotiation............ $ 53,000*
Legal—A lawyer will be involved in the preparation of the
letter of intent and the purchase or optioning of the
land. Here again the fee and time of payment will be
subject to negotiation............................. $ 3,000*

* Indicates the amount will vary and is subject to negotiation.

Phase III—Letter of Intent to Final Agreement

The object of this phase of negotiation is to prepare final plans and negotiate the actual purchase price. The costs involved are as follows:

Land—No additional cost..   0
Architect—Final plans will be required. This involves an additional
    two-fifths of the fee...$54,000*[2]
Legal—Review of final contract.....................................   0[2]

    * Indicates the amount will vary and is subject to negotiation.
    [2] Remaining one-fifth of architect's fee recognized by HAA covers the cost of architect's inspection of the project during construction.

Phase IV—Final Agreement to Sale

During this phase, the developer secures interim financing, constructs the buildings, and sells the project to the Local Housing Authority. The cash requirements will be as follows:

Land—Purchase price....................................$250,000 unless already acquired.
Architect—No additional cost..............................   0
Interim financing—The developer will probably have to pay a
    fee (probably two points) to secure interim financing......$ 73,000
Legal—Review and handling of construction financing and
    final closing...$ 5,000

B. FHA—CONVENTIONAL PROCESSING

Phase I—Determination of Suitability of Sponsor and Site

The objective of this phase is to secure FHA approval of the proposed developer and the type and location of the project proposed. If the site and the developer are acceptable, FHA will issue a *letter "B"* which means FHA has inspected and approved the site for the projected use and has determined that the developer is an acceptable sponsor. The letter encourages submission of formal application (Form 2013). FHA obtains an allocation of FNMA funds and has received regional FHA approval. It should be noted, however, that assurance of formal commitment is *not* given, which means, the developer is proceeding at his own risk. The costs involved are as follows:

Submit FHA Form 2012—No fee is required...................0
Land—The developer must control the land. If the land is
    controlled by public agency, no fee will be required.
    However if private property is involved, the land will
    have to be optioned or purchased......................Option $5,000
                                                        ($250,000 if cannot
                                                        negotiate option).
Architect—Preliminary sketches to permit a rough estimate of the number of units and determine the amount
    of the mortgage that be needed. However, since FHA
    does not require the submission of any plans, the
    amount of architectural work is a matter of the developer's discretion. The amount of the fee and the time of
    payment will be subject to negotiation..................$1,000*

Legal—Legal services will required to negotiate the option
or purchase of the land and to create the appropriate
nonprofit or limited distribution corporation. While it is
customary for the lawyer to wait until initial closing to
obtain his fee, this is a matter of negotiation............$2,000*

  * Indicates the amount will vary and is subject to negotiation.

Phase II—Submission of Application

The objective during this phase is to secure from FHA what is in effect a nonbinding conditional letter of commitment. FHA indicates the land value they will approve. Further, FHA evaluates preliminary plans and makes a rough estimate of construction costs and the approximate amount of the mortgage. Detailed plans are requested. Costs involved at this state are as follows:

Submit FHA Form 2013—FHA application fee (.15 percent of amount of
mortgage requested) is required....................................$ 6,000
Architect—Schematic drawings and outline specifications must be submitted with application. This will usually involve about two-fifths of
the architectural fee. Again, the time and amount of payment is a
matter for negotiation...$53,000*
Land—No additional money is required...............................   0
Legal Fee—No additional work is required...........................   0

  * Indicates the amount will vary and is subject to negotiation.

Phase III—Commitment

During this phase the requirement is to finish final drawings and obtain a quantity survey so that FHA can issue a formal commitment. After FHA reviews plans and estimate of costs, a commitment is issued. If the developer believes the commitment is too low, negotiations proceed. Once the developer receives an acceptable commitment, he takes it to FNMA and secures a commitment to purchase the mortgage.

Architect—Preparation of working drawings. This will require work equivalent to an additional two-fifths of the fee. If is usual for the architect to wait for initial closing to receive this payment..................   0*
Legal—No additional work is required................................   0
Quantity survey—Estimate of costs based on final drawings. This usually costs .05 percent of construction costs.........................$ 2,000
FHA commitment fee—When commitment is issued, a fee of .15 percent is required..$ 6,000
FNMA commitment fee—1 percent...................................$37,000

  * Indicates the amount will vary and is subject to negotiation.

Phase IV—Initial Closing

The objective here is to secure FHA approval of the entire project and to begin construction. At the initial closing the developer can draw down a substantial portion of all expenditures to date, *e.g.*, legal, architecture, land, application fees, to an amount which is the lesser of cost or allowance.

Architect—Architect paid additional two-fifths of fee allowed for plans.$ 54,000*[3]
Land—The developer will have to purchase the land. This usually
    takes place simultaneously with or just prior to the initial closing. . . .$250,000*
Legal—All of the FHA papers are drawn and the land is purchased . . . . .$ 4,000*
Off-site escrows and working capital—If any work has to be accom-
    plished to bring in the utilities or roads, this amount will have to be
    escrowed at the time of the initial closing. In addition FHA will re-
    quire 2 percent working capital . . . .$ 80,000*

    * Indicates the amount will vary and is subject to negotiation.
    [3] Remaining one-fifth of architect's fee recognized by FHA covers the cost of archi-
tect's inspection of the project during construction.

C. FHA—ACCELERATED MULTI-FAMILY PROCESSING (AMP)

Phase I—Issuance of Feasibility Letter

The determination of economic feasibility—the assessment of the costs and the rents to be allowed is one of the most critical steps in processing. Once FHA makes a determination of feasibility, financing is assured so long as the developer can bring the project in at the costs and rent level projected. In the conventional procedure, FHA postpones determination of economic feasibility until the middle of processing—after the preparation of detailed drawings and study of costs and land value are completed. This means the developer has expended a great deal of time and effort before securing any firm commitment from FHA.

The new accelerated multi-family processing requires FHA to make a determination of feasibility at an earlier stage. FHA estimates the rent levels which can be marketed and the construction and land costs which can be supported by such rentals. If the rent levels and mortgage amount contained in FHA's letter of feasibility are unacceptable, the developer is running a great risk in proceeding any further. Since the mortgage amount will be determined at an earlier stage, the developer should be more careful in developing his cost and rent structures. The costs involved in this stage are as follows:

Submit FHA Form 2013—This form will be submitted
    in all stages. In the first stage lump sum or per-
    centage cost estimates will be accepted. Detailed
    breakdowns are not required. No fee is required
    for the filing of this application   0
Land—The developer must control the land. If the
    land is controlled by a public agency, no fee will be
    required. However, if private property is involved,
    the land will have to be optioned or purchased . . . . . .Option $5,000
                                    $250,000 if option
                                    cannot be negotiated.

Architect—Preliminary sketches that permit an estimate of the number of units and determine the
cost of construction are advisable. Since FHA does
not require the submission of any plans at this
stage, the amount of architectural work is the developer's decision. Because the economic feasibility of the project is being determined at this stage,
it is advisable that the developer have a good idea
of costs...$2,500*
Legal—Legal services will be required to negotiate
the option or purchase of the land and to create
the appropriate nonprofit or limited distribution
corporation. While it is customary for the lawyer to
wait until initial closing to obtain his fee, this is a
matter of negotiation.............................$2,000*

  * Indicates the amount will vary and is subject to negotiation.

Phase II—Conditional Commitment

At this stage the mortgagee submits a formal application for conditional commitment (Form 2013). This application is accompanied by
detailed schematic drawings. An FHA application fee of .15 percent is
required. If the drawings and request for mortgage commitment conform
with the feasibility letter and are acceptable in detail, a conditional
mortgage commitment will be issued. The commitment is conditioned on
the development of final drawings which conform to FHA requirements
and are within the budget set forth in the conditional commitment. Since
FHA will have already approved the site, sponsor, type of project, and
general financial program (i.e., rent schedule, general land cost, and
construction cost), there should be few problems—all of the basic economic issues will have been resolved.

Submit FHA Form 2013—The form will be filled out in greater detail. Application and commitment fee of .30 percent will be required.........$12,000
Architect—Schematic drawings and outline specifications must be submitted with application. This will usually involve about two-fifths of
the architect's fee. Again, the time and amount of payment is a matter of negotiation...$51,500*
Land—No additional money is required................................. 0
Legal fee—No additional work is required............................. 0

  * Indicates the amount will vary and is subject to negotiation.

Phase III—Final Commitment

During this stage the object is to complete drawings and estimates of
costs so that FHA can certify that everything conforms with the conditional commitment and issue the final commitment. Once the developer
receives an acceptable commitment, he takes it to Fannie Mae and
secures a commitment to purchase the mortgage.

Architect—Preparation of working drawings. This will require work
equivalent to an additional two-fifths of the fee. It is usual for the
architect to wait for initial closing to receive his payment............$ 0*
Legal—No additional work is required................................$ 0*
FNMA commitment fee—1 percent...................................$37,000

　　* Indicates the amount will vary and is subject to negotiation.

Phase IV—Initial Closing

The objective here is to secure FHA approval of the entire project and
to begin construction. At initial closing the developer can draw down
expenditures for legal and organization, architecture, land, application
fees, quantity survey, to an amount which is the lesser of cost or
allowance.

Architecture—Architect paid remainder of fee for plans..............$ 54,000*[4]
Land—The developer will have to purchase the land. This usually
takes place simultaneously or just prior to the initial closing.........$245,000
Legal—All of the FHA papers are drawn and the land is purchased.....$ 4,000*
Off-site escrows and working capital—If any work has to be accomplished to bring in the utilities or roads, this amount will have to be
escrowed at the time of the initial closing. In addition FHA will require 2 percent working capital.[5]...................................$ 80,000*

　　* Indicates the amount will vary and is subject to negotiation.
　　[4] Remaining one-fifth of architect's fee recognized by FHA covers the cost of architect's inspection of the project during construction.
　　[5] Paid from mortgage proceeds in nonprofit cases.

HYDE PARK

Jack Wilson has just received a copy of a proposal for investing in Limited Partnership Interests in the Hyde Park Towers Urban Redevelopment Project in Chicago. With this information he planned to determine whether he should invest in the Hyde Park Project. Before making this decision, he wanted to consider what risks he would be incurring as an equity investor, the feasibility of the overall development, and the after-tax return that he could expect to earn on his investment. Other background information which would influence his decision is included in the following items of consideration.

Town Reconstruction Corporation

Town Reconstruction Corporation (TRC) was the developer of Hyde Park. A typical TRC project is financed as follows:

Each project is constructed and owned by a separate general partnership which purchases the land, and constructs, owns, operates, and finances the project. In the case of TRC's Hyde Park Project, the general partners are TRC and Conover Realty, the real estate division of a very reputable and well-known Wall Street investment banking firm. It is planned that Conover Realty privately place Limited Partnership Interests with equity investors in an amount equal to between 10% and 15% of the cost of each project. The remaining amount would be financed by a mortgage.

The equity investors would become limited partners and would receive Limited Partnership Interests entitling them to up to 90% of the income and losses until a certain rental level is achieved, and to at least 35% of the income and deductions thereafter.

Economic Conditions

As a result of the government's fearing that the economy might be expanding too rapidly, the Federal Reserve had recently initiated a tight money policy, and the Congress had suspended the double-declining balance method of depreciation.

In the last few months, the interest rate on projects such as this had increased by three fourths of 1%. Even though the current projections

349

for Hyde Park reflected this increase, the impact of additional changes are indicated by the following example: The three fourths of 1% increase amounted to approximately $138,000 additional interest cost in the first year of operation, and in excess of $4 million over the life of the mortgage.

The federal government suspended the right to use the double-declining balance method for determining depreciation until January 1, 1968. There was no assurance that this restriction would not be extended, as was done with the interest equalization tax. This reduced the attractiveness of an investment in the equity of a TRC project. Instead of recouping the equity investment in three to four years, it would be five to six years. TRC and Conover were able to get a specific example included in the Senate Finance Report on the H.R. 17607 bill which they believe will put Hyde Park under the wire as being a "binding contract" and thereby exempt it from the provision of the Act.

With these factors in mind, Mr. Wilson proceeded to review the financing proposal.

MEMORANDUM

Hyde Park Towers Urban Redevelopment Project: Limited Partnership Interests

Introduction and Highlights

1. A 136-acre area known as Hyde Park in downtown Chicago is being cleared and is in the process of being redeveloped as Hyde Park Towers.

2. The Project will contain a 30-story apartment building and two 17-story apartment buildings, underground parking facilities for 900 automobiles, and a small amount of commercial space for the convenience of residents. The total cost of the land and improvements is estimated at approximately $23,550,000.

3. The Project will be owned by a partnership called Hyde Park Redevelopment Company (Hyde Park). The general partners of the partnership are Conover Realty Corporation and Town Reconstruction Corporation (TRC). Conover Realty owns all the common stock of TRC. The Philadelphia Insurance Company owns all of the Participating Preferred Stock of TRC ($2,700,000 par value).

4. The land cost the City of Chicago approximately $30 per square foot and the price payable by Hyde Park is $6.50 per square foot. In July 1967, Hyde Park purchased approximately 6 acres of the Project site for $1,779,050 and by next June will purchase the remainder of such site for $353,138.50.

5. The Project site is adjacent to the Civic Center, which is a complex of 15 government office, court, and records buildings at the northern part

of the Central Business District. The magnificent new Music Center, a theater-in-the-Round, and a legitimate theater are located in the Civic Center. Two large new buildings were added to this complex in 1965—the new Federal Building and the new Water and Power Building, across First Street from Hyde Park. A new 40-story Union Bank Building was completed in 1966. A new Criminal Courts Building is contemplated.

6. Summary of Conclusions—High-Rise Apartment Housing Analysis, Parcel E, Hyde Park, Chicago, Illinois, prepared by Property Research Corporation:

There is no other residential development in the Central Area of Chicago in size or quality anything like the development planned by Town Reconstruction Company. At present there is very little other land in Central Chicago which is programmed for residential development. With a rash of new office buildings, Downtown Chicago has recently demonstrated that a recentralization trend is flowing. Plans for the growth of the Central Area visualize a 45 percent increase in floor area by 1980. The Central Area of Chicago is destined for a spectacular growth. With it will come an increasing demand for downtown housing. In our opinion there is definitely a market for residential development in the Central Area of Chicago and Parcel E is the best location in the downtown area to capture this market.

7. Hyde Park proposes to sell privately to investors $3 million of Limited Partnership Interests. It does not plan to consider investments of less than $100,000 per investor. The balance of the funds estimated to be needed will be financed by a first mortgage in the amount of $20,250,000 to Philadelphia and a capital contribution of approximately $300,000 by TRC. The mortgage loan is also a construction loan, and the first disbursement under the loan was used by Hyde Park to purchase approximately 6 acres of the Project site. The mortgage loan matures in 38 years and bears interest at the rate of 6½%. The mortgage loan is not a personal liability of Hyde Park or any partner therein, general or limited.

8. The Project is Phase I of an overall urban redevelopment project involving an aggregate of approximately 13.7 acres contemplated to be undertaken by Hyde Park.

9. The Investor Limited Partners will be allocated 90% of the profits and losses of Hyde Park through the year 1973.[1] They will then receive lesser percentages of profits and losses until the Project is 85% rented, after which time they will receive 35% of the profits and losses.

General

Hyde Park Redevelopment Company (Hyde Park), a limited partnership formed under the law of Illinois and with its Certificate of Limited Partnership filed in the state of Illinois, is sponsoring an urban redevel-

---

[1] References to years throughout this memorandum are to Hyde Park's fiscal year ending November 30.

opment project (the Project) in downtown Chicago known as Hyde Park Towers. The Project will contain a 30-story apartment building and two 17-story apartment buildings, underground parking facilities which will permit the parking of approximately 900 automobiles, and a small amount of commercial space for the convenience of residents. The Project is being constructed on a site which will consist of approximately 7 acres of land and will be part of a 136-acre area being redeveloped pursuant to a redevelopment plan adopted by the Community Redevelopment Agency of the City of Chicago, Illinois (the Community Redevelopment Agency). The total cost of the Project is estimated by Hyde Park and its general contractor, the Robert Higgins Construction Company of Chicago, at approximately $23,550,000.

The land for the Project is being obtained under, and the Project is to be constructed pursuant to, a Disposition and Development Agreement (the Land Disposition Contract) between the Community Redevelopment Agency and Hyde Park and Town Reconstruction Corporation (TRC), a Delaware corporation and a general partner of Hyde Park. Hyde Park will own the land, will construct the improvements thereon through a general contractor, and will operate the Project through TRC or some other managing agent.

The Land Disposition Contract contemplates that Hyde Park will acquire two additional parcels aggregating 6 acres of land thereunder and construct thereon two additional high-rise apartment buildings. The Project constitutes only Phase I of the overall urban redevelopment project proposed to be undertaken under the Land Disposition Contract. The additional parcels of land and the improvements to be constructed thereon are referred to below as the Remaining Projects.

Hyde Park proposes to obtain the funds for the Project:

1. From a first-mortgage loan (the Mortgage Loan) from the Philadelphia Insurance Company of $20,250,000. The Building Loan Agreement and Deed of Trust relating to the Mortgage Loan were entered into July 7, 1967, and disbursements have already been made.
2. From a capital contribution of approximately $300,000 by TRC which will be made by converting advances to and expenditures for the benefit of Hyde Park in such amount into a capital contribution.
3. From the contributions to the capital of Hyde Park of a restricted number of new investor limited partners (the Investor Limited Partners). To obtain their limited partnership interests (the Limited Partnership Interests), the Investor Limited Partners will agree to contribute an aggregate of $3 million.

The Investor Limited Partners will be allocated 90% of the profits and losses through the year 1973. They will then receive lesser percentages of profits and losses until the Project is 85% rented, after which time they will receive 35% of the profits and losses. The Investor Limited Partners will be paid a cash return which will depend on the apartment rents that can be achieved in the future. For federal income tax purposes it is estimated that the Investor Limited Partners' share of the excess of deductions over income will amount to approximately $1.2 million in the first five years. Exhibits showing projected operating results and projected allocations of income losses are attached to this memorandum.

The general partners of Hyde Park are TRC and Conover Realty Corporation, a New York corporation. Hyde Park also has two limited partners, which are TRC and Hyde Park Towers Investment Company, the latter being an Illinois partnership consisting of individuals presently directors and/or officers and/or employees and/or legal counsel for one or more of the corporate general partners. Conover Realty owns all the common stock of TRC. Philadelphia owns all the preferred stock of TRC ($2.70 million par value).

Hyde Park has engaged as the architect for the Project and the Remaining Projects Roscoe Aydelotte F.A.I.A. & Associates, architects and planning consultants of Chicago, Illinois. The construction of the Project is being carried out by the Robert Higgins Construction Company of Chicago.

Construction of the Project commenced on July 11, 1967, and Hyde Park's present plans call for completion by not later than June, 1969.

TRC will manage the completed Project for Hyde Park and will receive 4½% of gross rents and other income for such services.

Prospective Investor Limited Partners are not to construe the contents of this memorandum or any attachments hereto or any communications from Hyde Park or any of its partners as legal or tax advice. It is proposed that the law firm of Rieser, Olt, and Parker represent Hyde Park in the preparation and execution of instruments and documents for this transaction. The Investor Limited Partners should consult their own legal and tax advisors as to legal and tax consequences.

Capital Contributions

The Investor Limited Partners will acquire the Limited Partnership Interests when amendments providing for the Limited Partnership Interests are made to Hyde Park's agreement of limited partnership. It is expected that these amendments will be made in January, 1968.

At the time the Investor Limited Partners acquire the Limited Partnership Interests they will contribute to the capital of Hyde Park $400,000.

The Investor Limited Partners will make additional contributions (the Additional Capital Contributions) to the capital of Hyde Park in the amount of $500,000 in June, 1968, in the amount of $500,000 in December, 1968, and in the remaining amount of $1.6 million in June, 1969.

Estimated Costs and Financial Plan

It is estimated that the total cost of the Project will be approximately $23,550,000.

The estimate includes the amount of $17,273,000 as being the amount which will be paid by Hyde Park to its general contractor, the Robert Higgins Construction Company. This amount is based on a preliminary estimate by the general contractor, which is to prepare a final estimate in October, 1967. The preliminary estimate is $527,000 less than the guaranteed maximum cost in Hyde Park's construction contract with the general contractor, which guaranteed maximum cost is subject to increase in the event unforeseen or unusual soil conditions or foundation requirements are encountered.

The estimate includes $55,000 to be paid to Conover for arranging the investment by the Investor Limited Partners.

The estimate also includes approximately $1,360,000 heretofore paid or advanced by TRC on behalf of Hyde Park for costs of the Project, of which approximately $1,060,000 will be repaid to TRC from the proceeds of the Mortgage Loan and the capital contributions of the Investor Limited Partners and the balance of approximately $300,000 will become a capital contribution by TRC. It does not include a management fee to be paid to TRC for supervision and management of the construction of the Project in the amount of $20,000 per month from May, 1967 until the completion of the Project, not to exceed in the aggregate $500,000, which fee will be payable after completion of the Project on the contingent basis described below under the heading Hyde Park.

The estimate includes an allowance of approximately $285,000 for initial working capital. In this connection it is to be noted that the projected cash deficit from operations exceeds this amount by approximately $145,000, in the period January, 1969 through April, 1970. In the remaining months of 1970, this peak deficit is reduced to approximately $17,000.

Actual costs may vary from the estimates because of such contingencies as errors in estimation, increases in construction costs, and unforeseen delays and also because of increased cost of requirements imposed under the Land Disposition Contract.

The Mortgage Loan provides for Philadelphia lending to Hyde Park $20,250,000 (subject to downward adjustment in the event that certain costs of the Project are less than anticipated). The proceeds of the Mortgage Loan are disburseable from time to time to pay the costs of the site and of construction of the Project. The Mortgage Loan is for a term ending July 7, 2005, bears interest at the rate of 6½% per year, and is amortizable commencing in August, 1972 in the amounts of the principal components in substantially level monthly installments of principal and interest. The Mortgage Loan is not a personal liability of Hyde Park or any partner therein.

The Investor Limited Partners' contributions to capital will also be available to pay costs and expenses.

Hyde Park will have no committed sources of funds except as described in this memorandum. The general partners may but will not be obligated to advance funds, either as loans or as capital contributions, if the funds to be provided by the Mortgage Loan and the Investor Limited Partners are not sufficient.

Hyde Park

When the Investor Limited Partners acquire their Limited Partnership Interests in Hyde Park, the partners of Hyde Park will consist of (i) TRC and Conover Realty (the general partners), (ii) the Investor Limited Partners, and (iii) two other limited partners which will be TRC and Hyde Park Towers Investment Company. The capital account in which the partners will have interests in accordance with their capital contributions from time to time, will then consist of the contributions of the partners which in the case of the partners other than TRC and the Investor Limited Partners, will be small or nominal.

The Investor Limited Partners will be obligated to make the Additional Capital Contributions described above under the heading Capital Contributions. They will have no further liability in respect of Hyde Park except a statutory liability in certain events involving creditors of Hyde Park and then only to the extent of their capital contributions to Hyde Park which have been returned to them.

The proceeds of the Mortgage Loan and the capital contributions of the partners will be used by Hyde Park only to pay Permitted Costs. Such costs shall be (i) Hyde Park's costs and expenses of constructing and financing the Project consisting of its costs and expenses of acquiring the land for the Project and completing the improvements thereon including architect's and engineering fees, the costs and expenses of the carrying charges including real estate taxes and financing for the Project, the costs of preopening, advertising, and similar items; (ii) the amount of $55,000 to be paid to Conover Realty for its services in connection with the private placement of the Limited Partnership Interests; (iii) the costs and expenses of the formation of Hyde Park including the costs and expenses of the preparation of the Agreement of Limited Partnership and Certificate of Limited Partnership and necessary amendments to both; (iv) the costs and expenses of Hyde Park and TRC directly attributable to the preparation and execution of the Land Disposition Contract and any agreements in implementation thereof, the agreement with the architect and the construction contract with the general contractor and performance under each up to the completion of the Project; (v) the amount of the overhead of TRC properly allocable to any of the activities referred to in the foregoing prior to May, 1967; and (*vi*) amounts expended as initial working capital and in payment of any initial operating losses. The management fee to be paid to TRC for supervision and management of the construction of the Project (the TRC Construction Fee) in the amount of $20,000 per month from May, 1967 until the completion of the Project (not to exceed $500,000) shall not be a Permitted Cost.

The TRC Construction Fee will be paid after the completion of construction of the Project and the payment of all Permitted Costs, (*i*) from any amounts remaining of the proceeds of the Mortgage Loan and the capital contributions of the partners and (*ii*) from other gross receipts from all sources of Hyde Park to and including the year 1973, except that the Investor Limited Partners shall receive cash distributions of at least $50,000 in respect of the year 1970, $200,000 in respect of the year 1971, $150,000 in respect of the year 1972, and $100,000 in respect of the year 1973 before any amounts of their cash distributions in respect of any such year are used to pay the TRC Construction Fee. To the extent that payments of the TRC Construction Fee are made from gross receipts described in (*ii*) above, the amounts of such payments shall be credited to the capital accounts of the partner of Hyde Park who, except for the obligation to pay the TRC Construction Fee, would have been entitled to receive such amounts. In the event that the funds available from the sources referred to in (*i*) and (*ii*) above are not sufficient to pay all of the TRC Construction Fee the unpaid portion shall thereafter be deemed for all purposes to be a capital contribution on the part of TRC.

Except as hereinafter otherwise provided, Hyde Park's profits and losses and items of income, payment, and expense including depreciation shall be allocated to, and Hyde Park's distributions of cash will be made to, the Investor Limited Partners in accordance with subparagraphs (*a*), (*b*), and (*c*) below:

a) In respect of each year to and including 1973 the percentage will be 90%.

b) In respect of each year after the year 1973 in which the average percentage of rentable space rented during such year in the Project is as set forth in column (1) below, the applicable percentage will be the percentage set forth opposite such average percentage in column (2) below except that (*i*) in any such year in which such average percentage is less than such average percentage in any previous such year the applicable percentage will be the applicable percentage in that previous year, and (*ii*) if the average percentage of rentable space rented during any year prior to the year 1974 shall be 85% or more, such allocations and distributions shall be made without regard to this subparagraph (*b*).

(1)	(2)
Less than 81%.............................	.....90%
Less than 82% but not less than 81%.......	....79%
Less than 83% but not less than 82%.......	....68%
Less than 84% but not less than 83%.......	... 57%
Less than 85% but not less than 84%.......	....46%
85% or more...............................	....35%

c) In respect of any year as to which subparagraphs (*a*) or (*b*) shall not govern, the percentage will be 35%.

To the extent permitted by applicable law and regulations, Hyde Park will elect to take 200% declining-balance accelerated depreciation on each depreciable unit with respect to at least 12 full calendar years.

Except as otherwise provided below, Hyde Park will distribute to its partners semiannually all cash from operations not reasonably required for operating purposes.

As noted above, actual cash distributions to the Investor Limited Partners will not exceed $50,000 in respect of the year 1970, $200,000 in respect of the year 1971, $150,000 in respect of the year 1972, or $100,000 in respect of the year 1973, unless and until the TRC Construction Fee is paid.

Upon the sale of the Project (including any revesting of title in the Community Redevelopment Agency) or liquidation of Hyde Park, the Investor Limited Partners and the other limited partners will receive in priority to any payment to the general partners the total amount of their capital contributions to Hyde Park less any distributions previously made to them and, after all capital and the TRC Construction Fee (if any remains unpaid and not yet credited to capital) have been paid, the Investor Limited Partners will receive their then applicable percentage under (*a*), (*b*) or (*c*) above of any additional net proceeds. In such event, allocations of taxable gain shall be made in an appropriate manner to reflect previous allocations of profits and losses among the partners.

Hyde Park will keep its accounts on the accrual basis and will ascertain its profits and losses and payments of capital and other receipts and payments in accordance with generally accepted accounting principles. The Investor Limited Partners shall receive no interest on their capital contributions.

Except as contemplated below in this memorandum, Hyde Park will not amend substantially, consent to the impairment of or waive any of its substantial rights under or cancel or terminate the Land Disposition Contract.

Hyde Park will comply with the Land Disposition Contract so as not to be in default thereunder except that without the consent of the Investor Limited Partners Hyde Park will not take any action under the Land Disposition Contract in respect of any Remaining Project prior to the latest date specified in the Land Disposition Contract for the conveying of the land for such Remaining Project other than action required by the Land Disposition Contract to be taken prior to such date. Unless, at least 90 days in advance of the date for conveyance under the Land Disposition Contract of the land embraced in a Remaining Project, all of the Investor Limited Partners shall have irrevocably consented in writing to the acquisition of title thereto by Hyde Park, it shall make application to the Community Redevelopment Agency for approval of a transfer of all of the rights of Hyde Park with respect to such Remaining Project to another limited partnership; and if such approval is granted, Hyde Park shall so transfer its rights with respect to such Remaining Project provided Hyde Park is relieved of all further liability in respect of such Remaining Project under the Land Disposition Contract and the transferee pays to Hyde Park its costs and expenses and deposits which in accordance with generally accepted accounting principles are attributable to such Remaining Project. Each Investor Limited Partner will be given the opportunity to invest in any such transferee.

Without the consent of the Investor Limited Partners, Hyde Park will not borrow any amounts other than the Mortgage Loan or additional sums not to exceed $500,000 at any one time outstanding (and no such permitted borrowing will be a personal liability of any Investor Limited Partner therein).

Hyde Park will not engage in any transactions other than (i) the performance of the Land Disposition Contract as contemplated in this memorandum, and (ii) the financing, construction, and operation of the Project and all transactions reasonably related thereto, as contemplated in this memorandum.

After the amendment of the Certificate of Limited Partnership to reflect the admission of the Investor Limited Partners, the general partners will continue to maintain their respective interests in Hyde Park as set forth in the amended Certificate of Limited Partnership. Hyde Park will terminate on the bankruptcy, dissolution, transfer of partnership interest, or significant change in ownership (not resulting from transfers upon death, to a family trust or to charity) of a general partner.

A limited partner of Hyde Park may not withdraw his contribution or have the partnership dissolved.

Hyde Park will indemnify each of its general partners against any claims or liability incurred by it by reason of the fact that it was a general partner of Hyde Park, provided that the actions or omissions complained of were performed in good faith belief that it acted within the scope of its authority as contemplated in the Limited Partnership Agreement and that such general partner was not grossly negligent or liable for bad faith misconduct with respect to the actions or omissions complained of.

If any limited partner intends to sell his interest in Hyde Park, he will offer such interest to the other partners of Hyde Park. If such other partners do not notify such limited partner of their intention to purchase such interest within 30 days, such limited partner may then offer, within 90 days after giving such notice, to sell such interest to any person subject to the approval of the Community Redevelopment Agency upon terms and conditions not more favorable to the purchaser than those offered to such other partners.

Land Disposition Contract

The Land Disposition Contract was entered into by the Community Redevelopment Agency and Hyde Park and TRC as of February 23, 1966. While TRC is a principal signatory to the Land Disposition Contract, it is permitted to and will assign all its rights thereunder to Hyde Park.

The Land Disposition Contract, as implemented by an Implementation Agreement dated July 7, 1967, provides for the sale by the Community Redevelopment Agency to Hyde Park and TRC of four adjacent parcels of land in the Hyde Park area of downtown Chicago aggregating approximately 13.7 acres for $6.50 per square foot. In July, 1967, Hyde Park purchased a parcel of approximately 6 acres for the Project Site for $1,779,050 and by next June will purchase another parcel of approximately 1 acre to complete the Project Site for an additional $353,138.50.

Under the Land Disposition Contract, Hyde Park and TRC are obligated to develop the parcels in accordance with certain basic concept drawings and related documents. Detailed working drawings and other specifications also must be approved by the Community Redevelopment Agency. Hyde Park is obligated to commence the construction of the improvements to be made upon a parcel promptly after it acquires title to the parcel and to diligently prosecute such construction to completion.

Under the Land Disposition Contract, Hyde Park is not permitted to devote any parcel of land to any use other than the uses specified in the Land Disposition Contract. It may not, prior to the Community Redevelopment Agency's certifying completion of construction of the improvements on any parcel, sell or otherwise dispose of the whole or any part thereof without the approval of the Community Redevelopment Agency. It is not permitted, prior to the Community Redevelopment Agency's certifying completion of the construction of the improvements thereon, to mortgage any parcel except for the purpose of financing costs and expenses of land acquisition and the construction of improvements. The Community Redevelopment Agency has the right, among others, if Hyde Park fails to proceed with the construction of the improvements on any parcel after its purchase for a period of six months after notice, to revest title to the parcel in the Community Redevelopment Agency and to resell the same, reimbursing Hyde Park and TRC for their costs and expenses only if the proceeds thereof are sufficient to do so after paying the costs and expenses of the Community Redevelopment Agency.

The Land Disposition Contract requires, and Hyde Park and TRC have posted, a good-faith surety bond in the amount of $194,000, or 5% of the total purchase price of the four parcels. If Hyde Park and TRC default in the performance of the Land Disposition Contract with respect to a particular parcel or parcels prior to the conveyance of title to all parcels, the amount of the bond with respect to the parcel or parcels as to which default is made and for all unconveyed parcels will automatically become the sole property of the Community Redevelopment Agency and will be considered as liquidated damages for the default. Upon the Community Redevelopment Agency's certifying completion of the improvements to be made upon a particular parcel, the Community Redevelopment Agency will return to Hyde Park and TRC the portion of the bond with respect to such parcel.

The Land Disposition Contract contains provisions for extensions of time by reason of *force majeure* and permits Hyde Park and TRC to terminate their obligations with respect to a parcel and, if required by the Community Redevelopment Agency, other parcels if Hyde Park and TRC after due diligence fail to obtain specified financing for the land and improvements on such parcels.

The Land Disposition Contract may be terminated by the Community Redevelopment Agency if without its approval there is any significant change (voluntary or involuntary) in ownership of either Hyde Park or TRC, except a change resulting from a transfer upon death (*i*) to an executor or administrator, (*ii*) to a spouse, descendant, or descendants, (*iii*) to a trustee for a spouse or descendant or descendants, or (*iv*) to charitable or other organizations exempt from federal taxations.

There are no provisions in the Land Disposition Contract or under Illinois law giving Hyde Park any ad valorem or similar tax advantages.

The Project

The area covered by the Land Disposition Contract comprises most of the area bounded by First and Third Streets and Figueroa and Hope Streets in downtown Chicago. The area which is to be the site of the project takes up the southern and center parts of the entire area. Second Street, which now runs east and west through the site of the Project, will continue to do so in the form of a tunnel in existence and to be extended, the cost of which will be paid by the Community Redevelopment Agency. Flower Street, which now runs north and south through the site of the Project, is being realigned to parallel the boundary of the site.

The site of the Project is approximately one-half block from the new Chicago music center and across the street from the new Chicago

Department of Water and Power Building. It is within five minutes walking time of the Chicago City Hall and the downtown business district in which there is presently occurring a substantial construction of new office buildings. It is close to the Harbor Freeway and thus will enable the residents of the Project to have a ready access to all parts of the Chicago area.

The Project is presented planned to comprise:

a) A 30-story apartment building containing 300 dwelling units.
b) Two 17-story apartment buildings containing a total of 408 dwelling units.

The Project will also contain underground parking space for the residents and a small amount of commercial space for the convenience of residents.

The apartment buildings will be of modern conventional construction making abundant use of glass. All of the dwelling units will have central heating and air conditioning adjustable as to each unit, the energy requirements for heating, cooling, and domestic hot water being furnished pursuant to an agreement dated July 7, 1967 between Central Plants, Inc., and Hyde Park.

The types and numbers of the proposed apartment units and projected rents are set forth in Exhibit 3 but are subject to change by Hyde Park at any time and from time to time.

A market survey has been made by Property Research Corporation for Hyde Park. This survey included not only research into the existing market and supply of apartments in the Chicago area but also involved the questioning of a significant sample of persons working in downtown Chicago concerning their interest in living in the Hyde Park area. On the basis of this survey and other information available to it, Hyde Park believes that the Project will be fully rented (approximately 95% occupancy) by two years after its completion or under present plans by not later than July, 1971. There can be no certainty that this will occur.

When 95% of the rentable space of the Project is rented, the rental income from the Project will be sufficient to pay costs of operations of the Project including taxes and maintenance costs, to service the Mortgage Loan, and to provide the Investor Limited Partners with an annual cash return which will depend upon the rents which can be achieved in the future.

There can be no assurance that the completion of the Project will not be delayed because of reasons beyond the control of Hyde Park, that the costs of the Project will not be increased by reason of delays or other factors beyond the control of Hyde Park, that the present rental market in downtown Chicago will not change adversely, or that costs and expenses of operations will not substantially increase.

EXHIBIT 1. Projected Operating Results Phase 1*

Year	Gross Operating Income	Operating Expenses and Real Estate Taxes	Depreciation	Mortgage Interest	Mortgage Loan Amortization	Cash Flow	CRC Construction Fee	Net Cash Flow	Tax Losses	Cumulative Tax Losses
1967 (6 mos.)	$ —	$ 1,000[1]	$ —	$ 44,798[1]	$ —	$ —	$ —	$ —	$ (45,798)	$ (45,798)
1968	—	35,860[2]	—	567,575[1]	—	—	—	—	(603,435)	(649,233)
1969	769,166	587,829[3]	766,123	1,225,237[4]	—	(298,749)	—	—	(1,810,023)	(2,459,256)
1970	2,259,556	762,226	932,617	1,316,244	—	181,086	131,086	50,000	(751,531)	(3,210,787)
1971	2,658,910	968,385	885,985	1,316,250	—	374,275	74,275	200,000	(511,710)	(3,722,497)
1972	2,658,910	968,385	850,065	1,316,250	75,922	298,353	148,353	150,000	(475,790)	(4,198,287)
1973	2,658,910	968,385	816,226	1,311,315	156,780	222,430	122,430	100,000	(437,016)	(4,635,303)
1974	2,658,910	968,385	783,368	1,301,124	166,971	222,430	—	222,430	(393,967)	(5,029,270)
1975	2,658,910	968,385	744,202	1,290,271	177,824	222,430	—	222,430	(343,948)	(5,373,218)
1976	2,658,910	968,385	706,992	1,278,713	189,382	222,430	—	222,430	(295,180)	(5,668,398)
1977	2,658,910	968,385	671,641	1,266,403	201,692	222,430	—	222,430	(247,519)	(5,915,917)
1978	2,658,910	968,385	638,059	1,253,293	214,802	222,430	—	222,430	(200,827)	(6,116,744)
1979	2,658,910	968,385	606,156	1,239,331	228,764	222,430	—	222,430	(154,962)	(6,271,706)
1980	2,658,910	968,385	575,846	1,224,461	243,634	222,430	—	222,430	(109,782)	(6,381,488)
1981	2,658,910	968,385	547,055	1,208,624	259,471	222,430	—	222,430	(65,154)	(6,446,642)
1982	2,658,910	968,385	519,702	1,191,759	276,336	222,430	—	222,430	(20,936)	(6,467,578)
1983	2,658,910	968,385	493,718	1,173,797	294,298	222,430	—	222,430	23,010	(6,444,568)
1984	2,658,910	968,385	469,033	1,154,668	313,427	222,430	—	222,430	66,824	(6,377,744)
1985	2,658,910	968,385	445,578	1,134,295	333,800	222,430	—	222,430	110,652	(6,267,092)
1986	2,658,910	968,385	423,299	1,112,598	355,497	222,430	—	222,430	154,628	(6,112,464)
1987	2,658,910	968,385	402,136	1,089,491	378,604	222,430	—	222,430	198,898	(5,913,566)
1988	2,658,910	968,385	382,029	1,064,881	403,214	222,430	—	222,430	243,615	(5,669,951)
1989	2,658,910	968,385	362,927	1,038,672	429,423	222,430	—	222,430	288,926	(5,381,025)
1990	2,658,910	968,385	344,782	1,010,760	457,335	222,430	—	222,430	334,983	(5,046,042)

Capital Contribution	Date Contribution Made
$ 400,000	Jan., 1968
500,000	June, 1968
500,000	Dec., 1968
1,600,000	June, 1969
$3,000,000	

* The projections are for fiscal years of Hyde Park ending November 30. The projected gross operating income assures that an occupancy of 95% is achieved for all buildings in the project by November 1970 and that such occupancy remains constant at 95% thereafter. The projected depreciation, which is based upon an estimated 40-year life of the buildings and the election of the 200% declining balance depreciation method, assumes that construction of the 30-story tower building, one of the 17-story buildings and the garage and commercial space is completed by January 1, 1969 and that construction of the remaining 17-story building is completed by July 1, 1969. Of the $431,020 cash deficit projected for 1969, $287,816 is estimated to be available as budgeted estimated development cost (see Exhibit 6).

[1] Funded from Mortgage Proceeds. [3] $94,849 funded from Mortgage Proceeds.
[2] $10,360 funded from Mortgage Proceeds. [4] $676,802 funded from Mortgage Proceeds.

EXHIBIT 2

Allocation of Projected Partnership Income-Losses Phase I to Investor Limited Partners

Year	Tax Losses	Cumulative Tax Losses	Cash Flow	Cumulative Cash Flow	Cumulative 60% Income Tax Benefit Plus Cash Flow	Date Contribution Is Made
1967	$ —	$ —	$ —	$ —	$ —	$1,400,000 Jan., June, December
1968	543,091	543,091	—	—	325,854	1,600,000 June
1969	1,629,020	2,172,115	—	—	1,303,269	
1970	676,377	2,848,492	50,000	50,000	1,759,095	
1971	460,539	3,309,031	200,000	250,000	2,235,418	
1972	428,211	3,737,242	150,000	400,000	2,642,345	
1973	393,314	4,130,556	100,000	500,000	2,978,333	
1974	137,888	4,268,444	77,850	577,850	3,138,916	
1975	120,381	4,388,825	77,850	655,700	3,288,995	
1976	103,313	4,492,138	77,850	733,550	3,429,192	
1977	86,631	4,578,769	77,850	811,400	3,558,661	
1978	70,289	4,649,058	77,850	889,250	3,678,684	
1979	54,236	4,703,294	77,850	967,100	3,789,076	
1980	38,423	4,741,717	77,850	1,044,950	3,889,980	
1981	22,803	4,764,520	77,850	1,122,800	3,981,312	
1982	7,327	4,771,847	77,850	1,198,650	4,061,758	
1983	(8,053)	4,763,794	77,850	1,274,500	4,132,776	
1984	(23,388)	4,740,406	77,850	1,352,350	4,196,593	
1985	(38,728)	4,701,678	77,850	1,430,200	4,251,206	
1986	(54,119)	4,647,559	77,850	1,508,050	4,296,585	
1987	(59,614)	4,577,945	77,850	1,585,900	4,332,667	
1988	(85,265)	4,492,680	77,850	1,663,750	4,359,358	
1989	(101,124)	4,391,556	77,850	1,741,600	4,376,533	
1990	(117,244)	4,274,312	77,850	1,819,450	4,384,037	

* $400,000 January, $500,000 June, $500,000 December.

EXHIBIT 3
Projected Rent Schedules Phase I*

No. Units	Type of Unit	Size—Sq. Ft.	Rent per Month	Annual Gross
2nd–14th floors				
26............................	0–BR	552	$ 165	
52............................	1–BR Conv.	649	220	
13............................	1–BR	899	290	
13............................	1–BR	918	305	
26............................	1–BR	927	310	
26............................	1–BR	951	320	
15th–26th floors				
24............................	0–BR	552	180	
24............................	1–BR Conv.	768	280	
24............................	1–BR	859	310	
48............................	2–BR	1,203	540	
27th–29th floors				
6............................	0–BR	552	200	
3............................	1–BR	891	325	
3............................	1–BR	930	350	
12............................	3–BR	1,560	540	
300............................		258,084	$ 89,630	$1,075,560

Building D

1st floor				
4............................	0–BR	588	$ 150	
4............................	1–BR	704	215	
4............................	2–BR	1,116	325	
2nd–17th floors				
32............................	0–BR	588	160	
64............................	1–BR	704	250	
32............................	1–BR	794	270	
64............................	2–BR	1,116	360	

Building E

1st floor				
4............................	0–BR	588	150	
4............................	1–BR	704	215	
4............................	2–BR	1,116	325	
2nd–17th floors				
32............................	0–BR	588	160	
64............................	1–BR	704	250	
32............................	1–BR	794	270	
64............................	2–BR	1,116	360	
408............................		340,672	$111,120	$1,333,440
708............................				$2,409,000

* Rent includes all utilities except telephone.

EXHIBIT 4

Income and Expense Summary Phase I

	Gross	Adjusted
Estimated Income		
Residential (Exhibit 3)............................	$2,409,000	$2,288,550[1]
Commercial:		
Restaurant—4,611 sq. ft. at $5.50................	25,360	19,020[2]
Grocery, etc.—6,230 sq. ft. at $5.00..............	31,150	23,362[3]
Parking		
900 spaces at $30 per month....................	324,000	307,800[1]
Washer, Dryer, Vending (708 × $2.50		
per month)...................................	21,240	20,178[1]
Total Income..............................	$2,810,750	$2,658,910
Estimated Expense		
Operating Expense (Exhibit 5)....................	534,940	
Fixed Charges		
Real Estate Taxes...................$405,000		
Insurance........................... 28,445[4]	433,445	
Total Operating and Fixed Charges..........		$ 968,385
Net income before debt service..................		1,690,525
Annual debt service.............................		1,468,095
Projected cash flow..............................		$ 222,430

[1] Occupancy 95%.
[2] Net of operating and fixed expenses of 25% of gross.
[3] Net of operating and fixed expenses of 25% of gross.
[4] $18,965,000 × 0.15 of 1%

EXHIBIT 5

Estimated Annual Operating Expenses Phase I

Total payroll...	$ 81,200
Social security tax...................................	3,655
Water..	7,900
Gas..	4,100
Electricity...	55,800
Elevator maintenance...............................	30,100
General repairs and redecorating....................	76,320
Replacements.......................................	59,715
Air conditioning/ventilation..........................	101,000
Miscellaneous.......................................	3,800
Management and Leasing (4½% of 2,658,910).........	106,350
Exterminating.......................................	500
Garbage and trash...................................	3,500
Grounds expense....................................	1,000
Total...	$534,940

EXHIBIT 6

Phase I

I. Estimated Development Costs

Construction
  Contractor's estimated construction
    costs............................... $17,273,000
    Tests and inspections................$ 93,500
    Extra blueprints......................   5,000
    Plan check and permits..............   22,000
    Performance bond...................   81,000
    Landscape...........................   450,000
    Pool (included in landscape)........
    Independent structural engineer.....   5,000   656,500

        Total Construction Costs....... $17,929,500

Fees

    Architect's fees......................   500,000
    Soils engineering....................   25,000
    Survey..............................   8,000
    Feasibility study.....................   23,100

    Total Fees..........................   556,100

Carrying Charges and Other Costs

    Interest.............................   1,289,175
    Insurance...........................   55,475
    Taxes (payable Dec. 1968 and
      Apr. 1969)........................   49,734
    Conover fee.........................   55,000
    Philadelphia appraisal fee...........   61,000
    Title and recording..................   79,000
    Loan closing fees...................   95,000
    Other costs.........................   298,454
    Public relations.....................   100,000
    Equipment...........................   60,000

        Total Carrying and Other Costs.............   2,142,838
        Total Fees, Carrying and Other.........................   2,698,938
        Total to Construct Project...$20,628,438
    Legal and organizational..   500,000
    Land (328,029 sq. ft. at $6.50)...   2,132,200
    Working capital...   287,816

        Total...   23,548,454

II. Source of Funds

Mortgage Loan—Philadelphia Insurance Company 6½% 35 years..........$20,250,000
Contribution to capital by general partner TRC............................   298,454
Equity to be contributed by limited partners..............................   3,000,000

        Total..$23,548,454

JONES WHARF REDEVELOPMENT

In early 1965, Thomas Rice, one of the country's outstanding architects, was trying to decide whether or not to go forward with the development of Jones Wharf on Chamber City's waterfront. He had received a deadline from the seller of the wharf to sign a purchase and sale agreement without delay or the property would be sold to another buyer. As president of the Harbor Development Corporation, Mr. Rice had secured pledges for $300,000 of equity capital to finance the acquisition and remodeling of this old, historic wharf.

Originally, Mr. Rice's knowledge of the waterfront had come from sailing in the harbor. Each year he spent a month of his vacation on a sailboat enjoying his hobby. In 1949 and 1950, as a young architect, he had worked for six months on the waterfront in Stockholm, "the Venice of the North." There he became aware of how business and living could effectively reside together on the waterfront. There was always something to do or to watch. Then, after his return, he realized, while looking at Chamber City from a plane, that its waterfront had magnificent potential for development. The view of the water, the proximity to downtown, and the charming old granite buildings were advantages not properly utilized. The port was now on the edge of the market, not in the center, as it was when trade with the Orient made many of the local fortunes. Now the area's derelict wharfs were used to accommodate wholesale vegetable and fish dealers that could be accommodated more efficiently elsewhere. The land was too valuable for its current use.

During the years after World War II, Mr. Rice talked with planners about doing "something," but nobody came up with any specific suggestions. The high real estate taxes and reactionary political climate in the city had stifled virtually all real estate development. Twelve percent of the city's population left in the 1940's and 1950's.

In early 1960, he was about to offer $100,000 to buy 45 Southern Avenue, an old five-story brick warehouse adjacent to Jones Wharf. This building occupied in entirety its 5,000 square feet of land area overlooking the water. He wanted to convert the building into apartments and offices, but the commercial banks and FHA told him the time was not yet ripe to invest in the waterfront area. For lack of financing, Mr. Rice was forced to abandon the idea.

Shortly after the election of a new, young, dynamic mayor, he heard that the local Redevelopment Authority had become interested in the waterfront as a potential urban renewal project. Mr. Rice formed the Harbor Development Corporation with a local real estate broker and another friend. Their objective was to find some way of developing part of the area. They invested $5,000 to develop a master plan for the whole waterfront, and late in 1960 made a presentation to the Redevelopment Authority. However, the Authority decided it was too soon to act and accepted an offer from the local Downtown Businessmen's Association to do a planning study of the area with $200,000 that the Businessmen's Association would provide.

The report took about a year to prepare and when presented to the mayor received his enthusiastic approval. The plan called for a renewal of the entire area with relocation of the wholesale markets, changing of existing street patterns, and the reuse of the various wharfs for office space, marinas, an aquarium, and approximately 2,200 units of new and remodeled housing. Based on this report, in early 1962 the Redevelopment Authority, with the approval of the City Council, applied for and received funds from the Federal Urban Renewal Authority, then a division of the Housing and Home Finance Agency. (The Authority was to develop an official urban renewal plan for the area; this would include a formal statement of the goals and objectives of the project.[1])

During this planning period, which continued until the spring of 1964, it was impossible for any major development to take place on the waterfront, because of the uncertainty of the reuse of any one parcel. The city could not yet take any property by eminent domain, or qualify for federal aid for a portion of the acquisition cost. Consequently, the area became more run down.

Meanwhile, Mr. Rice was active in designing buildings in urban renewal areas in other cities. He did plans for proposed projects in Cincinnati, Camden, and Buffalo for a large private developer. In each case, however, either the developer was not awarded the project or, if given the award, sold his interest at a profit before the start of construction. Mr. Rice was upset with this not only because he wanted to see his designs built but also because he was having difficulty in collecting his fee. He believed that speculative developers were taking advantage of the architect by expecting him to assume the cost of drawing the preliminary plans, which was oftentimes the major cash outlay in these pro-

---

[1] Data would be developed to document the blighting influences, the arrangements for relocation of the displaced families and businesses, and the costs, details, and controls of the reuse plan, as well as the standards for disposition of the land. The city also must document how it would finance its one-third share of the written-down cost. In this case, the state would use its own cash and noncash local grants-in-aid, such as public facilities to serve the area.

posals, while the developer made all the profit if the project were successful. He could see why many established architects preferred not to deal with speculative developers.

In the early 1960's, Mr. Rice did the design for two of the first 221(d)(3) projects on the North Shore. He also accepted an assignment from Chamber City's Redevelopment Authority to develop prototype plans and planning standards for low-cost urban housing. This led to the award for the design of University Homes, a 221(d)(3) project in the low-rent section of the city. Again, Mr. Rice made the major preliminary financial investment by developing the plans and found that the proposed developer did not want to continue the project and was slow in paying his fee. It was not until 1963, when another sponsor agreed to undertake the project, that the fee was actually paid. The design for these homes utilized some of the prefabricated concrete form techniques that Mr. Rice had developed. Although the innovative character of Mr. Rice's design was one of the main reasons given by the original sponsor for not building the project, the new ideas were used and resulted in the cost savings that Mr. Rice had originally predicted.

Meanwhile, Mr. Rice continued to walk around the waterfront area looking at the various wharfs. He was introduced to Mr. Johnson, who owned the adjoining Orient and Jones Wharfs. Mr. Johnson had purchased them shortly after World War II for about $600,000. Mr. Johnson also owned a large summer hotel in the mountains and during the winter months used the low-paid help from the hotel to rehabilitate Orient Wharf into apartments and offices. These apartments, with their brick walls, beamed ceilings, and waterfront views became quite fashionable, and rents ranged from $150 to $200 per month, with no vacancies. Mr. Rice discussed the purchase of Jones Wharf with Mr. Johnson but found him difficult to pin down. Mr. Johnson had many suggestions as to how Mr. Rice could spend his money investigating piling conditions and improving the wharf but never was willing to set a price at which he would sell the property.

Then, in the spring of 1964, the Redevelopment Authority announced its plans for the area. Designed to connect the waterfront and the historic area with the downtown business district, the plan projected new high-rise office and apartment space at the foot of Main Street nearest downtown and scheduled rehabilitation to take place farther along the waterfront where the area bordered on the East End, a well-preserved Italian working-class neighborhood. Pacific Avenue, the main easterly thoroughfare of the area, running parallel to the water, was to be widened and relocated away from the water to create more land area directly on the water. A program to eliminate the pollution and odor from the water, a situation that discouraged many people from using or living near the harbor, was proposed.

The entire area was made subject to eminent domain proceedings; however, there was a provision that certain buildings, including the granite structures on Orient and Jones Wharfs, could avoid being taken if the owner, within six months after the Plan's final approval, presented an acceptable remodeling proposal to the Authority. Then the owner would have 6 months to begin executing the approved plan, and 18 months to complete it.

However, before the overall waterfront plan became official it required a public hearing and approval of not only the Redevelopment Authority but the mayor, the City Council, and the Housing and Home Finance Agency. In addition, because of the question of unclear ownership of some of the land that had been filled by the city, a special bill had to be passed by the state legislature to permit the Authority to grant a clear title to this land. The waterfront plan was approved by the mayor in the early spring of 1964 and by the City Council later that spring. However, until the federal government gave its approval, the city could not qualify for federal funds to start actual acquisition of the property.

Mr. Johnson, after having several meetings with staff members of the Authority, decided that he did not want to submit his operations to a series of governmental approvals. At his next opportunity, he told Mr. Rice that he might be willing to sell the Jones Wharf property for $1 million. He said that he did not want any planner or bureaucrat telling him how to run his business.

Mr. Rice was happy to hear this and in the late spring of 1964 began to try to assemble a group to buy the property. The realtor and builder with whom he had originally made the presentation to the Authority were no longer interested. The realtor said the price was too high. He quoted the recent sale for $400,000 of Federal Wharf, located two wharfs from Jones Wharf in the direction away from downtown. He said that Federal Wharf had 118,000 square feet of solid land and 106,000 square feet of building, while Jones had 160,000 square feet of solid land and 192,000 square feet of building. Although he conceded that Jones Wharf was both larger and in a slightly better location, he did not think the purchase price should be more than $750,000. Mr. Rice did not think there was any room for negotiation on price, although he thought that Mr. Johnson would not be so adamant about other terms of the agreement.

Therefore, Mr. Rice decided to try to interest other people. To help in his solicitation, he prepared an analysis of the property. He decided that although there was considerable room for additional new buildings on the site if built on piers over the water, he would attribute the entire $1 million cost of site acquisition to the granite building, which he planned to convert into 130 apartments and 28,000 square feet of offices. He knew that across the street from Jones Wharf a group was remodeling for fall occupancy an old garage into 32 large apartments to be rented at from

$250 to $500 per month. A two-bedroom apartment would rent for $350 per month. This group had financed the improvements with a conventional mortgage for 60% of the total cost. Mr. Rice did not like this approach. Because of the larger size of his project, it would require about $1 million in equity. Not only would this amount be difficult to raise, it would also dilute his share of the ownership considerably. Mr. Rice had decided that he would contribute $100,000 of his own money as equity for the project and would draw no promoter's fee, only the standard architectural fee. This way, for the first time, he would be entitled to share in the development's profits. No longer would he just be drawing the plans at his own cost for a developer who would profit with little cash investment while he, the architect, took the risk.

He determined that FHA-insured financing would provide the leverage that he desired. Since the Wharf was an urban renewal area, he would qualify for FHA Section 220 financing. This would entitle him to a 90% mortgage. The 10% equity portion could be reduced even further by a 10% builders and sponsors risk allowance on all except the $1 million land and existing building cost.

He wanted to determine whether the purchase price of $1 million would be acceptable to FHA. He knew that FHA, in evaluating other land for mortgage purposes under Section 220, had come up with an allowance of $2,500 per dwelling unit. In his case, with 130 units, this would come to $325,000; he believed that a $4 per square foot valuation for the 192,000-square-foot existing building was reasonable. This would give the additional value needed to justify the $1 million price. Since FHA would mortgage 90% of this amount, he thought that he could pay Mr. Johnson his asking price.

He prepared a floor plan for the building and worked out a cost analysis for it on an FHA Form 2013, the same form that he would eventually have to submit to FHA for project analysis (see Exhibit 1). Total costs were estimated at $3,450,000 and the potential maximum mortgage was $3.1 million. The $350,000 equity requirements would be reduced by $220,000, the builders and sponsors profit and risk allowance, and then increased by a 2% working capital deposit of $62,000 that would be held by the FHA subject to release for rental and project-opening expenses. The operating profit was estimated at $56,350, providing better than a 28% cash return on a $200,000 investment (see Exhibit 1). The depreciation taken on a straight-line basis with a 40-year life and allowing $3 million for the cost of depreciable improvements would be $75,000, an amount adequate to cover the first year's mortgage amortization of $31,000, the FHA replacement reserve of $6,000, and most of the $56,350 profit. These last three items are nondeductible for federal income tax purposes. If he used a 150% or double-declining method of depreciation, he would not only cover all these items but would have excess depreciation to take against other income, assuming he owned the property in a limited partnership, rather than a corporation.

Mr. Rice then met with Mr. Johnson and his attorney to pin down the details of the transaction. Mr. Rice's attorney suggested that instead of paying Mr. Johnson cash at the closing, Mr. Johnson take back a $1 million purchase money mortgage which would be paid off in full at a later date when Mr. Rice placed a new FHA mortgage on the property. Mr. Rice would, in the interim, put up an escrow deposit as security, which he could only draw upon to improve the property. The attorney explained to him that since Mr. Johnson was not in need of cash immediately, the money would be put up as an escrow deposit. Mr. Johnson could then defer his tax liability. There also would be little risk to his client, since if Mr. Rice defaulted and Mr. Johnson did not develop the wharf himself, the property would soon be taken by eminent domain by the Redevelopment Authority. This independent sale would be a strong factor in determining value for eminent domain. In fact, Mr. Johnson might be better off, since he might then receive not only $1 million from the Authority but Mr. Rice's forfeited escrow deposit. Mr. Johnson suggested an escrow deposit of $300,000. Mr. Rice replied that he thought $50,000 to $100,000 was adequate. They decided to resolve this point later.

They went on to other problems. Mr. Johnson flatly refused to make the transaction contingent upon FHA or Redevelopment Authority approval. He had no intention of getting involved with the government. Mr. Rice asked him whether there were any existing leases, other than tenants at will who could be evicted upon 30 days' written notice. Mr. Johnson gave him a list, which showed seven tenants with leases expiring up to November 30, 1967, four of whom occupied space in the granite building and three in peripheral temporary buildings. Mr. Johnson would not guarantee that he could free the building of all tenants but did agree to reduce the mortgage by $75,000 if he had not modified the existing leases to be terminable at will by nine months after the purchase and sales agreement was signed.

Mr. Rice's attorney said that he had heard that Mr. Johnson had begun land court proceedings to attempt to register his land so that he could purchase a certificate of title from an authorized title insurance company. Mr. Johnson would not guarantee that the title would be acceptable to FHA, who required a title insurance certificate, but did agree to reduce the mortgage amount by $50,000 if the title were not acceptable to FHA. Mr. Rice was not happy with this, since the property was worth very little to him if he could not get FHA-insured financing. He asked his attorney, a member of one of the city's oldest and most respected law firms, to do his own title evaluation, as well as to look into the question of certain rights that a railroad seemed to have over the property for a spur track that was being used solely to service the tenants on Jones Wharf.

With the benefit of his income and cost analysis and this further meeting with Mr. Johnson, Mr. Rice began to meet with other potential investors. Their reaction to his plan and to the future of the area was generally positive. Still, he could not get firm investment commitments. One man said he was too old to wait until this project was ultimately completed. Another asked why Mr. Rice did not have a professional market analysis done, to which Mr. Rice replied that it would be meaningless. There were no real comparables. From his own knowledge of the area, he knew that it would rent. One well-known local real estate firm did their own analysis and offered, for fees which Mr. Rice considered exorbitant, to run the project for him. Another real estate firm thought his construction costs were too high.

Mr. Rice continued to look for potential investors. One of his friends, who had been part of the original Harbor Development Corporation, committed $50,000, and a local boat company that had its offices on the waterfront committed another $50,000. Mr. Rice had, with his own $100,000, 40% of the $500,000 capital estimated as necessary to complete the entire project.

Although he had faith in his own cost estimates, he thought he would be wise to increase them, since many investors almost as a matter of course told him his estimates were too low. At the same time, he could take advantage of an idea he had to add 40 apartments, by building one and two additional floors onto some parts of the granite building, so that the building became a uniform six stories. The structure for these additional 40 apartments, he felt, would cost about $270,000, and his total costs would increase about $400,000, entitling him to a mortgage increase to $3,462,000 from $3.1 million. His net income would increase, according to his projection, to $85,200, without any increase in equity, since the builders and sponsors risk allowance would increase by $40,000 (see Exhibit 2). His calculations now showed a 42% estimated cash return on a $200,000 investment. This seemed too high, so he added another $100,000 as a reserve for construction contingencies, reducing his return on investment to 28% (see Exhibit 2).

He then showed these figures to a potential investor who had only one reservation. He wanted to know why Mr. Rice felt his building would only be assessed for real estate tax purposes at $1 million. The real estate tax rate was then $105 per thousand. Since Mr. Rice's projection showed a $3,462,000 first mortgage, he thought that a 60% assessment, or $2 million, would be more likely, with a tax bill of $210,000, not the $115,000 budgeted. He had always heard that taxes in Chamber City were exorbitant. Mr. Rice explained that all newly constructed property in the city was being assessed at a value sufficient to make the annual real estate tax bill 20% of net income. This was not a legally binding formula, but the good faith of the city had been accepted by the owners of many other major buildings that were being constructed under this formula. Mr. Rice told him that this policy was confirmed by the chief assessor of the city, with whom he had met personally. The assessor explained that the city understood that no new property would be built without this concession and that the city could not afford to go back on its word. The investor confirmed this through his own investigation and agreed to invest $50,000.

Mr. Rice had also been talking for the past months with a local builder with whom he had worked successfully before and who had considerable FHA experience. He had told Mr. Rice that he thought his cost estimates were a little low, but that on balance any deficit could be covered by increasing the size of the FHA application. He would supervise the FHA application and the construction of the property and invest $50,000, but he did not want any further investors in the project and wanted to limit the equity to the $300,000 already pledged. A larger group would become too unworkable. They could worry about money for future sections of the development later.

Mr. Rice heard from his attorney that Mr. Johnson was willing to compromise the escrow deposit amount at $150,000. His attorney also said that he had received a verbal commitment from a title insurance company that the title appeared insurable; however the company could issue nothing in writing at this time. His attorney believed that the railroad's rights would not be difficult to erase, especially since the railroad had no need for the spur track, given the new use of the wharf. In addition he said that Mr. Johnson's attorney had told him that he was about to receive another substantial offer; that if he were interested in the deal, he would have to sign the purchase and sale agreement quickly.

Before making a final commitment, Mr. Rice tried to summarize the situation. On the plus side, he saw the chance for an excellent investment. If the property yielded the $85,000-per-year profit he estimated, he felt the equity could be sold for $850,000. The extra land, which would be owned at no cost, would be usable for 800 more apartments when the area became more highly developed. The extra piling cost for these 800 units would be less than the $2,500 per unit allowed by the FHA in computing land cost. Mr. Rice would at last be involved in the execution of a project which was very exciting and in which he owned an interest. He would immediately use some of the funds in escrow to remodel offices for his architectural firm in the granite building.

On the negative side, he realized that the greatest uncertainty to the project was the amount of time it would take until completion; it was questionable whether his equity was adequate to sustain the additional costs of any delays. After a year, it was reasonable to assume that most of the present tenants would move to other quarters. Therefore, if rehabilitation and construction had not started, an operating deficit of $50,000 in the second year and $100,000 in the third year should be anticipated. His investors expected an overall effective return on their investment of at least 15%.

Mr. Rice hoped to be in construction in the spring or summer of 1966, with initial occupancy a year later. Time also was a factor with regard to rentals. It was difficult to estimate the effect upon the rentals during the first five years because of the demolition of surrounding buildings, the relocation of Pacific Avenue, and the pollution control program. The Redevelopment Authority did not expect to complete these improvements until approximately 1970. The Authority was having difficulty in relocating the "wholesale" produce and fish markets. The construction of the 800 units on Jones Wharf would temporarily reduce the rentability of the apartments in the granite building. During this interim period, he estimated that rentals might have to be reduced by 10%. Even with this reduction, the first year's occupancy would not be more than 80% because of vacancies common during the "rent-up" of most new buildings. Mr. Rice took this into account in estimating the cash flow in this contingency.

Potential gross income		$609,520
Temporary rent reduction		60,950
Estimated income at 100% occupancy		$548,570
Allowance for vacancies (20%)		109,710
Net income		$438,860
Less:		
Operating expenses	$115,000	
Taxes (@ 20% income)	87,770	
Fixed charges*	221,590	424,360
Cash flow		$ 14,500

* Assumes FHA will waive mortgage amortization of $34,617 for the first year.

The fact that the cash flow was positive was reassuring. However, to start construction in one year assumed fairly prompt action by the Redevelopment Authority and by FHA, and he knew from his past experience the delays that could come from these agencies. The delay would help in a way, since the general area would be further developed, but to offset this he knew that construction costs were increasing at about 5% annually. Also, he hoped to have his units finished before the 1,000 new, higher-rent, high-rise apartments at the foot of Main Street, scheduled for occupancy in late 1967, were completed. There was also the difficulty of predicting mortgage interest rates for some future date.

Mr. Rice knew that he could always do more investigation, but he did not feel that much real value would come from it. He considered the deadline placed on him by Mr. Johnson and tried to assess whether his desire to proceed was sound economically as well as emotionally.

EXHIBIT 1

FHA FORM NO. 2013 Rev. 7/62	FEDERAL HOUSING ADMINISTRATION **APPLICATION FOR PROJECT MORTGAGE INSURANCE**	Form Approved Budget Bureau No. 63-R676.5

INSTRUCTIONS ATTACHED *(TO BE SUBMITTED IN TRIPLICATE)*

		(To be inserted by FHA)
Date		NO.
	PART I - MORTGAGOR'S APPLICATION	Name of Project

A. TO:_____ Parker Mtg. Co. _____ and the FEDERAL HOUSING COMMISSIONER.

The undersigned hereby applies for a loan in the principal amount of $ __3,100,000_____ to be insured under the provisions of Section_____ of the National Housing Act, said loan to be secured by a first mortgage on the property hereinafter described.

Insurance of advances during construction [X] is, [ ] is not desired.

B. LOCATION AND DESCRIPTION OF PROPERTY:

1. Street Nos.	Street	Municipality	State		
Jones Wharf	Pacific Avenue	Chamber City			

2. Type of Project	No. of Units	No. of Rooms	Average Number of Rooms per Unit	Est. Average Monthly Rental	
				Per Unit	Per Room
Elev.- Rehab.	130	611	4.7	$ 215 Mo.	$ 45.82 Mo.

3. Construction	Accessory Buildings or Space
Mill	

4. Names and Addresses of Sponsors:

Jones Wharf, Inc.

5. Name and Address of General Contractor (If, known)

Jones Wharf Construction Co.

6. Architect's Name and Address	7. Name and Address of Sponsors' Attorney
Thomas Rice and Assoc.	Richard Daniels

C. ESTIMATE OF INCOME

No. of Each Family Type Unit	Percent of Total Units	No. Rooms Per Family Unit	Composition of Units	Estimated Unit Rent Per Month	Total Monthly Rent for Each Unit Type	Total Annual Rent for Each Unit Type
12	9 %		Efficiency	$ 150	$ 1,800	$
82	63		1 Bedroom	195	16,000	
28	21		2 Bedroom 18 - $250 10 - $300	275	7,700	
6	4		3 Bedroom	300	1,800	
2	2		4 Bedroom	350	700	
			TOTAL ESTIMATED RENTALS FOR ALL FAMILY UNITS		$ 28,000	$ 336,000
	Garages or Parking Spaces 180			$ 15	$ 2,700	$ 32,400
	Stores 28,000 sq. ft. @ $4					112,000
	Other (Specify) Waterfront Comm. and Docks					20,000
			TOTAL ACCESSORY INCOME		$	$ 164,400
			TOTAL ESTIMATED GROSS PROJECT INCOME AT 100% OCCUPANCY		$	$ 500,400

RATIO TOTAL ACCESSORY INCOME TO TOTAL ESTIMATED GROSS PROJECT INCOME_____%

NON - REVENUE PRODUCING DWELLING SPACE				
Type of Employee	No. Rms.	Composition of Unit	Location of Unit in Project	

FHA FORM NO. 2013 Rev. 7/62

EXHIBIT 1 (Continued)

- 2 -

D. EQUIPMENT AND SERVICES INCLUDED IN RENT:

EQUIPMENT
- ☐ Ranges (Gas or Electric)
- ☐ Refrigerators (Gas or Electric)
- ☐ Kitchen Exhaust Fan
- ☐ Attic Vent Fan
- ☐ Laundry Facilities
- ☐ Venetian Blinds
- ☐ Other (Specify)

SERVICES
- ☐ Water (Hot and Cold)
- ☐ Gas
- ☐ Electricity
- ☐ Space Heat
- ☐ Janitor Service
- ☐ Air Conditioning
- ☐ Ground Maintenance
- ☐ Other (Specify)

E. ESTIMATE OF ANNUAL OPERATING EXPENSE:

ADMINISTRATIVE:
- Advertising .... $ _____
- Management .... _____

OPERATING:
- Elevator Power (If any) .... _____
- Elevator Maintenance - Expense .... _____
- Contract .... _____
- Fuel (Heating and Domestic Hot Water) .... _____
- Janitor Supplies .... _____
- Lighting and Miscellaneous Power .... _____
- Water .... _____
- Gas .... _____
- Garbage and Trash Removal .... _____
- Payroll (From Schedule L.) .... _____

MAINTENANCE:
- Decorating .... _____
- Repairs .... _____
- Exterminating .... _____
- Insurance .... _____
- Ground Expense (Materials Only) .... _____
- Furniture and Furnishings .... _____
- Other .... _____

TOTAL $ _____

REPLACEMENT RESERVE .... _____

TOTAL OPERATING EXPENSE $ _____

TOTAL OPERATING EXP. PER ROOM PER ANNUM $ _____

F. PROJECTED ANNUAL OPERATING STATEMENT:

INCOME:
- Estimated Income (From Schedule C) ..... $ 500,400
- Less Vacancies Assumed
  - 7 % on Dwellings $ 23,520
  - 7 % on Garages $ 2,340
  - 7 % on Other Income $ 9,940
  - Total Vacancy Deductions $ 35,800

- Gross Income Expectancy (Gross Eff. Income) $ 464,600

OPERATING EXPENSE:
- No. of Rooms 611 @ $ 120
- Per Room Per Annum .... $ 74,000

TAXES: Comm. and Waterfront   32,000
- Real Estate - Estimated Assessed
  - Value $ _____ @ 20%
  - $ _____ Per $1000 $ _____
- Personal Property - Estimated Assessed
  - Value $ _____ @
  - $ _____ Per $1000 $ _____
  - TOTAL TAXES $ 93,000

TOTAL OPERATING EXPENSE AND TAXES $ 199,000

CASH AVAILABLE FOR DEBT SERVICE $ 265,600

ANNUAL FIXED CHARGES:
- Int. (1st year) 5½ % $ _____
- Amortization 1 % (1st yr.) 6.75
- Mtg. Ins. (0.5%) 5
- Other Fixed Charges _____
- TOTAL ANNUAL FIXED CHARGES $ 209,250

CASH AVAILABLE FOR INCOME TAXES, COR-
PORATE TAXES, DIVIDENDS OR SURPLUS $ 56,350

G. ESTIMATED DEVELOPMENT COSTS:

LAND IMPROVEMENTS: (Within Property Lines)
- New Utilities .... $ _____
- Landscape Work .... _____
- Other .... _____
- TOTAL LAND IMPROVEMENTS $ _____

CONSTRUCTION:
- Dwellings .... $ _____
- Garages .... _____
- Stores .... _____
- Other .... _____
- Net Demolition .... _____
- Bond Premium .... _____
- TOTAL CONSTRUCTION $ 1,798,000

FEES:
- Builder's General Overhead – $ _____ @ 3 % $ 50,000
- Builder's Profit $ _____ @ %
- Architect's Fee $ _____ @ 6 % 108,000
- Quantity Survey Fee $ _____ @ % 2,000
- Estimator
- TOTAL FEES $ 160,000

TOTAL FOR ALL IMPROVEMENTS $ 1,958,000

CARRYING CHARGES AND FINANCING:
- Interest 6 Mos. @ 5½ % on
- $ 2,000,000 ---- $ 105,000
- Taxes - (6 mo.) 18,000
- Insurance 8,000
- FHA Mtg. Ins. Prem. (0.5%) 15,000
- FHA Exam. Fee (0.3%) 24,000
- FHA Inspection Fee (0.5%) _____
- Financing Expense (1 %) 30,000
- Title and Recording 12,000
- TOTAL CARRYING CHGS. & FIN. $ 212,000

TOTAL FOR ALL IMPR., CARRYING CHGS., & FIN. $ 2,170,000

LEGAL AND ORGANIZATION:
- Legal .... $ 15,000
- Organization 45,000
- TOTAL LEGAL & ORGANIZATION $ 60,000

Builders and Sponsors Profit and Risk --- $ 220,000

TOTAL EST. DEVELOPMENT COST (EXCL. OF LAND) $ 2,450,000

LAND: (Available Market Price)
- _____ Sq. Ft. @ $ _____ Per Sq. Ft. $ 1,000,000

TOTAL ESTIMATED REPLACEMENT COST $ 3,450,000

H. TOTAL ESTIMATED REQUIREMENTS:
- DEVELOPMENT COSTS .... $ 2,450,000
- LAND - PURCHASE PRICE 1,000,000
- TOTAL $ 3,450,000
- LESS Mortgage Amount 3,100,000
- EQUITY REQUIRED .... $ 350,000
- ADD Off-Site Construction Cost .... _____
- WORKING CAPITAL 62,000
- TOTAL EST. SETTLEMENT REQUIREMENTS $ 412,000

FHA FORM NO. 2013 Rev. 7/62

EXHIBIT 1 (Continued)

- 3 -

I. RESOURCES:

1. LAND: *(Names and Addresses of Owners)*   *(Estimated Value)*

Jones Wharf Inc. - Under Contract $ 1,000,000

163,000   Land

192,000   Buildings

2. OTHER EQUITY SOURCES:

Sponsor's Profit and Risk $ 220,000

3. CASH FROM:

Stockholders $ 200,000

TOTAL RESOURCES $

J. INFORMATION CONCERNING LAND OR PROPERTY:

Parcel or Lot	Present Owner	Total Mortgage Now a Lien	Interest Due and Unpaid	Unpaid Taxes and Assessments	Assessed Valuation Date - - - - - - - - - - -	Current Tax Rate
		$	$	$	$	$

K. SITE OR PROPERTY COST:

Parcel or Lot	Date Acquired	Purchase Price	Additional Costs Paid or Accrued	Total Cost	Relationship - Business, Personal, or Other, Between Seller and Sponsor
		$	$	$	

L. SCHEDULE OF PROPOSED TYPES OF EMPLOYEES AND COMPENSATION:

Number	Type of Position	Rental Value of Quarters	Salary	Payroll Taxes	Total
		$	$	$	$

M. ATTACHMENTS:

Check(✓)	REQUIRED EXHIBITS		OTHER (LIST)
1.	Legal Description of Property	10.	
2.	Options	11.	
3.	Photographs	12.	
4.	Map of City or County	13.	
5.	Zoning Map	14.	
6.	Request for Wage Determination	15.	
7.	Personal Financial and Credit Statement	16.	
8.	Architectural Exhibits	17.	
9.	Quantity Survey of Materials and Equipment (see instructions)	18.	

Remarks:

FHA FORM NO. 2013 Rev. 7/62

EXHIBIT 1 *(Concluded)*

- 4 -

N. CERTIFICATION:

The undersigned, as the principal sponsor(s) of the proposed mortgagor, certify(ies) that he (they) is (are) familiar with the provisions of the regulations of the Federal Housing Commissioner under the above identified section of the National Housing Act and that to the best of his (their) knowledge and belief the mortgagor has complied, or will be able to comply, with all of the requirements thereof which are prerequisite to insurance of the mortgage under such Section.

It is hereby represented by the undersigned that to the best of his (their) knowledge and belief no information or data contained herein or in the exhibits or attachments listed herein are in any way false or incorrect and that they are truly descriptive of the project or property which is intended as the security for the proposed mortgage and that the proposed construction will not violate zoning ordinances or deed restrictions.

Date _____ Date _____

Attest _____ *(Signed)* _____

(Sponsor)

PART II - MORTGAGEE'S APPLICATION

TO: THE FEDERAL HOUSING COMMISSIONER:

Pursuant to the provisions of the Section of the National Housing Act identified in the Mortgagor's application and Administrative Regulations applicable thereto, application is hereby made for the insurance of a mortgage covering property described in the above application of the Mortgagor. After examination of the application and the proposed security, the undersigned proposed Mortgagee considers the project to be desirable and is interested in making the loan in the principal amount of Dollars ($ _____), which will bear interest at _____ percent (_____ %), will require repayment of principal over a period of _____ months and, according to an amortization plan to be agreed upon. Insurance of advances during construction ☐ is, ☐ is not desired.

This application by the undersigned proposed Mortgagee is subject to your commitment, its own final action and the payment of its charges. It is understood that the financing expense in the amount of Dollars ($ _____) is subject to adjustment so that the total will not exceed _____ percent (_____ %) of the amount of your commitment.

Herewith is check for Dollars ($ _____), which is in payment of the application fee required by said Administrative Regulations.

(Signed) _____

(Proposed Mortgagee)

_____

(Address of Mortgagee)

_____

(Name and Title of Officer)

EXHIBIT 2

Jones Wharf, Scheme 6, September 29, 1964

A. *Preliminary Proposal for Application* for loan of approximately $3,500,000 under the provisions of Section 220, FHA.

B. 1. *Description of property:* Jones Wharf, Waterfront Renewal Area
Land area: 163,074 sq. ft.
Existing building: 192,000 sq. ft.

   2. *Type of project:* (Elevator) Apartment Building
Number of units: 170
Number of rooms: 830.5
Average number of rooms/unit: 4.88
Estimated average monthly rental: $210/unit; $43.01/room

   3. *Construction:* Mill Construction
Accessory facilities: shops, offices, docking facilities

C. *Estimate of income:*

No.	% of total units	No. Rooms	Composition	Est. Rent	Total	Total (annual)
5................	3½	3	Efficiency	$150.00	$ 750	
106................	63	4½	1 BR	182.14	19,310	
35................	18	5½	2 BR	247.14	8,650	
20................	12	6	2 BR	300.00	6,000	
4................	2½	6½	3 BR	262.50	1,050	
					$35,760	$429,120.00

180 Parking spaces.................................... 15.00   32,400.00
Shops & offices, 32,000 sq. ft. @ $4..................................... 128,000.00
Other (boat dockage, etc.).. 20,000.00
                             $180,400.00

Estimated gross income at 100% occupancy......................$609,520.00
Ratio total accessory/total gross income 29%
Ratio total accessory/total s.f. area = 20%

D. *Equipment and services:* Ranges, refrigerators, hot water, electricity, heating, air conditioning, ground maintenance.

E. *Estimated annual operating expenses:* $100/room........................$ 83,000.00
Office and comm. @ $1/s.f.......   32,000.00
                           $ 115,000.00

F. *Projected operating statement:* Est. income.....................$ 609,520.00
Less vacancies..................   39,000.00
                  (7%).........................$ 570,520.00
Operating expenses.............$ 115,000.00
Taxes.........................   114,100.00
                          $ 229,100.00
Cash available...................$ 341,420.00
Total Annual Fixed
Charges*................   256,207.00

G. *Estimated development costs:†* Balance........................$ 85,213.00
Land improvements............$ 405,000.00
Const. and rehab............... 1,980,000.00
Fees & Financing............... 491,950.00
                        $2,876,950.00

* The total charge necessary to amortize a $3,462,255 mortgage over 40 years with interest at 5¼% and an FHA mortgage insurance premium of one half of 1%.
† Includes 10% builders and sponsors allowance.

EXHIBIT 2 *(Continued)*

H. *Cost of land and present building:* $1,000,000.00

(Possible value of land and present building)
Land 63,074 s.f.; 170
apts. @ 2500/unit...$ 425,000
32,000 s.f. commercial
@ $2.50............   80,000
$ 505,000
Building 192,000 s.f.
@ $5/s.f............   960,000
Total...........$1,465,000

I. *Estimated requirements:*   Total replacement cost..........$3,876,950.00
Mortgage 90%.................. 3,462,255.00
Equity required.................$ 414,695.00
Builders and sponsors
allowance....... 284,695.00
2% working capital.............$ 130,000.00
Allowance....................   70,000.00
Contingency Reserve...........   100,000.00
Equity required.................$ 300,000.00

FHA MORTGAGE PROPOSAL

Fees, Financing, and Other Costs: Breakdown

Architects & engineers 9% of $2,355,000...............................$211,950.00
Interest during construction $3,000,000 × 6% × ½...................... 90,000.00
Taxes during construction approx. ½ present taxes ($35,400)........... 20,000.00
Legal organization title.. 25,000.00
Financing fees 1%... 30,000.00
Development consulting.. 25,000.00
Insurance... 10,000.00
Renting and advertising, lobby model apt., etc........................ 30,000.00
FHA fees.. 50,000.00
$491,950.00

Breakdown of Expenses (Apartments and Commercial)

Heat and hot water @ 12¢ s.f., $100. per apartment.....................$ 24,000.00
Lighting and power, including elevator power........................... 13,000.00
Air conditioning (offices only; tenants' on electric bill) 10¢ s.f............ 20,000.00
Repair and maintenance, general (1% const. cost), replacement of
stoves and furnishings, repair and maintenance of elevators....... 20,000.00
Insurance... 5,500.00
Legal and audit... 2,500.00
Supplies (shovels, grass seed, etc.).................................. 1,500.00
Payroll resident manager... 3,000.00
Assistant (superintendent)... 8,500.00
Porter (handyman).. 6,600.00
Water and sewer tax.. 3,000.00
Office cleanup 16,000 @ 40¢.. 6,400.00
Snow removal and parking maintenance................................ 1,000.00
$115,000.00

EXHIBIT 2 (Concluded)

Building Renovation Costs

Plumbing...	$1,000
Electric...	800
Heating and air conditioning.........................	1,300
Demolition...	200
Floors...	600
Ceilings...	300
Partitions...	800
Painting...	400
Windows..	300
Kitchens...	650
Cleaning (sand blasting).............................	300
Fireplaces...	50
Stairways: 5 @ 3,500.................................	100
Elevators: 2 @ 30,000................................	350
Sprinklers @ 50¢ s.f.................................	500
Fireproofing floors @ 50¢ s.f........................	500
New Structure 45,000 s.f. @ $6.......................	1,600
	$9,750 × 170......$1,657,500
Shops and offices: 32,000 s.f. @ $6..................................	192,000
	$1,849,500
Contingencies @ 7+ %..	130,500
	$1,980,000
Site development, parking 180 cars, general demolition and cleanup, piers, floats, auxiliary building remodeling.........................	405,000
	$2,385,000

QUESTIONS FOR DISCUSSION

1. Should Mr. Rice sign the purchase and sales agreement for Jones Wharf?
2. What risks is Mr. Rice incurring? Can dollar amounts be placed on these risks?
3. What effect does the urban renewal process have upon the risk, timing, and financial return to the development in this case?
4. Has the city acted expeditiously in its planning process? What are the implications of its future actions on the commercial and residential rentability of the project?

SOUTHWEST
WASHINGTON

In January 1961, James Scheuer was trying to decide whether or not to become the developer of several Title I urban redevelopment projects in various large cities throughout the country. As a result of his experience in Title I as sponsor of Area B, a 1750-unit, 30-acre, $31-million residential project in Southwest Washington, a slum area of Washington, D.C., numerous redevelopment agencies had contacted him to ascertain his interest in projects in their communities. However, it had taken Mr. Scheuer six agonizing years to complete Capitol Park I, the first 402-unit apartment building in Southwest Washington; and he was just finishing the final plans for the next 900 units. Therefore, although he felt he had learned a great deal from his experience, he wanted to consider very carefully whether he should undertake future urban redevelopment projects, and if so, on what basis.

INDUSTRY BACKGROUND

Title I projects were being given considerable national publicity. On the one hand, many considered them the solution to rejuvenating the central cities, eliminating blighted neighborhoods, attracting back to the city the middle- and upper-middle-income families who had fled to the suburbs, and providing much-needed tax revenue for the cities. On the other hand, many criticized these projects because they uprooted existing neighborhoods of poor families without adequate provision for relocation and because the high-rent apartments being constructed did not serve the average city dweller. The private sponsor appeared to be making an outlandish profit.

The federal and local governments were attacked for using the power of eminent domain to acquire the site, providing cash subsidies to write down the cost of the land, and granting mortgage insurance to private developers of up to 97% of the total project cost.

Originally, Congress had passed the Housing Act of 1949, including Title I, which declared:

That the general welfare and security of the Nation and the health and living standards of its people require housing production and related commu-

383

nity development sufficient to remedy the serious housing shortage, the elimination of substandard and other inadequate housing through the clearance of slums and blighted areas, and the realization as soon as feasible of the goal of a decent home and a suitable living environment for every American family:

The act went on to say that:

(1) private enterprise shall be encouraged to serve as large a part of the total need as it can; (2) governmental assistance shall be utilized where feasible to enable private enterprise to serve more of the total need; . . .

Yet, in practice, the question still remained as to how much governmental assistance or incentive was required to bring private developers to build in Title I areas. Originally, it was felt that the assembly of the tract and the sale of the land at a written-down price would be adequate. However, there were two major problems. First, the character of a blighted neighborhood was such that few developers felt that middle-income families would be attracted to the area. As a result, the areas were made larger to provide enough land for the project to be able to create its own environment. Second, because of the increased project size the amount of funds required to develop the land mounted to the tens of millions of dollars. Land cost was a relatively insignificant percentage of total cost, normally less than 10%.

The life insurance companies were the only investors able to provide the funds and willing to accept a 6% return in contrast to the speculative builder's desire for a 15% to 20% return. Yet, insurance companies no longer were interested in becoming project sponsors. At the end of World War II, interest rates were low, and insurance companies, such as Metropolitan Life in Stuyvesant Town in New York City and New York Life in Lake Meadows in Chicago, were satisfied with the 4% to 5% return available from owning apartment projects that also met a widespread social need. Soon, though, alternative investment possibilities became more attractive to them. In addition, as landlords they became involved in such issues as housing integration and evictions, all of which led to unfavorable publicity. As a result, they were discouraged from undertaking new-project development. The last straw occurred in 1952 when New York's Board of Estimate, as a result of tenant pressure, broke its contract with Metropolitan Life and rejected an application for an increase in rents to cover rising operating costs. From that time, insurance companies preferred to take only the more traditional mortgage position and let others assume the public equity position.

As a result, the government was faced with the need to stimulate the noninstitutional investor, who would insist upon a high return and low equity requirements, to become involved in redeveloping slum areas. Recognizing this problem, Congress, as part of the Housing Act of 1954, passed a special assistance program for FHA, known as Section 220, to insure housing in urban renewal areas. This section directed FHA, to eliminate the "economic soundness" requirement for urban renewal areas and to evaluate an area assuming that it was rebuilt according to the official urban renewal plan. Traditionally, FHA was reluctant to take any risks. This was especially true in 1954, since Senator Capehart had just conducted a public investigation of the "windfall profits" made by many of the builders under FHA Section 608, even though both government officials and private builders understood at the time the bill was passed that such profits were intended in order to stimulate the production of housing. As a result of the probe, cash down payment requirements for sponsors were increased, a cost certification program was installed, and many builders and FHA officials were punished. Therefore, applications under Section 220 were being processed slowly, and few local officials would grant approval without firm orders from central FHA officials in Washington.

The problem was further complicated by the local FHA officials' basic distrust of central city loans insured by the FHA. Most FHA programs had been directed toward insuring single-family home developments in suburban areas. In the central city, land costs were high and large sites relatively scarce, and any clearance involved the difficult problem of relocation. The city environment was dirty and congested. Because of the low capital investment during the Depression of the 1930's and World War II, public facilities had deteriorated. Family living became less desirable because of the old schools, inadequate playgrounds, and danger of increasing traffic. Consumer demand was in the suburbs, not the city.

Yet, to counteract this trend, Congress further liberalized its Section 220 terms. Mortgage loan terms were extended to 40 years. To reduce the builder's cash needs, land cost was reimbursed at the start of construction rather than at the completion. A sponsor's noncash allowance of 10% was permitted to reduce the equity requirement. It became possible for a sponsor to build under this program for as little as 3% cash equity, since 97% of the funds were provided by an FHA-insured mortgage loan at 4½% to 5% interest. Since the investment was so small, the builder could be permitted a large return on his investment without much increase to the overall cost of the program. Also, as the percentage equity investment was small, it was hoped that many more developers would be able to become sponsors under the program.

Still, there was no rush to the program. The conventional real estate approach was to copy someone else's profit-making scheme after it had been proven. The newness of the Title I program and the area selected for development forced the sponsor to be an innovator, both in his ability to work within a new and complex matrix of government regulations and to create a new environment in a presently blighted area. James Scheuer's experience in southwest Washington took place in that atmosphere.

MASTER PLAN, DEVELOPMENT

Southwest Washington, a 550-acre triangle of land was located next to the Capitol and the Potomac River and had been for years one of the city's worst slums, housing low-income Negro families. Originally, at George Washington's urging, many of the city's leaders had bought homes there, and the area had been one of the city's most fashionable. However, James Creek, which ran into the river near the point, became an open sewer, and the nearby marshes became infested with malaria. Soon, only food and fish markets utilized the waterfront. Further isolation occurred through the placement of the Pennsylvania Railroad tracks in such a way as to cut off the area from the rest of the city. By 1860, Southwest was known as "the island." The only housing built there was dilapidated shacks for low-income Negroes.

There was considerable controversy as to the best reuse of the area. In 1950, John Nolen, then director of the National Capitol Planning Commission, urged that the site was "ideal for low-income families working in the terminal, the railroads, and the markets. These people must live somewhere." The commission drew up a plan based upon this approach.

Still, there were many who felt that this plan failed to appreciate the potential for upgrading the area because of its proximity to the Capitol. The railroad crossings could be hidden with overpasses. The swamps and drainage canal no longer existed. The waterfront could be cleaned up and the food and fish markets relocated. In 1952, the Redevelopment Land Agency hired two local, well-known architects, Mrs. Chloethiel Woodward Smith and Louis Justement, to make a comprehensive plan based upon the highest and best use of the site.

Their plan, published in 1953, showed a dramatically upgraded Southwest district. Yet, many prominent Washingtonians criticized the plan as too visionary. Financial men found the area unsuitable for middle-class families. Cheap walk-ups for Negroes were all that many builders visualized. Others objected privately on the grounds of the danger of forcing Negroes out of the ghettos, since they might try to move to "white" areas.

Finally, the "highest and best use" forces received a champion with the showmanship and ability to sell their approach. In February 1954, as the result of urging from the publisher of the Washington Post, William Zeckendorf, the New York developer, presented his master redevelopment plan for the whole area designed to give the city "the cosmopolitan atmosphere of a great world capital." He unveiled his scale model with brochures, press releases, and photographs before congressmen, businessmen, and the press. The plan followed the proposals of Mrs. Smith and

Mr. Justement in establishing a high-quality residential tone. It envisioned linking the area to the rest of the city through an overpass over the railroad tracks and the new Tenth Street Mall. Zeckendorf also proposed "L'Enfant Plaza," a complex of cultural, recreational, and commercial facilities, including government office buildings, clustered around a traffic-free pedestrian mall. This would be to Washington "what the Champs Elysees is to Paris and Piazza San Marco to Venice." Sidewalk cafes, fountains, theaters, skating rinks, dining and dancing, and a new waterfront filled out his dream.

Zeckendorf convinced local groups and other city officials that he could finance his dream and make it a reality. The *Washington Post* called the master plan "the most ambitious city rebuilding project ever attempted in America." It would counteract "the flight to the suburbs." Within a month a memorandum of understanding was drawn up between the District Redevelopment Land Agency and Zeckendorf's firm, Webb & Knapp, signifying his intent to undertake a large percentage of the 440-acre residential portion of the plan, subject only to the cooperation and coordination of the various government agencies who would build the concomitant office buildings.

SCHEUER'S ENTRY INTO REDEVELOPMENT

There were many other applicants for the remainder of the residential parcels. The most sought after was a 30-acre section called Area B, located next to Area C, the Zeckendorf land, but closer to the Capitol, and the proposed L'Enfant Plaza. Because of this location, it was expected to be one of the first parcels developed. A Norfolk, Virginia, building firm was given the award. However, in early 1955, the firm came under investigation by the Capehart Committee for several "608" projects, and decided to withdraw from Area B. John R. Searles, Jr., then executive director of the Redevelopment Land Agency, called several of the firms that had been interested the prior year, but none now wanted to become involved. Even Zeckendorf refused to expand his commitment. He stated that first the city had to insure that all the remaining sections would also go ahead. Area B had been cleared, but there was no buyer. This was typical of other Title I sites in Detroit and Baltimore. Mr. Searles was aware of the criticism that had been made of the local officials in those areas.

As a result, on the evening that the Washington papers announced in local headlines the official withdrawal of the Norfolk firm, Mr. Searles placed a call to New York to James H. Scheuer, a New York developer, to ask him if he would consider bidding for sponsorship of Area B. In 1952, Mr. Scheuer had joined a family business that had amassed a considerable fortune in real estate through the purchase of luxury apartment houses in Manhattan during the 1930's, when prices were at distressed levels. Prior to 1952, Scheuer had received graduate degrees in business administration and law and worked for the federal government in Washington. He was active in the New York Citizens Housing and Planning Council and in Democratic politics. He was interested in housing legislation and design and had received recognition from the National Urban League as the result of a successful integration of two state-assisted housing developments owned by his family. Earlier in 1955, Mr. Scheuer had met with Mr. Searles to discuss the new housing rehabilitation sections of the 1954 Housing Act. At that time, he had toured the Southwest Washington area, but since the sponsorship had already been awarded, his interest had been entirely academic.

His initial reaction, upon receiving Mr. Searles' new call, was favorable. He had been considering becoming involved in redevelopment work for sometime. He liked the idea of the government's assembling large tracts of centrally owned land, which a private developer alone could not assemble, and then reselling the land at a price low enough to permit an economically feasible development using the highest planning standards. The government's subsidy also included holding the land for the developer until he was ready to build, thus eliminating carrying charges, and included installing and paying for the necessary public facilities such as roads and sewers.

Specifically, Mr. Scheuer was attracted by the potential of this particular site. Its location only 500 yards from the Capitol was unsurpassed. The redevelopment master plan including the new government office buildings was a big asset. When complete, the area should have 20,000 office workers and 18,000 residents in 6,000 apartments, 1,000 of these units to be public housing. The mixture of high-rise apartments and town houses at various income levels was socially desirable and glamorous. As it was to Zeckendorf, the prestige of building in Washington was exciting to him.

From an economic standpoint, Washington, with its continual flow of government workers who preferred to rent rather than buy, was "depressionproof." Mr. Scheuer felt that 1,750 rental apartments should be absorbed quickly. He estimated that with a construction cost of $15,000 per unit, the project should cost $26.25 million. This would require an equity investment, because of the favorable FHA financing, available under Section 220, of only $800,000. He could expect an annual profit of $250 per unit. His total cash return would be $440,000 per year. This return would be tax sheltered by depreciation of $650,000 per year on a straight-line basis less approximately $400,000 amortization. By using the double declining-balance method of depreciation, his tax shelter would be even greater and could be used as a shelter for other income.

Mr. Scheuer, therefore, decided to accept Mr. Searles' invitation and offer himself as a potential sponsor to the Redevelopment Land Agency. However as soon as the news of his interest was reported in the papers, two local bidders decided to compete. In the light of this competition, Mr. Scheuer decided to make another prominent real estate figure his associate. He formed an equal partnership with Roger L. Stevens, a New York realtor and theatrical producer, who was also chairman of the Democratic Party's Finance Committee. They selected Chloethiel Smith as their architect.

The public criteria for awarding the sponsorship were to be the financial capability, development experience, and proposed plan of the three competitors. All agreed that the land price would be established as a result of the FHA appraisal and would not be an issue in the competition. Mr. Scheuer and Mr. Stevens appeared to have unlimited financial resources, but they lacked any development experience.

It was at that point that politics became crucial. All parties had had influential pressures exerted on their behalf, and the five-man board was deadlocked, with two voting for Scheuer, two for a Washington builder, and one undecided. This fifth, undecided member was Negro, and Scheuer and Stevens got word to him that even though Washington was a southern city, they had always planned to integrate their project. In October 1955, the Redevelopment Land Agency voted to award the sponsorship to Mr. Scheuer and Mr. Stevens.

GOVERNMENT NEGOTIATIONS

Once the vote was announced, Mr. Scheuer felt that the actual contract signing with the agency would be a formality and would quickly follow. However, although he had agreed to pay whatever land price was decided on by the FHA, the FHA itself got into a dispute with the Urban Renewal Administration (URA), another division of the Housing and Home Finance Agency (HHFA). The URA wanted the land price increased to minimize the amount of the federal write-down. The FHA wanted a low land price to keep rentals down in order to minimize the risk of default on their mortgage.

Months later, the two agreed on a price of $3 million for the 30 acres. Now Mr. Scheuer delayed the signing in an effort to convince the Redevelopment Land Agency to lease the land to them with an option to buy, rather than sell the land to them. His argument was that this was a common practice in real estate, and that as long as FHA would subordinate its mortgage to the land lease, the local agency would have no risk. The advantage to Mr. Scheuer was that Section 220 allowed a 10% builders-sponsors allowance on all costs except land. By leasing the land, he would reduce his equity requirements by 10% of $3 million, or $300,000. After considerable negotiation, he was able to satisfy the

District Redevelopment Agency, the URA, and the FHA. Finally, on July 2, 1956, the 50-page official land disposition agreement was signed.

The next stage was the preparation of a detailed site plan to submit to FHA for mortgage feasibility. Mr. Scheuer felt very strongly the need to create an especially attractive design to induce tenants to move to an area that heretofore had been considered a slum. Also, as he considered himself an investor interested in long-term profits, he wanted to own a building that would not become outdated as other new buildings were constructed. Lastly, he knew that the Redevelopment Land Agency expected him to establish a standard of excellence in design that would serve as an example for the rebirth of the area.

Mrs. Smith's design appeared to meet all of these tests. Through a mixture of town houses and five high-rise structures, a series of interim landscaped courts were created that interconnected the buildings and gave a park-like feeling to an urban setting. The first building, an eight-story, 402-unit apartment house, was to be built on stilts, enabling the creation of a glass-enclosed lobby looking out onto a lawn with landscaped walks, a lily pond, a sheltered barbecue pit, and groupings of chairs and tables. Full-grown trees were to be planted to give a finished look. Art objects would include animal sculptures on the lawn, a large tile mosaic by Leonni behind the pool, and a large metal screen structure by Harry Bertoia in the lobby. This courtyard would eventually be encircled by 80 town house units.

Before submitting this plan to the FHA, Mr. Scheuer first had to run the gauntlet of plan approval from four other government agencies—the district government, the Redevelopment Land Agency, the National Capitol Planning Commission, and the district's Fine Arts Commission—plus six district departments that each had to approve a particular facet of the development. One example of the type of problem that occurred was the question of commercial facilities that were to serve Area B. Because of the small size of the stores, this aspect of the development was not economic to the developer. Therefore, Mr. Zeckendorf proposed that all the small commercial areas for Southwest be consolidated into one larger community shopping center, which he would build on his adjoining property. After much discussion, all the parties and agencies agreed to this approach, and the change in plan was approved.

Other problems occurred when the Smith plan came into conflict with existing local regulations. The District Planning Commission finally agreed to a new approach to zoning for the site applying density standards on an overall project basis rather than the present single-lot, block basis. Five different agencies' sets of legal specifications for "light and air," dealing with building setbacks, had to be reconciled. Lack of information regarding the location of existing sewer lines, many of which were installed in pre-Civil War days, led to obvious planning difficulties.

Eventually, the redevelopment agency agreed to make a new survey so that Mrs. Smith could plan the sewer connections. Building height restrictions had to be changed so that a building on stilts would not use up one of its allowable floors by the stilts. The local highway department was planning an elevated road near the first apartment building that would block the view from the bottom three floors on one side. It took considerable discussion to convince the highway agency not to ruin the plan of the redevelopment agency, and to adjust its design. Lastly, minor local regulations seemed to provide an endless source of petty hinderances. The openings in the lattice work over the outside walls had to be made smaller to prevent starlings from flying through. The lily ponds were not approved except under the condition that the pond be stocked with a special mosquito-eating fish that would prevent the pools from breeding mosquitoes. Eventually, in February 1957, after seven months and an expenditure of $200,000 for architectural, legal, and other consultants' fees, the necessary local approvals were granted, and Mr. Scheuer was ready to make his official submission to the local FHA office for a test of feasibility for preliminary mortgage insurance commitment.

FHA[1]

Mr. Scheuer's submission for this portion requested a $5,605,000 mortgage for 40 years at the current interest rate of 4½%. This mortgage was 90% of his estimated total cost of $6,227,000 for the eight story, 402 unit building. The land was to be leased from the Redevelopment Agency for $42,000 per year. This lease payment was based upon 6% of the expected FHA land appraisal price of $700,000.

He summarized his total cost as follows:

Utilities	$ 30,000
Landscaping and exterior amenities	100,000
Total Exterior Improvements	$ 130,000
Construction cost	$4,875,000
Architects fee (4¼%) and builders offsite overhead	300,000
Other expenses*	355,000
Total Cash Costs	$5,660,000
10% builders-sponsors allowance	566,000
Total Project Cost	$6,226,000
Less: 90% mortgage	5,605,000
Net Equity Investment	$ 621,000

* Including interest during construction, 1.3% FHA fees, real estate taxes during construction, insurance, title and recording, legal, and organizational.

However, Mr. Scheuer realized that his actual cash investment would not be the same as the net equity investment figure shown on the FHA

[1] All figures used in this section are disguised.

application. First, the 10% builders-sponsors allowance did not have to be expended to be earned. Therefore, the $621,000 could be reduced by $566,000, theoretically leaving $55,000 as the total cash need. This assumes that the sponsor is also the builder and can utilize the total allowance himself. In this case, since neither Mr. Scheuer nor Mr. Stevens were builders, they had to engage an outside builder who would guarantee the construction cost to them, put up the performance bond required by the FHA, and supervise the actual construction. From their general inquiries, they felt a fee of about 4½% of the construction cost, or $220,000, would be standard for this type of project. Also, the FHA required a 2% working capital deposit of $112,000, which could be used for renting and promotional expenses. To agree to lease the land, the Redevelopment Authority had insisted upon a $100,000 deposit as a penalty if Mr. Scheuer failed to develop the remaining parcels. Lastly, there were approximately $50,000 of expenses that the initial FHA application did not cover but that were applicable to the remaining sections. The total of all of these cash requirements was $537,000.

Mr. Scheuer's income and expense allowance showed an annual return of only $38,000 (see Exhibit 1), or slightly over 7% on $537,000. However, Mr. Scheuer felt that rightfully $150,000 of the investment was applicable to the later projects and that the actual vacancies would be $24,000, only one half of the FHA allowance. This increased the actual cash return to $63,000 on an investment for this section of the project of $387,000. In addition, the annual depreciation generated on a 40-year double declining-balance basis of $300,000 per year was adequate to cover the mortgate amortization of $84,000, the projected profit of $63,000, and produce in the first-year excess depreciation of $153,000, which could be applied to other corporate income if this corporation could be combined with another income-producing one. There might be some problem in accomplishing this, since Mr. Stevens and he owned this corporation equally but did not have any other common investments. They also considered the value of tax losses during construction.

The FHA reviewed their application with considerable skepticism. Although the FHA knew that the Congress in establishing and then liberalizing Section 220 was attempting to encourage developers to work within urban renewal areas, the local field officers were still reluctant to take chances. The Capehart investigations did not criticize any bureaucrats who had turned down any Section 608 application or who had compelled a developer to increase his equity investment.

Mr. Scheuer's application contained several elements that seemed especially risky. First, the location, as was true of all urban redevelopment areas, had been a slum. Second, Mr. Scheuer's plan called for integrating the buildings racially, an idea that the chief underwriter felt was unfeasible for Washington, even in a more established area. Third, the architectural design was unusual, the most costly per-unit application ever received, and the FHA was reluctant to take chances on its public acceptance. Also, the 4¾% architect's fee was double the usual FHA allowance. Fourth, the mortgage application included $100,000 for art, amenities, and landscaping, which were not directly income producing and therefore, according to the local interpretation, should not be included as part of the mortgage. The FHA felt that the lower they kept the costs, the lower the rents would be, since debt service was over 50% of the total rental cost. The lower the rents, the less risk the project had of failing. Mr. Scheuer argued that the added costs were what would make the project attractive and insure its success. However, in August 1957, the local FHA office decided to hedge their bet by issuing a commitment of 82% or $5,105,000 rather than the requested 90%. This would be more than double the investor's required cash equity. In other words, they told Mr. Scheuer that they would agree to the added costs if the developer would pay for them.

At this point, the developers had the option of withdrawing from their agreement with the Redevelopment Agency, since it was conditional upon their receiving FHA approval. However, with a cost investment already of several hundred thousand dollars plus considerable time and with their prestige involved, Mr. Scheuer and Mr. Stevens decided to fight for a higher mortgage.

Their problem was further complicated by the increase in costs that occurred. Because the developers had never actually built an apartment house project before, they had based their figures upon very preliminary estimates by their architects. During the winter of 1957, it became apparent that actual construction costs would be 25% over their original estimates. Almost one third of this rise was inevitable, because of the general increase in construction costs since the estimates were first made. Much of the rest was caused by an inability to accurately estimate the cost of some of the design innovations. Another major problem came from the change in the money market. Market interest rates for this type of project were now 5¾% rather than 4¾%.

These factors resulted in a need to raise the monthly rents by $10 per room, from $32 to $42. Mr. Scheuer revised his mortgage application. The total costs were now:

Utilities	$ 40,000
Landscaping and exterior amenities	100,000
Total Exterior Improvements	$ 140,000
Construction cost	$6,170,000
Architectural fee (4¼%) and builders offsite overhead	350,000
Other expenses	440,000
Total Cash Cost	$7,100,000
Builders-sponsors allowance	710,000
Total Project Cost	$7,810,000
Less: 90% mortgage	7,020,000
Net Equity Investment	$ 790,000

The sponsors' cash investment was now:

```
Net equity investment...............................................$790,000
    Less: Builders-sponsors allowance................................ 710,000
                                                                     $ 80,000
Outside builders fee............................................... 280,000
2% working capital allowance....................................... 140,000
Project investment.................................................$500,000
Security with Redevelopment Agency................................ 100,000
Costs attributable to later projects...............................  50,000
                                                                    $650,000
```

Mr. Scheuer also prepared a new income and expense statement based upon the increased rents (see Exhibit 2). The potential profit of $49,000 plus $32,000 which was one half of the vacancies gave a return of $81,000 on a project investment of $500,000. The problem was to get the FHA officials to accept the higher costs and rents. Eventually, as a result of direction given from national FHA officials, who were anxious to see the project proceed, the local office began to change its attitude. Since a Section 220 mortgage was to be evaluated based upon the area being completely redeveloped, the FHA could minimize the problem of initial marketability and increase the percentage insured. Through a series of minor revisions, the mortgage level itself was increased. As an example, the reflecting pool was brought into coverage by placing one of the supporting columns of the "income-producing" exterior pavilions in the water. Mrs. Smith's 4¼% architectural fee was justified on the grounds that she would help supervise the overall project construction. Through such a series of devices, in April 1958, the mortgage was finally approved for the full amount of $7,020,000.

Only one last-minute hitch developed. A tight money market had developed, and lenders were not especially interested in FHA loans. Other markets provided higher returns. Finally, the president of the Federal City Council, an organization of district business leaders, and a prominent mortgage banker interceded to persuade John Hancock Life Insurance Company to grant to Capitol Park One the first private commitment for housing in an urban renewal area.

RENTAL PROBLEMS

Finally, in the spring of 1959, Mr. Scheuer was able to start his rental campaign. In fighting through the morass of government agencies and red tape, it had been difficult to keep sight of the fact that eventually the success of his project would be determined not by government approvals but by market acceptance of his apartments, as was the case with any private residential building. In this case, the problem was especially complicated by the fact that the public image of Southwest was as a slum, and most of the area, although cleared of its former structures, was still unattractive and open. Cab drivers were telling potential tenants moving to Washington from out of town, "I wouldn't rent there for anything. It's just a slum."

To counteract this, Mr. Scheuer was forced to spend $90,000 for promotion, approximately six times that budgeted by similar buildings in other sections of the city. Extra rental agents had to be hired to spend more time with potential tenants. Some concessions on leases had to be made. Tenants were told to try the area and were given leases which they could cancel upon 30-days' notice. Mr. Scheuer was delighted that he had fought the FHA and spent the extra money to create the parklike atmosphere. Otherwise, he felt he would have had no success in convincing tenants to move in at that time. The normal apartment house in an established area neither had as much open space to fill as he nor required the additional amenities.

An example of the extra expense he had to incur to provide a livable setting, was $10,000 to convert a basement area into a convenience grocery store that he rented for $1 a month. Originally, Mr. Zeckendorf was supposed to have completed his shopping center by that time. However, Mr. Zeckendorf's negotiations with various agencies and his willingness to allow Mr. Scheuer to be the pioneer had delayed his start. Since there were no acceptable shopping facilities nearby, and tenants would not move in without them, Mr. Scheuer was forced to spend not only the $10,000, but $2,000 legal fees to obtain a variance from the district zoning ordinance to permit a store in a residential building.

Another complication was in implementing the promise that the apartments would be integrated. During the first few weeks, Negroes comprised the large proportion of Sunday visitors. Most of them were not renters but prior residents of Southwest, coming to see the change in their old neighborhood. Still, the impression given to the public was that the bulk of the renters were Negro. The rental agents, Shannon and Lucks, the only major firm willing to handle the project, were unsure of how to handle the situation. Mr. Scheuer consulted with several local Negro leaders, who agreed that to achieve integration the project would have to be accepted first by the white community. Seventy-five percent occupancy should be reached before nonwhite tenants were accepted. Management explained its position frankly to those Negroes who had applied, and most agreed to stay on the waiting list.

However, when the building was 50% rented, the issue was forced by the application of a white man married to a Negro. The couple, both holding doctorate degrees, had been evicted from their previous apartment when the management learned that the woman was the man's wife, not his maid. They wanted to move to Capital Park I immediately. A lawyer, Joseph Rauh, former head of the liberal Americans for Democratic Action, took their case, and threatened Mr. Scheuer with court action. Although the complainants had no legal grounds, Mr. Scheuer was anxious to avoid the publicity, and agreed to let them in in a few months, and until then, pay the difference in rent for a furnished apartment hotel unit.

Actually, the high rents precluded most Negroes from moving in. Also, in Washington wealthier Negroes preferred to buy a home rather than rent. Still, the issue created considerable tension during the initial rental period. One agent was fired after being rude to the future dean of Howard University, who was "just looking." Eventually, though, to achieve a minimum 10% Negro occupancy, management had to solicit Negro organizations to send applicants.

Another problem was that of schools. The local elementary school would not be open for a year after Capitol Park I. This hurt initial rentals. Moreover, the initial attendance would primarily be from the Negro public housing projects nearby and might totally prevent white families with children from moving into the many town houses in the area designed for them. Finally, to solve this problem, Carl Hansen, the district's superintendent of schools, agreed to use the new Amidon School as a special one using new teaching techniques and to open it to any family in the city which would transport its children there.

Despite all of these efforts, when Capitol Park I was ready for occupancy in June 1959, only 18% of the units were rented. Some of the decrepit row houses still had not been taken down, and muggings and knifings were common. The public transportation system had not yet been arranged, and service was inadequate. To assist the developer, the FHA agreed to waive mortgage amortization payments until the building rented up. However, the sponsors had to invest another $150,000 to cover operational losses. A congressional investigation was begun to determine why the whole Southwest area was developing so slowly.

Finally, in the late fall of 1960, the building started to break even financially. Webb & Knapp's first two units were up and renting, the school and shopping center were in operation, and the general area was taking shape. After starting in April of 1958 with a 70% mortgage approval for the first 81 town houses that would complete the courtyard behind the first apartment house, Mr. Scheuer had gotten the percentage insured up to 90%. The government office buildings were approved and on the drawing board stage. FHA was revising its rules to permit these projects to be held by partnerships, thus enabling the partners to deduct from other income the operating losses due to heavy depreciation.

The national trend appeared favorable to urban apartment projects. The fastest-growing age brackets were those of older couples, young single adults, and childless young couples, all prime apartment candidates. This was coupled with a loosening of mortgage money and fast-rising land costs in the suburbs. However, in Washington there was the problem of increased competition from buildings in other, more established areas. Since the district adopted a new zoning ordinance late in

1958, which reduced the economic advantage of apartment house sites through greater limits on land coverage and density, many builders had filed plans and proceeded, increasing the competition at that time.

Also, because of the slowness of the urban redevelopment process and the poor relocation provisions of the existing residents, considerable public criticism arose on the part of groups representing the poor—politicians and sociologists. The national trend seemed to be toward rehabilitation rather than redevelopment, and toward lower-income rather than upper-income families. Mr. Stevens, 10 years older than Mr. Scheuer, had had enough. He wanted to sell the project. Mr. Scheuer did not, and as a result, he bought Mr. Stevens' 50% interest in Capitol Park I for his cost, which was one half of $650,000, plus $100,000 profit. In addition, it was arranged that HRH Construction Company, a large New York firm, would buy out Mr. Stevens' interest in the remainder and become Mr. Scheuer's partner. The construction firm would become the builder and contribute its builder's profit to the project to reduce cash equity requirements.

Mr. Scheuer was delighted. If all went well, for less than $2 million invested, he would have half interest in a 1,750-unit, $31 million development whose value should be increasing. However, he knew it would be many years before he would receive cash profits. The question now before him was whether, considering all the experience he had gained, he should attempt to apply it to Title I projects in other cities. If so, on what basis should it be, and what sort of investing and operating partners should he look for? Could he combine his desire to accomplish social objectives with that of making a reasonable economic return?

EXHIBIT 1

Projected Income and Expense
as of February 1957

Income

134 Efficiencies   @ $112/month
134 One-bedroom @ $145/month
134 Two-bedroom @ $185/month
402 Apartments

1,809 Rooms × $32 × 12 months	$695,000
Less: Vacancy @ 7%	49,000
Net Rental Income	$646,000

Expenses

Operating @ $100/room	$181,000	
Real estate taxes	35,000	
Land leasehold	42,000	
First mortgage*	350,000	
Total Expenses		608,000
Net Operating Income		$ 38,000

* Interest, 4½%; amortization, 1½%; mortgage insurance premium, one half of 1%.

EXHIBIT 2

**Southwest Washington
Projected Income and Expense
as of February 1958**

Income

134 Efficiencies   @ $142/month
134 One-bedroom @ $190/month
134 Two-bedroom @ $225/month
402 Apartments

1,809 Rooms × $42 × 12 months.....................................$917,000
    Less: Vacancy @ 7%... 64,000
Net Rental Income...$853,000

Expenses

Operating @ $115/room....................................$208,000
Real estate taxes... 45,000
Land leasehold... 42,000
First mortgage*... 509,000
    Total Expenses... 804,000
Net Operating Income...$ 49,000

  * 5¼% interest, 1½% amortization, ½% mortgage insurance premium.

QUESTIONS FOR DISCUSSION

1. How does this project and this type of development compare with other types of development projects? (Answer in terms of risk, rates, timing, taxes, equity requirements, etc.)
2. Do you feel this is an effective approach for the redevelopment of cities and the elimination of slums?
3. How would you encourage more developers to participate in urban renewal and low-income housing projects?
4. Also answer questions posed by Mr. Scheuer on page 397, at end of case, if you haven't already dealt with them.

WATERSIDE
DEVELOPMENT

In late 1960, Richard Ravitch, an executive and part owner of the HRH Construction Company, and Lewis Davis, an architect with the firm of Davis, Brody Associates, conceived the idea of building a major residential development on a platform extending over the East River in New York City. Historically, the waterfront had been used for shipping piers, warehouses, transfer stations, trucking companies, garages, and other structures needed to accommodate a major seaport. With the increasing use of other means of transporting freight and the relocation of the piers in the metropolitan area, the waterfront around Manhattan Island was no longer needed for shipping. The open space and excellent unobstructed view made the waterfront a better site for new high-rise apartment and office buildings than for industrial and warehousing facilities. The riverfront that Mr. Ravitch and Mr. Davis were considering was the East River shoreline between East 23rd and 30th Streets in New York City, directly across the Franklin D. Roosevelt Drive from Bellevue Hospital and the New York University Medical Center. It was dotted with rotting piers. Mr. Ravitch and Mr. Davis were certain that a major housing development on a platform extending out into the East River would provide much needed, attractively located housing and would contribute to the improvement of the area.

They proceeded to determine which governmental body controlled the East River waterway. They found that normally, the U.S. Army Corps of Engineers has control over navigable waterways. However, in this case, the area over which they proposed to build was inside the U.S. pierhead line and therefore, did not come under control of the Army Corps of Engineers but the City of New York.

They also checked the zoning of the property and discovered that the area had previously been zoned for high-rise apartments and commercial usage. However, it had been changed to M–2 a few years earlier to permit its use as a hydrofoil pier. It was no longer being used for this purpose, and Mr. Ravitch felt that it would not be too difficult to have the property rezoned to its original zoning regulation.

In the process Mr. Ravitch also considered building a commercial development on this site but felt that the site was too small and isolated to be used for this purpose.

399

As the zoning and control of the rights to this "property" above the East River were in the hands of the city, Messrs. Ravitch and Davis approached James Felt, head of the City Planning Commission. When presented with the idea, Mr. Felt's reaction was that the proposal of a housing development on a platform above the East River was too visionary and impractical. At this point, and because of other business pressures, Messrs. Ravitch and Davis shelved the idea.

In the interim, among the many properties, costing in total many millions of dollars, for which HRH was the general contractor were two which had a bearing on the proposed project. One was the construction of a Gulf Oil Company pier, service station, and parking garage on a platform over the East River near East 23rd Street, not far from the proposed development. This convinced HRH that construction of buildings on a platform was feasible. In addition, HRH Construction Company and Davis, Brody Associates were working together with the Housing and Redevelopment Board on a total neighborhood plan for the Bellevue Area from 23rd to 30th Streets, between 2nd Avenue and F.D.R. Drive (the East River). They were also the designers and builders of houses in the Bellevue South Urban Renewal area, a nonprofit project, sponsored by the Phipps Foundation.

In the summer of 1964, Mr. Ravitch came across a speech delivered by David Ballard, who was then head of the City Planning Commission, in which Mr. Ballard discussed the poor use and waste of the waterfront in New York City. He pointed out the isolation of the city from its riverfront by the highways running around the periphery of Manhattan Island. Mr. Ravitch arranged a meeting with Mr. Ballard, who was very much impressed with the proposed development.

Mr. Ravitch then approached the city's Department of Marine and Aviation, which he was told had the right to lease this "property." The Commissioner of Marine and Aviation was not overly enthusiastic about the proposal. He had had little experience with housing developments and the leasing of air rights above the river or of offshore property. There was a question of whether he would ever approve a long-term lease on this property. Mr. Ravitch also discovered that the city was not empowered to enter into leases for periods longer than 50 years. He felt that he would need a much longer-term lease in order to obtain the type of financing in which he was interested.

Mr. Ravitch then considered the Redevelopment Companies Law, Article V of the Private Housing Finance Law of the State of New York, which empowered the city to enter into longer-term leases on city land and grant real estate tax abatements. This law was passed in the early postwar period in order to assist life insurance companies that were interested in building much needed large housing developments, such as Peter Cooper Village and Stuyvesant Town. The law's legal basis was

Article 18 of the New York State Constitution, which allowed the city to acquire and resell or lease land where the intent was to clear, replan, reconstruct, and rehabilitate a substandard or unsanitary area. Therefore, this law not only permitted long-term leases but also made it possible for the city to enter into a lease with Mr. Ravitch for the air rights above the East River between 23rd and 30th Streets and F.D.R. Drive and the U.S. pierhead line. There was no requirement under this law for Mr. Ravitch to compete with other developers at a public auction for this property. As a result, the lease could be negotiated directly between Mr. Ravitch and the city. To qualify under the Redevelopment Companies Act, there had to be a public purpose, such as the furnishing of middle- and low-income housing in short supply. The city could then employ its right of eminent domain to acquire property and could agree to abate real estate taxes for various periods. These were the two rights which were used to assist the construction of the above-mentioned Peter Cooper Village and Stuyvesant Town. However, in return the developer's profits on such projects must be limited to 6% of total equity.

Mr. Ravitch tried to have the control of the property assigned by the mayor from the Commissioner of Marine and Aviation to the Redevelopment Agency where he could obtain the benefits of this act. The Commissioner insisted that this property was under his control. Mayor Robert Wagner did not make the decision as to which department would be given authority over the matter.

At this point, another problem cropped up. Mr. Ravitch's attorney discovered an old law which gave the U.S. government the right to reclaim any waterway it considered necessary for navigation, without compensating the owner. Under these circumstances, it would be impossible to obtain mortgage financing, although it was most unlikely that the federal government would ever exercise this power of confiscating property without compensating the owner.

Mr. Ravitch approached various congressmen and senators to introduce legislation to prohibit the federal government from expropriating waterfront improvements without compensation. Congressman Emanuel Celler, chairman of the House Judiciary Committee, was persuaded to introduce the Rivers and Harbors Act of 1965, which specifically established the East River waterfront between 17th and 30th Streets as nonnavigable for purposes of federal law. This legislation was enacted in 1965 with the assistance of many New York congressmen and friends of Mr. Ravitch and his associates, along with the help of former Mayor Robert Wagner. The enactment of this law made it possible for a developer to get title insurance on the property, a requisite for obtaining mortgage financing.

By this time, Mayor John Lindsay had been elected in New York City. Mr. Ravitch approached the new mayor with his proposed Waterside

Development. Mayor Lindsay liked the idea, but insisted upon adding the requirements that provision be made in the new development for low-income families and that the project contain families with diverse incomes. With this understanding in 1966, Mayor Lindsay gave the City Redevelopment Agency the authority over the project and excluded the City Department of Marine and Aviation.

Now Mr. Ravitch and his associates undertook the task of preparing a more detailed plan of the development, including the number and type of housing units, the capital requirements and the cash flow after completion of the project. It was over five years since the idea for the project had first occurred to Mr. Ravitch, and he still was unsure whether he would ever receive any compensation for his time or idea.

At this point, he had taken the idea to the mayor and to the Housing Redevelopment Board, both of whom had supported it. Planning control had been wrested from the Department of Marine and Aviation, which had jurisdiction over the waterfront. Legal ownership of offshore land had been determined. A federal law had been passed declaring the waters of the area nonnavigable to avoid the technicality of seizure without compensation for obstruction of navigation. Mr. Ravitch had commended the physical planning for the project.

Mr. Ravitch proposed that his company, the Waterside Redevelopment Company, lease the property from the city for a period of 99 years, at which time the offshore rights and all structures on it would revert to the city, and the city would then have full title to the property. Under the State Redevelopment Companies Law, the developers would pay the city $404,500 a year in lieu of rent on the offshore land and real estate taxes for both land and building. If the developers chose to make distributions in excess of the 6%, the subsidy would be stopped, and annual payments to the city of 6% of the full assessed value of the property would become due. There was to be no charge for the air rights, although the cost of the platform on which the project was to be built was estimated at $22 per square foot. Land cost in the area was $50 per square foot.

Meanwhile, Mr. Ravitch suggested to the United Nations School, which was not officially connected to the U.N., that it locate at the proposed site. Rather than work with Mr. Ravitch and join the development, the officials of the U.N. School immediately applied directly to the city for the land between 23rd and 25th Streets, which Mr. Ravitch had proposed be included in the Waterside Development. The city awarded this property to the U.N. School, thereby reducing the total area of the proposed Waterside Development to the area between 25th and 30th Streets.

After this setback, an obstacle course was run through city and local agencies, boards, committees, and institutions, but finally problems were being solved. Open space and traffic patterns were worked out for the adjoining U.N. School. The architects for the scheduled expansion plans at Bellevue and New York University Hospitals just across the East River Drive began to coordinate their planning with his. "What turned the trick at the end of five years is discouragingly simple: sponsorship at the top. Without it, bureaucracy produces no plans of stature and no bold designs."

"The proposal got nowhere under the previous administration," said Mr. Davis. "This thing had been dead a hundred times. It now has the active backing of Housing and Development Administrator Jason Nathan and of Mayor John Lindsay."

The technical plan for the development involved the construction of the buildings on a wedge-shaped platform (above the high-water mark), resting on piles in a bend in the East River between 25th and 30th Streets. The physical plan included 267,000 square feet of site area, of which 150,000 would be set aside for park and recreational purposes and would be open to the public.

Parking for 740 cars would be provided on a second level underneath the main level of the platform. A pedestrian bridge over the East River Drive at 25th Street and two vehicular underpasses at 23rd and 30th Streets would provide access not only for residents but for others who wanted to enjoy a waterfront promenade and the boat moorings that would encircle the platform.

The proposal showed 1,118 apartments in three 35-story buildings and 48 town houses, each containing two duplexes. Financing would be provided under Section 220 of the Federal Housing Administration, which issues loans equal to 90% of the "cost" of a project at a maximum interest rate of 6% repayable over a 40-year term. This specific section of the insurance program was designed for middle-income housing in an urban renewal area. Since Section 220 is applicable only in urban renewal areas, Mr. Davis planned to ask the city to designate the site as eligible for urban renewal without the normal federal and city cash subsidies. HRH Construction then estimated the following cost schedule for this section of the project.

Estimated Cost of the Project

Estimated construction cost	$26,900,000
Net demolition	40,000
Architectural, engineering, overhead—2% +	750,000
Interest during construction @ 5½%	2,153,000*
Payments to city during construction	106,000
Insurance and bond premium	250,000
FHA and city fees (2%)	626,000
Financing fees (2%)	626,000
Title and recording	80,000
Legal, organization, accounting	100,000
Builders and sponsors allowance	3,163,000
Total Cost	$34,794,000*
Less: Mortgage—90%	31,314,000
Equity investment	$ 3,480,000
Working Capital (2%)	628,000
Total Equity (including Builders and Sponsors allowance)	$ 4,108,000*

* At an interest cost of 6% during construction, the development cost increases to $35,030,000; the mortgage to $31,532,000; and the total equity increases to $4,135,000. It was probable that a 5½% interest rate would be obtained. This is the basis for the above analysis.

The apartments would be broken down into the categories shown in the accompanying table.

Apt. Size No. of Bedrooms	No. of Apts.	No. of Rooms per Apt.*	Total No. of Rooms
Three High-Rise Apartment Buildings Combined			
0	214	3	642
1	464	4	1,856
2	332	5	1,660
3	60	6½	390
Total	1,070 Apts.		4,548
Town Houses			
3	48	7	336
Grand Total	1,118		4,884

* As per-room count designations under Mitchell Lama Limited Dividend Housing Law.

Using these figures, Mr. Ravitch computed an estimated income statement as follows:

Expenses to Be Covered—@ 5½% Interest Rate

Debt servicing of mortgage—$31,314,000 × 7% (interest @ 5½%, FHA insurance ½%, amortization 1%)	$2,192,000
Maintenance and operating expenses (including reserves)	530,000
Annual payments to city	404,500
Return on equity—$4,106,000 × 6% limited dividend	246,500
Total Income Required to Cover Expenses and Provide 6% Return on Equity	$3,373,000*

Income

Nonresidential income

(1) Commercial and professional space

54,500 sq. ft. @ $5..............................	$272,500	
Less: 10% for vacancies.......................	27,000	245,500

(2) Parking

50 outdoor spaces @ $30/mo. × 12 months.......	$ 18,000	
700 indoor spaces @ $40/mo. × 12 months.......	336,000	
Total Parking Income.....................	$354,000	
Less: 10% vacancies............................	35,500	318,500

(3) Miscellaneous income—1,118 Apts. × $25/Apt./year..........	28,000
Total Nonresidential Income...........................	$ 592,000
Total Income Required to Cover Expenses	
@ 5½% Interest...	$3,373,000
Total Estimated Nonresidential Income.....................	−592,000
Net income required from apartments...........................	$2,781,000
Plus: Estimated apartment vacancies—5%.....................	146,000
Gross annual apartment rent roll...............................	$2,927,000

$$\text{Average rent/room/month } \frac{\$2,927,500}{4,884 \text{ rooms} \times 12} = \$49.95\dagger$$

* Expenses to be covered @ 6% interest rate.

Debt servicing—$31,532,000 × 7½%..........................	$2,365,000
Maintenance and operating (including reserve)..............	530,000
Annual payment to city...	404,500
Return on $4,135,000 equity @ 6%...........................	248,000
Income required if Interest at 6%...........................	$3,547,500

†At the 6% interest rate, the required income from apartments would be $2,955,500 or $53.09 per room per month.

Mr. Ravitch derived his apartment rental figure by estimating all his expenses plus a conservative allowance for vacancies, plus a 6% return on his estimated investment. The 6% return figure was employed because the company was being set up as a limited-profit housing company. Also, for that reason, the nonresidential income was used to reduce the residential rents. The developers had the right to convert the property to a normal profit-making company. However, in that event the rent charged by the city would jump to 6% of the full assessed value, or approximately $2 million per annum, instead of the $404,500 rental under the limited-dividend profit proposal. Of course, even under the limited-distribution proposal, the rate of return would increase should the assumed vacancy rate fall or should expenses be below the estimated level.

Mr. Ravitch then reversed his analysis from a cost approach to a market analysis, to see whether the rental levels necessary to cover his costs were practical. The proposed or computed monthly rental levels of $49–53 per room appeared inordinately low compared to relative rents on similar apartments. At this level, it was unlikely that there would be any vacancies. More probably, there would be a substantial waiting list, especially so because of the unique location, attractive design, and community plan; therefore, he concluded that the project was economically feasible.

Mr. Ravitch's proposal was dependent upon having this area designated as an Urban Renewal Area, thus enabling it to obtain the advantage of Section 220 financing. The cost included an allowance of $3,163,000 for builders and sponsors allowance or profit, which could be used as part of the $4,106,000 equity requirement. Under this assumption, the developers-sponsors investment would be reduced to approximately $1 million in this portion of the project. The leverage would provide the developer with major tax advantages, since he could depreciate the entire cost of the project over a 40-year period (no allowance for land, since leased) at the double declining-balance method, while the mortgage amortization, a nondeductible expense for tax purposes, started at 1%. In addition, the allowable return would be calculated on the total equity figure, including the noncash builders and sponsors allowance.

However, in order to justify the project to the city and obtain a low rental figure of $404,500 for the property, the sponsor was required to build housing for the low-income group. He proposed to build the number of "low-income" apartments shown in the accompanying table.

Below-Market-Rate Structure Apartments

No. of Bedrooms	Total No. of Apt. Units	Total No. of Rooms per Apt.	Total Number of Rooms
0	70	2½	175
1	105	3½	367½
2	140	4½	630
3	35	6	210
Total	350		1,382½

He then estimated the construction cost for these apartments.

Estimated Construction Costs

Estimated construction cost (including builders and sponsors fee)	$5,800,000
Architectural, engineering, overhead	300,000
Interest during construction	336,700
Payments to city during construction	2,000
Insurance and bond premium	80,000
FHA and city fees (1.2%)	73,500
Financing fees (FNMA—2½%)	153,000
Title and recording fee	21,500
Legal and organization	35,000
Total Estimated Development Cost	$6,801,700
Mortgage—90%	6,121,500
Equity requirement	$ 680,200
2% working capital	122,400
Total Equity	$ 802,600

The sponsor estimated his operating costs to determine the apartment rental rates. Since this was housing for low-income families, he proposed to build this project with a federally insured mortgage, specifically FHA,

Section 221(d)(3), which was promulgated for the construction of lower-income subsidized housing. Under this program, the developer, a limited distribution company, is entitled to a mortgage equal to 90% of his costs for a term of 40 years at an interest rate of 3% and a constant payment for interest and debt amortization of 4.2958%. The FHA waives its one half of 1% mortgage insurance premium. The low debt-servicing cost would necessitate that FNMA purchase the mortgage, since no private lender would supply funds at a 3% interest rate at this time. The low debt-servicing cost, combined with the elimination of all real estate taxes and land rent for this part of the project, enables the developer to rent the apartments at below normal rentals. To insure that the lower-middle-income tenants receive the benefits of this housing, the mortgage cannot be prepaid for 20 years, and rentals are controlled.

Mr. Ravitch estimated operating costs as follows:

Mortgage debt servicing—$6,121,500 @ $4.2958%.	$263,000
Maintenance and operating (including replacement reserve)	150,000
Payment to New York City.	1,000
Return on equity—$802,600 @ 6%.	48,000
Estimated income required.	$462,000
Nonresidential income estimate—	
350 apts. @ $25/apt./annum.	−8,750
	$453,250
Add 5% vacancy.	23,750
Annual rent roll.	$477,000

$$\text{Average rent/Mitchell Lama room} = \frac{\$477,000}{1382.5 \times 12 \text{ mo.}} = \$28.75/\text{room/month}$$

At this $28.75 monthly rental per room, there would be a great demand for the apartments, although the apartments would be restricted to families in the lower-middle-income categories (see Exhibit 1). About 70 of the apartments, or 20% would be rented to low-income families at an even lower rent, $18 per room. Either the New York City Housing Authority would lease the apartments and rerent them to public housing clients at about $18 per room per month, with the federal government making up the difference, or the federal government would provide rent supplements directly to the owner, in which case the owner would select the tenants. (The Housing and Urban Development Act of 1965 authorized a new program of rent supplements for low-income families and individuals.)

Mr. Ravitch was interested in obtaining funds for the financing of the project. His builders and sponsors allowance would provide much of the equity for the project. In addition, he thought that $2 million–$2.5 million in cash would probably be required, although it was probable that the cash investment upon completion of this project would be $1.5 million, since much of the 2% working capital allowance might not be needed. He approached a major investor to provide the cash portion of the equity. The prospective investor was concerned with the limitation of the profit distribution to 6%. He was aware that the 6% allowable return was based upon an assumed investment which included the builders and sponsors profit. The builders and sponsors allowance was $3,163,000 on the middle-income housing portion of the project. While the cost schedule for the low-income building did not specifically show any allowance for builders and sponsors profit, he estimated that it would probably be approximately $620,000. Thus, while an investment of $2 million–$2.5 million would be required during construction, the $1.5 million required equity upon completion of construction would be a very conservative figure.

The proposed investor was most interested in the excess book losses generated by the property for tax purposes. The investors in his group were in an extremely high tax bracket, well above the 50% corporate tax rate. Excess losses generated by depreciation were of great value to them. The high leverage created by owning with an investment of $1.5 million property with an estimated cost of over $41 million, would give them an excellent tax-loss situation, since they would also be entitled to use the double declining-balance method of depreciation and a 40-year depreciable life and be permitted to depreciate the entire cost, since there was no land included. They expected that HRH Construction Company would allow them to set up a situation where the financing group would be entitled to the entire depreciation and one half of the cash income (cash flow) generated by the property, since HRH did not have a need for the tax shield.

The prospective investor knew that the Waterside Development plan would have to be submitted to the City Planning Commission and Board of Estimate for approval of the entire transaction, including the terms of the proposed city lease and the zoning changes. They did not feel that this would be a major problem. The integration of economic levels represented a commitment by the Lindsay administration to scatter low-cost housing among middle-income families. Although Jason R. Nathan, administrator of housing and development, said that middle-income families would live in the same building as poor families, and since this was the basis for the city's support of the project, the proposed investors thought that this might create rental problems. The developers nevertheless argued that at the proposed, below-normal rental levels, occupancy of the units would never be a problem.

As Mr. Nathan had said, "We're giving them a good housing buy, and there should be no question of marketability."

The request that the city designate the site as eligible for urban renewal without the normal federal cash subsidies in order to qualify as a borrower under the FHA Section 220 was certain to be granted, along with federal government approval, according to Mr. Nathan.

The investors realized that, in fact, the entire project was being subsidized through the federal mortgage insurance program, the FNMA mortgages for the lower-income section, the city's contribution of air rights, and real estate tax abatement. The project would normally produce $800,000 a year in taxes rather than the $404,500 payment. Therefore, the developers, in effect, would pay no rent for the land and receive a 50% tax abatement. In turn, the developers would be limited to a 6% return on their investment, giving the occupants of the building the advantage of the subsidy through lower rents.

The size of the city subsidy, even though through lost revenue rather than cash, indicates the difficulty of building apartments in New York City at "reasonable" rents. This project might very well have been undertaken without any subsidy, but only if built for upper-income tenants with rentals of about $75 per room. Housing experts noted that subsidies are necessary if private investment is going to produce middle-income housing in the city. Mayor Lindsay acknowledged the problem when he said, "We are placing a great stress on public and private cooperation to build housing that people can afford. And to do that we have to use our tax power to cut costs." This development also involved no relocation of existing tenancy, since the site was dotted with rotting piers and produced no tax revenue. The shoreline is directly across the F.D.R. Drive from Bellevue Hospital and the New York University Medical Center. No existing taxpaying property would have its view of the river blocked.

The investors realized that the above line of thinking should result in rapid approval of the proposed Waterside project by the City Planning Commission and Board of Estimate. While Waterside was the product of five years of hard, frustrating work that included overcoming a myriad of barriers of interdepartmental conflict and delay, it now appeared to have strong government support.

The project is a trend-setter for New York in every sense of the term. It is an urban concept that utilizes the waterfront for housing and recreation in a distinctly urban way. The design level is able, sophisticated and creative.

The standard that is established for mixed housing, commercial, recreational and open-space uses, in a coordinated, multilevel complex with parking and facilities underground, is found in leading design publications, and is beginning to appear in other cities. It is still only on paper in New York.

This could be the city's first large-scale breakthrough from the norm of sterile housing clichés and arid open space that has been the bureaucratic or easy-profit formula. Waterside would be a standard-setting development for any waterfront city in the world. It achieves this status because it does not use the currently popular idea of fountain-studded plazas, pedestrian walkways along the water, and cafes and shops as detached gimmicks with easy eye-appeal, but as sound instruments of the highest level of comprehensive planning. These stylish amenities are set into a solid functional framework of pedestrian and vehicular circulation, parking and servicing.

Just how sophisticated and comprehensive that planning is can be seen in the fact that, unlike Lincoln Center, for example, it does not stop at its traffic boundaries. Meant to be a city facility, rather than a purely local one, the development will be connected with the community across the East River Drive.[1]

And finally, unlike many urban renewal projects, Waterfront Development would create 1,450 housing units without disrupting the life of one single family or costing one job or loss of business. It was to be the first planned development in New York City to serve all income levels.

While the members of the investor group were almost certain that approval would be obtained, they were aware of the time lag involved. While it was already the middle of 1966, they would not obtain approval of the City Planning Commission until March 1967, and then of the Board of Estimate in July 1967. These approvals to: (1) rezone the property to permit the construction of high-rise apartments and diverse commercial facilities including a movie house, (2) approve the area as a Title 1 project (with no federal cash subsidy), and (3) approve the terms of the lease and tax abatement. Hopefully, by the fall of 1967, preliminary approval of the mortgage insurance for the project by the FHA should have been received and by the spring of 1968, final FHA approval should have been granted. Construction would, therefore, commence in the summer of 1968, if all proceeded smoothly.

Mr. Ravitch explained the need to change to C2–7 zoning to permit the construction of a movie theater and boat docking and to allow the use of tower regulations in high-rise structures to achieve the maximum allowable floor area. However, the total floor area and population density was not to exceed the minimum permitted in an R–8 zoning district. This zoning would allow construction according to the plans previously described.

According to this plan, 1,500 apartments with 6,000 rooms containing 15.7 million cubic feet or 1.5 million square feet of space, exclusive of cellars, balconies, stores, offices, and garages would be built. The site would house 4,200 people, with 680 persons per acre. Only 25% of the site would be covered by structures, the remainder being open space, recreation area, piazzas, walkways, sitting areas, playgrounds, and boat dockings. The property would also provide off-street parking for 50% of the number of dwelling units. The site plan had four tall towers, 48 town houses, shops, a theater, and a restaurant surrounding a large plaza, which descended in several terraces to the river 25 feet below the main level.

The investors were confident that HRH Construction Company and Davis, Brody Associates could convert the plan into reality at below the estimated costs furnished, although the longer the time period until construction commenced, the more risk of increases in costs.

---

[1] *The New York Times*, December 20, 1966.

The architects were now also working with Housing and Redevelop ment Board on a total neighborhood plan for the Bellevue area from 23rd to 30th Streets, between Second Avenue and the Drive. They were also the designers of houses in the Bellevue South urban renewal area and of a middle-income cooperative, Riverbend, under construction on Fifth Avenue from 138th to 142nd Street.

The prospective investors were concerned about the possibility that the double declining-balance method of depreciation might be elimi- nated for a period of one to two years, at which time they could only use the 150% declining-balance method for the life of the property, even if the law were reversed at a later date. If this were to happen, they wondered whether this would change their investment decision, and if they did invest and such a prohibition were introduced, should they delay construction until the double declining-balance method of depre- ciation was reintroduced.

Once the project's depreciation began to be inadequate to cover the net income and mortgage amortization, the likelihood of sale at a sub- stantial profit was small, because of the limited-dividend nature of the development. The advantage of low amortization during the early years, while beneficial to producing tax losses, was not building up equity at a fast rate. Even after 10 years, the Section 221(d)(3) mortgage would only have been reduced about 15%, and the Section 220 mortgage about 11%. The result of this was that since income was controlled, there would not be a sufficiently great enough increase in cash flow to warrant refining the mortgage to a higher level through conventional terms. The terms of the FHA mortgages were too desirable.

EXHIBIT 1

**Federal Housing Administration
100 Boylston Street
Boston, Massachusetts 02116**

February 1, 1967

GENTLEMEN:

The rent and income limitations for Boston* under Section 221 (d)(3) below market interest rate program are as follows (3 percent):

No. in Family	No. of Bedrooms	Maximum Monthly Housing Expense	Maximum Annual Income
1	Efficiency	$ 95.00	$ 5,700
2	1	115.83	6,950
3 & 4	2	135.83	8,150
5 & 6	3	155.83	9,350
7 or more	4	176.67	10,600

* New York's figures are similar to Boston's.

Maximum housing expense represents monthly rental with all utilities provided. Single-person occupancy permitted *only* for elderly (i.e., over 62 years old) and for physically handicapped.

It would be appreciated if you would sign one copy of this letter as indicated on the bottom and return it to our office.

Very truly yours,
JOHN W. FLYNN
Director

I have reviewed the rent and income limitations under 221 (d)(3) below market interest rate program.

Signature:

QUESTIONS

1. What return can the investor expect as a return on his investment both from a cash and after-tax point of view? Assume that the investment is $2.5 million for three years and $1.5 million thereafter, with the developer sharing after three years in 50% of the cash flow but none of the tax benefits. The construction period is two years. Assume the project is sold at the end of 10 years on a basis providing an 8% cash pretax return on equity to the new investor.

2. How would this return change if the tax laws were changed to permit only 150% declining-balance depreciation rather than the double declining-balance method?

3. What is the cash flow return to the developer? Is this worth the work that has been involved?

4. From a public policy viewpoint, does this development satisfy public purpose? What subsidies are involved? Should the city and/or federal government grant assistance of the type requested?

5. Could the project be built without the benefit of federal insurance and loan programs? What accounts for the difference in rent between buildings insured under Section 221 (d)(3) and Section 220? What would the rents have been with no subsidy?

6. Appraise the risk and complexities of launching such a new concept where the success is so dependent upon governmental assistance of the type requested. What agencies were involved?

PART V

**Development—
Government
Programs—
Low-Income Housing**

CROWN HEIGHTS

In May 1968, Lawrence Baldwin was offered the opportunity to purchase four six-story elevatored buildings containing 335 apartments for $1,450,000. The buildings were being offered by Arthur Rogers, a Brooklyn real estate broker and property owner, who had received the listing from a Brooklyn commercial bank. The bank was acting as a trustee for an estate and was anxious to liquidate the properties.

The buildings were located within eight blocks of one another in Crown Heights, a changing area of Brooklyn, N.Y., near the junction of the East Flatbush and Brownsville sections. Until the 1950's, the area had been one of the most desirable in Brooklyn. Upper-middle-income families occupied the apartment buildings and the three-story, well-kept brownstone apartments that characterized the area. Since the apartments were under rent control, the rentals were low and there were no vacancies. The neighborhood had many parks, good schools, and shops, and most of the families as well as the landlords had lived there for two to three generations.

However, during the 1950's, many of the families began to move to the suburbs. With the neighborhood starting to break up, many landlords began to look at ways of increasing their return. Under rent control in New York City, rents in older apartments could not be raised except to cover increased operating costs or when an apartment was vacated and a new tenant occupied the apartment. In the latter case, the landlord was entitled to a 15% rent increase.

Since rents in most apartments at that time averaged only $60 per month, the landlords had no trouble rerenting them for $69 per month when vacancies occurred. Similar units in new buildings in other sections of Brooklyn were renting at from $150 to $200. As a result, the landlords of the rent-controlled buildings found themselves besieged with applicants for any apartment that became vacant. The new arrivals were less wealthy, but still took care of their apartments.

Because of low rents, the landlords normally did little to repair their properties; they expected the tenants to keep up their apartments. Until the 1950's, the tenants did so, oftentimes modernizing their kitchens and bathrooms as well as redecorating their apartments. However, as the units began to turn over more rapidly, there was little incentive for the new occupants to make long-term investments in their apartments. On the East Side of Manhattan, in many of the older rent-controlled build-ings, property owners had created cooperatives which allowed the ten-ants to buy their apartments. In Brooklyn, though, the trend was to move out of the area rather than upgrade it.

Many of the landlords were moving from Brooklyn and because of the distance became less interested in their properties. Speculators who specialized in purchasing rent-controlled buildings began to offer these now-absentee owners what appeared to be high prices, since the return on the new owner's equity would be only 1% to 3%, after mortgage payments. There were several reasons for this high multiple. First, be-cause of the low rents, the return was practically guaranteed. Second, there was the expectation of raising rents by 15% when vacancies occurred. And third, there was the hope that someday rent control might be lifted, enabling the landlord to obtain full market rents. However, in New York, rent control had been very much of a political issue, and the tens of thousands of families taking advantage of these lower rents had been able to pressure the public officials to retain the law. They were supported by many who argued that if rent controls were lifted, there would be thousands of poor people thrown out into the streets or put on public welfare.

In Brooklyn, the rate of deterioration of the apartments was greatly accelerated because of the racial question. Prior to the late 1950's, few Negroes had lived on the Crown Heights side of Eastern Parkway. However, the vast influx of Negroes from the South overcrowded the older Negro areas and forced them to expand to other sections. Because of their high unemployment rate and low economic position, the Negroes could not afford to be selective in their housing choice and were forced into the least desirable, low-rent buildings. Ebbets Field, located close by and long the home of the Brooklyn Dodgers, was sold to a large real estate firm, which announced plans to construct a low-rent housing project on the site utilizing the New York State Mitchell-Lama low-cost financing program.

On Crown Street, three small apartment buildings sold to a profes-sional blockbuster were resold to Negro families, who occupied the apartments. There was a mushrooming effect. Gradually, other landlords began to get nervous, and the speculator bought their buildings, too, at discount prices. The new landlords filled all vacancies with Negro fami-lies, some in the lower-income categories. As this occurred, the older families in the neighborhood began to move out in larger numbers. After the first few reports of muggings and robberies, many white families wanted to move out of the area altogether, rather than attempt to stay and to maintain the area. For the first time in decades, there were one or two store vacancies on the street. Prices began to decrease despite the in-crease in rents.

Those landlords who did retain their buildings often turned them over to management firms who specialized in increasing the return on rent-controlled buildings. These firms were accustomed to collecting rents weekly from less reliable tenants, ignoring their complaints, and maximizing the turnover. Rents were from $60 to $70 per month to $100 per month. Since the landlords did no repairs, their operating profits went up considerably. Because the Negro tenants had little choice of places to which they could move, and had little faith in the city's willingness to help them, they did not complain about their treatment.

To avoid rent control altogether, some speculators began to turn their buildings into boardinghouses, breaking up the large apartments into one- or two-room units. The monthly rents were kept at $60 to $70 per unit, but there were now twice as many units in the same building. The city did not object too strenuously to this process, since the welfare department was utilizing these lower-rent units to handle the city's increasing welfare rolls, which had risen to over 700,000 people by 1967 and were expected to reach 1 million people by 1970. Also, the city was able to take advantage of the higher rent rolls in the short run, by increasing the property assessments for real estate tax purposes.

Yet, in spite of the increase in profits, the selling prices of buildings in the area declined. The type of investor interested in the area no longer would accept a low cash return. He was not willing to pay for future growth. Also, although the properties had a more active turnover, there was less cash involved. The seller took back large purchase money mortgages. This became necessary not only because of the character of the new buyers but also because of the unwillingness of banks to refinance or renew existing mortgages. Those institutional lenders willing to consider making loans in the area demanded higher interest rates and faster amortization, thus absorbing much of the increase in cash flow.

Mr. Baldwin visited the four buildings offered by the bank together with Mr. Rogers. His initial reaction was one of shock. Mr. Baldwin's office was in Manhattan and his home was on Long Island. Although he owned other property, he was not aware that conditions like this existed in New York. Many of the buildings in the neighborhood had broken windows, beer cans in the lobby, rags stuffed in pipes where radiators had been removed, and a smell that kept him from getting beyond the entrance. The city seemed to be providing no services to the area. He was especially disappointed because he had lived in the neighborhood only five years ago, when it still had charm.

In spite of the physical surroundings, Mr. Baldwin was attracted by the 30% cash return on equity these properties appeared to offer, as opposed to buildings located in Manhattan where the return was from 0% to 6%. The buildings being offered by the bank had an official asking price of $1,650,000, but Mr. Rogers said that bank officials had told him that they would accept a price of $1,450,000 subject to existing first mortgages of $1 million. The seller would take back a $225,000 purchase money second mortgage at 6% interest with a 10-year repayment schedule, but maturing in 5 years. The balance of the purchase price, $225,000, was to be paid in cash. Mr. Baldwin summarized the setup furnished him on these buildings (see Exhibits 1 and 2). He added allowances for vacancies and management not shown on the original statement.

Rental income..		$400,500
Less:		
Real estate tax..	$81,950	
Operating expense....................................	65,850	
Repairs at 8%...	32,000	
Vacancy at 4%..	16,000	
Management at 4½%.................................	18,000	
Total Operating Expenses...........................		213,800
Net before Financing......................................		$186,700
Less:		
First mortgage payment...............................		(88,000)
Second mortgage payment............................		(34,000)
Net Income...		$ 64,700

Mr. Baldwin asked Mr. Rogers why he did not buy the properties himself. A 30% cash return plus the high mortgage amortization was very good, especially for Mr. Rogers, who was active in the real estate business. Mr. Rogers said that he did like the properties, but he did not have the $225,000 cash. Normally, he said, a private individual would not require as heavy a down payment as the bank was requiring. He told Mr. Baldwin that the bank had offered him a $25,000 commission, which he would be willing to reinvest in the property to become Mr. Baldwin's partner. He would manage the property for the 4½% fee. Since Mr. Rogers would have an interest in the property, Mr. Baldwin could be sure that he would take care of the buildings properly. Mr. Baldwin was not anxious to have an unknown partner, but, on the other hand, he knew he could not manage the buildings himself. He liked the idea of giving Mr. Rogers an incentive. Whether the investment of a $25,000 commission was enough of a commitment on Mr. Rogers' part, he was not sure.

Another question Mr. Baldwin had was the risk of being unable to refinance the $840,000 balance due on the first mortgage, which would come due only 4⅓ years after the properties were purchased. Mr. Rogers said that he felt the risk was minimal because of the heavy amortization of the mortgages. At the end of the 4⅓-year period, the first mortgage would be reduced by $160,000 and the second by $95,000. At that time, a new $970,000 first mortgage would refinance both the first and the second mortgages. The present payments of $122,000 on the two existing mortgages would be available for the new mortgage. Even assuming a rise in interest rates to 7%, the new mortgage could be repaid in under 10 years.

Mr. Baldwin expressed a fear as to the income tax consequences of the heavy amortization. He wondered whether the depreciation would be adequate to cover these amounts. He calculated that of the $1,450,000 price, $150,000 would be allocable to the land, leaving $1.3 million to depreciate over a 20-year period. Using a 150% declining-balance rate, this would result in total depreciation charges of $375,000 during the 4½-year period. The tax liability for 4½ years would be:

Cash income	$ 280,000
Amortization of 1st and 2nd mortgages	255,000
Gross taxable income	$ 535,000
Depreciation	(375,000)
Net taxable income	$ 160,000
Income tax at 50%	(80,000)
Net income	$ 80,000

This $80,000 tax liability would reduce the cash income from $280,000 over the period, or to $46,500 annually. On a percentage basis, this reduced the return from 30% to approximately 20%.

Mr. Rogers suggested that since he had ample depreciation on his other properties to cover the excess income on this one, perhaps they could take another approach to purchasing the property. After Mr. Baldwin had purchased the property for $1,450,000 subject to the first mortgage of $1 million, and the second of $225,000, he would sell Mr. Rogers a 30-year leasehold on the property for $200,000. The payment would be made $25,000 in cash and $175,000 in the form of a purchase money mortgage for 4½ years at 6% interest. The annual carrying cost of this mortgage would be $46,000. Mr. Rogers would pay Mr. Baldwin the $186,700 net before financing, $140,700 in the form of leasehold rent and $46,000 as repayment of the $175,000 purchase money mortgage. He would also pay Mr. Baldwin 50% of the income above $186,700 during the first 4½ years, and thereafter 50% of the income over $140,700.

Mr. Baldwin examined the tax consequences during the first 4½ years of this suggestion. On the one hand, his depreciable base was reduced from $1.3 million to $1.1 million, reducing the depreciation over the period from $375,000 to $317,000. On the other hand, the $280,000 of income subject to taxation would be reduced by the $175,000 that is a repayment of the leasehold mortgage. He did a new tax summary.

Cash income	$ 105,000
Amortization of 1st and 2nd mortgages	255,000
Gross taxable income	$ 360,000
Depreciation	(317,000)
Net taxable income	$ 43,000
Income tax at 50%	21,500
Net income	$ 21,500

His actual cash income would be $105,000 less the $21,500 tax liability plus the $175,000 repayment of the leasehold mortgage, or $258,000. This compared with $200,000 using the previous alternative. On an annual basis, his return on his $200,000 investment would be increased from $46,500 to $60,000, merely through a different financing arrangement.

Mr. Baldwin reviewed these two alternatives in the light of the risks of the overall project. It was almost impossible to quantify the risk of refinancing the mortgage at the end of the 4½ years. So much depended upon the condition of the neighborhood and the money market at that point. As an example, a new lender might require him to spend $250,000 to remodel the kitchens in all the 335 apartments. He did have one advantage. If conditions were bad, the present first-mortgage lender might hesitate to call the mortgage, since he would not want the headache of running the property himself. This might not be true of the purchase money mortgage lender.

Mr. Baldwin knew that his repair allowance of $32,000 could very well be inadequate to keep the apartments in condition if the nature of occupancy deteriorated or the city decided to enforce its health and building codes. On the other hand, his properties were assessed for tax purposes at $1,702,000. Most properties in New York were assessed at 80% of value. Since he would be purchasing the property for $1,450,000, he could go to court and argue that his assessment should be 80% of $1,450,000 or $1,160,000. If he were successful, his tax bill would be reduced from $82,000 to $56,000. In effect, the city would be the major loser as a result of rent control. Still, a court fight might take two to three years, and the result was always uncertain. In the meanwhile, the city could get sticky about enforcing building codes on his properties.

Another potential problem to Mr. Baldwin might be Mr. Rogers. Although Mr. Rogers seemed honest, he knew that the type of person accustomed to dealing in slum property must be "hard-nosed." Since Mr. Rogers' investment was only his commission, he could easily drop his interest and leave Mr. Baldwin with the problem of finding a new manager whom he could trust. He not only did not want to collect rents or to manage the property himself, but did not want to have his name associated publicly with it. He could visualize his friends' reaction to seeing his name in *The New York Times* as a "slum lord."

He knew that rent control had been necessary in times of housing shortages when no new buildings could be built. This was true during World War II. It appeared to him, though, that the continuation of rent control beyond such a crisis had led only to the deterioration of property. Whether the social pressures were such that the neighborhoods would have deteriorated in any case was a question he was unable to answer. He saw now, however, that the city was being forced to go into formerly desirable areas, such as Crown Street, and spend vast sums of government money to renew them to the same condition they had been only 20 years earlier.

This suggested to Mr. Baldwin the alternative of refinancing his property at the end of the 4⅓-year period through a mortgage insured by the Federal Housing Administration (FHA). He found that his property would probably be eligible for a below-market interest rate loan under FHA Section 221(d)3 if the buildings were completely rehabilitated to FHA standards. Under this program, the developer would receive a 40-year loan at an interest rate of 3% with a constant payment for interest and debt amortization of 4.2958%. In return for this loan, the developer was required to limit his rent levels and consequently his profits, so that for a minimum period of 20 years, the income tenants for whom the program was designed would be able to take advantage of the subsidy.[1]

Mr. Baldwin did a cost analysis based on taking this approach at the end of 4⅓ years. He assumed that the FHA would appraise the existing buildings for inclusion in the new mortgage at $1,200,000. He felt that this was conservative considering that his purchase price was $1,450,000.

Existing building cost	$ 1,200,000
Renovation—335 apartments @ $10,000	3,350,000
Builders and sponsors allowance on renovations	335,000
Total Project Cost	$ 4,885,000
90% mortgage	(4,395,000)
Equity requirement	$ 490,000*

*The builders and sponsors allowance could be used to reduce the equity requirement.

Mortgage debt servicing—$4,395,000 @ 4.2958%	$188,000
Maintenance and operation @ $400/unit	134,000
Real estate taxes @ 15%	67,000
Return on equity permitted	25,000
	$414,000
Plus 5% vacancy	21,000
Annual rent roll	$435,000*

*Average rent per apartment $435,000 ÷ 335 = $1,298 per year or $108 per month.

Mr. Baldwin was amazed. His calculations showed that he could spend $10,000 per unit on building renovation and still have to increase rents only $8 per month, from $100 to $108. Even if he did the renovation based on his purchase price of $1,450,000, assuming the FHA appraiser would allow it, the rents would only have to increase to an average $118

---

[1] Under the 1969 tax reform law, an investor is allowed a rapid five-year depreciation write-off on all rehabilitation expenditures. While not explicitly considered by Mr. Baldwin in his following calculations, the financial returns are increased by this special write-off.

per month. His return, however, would be limited to $25,000 per year at 95% occupancy, or $47,000 at 100% occupancy, with no cash investment. This compared with the potential of running the building in its present condition, with a return of $60,000 on a $200,000 investment.

Mr. Baldwin could see certain drawbacks to the rehabilitation approach. To process the property through FHA could take two to three years, and even then there was the risk of its not being approved. The government program itself could be changed, or the appropriation for the subsidy to pay the difference between the 3% interest rate and the government borrowing rate could be withheld. Besides, Mr. Baldwin believed there was something artificial about giving a 40-year mortgage for improvements that would probably not last more than 10 to 20 years, or even less, given the nature of the potential tenants.

Therefore, although the FHA mortgage might be an excellent way to combine a social purpose with a reasonable financial return, he could not count on it. He must make his prime decision based upon the alternatives available to him to operate the properties in their present condition. He must contrast the opportunity to make a high cash return with the problems of investing in a slum area. His friends told him that this area of Brooklyn might be 100% Negro in five years. There might be riots. The tenants could stage a rent strike, reducing his income to zero unless he improved the property. FHA or conventional, the people living in the area might not have the income to pay their rent. Still, he could not see how the city could sit by and see the neighborhood and the city services continue to deteriorate. The federal government's commitment was to aid the Negro. With Mr. Rogers as his partner, he might be able to take advantage of the situation.

EXHIBIT 1

Crown Properties
Description of Properties

	150 Crown St.	712 Crown St.	7 Balfour Pl.	1041 Bushwick Ave.	Total
Apartments*					
1½ rooms...............	14	—	—	—	14
2 "	6	—	1	1	8
2½ "	10	12	—	—	22
3 "	63	48	21	25	157
3½ "	6	—	—	1	7
4 "	20	30	10	18	78
5 "	5	22	6	3	36
6 "	—	12	1	—	13
Total Apartments...	124	124	39	48	335
Total Rooms........	373	476	141	167.5	1,157.5
Average rent/apt./yr......					$1,195
Average rent/apt./mo.....					100
Average rent/room/yr.....					346
Assessment..............	$625,000	$630,000	$207,000	$240,000	$1,702,000
First mortgage					
Amount...............	$370,000	$390,000	$105,000	$135,000	$1,000,000
Interest rate...........	5½%	5½%	5½%	5½%	5½%
Due date..............	9/72	9/72	8/72	8/72	9/72
Quarterly payment† ..	$ 8,500	$ 9,000	$ 2,000	$ 2,500	$ 22,000
Plot size.................	217.4′ × 80′	200′ × 135′	70′ × 130′	100′ × 100′	54,500 sq. ft.

* All buildings—six-story with elevator.
† Equivalent of payment for 5½% mortgage for 18 years.

EXHIBIT 2

Crown Properties
Income and Expenses

	150 Crown St.	712 Crown St.	7 Balfour Pl.	1041 Bushwick Ave.	Total
Rental income.................	$143,200	$150,300	$47,500	$59,500	$400,500
Less expenses					
Taxes......................	$ 30,000	$ 30,250	$10,000	$11,700	$ 81,950
Water-sewer.................	2,445	1,800	806	638	5,689
Insurance...................	4,795	3,544	2,800	1,322	12,461
Help.......................	6,600	6,600	2,600	2,750	18,550
Electricity..................	2,000	9,500	800	1,000	13,300
Fuel.......................	7,400	3,150	2,000	3,300	15,850
Repairs....................	12,000	11,500	3,500	5,000	32,000
Total Expenses..........	$ 65,240	$ 66,344	$22,506	$25,710	$179,800
Net before financing..........	$ 77,960	$ 83,956	$24,994	$33,790	$220,700
Less: First mortgage payments.................	34,000	36,000	8,000	10,000	88,000
	$ 43,960	$ 47,956	$16,994	$23,790	$132,700

OLD TOWN GARDENS I

In the fall of 1966, Mr. Gene Coleman, a partner in Hanover Equities had just returned from Old Town Gardens (OTG), an apartment complex which Hanover owned and operated. While there he had witnessed a line of 23 demonstrators marching in front of the manager's office and carrying signs that read: "OTG—This Year's Disaster Area," "Falling Plaster Means Disaster," and "We Want Safety, Racial Balance, Fair and Standard Rents, and Maintenance." This was just one of many incidents which had plagued Mr. Coleman since he had put together the syndication to purchase OTG in 1960.

The financial return on the property had continually declined since 1960; if this trend were to continue, it was inevitable that OTG would soon face bankruptcy. As Mr. Coleman reflected on his experience with the property, he tried to determine where he had gone astray. Some of the questions he hoped to answer were: Was the failure due to the way the property had been managed? Was it related to the fact that he lived in New York but the property was located in Chicago? Since 1962, the racial composition of the apartments had changed from virtually all white to an estimated 75% Negro. Had this integration been properly implemented? Is it possible that the area around the complex had been changing so rapidly that there was little that could have been done to change what had happened to the project? Should more money have been invested in the property to improve its physical condition or would this have been only throwing good money after bad? Mr. Coleman thought that answering these questions might keep him from making similar mistakes in the management of his other properties and also might help him decide on what future action he should take to improve the situation at OTG.

DESCRIPTION OF THE COMPLEX

Old Town Gardens was built in the late 1920's by the Marshall Field estate in an area cleared out of what was then a run-down Italian neighborhood. The development, the first such renewal project in the country, was launched as a social experiment. Good housing would be provided at reasonable rents in hopes that improvement would spread to the surrounding area.

The property is located in Chicago's Near North Side and is convenient to all forms of bus and elevated transportation and major traffic arteries. Less than two miles northward from the Loop area, the development is within half a mile of Lincoln Park with its museums, zoo, ball field, lakes, and restaurants, and within close proximity to the Lake Michigan beaches.

OTG covers more than three city blocks, of which approximately 4 acres are devoted to buildings and the balance to gardens. The land parcel is rectangular in shape and bounded by an area free of bisecting streets on North Sedgwick Street, Blackhawk Street, Hudson Street, and Evergreen Avenue. It contains 247,358 square feet, and an additional site, used for the garage and heating buildings, occupies approximately 22,946 square feet. The improvements on the property consist of 12 brick buildings of reinforced concrete construction. Ten of the buildings are five-story and basement fireproof store and apartment buildings; one is a four-story garage for 103 cars, and one is a heating building. The buildings do not have elevators and are not air conditioned. Each apartment building has a laundry and storage rooms, and eight have roof gardens and sun-rooms; one has a large meeting room, accommodating 100 or more people, and equipped with cloakroom, kitchen and washrooms. Another of the apartment buildings has two large recreation rooms, one of which is equipped and operated as a nursery. All of these facilities are maintained for the exclusive use of the tenants. The buildings contain 684 apartments with an aggregate of 2,808 rooms; 16 of the apartments contain 3½ rooms, 343 contain 4 rooms, 288 contain 5 rooms, and 37 contain 6 rooms.

The project, originally known as the Marshall Field Garden Apartments, was operated by the Field Estate until 1942, when it was sold to Randolph Bohrer and renamed the Town and Garden Apartments. In 1955, the apartments were sold to a group of investors organized by Arthur Rubloff & Co., a major midwestern real estate firm located in Chicago. The Rubloff firm also managed the project, which was renamed the Old Town Garden Apartments.

MANAGEMENT UNDER ARTHUR RUBLOFF

During the Rubloff management, the project experienced virtually 100% occupancy, as it had continued to do since 1939, and a 99% rent collection rate. Rubloff attributed this record to several factors: excellent value for the money, a strict maintenance policy, the provision of desired amenities, and the creation of a social atmosphere within the apartment complex.

When the property was acquired in 1955, the average rent per room was $21. This was gradually increased to only $24 per room by 1960, even though there were no rent control laws in Chicago. Apartments were equal to or larger than the size of apartments in new construction which were being rented at substantially higher rates. Furthermore, Chicago had no comparable development—one that was a multiple-dwelling community located in the heart of the city and having within its perimeter landscaped gardens, recreational accommodations, and shopping facilities.

A strict maintenance policy which provided for regularly scheduled painting, garden and grounds service, thorough cleaning of the common areas, and prompt reply to tenant complaints kept the building in good physical condition and the tenants happy.

Rubloff's management policy was indicated by the following statement made by one of its executives: "We endeavor in any large apartment complex to encourage couples to make friends with other couples, have a man meet other men, and a woman meet other women. In so many apartments the atmosphere is so impersonal; people can live and die and no one else knows the difference. This is what we always strive to do, and we feel that we did it extremely successfully at Old Town Gardens . . . we had that building so gimmicked up!"

Among the social activities set up by Rubloff was a bridge club which met three nights a week. Prizes and an attendant who scheduled and supervised the games were provided. The project had its own women's club, garden club, and girl and boy scout units, which met in the auditorium and recreational rooms. Amateur plays were regularly produced. A photography and woodworking shop was outfitted for the tenants' use. Space was provided for a self-service library, which was available to the tenants 24 hours a day. A college student was hired to catalog and reshelve the books on a part-time basis. Initially 1,000 paperback books were purchased by Rubloff. The tenants personally donated 14,000 additional books.

Over the years, the development became an almost self-sufficient community, with the reputation of being a honeymoon spot for wealthy young North Shore couples. The community published its own newspaper, had its own acting group, conducted social events, flooded the basketball court in winter for ice skating, and filled the nursery with residents' children.

In the late 1950's, Rubloff became involved in the development of Carl Sandburg Village, an ambitious $40 million project consisting of six 27-story high-rise apartment buildings, two 10-story cooperative apartment buildings, and 81 townhouses. The apartments were aimed at middle- to upper-income families and were to replace a generally blighted area. The site was located less than a half mile to the east of Old Town Gardens.

Even though OTG continued to attract middle-income white families, experience a low turnover rate, and maintain a waiting list of prospective tenants without offering any concessions, the neighborhood was rapidly deteriorating. There even existed some tension between tenants and the residents of the area, who often resented the brick fortress of outsiders that had been placed in their midst.

Consequently, in conjunction with the planned Sandburg project Rubloff initiated a rehabilitation program for the area. Even though the state was going to help to a limited extent, most of the work was to be handled

Old Town Gardens Apartments

privately. The plan was not only to rehabilitate the surrounding properties by offering low-cost architectural service, helping get mortgage funds, and aiding in construction but also to modernize the Old Town apartments. This was to include updated kitchens and baths, improved plumbing and heating facilities, and a renovated façade. It was believed that even though the tenants did not appear to be dissatisfied with the facilities, the improvements would be necessary if the apartments were to continue to be competitive in the future.

These plans encountered opposition from two groups. First, many of the local merchants and landlords did not want to upset the status quo of the neighborhood. Financially, they believed that they had little, if anything, to gain. The landlords probably would not be able to increase their rents enough to justify the additional investment in their properties; they could earn a considerably higher return instead by acquiring more of the same kind of properties and operating them with no improvements. The turnover of property in the neighborhood was rapidly increasing as the elderly German and Italian population were either moving out of the area because of the increasing Negro population or dying of old age. This naturally tended to push the price of properties further downward, thus making them more attractive investment opportunities. Second, some of the investors in the Rubloff-OTG syndicate opposed their making any additional commitment in the project—especially since it meant that they would have to become so involved in the rehabilitation of the entire neighborhood.

SALE OF OTG TO HANOVER EQUITIES

In the fall of 1959, when the merchants and landlords as well as Rubloff's own investors were pressuring him not to proceed with the rehabilitation, Hanover Equities made an offer to purchase OTG. Rubloff decided, with the approval of his investors, that it was in his best interests to sell the complex.

During the five years under his management, the apartments had shown an increasingly improving return (see Exhibit 1); the terms of the sale now provided for the recognition of a substantial capital gain. The investment of the Rubloff group in OTG was $742,500. The final terms of the sale provided for $1,137,500 in cash and a $1,650,000 purchase money mortgage. The 6% second-mortgage notes were repayable in monthly installments of $11,000 (covering both interest and amortization) for 10 years with a balloon payment of $1,210,000 due at the end of the 10 years.

Hanover assumed an existing first mortgage with a principal balance of $1,350,000. This mortgage required annual amortization payments of $50,000 plus 3½% per annum interest, and a balloon payment of $1 million due on December 1, 1966.

In order to finance the acquisition, Hanover Equities syndicated the property. The partners provided $30,000 and raised an additional $1,320,000 by selling 264 limited-partnership interests of $5,000 each. From the proceeds of the issue, $212,500 was deducted for underwriting commissions of $71,280 (handled by Hanover), broker's commission payable to Rubloff of $37,500, and sponsor's (Hanover's) expenses and profit of $103,720. The limited partnerships were to receive the benefits of tax losses and an annual cash payment of $550 per $5,000 interest.

In summary, the purchase price of the property was:

```
Cash to Rubloff group.......................................$1,137,500
Purchase money mortgage taken by Rubloff investors...... 1,650,000
Balance due on first mortgage............................. 1,350,000
Expenses of issue, etc.....................................   212,500
     Total................................................$4,350,000*
```

    * Of this, $4,230,000 could be allocated to depreciable assets.

Hanover then took a net lease on the property from the syndicate for an initial term of 20 years with options to renew on the same terms and conditions for three additional terms of 23 years each. The lease provided for annual net basic rent of $148,500 plus additional rental in an amount equal to the annual payments for interest and amortization of the mortgages assumed in the purchase of the property. In the event that the gross rental income of the property exceeded $1,275,000 in any calendar year, the limited-partnership interests were to be paid 25% of that amount.

When asked why he was attracted to the OTG investment, Mr. Coleman said that he was influenced by two factors. First, the past record of the apartments was exceptional. The vacancies were virtually zero, collections were very high, and the turnover was low. More important than this was the potential for raising rents. The current schedule was definitely below what existed in the Chicago market. He did recognize, however, that certain improvements costing nearly $500,000 would have to be made in the near future in order to justify partially this increase in rents.

MANAGEMENT UNDER HANOVER OWNERSHIP

Since Mr. Coleman and his partners lived in New York City, they were unable to assume the responsibility of personally managing the property. They therefore contracted with the Rubloff firm to continue managing the apartments but switched to Baird and Warner, another Chicago real estate firm, within a few months.

One of the first changes made was to increase rents by 12%. This was justified to the tenants by explaining that there were higher financing charges under the new ownership, that real estate taxes had increased due to an increased valuation on the property, and that the new investors required a certain minimum return on their investment.

Except for those who were on a fixed income and could not afford any increase, most of the tenants grudgingly accepted the higher rents. To further aggravate the situation, however, no visible improvements were made to facilities. The only change noticed was that some of the larger apartments were being divided into smaller units.

Even though Baird and Warner was given instructions to continue most of the social activities which Rubloff had pioneered (the out-of-pocket costs were minimal), they were not nearly so successful. Now these gatherings provided an opportunity for the tenants to sit around and complain about the "deteriorating condition" of the building. In fact, the apartments were still being maintained at standards similar to the past; however, with the increased rents, the tenants had set their own standards higher and thought that considerable improvements were needed. They could not understand why they should have to pay more rent just because some group from New York had higher financing costs.

This dissatisfaction resulted in a gradual increase in turnover. Costs for redecorating apartments and obtaining new leases increased accordingly. By 1962, nearly 175 of the 684 apartments were vacant. Hanover was finding it increasingly difficult to meet all its financial commitments on the complex. They asked the first- and second-mortgage lenders to waive the amortization payments but were refused.

Pressure was now being put on the OTG management to integrate the property. The area surrounding it was by this time largely Negro. CORE and other Negro groups began to demonstrate for integration in front of the buildings. Substantial press and television coverage was devoted to their cause. Finally, Mr. Coleman flew to Chicago to discuss the charges made against the OTG management. He was accompanied by a Negro attorney who was experienced in such matters. Mr. Coleman confronted the CORE leaders by saying, "Our policy has been and always will be to accept any and all qualified Negroes who apply." The CORE leaders, half of whom were whites who claimed that they had lived with the Negroes for 10 years and thus really knew how they felt, were surprised by his response. From then on, Hanover experienced little difficulty from the Negro leaders.

While in Chicago, Mr. Coleman discovered that Baird and Warner had not been processing Negro applications with the same standards as used for whites. Due to this, and a general dissatisfaction with their performance as evidenced by the high vacancies at OTG, he terminated Baird and Warner's contract. In their place he hired Sam Lane to fill the position of resident manager. Mr. Coleman planned to take a more active role in OTG's management from his office in the Pan American building in New York City. He and his partners were managing nearly 4,000 apartment units, most of which were located in the New York City area.

An immediate campaign was started to fill the vacancies at OTG. Half-page ads were placed in the Sunday newspapers and also in local Negro papers. Promotional material was distributed in the post offices and other government installations in hopes of attracting Negro civil service workers. These ads portrayed integrated living by showing a picture of a white and Negro couple talking together. Concessions such as television sets or free rent for two to three months were also featured in order to induce people to sign a lease.

The OTG advertising campaign, focusing on the slogan "integrated living," received high praise from the metropolitan press. Mr. Lane had consulted with Chicago's Urban League and several civil rights groups before launching the campaign. Some of the Urban League workers were retained by OTG to aid in the integrating process. This relationship quickly deteriorated, however, when the Urban League personnel began to suspect that they were being used as salesmen rather than consultants.

The vacancy rate began to decline. Once the very liberal integration policy was publicly announced, Negroes were very anxious to move into what had in the past been a relatively prestigious complex. In addition, rents were low enough that they could afford it.

Hanover's original goal was to obtain a 30% Negro–70% white balance within the building. The whites, however, began flooding out, and within a year the balance was 50–50. There appeared to be no way of closing the flood gates. Furthermore, some of the original Negro tenants moved out because they wanted to live in a white community. At one point a committee was formed by Negro tenants who were concerned about the increasing percentage of Negroes living in OTG. A Negro and a white co-chaired the short-lived organization.

By late 1964, Hanover began to reexamine the attractiveness of the OTG investment. To date it had definitely been a bad mark on their record. (See Exhibit 1 for financial performance.) Management of the property required a disproportionate share of their time. Collecting rents had turned into a major task requiring constant attention. Many tenants were personally visited weekly in order to insure that OTG obtained its share of the tenant's earnings; otherwise, the tenant may have spent it on other items by the time the end of the month came around. Hanover also suspected that in their absence they were being abused by various individuals and concerns who were performing maintenance and decorating services for them.

The partners suggested that rehabilitating the project under the FHA 221(d)(3) program might be the easiest way out. This program provided low-cost mortgage funds for the construction or rehabilitation of low-income housing. Either they or another group could sponsor the project.

Several organizations were actively sought to do the rehabilitation. One of the Hanover partners even went so far as to contribute $25,000 to a charitable organization to cover expenses which would be incurred in preparing a 221(d)(3) application. This organization encountered so many obstacles, particularly in getting low-interest funds appropriated by the FHA, that it eventually withdrew its offer.

Even though his partners wanted to sell, Mr. Coleman was reluctant to dispose of the property at this time; he reasoned that it had finally made a turn for the better and would be a good money-maker in the future. Furthermore, since the FHA regulates the maximum income which a tenant can earn and still remain in the building, some of the tenants were opposing a 221(d)(3) because they feared that they would be forced to leave.

THE 1966 RENT STRIKE

Hanover continued to own and manage OTG in 1966. No major changes had been made in the facilities because they had been unable to obtain additional financing and were still finding it difficult to meet their fixed commitments. A fire which had destroyed some of the garbage chutes and resulted in considerable inconvenience to the tenants and in cluttered halls, triggered picketing outside the OTG management offices and a rent strike. Extensive press and television coverage was again focused on OTG and its tenants, who had organized themselves as the Tenants Action Council of Old Town Garden Apartments (TAC).

Eventually over 150 eviction notices were sent to tenants who were withholding rents. In early September, the belongings of three evicted tenants were forcibly returned to their apartments by strike supporters. Six men were arrested and charged with criminal trespass. During the night over 300 supporters sang freedom songs as they conducted an all-night vigil. Dr. Martin Luther King, Jr., made an appearance in support of their cause (see Exhibit 2 for newspaper coverage).

EXHIBIT 1

Income Statement

	Fiscal Years Ended August 1			10 Mos. Ended	Fiscal Years Ended June 30				
	1957	1958	1959	6/30/60	1961	1962	1963	1964	1965
Gross income from rentals, garage, etc.	$857,000	$371,000	$952,000	$800,000	$950,000	$ 940,000	$ 935,000	$ 920,000	N.A.
Expenses:									
Operating expenses	$355,000	$326,000	$312,000	$290,000	$355,000	$ 385,000	$ 405,000	$ 410,000	N.A.
Tenant welfare	4,000	4,000	3,500	3,000	3,000	2,500	—	—	N.A.
Real estate taxes	132,000	132,000	153,000	125,000	165,000	158,000	152,000	152,000	N.A.
Garage expenses	—	—	39,000	32,000	39,000	41,000	35,000	38,000	N.A.
Adm. & renting exp.	201,000	205,000	210,000	180,000	430,000	450,000	490,000	495,000	N.A.
	$692,000	$667,000	$717,500	$630,000	$992,000	$1,036,500	$1,082,000	$1,095,000	
Income from operations before depreciation, interest and other items	$165,000	$204,000	$234,000	$170,000	$(42,000)	$ (96,500)	$ (147,000)	$ (175,000)	N.A.

N.A. = Figures not available for this year or the fiscal year 1966.

EXHIBIT 2
Newspaper Coverage

A Garden . . . or Just an Arena?*

By Mary Knoblauch

"CLEANLINESS AND excellence of building condition have always been outstanding features of Old Town Gardens . . . Chicago's leading integrated apartments at moderate rentals," reads the advertising brochure.

Police in the 18th district call it "The Arena," an ironic nickname for what was once the most desirable middle income housing on Chicago's near north side.

Opened in 1929, the 10-building, 628-apartment complex rims a 2-block area bounded by Sedgwick, Blackhawk, Hudson, and Evergreen streets. Inside the wall of buildings is a spacious, grassy garden area and children's playground.

But the peaceful garden is misleading. Tomorrow 260 tenants of the buildings will begin a rent strike aimed at forcing the buildings' owner to redress tenant grievances.

JUST 2 BLOCKS away are the southern outposts of Wells street's glitter gulch. Across the street on Sedgwick is Poor Richard's, the newest mecca for the folk music crowd. But Old Town's bright lights have not conquered the slums and decaying buildings that surround Old Town Gardens.

The apartments themselves are still attractive on the outside. Bushes are clipped, and ivy climbs the yellow brick walls. But women don't use the basement laundry rooms, one to a building. Too many attempted and successful rapes and muggings have scared them away.

There are double entrance doors, and tenants must buzz to let visitors thru the inner door. But open, screenless windows in the hallway are an invitation for prowlers to enter at will. The basement passageways are full of niches and crannies where a half-dozen attackers could lie in wait for a victim.

THE MANAGEMENT provides a guard service, but so far it has been unable to make many of the tenants feel safe in their buildings. Jimmy marks on doors and mailboxes are evident.

The complex was built by the Marshall Field estate to provide working people with good quality, reasonable city living. In 1954 it was sold to a group of investors headed by Arthur Rubloff and company, who sold it 6 years later to the Hanover Equity company, an absentee landlord based in New York.

In 1963 the complex was integrated. Today about 62 percent of the tenants are Negro, and the remaining white tenants are mostly concentrated in a few buildings.

The Tenants Action Council [T. A. C.], the association of tenants sponsoring the rent strike, has prepared a list of renovation projects for the complex.

"BASICALLY THESE buildings are sound," said Dave McCullough, an electronics engineer and one of the leaders of T. A. C. "But they need work to keep them from deteriorating further. These buildings are what the west side was 10 or 20 years ago." He pointed to the peeling paint on window frames, missing screens, BB holes in door panes.

---

* Reprinted with permission from Chicago American, Sunday, July 31, 1966.

EXHIBIT 2 (Continued)

T. A. C. has listed other preventive maintenance projects:

The wiring is deteriorated and inadequate for today's appliance-oriented housekeeping. A heavy rain often knocks out the lights in an entire building because of the worn electrical insultation. T. A. C. wants new wiring.

T. A. C. wants the building management to increase the guard service and state in writing how often apartments are to be redecorated.

T. A. C. also recommends installation of an intercom system so tenants may know whom they are admitting when they open their door.

It also wants the management to adopt a new lease, drawn up for T. A. C. by its legal advisers. This lease spells out management's responsibilities to the tenants, as well as vice versa.

In return for all this, T. A. C. promises that it will see to it that tenants do their part in apartment upkeep.

T. A. C. will also picket the rental office during the rent strike.

Legal assistance has been provided for T. A. C. by the Coordinating Council of Community Organizations, the Southern Christian Leadership council, the United Auto Workers, and the industrial union division of the AFL-CIO, McCullough said. The latter will also provide some pickets for the duration of the rent strike, because they are interested in T. A. C.'s attempt to form a tenants' union which will bargain collectively with the landlord.

BASICALLY, T. A. C. wants to keep the Old Town Gardens from turning into what they feel will be just another jam-packed slum. Already the buildings' halls have a faint smell of bad plumbing and old cooking, and roaches are a common complaint. Tomorrow the real battle begins.

Rent Strike Sit-in Hits Old Town Apt. Office*

By Robert Dishon

Sixteen demonstrators Friday staged a sit-in at the rental office of the Old Town Gardens apartment project to dramatize a rent strike.

They sat on the floor and on desks in the office of Town and Garden Apartments Inc., 1448 N. Sedgwick, as office personnel scurried about clearing off desks.

The sit-ins sang freedom songs in unison with about 50 other demonstrators clustered outside the office.

The group had marched to the office carrying the furniture of one of three tenants evicted Thursday. They stacked it just outside the office.

The Rev. James Orange, 24, of 1550 S. Hamlin, one of those taking part in the sit-in, said the group would stay "until we are either asked to leave or arrested."

Orange identified himself as a field worker for Dr. Martin Luther King's Southern Christian Leadership Conference.

DR. KING Thursday threw the support of his Chicago Freedom Movement behind the rent strike.

He will address a rally for tenants at 8 p.m. Friday in the Olivet Community Center, 1441 N. Cleveland.

---

* Reprinted with permission from the *Chicago Daily News*, September 2, 1966.

EXHIBIT 2 (Concluded)

The decision to support the strike was made Thursday in an all-day conference of civil rights leaders at a United Auto Workers Union camp in Ottawa, Ill.

"This is a significant new development in the Chicago Freedom Movement's struggle to end slums," said the Rev. Andrew Young, one of Dr. King's top aides.

FRIDAY night's rally is being sponsored by the Tenants Action Council (TAC), the Old Town Gardens group that is seeking management recognition as a bargaining agent.

Other civil rights leaders scheduled to speak at the rally include Mr. Young; Albert Raby, convenor of the Co-ordinating Council of Community Organizations, and two other King aides, the Rev. Jesse Jackson and the Rev. James Bevel.

A TAC spokesman said four more families were scheduled to be evicted Friday.

Among those evicted Thursday were Robert and Barbara Smith, who celebrated their first wedding anniversary Sunday.

Friday they weren't sure when they'd be able to collect their furniture and belongings and move back in.

Some of their things were scattered among friends, but most of their furniture stood all night in front of their building at 1414 N. Sedgwick.

A handsome new $400 sofa was badly damaged. Records were broken. Household articles were lost.

Smith, 28, is a consultant for the Illinois Commission on Human Relations, and his wife, 23, is a clerk and receptionist at Roosevelt University.

TENANTS IN the 10-building complex on the Near North Side began a rent strike Aug. 1. They say they fear declining building maintenance will turn the integrated project into a slum.

The management obtained eviction orders against 141 tenants and Thursday a team of professional movers, supervised by Circuit Court bailiff Paul Ganno, appeared at the door of the Smiths' third-floor apartment.

When they had hauled the last of the couple's belongings out to the sidewalk, a group of tenants and sympathizers carried them back up.

A LARGE crowd gathered as the movers began ousting Linda Johnson, 28, a social worker and vice chairman of TAC, from her fourth-floor apartment at 1423 Hudson and Virgil Crandall, 28, an insurance man, from his flat on the first floor.

Placards bobbed and the crowd sang protest songs as policemen arrived to block efforts to return furniture to the two apartments.

MEANWHILE, Mr. Young disclosed that Dr. King is thinking about "closing his house in Atlanta and moving to Chicago to stay."

Mr. Young said Dr. King believes there is "so much to do in Chicago" that he feels his full-time presence is needed here.

He said Dr. King told him on a recent plane trip from Atlanta to Chicago:

"I can see no excuse for not closing down our whole house in Atlanta and coming up here (Chicago) to stay."

OLD TOWN GARDENS II

In October 1968, Arthur Rubloff was trying to determine what recommendation he should make to his clients on their investment in Old Town Gardens (OTG), an apartment complex in Chicago's Near North Side. Currently before him was a proposal to rehabilitate the apartments under the Federal Housing Administration's Section 221(d)(3).

After selling the property in 1960, Rubloff's only interest in OTG had been a second mortgage which the Rubloff-OTG syndicate held. In 1966, when the tenants engaged in a rent strike (see OTG I), the Rubloff group was dragged into the public eye because the protestors charged that the second-mortgage holders were also liable for the conditions which existed at OTG.

Subsequently, Hanover Equities, the owner of OTG, defaulted on both the first and second mortgage. As a result of the foreclosure proceedings, the Rubloff investors were put in the position of having to redeem the first mortgage; otherwise they would forfeit any claim which they had to the property.

THE 1966 RENT STRIKE

Under the terms of the purchase money mortgage, Hanover could default by either failing to make the monthly interest and amortization payment of $11,000 or permitting "economic waste" of the property. "Economic waste" is defined as allowing the property to deteriorate without performing the normal maintenance function; in reality, establishing economic waste is difficult. By early 1966, when friction between Hanover and the tenants was building up, it was Rubloff's opinion that Hanover had not yet committed "economic waste." The following inter-office communication relates the conditions which Rubloff witnessed at OTG in 1966:

Per your request, I visited Town and Garden on Friday, April 8. My first visit was with Jim Kerner, who is still chief janitor. As you know, Jim knows more of the intricacies of the building than anyone else there. He was very willing to offer any information concerning the building.

The sign carriers are demonstrating from 6 P.M. on Saturdays and Sundays. The leaders are the Rev. Smith from Underwood Institute, Joan Jedel, a Mrs. Blacker, and Linda Peach, who seems to be one of the organizers. Tom Boyd, who is a tenant from our time of management, is presently the editor of the

Garden Topics. From all appearances, he is on the payroll or is a "friend" of the present management. He has been acting as an intermediary between the tenants and the management. He also is the Democratic precinct captain for the area.

I met him on the street, and he stated that the tenants picketing who live in the building are "pigs"; however, he added that professional picketers were being used. This differs from Jim's statement that the picketers were tenants of the building; however, at one time a list of the picketers was taken and a City inspector called in to visit the apartments of the sign carriers regarding their complaints of falling plaster—no maintenance—slum dwelling, etc. Strangely enough, the City inspectors were refused admittance to all apartments of the sign carriers. Tom Boyd stated that he showed his apartment to the City inspectors to prove that the apartments were up to standard, and the picketers refused the City inspector admittance as they did not want it known in what condition they kept their apartments in regard to housekeeping and cleanliness.

The dissident group prints their own paper, and they have an organization called T.A.C., which stands for Tenants Action Committee. It is difficult to walk anywhere on the Town and Garden property without seeing a T.A.C. sticker on walls, windows, in fact, everywhere. There were literally hundreds pasted on the property.

Jim informed me that a few small fires have occurred as a result of the management turning electricity off for nonpayment of rent. Because of this, tenants have resorted to the use of candles, which evidently have been knocked over accidentally, resulting in fires.

There are still building representatives who meet monthly; however management is not represented. I noted on the 5th floor kitchen of Building 9, that the screen has been torn down both sides and across the bottom. Jim said that the occupants do not use the dumb waiter for garbage disposal, but merely use the kitchen window, which necessitates an almost daily clean up of the garden below this window. In line with this, he stated that he has seen poor credit reports on prospective tenants who are nevertheless given apartments within the property. He feels screening is at a minimum, and it merely takes cash in hand for the first month's rent to get an apartment in the building.

Approximately 50% of the screens were left on the windows through the winter, and no thought has been given to repair either the stored screens or the ones which were left in place. Jim said that recently Cayce Exterminating has been called in as exterminators. Robert Cayce stated that he was amazed to see that the basement areas were so clean. It was further stated by a member of Cayce's staff that it was unfortunate that the apartments were not kept as clean by the tenants as the basements were by the building personnel.

The building employees feel that there is a strong "I don't care" attitude on the part of the management. Previously, on the dumb waiters, we had an individual garbage container for each apartment per 5-floor tier. With a lowering of tenancy, it was found that the individual containers were no longer being used. The individual containers were removed, and one large container was placed within the dumb waiter for garbage disposal. Within the last few months, this large container has also ceased to be used. In many cases, a tenant now merely opens the dumb waiter door and disposes of the garbage by throwing it down the shaft. There have been several near misses when janitors have been emptying the garbage into the shaft with no regard to who is below.

It is most unfortunate that things are developing as they are, as my observation was that even old-time employees who formerly had a great personal pride in the building are taking on an "I don't care" attitude. This is a natural attitude as the employees cannot be expected to take pride in something that the management feels no pride in.

Still concerned about possible deterioration of the property and also the adverse publicity which it was generating, Rubloff asked his attorney to meet with representatives of the Tenants Action Committee. His report was as follows:

I met with members of the Tenants Action Committee on last Saturday afternoon in my office. There were three in number. Also in attendance at my invitation was Mr. Ernest Jackson. We spent a full two hours going over all the details of their grievances. Each of their 14 points were discussed and treated separately. Without attempting to set out in detail the nature of the complaint and the queries and information made and obtained in relation to said complaints, it was our opinion as lawyers that for the most part these were administrative complaints having to do with the number of janitors employed; number of guards employed; duties of maintenance men; publishing of rent schedule; rewording of lease; installation of an intercom system; removal of garbage, etc., that were in no way directly related to the establishment of "economic waste."

Both Mr. Jackson and myself attempted to procure specific and actionable information having to do with the actual physical condition of the exterior of the premises and the interior of the apartments. The committee advised us they had not come prepared to furnish us with this information but did volunteer that some such conditions existed. They have promised to list and photograph these conditions for us, such as they may be and get this information to this office in a reasonably short period of time. I have some doubts as to whether the extent of such information relating to waste and deterioration will be as readily available as they state. I think it became evident to Mr. Jackson and myself that while the tenants and their authorized representatives have sufficient cause for complaint to warrant concerted action, nevertheless the nature of their demands in many instances smacks of socialistic philosophy that takes them over and beyond their legal rights as established by their contract and by the law. A brief illustration of this has to do with their demand that the lease be rewritten to suit the convenience of the tenant rather than act as a protection for the landlord against the acts of the tenants, and their further demand that all rents be uniform and that a rent schedule be posted and that management give them a breakdown of the number and nature of the complaints received in relation to the guard service, and the number of hours worked by employees and maintenance men, etc. These are items which if presented independently to a court on a complaint relating thereto, could not warrant the granting of equitable or legal relief. Naturally they are cumulative in relation to the existence of waste, if waste can first be proven.

Suffice it to say, however, that as a consequence of these activities by T.A.C. and of their picketing, management has made various concessions and changes which should result in improved administrative facilities. Philosophically, sometimes agitators will continue to agitate simply for the sake of disturbance and publicity. I have not reached a conclusion that such is the case here, but I would think that having attained a certain degree of correction, such as change in extermination policies, improvement of garbage removal, cleaning up of laundry facilities (which is being done), and providing new equipment therein, that they would modify their demands and mollify their agitation so that a cooperative basis between Committee and management can ultimately result. So far, this does not seem to have occurred even though some progress as above detailed, has been made.

The matter that most disturbs me, and that cannot become a subject of open public discussion (at least for the present), is the imbalance of integration which has now occurred in said premises. A year ago when I made my report to you, I advised that integration was being maintained on an approximate 50% level. Presently, I am advised that level has changed to 70% Negro and 30% white, and that the turnover is increasingly large. It becomes obvious to me, and I am sure to you, that as the white tenants (encouraged and induced by the imbalance of integration), leave the premises, they are for the most part being replaced with Negroes, and what has occurred in most ventures of this kind will occur here, namely that the premises will become even more heavily out of racial balance. I think that the pressures on Hanover for constant maximum income will continue to accelerate the situation described.

However, even if we should reach the conclusion that no cause of action presently exists by virtue of the absence of "economic waste," the matter will be brought to a crisis shortly. Hanover is faced with the refinancing of this project within the next several months inasmuch as the balloon note of New England Mutual becomes due on December 31, 1966. We will be asked to subordinate to a new mortgage. If their financing is obtained in the East and they pay enough for it, they might not have any problem unless the investigation of the proposed lender picks up the publicity that has been somewhat nationally publicized in relation to the premises. It would appear to me, however, that any responsible lender who is willing to risk more than a million dollars, will seek a "condition report" of the premises, both interior and exterior, and this may require Hanover to put them in such physical shape as will keep our security at a better level.

Just as a conclusion, I suppose you may have seen the television broadcast of Sunday night on Channel 5 which contained as a 10 o'clock news item, pictures of a large delegation picketing the home of Sam Lane. Many of these pickets were obviously, from their placards, residents of Old Town, and they were predominantly Negro. It appears as though they have picked up infor mation that associates Sam Lane either as owner or partner in Ed Realty, which is managing other slum property, and they have issued bulletins describing said slum property so as to create a horror picture. The cumulative effect of all of this activity is not doing any good for Town and Garden.

In September, even though Arthur Rubloff personally held only a small percentage of the second mortgage and neither he nor his investors were involved in the management of OTG, the Rubloff firm received an open letter from T.A.C. The letter, which attempted to hold Rubloff responsible for the "conditions" at OTG, was widely publicized in all the news media. The content of this letter was:

We are tenants of the Old Town Garden Apartments, a Near Northside complex of 628 units. We CARE about our homes, our community, our city. Do you?

You and your fellow investors hold a large second mortgage on our homes. If for no other reason, you should be concerned about your investment. Why do you allow a New York firm to siphon large profits from our building and return little or no services?

Our buildings are becoming a dangerous SLUM!! They have antiquated electrical wiring, falling plaster, peeling paint, faulty plumbing, substandard maintenance, discriminatory rent schedules and worst of all, they are now roach infested.

You could reverse this trend. Could it be you are unaware of our problem, or are you indifferent?

In any case, your inaction allows large profits for a New York concern while creating another slum for Chicago. If this can happen to us, it can happen to the tenants in any large building in our city. Why should Chicago become a slum so that New York can profit?

Mr. Rubloff, are you really a concerned Chicagoan? WE are!

Mr. Rubloff's reply was delivered by telegram:

TENANT ACTION COUNCIL
TOWN & GARDEN APARTMENTS
C/O THOMAS McBRIDE, COORDINATOR
1368 NORTH SEDGWICK
CHICAGO, ILLINOIS

AS A CHICAGOAN WHOSE EFFORTS HAVE LONG BEEN DI-RECTED TOWARD HELPING BUILD AND MAINTAIN A CITY WHICH PROVIDES GOOD LIVING AND WHOLESOME ENVIRONMENT FOR ALL OF ITS CITIZENS, I REGRET THAT NEITHER I NOR ARTHUR RU-BLOFF & CO. POSSESS LEGAL RIGHTS OR AUTHORITY TO ASSIST YOUR GROUP IN RESOLVING PROBLEMS WHICH YOUR MEMBERS FEEL EXIST UNDER THE PRESENT MANAGEMENT OF TOWN AND GARDEN APARTMENTS. HAVING DIVESTED OURSELVES FROM MANAGEMENT AND OPERATION OF TOWN AND GARDEN APART-

MENTS IN 1959 AND HAVING NO OWNERSHIP IN THIS PROPERTY, THERE EXISTS NO BASIS FOR US, AS OUTSIDERS, TO NEGOTIATE WITH YOUR GROUP WITH RESPECT TO GRIEVANCES IN THE CONTROVERSY THAT CURRENTLY EXISTS BETWEEN YOUR TENANT GROUP AND THE OWNERS.

AS HOLDER OF AN EXTREMELY SMALL PORTION OF A SECOND MORTGAGE LOAN, WHICH CONSTITUTED PART OF THE SALE TO THE PRESENT OWNERS IN 1959, MY MINORITY INTEREST IN THE SECOND MORTGAGE LOAN IN NO WAY CONSTITUTES PARTIAL OWNERSHIP AND ENTITLES ME TO NO VOICE NOR PARTICIPATION IN THE MANAGEMENT OR PROFITS OF THIS OPERATION.

ARTHUR RUBLOFF

T.A.C. at the same time began picketing the downtown offices of the Rubloff firm and also his Carl Sandburg Village. Both of these demonstrations were extensively covered on television. In Exhibit 1 are reprints of two articles which appeared in Chicago newspapers.

HANOVER DEFAULTS ON MORTGAGES

Hanover defaulted on both the first and second mortgage in December 1966. The first mortgage, held by New England Mutual, matured; Hanover was unable to refinance the $1 million balloon payment then due. It also failed to make the annual payment due on the Rubloff group's second mortgage. Proceedings were begun in the Circuit Court of Cook County to foreclose both mortgages. A foreclosure decree on the second mortgage was entered on May 15, 1967, establishing the second-mortgage indebtedness as $1,443,612.58 (principal—$1,388,448,04; interest—$32,889.46; attorneys' fees and costs—$22,275.08). On June 13, 1967, a sale was held in conformance to the foreclosure decree. In order to protect their interests, the Rubloff group bid $1 million for the property and successfully acquired title to the property subject to the first mortgage and current real estate taxes.

A foreclosure decree on the first mortgage was then entered on September 19, 1967, establishing the first-mortgage debt at $1,091,110.27. On October 26, 1967, a sale was held under the first-mortgage foreclosure decree. New England Mutual, holder of the first mortgage, bid the full amount of the mortgage debt and was subsequently issued a certificate of sale for the property.

Under Illinois law, Rubloff had one year (until October 26, 1968) to redeem from the first-mortgage foreclosure sale. In other words, the Rubloff group would have to purchase the property from New England Mutual for $1,091,110.27 plus interest at 6% per annum; otherwise, they would have no further claim on the property.

PROPOSED REHABILITATION

Currently, the entire Old Town neighborhood was undergoing extensive change. Four blocks to the east of OTG, along North Wells Street, the commercial properties, which included distinctive shops, boutiques, and restaurants, had been restored to their original charm. The Victorian residences were being acquired and remodeled by upper-middle-income families and were responsible for attracting many new and desirable people to live and shop in Old Town. The successful completion of Carl Sandburg Village, an award-winning Rubloff apartment project, had been the catalyst in bringing these changes about. Over all, the area's rebirth can be compared with the similar redevelopment of Beacon Hill in Boston or Greenwich Village in New York City.

The elevated tracks of the local transit authority still acted as a natural barrier between the OTG site and the renovated area. However, within one-half mile to the west of OTG, the completion of a large public housing project would further stabilize this section.

Recognizing the effect that these changes would have on the desirability of Old Town, Rubloff was trying to determine whether it was economically attractive to rehabilitate the existing buildings. The remodeling would include building a new heating plant, new baths and kitchens, rejuvenating all windows, redecorating all apartments and service areas, and providing new floor covering, new electrical service, and adequate closet space. Every effort would be made to upgrade the architecture of the buildings in order to improve the character and atmosphere of the complex. Exhibit 2 is the architect's summary of the work to be done.

Since this the apartments were going to continue to be rented to low-income families, Rubloff proposed to finance the rehabilitation with a federally insured mortgage, specifically FHA, section 221(d)(3). Under this program the developer, a limited-distribution company, is entitled to a mortgage equal to 90% of his "costs" for a term of 40 years at an interest rate of 3% and a constant payment for interest and debt amortization of 4.2958%. The FHA waives its one half of 1% mortgage insurance premium. This low interest rate necessitates FNMA to purchase the mortgage, since no private lender would supply funds at a 3% rate.

The following cost schedule and financial structure was prepared for the rehabilitation.

Estimated Cost of the Rehabilitation

New entry gates and security requirements................$	450,000
Interior revisions to apartments...........................	2,278,000
Rehabilitation of service areas and exterior improvements..	1,100,000
New electrical and heating systems.......................	2,282,000
Estimated construction costs.......................$	6,110,000
Builder's general overhead @ 2%.........................	122,000
Architectural and survey fees............................	50,000
Interest during rehabilitation @ 6¾%....................	690,000
Taxes...	109,000
FHA and FNMA fees......................................	161,000
Insurance and bond premium...........................	55,000
Financing expense......................................	193,000
Title and recording.....................................	5,000
Legal and organization..................................	50,000
Builders and sponsors profit and risk.....................	755,000
Acquisition price of land and existing buildings............	2,400,000*
Total Cost..$	10,700,000
Less: Mortgage @ 90%.................................	9,630,000
Equity investment.......................................$	1,070,000
Working capital—2%....................................	214,000
Total Equity..$	1,284,000

* Includes redemption of first mortgage, investment in second mortgage, and carrying costs incurred prior to the start of the rehabilitation.

The remodeled apartments and commercial facilities would provide revenues as follows:

Type of Unit	No. of Units	Monthly rent per Unit	Annual Rent Full Occupancy
1 BR.................................	48	$116	$ 67,000
2 BR.................................	532	140	894,000
3 BR.................................	38	156	71,000
Total Residential Income.................................			$ 1,032,000
Garage, office, and store income...........................			38,000
Electricity income..			48,000
			$ 1,118,000
Less:—Estimated vacancies @ 7%......................			78,000
Total Estimated Income............................			$ 1,040,000
Expenses to be covered			
Debt servicing of mortgage—3% interest plus 1.295% amortization..			413,000
Maintenance and operating expenses...................			360,000
Taxes..			190,000
Total Expenses and Debt Service....................			$ 963,000
Return on equity (6% of $1,284,000).......................			$ 77,000

The "costs" defined by FHA included an allowance of $755,000 for builders and sponsors allowance; this could be used as part of the $1,284,000 equity requirement. Under this assumption, the sponsors would have an investment of approximately $529,000. This leverage would provide major tax advantages, since the developer would be permitted to depreciate the cost of the project improvements on a straight-line basis using a special five-year useful life period. The 125% declining-balance method could also be employed for the existing structural shell of the building. The mortgage amortization, a nondeductible expense for tax purposes, started at 1%. The allowable return would be calculated on the total equity figure, including the noncash builders and sponsors allowance.

In return for these incentives the government imposed the following restrictions on the developer:

1. Tenants eligible for rental of the units are limited to those earning a specified maximum annual income.
2. Rental rates are controlled by the FHA.
3. Cash dividends are limited to 6% of Total Equity.
4. In order to insure that lower rental housing continues to be available, the loan cannot be repaid for 20 years.

Even though Mr. Rubloff thought that rehabilitating OTG under the 221(d)(3) program might be financially attractive, he wondered if it would be worth all the "red tape" involved. He knew that congressional appropriations to the program had been minimized as a result of the Vietnam War. With construction costs increasing at an annual rate of 10%, he wondered whether it might be more attractive to finance the rehabilitation with conventional sources and then be able to start work immediately. He thought that he could get a 7% interest rate, payable over 25 years, for 80% of the estimated cost. He also believed that he could successfully increase the rents 10% over the proposed schedule under the 221(d)(3) program; even at this increased rate, the rental structure would be very competitive in the market.

EXHIBIT 1
News Coverage

CARL SANDBURG VILLAGE IS SCENE OF MARCH*

Al Raby, convenor of the Coordinating Council of Community organizations, and 50 members of the Tenants Action Council marched around Carl Sandburg village yesterday to protest what they called the deterioration of the Old Town Garden apartments.

Carl Sandburg village was selected as the target of the protest march because it was developed by the Arthur Rubloff & Company, a realty firm which holds the second mortgage on the Old Town Garden complex, said David McCullough, 27, of 1368 Sedgwick St., T.A.C. direct action coordinator.

---

* Reprinted from the *Chicago Tribune*, September 6, 1966, courtesy the *Chicago Tribune*.

EXHIBIT 1 (Continued)

Wants Pressure Used

"Rubloff, as head of the 17-man group of financiers holding the second mortgage, could exert pressure on the owners to make repairs and check the deterioration of the apartments," McCullough asserted.

Rubloff said the firm which bears his name "has absolutely no interest whatsoever" in the Old Town Garden apartments. "I—not Arthur Rubloff & Company—own an infinitesimally small interest in a second mortgage on the apartments," Rubloff said.

Rubloff, who labeled attempts to connect him directly with ownership of the buildings as irresponsible, said his interest does not allow him to dictate how the apartments should be managed.

Withhold Their Rent

On Aug. 1, 347 tenants in the 684-unit complex in the 1400 block of Sedgwick street withheld their rent to protest management of the buildings. The complex is owned by Hanover Equities corporation, New York City.

McCullough said T.A.C. plans to park a truck loaded with furniture of an evicted family in front of City Hall later this week to prod city officials into taking a stand in the group's fight.

Rubloff Calls TAC Pickets "Irresponsible"

Arthur Rubloff Wednesday characterized as "irresponsible" the Tuesday picketing of his Loop offices by the Tenants Action Council of Old Town Garden Apartments.

Although he is one of a group of Chicagoans who hold a 10-year, $1,500,000 second mortgage on the Near North apartments, Rubloff said he had not served as rental agent since 1959 when the project was sold to Hanover Equities, an Eastern concern.

"I have no control over the present owners. I couldn't do anything, if I wanted," Rubloff declared.

"Met Payments Promptly"

"They have met their payments promptly on interest and principal. I can't foreclose on any mortgage."

He said that after hearing rumors, he sent engineers from his firm to inspect the property, as late as two weeks ago. They found no "waste," he said. (He was using the term in a legal sense, referring to property wastage for which owners might be responsible.)

"There was nothing we could do; nothing we could hang our hats on," he added. The veteran real estate operator, developer of Carl Sandburg Village and manager of many Chicago properties said, "the rents at Old Town Garden are very low. This economic factor may determine the quality of maintenance."

EXHIBIT 1 (Concluded)

Rubloff said he believes there is nothing more degrading than to be considered a slum landlord. It was in that connection that he labeled the TAC picketing "irresponsible."

The Old Town Garden tenants have recourse, said Rubloff. "They pay very little rent. If they are dissatisfied, they can move.

"If they could get what they want, there would be no real estate business in America."

Relates Meeting

A T.A.C. spokesman, co-ordinator David McCullough of 1368 N. Sedgwick, said it was incorrect for Rubloff "to equate picketing with irresponsibility. We contacted Mr. Rubloff by letter three months ago, later met with his lawyers and requested an inspection of the buildings."

He said when T.A.C. first picketed Rubloff's offices a week ago, a lawyer for Rubloff talked on the street with T.A.C. officers. McCullough said the lawyer told them that Rubloff that day had sent a telegram to Hanover Equities asking that a representative meet him on the issue.

"His lawyers have never denied Mr. Rubloff's interest and responsibility as a second mortgagor for the property," McCullough said.

EXHIBIT 2

Proposed Rehabilitation

Old Town Garden Apartments
Notes Re: *Architectural Rehabilitation*

Housing Block

> Size–263'-9" $\times$ 938'-10" = 247,265 S.F. = 5.676 acres
>
> Zoned West ½–R-5 = 400 SF/DU . . . . .307 DU
> East ½–B 4-3-400 SF/DU . . . . .307 DU
> Permitted under present zoning . . . .$\overline{614}$ DU
> Total apts. in existing housing block . . . . .628 DU

Garage Site Across Street

> 75' $\times$ 204' plus 75' $\times$ 102' = 22,950 SF = .526 acres
> Zoned C 1-3
> C 1-3 = FAR-3
> Parking required by zoning = 75% = 470 cars.

A. Re: *Parking*

Available in present garage—163 cars on 4 levels. Because there is available on-street parking, and also parking in public lots to the west, it is proposed to not increase the off-street parking at the present time. This decision results from the fact that the present off-street (garage) parking is under-used now. Only about 120 spaces are now rented.

EXHIBIT 2 (Continued)

B. Re: *General Development Plan Residential*

1. New heating plant arrangement so that costs are normal for low-rise housing.
2. Reorganize building maintenance so janitor costs are normal for low-rise housing.
3. Re-furnish apartments for tenant appeal, and so maintenance costs are minimum, i.e. interior work should bring units to first class, like-new condition.

   a) New baths to include: ceramic tile, tub, lavatory, vanity cabinet.
   b) New kitchens to include: cabinets, refrigerator, range and space for washer, dryer and dish washer.
   c) Stairwells—minor changes.
   d) New call and communication system.
   e) New decorating.
   f) Rehabilitate all windows and weather strip.
   g) Hot water radiation.
   h) New first class electrical service to Chicago Code new construction standards.
   i) New trash chutes to replace garbage dumb waiter system.
   j) Adequate closets.
   k) Some combined LR & DR, but present plans may be preferable in some cases.
   l) Floor covering: new vinyl asbestos in kitchen; new ceramic tile in baths.

C. Re: *Public Spaces*

1. Rationalize entrance control pattern.
2. Develop adequate child care facility (Day Care).
3. Develop adequate crafts rooms.
4. Develop attractive adult community room and auditorium.
5. Make stores attractive for studio, gallery, small commercial, or office tenants. The Sedgwick stores cannot be residential type studios under B 4–5 Zoning.
6. Develop the court area landscape to high standards.

D. Re: *Financial Plan*

1. Preliminary d-3 projections indicate a workable project with replacement cost at $10,800,000 = $9,800,000 mtg. equals $15,500 per D.U.

   a) The above is based on new mortgage to cover mortgage at $1,050,000; 2nd mortgage $1,450,000 equity at approximately $300,000 = $2,800,000.
   b) F.H.A. redeveloped equity undetermined. This will be resolved in part from builders-sponsors profits and risk, and compensation for some equity other than the second mortgage (possibly $300,000 as above).

EXHIBIT 2 (Continued)

2. The above preliminary projections are made on the basis of maximum 221 d-3 rents. There is a high percentage of 1-bedroom apartments (58%). It should be noted that the 1-bedroom units average 3¾ rooms, higher than most new projects.

E. Re: *General Architecture*

The objective within apartments is to produce units with desirable rental characteristics—good room layouts—good kitchens and baths.

A major expenditure should be directed toward making exciting architectural additions or revisions to the project so that the whole character and atmosphere is much upgraded.

F. Re: *Garage*

The available parking spaces in the existing garage are 163 cars. The Chicago Code requires 75% of 628 DU = 470 cars.

The present parking demand for garage spaces is about 120 cars. The garage requires so much personnel that it is uneconomic to operate. Because the operating picture would not improve much if more garage space were added, it is recommended that the parking provisions be developed off-site on land to become available thru community and city programs. Actually there is sufficient on-street parking to serve the project.

G. Re: *Elevators*

The installation of elevators to apartments was considered, and judged not feasible because of the large number of elevators required: and the difficulty of installation. Each of the 10 buildings contains between 60 and 66 apartments served from five-stair halls. Elevator service would necessitate 50 elevators for 628 apartments, an abnormal ratio.

H. Re: *Entry Gates and Central Security Station*

The problem of tenant security in the changing neighborhood has been a matter of concern to the management of the project. This problem requires a solution which will satisfy the security requirements and at the same time not be unworkable to the management. The solution is to employ a system of enclosed gates provided for the purpose of surveying each entrant to the apartment complex. One set of gates at the main entrance to each building provides a heated station which contains an Apartment Call Panel for each building; an electrically operated door; and a closed circuit television camera to survey each entrant.

Other gates are provided at intermediate points between buildings. These are similar except that the Apartment Call Panel provides for communication with all other buildings in the project.

This system of gates would serve the tenant's need to enter the project from the street quickly. The controlled surveillance of any entrant could be maintained at a central station requiring a minimum of personnel.

The central security station would best be located within management

EXHIBIT 2 (Concluded)

offices either in or near the project. This station would contain the television monitor and other equipment related to security.

I. Re: *Vacancy Rate of Fifth-Floor Apartments*

The current Vacancy Schedule shown elsewhere in this report indicates that the upper floor apartments do not suffer because of their location in the buildings. A nominal decrease in rental for the upper apartments should serve to offset the higher location.

PLAZA DRIVE
APARTMENTS

Mr. James Allison had just received the following memorandum material from H. D. Davis & Co. outlining a proposed limited partnership investment in a federal government "221(d)(3)" subsidized housing project. Mr. Allison had dealt extensively with H. D. Davis & Co., a very well-known investment banking firm that provided a full-range of financial services and opportunities for its clients. In this particular investment proposal, Mr. Allison was interested in assessing the risks related to the excellent returns that were seemingly available to a high-tax-bracket investor such as himself.

In the first instance, he wondered if the market for urban renewal housing units was sufficient to absorb the added supply of 200 additional units in the proposed area. Even if a potential market were available, Mr. Allison did not know if the rental ranges provided for in the memorandum would be satisfactory for low-income tenants or whether rent levels would be high enough to offset future increased expenses and taxes which did not seem to be reflected in the financial projections.

Mr. Allison was aware of the reputations of Hampton Enterprises and Burton Builders. Both firms were well respected and financially strong companies that had extensive experience in the construction and financial arrangements related to "221(d)(3)" projects. He was concerned, however, about the later management of the property and the tenant selection procedure to be employed. He felt that the tenant structure should be integrated and that, as nearly as possible, proper screening should be effected to get a desirable tenant group that would aid in keeping the apartments maintained properly for the realization of projected revenues.

Mr. Allison had other questions that he felt he could get help on from some of his business associates. He was convinced that Grimm, Marsh, and Dodd's legal opinion related to ownership and allocation of losses was correct. Nevertheless, he felt that he would check the tax consequences with his attorney. He also wanted to find out more about FHA regulations and loan requirements before he made a decision. Last of all, Mr. Allison wanted some assistance in reaching a conclusion about the return on investment calculations provided in the financial work by the large accounting firm of Young & Young.

He hoped to find an answer to these questions, and any other problem areas proposed by his business associates within the next few weeks. At that time, he would have to make a final decision about the investment of his capital in the proposed limited partnership interest.

MEMORANDUM PROPOSAL FOR URBAN RENEWAL "221(d)(3)" HOUSING PROJECT LIMITED-PARTNERSHIP INTERESTS
(Eight Units at $53,500 Each)[1]

Purpose: Proceeds will be used to acquire approximately 18 acres on Plaza Drive in St. Louis, Missouri, and to construct thereon 16 buildings containing a total of 202 apartment housing units.

    The buildings will have a gross floor area of 207,542 square feet and a net rentable area of 76,528 square feet. There will be 6 one-bedroom units, 140 two-bedroom units and 56 three-bedroom units. Monthly rentals will range from $85.75 to $116.

Total Cost:

a)	The Partnership	$ 428,000
b)	The Lenders	2,786,700
c)	Total	$3,214,700

Developer: Hampton Enterprises.
Builder: Burton Builders, Inc.
Architect: Young-Carlisle Associates.
General Partners:
    a) Hampton Properties, Inc. (a subsidiary of Hampton Enterprises).
    b) Burton Builders, Inc.
Mortgagee: Government National Mortgage Association (permanent financing).
Takedown of Monies:
    a) Admission as limited partner (on or about January 1970) = $15,000
    b) On or about July 1970 = $12,000
    c) On or about January 1971 = $12,000
    d) On or about July 1971 = $14,500 (approximately)[1]
Allocation of Benefits:
    a) Limited partners receive 100% of the cash flow, and profits and losses through approximately the 25th year.
    b) Thereafter, limited partners receive 50% (Hampton Ventures and Burton Builders, Inc., receive the other 50%) of the cash flow, profits and losses.
    c) Limited partners receive 50% of the residual proceeds upon the sale of the Project.

---

[1] Subject to reduction in the event the principal amount of the mortgage at final endorsement is reduced by more than $29,000.

Rate of Return: *Based on the assumptions contained in this memorandum,* it is estimated that the limited-partnership interests will earn the following after-tax annual rates of return:

Limited Partner's Tax Bracket	After-Tax Annual Rate of Return
50%	14.0%
70%	23.0%

Other:

a) Construction Guaranties: Hampton Properties and Burton will furnish any additional funds necessary to complete construction. Such additional funds will be evidenced by Residual Receipts Obligations and will not change the respective interests of the partners.

b) Subordinated Loans: In the event that the partnership should require funds for normal operating expenses in addition to funds provided by rental income, Hampton Properties and Burton agree to make subordinated loans up to certain limits.

Description of the Project

This memorandum summarizes a proposed transaction in which a group of individual or corporate investors (the Investors) will acquire all the limited-partnership interests in a limited partnership (the Partnership) organized to construct and operate a "221(d)(3)" housing project (the Project) in St. Louis, Missouri consisting of 202 housing units in 16 garden apartment buildings. The general partners of the Partnership are Hampton Properties, Inc. (Properties), which is a subsidiary corporation of Hampton Enterprises (Hampton) and Burton Builders, Inc. (Burton) a corporation owned by Elliot Burton.

The land on which the Project is to be built is located on Plaza Drive in St. Louis, Missouri, and is presently owned by Hampton Enterprises. The general contractor of the Project is Burton Builders, Inc.

Construction of the Project will begin on February 1, 1970, and, based upon present projections, it is anticipated that construction will be completed in approximately 18 months.

A commitment to furnish construction financing for the Project in the principal amount of $2,786,700 (the construction loan) and bearing interest at the rate of 7.5% per annum has been issued by the Loan Association of St. Louis. In addition, two discount points will be amortized over the construction period. The Partnership will pay the two discount points to be amortized over the construction period after the investors have been admitted as the limited partners, and the projections and statements concerning tax consequences and rates of return in this memorandum and accompanying exhibits have been computed assuming that such admission will occur prior to the payment of such discount points.

Permanent financing in the amount of the construction loan will be supplied by the Government National Mortgage Association (GNMA). Such financing will bear interest at the rate of 3% per annum. One discount point will be amortized over the 40 years during which the mortgage on the Project is amortized.

The FHA will insure the mortgage note (the Mortgage Note) evidencing the loan, including advances under the Mortgage Note during the construction period. In return for the reduction of economic risk afforded by the FHA insurance, the Partnership must operate the Project subject to FHA regulations, one of which limits the distribution of cash flow. The limitation is presently a 6% before-tax return on equity. Equity is defined in the following manner: Equity is 11.11% of the maximum amount of the Mortgage Note or $309,602. Therefore, maximum cash flow available for distribution is 6% of $309,602 or $18,576.

Until the Investors have recouped from cash flow from normal operations and from other cash distributions of the Partnership an amount equal to their investment in the Partnership, including H. D. Davis & Co., fees and expenses, 100% of the profits and losses of the Partnership and 100% of the cash flow permitted to be distributed (i.e., under the present 6% limitation—$18,576) will be distributed to the Investors. Thereafter, the Investors' interest in the profits and losses and cash flow of the Partnership will be reduced to 50%, and Properties' and Burton's interest will be 50%. The net proceeds of any sale or refinancing of the Project or any portion thereof prior to, or in connection with, any liquidation of the Partnership will be distributed after payment of, or reservation for, Partnership debts and liabilities, in the following order of priority, (i) to the payment of the Subordinated Loans (hereinafter defined); (ii) to the payment to the Investors of amounts equal to their investment in the Partnership, less any previous distributions; (iii) to the payment of Residual Receipts Obligations (hereinafter defined); and (iv) 50% to Properties and Burton and 50% to the Investors.

Profits and losses will be determined in accordance with the accounting methods followed by the Partnership for federal income tax purposes. To the extent advantageous to the partners and permitted by applicable laws and regulations, the Partnership will use accelerated depreciation methods, and will elect to treat as an expense, for tax purposes, all interest and real estate taxes during the period of construction. The Partnership will be on the accrual basis, and its fiscal year will be the calendar year. Each partner will be furnished annually with financial statements of the Partnership and all necessary tax information, prepared by any independent certified public accountant as may be selected by the general partners and with the prior written consent of at least 51% of the limited partners.

Properties and Burton will be responsible for all dealings with and compliance with the rules and regulations of the FHA, including the approval and allocation of funds by the FHA. In the event that the loan and the capital contributions of the Investors are not sufficient to complete the Project to the satisfaction of the FHA, GNMA, and any other appropriate agency. Properties and Burton have jointly and severally agreed to provide advances to satisfy the costs of construction, interest charges, and all other expenses relating to the construction of the Project. Such advances will be evidenced by certain obligations of the Partnership (Residual Receipts Obligations) which will be reimbursed upon distribution of the assets of the Partnership. Payment of such advances by Properties and/or Burton will not change the respective interests of the partners in the Partnership and will not affect the obligation of Properties and Burton to make Subordinated Loans (as hereinafter defined) to the Partnership after completion of construction.

If the Partnership should require funds for normal operating expenses after completion of construction, Properties and Burton have agreed jointly and severally to lend funds (Subordinated Loans) to the Partnership on a declining basis. The Subordinated Loans will be evidenced by notes which will be payable out of cash flow before distribution of cash flow to the partners and also out of any other available funds of the Partnership before distributions to the partners. The Subordinated Loans will bear interest at the prime rate from time to time in effect at the bank in which the Partnership maintains its major accounts.

Supervision of the Project will be the responsibility of Properties and Burton. The Limited Partnership Agreement provides that these general partners have the sole right to manage the business of the Partnership. However, the Limited Partnership Agreement provides that the general partners may sell or refinance the Project only with the prior written consent of 51% in interest of the limited partners.

The two sources of funds for the Project are (1) the Investors as limited partners providing $428,000 and (2) GNMA providing $2,786,700 for a total of $3,214,700. Such funds are expected to be applied as follows: the land—$36,612; improvements to the land—$423,600; construction of the Project—$2,063,712; closing expenses—$81,817; carrying charges—$212,486; and payments to Properties and Burton and H. D. Davis & Company—$428,000.

In order to acquire a $53,500-unit investment in the Partnership (a Partnership Investment Unit), each Investor will be required to contribute to the Partnership on or about the date of his admission as a limited partner $15,000 to cover his proportionate share of incurred and pending expenses of the Partnership including H. D. Davis & Co. fee. Based upon present projections, an Investor subscribing to a Partnership Investment

Unit will be required to make three additional installments of his contribution as follows: Two installments during the construction of $12,000 each, and a final installment, upon the final insurance endorsement (Final Endorsement) of the Mortgage Note by the FHA, which is projected to be $14,500. The total amount which the Investors will be required to contribute to the Partnership (not including that portion of their capital contribution paid by the Partnership to H. D. Davis & Co.) will be equal to 11.1% of the principal amount of the Mortgage Note at the initial insurance endorsement (Initial Endorsement) of the Mortgage Note by the FHA. In the event the principal amount of the Mortgage Note at Final Endorsement is reduced by $29,000 or more, the limited partners' capital contributions will be reduced by 11.1% of the reduction in excess of $29,000.

The amounts paid to H. D. Davis & Co. will be used to pay the expenses of the transaction, including counsel fees for the Investors, charges with respect to the review of the attached tables by Thomas & Thomas, printing costs and the like, and its fee. The Limited Partnership Agreement will provide that, should any Investor fail to contribute an installment when due, the remaining Investors, as limited partners (or the general partners if the remaining limited partners do not do so), will have the option to purchase his interest at 10% of the amount of his interest then shown on the books of the Partnership.

Economic Benefits

The economic incentives for investment in the Partnership are (1) an annual cash return, (2) the availability of cash from a refinancing and (3) 50% of the proceeds from the sale of the residuals.

1. *Cash Return*

It is expected that an Investor will receive a cash flow from operations of approximately 4.3% per annum on his capital contributions to the Partnership until Investment Recovery. The amount of cash flow which may be distributed annually to the Investors is presently limited by FHA regulations to 6% of the total equity (which is 11.11% of the Mortgage Note), and under this limitation, the Investment Recovery on a cash return basis will not occur prior to the 25th year after completion of construction under present regulations at the present amount of Mortgage Note. However, in the event the FHA amends its regulations to permit larger distributions, the cash flow to the investors will be increased and Investment Recovery will be accelerated accordingly. After Investment Recovery, an Investor will receive a cash flow from operations of approximately 2.1% per annum on his capital contribution to the Partnership.

2. Refinancing

After 20 years from the Final Endorsement, refinancing of the mortgage is permitted without prior FHA approval. Under present laws and pursuant to the Partnership agreement, 50% of the excess cash generated from such a refinancing would be distributed to the Investors without tax consequences after such proceeds have been applied to Investment Recovery and to pay the outstanding Subordinated Loans and Residual Receipts Obligations.

3. Residual Values

The Investors will be entitled to 50% of the balance of the proceeds from the sale of the residuals after such proceeds have been applied to Investment Recovery and to pay the outstanding Residual Receipts Obligation and Subordinated Loans. However, no assurance can be given as to the value of the residuals.

Each Investor will be required to represent that his contribution to the Partnership is being made for investment without any view to the distribution thereof.

Each investor will receive an opinion of Messrs. Grimm, Marsh & Dodd to the effect that (1) the Partnership will be considered the owner of the Project for federal tax purposes and (2) subsequent to becoming a limited partner in the Partnership, such Investor will be entitled to deduct his allocable share of the Partnership losses, including Partnership losses attributable to allowable interest and depreciation deductions.

Return Analysis and Federal Tax Implications

General

The computations and tax sections set forth in this memorandum are for convenience only. Each Investor should seek, and must depend upon, the advice of his tax counsel or accountants with respect to his investment in the Partnership (and be responsible for the fees of such counsel and accountants). H. D. Davis & Co., Messrs. Grimm, Marsh & Dodd, and Thomas & Thomas assume no responsibility for the tax consequences of this transaction.

The various schedules, projections, and statements concerning tax consequences and analytical presentations contained herein are set forth only for the purposes of convenience and illustration. It should be noted that such computations have been based upon the provisions of the Tax Reform Act of 1969. The act provides that for taxable years beginning after 1971, the maximum capital gains rate will be 25% of the first $50,000 of gains in any one year and 35% of the gains in excess of such

$50,000. In computing the amount of capital gains tax attributable to each Investor on disposition of the project, it has been assumed that each Investor has no capital gains in the year of disposition other than those arising from such disposition.

It should further be noted that the computations herein do not take into account two items of tax preference which are present in the Partnership: (1) the difference between the amount of depreciation to be claimed by the Partnership under accelerated methods of depreciation and the amount of depreciation which would be allowable under the straight-line method, and (2) any capital gains arising upon the sale of Partnership property. Each Investor should consult his own tax counsel to determine the effect of these two tax preferences on his particular tax situation.

Exhibit 1 sets forth the projection of income, expenses and resulting cash flow from the Partnership's operation of the Project and the cash flow available for distribution to the Partnership for each year during the 25-year period in which it is assumed the Partnership retains ownership of the Project, as discussed below. Exhibits 2 and 3 set forth the federal income tax consequences of a $53,500 Partnership Investment Unit. For purposes of illustration, the tax consequences applicable to a taxpayer in a 50% and 70% tax bracket have been set forth.

Rate of Return

The rate-of-return method of analytical approach assumes that all cash generated, resulting from both cash flows and tax savings realized by an Investor after return of his capital investment, plus a 14.0% return in the case of an Investor in the 50% tax bracket and a 23.0% return in the case of an Investor in the 70% tax bracket, is used to establish an account from which cash can be withdrawn in an amount sufficient to cover the taxes of such Investors attributable to the sale of the Project by the Partnership at the end of the 25th year after completion of construction. The amount of such taxes per Partnership Investment Unit would be approximately $32,478.22 to an Investor in the 50% tax bracket and approximately $40,469.51 to an Investor in the 70% tax bracket, assuming a sale at the end of the year for $1 above the unamortized balance of the Mortgage Note.

However, by this approach, it is assumed that tax savings are not contributed to the voluntary fund until as late a point in time as necessary. As illustrated in columns "E" and "J" of Exhibit 3, this point does not occur until approximately 11.75 years after the final equity contribution, in the case of an Investor in the 50% tax bracket and approximately 10.75 years in the case of an Investor in the 70% bracket. Thereafter, all remaining tax savings and the approximate 4.3 annual cash flow return are contributed to the voluntary fund, which it is assumed will be invested at a 4.5% after-tax yield. The voluntary fund will be sufficient to pay the taxes resulting from the sale of the Project as discussed above. The net effect of the foregoing is to leave the Investor with the cash flows and tax savings received during the earlier years equal to the total amounts set forth in columns "B" and "C" of Schedule C in the case of the 50% tax bracket Investor and in columns "G" and "H" in the case of the 70%-tax-bracket Investor.

EXHIBIT 1

Projection of Cash Requirements and Sources from Beginning of Development Through 1995*

	1970	1971	1971	1972	1973	1974
Income.....			67,342.5	269,370.0	269,370.0	269,370.0
Rent at full occupancy less 5% vacancy allowance..			3,395.6	13,582.5	13,582.5	13,582.5
Total Income..			63,946.9	255,787.5	255,787.5	255,787.5
Expenses						
Interest (A)..	61542.8	92448.3	20,877.8	82,825.1	81,703.1	80,547.1
Depreciation (B)..			46,595.4	184,751.8	178,232.2	171,712.6
Operating expenses..	38112.8	24256.3	26,619.5	106,478.0	106,478.0	106,478.0
Total Expenses..	99655.6	116,704.6	94,092.6	374,054.8	366,413.3	358,737.6
Taxable income (loss)..	(99655.6)	(116,704.6)	(30,145.7)	(118,267.3)	(110,625.8)	(102,950.1)
Cash flow from operations†..			16,449.7	66,484.4	67,606.4	68,762.4
Less: Additional cash requirements						
Mortgage principal payments..			9,050.2	36,886.4	38,008.3	39,164.4
Replacement reserve (C)..			2,755.5	11,022.0	11,022.0	11,022.0
Total Additional Cash Requirements..			11,805.7	47,908.4	49,030.3	50,186.4
Cash Flow Available for Distribution (D)..			4,644.0	18,576.1	18,576.1	18,576.1

	1975	1976	1977	1978	1979	1980
Income..	269,370.0	269,370.0	269,370.0	269,370.0	269,370.0	269,370.0
Rent at full occupancy less 5% vacancy allowance..	13,582.5	13,582.5	13,582.5	13,582.5	13,582.5	13,582.5
Total Income..	255,787.5	255,787.5	255,787.5	255,787.5	255,787.5	255,787.5
Expenses						
Interest (A)..	79,355.8	78,128.4	76,863.6	75,560.3	74,217.4	72,833.7
Depreciation (B)..	165,193.0	158,673.3	152,153.7	145,634.1	139,114.5	132,594.9
Operating expenses..	106,478.0	106,478.0	106,478.0	106,478.0	106,478.0	106,478.0
Total Expenses..	351,026.8	343,279.7	335,495.3	327,672.5	319,810.0	311,906.6
Taxable income (loss)..	(95,239.3)	(87,492.2)	(79,707.8)	(71,885.0)	(64,022.5)	(56,119.1)
Cash flow from operations†..	69,953.7	71,181.1	72,445.9	73,749.2	75,092.1	76,475.8
Less: Additional cash requirements						
Mortgage principal payments..	40,355.6	41,583.0	42,847.8	44,151.1	45,494.0	46,877.7
Replacement reserve (C)..	11,022.0	11,022.0	11,022.0	11,022.0	11,022.0	11,022.0
Total Additional Cash Requirements..	51,377.6	52,605.0	53,869.8	55,173.1	56,516.0	57,899.7
Cash Flow Available for Distribution (D)..	18,576.1	18,576.1	18,576.1	18,576.1	18,576.1	18,576.1

	1981	1982	1983	1984	1985
Income					
Rent at full occupancy less 5% vacancy allowance	269,370.0	269,370.0	269,370.0	269,370.0	269,370.0
	13,582.5	13,582.5	13,582.5	13,582.5	13,582.5
Total Income	255,787.5	255,787.5	255,787.5	255,787.5	255,787.5
Expenses					
Interest (A)	71,407.9	69,938.7	68,424.8	66,864.8	65,257.5
Depreciation (B)	126,075.3	119,555.7	113,036.1	106,843.1	101,630.2
Operating expenses	106,478.0	106,478.0	106,478.0	106,478.0	106,478.0
Total Expenses	303,961.2	295,972.4	287,938.9	280,186.0	273,365.7
Taxable income (loss)	(48,173.7)	(40,184.9)	(32,151.4)	(24,398.5)	(17,578.2)
Cash flow from operations†	77,901.6	79,370.8	80,884.7	82,444.7	84,052.0
Less: Additional cash requirements					
Mortgage principal payments	48,303.6	49,772.8	51,286.6	52,846.6	54,454.0
Replacement reserve (C)	11,022.0	11,022.0	11,022.0	11,022.0	1,022.0
Total Additional Cash Requirements	59,325.6	60,794.8	62,308.6	63,868.6	65,476.0
Cash Flow Available for Distribution (D)	18,576.1	18,576.1	18,576.1	18,576.1	18,576.1

	1986	1987	1988	1989	1990	1991
Income						
Rent at full occupancy less 5% vacancy allowance	269,370.0	269,370.0	269,370.0	269,370.0	269,370.0	269,370.0
	13,582.5	13,582.5	13,582.5	13,582.5	13,582.5	13,582.5
Total Income	255,787.5	255,787.5	255,787.5	255,787.5	255,787.5	255,787.5
Expenses						
Interest (A)	63,601.2	61,894.5	60,136.0	58,324.0	56,456.8	54,532.8
Depreciation (B)	96,417.2	91,204.3	85,991.3	80,778.4	75,565.4	70,352.5
Operating Expenses	106,478.0	106,478.0	106,478.0	106,478.0	106,478.0	106,478.0
Total Expenses	266,496.4	259,576.8	252,605.3	245,580.4	238,500.2	231,363.3
Taxable income (loss)	(10,708.9)	(3,789.3)	3,182.2	10,207.1	17,287.3	24,424.2
Cash flow from operations†	85,708.3	87,414.9	89,173.5	90,985.5	92,852.7	94,776.7
Less: Additional cash requirements						
Mortgage principal payments	56,110.2	57,816.9	59,575.4	61,387.5	63,254.6	65,178.6
Replacement reserve (C)	11,022.0	11,022.0	11,022.0	11,022.0	11,022.0	11,022.0
Total Additional Cash Requirements	67,132.2	68,838.9	70,597.4	72,409.5	74,276.6	76,200.6
Cash Flow Available for Distribution (D)	18,576.1	18,576.1	18,576.1	18,576.1	18,576.1	18,576.1

* The assumed date of disposition of the Project is the end of calendar year 1995.
† Cash flow from operations equal total income minus total expenses other than depreciation, which is a noncash expense. For example, in 1971, cash flow from operations in the amount of $16,449.70 is derived as follows: $63,946.90 − ($94,092.60 − $46,595.40) = $63,946.90 − $47,497.20 = $16,449.70.

EXHIBIT 1 (Continued)

	1992	1993	1994	1995
Income..................................				
Rent at full occupancy less 5% vacancy allowance.....	269,370.0	269,370.0	269,370.0	269,370.0
	13,582.5	13,582.5	13,852.5	13,852.5
Total Income..............................	255,787.5	255,787.5	255,787.5	255,787.5
Expenses				
Interest (A)...............................	52,550.4	50,507.6	48,402.7	46,233.8
Depreciation (B)..........................	65,165.0	60,054.1	54,943.1	49,832.1
Operating expenses........................	106,478.0	106,478.0	106,478.0	106,478.0
Total Expenses........................	224,193.4	217,039.7	209,823.8	202,543.9
Taxable income (loss)......................	31,594.1	38,747.8	45,963.7	53,243.6
Cash flow from operations†.................	96,759.1	98,801.9	100,906.8	103,075.7
Less additional cash requirements				
Mortgage principal payments..............	67,161.0	69,203.8	71,308.7	73,477.6
Replacement reserve (C).................	11,022.0	11,022.0	11,022.0	11,022.0
Total Additional Cash Requirements.....	78,183.0	80,225.8	82,330.7	84,499.6
Cash Flow Available for Distribution (D).....	18,576.1	18,576.1	18,576.1	18,576.1

† Cash flow from operations equal total income minus total expenses other than depreciation, which is a noncash expense. For example, in 1971, cash flow from operations in the amount of $16,449.70 is derived as follows: $63,946.90 − ($94,092.60 − $46,595.40) = $63,946.90 − $47,497.20 = $16,449.70.

Footnotes to Exhibit 1

(A) Computation of interest on the loan assumes a linear takedown schedule over the estimated 18-month construction period. For purposes of illustration, Exhibit 1 indicates that the 18-month construction period is completed on July 30, 1970, and that the allocation of such construction interest to the Investors commences in the ninth month of such construction period.

(B) Depreciation expense was calculated using the sum-of-years'-digits method of depreciation for the life of the asset. The following is a summary of the depreciable property:

1. Building:

Total All Improvements.......................	$2,329,454.00	
Architect fees and FHA inspection fee......	102,339.00	
Title and recording........................	10,920.00	
Legal expense (organizational).............	14,200.00	
Allocable proportion of payments to Properties, Burton, and H. D. Davis & Co......	410,349.00	
Total for Building........................	$2,867,262.00	33-year life

2. Kitchen equipment...........................

Allocable proportion of payments to ventures, etc....	$ 87,333.00	
Total Kitchen Equipment..................	14,586.00	
	$ 101,919.00	12-year life

3. Landscaping.................................

Allocable proportion of payments to ventures, etc....	$ 18,348.00	
Total Landscaping........................	3,065.00	
	$ 21,413.00	20-year life

(C) Replacement Reserve. It is assumed that the Replacement Reserve is invested in a 2% after-tax fund. One replacement is made in 1985 for $110,000. These funds are used to replace kitchen equipment and other items. One replacement is transferred to the new owners as one of the assets that they have purchased. The balance in the Replacement Reserve at the date of disposition is transferred to the new owners as one of the assets that they have purchased.

	1971	1972	1973	1974	1975	1976
1. Replacement Reserve additions	2,755.5	11,022.0	11,022.0	11,022.0	11,022.0	11,022.0
2. Income on Replacement Reserve		138.5	363.4	592.8	826.8	1,065.6
3. Less: Replacements		0	0	0	0	0
4. Total Replacement Reserve	2,755.5	13,916.0	25,301.3	39,616.1	48,764.9	60,852.5

	1977	1978	1979	1980	1981
1.	11,022.0	11,022.0	11,022.0	11,022.0	11,022.0
2.	1,309.1	1,557.6	1,811.1	2,069.7	2,333.5
3.	0	0	0	0	0
4.	73,183.6	85,761.3	98,596.4	111,688.1	125,043.6

	1982	1983	1984	1985	1986
1.	11,022.0	11,022.0	11,022.0	11,022.0	11,022.0
2.	2,602.6	2,877.2	3,157.3	1,784.7	1,484.5
3.	0	0	0	110,000.0	0
4.	138,668.2	152,557.4	166,746.7	69,553.4	82,059.8

	1987	1988	1989	1990	1991
1.	11,022.0	11,022.0	11,022.0	11,022.0	11,022.0
2.	1,736.5	1,993.6	2,255.8	2,523.4	2,756.4
3.	0	0	0	0	0
4.	94,818.3	107,833.9	121,111.8	134,657.2	148,475.5

	1992	1993	1994	1995
1.	11,022.0	11,022.0	11,022.0	11,022.0
2.	3,074.8	3,358.9	3,648.6	3,944.3
3.	0	0	0	0
4.	162,572.3	176,953.2	191,623.8	206,590.1

(D) This amount represents cash flow available for distribution to the entire Partnership. The limited dividend of $18,576 goes to the Investor until Investment Recovery on a cash return basis. After Investment Recovery, 50% of the $18,576 or $9,288 goes to the Investors and 50% to Properties and Burton. An individual investor's share is 12.5% of $18,576 or $2,322 prior to Investment Recovery and after Investment Recovery is $1,161 (See column A of Schedule B).

EXHIBIT 2

Projection of Taxable Income and Cash Generated per Partnership Investment Unit
(one unit = 12.5% of the project)

Year	A Cash* Flow	B Taxable† Income	C Tax Savings 50%	D Tax Savings 70%	E Cash Generated‡ 50% (A + C)	F Cash Generated‡ 70% (A + D)
1970........	0	−12,456.99	6,228.50	8,719.90	6,228.50	8,719.90
1971........	0	−14,587.71	7,293.86	10,211.40	7,293.86	10,211.40
1971........	580.50	− 3,768.21	1,884.11	2,637.75	2,464.67	3,218.25
1972........	2,322.01	−14,783.42	7,391.71	10,348.39	9,713.72	12,670.40
1973........	2,322.01	−13,828.22	6,914.11	9,679.76	9,236.12	12,001.77
1974........	2,322.01	−12,868.76	6,434.38	9,008.14	8,756.39	11,330.14
1975........	2,322.01	−11,904.91	5,952.46	8,333.44	8,274.47	10,655.45
1976........	2,322.01	−10,936.53	5,468.26	7,655.57	7,790.27	9,977.58
1977........	2,322.01	− 9,963.48	4,981.74	6,974.44	7,303.75	9,296.44
1978........	2,322.01	− 8,985.62	4,492.81	6,289.93	6,814.82	8,611.94
1979........	2,322.01	− 8,002.81	4,001.40	5,601.97	6,323.41	7,923.97
1980........	2,322.01	− 7,014.89	3,507.44	4,910.42	5,829.45	7,323.43
1981........	2,322.01	− 6,021.71	3,010.85	4,215.20	5,322.86	6,537.21
1982........	2,322.01	− 5,023.11	2,511.55	3,516.18	4,833.56	5,838.18
1983........	2,322.01	− 4,018.92	2,009.46	2,813.24	4,331.47	5,135.25
1984........	2,322.01	− 3,049.81	1,524.91	2,134.87	3,846.92	4,456.88
1985........	2,322.01	− 2,197.27	1,098.64	1,538.09	3,420.64	3,860.10
1986........	2,322.01	− 1,338.62	669.31	937.03	2,991.32	3,259.04
1987........	2,322.01	− 473.67	236.83	331.57	2,558.84	2,653.58
1988........	2,322.01	397.77	− 198.88	− 278.44	2,123.12	2,043.57
1989........	2,322.01	1,275.89	− 637.95	− 893.13	1,684.06	1,428.88
1990........	2,322.01	2,160.91	−1,080.45	−1,512.63	1,241.56	809.37
1991........	2,322.01	3,053.02	−1,526.51	−2,137.11	795.50	184.90
1992........	2,322.01	3,949.26	−1,974.63	−2,764.48	347.38	− 442.47
1993........	2,322.01	4,843.48	−2,421.74	−3,390.44	− 99.73	−1,068.43
1994........	2,322.01	5,745.46	−2,872.73	−4,021.83	−550.72	−1,699.82
1995........	1,161.00	3,327.73	−1,663.86	−2,329.41	−502.86	−1,168.40

† The minus signs before the figures in this column indicate an Investor's proportionate share of tax losses resulting from the excess of total expenses (including depreciation) over total income in the Project.

‡ Cash generated is equal to the sum of (i) cash flow (column "A") and (ii) tax savings (column "C" for a 50%-tax-bracket Investor and column "D" for a 70%-tax-bracket Investor.

* After Investment Recovery in 1994, one unit of investment in the partnership will equal 12.5% of 50% of the Project.

EXHIBIT 3
50% Tax Bracket
Return on Investment with Assumed Reserve Fund
Invested at 4½% After Taxes to Fund Future Tax Payments

	A	B	C	D	E Reserve Fund (B)		
Year	Cash Generated	Return on Investment* at 14%	Return of Investment	Unrecovered Investment	Benefits Invested and Tax Payments	Assumed 4½% After-Tax Income	Fund Balance
1970	6,228.50	2,568.47	− 8 339.97*	23,339.97	0	0	0
1971	7,293.86	2,773.54	− 21 979.68*	45,319.66	0	0	0
1971	2,464.61	1,585.30	879.31	44,440.35	0	0	0
1972	9,713.72	6,030.45	3 683.27	40,757.09	0	0	0
1973	9,236.12	5,513.05	3 723.07	37,034.02	0	0	0
1974	8,756.39	4,989.90	3 766.49	33,267.52	0	0	0
1975	8,274.47	4,460.46	3 814.00	29,453.52	0	0	0
1976	7,790.27	3,924.14	3 866.13	25,587.39	0	0	0
1977	7,303.75	3,380.26	3 923.43	21,663.90	0	0	0
1978	6,814.82	2,828.06	3 986.76	17,677.14	0	0	0
1979	6,323.41	2,266.65	4 056.76	13,620.38	0	0	0
1980	5,829.45	1,695.07	4 134.38	9,486.00	0	0	0
1981	5,332.86	1,112.18	4 220.68	5,265.32	0	0	0
1982	4,833.56	516.71	4 316.85	948.46	0	0	0
1983	4,331.47	33.18	948.46	0	3,349.83	40.14	3,389.97
1984	3,846.92	0	0	0	3,846.92	220.55	7,457.43
1985	3,420.64	0	0	0	3,420.64	399.45	11,277.52
1986	2,991.32	0	0	0	2,991.32	566.97	14,835.82
1987	2,558.84	0	0	0	2,558.84	722.47	18,117.13
1988	2,123.12	0	0	0	2,123.12	865.23	21,105.48
1989	1,684.06	0	0	0	1,684.06	994.53	23,784.07
1990	1,241.56	0	0	0	1,241.56	1,109.59	26,135.22
1991	795.50	0	0	0	795.50	1,209.51	28,140.32
1992	347.38	0	0	0	347.38	1,293.75	28,781.45
1993	− 99.73	0	0	0	− 99.73	1,361.26	31,042.98
1994	− 550.72	0	0	0	− 550.72	1,411.32	31,903.57
1995	− 502.86	0	0	0	− 32,981.08	1,451.52	374.02

* See notes to Exhibit 3.

EXHIBIT 3 (Continued)
70% Tax Bracket

	F	G	H	I	J Reserve Fund (B)		
		Return on			Benefited	Assumed 4½%	
	Cash	Investment*	Return of	Unrecovered	Invested and	After-Tax	Fund
Year	Generated	at 23%	Investment	Investment	Tax Payments	Income	Balance
1970.........	8,719.90	4,093.01	– 7,373.11	22,373.11	0	0	0
1971.........	10,211.40	4,339.54	–20,628.14*	43,001.26	0	0	0
1971.........	3,218.25	2,451.16	767.10	42,234.16	0	0	0
1972.........	12,670.40	9,359.71	3,310.69	38,923.47	0	0	0
1973.........	12,001.77	8,597.19	3,404.58	35,518.89	0	0	0
1974.........	11,330.14	7,811.63	3,518.52	32,000.38	0	0	0
1975.........	10,655.45	6,998.05	3,657.40	28,342.98	0	0	0
1976.........	9,977.58	6,150.28	3,827.30	24,515.68	0	0	0
1977.........	9,296.44	5,260.62	4,035.83	20,479.86	0	0	0
1978.........	8,611.94	4,319.49	4,292.45	16,187.45	0	0	0
1979.........	7,923.97	3,314.96	4,609.01	11,578.39	0	0	0
1980.........	7,232.43	2,232.16	5,000.27	6,578.12	0	0	0
1981.........	6,537.21	1,052.55	5,484.65	1,093.46	0	0	0
1982.........	5,838.18	62.33	1,093.46	0	4,682.39	59.81	4,742.20
1983.........	5,135.25	0	0	0	5,135.25	304.34	10,181.79
1984.........	4,456.88	0	0	0	4,456.88	541.75	15,180.42
1985.........	3,860.10	0	0	0	3,860.10	760.36	19,800.88
1986.........	3,259.04	0	0	0	3,259.04	961.60	24,021.52
1987.........	2,653.58	0	0	0	2,653.58	1,144.46	27,819.56
1988.........	2,043.57	0	0	0	2,043.57	1,307.91	31,171.04
1989.........	1,428.88	0	0	0	1,428.88	1,450.84	34,050.76
1990.........	809.37	0	0	0	809.37	1,572.10	36,432.24
1991.........	184.90	0	0	0	184.90	1,670.47	38,287.60
1992.........	442.47	0	0	0	442.47	1,744.71	39,589.84
1993.........	–1,068.43	0	0	0	– 1,068.43	1,793.67	40,315.08
1994.........	–1,699.82	0	0	0	– 1,699.82	1,816.12	40,431.39
1995.........	–1,168.40	0	0	0	–41,637.91 (D)	1,830.48	623.96

Footnotes to Exhibit 3

* It is assumed that an Investor makes his first installment of $15,000 at the beginning of construction, his second installment of $12,000 in July, 1970, his third installment of $12,000 in January, 1971, and the final installment of $14,500 in July, 1971.

(A) It is assumed that cash generated is applied quarterly in the following manner: first to return on investment at the indicated annual rate of return and second to reduce the Unrecovered Investment.

(B) Represents the amount of benefits required to be funded which, with interest compounded quarterly at the indicated rate after-tax, will be sufficient to pay the indicated taxes on a quarterly basis.

(C) Includes $502.86 of ordinary income taxes (the amount by which taxable income exceed cash flow in 1995) and $32,478.22 of tax liability derived as follows:

I. Capital Gains Tax

Assumed sales price of Project at end of 25th year after completion of construction.	$ 1.00
Add 12.5% Unamortized Loan Balance.	187,642.95
Total Sales Price.	$187,643.95
Less: 12.5% value of Replacement Reserve.	$ 25,823.76
Less: 12.5% cost of land.	4,576.50
Less: 12.5% undepreciated book value of building (straight-line).	27,311.82
	$129,912.87
Capital gains tax at 25% or taxes due on sale.	$ 32,478.22

(D) Includes $1,168.40 of ordinary income taxes (the amount by which taxes payable on taxable income exceed cash flow in 1995) and $40,469.51 of tax liability derived as follows:

I. Capital Gains Tax

Assumed sales price of Project at end of 25th year after completion of construction.	$ 1.00
Add 12.5% unamortized loan balance.	187,642.95
Total Sales Price.	$187,643.95
Less: 12.5% value of Replacement Reserve.	$ 25,823.76
Less: 12.5% cost of land.	4,576.50
Less: 12.5% undepreciated book value of building and replacements.	27,311.82
	$129,912.87
Capital gains tax at 25% on first $50,000 of gain.	$ 12,500.00
Capital gains tax at 35% on balance of gain ($79,912.87).	$ 27,969.51
Total Taxes Due on Sale.	$ 40,469.51

PART VI

New Town
Development

COLUMBIA I

In October 1962, the staff of the Connecticut General Life Insurance Company was attempting to evaluate the plan of James Rouse, president of Community Research and Development, Inc. (CRD), for the creation of a new city, Columbia, in Howard County, Maryland. Columbia was eventually to provide homes for 100,000 people plus commercial, industrial, and public facilities necessary to support them. To implement the plan would require the acquisition of over 12,000 acres of land, the planning and rezoning of the site, development financing of at least $50 million, and the assembly of an organization capable of carrying out this intricate task. Mr. Rouse had requested that Connecticut General provide the necessary financing and receive a 50% interest in the project. Connecticut General was unsure of the action it should take.

CRD itself was formed in 1957 by Mr. Rouse as a real estate development company. The management for the company was performed by the James W. Rouse & Co. (JWR), which also owned 30% of the company's stock. Started in 1939 in Baltimore, Maryland, JWR was one of the larger mortgage brokerage firms in the United States, servicing approximately $250 million of mortgages for various financial institutions. The company received fees from the borrower for placing or originating mortgages and subsequently from the lender for collecting and servicing the loan. In the year ending May 31, 1962, gross revenues had reached $1,295,000 and earnings before taxes $168,000. After World War II, the company began to specialize in the placement of government-insured residential mortgages. As these mortgages were traded on a national basis, the company opened offices in other sections of the country.

Then, as the trend to shopping center development became more prevalent, JWR became active in the placement of commercial mortgages for these centers. Convinced that there was a trend toward larger-sized regional shopping centers, built with enclosed malls, Mr. Rouse formed CRD to act as a developer specializing in this area. The enclosed mall design involves locating a number of stores on both sides of a pedestrian mall with the store fronts facing on the mall. The mall is roofed over and completely enclosed, heated, air conditioned, and landscaped to provide a more comfortable shopping environment. By October 1962, the firm had opened six shopping centers of this type. The average size of each center was 360,000 leasable square feet. In May 1962,

CRD's net cash flow from operations was $142,000, before depreciation and income taxes but after mortgage amortization, but in the next fiscal year, as a result of the opening of several additional shopping centers, the net cash flow was expected to reach $375,000.

CRD had also recently purchased a 72-acre site in the Roland Park Section of Baltimore at a price of $4 million. The site, one half of the Baltimore Country Club golf course, was planned as a small upper-income community with 600 town houses, 600 rental units, a village square, recreation areas, an inn, and an office building. The project, named Cross Keys, was the company's first venture outside shopping centers and into a mixed-use development.

NEW TOWNS

However, Mr. Rouse had been interested for some time in the development of planned communities. He had traveled extensively throughout the country and felt that the current suburban growth trends represented a wasteful and inefficient use of resources that contributed to the creation of an environment without amenities and filled with potential social hazards. Valuable tidelands and wetlands were being consumed. High-quality farmland was being submerged at the rate of 375 acres per day. The water supply was diminishing and becoming polluted through industrial waste and inadequate sewage systems. The recreation needs of our population were unsatisfied, and because of the growing shortage of well-located land, it was becoming increasingly expensive to satisfy these needs. With 25% of the national population, the Northeast had only 4% of the total recreational acreage. Once preempted by urban sprawl, the amenities of open space and undeveloped land became irretrievably lost.

Mr. Rouse felt that the problem was more than physical. There was a considerable social and psychological human toll that resulted from monotonous suburbs with little diversity of opportunity or human contact, from longer commuting time, and from inadequate facilities. The cost of providing and updating schools and other facilities was becoming a financial burden to the local communities, and as a result real estate tax rates were rising. Originally, families had fled from the cities to avoid congestion. In the cities, automobiles jammed the streets. There was no place for children to play. Schools were inadequate, and little was being done to improve them. Neighborhoods were breaking up. Life was becoming anonymous. There was crime in the streets, few playgrounds, and no place to walk. The poor and deteriorating mass transit systems made the scattered facilities even less accessible, and inadequate parking space made car ownership difficult. Because of a preponderance of apartment houses, there was little opportunity for homeownership.

However, to the surprise of the millions of families who moved to the suburbs after World War II, the suburbs were soon suffering from many of the same problems of congestion which these families had hoped to escape. The suburbs had not planned the needed public facilities and transportation systems. The suburban zoning codes established density on a per-acre basis rather than on a cluster basis. This resulted in monotonous, identical housing projects, which used up virtually all of the site. On the other hand, cluster zoning, which permitted homes to be clustered on part of the site, resulted in a more economic development, with most of the land left open for public use.

Mr. Rouse believed that both cities and suburbs had lost their human scale, failing to "produce an environment in which various institutions could work for humans in a creative way." He saw an opportunity for a sensitive businessman to utilize the skills and flexibility of private enterprise to achieve a better solution. Local government had been too weak to change development patterns. State governments had been decreasing in importance for the past 100 years, and the federal response to urban problems had normally been strong policy statements with weak following legislation. Furthermore, federal powers were inadequate to correct the problems singlehandedly. Up until now, building new communities had not been a business. The average homebuilder built only 17 homes per year, and very few built in the thousands. Mr. Rouse was convinced that "the surest way to make the American city what it ought to be is to demonstrate that it's enormously profitable to do it a better way." He was not interested merely in building a monument. He believed that market conditions were ripe for him as a businessman to become involved in city building.

The U.S. population was expected to increase from 180 million in 1960 to 262 million in 1985 and to 360 million in the year 2000. Historically, out of a total population increase of 30 million in the period 1910 to 1930, the largest portion, 6.5 million people, came in cities of over 1 million (See Exhibit 1). Between 1930 and 1960, cities of that size grew by only 2.5 million. Meanwhile, towns and cities of 50,000 to 100,000 grew by 6.5 million, places of 25,000 to 50,000 by 8.3 million, and places of 10,000 to 25,000 by 8.7 million, all out of a total population increase of 57 million. Therefore, not only did demographic data show an overall population increase, but Mr. Rouse was certain that he could predict that the bulk of that increase would be located on the urban fringes. By the year 2000, the total urban population including cities and suburbs was expected to reach 250 million, 190 million of whom were expected to live and work on these urban fringes, compared with 40 million in 1960. This incremental increase of 150 million would be equal to the entire population of the United States in 1950.

Therefore, Mr. Rouse felt that the growth in population, and the dissatisfaction with cities and the existing suburbs, presented an excellent market potential. In traveling around the world, he became convinced that a "new community" was the proper mechanism to take advantage of this potential. A planned community could be based upon prescriptive rather than repetitive or reactive forms of urban development, and could offer new opportunities to develop land economically, and in a manner that would provide a stimulating environment and relate to human needs. Mr. Rouse believed that in smaller towns, broader friendships and feelings of responsibility were developed. Communities were not "works of art" but "gardens in which we are a growing people and civilization." New communities have no "locked-in" decisions in basic facilities and structural plants that impede similar experimentation in old, densely settled cities. Moreover, the new community can plan facilities on a broader, more flexible scale because of the knowledge of its future size. As an example, economies of scale can be obtained in designing and locating sewage treatment plants, solid-waste disposal facilities, and public transportation and road networks.

The idea of planned communities is not new. In this country, Washington, D.C., and Philadelphia, Pennsylvania, started with master plans. There are now new town movements in England, France, Holland, and Scandinavia. These movements are primarily based upon the principles of the Garden City Association founded by Ebenezer Howard in England at the turn of this century. Between 1902 and 1919, a small group of investors, led by Howard, laid the foundations for two new towns in the country north of London. Successful in attracting both people and jobs, these private communities lagged because of lack of adequate capital for basic facilities. In England, the New Towns Act of 1946 was passed by Parliament to provide a broad range of subsidies and assistance through special public new town development corporations. Many were successfully built in subsequent years under this program.

In the United States, in 1918, the U.S. Housing Corporation of the Department of Labor built several projects that included a coordinated housing, industrial, and transportation scheme. These projects were later sold to private buyers. In the late 1920's, a private group influenced by Howard, and led by Clarence Stein, planned and built a new town, Radburn, N.J. The design for this town used cul-de-sac streets and connecting greenways to create a "garden" atmosphere in a mixed-use development involving residential, commercial, industrial, and public uses. However, because of a shortage of private capital during the depression, Radburn never expanded to its projected size.

During the 1930's, three open-space communities with low-income rental housing were built by the Resettlement Administration of the U.S. Department of Agriculture. The three—Greenbelt, Maryland; Greenhills, Ohio; and Greendale, Wisconsin—were all located near primary employment facilities and within commuting distance of large central cities. The purpose of their site planning was to test the greenbelt buffer concept as a solution for integrating the physical realities of the rural areas with those of the urban community. Greenbelts, which were open landscaped areas, were used to separate uses within a development and to separate the new town from adjacent towns. This prevented the creation of sprawl, where one identical-looking community ran on into another. The dwellings were clustered about open space with pedestrian underpasses to community facilities and shops, which included resident consumer cooperatives.

It is the integration of superior site planning with community facility shopping and employment centers that some feel has characterized the concept of "new towns" as we know them today. Others, such as the developers of Irvine Ranch, California, regard self-sufficiency as another essential. However, the population of each of the greenbelt towns was only 5,000 to 7,500 persons, obviously not enough to be self-sufficient. Mr. Rouse's analysis led him to believe that to be able to offer the variety of activities and institutions of a city, a population of approximately 100,000 was required. If smaller, the city could not support urban ameni- ties such as cultural facilities, colleges, professional athletic teams, res- taurants, and theaters. If larger, it would lose the sense of personal control and participation that gave human scale to a community. Racine, Wisconsin, and Charlotte, North Carolina, had populations of this size, and appeared able to support anything except perhaps a big-league baseball team and a symphony orchestra.

The new cities being planned in the United States were all relatively large: Reston, Virginia—75,000 people on 7,180 acres; Laguna Niguel, California—40,000 people on 7,100 acres; El Dorado Hills, California— 75,000 people on 9,800 acres; Clear Lake City, Texas—180,000 people on 15,000 acres; and Irvine Ranch, California—300,000 people on 93,000 acres. Through size, the developers hoped to be able to offer a higher quality of services and amenities, by spreading the costs of artificial lakes, golf courses, open spaces, community colleges, health clinics and recreation buildings over the thousands of people who will live there. Good design can be more economical and attractive. As an example, in Bridgeport, Connecticut, with a population of 100,000, 23% of the land is dedicated to streets. In a planned development, 8% to 10% of the area should be adequate for streets, thus freeing the extra land for parks and open space. The size of the projects also was expected to lead to the use of better professionals, whose designs could be more innovative, thus developing new systems for transportation, communication, health serv- ices, and other methods of organizing the community.

Yet, Mr. Rouse was aware that as glamorous as new city building appeared to be, few believed that it could be profitable as a business. There was no established blueprint to follow, and each of the new cities appeared to be faltering for a different reason. El Dorado Hills, California, had based its development on the projected expansion in employment of Aerojet-General from 20,000 to 30,000 employees. Instead, there was a reduction in defense spending, and the company was forced to cut back to 10,000 employees. Laguna Niguel found that the cost of offsite utilities ran to $20 million, far more than projected. Clear Lake City, Texas, was being developed on land next to the Houston Space Center. The Space Center developed more slowly than expected, and the company's market research program was poor, having recommended the building of California-style houses that had little appeal to Texas buyers.

The problems of Reston, Virginia, were of the greatest interest to Mr. Rouse, partially because of its proximity to Washington, D.C. (a 21-mile drive) and partially because of the ambitious master plan of Robert Simon, its developer. Mr. Simon regarded his master plan, which divided the wooded and rolling tract into seven villages, plus a downtown and industrial area, as the blueprint for the future. Children would walk to school without crossing auto-used roads. A variety of single-family houses, town houses, and apartments would overlook trees and lakes. Telephone lines and TV antennas would be hidden. A "high-density sinew" running through the area containing most of the major uses of Reston would put the surrounding recreation areas—including two lakes, golf courses, swimming pools, and wooded trails—within walking distance of one another. Mr. Simon hoped to meet contemporary needs for a "decent stimulating environment for the working man with leisure." This deep-set concern for human needs made a profound impression on Mr. Rouse.

Mr. Rouse's background was heavily oriented toward public service. He had been a member of President Eisenhower's Advisory Committee on Housing, which produced many of the recommendations emphasizing the rehabilitation of neighborhoods, as well as the elimination of slums, which led to the 1954 Housing Act. From 1958 to 1960, he was president and chairman of the board of directors of Action, a group organized to help the renewal of poorer neighborhoods, originally called the American Council to Improve Our Neighborhoods. Locally, in 1961, he was chairman of the Subcommittee of the Maryland State Commission which drafted the legislation establishing the Regional Planning Council in the Baltimore metropolitan area. He had also been chairman of the Greater Baltimore Committee.

While admiring Mr. Simon's purpose, Mr. Rouse felt that Reston would be unsuccessful financially, despite the excitement of the development. The project was underfinanced. The $14 million raw land cost was only a small part of the total cost involved, and Mr. Simon was having difficulty raising equity funds. He appeared to be too heavily influenced by architects, who put architectural excellence ahead of cost considerations. This concern for "avant-garde" design led to the decision to market modern architecture, a strategy Mr. Rouse felt was wrong for the East, when dealing with volume sales. The location itself had been hurt by the failure to obtain an access road off the new highway leading from Dulles Airport to downtown Washington. As a result, the driving time to Washington remained at the original 45 minutes, rather than the projected 25 minutes when the project began. This affected not only the residential but also the commercial and industrial potential of the site. Furthermore, the developer's cost control system and cash flow projections were inadequate, and the company lacked management depth, especially in the construction area.

In setting up his own new town, Mr. Rouse hoped to avoid these mistakes as well as those that had slowed down other new towns. He had to find land that could be bought at a low price, and then reused quickly for uses that warranted higher per-acre selling prices. Otherwise, the carrying charges of holding the land would drastically reduce profit potential. Assuming no sale, for example, to make a 20% pretax return, land value would have to double every four years, assuming that the land cost was financed with 100% equity. Assuming two-thirds debt financing at 6% and one-third equity financing at 20%, the land value would have to double every 9½ years. Although there was an advantage to leverage, the developer would be forced to carry the cost of debt servicing during the development period.

HOWARD COUNTY

In May 1962, one of the members of CRD's board of directors heard that 1,000 contiguous acres located between Baltimore and Washington were available in Howard County at a price per acre of $600. The seller was willing to take back a purchase money mortgage for two thirds of the selling price. The director suggested the purchase of this land as an investment with some of the company's excess cash. The parcel was located 45 minutes driving time from Cross Keys. Howard County was the least developed of the five Maryland counties, which together with the city of Baltimore formed the Baltimore Standard Metropolitan Statistical Area (SMSA) (see Exhibit 2). Statistics showed that these five counties had added 1 million people to its population between 1940 and 1960 to reach a total population of 1,433,437 in 1960. Howard County's population, although small, had more than doubled during that period to 36,152, and was expected to reach 50,000 by 1965. Although in 1959 the percentage of land in the county used for farms was still 60.2% of the county's 150,000 acres, this percentage was down from 74.8% in 1954. Average farmland values during that period had risen from $248 per acre to $517 per acre, and assessed value had tripled.

One of the directors raised questions concerning the factors that had kept land values in the area from increasing further. There appeared to be three primary reasons. First, there were no major roads through the county, so that driving time to Baltimore and Washington was still fairly long. Most of the people who lived in the Baltimore-Washington area commuted to one of the core cities to work and had located closer to these cities. However, new major highways were under construction. Second, since most of the area was still farmland, the development cost for roads and sewers was quite high, and the quality of municipal services was low, all of which discouraged suburban development. Third, the political climate was one of resistance to any change. The county's residents were mainly farmers and exurbanites, who had moved there to avoid the trend toward urbanization. The Republicans were favored to unseat the incumbent Democratic county commissioners, based on the Republicans' pledge to oppose the rezoning of minimum lot sizes from ½ acre to ¼ acre, thus limiting the growth of the area and inhibiting the use and ultimate price of the land.

In spite of these factors, Mr. Rouse felt that the land should be purchased. He said that growth of the area was inevitable and would come fairly quickly after the completion of the new highways in the next five to eight years. This site, unlike Reston, had access from two sides, from Baltimore as well as Washington. The Baltimore-Washington metropolitan areas contained 4.5 million people. These two core cities were only 35 miles apart, with an excellent system of roadways connecting two peripheral beltways 20 miles apart. With a 36.7% increase in population from 1950 to 1960, the Washington SMSA was the fastest-growing area in the Northeast. In the last 20 years, Washington had added the equivalent of a city larger than Atlanta to its population and was expected to add the equivalent of a city larger than Baltimore in the next 20 years. In the same period, Baltimore added a city larger than Denver and should add in the next 20 years one larger than Dallas. The corridor between the two cities had added over 1 million people in the prior 15 years.

Therefore, in spite of some opposition to the purchase of land not ready for immediate reuse, the board of CRD authorized the purchase of 1,000 acres for $600,000. Just prior to settlement in September 1962, 428 acres adjoining the initial 1,000 acres were offered for sale. The company arranged to purchase this parcel for $400,000 with $105,000 payable in cash and the balance due in 90 days. Mr. Rouse felt that his company had used its excess cash in an investment that offered little risk and great potential.

It was at this point that Mr. Rouse began to realize the possibility of assembling a much larger tract which would provide the opportunity of embarking on his dream to create a new town. Many of the local farmers were willing to leave the county because of the changes that appeared to be coming in the character of the area. Land prices of $1,000 per acre seemed high to them, considering that many had purchased their land originally at under $50 to $100 per acre. Also, in Maryland, as in the rest of the country, small farmers were unable to compete efficiently with large 5,000- to 10,000-acre farms in the Midwest and Far West. Mr. Rouse felt that once the full potential of the new highways was understood, and other developers began to come into Howard County, prices of $3,000 per acre would become normal.

There were many implications to a larger land purchase. In buying 500 to 1,000 acres, one could normally get a purchase money mortgage for at least two thirds of the cost for two to five or more years. The cash equity requirement was within CRD's capability, and the carrying charges for two to three years were not too great. In addition, the size of the parcel was such that it was easily resalable to the average homebuilder before the expiration of the purchase money mortgage. If Mr. Rouse was correct in his judgment that the land price would at least double in the next three years, and assuming that the carrying cost of the land was 10% per year, the profit on a purchase of 1 acre at $1,000 and sold for $2,000 at the end of the three-year period would be $700. However, if the original equity portion were only $300, and the carrying cost $300, the investor would more than double his $600 investment. At a selling price of $3,000 per acre, the investor would more than quadruple his $600 investment.

A bigger parcel had a different set of problems. If Mr. Rouse were to accomplish his dream of creating a new city for 100,000 persons, he projected that he would need at least 12,000 acres. There were few potential buyers for a parcel that size. Even Levitt & Sons, the country's largest homebuilder, rarely purchased more than 2,500 to 3,000 acres in one place at one time. The carrying cost of so large a parcel was considered prohibitive in relation to the estimated time required to sell off the entire parcel. To be resold quickly, the parcel would have to be broken up for sale to several builders. This could not be done quickly, since builders would fear the competition of putting too much land up for development at one time. Second, the builders would tend to want to buy the best parcels, leaving the least desirable sections. Third, in breaking up the land the owner would lose the opportunity for capital gains tax treatment.

Since few landowners in the Howard County area owned more than a few hundred acres, the assembly of the land required simultaneous negotiations with many sellers. The price of $600 to $1,000 per acre was possible at the present time, when purchasing one or two tracts, but on a larger scale the activity would tend to push up prices. Also, in assembling a large tract, which would be held for a long period, the normal short-term purchase money mortgages became unsatisfactory. The purchaser would, therefore, have to arrange not only equity but debt financing in advance. Assuming the purchase of 12,000 acres at an average projected per-acre price of $1,500, there would be a requirement for $18 million of financing. Traditional bank financing for land purchases when available, was limited to a maximum of 50% of value. Mr. Rouse knew that CRD did not have more than $1 million of its own capital to put into this project, of which $300,000 had already been committed for the purchase of the 1,428 acres.

In addition, there were the costs of carrying and developing the land. The cost of interest at 7%, insurance, and real estate taxes could amount to $1.8 million per year on an $18 million purchase. Then, there were the costs of developing such a parcel, including roads, sewage systems, and utilities. One of the reasons for creating a new city was to effect economies of scale. However, this implied heavier initial costs, which would then be amortized over a large number of users. As an example, a sewage treatment plant alone could cost $6 million. Cabot, Cabot, and Forbes, in developing Laguna Niguel, spent $20 million for offsite utilities alone. Mr. Rouse could see the need immediately for $25 million and shortly for another $25 million to undertake the development.

There were few private individuals willing to invest funds of that size. Large industrial corporations, if interested, would probably not be willing to permit CRD to control such a project, which Mr. Rouse felt was essential. Institutional investors appeared the only source. However, few were interested in real estate loans unless backed by a predictable stream of income, such as in a shopping center, office building, or apartment house. Most land loans also were repaid on a partial basis as each parcel was sold. If a developer had to use his sales income to repay the lender, obviously less money was available for future development of the site. Therefore, Mr. Rouse realized the need for an institutional lender who would treat the project as an investment rather than a loan. He was aware of the problem Robert Simon, developer of Reston, got himself into by arranging to purchase the land before arranging his financing. Mr. Simon still had not secured his financing and was apt to have to give up his idea at a considerable personal financial loss.

Therefore, Mr. Rouse decided that he did not want to proceed further without securing his financing. In December 1962, after an unsuccessful first attempt, Mr. Rouse contacted the Connecticut General Life Insurance Company. This firm had previously provided funds for a number of CRD's successful commercial developments, and JWR had acted as a mortgage correspondent for the Connecticut General in some areas. Mr. Rouse felt that Frazier Wilde, the chairman of the board of the insurance company, had both the imagination and understanding to be attracted by this idea.

LAND ACQUISITION

During the next month, Connecticut General investigated the area thoroughly. It agreed with Mr. Rouse that the location was a good one because it would draw people from the Baltimore and Washington markets. The company had mixed feelings, though, about a project that contemplated acquisition of 12,000 to 15,000 of the county's 150,000 acres. On the one hand, it appeared logical to assume that the overall price level of land in the area would increase. On the other, a parcel of this size would be difficult to resell if the new town development did not prove feasible. Mr. Rouse said that, in his judgment, the assembly of the land alone would result in the whole being worth more than the sum of the parts, since the area could then have the planning flexibility to maximize development opportunities.

Connecticut General also raised the question of what would happen if Mr. Rouse were able to acquire only 5,000 acres or 8,000 acres or if the acreage were too scattered to permit proper planning. After all, to assemble the full site would require the purchase of over 150 parcels. If only 5,000 to 8,000 acres were acquired, the site would be neither big enough for a new town nor small enough to sell to a large builder. Mr. Rouse recognized the problem but said that he could not make the individual purchases contingent upon the purchase of the full acreage. He would have to commit himself to the smaller acreage, or he would not be able to act quickly. The longer the acquisition period, the more likely the remaining landowners would recognize his purpose and become holdouts for higher prices or not sell at all. He thought that an average price of $1,500 per acre was reasonable. This was over twice the price level of his present purchases and would give him the maneuverability to purchase some more expensive parcels which were essential to a properly planned development.

As an example, Mr. Rouse felt it was especially important to purchase the higher-priced, commercially zoned parcels on the highways, both to control the visual entrances to the site and to enable him to "marshal the market" for his own shopping center, by eliminating competition. Yet, at an average price of $1,500 per acre, Mr. Rouse was convinced that Connecticut General would not lose money on the transaction, since similar land in adjacent counties was selling for $3,000 to $5,000 per acre. It was only a matter of time for these prices to be paid in Howard County. Connecticut General questioned the value of comparable land prices, since other counties were more receptive to residential tract developers and would grant the necessary zoning changes and permits required by the developer. Although Connecticut General was normally satisfied with a 6% return on mortgage investments, the company looked to a 10% return in equity situations. The time of the holding period was thus crucial to the overall return.

Another question the insurance company raised was whether the fact that there were already 2,200 homes with 8,000 residents living in the general area would prove to be a major disadvantage to the planning of the area. A "Swiss cheese" type of development with pockets of existing uses left seemed a problem. Mr. Rouse felt that the proposed area was large enough to be planned with these homes. To a certain extent, their existence would prove an advantage both in providing an immediate market for his commercial facilities and demonstrating the market already for homes in the area. Also, since it was no longer a practical possibility to acquire the land as a contiguous parcel, he could bypass the holdouts who resisted selling or who demanded too high a price without disrupting his planning for the site. Since it was obvious that word of his activities could not be kept secret for very long, it was important that potential sellers did not get the impression that their site was crucial to his plan. The planning problem of fitting the holdout parcels into the development would have to be overcome later.

The insurance company also questioned the strategy for purchasing the land. Mr. Rouse said that there were two approaches. Either the land could be bought in the name of the principals or through the use of straws or nominees, who would disguise the identity of the real purchaser. The first approach had the advantage of insuring the seller that the purchaser was financially responsible and would complete the purchase; however, it might also give the seller the attitude that since the purchaser was wealthy, he would pay more for the land. Mr. Rouse leaned toward the secrecy approach, since he felt he would meet less seller resistance if it did not appear that the land was being assembled by one individual with large-scale development plans. He would create dummy corporations to serve as straws or nominees. Each would be represented by a separate lawyer and realtor, who did not know the identity of the real client. By giving his corporations names characteristic of small suburban divisions, such as Serenity Acres, Cedar Farms, and Potomac Estates, he would try to give the impression that the buyers were small housebuilders. As a further check, he would run the whole acquisition operation from the office in Baltimore of his attorney, Jack Jones. He would tell very few in the CRD organization of his plans.

The insurance company could see the validity to this approach but questioned the ethics involved in the decision. As a public corporation, Connecticut General did not want to be criticized later for "swindling" small farmers out of their land, even though it was a common industry practice to hide the identity of the real purchaser. The company saw a further disadvantage that at a later date, when the identity of the principals was revealed, the county's residents might resent their clandestine approach, and refuse to cooperate in giving the necessary approvals for zoning changes and overall planning.

This was especially important because the residents were already up in arms about the possibility of any zoning change. In this case, the developer would be requesting permission to build on 10% of the county's land a city with apartments, industrial, commercial, and other public facilities that would completely change the character of the county. Mr. Rouse admitted that zoning and the obtaining of other local approvals was the key to the project. He said he would prefer to be able to buy the land subject to the zoning change required to develop the project according to a master plan for a new town; but in a multiparcel acquisition, as opposed to a single-parcel acquisition, this was difficult, since if the sale were conditional, and if the developer's real intentions were known, the land prices would rise. This in itself might be satisfactory if the risk were minimized, but Mr. Rouse did not think he could convince all 150 sellers to follow this approach. There would be many parcels he would not be able to purchase conditional upon a zoning change.

ZONING

Presently most of the land was zoned single-family residential with a permitted density of two single-family homes per acre. Mr. Rouse hoped eventually to secure five major assurances from the local county government:

1. Zoning permitting higher residential densities and industrial and commercial uses.
2. The authority to create a special entity that could issue tax-exempt bonds for major roads and utilities on the site.
3. The assurance that at public expense, peripheral roads and utilities adequate to handle a development of this size be brought to the site.
4. A legal basis that would guarantee to the developer that he would not, over the long-term development period, be forced to change zoning and other controls as the result of pressure from either the county or his own residents.
5. A commitment to improve the level of municipal services so that the project could attract residents.

The most crucial of these points was the first, the change in zoning, since commercial and industrial uses could increase the sales price per acre from $1,500 per acre to $10,000 to $40,000 per acre. Connecticut General wanted to know why Rouse expected the county to change the zoning, especially since the county and its residents appeared anxious to maintain the rural character of the area. In the next election the county commissioners were expected to be unseated because of their willingness to reduce zoning requirements to permit single-family houses on ¼-acre lots rather than ½-acre lots. Mr. Rouse said that there were two major selling points that he could employ to induce the county to change the zoning. First, the higher uses created more tax revenue for the county from shopping centers, office buildings, and industrial parks which demanded little in the way of municipal services. Real estate taxes in the county were now rising rapidly because of the large lots, scattered housing, and many school-age children. Garbage, police, sewer, water, and school bussing costs were all high because of the low densities. Schools were filled. Fire protection was inadequate. Rural roads were already crowded with commuter traffic. Parks, recreation, cultural, and hospital facilities were unsatisfactory. To rectify these situations, more money was required, and an expanding tax base was essential to raising this money. Although the county residents liked the rural atmosphere, most also wanted a higher level of municipal services.

Besides the financial argument, Mr. Rouse thought that the qualitative one of establishing proper standards for growth and development was equally important. After all, the residents of Howard County could see from looking at adjacent counties that growth was inevitable. It was only a question of how growth should occur. Rouse felt he could convince the county that suburban sprawl was not inevitable. The land did not have to be divided into small residential lots, huge shopping centers, massive parking lots, and sprawling highways. The problem was that existing zoning codes encouraged the misuse of land, and a new approach to zoning was necessary.

Originally, zoning codes were established in the late 1800's as safety measures to permit firemen to get through with their hoses, to help prevent the spread of fires, and to assure proper ventilation and sunlight. The controls established were essentially related to building setback and separation. Even earlier, regulations were established to prohibit specific menaces, such as gunpowder in certain colonial villages, slaughterhouses in 1692 in Massachusetts, and Chinese laundries in California in the late 1800's. During the early 1900's, land-use regulations were added in an attempt to create more attractive, functional communities. Essentially, the purpose was to separate the areas where people lived from the ugly, polluted industrial areas where they worked and the traffic-congested areas where they shopped. In 1916, the first comprehensive zoning plan was approved in New York City, although it was not given final judicial approval by the U.S. Supreme Court until 1926 as the result of the *Village of Euclid* v. *Ambler Realty Company* case. The basis for the decision was that zoning was a legitimate use of the police power of the state. There was a public need for some form of control through land-use regulation to prevent the chaotic growth of a community.

However, in practice, zoning had become primarily a negative control. It limits what can be developed on a site but does not guarantee that a desired use actually will result. Zoning has become means for local communities to resist change, to keep out "undesirable" people and uses. Local politicians have used their power to change zoning to award favors to their friends, by permitting higher economic uses that increase the value of particular parcels. Meanwhile, existing requirements often result in a waste of land, money, and time. Large front lawns are of little value to the public, since they are not open to public use, and on the other hand are of little value to the homeowner because they are open to public view. Backyards are often too large just for sunbathing and barbecues while too small for playing fields. By stretching out the space required for homes through yard and setback requirements, the length and thus the cost of roads and utilities is increased. People have to spend more time traveling to school, to work, to shopping. A second car becomes an essential to suburban living.

Yet, the answer to such poor planning, cluster zoning, had met considerable resistance from local communities. Cluster zoning controls the overall density in terms of units per acre, but does not dictate the placement of the units on the site. Thus, where ½-acre zoning exists on a 100-acre tract the county would permit 200 units to be built on 20 acres, so long as 80 acres remain open land available for community use. Theoretically, the builder would then be putting more land into public open space, preserving the natural and physical amenities of the land and minimizing his site development cost, without any overall increase in the number of units built. In actuality, most builders also use the device as a means of increasing the overall density, or of using the land not now needed to achieve the total residential density, for income-producing uses ranging from a golf course to commercial or industrial buildings. The question was whether the developer could convince the local community that these other uses were also of advantage to the community.

Mr. Rouse felt that he could prove the financial advantage of his new city to Howard County. He knew that Reston, with 70,000 people, projected a total cost of over $700 million. On this basis, Columbia, with a projected population of 100,000, should cost $1 billion. Assessed at 60% of value and taxed at the current Howard County $2.55/$1,000 rate, Columbia should produce over $15 million in annual tax revenue to the county, or $150 per capita. Since the present rate of county expenditure per capita was only $118, Columbia should, therefore, result in a profit to the other residents of the county. Mr. Rouse was aware that he was assuming the present per capita rate of expenditure to continue, which ran counter to the experience in neighboring counties where, because of rising demand for services, the cost per capita was already $200. Mr. Rouse hoped that the county would recognize that growth was in any case inevitable and that his development approach was more beneficial to the county than an approach built under existing zoning.

Mr. Rouse explained to Connecticut General that he had used the comparative technique very effectively in changing the zoning for his village of Cross Keys. Cross Keys was a 72-acre site in the Roland Park Section of Baltimore purchased at a price of $4 million. The parcel, one half of the Baltimore Country Club golf course, was planned as a small upper-income community with 600 town houses, 600 rental units, a village square, recreation areas, an inn, and an office building. The project was the company's first venture outside shopping centers and into a mixed-use development. There, he had held a series of neighborhood meetings at which he presented not only his own plan but an obviously unsatisfactory one that would be permitted under the existing zoning. He showed how his plan would fit in with the existing upper-income neighborhood and existing municipal facilities. He said that he had learned the need to work closely with the local residents. His willingness to cooperate with reasonable suggestions from the residents had been effective in making them feel that they had a part in forming his final plan. As a result, he had achieved a zone change that many had felt would be impossible to obtain.

Connecticut General's reaction was that the situation in Howard County was different in that the area was much larger. As opposed to Cross Keys, where the upper-income apartments and prestige shopping center were compatible with the image the local residents had of their area, Columbia would drastically change the character of Howard County and would require totally new municipal services. The political situation in Howard County was certainly antideveloper, and as logical and persuasive a salesman as Mr. Rouse was, Connecticut General was unsure as to his chances for success.

Another factor Mr. Rouse thought would work in their favor was that Robert Simon had just received approval for a new Residential Planned Community (RPC) zoning from Fairfax County, Virginia, which permitted the plan for Reston to be built (see Exhibit 3). The RPC zoning was based on population density distribution. Although 60 people per acre would be permitted in some sections, the overall density could not exceed 13 per gross residential acre, as opposed to 11 people under existing zoning. The main key was the permission for mixed land use on much of the land, freed up by the cluster principle, enabling the developer to obtain higher prices from sale of land for industrial and commercial purposes.

The political battle over this zone change had received considerable national publicity. When the local commissioners had indicated that they were opposed to the new zoning, the *Washington Post* printed many articles and editorials supporting Reston. These articles resulted in such a tremendous local support for the planned-community concept that the local commissioners were forced to change their stand. Mr. Rouse was sure that this would have an influence on the commissioners of Howard County, although he knew of many other situations throughout the country where popular opinion could not be mustered for equally valid proposals.

MARKET PLANNING

Mr. Rouse was convinced, too, of the need to plan his project employing the highest possible standards both to obtain the zoning and, even more so, "to produce an environment in which various institutions can work for humans in a creative way." He hoped to bring in experts from many fields to "apply the social sciences to the actual design and operation of a new community better than it has been done before." Connecticut General questioned whether such an approach would be economic. Also, would the result be merely an array of institutions? Admittedly, institutions are important to the character of a city, but isn't the key the "ambience" that gives an area such as Georgetown its individuality? Is this something that can be created or manufactured? Wouldn't the result more likely be a glorified large-scale subdivision similar to other suburbs?

Mr. Rouse disagreed. He felt that a city could be designed so that the individual residents could feel a sense of identity. Women could be helped to overcome the sense of isolation and frustration common to much of suburbia. People benefit from living in communities that are mixed economically and racially. New transportation systems integrated with the basic site plan could eliminate the need for a second car. Adequate and convenient recreational facilities would bring more people outdoors. Comprehensive community health plans could reduce the cost of medical care. The forms of government would vary depending upon the function it performed. There was no reason not to "demonstrate the applicability of the behavioral sciences under actual operating conditions." Admittedly, all these ideas would have to be costed out by engineers and economists, but Mr. Rouse said that it was his judgment that the potential buyer would prefer to live in Columbia rather than a normal subdivision, specifically because it would offer a better way of life. In addition, the high quality of community amenities was especially important to attract people in the case of Columbia, because of its distance from the centers of Baltimore and Washington and its location in a less developed area.

Connecticut General was concerned with the cost of these proposed amenities and services. If they were costly, Columbia would have to be an upper-middle-income community. Furthermore, was the potential buyer willing to pay for the services, and, if so, how much? Mr. Rouse thought that the commercial and industrial land sales at higher prices would compensate for many of these costs, and without the residential amenities the community would not permit the higher and more valuable land uses. From a residential sales standpoint, although 25,000 to 30,000 units was a large undertaking, it only represented 2% to 3% of the total Baltimore-Washington metropolitan market for the next 20 years, and 15% of the projected market for the next 15 years for the corridor between the two cities. He felt Columbia would compete effectively in this market. The thought of having to sell one of every seven families who wanted to live in this large corridor area seemed an immense task to the insurance company officials.

FINANCING

The company also questioned the potential profitability of the project. Mr. Rouse explained that at this point in time it was difficult to establish a set of firm, meaningful figures. Until the land was purchased, a site plan could not be drawn, nor could the land be divided into residential, commercial, office, industrial, and other uses. The users also depended upon the zoning restrictions, which also were unknown. If Mr. Rouse were forced to make an assumption, he would do so on the following basis:

Projected Profit Analysis
($ million)

```
Income
  12,000 acres × 80% salable @ $15,000 average
    (range—$1,500 to $100,000)                        =        $144
Expenses
  Land—12,000 acres              @ $1,500/acre = $18
  Townwide development*          @ $1,500/acre =  18
  Land finishing†                @ $2,000/acre =  24
  Planning, sales administration @ $1,000/acre =  12
  Financing                      @ $1,500/acre =  18
                                                            ─────
                                                              90
Net Profit before Taxes                                     $ 54‡
```

  * General roads and utilities paid for by developer.
  † On-site utilities, grading, landscaping, local streets.
  ‡ Not including profit on income-producing property.

However, not only was it difficult to estimate income; the expenses were equally uncertain. The land cost would naturally vary, depending upon the number of acres purchased. Mr. Rouse included a cost for townwide roads and utilities, although he hoped to be able to form a separate Community Improvement District, which would issue its own bonds to finance these improvements as was often done in California.

The bonds would be repaid from user charges on the utilities. However, at this time he did not know whether these bonds would affect the borrowing credit of the county and would be permitted by the county.

On the other hand, Mr. Rouse did feel that he would be able to form a Homeowner's Association, similar to the one created at Reston, to handle the maintenance cost of many of the community facilities. He also anticipated that this Association would bear the initial $15 million construction cost of these facilities and thus did not include this cost in his estimate, although the developer might have to loan the funds initially to the Association. The county itself would handle the cost and administration of schools, police, fire, garbage pickup, and other municipal services. The Homeowner's Association would be responsible for operating and maintaining such community facilities as neighborhood centers, lakes, recreational areas, and parks. The dues to the Association, which would probably be about $100 per year per family, would cover these costs and gradually repay the loan for the construction costs. The expenditure for planning, sales, and administration of $12 million amounted to approximately 8.3% of gross income, a figure Mr. Rouse judged to be reasonable in the light of the experience of such land development companies as Levitt & Sons.

In spite of the apparent general lack of competent managerial personnel in this industry, Mr. Rouse expected that the excitement of the project would enable him to hire the wide range of staff personnel necessary to implement the project. However, the supervision and training of the personnel and top management's limited experience in new towns were considered to be potential problems, although Rouse felt that his general shopping center and his Cross Keys experience would be most useful. The financing expense naturally depended upon the amount of money needed, the period the loan would be outstanding, and the interest rate.

He then evaluated his need for funds from the Connecticut General over the period. Much depended upon the success in establishing a source for the proposed bonds of the Community Improvement District and Homeowner's Association. Although the cash outflow was long term, at least 5 to 10 years, it would be especially heavy in the early years, because of the need to pay all cash for the land; to acquire all the land initially; to install a large percentage of roads, utilities, and amenities early in the development period; and to achieve economies of scale. It was also essential to make these expenditures to give credibility to the total plan, so that a potential home buyer would believe that he would receive what the rental brochure promised. Mr. Rouse estimated his need would be $18 million for the land alone, plus carrying costs of 10% per year for two years, and planning, engineering, legal, and organizational expenses of $1 million. To be safe, he requested an initial commitment of

$25 million from Connecticut General until the planning and zoning phases were complete and construction was ready to commence, and then a further commitment within three years of another $25 million for actual site improvements, such as sewers, roads, and lakes.

Mr. Rouse was very much concerned that Columbia be adequately financed so that the project would proceed in sequence and that the needed public facilities existed at such time as the residents moved in, not two years later as was the case in many developments. The new city must appear a reality to the potential buyers. In addition, there were cost savings in putting in a sewer system for the entire project. Mr. Rouse asked that the lender defer interest payments until later years. He also suggested that contrary to normal industry practice where the loan was repaid as the land was sold, the developer be permitted to use his land sales revenue for further site development and not be forced to repay the loan until the cash flow permitted. Mr. Rouse's reason for this suggestion was that the remaining land became more valuable as the community developed, since the money was being used in the project, and thereby enhanced the lender's security. Since the sale prices for the remaining land increased, there was little risk to the lender's capital in waiting, although the overall return certainly depended upon expeditious development. The longer the time period, the higher the carrying charges, which gave the borrower the incentive to repay the loan as quickly as possible. As an estimate he thought that over a 15-year period the loan might be repaid from the 8th through the 12th year. At that time, the cash flow should be more than enough to cover further development expenses. The developer's profit would come during the last three years.

He initially requested from Connecticut General that the loan bear a 10% interest rate, which was 3½% above market, because the loan was for 100% of cost and the repayment schedule was deferred. In this case, Connecticut General would receive none of the equity. The insurance company would be secure in that after the assembly and rezoning of the land, the land value would more than double, putting the land loan at 50% of value.

The insurance company had several problems with this proposal. To a certain extent, it felt that despite the fact that its investment was a loan, its situation was in reality an equity one. If the land sales did not go as projected, there was the possibility of the company being forced to become the developer. This in itself could be a problem, since Connecticut General would then have to go out and hire a developer such as Rouse to run the project for it. Therefore, since the insurance company was taking the risk, it might be more profitable to lower the interest rate on the loan to 8%, and take 50% of the equity. Then, if the development went better than anticipated, the company had an opportunity to realize a far greater return. There was also the possibility of the development company in which Connecticut General would participate owning some of the profitable income-producing property, such as the shopping center, office buildings, or apartment houses. The alternative approach to reducing the lender's risk of requiring Rouse to put up $5 million to $10 million of the $50 million was unrealistic, since Rouse did not have more than $1 million of capital available for this venture. The insurance company believed, though, that Rouse should be required to spend that money for initial planning, legal, and zoning expenses because this was the time of highest risk. Rouse was prepared to accept these changes, if Connecticut General agreed to provide the money for the initial land acquisition.

The next question was one of the extent of the commitment at this time. Considering the uncertainties of land acquisition, planning, and zoning, should the commitment go beyond the acquisition stages? On the one hand, the last $25 million would probably be needed to develop Columbia, and Mr. Rouse was going into this venture for that reason. On the other hand, since land acquisition and zoning were not guaranteed, Connecticut General felt justified in asking for another review once the plans could be finalized and more detailed financial estimates could be made. The insurance company did not want Mr. Rouse to be unaware of the possibility that the company might not go forward. It might want the loan repaid, or decide to ask Mr. Rouse to find another investor for the last $25 million, and reduce its ownership share to 25%.

Connecticut General was still left with the risk of what to do if Mr. Rouse could not find new financing. Therefore, it wanted to feel confident that the basic land value supported the loan. On the one hand, the size of the parcel was a disadvantage. All the land might not be acquired. Zoning could be refused. The secrecy involved in acquisition could create public repercussions. On the other hand, the land appeared to be well located and available at reasonable prices. The potential of creating a new city was exciting. It appeared to offer the opportunity to make a social contribution as well as a financial gain.

Yet, thus far, the experience of private developers in making money from new town development was not positive. Whereas the risk seemed minimal of the raw land prices decreasing, the large expenditures for site development and community facilities required to build a new town could be lost if the potential home buyer was unwilling to pay for this cost. A large market of upper-middle-income home buyers had to exist for a peripheral, untested location. The developer was at the mercy of the local government for zoning for establishment of a Community Improvement District, for maintaining a high level of municipal services, and for the myriad of local licenses and approvals necessary to complete the project. It was not yet proven that the way of life so forcefully proposed by Mr. Rouse for Columbia was what people wanted if they had to pay for it. Perhaps the formlessness of suburbia was an advantage to some people. After all, if people wanted more from suburban life, wouldn't they have forced the developers and local governments to have provided it? New towns were supposed to be integrated by income and race. There was a question as to whether this was desirable, especially in the Washington area which was more a southern than a northern city. Market studies to determine all these points seemed meaningless, since no real comparables existed.

The insurance company also questioned the concept of a new city itself. Would people want to work where they lived, or would the proximity destroy the suburban atmosphere that most people appeared to prefer? On the other hand, how self-sufficient could a new community be in attracting industry without an existing labor force; or commercially profitable without an existing market? The higher prices came from these land sales. It appeared that Columbia had a better chance than most to succeed, specifically because, located between Baltimore and Washington, it did not have to be self-sufficient. It could draw from both of these growth areas. Mr. Rouse agreed that a new town had little chance for success if built in the wilderness. The 8,000 existing residents now living in the project area would at least provide an initial market for a neighborhood, if not a regional, shopping center, and industry could draw employees from nearby communities.

The insurance company did not want to underestimate the organizational problems of managing a new city as opposed to a conventional real estate project. Not only were lawyers, engineers, architects, builders, salesmen, market analysts, and accountants required for the different types of uses, but political scientists, sociologists, doctors, communication engineers, and a multitude of other experts were needed to create the physical, social, and political infrastructure of the new community. Mr. Rouse appeared to understand this problem, but could he attract qualified personnel and establish a cost control system to provide the necessary information to evaluate their performance and control such an overwhelming and enormous task? In three years, could he create town houses, office buildings, and the start of a major downtown in an area now used only for farmland?

Connecticut General had a great deal of faith in James Rouse. However, the question was whether or not any man would be able to accomplish without public subsidies, but at a profit, the creation of a new city. If the insurance company did decide to go ahead, what should be its role? What ground rules should be established as to its participation in the ownership of the development company? How should its position relate to the timing, control, and execution of the project in the initial stages of land acquisition, planning, and zoning, and then later during the actual development of the site? Should there be an agreement in advance as to what would happen if the insurance company went ahead with the first phase but not the second? Mr. Wilde requested specific records from his staff concerning these problems.

EXHIBIT 1

Statistical Abstract of the United States

No. 12. Urban and Rural Places and Population, by Size of Place: 1910 to 1960

[Prior to 1960, excludes Alaska and Hawaii. "Previous urban definition" refers to the definition used prior to 1950 when a number of large and densely settled places were not included as urban because they were not incorporated. In 1950, the Bureau of the Census adopted the concept of the urbanized area and delineated boundaries for unincorporated places. All the population residing in urban-fringe areas and in unincorporated places of 2,500 or more is classified as urban according to the "current" definition. See also *Historical Statistics, Colonial Times to 1957*, series A 181–209]

CLASS AND SIZE	1910	1920	1930	1940	1950 Previous urban definition	1950 Current urban definition	1960 Previous urban definition	1960 Current urban definition
PLACES								
Urban [1]	2,262	2,722	[1] 3,165	3,464	4,054	4,741	5,022	6,041
Places of 1,000,000 or more	3	3	5	5	5	5	5	5
Places of 500,000 to 1,000,000	5	9	8	9	13	13	16	16
Places of 250,000 to 500,000	11	13	24	23	23	23	30	30
Places of 100,000 to 250,000	31	43	56	55	67	65	80	81
Places of 50,000 to 100,000	59	76	98	107	129	126	203	201
Places of 25,000 to 50,000	119	143	185	213	283	252	427	432
Places of 10,000 to 25,000	369	465	606	665	831	778	1,140	1,134
Places of 5,000 to 10,000	605	715	851	965	1,129	1,176	1,326	1,394
Places of 2,500 to 5,000	1,060	1,255	1,332	1,422	1,574	1,846	1,799	2,152
Places under 2,500	(X)	(X)	(X)	(X)	(X)	457	(X)	596
Rural	11,830	12,855	13,433	13,288	13,235	13,807	13,418	13,749
Places of 1,000 to 2,500	2,717	3,030	3,087	3,205	3,404	4,158	3,545	4,151
Places under 1,000	9,113	9,825	10,346	10,083	9,831	9,649	9,873	9,598
POPULATION (1,000)								
United States	91,972	105,711	122,775	131,669	150,697	150,697	179,323	179,323
Urban	41,999	54,158	68,955	74,424	89,749	96,468	113,056	125,269
Places of 1,000,000 or more	8,501	10,146	15,065	15,911	17,404	17,404	17,484	17,484
Places of 500,000 to 1,000,000	3,011	6,224	5,764	6,457	9,187	9,187	11,111	11,111
Places of 250,000 to 500,000	3,950	4,541	7,956	7,828	8,242	8,242	10,766	10,766
Places of 100,000 to 250,000	4,840	6,519	7,541	7,793	9,724	9,479	11,548	11,652
Places of 50,000 to 100,000	4,179	5,265	6,491	7,344	9,138	8,931	13,959	13,836
Places of 25,000 to 50,000	4,023	5,075	6,426	7,417	9,876	8,808	14,776	14,951
Places of 10,000 to 25,000	5,549	7,035	9,097	9,967	12,768	11,867	17,731	17,568
Places of 5,000 to 10,000	4,217	4,968	5,897	6,682	7,832	8,139	9,350	9,780
Places of 2,500 to 5,000	3,728	4,386	4,718	5,026	5,579	6,490	6,332	7,580
Places under 2,500	(X)	(X)	(X)	(X)	(X)	578	(X)	690
Unincorporated parts of urbanized areas	(X)	(X)	(X)	(X)	(X)	7,344	(X)	9,851
Rural	49,973	51,553	53,820	57,246	60,948	54,230	66,267	54,054
Places of 1,000 to 2,500	4,234	4,712	4,821	5,027	5,383	6,473	5,616	6,497
Places under 1,000	3,930	4,255	4,363	4,316	4,129	4,031	4,032	3,894
Other rural	41,809	42,586	44,637	47,903	51,437	43,725	56,619	43,664
PERCENT OF TOTAL POPULATION								
United States	100.0	100.0	100.0	100.0	100.0	100.0	100.0	100.0
Urban	45.7	51.2	56.2	56.5	59.6	64.0	63.0	69.9
Places of 1,000,000 or more	9.2	9.6	12.3	12.1	11.5	11.5	9.8	9.8
Places of 500,000 to 1,000,000	3.3	5.9	4.7	4.9	6.1	6.1	6.2	6.2
Places of 250,000 to 500,000	4.3	4.3	6.5	5.9	5.5	5.5	6.0	6.0
Places of 100,000 to 250,000	5.3	6.2	6.1	5.9	6.5	6.3	6.4	6.5
Places of 50,000 to 100,000	4.5	5.0	5.3	5.6	6.1	5.9	7.8	7.7
Places of 25,000 to 50,000	4.4	4.8	5.2	5.6	6.6	5.8	8.2	8.3
Places of 10,000 to 25,000	6.0	6.7	7.4	7.6	8.5	7.9	9.9	9.8
Places of 5,000 to 10,000	4.6	4.7	4.8	5.1	5.2	5.4	5.2	5.5
Places of 2,500 to 5,000	4.1	4.1	3.8	3.8	3.7	4.3	3.5	4.2
Places under 2,500	(X)	(X)	(X)	(X)	(X)	0.4	(X)	0.4
Unincorporated parts of urbanized areas	(X)	(X)	(X)	(X)	(X)	4.9	(X)	5.5
Rural	54.3	48.8	43.8	43.5	40.4	36.0	37.0	30.1
Places of 1,000 to 2,500	4.6	4.5	3.9	3.8	3.6	4.3	3.1	3.6
Places under 1,000	4.3	4.0	3.6	3.3	2.7	2.7	2.2	2.2
Other rural	45.5	40.3	36.4	36.4	34.1	29.0	31.6	24.3

X   Not applicable.
[1] Bluefield, Va., and Bluefield, W. Va.; Bristol, Tenn., and Bristol, Va.; Delmar, Del., and Delmar, Md.; Harrison, Ohio, and West Harrison, Ind.; Junction City, Ark., and Junction City, La.; Texarkana, Ark., and Texarkana, Tex.; Texhoma, Okla., and Texhoma, Tex.; and Union City, Ind., and Union City, Ohio, were counted as separate incorporated places in all years except 1930 when each pair was counted as a single place.

Source: Dept. of Commerce, Bureau of the Census; *U.S. Census of Population: 1960*, Vol. I.

EXHIBIT 2. Maryland County Economic Data Book, Maryland State Planning Department, April 1, 1964

Counties	Howard	Anne Arundel	Baltimore	Montgomery	Prince George	State of Maryland
Population						
1964*	48,000					3,100,687
1960	36,152	206,634	492,428	340,928	357,395	2,343,001
1950	23,119	117,392	270,273	164,401	194,182	1,821,244
1940	17,175	68,375	155,825	83,912	89,490	1,631,526
1930	16,169	55,167	124,565	49,206	60,095	1,149,661
1920	15,826	43,408	78,817	34,921	43,347	863,003
No. of households—1960	9,549	51,180	134,558	92,433	94,995	
Population (sq. mi.)—1960	144.6	495.6	809.6	691.5	736.9	314.0
Land area (sq. mi.)	250	417	608	493	485	9,874
Family median income—1960	$ 6,401	$ 6,503	$ 7,098	$ 9,317	$ 7,471	$ 6,309
Effective buying—1962						
Total (in millions)	$ 81.6	$ 464.78	$ 1,320	$ 1,236	$ 920	$ 7,199
Per household	$ 7,923	$ 8,183	$ 8,750	$ 11,761	$ 8,570	$ 7,852
Property assessed value—(in millions)						
1963*	$ 161.5	$ 572.15	$ 1,963	$ 1,743	$ 1,205	$10,752
1956	$ 53.1	$ 282.6	$ 1,274	$ 900.6	$ 561	$ 7,207
1959—Agriculture						
Number of farms	618	961	1,361	973	1,251	25,122
Per cent of county	60.2%	30.6%	34.1%	53.7%	40.1%	54.7%
Average size farms/acre	155.9	85.1	110.1	174.3	99.4	137.6
Average value/farm	$77,352	$40,579	$76,097	$106,728	$53,076	$36,461
Average value/acre	$ 517.04	$ 499.06	$ 720.97	$ 680.09	$ 595.06	$ 276.22
1954—Agriculture						
Number of farms	881	1,187	2,331	1,455	1,786	32,500
Percent of county	74.8%	38.2%	52.8%	62.4%	51.4%	61.6%
Average size farm/acre	136.4	85.9	89.0	135.6	89.4	119.9
Average value/farm	$32,835	$22,510	$29,431	$ 38,030	$28,809	$20,342
Average value/acre	$ 248.30	$ 262.11	$ 368.31	$ 300.72	$ 361.82	$ 177.02
Motor vehicles registered						
1962	18,791	85,811	220,644	178,607	174,668	1,290,380
1955	11,618	52,997	145,522	107,757	107,297	968,064
Water acreage (sq. mi.)	1	41	30	13	11	203
State and fed. owned land—(sq. mi.)	8.2	5.6	12.5	5.0	26.0	40.0

* Projected.

EXHIBIT 3

Fairfax County Zoning Ordinance
Appendix C: Local Ordinances

1. RESIDENTIAL PLANNED COMMUNITY ORDINANCE, FAIRFAX COUNTY, VIRGINIA (ADOPTED JULY 18, 1962)

(A) Purpose and Intent

The RPC District (Residential Planned Community) is intended to permit in accordance with the master plan the development of planned satellite communities containing not less than 750 contiguous acres under one ownership or control in those areas of the County provided with sanitary sewers, sewage disposal facilities, adequate highway access and public water supply. Within such planned communities, the location of all residential, commercial, industrial and governmental uses, school sites, parks, playgrounds, recreation areas, parking areas and other open spaces shall be controlled in such a manner as to permit a variety of housing accommodations and land uses in orderly relationship to one another. Such planned communities, when approved, shall constitute a part of the master plan for the County as a whole, and the preliminary consideration of such planned communities by the Planning Commission shall be based on recognition of this requirement.

(B) Procedure for Establishment

(1) Following approval of a satellite community as a part of the master plan of the County, the Board of County Supervisors may create within such planned location an RPC District containing a minimum land area of not less than 750 acres under one ownership or control. Additional land area may be added to an existing RPC District if it is adjacent or forms a logical addition to an existing RPC District. The procedure for an addition shall be the same as if an original application were filed, and all of the requirements of this article shall apply except the minimum acreage requirement of 750 acres.

(2) The applicant shall furnish with his application for rezoning 15 copies of a preliminary plan, prepared or certified by a surveyor or engineer duly authorized the the State to practice as such, showing the proposed general layout, the general location of the various types of land uses, the proposed densities of population in residential areas, a major thoroughfare plan, a public utility plan, a storm drainage plan and a plan showing the location of recreation spaces, parks, schools and other public or community uses.

(3) Following approval by the Planning Commission and the Board of County Supervisors of a preliminary plan, the applicant shall furnish 15 copies of a final plan of any section of not less than 100 acres of the land shown on the preliminary plan, prepared or certified by a surveyor or engineer duly authorized by the State to practice as such, showing the layout of all major and local thoroughfares and local streets, the location of all buildings, parking areas, pedestrian ways, utility easements, lot lines, open spaces, parks, recrea-

EXHIBIT 3 *(Continued)*

tion areas, school sites, playgrounds, the proposed use of all buildings and the metes and bounds of all dedicated areas and lots. The applicant shall also furnish a proposed deed of dedication including restrictions safeguarding the use of open spaces and preventing encroachment upon open spaces between buildings. The applicant shall furnish a deed, or deeds, to land determined by the County to be needed for public elementary and intermediate school purposes. When the final plan and deed of dedication shall have been approved by the Planning Commission as being in conformity with this section and with any changes or requirements of the Board of County Supervisors on the preliminary plan and it has been determined that the applicant has complied with the requirements of Chapter 23 of the Code of Fairfax County (which is the Subdivision Control Ordinance) whether or not it is a subdivision, it shall be approved for recordation and recorded. Thereafter, no modification may be made in any final plan except by an amended final plan submitted as provided for the original plan.

(C) Permitted Population Density

(1) Overall Density

The overall population density shown on the master plan for development as an RPC District and associated industrial and commercial uses shall not exceed an average density of 11 persons per acre. In computing population density, a factor of 3.7 persons shall be used per one family dwelling, 3.0 persons per garden type apartment unit or town house and 1.5 persons per high rise apartment unit.

(2) Types of Density

Three residential density areas shall be permitted in an RPC zone in the locations shown on the master plan. Such density areas shall be designated low, medium and high.

a. The population density within a low density area shall not exceed 3.8 persons per acre of gross residential area.

b. The population density within a medium density area shall not exceed 14 persons per acre of gross residential area.

c. The population density within a high density area shall not exceed 60 persons per acre of gross residential area.

(3) Computation of Density

In computing average density on any final plan of a part of an RPC District, which district at the time of its creation was under one ownership or control, any excess in land area over that required to support an average density of 13 persons per acre of gross residential area in any final plan previously recorded may be included. In other words, as each successive final plan is submitted, the overall density of all areas shown on recorded final plans within the proposed RPC District as shown on the master plan shall be recomputed so that the average population density of the developed areas within the re-

EXHIBIT 3 *(Concluded)*

corded sections of the RPC zone shall never at any time in the history of the development exceed a density of 13 persons per acre.

(D) Uses Permissible

(1) All uses permitted by right or by special permit in any district except RM-3, C-D, CDM, C-G or industrial shall be permitted in an RPC District. Not more than 1.5 acres per 1,000 persons may be used for uses permissible in the C-N zone. Uses permissible in a C-N zone may be located within the same building as multi-family dwellings provided the C-N uses is on a separate floor or its entrance is on a separate side of the building from the residential entrance. Motels shall also be permitted subject to the provisions contained in the CDM District.

(2) Uses in an RPC District shall be permissible only in the location shown on the approved preliminary plan required by Section 30–68.2(b).

(3) The initial use of any area within an RPC District shall be shown by the plan required in Section 30–68.2(b). Thereafter the use of neighborhood commercial property shall be governed by the uses allowed in the C-N District, the use of all dwelling units shall be governed by the uses allowed in the R-12.5 District, except that no use shall be denied solely because a particular lot has less than the minimum area, less than the minimum setback, less than the minimum frontage, or less than the minimum parking requirements in the C-N or R-12.5 District, provided the minimum parking requirements are met in a different location, as the case may be.

(E) Lot Sizes and Building Location Requirements

The location of all structures shall be as shown on final plans required by Section 30–68.2(b). The proposed location and arrangement of structures shall not be detrimental to existing or prospective adjacent dwellings or to the existing or prospective development of the neighborhood. Open spaces between structures shall be protected where necessary by adequate covenants, running with the land, conveyances or dedications. There shall be no minimum lot size, no minimum setback lines, no maximum percentage of lot coverage and no minimum lot width in an RPC District. However, every single family dwelling shall have access to a public street, court, walkway or other area dedicated to public use and no single family dwelling (except a town house or semi-detached dwelling) and no addition to any single family dwelling shall be erected within a distance of less than 24 feet from any other single family dwelling.

COLUMBIA II

In the fall of 1965, James Rouse was concerned with the problem of implementing his development plan for Columbia. Columbia was a new city for 110,000 people being developed by Howard Research and Development Corporation (HRD) on 15,000 acres between Baltimore, Maryland, and Washington, D.C. HRD was owned equally by the Connecticut General Life Insurance Company and the Rouse Company, formerly called Community Research and Development, Inc.[1] Mr. Rouse's problem was the establishment of a management group and of controls that could effectively build a new city in an undeveloped area that would eventually cost over $1¼ billion and take close to 15 years to complete. The problems of obtaining approvals of local government; attracting residential, industrial, and commercial tenants; providing adequate construction and permanent financing; and adapting to changing local and national economic conditions were more complicated and risky because of the size of this project. Even the largest home builders in the United States rarely attempted development of more than 2,000 to 3,000 acres in one location.

Mr. Rouse had been aware of the difficulties involved when he first decided to assemble the land. He felt that the scale of the project was even more of an advantage than a disadvantage. He would have the opportunity to create a better way of life that would attract people to Columbia. Because of the size, he could amortize the cost of amenities beyond those offered by normal subdivisions. Not only, under the master plan, would Columbia have the usual swimming pools, shopping centers, and play areas, but it would also have neighborhood community centers, a bustling downtown, parks and lakes, cultural centers, everything except a symphony orchestra and a big-league baseball team. By planning in advance, Mr. Rouse could obtain the cost advantages of installing large-scale utility and road systems. The scope and innovative nature of

---

[1] On June 10, 1966, Community Research and Development (CRD) acquired the stock of James W. Rouse & Co., Inc., a mortgage banking firm, for 691,235 shares of common stock and 25,000 shares of $100 convertible preferred stock. The name of the company was changed to the Rouse Company. Thirty percent of the stock of CRD had been owned by James W. Rouse & Co., and James Rouse had been president and chief operating officer of both firms. The surviving corporation had outstanding 2,889,945 shares of common stock.

the project was such that it was certain to attract local and national attention, facilitating the marketing of the land. He also felt that this publicity would enable him to attract the best professionals to his organization. Traditionally, in the real estate industry, few integrated firms existed. Most firms maintained a small permanent organization and relied upon outside consultants for legal, architectural, engineering, financial, construction, and marketing advice. Mr. Rouse doubted whether a project such as Columbia could be operated on such a basis.

BACKGROUND

During the early stages of the project, Mr. Rouse had been able to keep control within a small group. He had attempted to structure the project so as to minimize the risks that endangered the profitability of other new town developers. In 1962, Mr. Rouse had determined the possibility of assembling a large tract of land in Howard County. Howard County appeared to be on the verge of large-scale growth because of its location in the Baltimore-Washington corridor, which had added 1 million people between 1940 and 1960 and was expected to add another million people in the next 15 years. New roads were practically complete, which would minimize Howard County's major disadvantage, its long driving time to Baltimore and Washington. Therefore, Mr. Rouse knew that a new city in such a location would not have to be self-sufficient, especially in its early years, but could draw upon the surrounding areas.

However, before attempting to assemble the land, Mr. Rouse secured the necessary preliminary financing from the Connecticut General Life Insurance Company. This company agreed to loan $18 million for land acquisition based upon an average acreage cost of no more than $1,500, with collateral in the form of an 8% first deed-of-trust note with principal and interest both due April 30, 1967. Then, after the site was assembled and planned, the insurance company intended to negotiate the conversion of its short-term loan to a more permanent financing arrangement which would also include an equity participation.

Mr. Rouse then began to assemble the land. He worked through various front organizations, straws, dummy corporations, and nominees, each of which was represented by a separate lawyer and realtor who did not know the identity of the real client. Almost none of his employees knew of this project. Mr. Rouse's purpose was to keep down the land price, and prevent holdouts, who might get an exaggerated view of their land value if they knew that the purchaser was a large development corporation.

However, it quickly became apparent that a considerable amount of land in the area was changing hands. Various rumors began to circulate. One was that the land was to be used for an African diplomatic colony;

another that British or Russian money was behind the purchases; and a third that the site was to be used as a United Nations cemetery.

Mr. Rouse realized that he would have to accelerate his buying efforts. Secret strategy meetings to make rapid decisions were held daily in hotel rooms and out-of-the way places. This was essential, since each purchase presented a separate problem necessitating an individual solution. Some sellers were paid cash. Others did not want cash for tax reasons, and installment sales were negotiated. Some preferred to lease their land, while others wanted to sell the land but wanted the right to live on their property for the rest of their lives. Rouse was able to capitalize on the Maryland real estate tax laws which gave preferential treatment to farmland, by arranging for many of the farmers to continue to work their farms on an annual lease basis. Without this arrangement, Rouse was afraid that once the land was rezoned, the county would reassess the land based upon the new higher land use, even though much of the land would not be developed for some years. Many of the sites had title problems which had to be cleared up before the purchase took place. On some parcels he was able to acquire options, but on others he had to take title immediately.

In general, Mr. Rouse found that he was able to act more quickly and at a better price through an all-cash offer. If the pay period were long, he was not able to maintain his average price at $1,500 per acre. Four persons who held a total of 1,500 acres did not want to sell at that time. One parcel of 20 acres along the highway zoned for commercial purposes was bought, but at a price of $15,000 per acre because of the zoning. Finally, Mr. Rouse was forced to pay $3,000 per acre for a 1,000-acre farm and he recognized that additional land could not be purchased for less than that price. If he continued to acquire land, he would exceed his $1,500 per-acre average.

However, by this time, October 1963, nine months after he had begun, Mr. Rouse had dealt with 328 individual owners in making 165 separate purchases. He had acquired slightly under 15,000 acres in his target area at an average cost of $1,450 per acre. Connecticut General had advanced approximately $18 million, and he had financed the remainder through purchase money mortgages. His firm's cost was only $750,000 for planning and preacquisition expenses.

Also, the rumors being circulated were beginning to arouse public opinion, and Mr. Rouse realized that he must make his intentions clear. Otherwise, the atmosphere would become so negative that when he applied for a zone change, he would be voted down no matter what he proposed.

Therefore, on October 31, 1963, Mr. Rouse made an appearance before the County Commissioners of Howard County to announce that HRD had purchased approximately 15,000 acres of land in the county.

This comprised 10% of the county. Mr. Rouse was careful to explain the background of the principals owning HRD, and its intention to develop the site, which would be called Columbia, according to the highest possible standards. He realized that he would need the assistance and approval of the commissioners in many areas, and he intended to work with local citizen associations to coordinate his planning with their needs. Mr. Rouse said that he hoped the county would take no precipitous action during his planning, which should take at least nine months.

Mr. Rouse's announcement was particularly shocking to the Republican County Commissioners, since they had just been elected to office on a platform emphasizing opposition to any high-density development for the area. Their election had exemplified the public attitude toward change. It did not appear likely that the residents of the county, predominantly farmers or exurbanites who had moved to Howard County to avoid urban living, would approve a plan that would triple the county's population. Mr. Rouse, however, hoped through the high quality of his planning process to defer any legal action on the site until he could present his plan.

Although he had not officially begun the detailed planning of the property, Mr. Rouse had selected William Finley as project director of Columbia in the fall of 1962. Mr. Finley was assigned the special responsibility of supervising the project planning. In 1949, he had received the first Bachelor's and Master's degrees given by the department of city planning at the University of California. Since that time, he had worked in local government, first as planning director for Richmond, California, and then as director of the National Capital Planning Commission, Washington, D.C. At CRD he had first assisted in the development of the Village of Cross Keys, a smaller project of the company, combining higher-income residential, office, and retail uses. In the spring of 1963, Mr. Finley hired Morton Hoppenfeld as chief designer for Columbia. Mr. Hoppenfeld had been chief of special area planning for the Philadelphia Planning Commission and later urban designer for the Capital Planning Commission under Mr. Finley. Both men had come to the project excited by Mr. Rouse's vision and the potential of the site.

Mr. Rouse's philosophy was based on the premise that planning must relate to people. He said: "It should be possible to produce an environment in which various institutions can work for humans in a creative way. Planners too often propose the creation of 'great environments' unrelated to the real needs and aspirations of the people who will live there. The architect must be a social servant. Serious social problems are created by the disproportionate scale of our cities. In a small town, broader friendships and feelings of responsibility are developed. Communities should not be 'works of art' but gardens in which we are a growing people and civilization."

To implement Rouse's ideas, Mr. Hoppenfeld suggested the creation of a "work group" of individuals representing various disciplines, primarily in the social sciences, who could assist the land planners in developing a community plan. This effort to coordinate social with physical planning was to be the major guideline for the creation of Columbia.

During the summer and fall of 1963, a 14-member work group was formed, representing a number of occupations and academic disciplines. The members were:

Henry Bain, Jr.—Consultant in Public Administration and Business
Antonia Handler Chayes—Technical Secretary to Committee on Education, President's Commission on Women
Robert Crawford—Commissioner of Recreation for Philadelphia
Dr. Leonard Duhl—Psychiatrist at the National Institute of Public Health
Nelson Foote—Sociologist and Manager of Consumer and Public Relations, General Electric Company
Herbert Gans—Professor of Sociology at Columbia
Robert M. Gladstone—President, Robert M. Gladstone and Associates, economic research and market analysts
Christopher Jencks—Education specialist and education editor of the *New Republic*
Dr. Paul Lemkau—Professor of Public Health and Psychiatry at Johns Hopkins
Donald Michael—Chairman and Resident Fellow at the Institute for Policy Studies, Washington, D.C.
Chester Rapkin—Professor of City Planning, University of Pennsylvania
Wayne Thompson—City Manager of Oakland, California
Alan Voorhees—Transportation Consultant
Stephen B. Withey—Professor of Psychology, University of Michigan

The purpose of the group was to "apply the social sciences to the actual design and operation of a new community better than it has been done before." The members of the work group were initially suspicious. They feared that they were being used mainly as "window dressing" to obtain a zone change. Mr. Rouse's enthusiasm forced them to think more positively. He convinced them of his desire to create something better than the normal suburb. He wanted: (1) to build a complete city as far as possible, containing all elements that might normally be located in a community of approximately 100,000 persons for the Washington-Baltimore region; (2) to "respect" the land by giving full expression to terrain, tree and plant life, soil conditions, existing bodies of water, and other natural features; (3) to emphasize the needs and growth of people in the community in terms of social, educational, cultural, political, recreational, and economic factors; and (4) to respond fully to marketplace requirements in planning and programming the development.

The problem of the group was to take these general objectives and translate them into specific services, specifying the level of services to be provided, the physical facilities required to provide these services, the overall costs of the services and facilities and the specific areas of interaction of these services with other aspects of the community. The group attempted to answer many of the criticisms leveled at existing suburbs. How can a woman be helped to overcome the sense of isolation and frustration common to much of suburbia? Can she be something beyond a housewife and chauffeur for her children? Do buyers benefit from neighborhoods that are mixed economically and/or racially? Could a government be designed that would not be monolithic in concept but that could vary depending upon the function it performs? How can one offer diversity of opportunity in shopping, job opportunities, and communications?

These questions all were related to economics. The proposed services and facilities might impose too heavy a financial burden on either the developer or the residents. Which would the residents want enough to pay for, and how much would they pay? The services, roads, and utilities must be provided early enough to give the potential buyer confidence that the community would be completed as planned, but on the other hand the developer wanted to minimize his capital expenditures during the early years until the marketing pace picked up.

To aid the work group in their deliberating, 110 officials, advisors, and consultants were called in during the planning of Columbia (see Exhibit 1).

The final recommendations were not revolutionary, and certain outsiders felt that Columbia was only a slightly better suburb. The work group recommended social homogeneity at the neighborhood level to prevent the typical "keep up with the Joneses" financial competition. The criticism that mini-ghettos were in effect being created was countered by the argument that families wanted the sense of belonging which came from living with people who made them comfortable. This sense of security was carried into the architectural design, which Mr. Rouse felt should not be too "avant-garde," a criticism that had been leveled at Reston. Half of the housing was to consist of single-family homes and the other half higher-density apartments and town houses. The overall density for the 15,000 acres was to be less than 7 persons per acre as contrasted with 10 per acre in Reston and other new cities.

The attempt was conservative, to build upon and improve existing suburban life, by offering amenities, better organized from the standpoint of accessibility and from the standpoint of preserving the natural beauty of the area. Specifically, the work group recommended that:

1. The neighborhood and village schools be within easy safe walking distance and in phase with the development.
2. The neighborhoods have swimming pools, tennis courts, play fields,

tot lots, and "corner" neighborhood stores that would serve to sell certain commodities and drugs as well as serve as a neighborhood meeting area.

3. The village centers have, in one general area, stores, doctors' offices, churches, a library, community hall, high school, middle school, play fields.
4. There be an open-space system with walks, bicycle paths, and riding trails spacing and connecting the neighborhoods and villages.
5. A major recreational system be established for all of Columbia, including lakes for boating and fishing, big parks with camping sites, picnic grounds, nature trails, riding stables, bridle paths and golf courses.
6. The town center have department stores, fine shops, restaurants, movies, theater, concert halls, hotels and inns, office building, a community college hospital, stadium, music and art schools, and public squares and parks.
7. Employment centers be built with major industrial plants, warehouses, distribution facilities, research and development centers and regional offices.
8. A transportation system be developed, including:
    a) Minibuses with their own right-of-way connecting village centers, the downtown and employment and recreation centers. Bus stops be within a two-minute walk of 40% of the units and be spaced to travel five minutes apart at a cost of 10 cents a ride.
    b) Separate routes for pedestrians, bicyclists, and automobiles.
    c) Special major streets where automobiles could move freely without interference of pedestrians, bicycles, driveways, or parking.
9. A communication network which would involve a closed circuit educational TV system to each dwelling, Columbia newspapers, radio and TV stations, and extensive adult education and vocational training programs.
10. A serious attempt be made to make community institutions and facilities more useful in serving people of Columbia through a Community Services Center that would represent people and communicate their needs to each other.

These recommendations formed the basis for the physical planning for Columbia. Mr. Rouse and Mr. Finley felt that their plan was not a "glorified subdivision" typical of large home builders and would not be treated as such when HRD made its zoning presentation to the county. The land was not optioned but acquired in advance in its entirety. This gave credibility to the total plan. Columbia itself would have a great diversity of homes and income types, with the actual home building done by a number of outside builders. To achieve a sense of self-sufficiency, the complex included commercial and industrial development on a far larger scale than found in the standard, less-integrated subdivision. The community would provide 30,000 jobs within its borders. The long 15-year development period automatically required the developer to adopt a broader perspective. Whereas the normal subdivider merely receives his zoning and building approvals once in an area and then proceeds on his own, HRD expected to deal with public agencies throughout the growth of the city, both from the standpoint of legal approvals and from that of establishing and maintaining the level of community services. Also, since HRD intended to own much of downtown Columbia itself as well as some of the multifamily projects, the company's initial financial commitment was greater, since to achieve market confidence, more roads, utilities, and amenities would be installed earlier in the development period. Lastly, the quality of development would be better. The size of the project permitted the hiring of a better staff, including more planners and outside experts. The developer became a merchant of a total environment: political, economic, social, and physical.

The problem now became a tactical one, as to the best way to convince the residents of Howard County and the County Commissioners that a zone change to permit Columbia was desirable. This was especially difficult because the mood of the residents as expressed in the recent election was to maintain the status quo. Normally, zoning fights became a battleground between builders anxious to utilize the land to greater economic advantage and local residents fighting any change to their community. Zoning is primarily a negative control. It limits what can be developed on a site but does not guarantee that a desired use actually would be built. Mr. Rouse wanted to prove that zoning could be used in a positive manner to encourage the best in community development through better and more flexible land-use control.

The economic advantages to Mr. Rouse of more intense zoning are easily apparent. Under present zoning he could build 30,000 units on 15,000 acres, which would result in a per-unit raw land cost of $750. His new plan called for the 30,000 units to be built on 50% of the land, correspondingly reducing the per-unit land cost by 50%. There were further cost advantages to him in that with the greater density the length of the roads and sewers would be reduced.

As to the remaining 50% of the land, Mr. Rouse was willing to leave 25% for public parks and open space, such as golf courses, in order to receive approval for industrial and commercial zoning on the remaining 25%.

Lastly, although Mr. Rouse considered his $1,500 per-acre purchase price as cheap even at that time, he knew that he would not be able under existing zoning to find a buyer for 15,000 acres, because of the difficulty in absorbing 30,000 units in Howard County without any concomitant increase in industrial and commercial development. Also, if the zoning change was denied, Connecticut General would probably request that its $18 million loan be repaid upon expiration in 1967. Therefore, Mr. Rouse attached great importance to his proposal on November 1964, to the Howard County Planning Commission. He requested a planned community ordinance, such as was created in Fairfax County, Virginia, in 1962 (see Exhibit 3 in Columbia I). Mr. Rouse's objectives were essentially fourfold:

1. Zoning which permitted greater planning flexibility, higher residential densities, and industrial and commercial uses.
2. The authority to create a special entity that could issue tax-exempt bonds for major roads and utilities on the site.
3. The assurance that peripheral roads and utilities adequate to handle a development of this size be brought to the site.
4. A legal basis that would guarantee to the developer that he could not, over the projected 15-year development period, be forced to change zoning and other controls as the result of pressure from either the county or his own residents.

Mr. Rouse began his campaign by sending a copy of the brochure he presented to the County Commissioners to every public official and homeowner in Howard County. His experience in changing the zone for his Village of Cross Keys in the Roland Park Section of Baltimore had taught him the need to work closely with the local residents. There he had held a series of neighborhood meetings at which he presented not only his own plan but an obviously unsatisfactory one that was permitted under the existing zoning. He showed how his plan would fit in with the existing neighborhood and municipal facilities. His natural persuasiveness, plus his willingness to cooperate with reasonable suggestions from the residents, had been effective in making the local residents feel that they had had a part in forming his final plan.

The brochure for Columbia attempted to make three basic points: (1) suburban expansion into Howard County was inevitable; (2) there were problems to this growth; and (3) Columbia would do a better job of solving these problems than any other practical alternative.

In regard to the inevitability of expansion, the brochure presented the population statistics for the area.

Population Statistics

	Five Corridor Counties	Metropolitan Baltimore	Metropolitan Washington
1950	769,347	1,405,399	1,507,900
1960	1,433,000	1,727,023	2,314,310
1980*	2,805,000	2,400,000	3,638,000

* Estimated.

By next listing the problems of this growth, Mr. Rouse showed his awareness and understanding of the concerns of the residents toward development trends similar to those in other counties. The results had been spiraling taxes, the waste and abuse of the land, monotonous suburbs, inconveniently located facilities, and unsightly development. Mr. Rouse tried to point out that already in Howard County the schools were overcrowded, rural roads crowded, and fire protection and other municipal services inadequate. Yet, he knew that the low level of municipal services was to a certain extent deliberate. It kept down growth and kept down property taxes for the present residents. The per capita expenditures in Howard County were only $118 as compared with over $200 in neighboring counties.

Mr. Rouse was aware that he could not attract a large number of home buyers without a higher level of services, and he knew that it would be naïve to pretend that the services proposed for Columbia would not increase expenditures. But, he attempted to show the county that Columbia would not only be self-supporting but produce excess tax revenue. Put in another way, if Columbia had been built in 1965, taxes could have been reduced by 40%, or services increased to $157 per person. The major reason for this difference was that only 16% of Howard's existing tax base was nonresidential, while 40% of Columbia's was anticipated to be.

There was considerable controversy over the financial issue, since many claimed that once the county changed its attitude, the cost of services would rise to the $200-per-person level of other counties, and the tax rate in Howard County would have to increase substantially. Also, there was no guarantee that Columbia would get the commercial and industrial users that would provide the tax surplus. In addition, if Columbia succeeded in attracting 100,000 residents, the existing voters would be outnumbered, and the existing officeholders might be voted out.

Mr. Rouse continued to take a positive approach. The brochure said that in Columbia, "The single purpose was to take advantage of every opportunity to preserve and enhance the land as a beautiful and useful asset of the community." His aim was to permit better land use; utilize modern town planning techniques; promote safety in streets through separation of pedestrian and automobile traffic; prevent wasted time and money in useless traffic movement through proper location of all facilities; prevent wasteful duplication of services through multiple use of facilities; create spaciousness through well-located open spaces; and encourage civic responsibility through personal relationship of inhabitant and community.

Specifically, the new town zoning ordinance overall required that the community must be economically and culturally self-sufficient with a minimum size of 2,500 acres; with public facilities, including transportation, water, and sewers, provided; and with a maximum overall dwelling density of 2.5 per acre, including single-family, low-density of 2 units per acre, medium density of 4 units per acre, and apartments at 15 units per acre. The community must be built in accordance with the use plan. The minimum floor area for homes and town houses was 1,050 square feet. There were to be controls for off-street parking, signs, set backs, and industrial use. The land-use requirements were as shown.

Type	Minimum % Area	Maximum % Area
Open space	20%	NA*
Single-family low	15%	NA
Single-family medium	25%	NA
Apartments	NA	10%
Commercial	2%	10%
Industrial	10%	10%
Other	NA	15%

* NA = None Applicable.

The county officials' first reaction to the plan was negative. In February 1965, the County Commissioners released a memorandum from their attorney declaring that a Planned Community Ordinance was illegal under Maryland law. The county representatives also argued that a special tax district, which HRD wanted to have formed, would seriously impair the bonding capacity of the county, resulting in higher taxes to all county residents. Lastly, the officials were concerned that the extra services proposed for Columbia became a tax burden on the present residents.

Mr. Rouse was somewhat disturbed by this initial reaction, but realized that the County Commissioners for political reasons could not approve his zoning change without a fight. His attorneys advised him that the county's point as to the separate district for bonding purposes was a valid one, and HRD might have to bear all the costs for roads and utilities themselves, a cost that at that time was estimated at over $20 million.

To solve the problems of the developer's maintenance of control of the development during the construction period and to insure that Columbia's services would not be a burden on the county, the decision was made to form the nonprofit Columbia Park and Recreation Association (CPRA). The CPRA had its basis in the Maryland tradition of deed and agreement for property assessment, whereby a predetermined amount is paid annually to the Association by the property owners. To enforce this agreement, the Association had to create what in effect was a first lien upon the property.

The organization of the Association would be headed at the outset by a seven-member board of directors, all of whom would be appointed by HRD; two would be ex officio. As the project proceeded, additional members would be elected to the board until the residents themselves had control. There would also be an overall advisory council of residents to the board.

The function of the CPRA would essentially be fourfold: (1) building and maintaining the parks, pools, courts, marinas, lakes, and community buildings; (2) operating preschool and child-care centers; (3) providing maintenance for all public and park landscaping, and operating the minibus system and other conveniences for public areas; and (4) coordinating with Howard County's unified county government in the areas in which the county provides services to Columbia. The county still had the major responsibility for education, police, fire protection, justice, health, planning, zoning, building inspection, and public utility departments.

Another area in which Mr. Rouse modified his approach was in the relationship of the zoning requested for Columbia to other builders and landowners. Originally, since he did not want to appear to be making a proposal that would give advantages applicable only to Columbia, the minimum area eligible for consideration was reduced to 750 acres, and the overall permitted residential density was four dwelling units per acre. This was in spite of Columbia's size of 15,000 acres and proposed density of two units per acre. However, many local residents objected strenuously to any measures that would encourage other builders who might be less reputable. As a result, the minimum acreage was increased to 2,500 acres and the maximum density to 2.5 units per acre. A separate zoning classification with separate regulations for parcels of from 750 to 2,500 acres was proposed and eventually approved.

The county officials asked if HRD could tie the residential building to the number of jobs provided by new industries, or if he could accept approval for a section of the project until more experience was available. Mr. Rouse felt he could not accept such restrictions. For the overall concept of a new city to work, potential tenants must be assured that the project in totality would be built. Also, he had to make certain economic decisions that were based upon the size of the total project. As an example, a sewer line to service the whole city might cost $4 million. To install smaller lines now for $2 million and increase their capacity later might eventually cost $6 million. He was willing to take the risk of spending $4 million now, if he knew he could proceed at his option.

Mr. Rouse gave the local residents every opportunity to see the plan and ask questions about it. An exhibit was set up that was visited by 5,000 people in seven months. Over the next months, over 500 meetings of six or more people were held. Mr. Rouse's group sent speakers to every group that would hear them. They canvassed virtually every organization in the county.

In June 1965, Mr. Rouse was rewarded for his effort with the adoption of the New Town district zoning. Ninety days later, the county approved the plan for Columbia under this zoning. At the public hearing held to discuss the change, every major civic group had announced its support for Columbia. The only person who had spoken against the plan said that he did so only as a private citizen. He said that if he were an official of the county, he would have voted for its adoption.

Soon thereafter, Connecticut General decided that it was interested in converting its loan to a permanent basis, based upon the development of Columbia as a new town. However, the insurance firm decided it was only willing to furnish one half of the $50 million that was estimated as the developer's cash needs. Therefore, the Teachers Insurance and Annuity Association of America was asked to participate. Because of the increased risk resulting from the high debt-to-equity ratio, the interest was initially proposed at 8½% which was 2% above standard mortgage rates at that time. The president of Teachers commissioned a new appraisal of the land based on its value as a single site with the new zoning. The appraisal valued the land in its undeveloped state at $60 million. An agreement was reached whereby the interest rate in Teachers' portion of the loan would be reduced to 6½%; in return, Teachers would be given a 15-year option to purchase 10% of the presently outstanding stock of HRD from the two stockholders for $3 million.

In December 1965, a final agreement was reached whereby Connecticut General contributed $25 million, Teachers $15 million, and the Chase Manhattan Bank of New York $10 million to a maximum loan of $50 million. The term was for 10 years at an average rate of 7.3%. In December 1971, 5% of the loan would become due, then 8% in December 1972, 12% in December 1973, 10% in December 1974, and the remaining 65% in December 1975. Other than payments due under the above schedule, HRD could sell land without the normal principal repayment required by most lenders on raw land, provided that the sales price be in accordance with a previously agreed-upon land sale price and provided that the money be retained by HRD for further development of other areas of the site.

HRD was capitalized with $1.5 million contributed equally by Connecticut General and Rouse. The stock itself was pledged as security for the loan. Three of the five directors of HRD were elected by Connecticut General. However, Rouse received a contract on a cost basis to operate, implement, and manage the development at least until December 31, 1970.

One problem that was never resolved by any of the parties was the determination of a return on investment for their respective interests in the project. First, what was the investment: the $1.5 million paid for the stock, the $50 million loan commitment, or the equity plus the overage loan balance, a balance which was difficult to determine at this time? Some, but not all of the loan, should rightfully be considered as equity. But then, what was the investment of Rouse for its share? Even though its expenses were being covered, was there a factor that should be computed for loss of alternative opportunity, since Mr. Rouse and many other key employees of his company were engaged almost full time on this project. One approach that was discussed was that the profit today was the present value of the right to receive $80 million in 15 years, discounted back at an appropriate rate. The problem was further complicated by the uncertainty of the income tax consequences. There was no question but that HRD was a land developer and would be subject to taxation at corporate rather than capital gains rates. But, there was a further problem in distributing the money to the stockholders at the end of the project without additional taxes. Possible alternatives included mergers, buyouts, or retention of HRD to develop other properties. The most desirable alternative today might change because of new tax laws in effect at the end of 15 years. The investment properties owned by HRD also might provide excess depreciation to shield some of the other income.

These income-producing properties would also create an equity value. Columbia Development Corporation, a wholly owned subsidiary of HRD, was formed to own the town center, including the shopping area of 1 million square feet, and the office area of 700,000 square feet plus some commercial space in other areas; 500,000 square feet of industrial space, and 2,000 apartment units. The total annual revenue from these investments was expected to reach $3 million by the end of 15 years, which, capitalized at a 10% rate, would be $30 million.

Lastly, the present projections were based upon a 15-year development period. Many of the costs for Columbia had already been fixed; thus, the trend towards inflation and area growth would work to their benefit.

But, delays might create the need for additional funds, resulting in higher carrying charges, and lengthening the period before the developers began to make a profit.

Mr. Rouse believed that a properly conceived financial plan should provide a means for operating control and evaluation of his complex project to minimize these potential problems. This plan must relate changes in market demand and cost. It must assist management in systematically identifying and classifying projected proceeds and expenditures for the development period; in determining the maximum financing required for land development; in estimating the net proceeds from land development before income taxes; in establishing guidelines for the preparation of annual development budgets; in establishing the development pace; and in establishing specifications for land development. The information would also be used for tax planning, project scheduling, estimating staff requirements, marketing strategy, and almost every other segment of the project.

The Columbia Economic Model (CEM) was considered a key to the financial success of the project and the most important financial control tool for the Columbia management (see Exhibit 2). The model itself was not very sophisticated. It used neither simulation techniques not probabilistic theory to derive its output. Rather, it was an extended cash flow forecasting device which included a number of assumptions each of which was continuously examined for appropriateness and validity.

The model was important because it gave the new community legitimacy as a business enterprise by helping to insure that cost-control and cash projections were adequately stressed. In addition, the CEM was an integrating force for the entire organization. It could be utilized to examine fully the complex implications of changes in development pace, costs, and other factors related to the total Columbia project. This type of management in a huge and complex project could not, obviously, be accomplished efficiently by any one individual executive without the aid of the model and other organizational members.

EXHIBIT 1

Advisors and Consultants to the Rouse Company in the Planning of Columbia

PRIMARY ADVISORS

Dr. Henry M. Bain, Jr., Public Administration
Chevy Chase, Maryland
Antonia Chayes, Family Life
Washington, D.C.
Robert W. Crawford, Recreation System
Commissioner, Department of Recreation
Philadelphia, Pennsylvania
Dr. Nelson F. Foote, Community Structure
Manager of Consumer and Public Relations Research Program
General Electric Company, New York, N.Y.
Dr. Herbert J. Gans, Community Structure
Columbia University
Robert M. Gladstone, Economics and Housing Market
Washington, D.C.
Christopher S. Jencks, Education
Fellow, Institute for Policy Studies
Washington, D.C.
Dr. Paul V. Lemkau, Health Systems
The Johns Hopkins University
Dr. Donald N. Michael, Chairman
Resident Fellow, Institute for Policy Studies
Washington, D.C.
Dr. Chester Rapkin, Housing
Professor, Wharton School and Institute for Urban Studies
University of Pennsylvania
Wayne E. Thompson, Local Government and Administration
The Dayton Company
Minneapolis, Minnesota
Alan M. Voorhees, Traffic and Transportation
Washington, D.C.
Dr. Stephen B. Withey, Communication in the Community
University of Michigan

GENERAL ADVISORS

Edwin Castagna, Library Systems
Director, Enoch Pratt Free Library
Baltimore, Maryland
Guido Crocetti, Health Systems
The Johns Hopkins University
Dr. Leonard J. Duhl, Community Social Structure

Department of Housing and Urban Development
Washington, D.C.
Paul B. Sears, Ecology
Professor, Department of Botany
Yale University
Dr. Herbert F. Striner, Employment Opportunities
Director of Planning, Upjohn Institute for Employment Research, Washington, D.C.

MEMBERS OF DR. LEMKAU'S ADVISORY COMMITTEE ON HEALTH SYSTEMS

Dr. Nicholas G. Alexiou, School Health Programs
Dr. Howard Ennes, Health, Education & Community Organization Development
Dr. Ruth B. Freeman, Public Health Nursing
Dr. Herbert Klarman, Medical Care
Dr. Verl Lewis, Community Welfare Service
Dr. Burton R. Pollack, Dental Health
Dr. Theodore R. Shrop, Local Health Organization
Dr. John Whitridge, Jr., Maternal & Child Health Programs
Dr. Charles M. Wylie, Public Health Administration

THE ARTS

Dr. Stanley Cavell
Department of Philosophy
Harvard University
Hyman Faine
National Executive Secretary
American Guild of Musical Artists
New York, N.Y.
Hugh Hardy, *Architect*
New York, N.Y.
Dr. Esther Jackson, *Director of Education*
New York Shakespeare Festival
Bernard Joy, *Designer*
New York, N.Y.
Dr. Charles Kent, *Director*
The Peabody Conservatory
of the City of Baltimore
Eugene W. Leake, *President*
The Maryland Institute

EXHIBIT 1 (Continued)

Milton Lyon, *Director*
  Department to Extend the Professional
  Theatre Actors' Equity Foundation
Charles Parkhurst, *Director*
  Baltimore Museum of Art
Bennard Perlman
  Art Consultants of Baltimore
John Ruddley
  County Director of Art
  Westchester Workshop

COMMUNICATIONS

Bison Associates
  Boston, Massachusetts
T. Wilson Cahall
  Administrative Assistant to Superinten-
  dent of Schools
  Washington County Board of Education
  Hagerstown, Maryland
Professor Arthur Hungerford
  Associate Professor of Speech for Radio
  and Television
  Pennsylvania State University
Robert C. Snider, *Assistant Executive*
Secretary
  National Education Association

COMMUNITY INVENTORY, CHARLOTTE, N.C.

Donald C. Sanders
  Charlotte, North Carolina

COMMUNITY INVENTORY, RACINE, WISCONSIN

John M. Ducey, *President*
  Institute of Urban Life
  Chicago, Illinois

CONFERENCE CENTER

Dr. Jess E. Burkett
  College of Continuing Education
  The University of Oklahoma
James D. Landon, *Manager*
  Onchiota Conference Center
  Sterling Forest, New York
Ralph Showalter, *Executive Director*
  Social Development Corporation
  Washington, D.C.

EDUCATION

Dr. George Packer Berry, *Retired Dean*
  Harvard Medical School
Dr. Kenneth E. Boulding, *Professor of Eco-*
nomics
  The University of Michigan

Sadie D. Ginsberg, *Instructor and Con-*
sultant
  Early Childhood Education
  University of Maryland
Dr. Wesley Hotchkiss, *General Secretary*
  Division of Higher Education
  United Church of Christ
  New York, New York
Dr. A. A. Liverright, *Director*
  Center for the Study of Liberal Education
  for Adults
  Boston, Massachusetts
Robert A. Luke, *Director*
  Adult Education Service
  National Education Association
Dr. Earl J. McGrath, *Executive Officer*
  Institute of Higher Education
  Teachers' College
  Columbia University
Lester W. Nelson
  Educator, formerly with Ford Foundation
  Baltimore, Maryland
Dr. Bernice Neugarten
  Committee on Human Development
  University of Chicago
Dr. David Popenoe, *Research Director*
  The Urban Studies Center
  Rutgers University
Daniel Robinson, *Partner*
  Peat, Marwick, & Mitchell
  New York, New York
George Y. Rusk
  Baltimore, Maryland
Alvin Toffler
  New York, New York
Sidney Wallach, *Executive Director*
  Oliver Wendell Holmes Association

ENERGY SYSTEMS

Albert B. Gipe & Associates
  Baltimore, Maryland

FAMILY LIFE

Dr. Joel Elkes, *Director*
  Department of Psychiatry and Behavioral
  Sciences
  The Johns Hopkins University
Dr. Ruth H. Useem, *Professor*
  Department of Sociology
  Michigan State University

FEDERAL INSTALLATIONS

Robert Plavnick
  Washington, D.C.

FORESTRY

Gerald Williams
  Westminster, Maryland

EXHIBIT 1 (*Continued*)

GOLF COURSE LOCATION AND DESIGN

Edmund B. Ault
Silver Spring, Maryland

HIGHWAY ENGINEERING

Green Associates, Inc.
Baltimore, Maryland
Rummel, Klepper & Kahl
Baltimore, Maryland

INDUSTRIAL LAND AND PROGRAM EVALUATION

Fantus Area Research, Inc. and
The Fantus Company
New York, New York

INDUSTRIAL LAND DEVELOPMENT

James M. Rice Associates
Maywood, New Jersey

LAND DEVELOPMENT ENGINEERING

C. D. Messick, Jr. & Associates
Annapolis, Maryland
Purdum & Jeschke
Ellicott City, Maryland
Geo. Wm. Stephens, Jr. &
Associates, Inc.
Towson, Maryland

LANDSCAPE DESIGN

Gerald M. Cope
Philadelphia, Pennsylvania

LAND USE REGULATIONS

David W. Craig
Pittsburgh, Pennsylvania
Lewis Elston
Silver Spring, Maryland
Charles E. Hogg
Ellicott City, Maryland

LAND USE REGULATIONS AND LOCAL GOVERNMENT

William A. Doebele, Jr., *Professor*
Department of City and Regional Planning
Harvard University

LEGAL COUNSEL

David E. Belcher
Charles C. G. Evans
John Martin Jones, Jr.
Piper & Marbury
Baltimore, Maryland

LOCAL GVERNMENT AND FINANCE

Charles M. Haar, *Professor*
Harvard Law School
Harvard University
Richard Netzer
Graduate School of Public Administration
New York University
Paul S. Sarbanes
Charter Revision Commission of Baltimore City

MARKET RESEARCH

Carl Norcross
Goodkin-Norcross Research Corporation
Washington, D.C.

MUNICIPAL FINANCE

Wain Wright & Ramsey, Inc.
New York, New York

NEW TOWN DEVELOPMENT

Thomas McDade
Housing and Home Finance Agency
Washington, D.C.
Wyndham Thomas, Esq., *Director*
Town and Country Planning Association
London, England

OPINION SURVEYS

Sidney Hollander Associates
Baltimore, Maryland

PROPERTY SURVEYS

Maps, Inc.
Baltimore, Maryland

PUBLIC ADMINISTRATION

John A. Donaho & Associates
Baltimore, Maryland

RAILROAD ENGINEERING

James Crockett Associates
Baltimore, Maryland

RECREATION

Milton Costello
Wantagh, New York
Dr. M. Alexander Gabrielsen
New York University
Bernard Kreh
Miami, Florida
Ira Rigger
Baltimore, Maryland

EXHIBIT 1 *(Continued)*

SEWER, WATER, AND UTILITIES ENGINEERING

Jerome B. Wolff
  Towson, Maryland

SOIL STRUCTURE

Robert P. Balter
  *Soil and Foundation Consultants, Inc.
  Baltimore, Maryland*

STREAM VALLEY PLANNING

Dr. M. Gordon Wolman, *Chairman
  Department of Geography
  The John Hopkins University*

TRAFFIC AND TRANSPORATION

Robert Morris
  Baltimore, Maryland
Robert Pollack
  *Manager of Operations
  Cleveland Transit System*

TRAFFIC ENGINEERING

Wilbur Smith & Associates
  New Haven, Connecticut

TREE FARMING

Dr. Thomas Cannon
  University of North Carolina

UTILITY SYSTEMS PLANNING

Dr. Abel Wolman
  *Professor Emeritus of Sanitary
  Engineering
  The Johns Hopkins University*

CONSULTANTS AND ADMINISTRA-TORS FOR RELIGIOUS GROUPS IN THE PLANNING OF COLUMBIA

Dr. Stanley J. Hallett, *Executive Secretary
  Department of Church Planning
  Church Federation of Greater Chicago*
Brother Anthony Ipsaro, S. M.
  *Superintendent of Baltimore
  Archdiocesan Schools*
Dr. Louis Kaplan, *President
  Baltimore Hebrew College*
Reverend William J. Lee, S. F.
  *Rector, St. Mary's Seminary College
  Baltimore, Maryland*
Dr. Leon Sachs, *Executive Director
  Baltimore Jewish Council*

Reverend Clarence Sinclair
  *Mission Development Committee
  for Columbia*
Reverend John Wagner, *Director
  Commission on Urban Life
  National Council of Churches*
Louise Yolton
  *Mission Development Committee for
  Columbia*

CONSULTANTS TO THE BOARD OF LIBRARY TRUSTEES OF HOWARD COUNTY AND THE STATE DEPARTMENT OF EDUCATION

Dr. Richard Darling
  *Supervisor of Library Services
  Montgomery County Public Schools*
Dr. Harold Goldstein
  *Graduate School of Library Science
  University of Illinois*
Dr. Philip Lewis, *Director
  Research, Development, and Special
  Projects
  Chicago Board of Education*
Dr. C. Walter Stone
  *Director of Libraries
  University of Pittsburgh*

CONSULTANTS TO THE STATE AND LOCAL BOARDS OF EDUCATION

Dr. William Alexander, *Professor of Educa-
  tion
  Graduate School of Education
  University of Florida*
Dr. Robert H. Anderson, *Professor
  of Education
  Graduate School of Education
  Harvard University*
Dr. Calvin Stillman, *Vice President
  Broadcasting Foundation of America*
Dr. Richard Wynn
  *Professor of Educational Administration
  Graduate School of Education
  University of Pittsburgh*

SPECIALISTS FROM THE JOHNS HOPKINS MEDICAL INSTITUTIONS IN THE DEVELOPMENT OF HEALTH FACILITIES

Dr. Joseph Sadusk
  *Associate Dean for Community Medicine
  The Johns Hopkins University School of
  Medicine*
William F. Towle
  The Johns Hopkins Medical Institutions

EXHIBIT 2

Economic Model

INTRODUCTION

The CEM is used as a management tool primarily to:

1. Systematically identify and classify projected proceeds and expenditures for the development period.
2. Determine the maximum financing required for land development.
3. Estimate the net proceeds from land development before income taxes.
4. Establish guidelines for the preparation of annual development budgets.
5. Establish development pace.
6. Establish specifications for land development.

Information developed in the preparation of the CEM is also used for:

1. Tax planning.
2. Project scheduling.
3. Estimating staff requirements.
4. Marketing strategy.
5. Almost every other segment of the project.

The CEM does not:

1. Determine or project a rate of return on invested capital.
2. Include any projections on properties to be developed by wholly owned subsidiaries for our own account except that:
    a) Land is "sold" at full value to subsidiaries.
    b) A working capital requirement for subsidiaries is included in the determination of maximum financing requirements.
3. Provide for inflation; all dollars are current dollars. Increased prices are assumed to result from development rather than inflation.
4. Determine or project profit on major categories of land disposition.
5. Determine or prorate costs to specific geographic areas.

PREPARATION

The CEM is updated every quarter. The preparation process has recently been computerized, and we now have the capability of preparing all or any part of the model at anytime.

Responsibility is assigned for every assumption used in the preparation of the CEM. Prior to the preparation of the CEM, each person responsible for assumptions is requested to review and update them in accordance with current programs. Revisions to assumptions are made for favorable or unfavorable reasons including:

1. Current cost projections.
2. Schedules.
3. Market reaction.
4. Specification revisions.

EXHIBIT 2 *(Continued)*

A preliminary review of assumptions is made by management before the revised calculation of the CEM is made to determine that the assumptions are reasonable.

Management then reviews the updated CEM giving particular attention to:

1. Assumption revision (which are highlighted).
2. Projected peak debt.
3. Net proceeds from development.

Management approves or revises assumptions and additional CEM calculations are made until the results are satisfactory. The CEM is then distributed to all department heads working on Columbia.

Every major development decision is referenced to the CEM to determine its consistency with approved management development policy. Certain projects have been delayed or eliminated because they have not been previously included in the CEM. Other projects have been approved and then included within the CEM.

The contents of the CEM include:

1. Assumptions
2. Economic Model Years
3. Net Proceeds From Development
4. Land and Development Costs
5. Composite Financing Position
6. CA Cash Accounting
7. CA Operating Expenses
8. CA Capital Costs
9. HRD Cash Accounting
10. Consolidated Land Sales Proceeds
11. Residential Sales Proceeds
12. Residential Sales Prices
13. Pace of Residential Development
14. Residential Land Usage
15. Commercial and Industrial Development Land Proceeds
16. Commercial and Industrial Pace and Prices
17. Public Land Sales Proceeds
18. Public Land Sales Pace and Prices
19. HRD Town Development and Administrative Costs
20. HRD Residential Lot and Industrial Land Development Costs
21. HRD Residential Lot Development Costs

EXPLANATION OF CEM CONTENTS

Assumptions. All of the assumptions, which are the basis for the financial projections, are detailed at the front of the CEM.

Assumptions include such items as:

1. Development programs.
2. Marketing strategy.
3. Schedules.

EXHIBIT 2 (Continued)

4. Cultural programs.
5. Cash flow.
6. Financing costs.
7. Special considerations.

Economic Model Years. The CEM is based on a 15-year development program. Each CEM year corresponds with the company's fiscal and budget year. CEM figures are, therefore, consistent with financial statements and budget reports.

Net Proceeds from Development. Gross land sales proceeds and miscellaneous income (timber sales, etc.) less land and development costs reflect net proceeds from development before income tax. The CEM is utilized for income tax planning but does not reflect projected income taxes.

Land and Development Costs. Actual land and predevelopment costs are reflected. Development costs include actual costs to date and projected costs for the remaining development period. Development costs by category include:

A. Townwide costs. This category includes:
    1. Roads.
    2. Major utilities.
    3. Administrative expenses.
    4. Real estate taxes.
    5. Leasehold payments.
    6. Special items.
B. Land finishing costs—includes intract costs (as outlined later).
C. Financing costs.

Composite Financing Position. Composite debt is limited under the terms of the financing documents. This projection must, therefore, be within those limitations and is the net of land acquisition, predevelopment, and development costs less land sales proceeds and invested capital.

CA Cash Accounting. The Columbia Park and Recreation Association (CA) is the nonprofit corporation formed for the purpose of creating, maintaining, and operating community facilities in Columbia.

The accounting for CA in the CEM is segregated because:

1. It has no effect on net proceeds from development.
2. There are separate limitations on CA financing.
3. CA represents a different type of responsibility as compared to the responsibility for land development.

CA cash accounting summarizes revenues from assessments, capital costs, operating and financing costs.

CA Operating Projections. CA operating projections include:

1. Recreation programs (golf, tennis, etc.).
2. Cultural programs.
3. Day-care center.
4. Public works.
5. Administration.

EXHIBIT 2 (Continued)

CA Capital Costs. Capital costs include such items as:

1. Neighborhood and village centers.
2. Tennis clubs.
3. Day-care center.
4. Plazas and squares.
5. Parks and equestrian trails.
6. Lakes and marinas.
7. Transit system.
8. Public safety equipment.
9. Public works equipment.

HRD Cash Accounting. This summary is the basis for calculating financing costs. Assumptions are made as to cash flow from land sales and development costs during each development year. For example, development costs may be projected at $5 million for a development year, and the assumption may be made that all of this will occur in the first three months of that year.

Consolidated Land Sales Proceeds. Land sales proceeds are identified under:

1. Residential.
2. Commercial.
3. Industrial.
4. Public.
5. Other.

Proceeds are determined by multiplying projected unit pace by projected unit price. Each category of sales includes a separate section for pace and price.

Residential Sales Proceeds. Residential proceeds are further categorized as:

1. "Detached" houses.
2. Town houses.
3. Garden apartments.
4. Mid-rise apartments.
5. High-rise apartments.

Residential Sales Prices. Prices are established for development years 1–5, 6–10, and 11–15 for each category. They are shown for finished and "unfinished" sites and are expressed in dwelling unit or acre terms.

Pace of Residential Development and Residential Land Usage. Disposition of residential land is shown for each development year by acres and dwelling units. The pace reflected is assumed to be units sold. The costs connected with these units, therefore, precede disposition.

Commercial and Industrial Pace and Proceeds. Commercial land is divided into geographic areas including:

1. Town center.
2. Village centers.

EXHIBIT 2 (Continued)

3. Neighborhood centers.
4. Townwide.

These sites include:

1. Retail.
2. Office.
3. Opportunity.
4. Other.

Industrial sites are similarly divided into use categories.

Prices are established for five-year periods.

Public Land Sales Proceeds. The disposition pace and price (if applicable) for public land sales include:

1. Schools.
2. Hospital.
3. Churches.
4. College.
5. State and federal highway programs.
6. Other.

Prices are established for five-year periods.

Townwide Development and Administrative Costs. Development costs are further defined into such items as:

1. Sewer.
2. Water.
3. Salaries and overhead.
4. Advertising and promotion.
5. Legal expenses.

Residential Lot and Industrial Land Development Costs. The cost of intract utilities, streets, etc., are determined by applying unit "finishing" costs to the number of units assumed to be "finished" in each development year. Units are assumed to be finished and sold in the same development year, but costs are assumed to be in the beginning of the year and proceeds at the end of the year.

It is not assumed that all land will be sold as "finished" land, and it is therefore more practical to project finishing costs as a function of units to be sold as finished units rather than on a geographic area basis.

Lot Development Costs. Assumptions on the specifications of a finished lot are made and costed for:

1. Acre and larger sites.
2. One-half-acre sites.
3. One-fourth-acre sites.
4. Town house sites.

EXHIBIT 2 *(Concluded)*

Specifications include:

1. Streets.
2. Sidewalks.
3. Landscaping.
4. Storm drainage.
5. Engineering.
6. Overhead.
7. Utilities.

PART VII

Corporations in
Real Estate

WEBB & KNAPP—
AND ZECKENDORF

John McDonald

A Wall Streeter, sitting next to William Zeckendorf, the celebrated financial wizard of the real-estate world, at La Florida restaurant in Havana on January 7 last, was asked by another member of the party what the Street would like to know most about Zeckendorf. He replied right off and virtually in Zeckendorf's ear:

"Can he ride a bear market?"

Zeckendorf laughed and said nothing. But he was in the course of making a New Year's resolution concerning this very subject.

Perhaps the question has invaded the conscious and unconscious of every man in the Street about every other man and company in the U.S., but it is especially relevant to one like Zeckendorf whose rise has been so fast as to be almost unbelievable and who has seemed to be holding on to his luck charm and betting on a repetition of past triumphs.

President, principal owner, and impresario of the real-estate company, Webb & Knapp, Inc., William Zeckendorf has put on what is probably the finest solo performance in speculative finance in recent history. A trader and producer, he has dealt in the grand manner with the design, development, and redevelopment of buildings, with the future of cities and the potentials of land. Financially, he has dealt in borrowed money, rent, and capital appreciation; and since his unique company (a company of capital in real estate) is listed on the American Stock Exchange, and since he goes to Wall Street (and elsewhere) to borrow a lot of money, and since he has made a lot of money in an unfailingly spectacular way, the eyes of Wall Street are on him with envy, and curiosity as to his future.

Zeckendorf's financial performance in sum is his raising the net assets of Webb & Knapp by bootstrap from a minus $127,000 in 1942 to about $75 million net worth (Webb & Knapp appraisal) in January, 1954. The $75 million represents a controlling leverage on about $250 million worth of brick, mortar, land, and other holdings.

* Reprinted from the March, 1954 issue of *Fortune* Magazine by special permission; © 1954 Time Inc.

This includes a substantial interest in a vast array of properties ranging from such gilt-edged land improvements in New York City as the Chrysler and Graybar buildings, the Airlines Terminal Building, 1 and 2 Park, 270 Park, 383–385 Madison, where Webb & Knapp has its chic penthouse offices, 711 Fifth, 1407 Broadway (a new forty-one-story office building that in January was being sold off), a twenty-five-story office building under construction between Macy's and Gimbels, and other Manhattan properties; Roosevelt Field (a $60-million Long Island industrial and retail project under development on the site of a former airport), 500,000 square feet of potential retail land in Flushing, Long Island; projects active or forthcoming at Camden, Philadelphia, Atlanta, Denver (a $38-million group of projects, including a $15-million twenty-two-story office building under construction), San Diego (an $8-million defense housing project), San Francisco (a piece of Nob Hill), and other places; numerous pieces of undeveloped urban, suburban, and rural land such as a tract the size of Manhattan Island within the city limits of Los Angeles and 62,000 acres of potential farmland in the Florida Everglades. Webb & Knapp has $60 million of construction currently under way across the country. All together it is a beautiful real-estate empire, and that part of it which is developed has tenants who comprise a substantial sampling of the bluebook of American industry.

Zeckendorf's personal assets include the entire issue of Webb & Knapp's second preferred stock—one million shares with a liquidating value of $27,250,000; about six million shares of Webb & Knapp's 20 million shares of common stock, selling on the market at around 85 cents on January 20; and perhaps $5 million outside of Webb & Knapp. This is a total of about $37 million. (It is possible on Zeckendorf's appraisal to put the liquidating value of the common at twice 85 cents, for a total of about $42 million in personal assets.) And he has made several millionaires among his co-venturers and former fellow stockholders to an aggregate amount of more than $25 million during the time he put his fortune together. Not bad, considering that this has been a period with the highest tax handicap in U.S. history, and that twelve years ago Zeckendorf had no assets.

Being both rich and famous, Zeckendorf needs no praise. But what about the question asked at La Florida? Can he be expected to ride a bear as well as a bull? This is really two questions, namely: Is he as good as he has been lucky? And what, objectively, is the situation of Webb & Knapp?

ZECKENDORF: HIS TALENTS

Webb & Knapp is a rapidly changing company. For ten years beginning in the early Forties Zeckendorf took it and himself on the road to fame and fortune mainly on a policy of trading for capital appreciation.

After merging with American Superpower (an investment trust dealing in utility securities) in 1952, Webb & Knapp became a listed company; and with the advent of public stockholders, Zeckendorf shifted to a policy of developing recurring earnings along with trading for capital appreciation, and began to build a substantial corporation on the expectation of permanence and growth. A new major change of policy completes this evolution of Webb & Knapp away from its past. This was contained in Zeckendorf's 1954 New Year's resolution, which he formulated in a Super Connie between Miami and Cleveland the day following the conversation at La Florida—of which more later. First, how good is he?

Some men are born with money (Zeckendorf was not), and some with other gifts; and for the appreciation of either, one can look to the parable of the ten talents. Zeckendorf is a gifted man. He has a mind of unusual caliber in intuition, rough calculating ability, and resourcefulness; and an imagination that can take fire without appreciable loss of discipline. He once played bridge in such company as Theodore Lightner and Oswald Jacoby, but for years he has given his sole attention to business. He is big, six feet and over 200 pounds, with a broad ingenuous face and manner; and tireless, working himself under pressure and with pleasure at a rate of about ninety hours a week. He sleeps six hours, is up at seven in the morning, is instantly at work and never not working, even in Havana or Hawaii where he occasionally indulges a taste for fishing and sunning in exotic surroundings.

Zeckendorf theorizes more than most businessmen, but limits his generalizations to what can be applied to a concrete problem. The quality of his mind lies in his ability to handle a number of diverse strands of thought corresponding to realities and to bring them together simultaneously in the concept of a deal. His memory is prodigious. He works extemporaneously (doodling a design of the interconnectedness of things) and makes public speeches without formal preparation. In addition to having all of Webb & Knapp's properties at his fingertips he says that he knows all he needs to know (and that includes financial structure) about every major piece of property on Manhattan Island. He has a gift for off-the-cuff appraisal. When Robert J. McKim, president of Associated Dry Goods Corp., owners of what was then McCreery's department store, went to him at his home one Saturday morning last summer and said, "What will you give me for the McCreery store building on Thirty-fourth Street?" Zeckendorf figured for a few minutes and said $5,500,000, which proved to be within 4 percent of the book value. McKim called his lawyer to come up and that afternoon they initialed the deal under which Zeckendorf was to put up $1 million. Within a month Zeckendorf had leased the property to Ohrbach's on a basis that would generate a $2-million profit, and some residual values.

There are many such anecdotes about Zeckendorf that give his trading a magical aura, and that have made him legendary. And he actually has a nice turn of mind, as indicated, for example, in what he wrote recently to the head of a large corporation to whom he offered for sale a great building for a large number of millions of dollars. The letter was only eight lines long and concluded, "I know that there are many details to be considered, but simplicity is of the essence." A mathematician writing to another mathematician would have reduced it to one line and called it an elegant equation. Eight was elegance for this deal in verbal longhand.

Zeckendorf has gifts, too, of nerve, wit, and presence. He has the nerve not to look at the zeros in a million dollars. The number is one, and fifty million is fifty. (This is not unusual among bankers or government officials, but in a private trader it is something to see.) He will settle any deal on the back of an envelope. A trader's wry wit and a natural gaiety, ebullience, and buoyancy cushion his nerve. But at times he is given to volatile expressions of anger. His mistakes he writes off without qualm. He can be sentimental, and he is heavily engaged in philanthropy. If he has any valleys of the spirit, he does not show them.

STAR AND PRODUCER

Paradoxically, Zeckendorf is both very sure of himself and willing to listen carefully to what others have to say. He has a strong sporting attitude that governs his business ethic. He says he never tries to buy at the low or sell at the high, for he wishes to leave a trail of good feeling and good will. It is a fact that with all his triumphs in trading he is widely esteemed in his markets and community. Though he moves swiftly from person to person through a day's dealings, and can be brusque with other traders when a deal does not appeal to him, he has an engaging personality that, combined with mastery of his business, gives a commanding effect. His life, with a telephone perpetually in his ear even while he rides in his Cadillac limousine (license WZ-1), might seem like a grand affectation, but it is sincere showmanship. Like many great showmen, he is without personal affectation.

Showmanship is essential in modern real-estate trading. The old-time, staid, inconspicuous real-estate firm set the mode for a different era, when the trade was closer knit, the activity less intense, narrower in scope, and mainly regional. Today a trader like Zeckendorf, operating on a national scale, would not find his market if he had to do all the looking. The successful young traders today—like Hollywood stars—engage publicity men to make their names known. Zeckendorf has done so, although his deals have a way of making news on their own.

Finding deals is a search problem, and the best economy of the search is to have the deals come to you. Furthermore, when a big deal is offered, the principals and brokers want to deal with a *name;* and how many big names are there? Four or five, of which in marquee lights Zeckendorf's is now the brightest. Today Zeckendorf's office is itself a market with deals being offered to him by brokers all over the country.

RISING STAR

Zeckendorf was known in New York real estate in the Thirties as a comer. His talents were recognized, depression fashion, in 1938 when he was offered $9,000 a year and a one-quarter interest in Webb & Knapp, then a real-estate consultant firm. The quarter interest had a liquidating value of less than zero, and Zeckendorf was then making about $20,000 a year on his own. He went in, however, with a sense for the value of the Webb & Knapp name and market connections. From then on the firm had an engine. But money did not show until wartime, when Zeckendorf took over the management of Vincent Astor's $50-million real-estate portfolio. Zeckendorf's star (and Astor's money) then went straight up. It first appeared in public view when (with commissions obtained from the Astor account) he assembled the Manhattan properties that became the site of the United Nations. The U.N. deal cost Webb & Knapp a number of millions that it might otherwise have made had Zeckendorf turned it on a strictly commercial basis, but it made him famous. It also revealed a pattern of thought and action that animated many Zeckendorf deals.

It was a simple deal, essentially. The far East Side of Manhattan north of Forty-second Street was the old slaughterhouse district. For blocks around it, land sold from $2 to $5 a square foot, while three blocks farther away, near Grand Central, it fetched as high as $300 a square foot. Zeckendorf one day was offered the slaughterhouses at $17 a square foot. He replied that he could buy land around there for less than $5. But the price stood, and Zeckendorf reflected, and smelled. It dawned on him then that the smell was built into the $5 price, and that without the smell and with a great new development in east-central Manhattan on the site of the slaughterhouses, the land around would be worth—no one knew how much. He bought the slaughterhouses and as much land around as he could get (seventeen acres). It was one of the finest real-estate deals anyone ever made. The U.N. was then looking for a site and was ready to leave New York to find one. Zeckendorf agreed to sell this magnificent plot to the U.N. at a modest profit, and John D. Rockefeller, Jr. donated the money to the U.N. to make the purchase.

MACY-GIMBEL AISLEWAY

About the same time Zeckendorf began to eye the nondescript parcels of property on Thirty-third and Thirty-fourth streets between Macy's and Gimbels, all separate buildings, separately owned, and run down.

On the same principle as applied in the U.N. deal, he saw that these parcels assembled into one large plot with the old buildings removed would make a through merchandise mart between the two great department stores. This one took a long time but he finally got 74,273 square feet in the block including enough contiguous land on both streets to make a single plot of 36,340 square feet; and on the latter the Webb & Knapp construction company is now erecting a $12-million twenty-five-story office building, the first floor of which will house Woolworth, and an A. S. Beck (shoe) store. Woolworth's store, with over a mile of linear counter space running straight through the block, like an arcade of aisles between Macy's and Gimbels, will be its largest in the country. The only problem Woolworth anticipates is how to keep the merchandise moving onto the counters as fast as it moves off.

Similarly Zeckendorf has changed lofts and residences into offices, obsolete and semi-obsolete office buildings into modern office buildings, low-grade warehouses into high-grade warehouses, a riding academy into a TV broadcasting studio, airports into industrial workshops and shopping centers—not dreams but workable propositions.

VISION AND DESIGN

He is not without dreams either, and if he has his way the U.S. will have a new look in his generation. He looks out over the scene of peripheral growth and downtown decay in American cities today and groans—with pleasure at the opportunities. Growth of population and increasing speed of transportation, he believes, have changed the nature of real estate. Unlike most trend observers, he believes that suburban life will eventually become obsolete, urban life will be restored, and rural development will come along with the helicopter.

He does not think much, however, of the outburst of office building in New York City today: with few exceptions he appraises it economically and aesthetically as a hit-and-run business. His own new Denver building he believes to be the best office building yet built on an investment basis (such elegant office buildings as Lever House in New York, General Petroleum in Los Angeles, and the like, he considers to be institutional monuments). He hopes soon to build his revolutionary circular apartment building, the "Helix," created by his chief designer, Ieoh Ming Pei. In general he is dedicated to the proposition that the conflict between aesthetics and economics in architecture can be resolved, and he expects to be one of the principal catalysts of that resolution.

Thus here is an avowed speculator of a new school: for while Zeckendorf can turn a deal in classic style, he can do something else that involves an insight into what things could be as well as what they are. Roger Stevens, who turned the Empire State deal and appears to be on the way to becoming the next Shubert on Broadway—and Zeckendorf's nearest rival among younger men for the laurels in the real-estate world —says of Zeckendorf, "Most people in real estate don't realize that World War I is over, but Zeckendorf is thinking of tomorrow." Real estate grew haphazardly and, being by nature fixed to a place, was unresponsive to the great changes in American industrial, office, and personal life. Zeckendorf has seen the possibilities of adapting real estate to the requirements of change.

THE "HAWAIIAN TECHNIQUE"

In the characteristic Zeckendorf deal, he does not sell precisely what he buys either physically or financially. This has been the key to his operation and its success. He processes the real estate with physical development, often with a recognition of the interdependence of the value of neighboring properties and of combinations of properties; and he merchandises real-estate investments on a principle similar to that which governs the distinctions in the sale of risks in corporate securities —i.e., on an analogy with common and preferred stocks, debentures, etc., or what Zeckendorf calls "the Hawaiian technique," because he thought of it while bonefishing in Hawaii. Aside from inflation, these two creative procedures have brought Webb & Knapp its greatest gains; and they are the basis of Zeckendorf's pride in being a producer as well as a trader.

The "Hawaiian technique" for selling a variety of investment risks in a single building has shown itself in part in most of Zeckendorf's past deals, but it came into focus as a financial conception last year in the following way: Webb & Knapp had a 40 per cent interest in the corporation that owned 2 Park Avenue, a twenty-five-story office building occupying the entire block front on the west side of Park Avenue from Thirty-second to Thirty-third streets, appraised in 1951 by the Charles F. Noyes Co. at $9,158,000. Zeckendorf thought it was time to sell, and figured the building was then worth roughly $10 million. The other interests, however, at first did not want to sell. Zeckendorf told them, "Don't do nothing. Either buy me out or sell to me." And he offered to buy at a valuation of $10 million or sell at a valuation of $9,500,000 (his theory being that the whole was worth more than the separate parts). The other owners sold options to Webb & Knapp (and others) to buy all their stock in the corporation and the closing was set for a future date.

Zeckendorf went off fishing in Hawaii, but remained concerned about the financing and sale, for there were two mortgages to be refinanced and other complications. He was casting in the surf off Oahu when he started to reflect that the usual $10-million U.S. corporation is not divided simply into mortgage and equity but into common stock, one or two preferreds, debentures, first-mortgage bonds, bank loans, accounts receivable serviced by a factor, warrants to buy common stock, and so on; and these represented the various classes of investors, each investor seeking out just what suited his requirements, taste in risks, and tax status. It also occurred to him that if these various corporate risks were sold in a lump to a single buyer, he would not be willing to pay as much for them as separate buyers who could pick what they particularly wanted.

MERCHANDISING RISK

Why not, he thought, create as many classes of investors in real estate as possible and sell that way at perhaps a higher price? With this brainstorm, he got out of the water, laid down his rod, went to his cabin, called New York, and in a two-hour conversation told his office to call off the pending refinancing of 2 Park and instead to call up a certain group and tell them this: This property yields about $1 million net a year and it has a potential of additional earning power of as much as $750,000 through increased rents. Tell them that a lease, at $600,000 net, producing a profit of $400,000, can be acquired for $5 million, $1,500,000 cash and a $3,500,000 mortgage. The owner of the $1,500,000 equity, thought Zeckendorf, would be the common stockholder: if rents went up, he gained; if down, he lost. The $3,500,000 mortgage holder would be in effect the preferred stockholder.

Now, said Zeckendorf, go to a mortgagee and say we want to borrow some money. Sell him a $6,750,000 first mortgage on the fee (land and building) at 4.5 per cent. And what of the fee itself that represented part of Webb & Knapp's profit? Zeckendorf soon afterward carved out a second mortgage of $2,250,000, which he put up as part of the collateral on the Chrysler-Graybar deal, along with the $3,500,000 leasehold mortgage. He still owns the fee to the 2 Park property!

Zeckendorf has been offered $1,200,000 for the fee. The offer was from someone for whom the fee would be most suitable. This would have to be someone who needs a conservative security, substantial depreciation, and leverage (depreciation on the smallest amount of equity investment). The security was the $600,000 income on the lease, backed up by a $400,000 cushion of earnings. Notice the result, said Zeckendorf, if we sell the fee subject to the $6,750,000 and $2,250,000 mortgages and take $1,200,000 cash. The fee owner, receiving $600,000 and paying $495,000, would realize $105,000 income on a $1,200,000 investment, which, with a depreciation of about $300,000 a year, would be tax free.

Now for the addition: In the deal the leaseholder put up, in cash and a mortgage on the lease, $5 million. Webb & Knapp obtained $6,750,000 from the first mortgagee of the fee and another $2,250,000 from the second mortgage, or a total of $14 million. It still owned the fee for which it has been offered $1,200,000 in cash and mortgages, or in sum, $15,200,000 for a building that Zeckendorf had been willing to sell on a $9,500,000 basis. True the profit ($5,200,000) is in the form of paper, which would sell at a substantial discount in the open market, but Zeckendorf caused it to act like cash by using it as collateral in obtaining the equity in the Chrysler and Graybar buildings. He is now in the process of selling 1407 Broadway, involving about $30 million, by the Hawaiian technique.

NOT A BAD DAY'S FISHING

How, one might ask, does Zeckendorf find everyone, and how does he get people to buy or sell? To the first question the answer is, he knows the market and the market knows him. The answer to the second is that very often people are compelled to buy or sell for tax reasons. The corporations owning the Chrysler and Graybar buildings had no depreciation and were suffering from big corporation taxes. Two Park likewise. The corporation owning the latter had not paid a dividend in fifteen years.

SUPERMAN AND SUPERPOWER

In 1952, Zeckendorf merged Webb & Knapp into American Superpower. Like most of his deals, it had complications. Suffice it to say the following. Between 1947 and 1949, Zeckendorf bought out his partners in Webb & Knapp at a nice profit for them (nearly $10 million) and got himself considerably in hock in the process. He emerged, however, as sole owner of an empire that on the Noyes appraisal in 1951 had a net worth of about $42 million. It was represented by 333 shares of non-liquid Webb & Knapp stock. For personal estate reasons, and because he wished to be in a position to pay off his indebtedness, Zeckendorf wanted a public stock listing, and he was never one not to want $10 million more of working capital, or to overlook a nice carry-forward of capital losses. Superpower provided all these benefits; and the merger improved the liquidating value of Superpower's 63,000 preference shares (now Webb & Knapp first preference with a claim on the assets of $13,167,000) and gave worth to its common, which before had a deficit worth.

Zeckendorf took the second preferred issue of one million shares, worth about $25 million on liquidation, and 11,707,004 of the 20 million shares of common (35 million authorized). He took a personal paper loss of about $10 million in the merger ($42 million in the former Webb & Knapp, down to $32 million in the new one); or to put it another way, Zeckendorf "paid" about $1.50 a share for his 11 million-odd shares of the new "60-cent" common. He figures the intangibles (and tangibles) were worth it. It was one of those reverse mergers, American Superpower first changing its name to Webb & Knapp, Inc. (a Delaware corporation), and then "absorbing" Webb & Knapp, Inc. (a New York corporation), of which one of the participants is reported to have said, "Superpower didn't absorb Webb & Knapp. Superman swallowed Superpower."

NEW ORGANIZATION

The merger put new responsibilities on Zeckendorf. He had then to build a permanent organization. Of course, on the one hand, he already had an organization and, on the other, he was not going to cease being the star of the show; yet the difference was perceptible and Webb & Knapp today is a substantial organization without which Zeckendorf's present operations would not be possible.

He has an able team of nineteen executive specialists, and a number of consultants, covering the fields of law, finance, taxation, property development (industrial, office, retail shopping, rural, etc.), administration, design, construction, leasing, real-estate management, and the like, all together an organization with 211 employees in the New York office and an additional 1,547 employees engaged directly and indirectly in operating the properties owned, controlled, or managed by Webb & Knapp—a quite large company, perhaps the largest, in the real-estate field.

Webb & Knapp's rapid growth and the peculiarity that it consists of a large number of discrete projects have brought on a number of management problems. The company needs at once more decentralization and a more simplified centralization, without which its expansion must be limited to the number of different subdivisions that one man can carry in his head. Any one of Webb & Knapp's major development properties is enough to keep one man busy—and indeed some do. Arthur G. Rydstrom, senior vice president and former banker, sits in Denver and occupies himself with that project. For some time now Vice President Robert W. Shepard has given most of his time to the Thirty-fourth Street (New York City) development; Vice President Herbert I. Silverson to Roosevelt Field (Long Island), of which he is president; Maurice Iserman, vice president and general counsel, and one of the best-known real-estate lawyers in the country, occupies himself considerably (along with Webb & Knapp's two resident lawyers) with whatever deal or project is being currently negotiated. Zeckendorf's twenty-four-year-old son, William Jr., who grew up with real estate and is just back from Korea, plans to give much of his time to the Florida development. Ieoh Ming Pei, designer, and his staff sit up in a studio on the roof of 383 Madison drawing pictures of office buildings, factories, and apartment houses of the future along with some immediately realizable conceptions. Pei, says Zeckendorf, is the key to Webb & Knapp's design thinking.

EARTHY AND CELESTIAL

Thus Webb & Knapp, being an organization not of remote financiers but of earthy (and celestial) real-estate men and designers who live with the properties, can do things an individual could not. They finance, buy, develop, plan, design, assemble, build, lease, manage, and sell all kinds of land and buildings for all kinds of purposes (which they must become intimately acquainted with); and an odd miscellany of tankers, a railroad, oil leases and an oil well, a department store in Denver, Charlie Chaplin's Hollywood studio, and what not that Webb & Knapp happened to pick up in one deal or another. (Zeckendorf is also the real-estate consultant of the Rockefellers and Time Inc.) With this organization behind him, Zeckendorf has an incomparable situation in the real-estate field as regards both practical operation and market knowledge. His policy is to manage—and thus protect the value of every Webb & Knapp property, including even those, like 1 and 2 Park Avenue, on which the company holds mortgages.

RUGGED YEAR

With $60 million in construction work going on in 1953; and nine major deals (five department stores besides McCreery's, Chrysler-Graybar, the Terminal Warehouse in Philadelphia, and 1407 Broadway) and other minor ones swung between September and December alone, Webb & Knapp had the busiest year in its history, and Zeckendorf his most rugged. For once, at New Year's, he admitted to an awareness of a certain amount of effort.

Webb & Knapp also ended the year long on property and short on cash. Its net quick position on September 30, 1953, was in round numbers $1,660,000 cash against a short-term debt (notes payable within a year) of $10,470,000, and it had not changed materially by the year's end—on the face of it a remarkably adverse ratio. And this brings the story back to the New Year's resolution with which it began.

It is difficult in real estate to cite the volume of business in the usual way. In the deals in which Webb & Knapp participated as a principal in 1953, taking as volume the purchase and sale of properties, financing and refinancing, leasing and re-leasing, and the construction of new buildings, the company did about $500 million worth of business. In this type of computation, however, the Chrysler-Graybar deal, with all its intermediate capital transactions, was not $52 million (the sale price) but $120 million, so the figure is not a clearly informative one. It is also difficult to evaluate the significance of the company's current income. Net income after taxes for 1953 is estimated at $1,500,000. This covers dividends and other requirements of the preference stock ($378,000 dividend plus 25 per cent of the balance for arrears) and increased the net worth by $917,000 against which the second preferred (one million shares at $1.50 dividend) will have an eventual claim. But the company's greatest gains do not appear in the income account.

FANTASTIC GAIN

From the time of the merger in July, 1952, Webb & Knapp's net worth on its appraisal increased from $52 million to $60 million by April 30, 1953, and to $75 million by December 31, 1953, a fantastic appreciation of $23 million in eighteen months, in which only one of the elements—and a minor one—was inflation. After all debt except potential taxes on appreciation of the value of properties, Webb & Knapp has a theoretical $54-million unrealized profit, and naturally Zeckendorf says, "I don't like to ring the cash register any more than necessary." A tax on this profit may never occur, for in the event of total liquidation it would go direct to the stockholders without a company tax, but with a personal capital gain over the cost of the stock.

There are of course many prior liens against most of the Webb & Knapp properties. These are mainly first mortgages and ground rents, and some bank loans. Most of the mortgages are "without recourse," that is, on terms in which the lender looks to the corpus of the collateral and not to Webb & Knapp. Bank loans (against pledged assets) are used only on a short-term interim basis. There is, however, about $15 million in liens against the company itself on its general credit; and as a matter of routine business the company also uses its general credit at times to guarantee various types of payment, as in Denver where the quarterly payments on the building loan are guaranteed until a sufficient number of leases can be assigned to release the company from this obligation. In short, Webb & Knapp deals primarily in equities on calculated risk. From this it profits proportionately when the market goes up. Contrariwise it stands to lose more if the position is maintained and the market goes down. How much of a recession, then, can Webb & Knapp stand? Could Zeckendorf make an orderly retreat if he had to?

If this were any company but Webb & Knapp its formal balance-sheet position would look bad. For while the net worth of the assets has been soaring, the cash position is poor and the income on $75 million in equities is low. However, since Webb & Knapp has only salable goods in the "inventory" it is obvious that the adverse cash position could change by the sale of equities; and as the non-productive properties under construction are completed and thereby converted into productive assets, the short-term (construction-loan) debt is converted into long-term (mortgage) debt amortizable out of earnings. In other words, with all those deals and $60 million in construction in 1953, Webb & Knapp ended the year in a squeeze as tight as the *Queen Elizabeth* passing through the Panama Canal.

PUZZLED MARKET

Webb & Knapp evidently has puzzled the stock market, and well it might. The market has no doubts regarding the preference stock (though because of the piled-up arrears it, like many preferred stocks, is better in the portfolio of corporations than of individuals, the former being taxed at a lower rate on dividends). The preference stock has been selling at about 80 per cent of its value (including arrears) at a yield of less than 3.5 per cent a high market rating indeed—and Webb & Knapp is able to use the arrears as working capital at no interest and with no calling date other than a sometime moral one.

But the common stock, which was worth in liquidation value 60 cents a share at the time of the merger and sold as high as $1.62½ in 1952, has been selling (January, 1954) at about 85 cents a share despite Zeckendorf's estimate of a current liquidating value of about $1.75 a share. This reversal may in part be due to the market's weakness in 1953 and to the depressive effect of Zeckendorf's own sale of three million shares, or to the fads and fashions of the security market, to doubt about Zeckendorf's future, or some combination of these factors.

More important in the market estimate, however, in Zeckendorf's opinion, is a lack of knowledge of the company, and in particular of how to read its labyrinthian balance sheet. The net quick position, he says, which ordinarily is an important consideration, has little meaning in regard to Webb & Knapp, for that position can change from day to day twenty to one either way. Webb & Knapp is a company of capital assets comparable to an investment trust; and its real estate, he says, is not comparable to an industrial company's fixed-assets position. The real estate is inventory, with present or potential earning power, and it has a ready cash market. The key to reading the balance sheet correctly, he says, is to view the inventory "not as things we use but as things for sale."

Webb & Knapp's appraisal of its liquidating value . . . is comprised of figures at which Webb & Knapp believes it can sell for cash in the present market. Zeckendorf says that such figures change periodically, but that the net realization from sale of properties in the past has on balance been greater than the appraisals. He points out that his customers' market is not primarily among real-estate or hotel men, but among investors in other fields who are looking for a capital gain or return on investment: insurance companies, pension funds, merchants, retired investors, individuals, families, snydicates, and corporations. Among the corporations that have bought properties from him for their own use, he cites the United Nations, General Foods, Standard Brands, Bethlehem Steel, Woolworth, C.B.S., A.B.C., Walgreen Co., Holland-America Line, East Asiatic Co., Time Inc., Allied Stores, Gimbel Brothers. Among those that have bought from him for investment, he cites Prudential Insurance, Metropolitan Life, Penn Mutual, Connecticut General, New England Mutual. Thus does he view his market; and his buying and selling he sees not as simply trading among traders, but as a service to investors and users of real estate.

Zeckendorf has no personal conviction that recession necessarily lies ahead; and a 10 per cent recession he believes would have no effect on Webb & Knapp. But it is evident that he put his own house in order when he sold some of his common stock on the grounds that he wanted to get himself out of debt for the first time in his life, especially out of the last of the heavy debt he contracted when he bought out his partners in 1949. That was the biggest risk he ever took, as anyone will agree who remembers the uncertainties of that period.

NEW YEAR'S RESOLUTION

His New Year's resolution has the customary Zeckendorf flair for making a turn and proceeding with force. It has five parts: (1) to stop expanding in the old way; (2) to sell off a few properties to improve the balance sheet as regards cash and debt; (3) to develop new concepts and design new structures on the land now owned by Webb & Knapp; (4) to execute them through Webb & Knapp's construction company; and (5) to tighten his organization for administering the properties efficiently. In general this means to consolidate the gains and exploit them in a different way. It means that he is out of the market for all but self-financing deals (like Chrysler-Graybar).

According to this new plan, Webb & Knapp will become more a development than a trading company, though development itself has some speculative aspects suitable to Zeckendorf's temperament. Webb & Knapp has acquired enough properties, in his opinion, to warrant a half-billion dollars of development.

As a hedge, the new policy has a rationale calculated to suit the peculiarities of the real-estate business. Since Webb & Knapp does its own designing, building, and development work, recession to Zeckendorf means, on the favorable side, lower costs of construction and easier and cheaper money. (Construction in real estate is equivalent to a short sale in securities: you budget at x dollars and you make a speculative profit if you come in under it. If things go on up, the old and new properties will

The Remarkable Assets of Webb & Knapp

This table, drawn at FORTUNE'S request, shows publicly for the first time the corpus of Webb & Knapp: a breakdown of the company's properties, the company's appraisal of their market value, a computation of the company's net worth, and the unrealized appreciation over the book value, as of September 30, 1953 (virtually unchanged by January, 1954). It should be noted that the appraisal of each property is limited to Webb & Knapp's percentage of ownership. In sum, the table shows Webb & Knapp's $76,692,000 equity in $251,143,000 worth of properties, and its $54,403,000 paper profit.

Real Estate		Type of holding	Percentage of ownership	Company's appraisal of its gross percentage
Chrysler and Graybar Bldgs.	New York, N. Y.	Fee and Leasehold	75	$ 44,700,000
Chrysler and Graybar Bldgs.	New York, N. Y.	Land under leasehold	75	12,000,000
383/5 Madison Avenue	New York, N. Y.	Lease privilege	100	4,000,000
383/5 Madison Avenue	New York, N. Y.	Land under leasehold	100	6,000,000
1407 Broadway	New York, N. Y.	Fee	100	26,000,000
Roosevelt Field	Hempstead, N. Y.	Fee	61.87	14,230,000
Camden Airport	Camden, N. J.			
Camp Ono	San Bernardino, Calif.			
1½-9 W. 34th Street	New York, N. Y.	75% interest in fee		
78 parcels	Flushing, N. Y.	Fee and leasehold	100	11,300,000
Bach Building	Flushing, N. Y.	Land under leasehold	100	1,000,000
2 Park Avenue	New York, N. Y.	Fee	100	10,250,000
Airlines Terminal	New York, N. Y.	Fee	100	6,500,000
West 33rd & 34th Streets	New York, N. Y.	Fee and leasehold	65	13,796,000
Clairemont Gardens Apts.	San Diego, Calif.	Fee	100	6,941,000
270 Park Avenue	New York, N. Y.	Leasehold	100	7,000,000
270 Park Avenue	New York, N. Y.	Land under leasehold	100	6,000,000
Terminal warehouse	Philadelphia, Pa.	Fee and leasehold	100	5,125,000
Terminal commerce Bldg.	Philadelphia, Pa.	Fee	100	4,675,000
Hampton Gardens Apts.	St. Louis, Mo.	Leasehold	100	5,000,000
Hampton Village	St. Louis, Mo.	Fee	50	3,250,000
Vacant land	Mountain Park, Calif.	Fee	87.50	2,625,000
Shopping centers	Levittown, N. Y.	Fee	100	3,000,000
Various parcels	Denver, Colo.	Fee and leasehold	Various	7,183,000
Various parcels	Denver, Colo.	Land under leasehold	Various	600,000
Indian Trail Ranch	West Palm Beach, Florida	Fee	52.4	1,336,000
Times Square Post Office	New York, N. Y.	Fee	100	2,700,000
Merchandise Mart	San Francisco, Calif.	Leasehold	24.5	368,000
Merchandise Mart	San Francisco, Calif.	Land and building under leasehold	24.5	1,568,000
All other	Various	Fee and leasehold	Various	12,364,000
Total Real Estate				$219,511,000

Miscellaneous Investments

4 tankers		Fee	100	6,462,000
1 freighter and 1 tanker		Fee	48.9	1,083,000
Other			Various	24,087,000
Total: gross value				$251,143,000

Less Land under leaseholds	27,168,000	
Due on contracts to purchase*	72,141,000	
Encumbrances on real estate owned	48,190,687	
Other liabilities	26,951,313	$174,451,000
Net worth		76,692,000
Less book value		22,289,000
Unrealized expected gain, on Webb & Knapp's appraisal		$ 54,403,000

*These purchases have been completed since September 30, 1953, and paid for by cash, mortgage or leasehold undertaking. Hence in January, 1954, this item would be absorbed into "Encumbrances" and "Other liabilities."

appreciate; if things go down, Zeckendorf expects to ride the escalator of cheaper construction and cheap money.

Come what may, Zeckendorf's program is to spend for development.

Capital for this program will come from earnings, sales of property, and, of course, from borrowings. And perhaps Zeckendorf will seek new infusions of equity capital. What he is most concerned about is the availability of money and interest rates, the former more than the latter, for the level of the interest rate affects only the spread between income and the interest rate on mortgages, whereas the availability determines whether a deal is on or off. The quintessence of his business has been to take this spread, improve the income, and capitalize it out at ten or twelve times the increase. This will continue to be the case in development work.

THE PROGRAM

Among the developments for 1954 are such varied items as Webb & Knapp's 500,000 square feet of potential retail land in Flushing, Long Island; the continuation of the $60-million development at Roosevelt Field, Long Island, where Macy's is coming in as the core of a shopping center alongside the industrial development; the continuation of the Denver development with the construction of a new Statler hotel and other buildings; the conversion of the Everglades property into range and farmland (with a chip on the possibility of Florida oil); and the first projects for Parkon, Inc., an automatic, vertical parking system that Webb & Knapp is developing in cooperation with Otis Elevator (which may solve city parking problems but still leave Zeckendorf puzzling over what to do about the congestion in city streets). Webb & Knapp also has a $200,000 option on the "land" (i.e. air) over the Pennsylvania Railroad tracks in west-central Manhattan, on which he proposes to build the largest office and merchandising building in the world (seven million square feet as compared with Empire State Building's 2,200,000). This deal, involving a potential $100 million, however, depends on a number of decisions including a pending post-office lease. And numerous other projects are in work or forthcoming.

Thus Zeckendorf is for certain betting against a '32, but he is taking a hedge of his own design against the possibility of something less severe. It remains to be seen whether he can restrain himself from engaging in a good trade for the trade's sake when he sees one, and prevent himself from getting overloaded with prize deals as he did in late 1953. He needs now only to manage success itself.

NEW CITIES FOR OLD*

William Zeckendorf

1

IIow can we keep cities that represent the toil and sweat and invested labor and invested capital of generations from becoming ghost towns? It is wonderful to talk about going out into the country—as I see some of you have done here—to build a perfect city on a plateau; I don't say that that is easy, but I do say that it is much more of a challenge for somebody to tell you, "Here is a city in which there are five billion dollars or more invested. Try to save it from disintegration and economic blight, which cannot miss if you do not do something about the core which you are permitting to rot; never mind doing something gaily and theoretically about the periphery."

We are all building these wonderful means of ingress to and egress from the central and urban areas, which simply means that we are developing easier and easier means of escape. They are roads from, not to, because people come to the town for reasons of necessity and leave it as fast as they can. That is the really greatest challenge that we've got in this country. People speak of inflation and of the results that will follow inflation, of economic and social waste and the fact that we are going to pass on to generations to come the errors of our ways through high debt, inflated money, dislocated economy. That is nothing compared with what is going on by attrition; attrition in the sense that the cities of the country are being permitted to die on the vine; cities that have been built and paid for, cities against which billions of dollars of municipal bonds have been levied in good faith and bought by citizens who have saved their life's labors to invest in these municipal securities and mortgage bonds, and indirectly through the life insurance companies which rein-

Although he was born in Paris, Illinois, and his grandparents hailed from Arizona, New York claimed William Zeckendorf at the age of two, and in the driving force of his maturity he has had much to contribute to the rejuvenation of that city. Now in his forty-sixth year, he is the President of Webb & Knapp, real-estate developers, who invest and finance for their own account and who have put new life into old property in many metropolitan areas across the country. This article is an enlargement of a talk which Mr. Zeckendorf gave before the Harvard School of Design.

vest their savings to make these cities go. If this attrition continues, these savings are going to be wiped out.

Inflation has almost no greater threat than the threat that has taken place in cities like Boston, one of the worst examples I know. Our firm is so concerned about Boston that it would not buy any real estate here. It is no joke. We believe that Boston, with its tax rate what it is and justified because of the expense in comparison with the potential revenue, is going to go broke.

You have already put through a semiconfiscation of private property by your levied tax. Your tax rate is such and your assessment rate is such in the City of Boston that you have practically confiscated the assets already. It is not something that you have to wait around for. And the first depression will find half the city on the town tax roll, because only the high occupancy, the extraordinarily high rents due to a scarcity resulting from an unusual situation, make it possible to run these properties and pay the taxes and operating charges with some modest return on the investment. You have a town here that is completely dislocated, where your people work in one community and spend their money in another community that pays nothing to the town in which their labors are expended. There are other cities in this same dilemma. But Boston is an outstanding example.

I want to talk about the possible cure. That is more important. The cure, in my opinion, is really the greatest challenge to the imagination, much more challenging than going out in a pasture and building a city, and much more satisfying from a constructive and a creative standpoint than abandoning the core to eventual ruin—anybody can do that if given enough boondoggling subsidy. But it takes real thinking, real energy, courage, and imagination to work within the confines of an existing problem. As a matter of fact, you will find in your experience, as you go into architectural life, that the greatest results you can get in ingenuity are those which are dictated in alterations where the restrictions of existing conditions force you to do things that you would never do if you had a completely free hand. Working within limitations will often produce more striking results, because of the provocative problems that arise, than if you have no limitations.

2

Let me give you three examples of constructive developments which our firm has put through in the heart of New York City. The first begins on the day a broker called and offered us at a price of $700,000 the old riding academy at 66th Street running through to 67th Street just west of Central Park West, a piece of property consisting of some 40,000 square feet. We turned down the offer with the comment that it was impossible at that price—we could not afford to build apartments in that area at that square foot figure—to which the broker responded that the buildings themselves were very valuable. We pointed out that we would pay more for the property demolished than with the buildings on it, as they had outlived their usefulness, and let it go at that.

Some weeks later I happened to be driving through 66th Street, and what follows illustrates the old adage that it is better to be lucky than smart. Because of a traffic jam my car was stalled in front of the academy. I decided that as long as I was there I might as well take a look at the property. I noted that the main building—the riding arena—was 92 × 200 with a great high vaulted ceiling and no interior columns. I said to myself, here is a perfect place for a television studio. Upon my return to the office I called the broker and we bought the property at his price, $700,000 with 20 per cent cash, balance on purchase money mortgage.

We circularized all the radio companies immediately, offering the property for television purposes, and to our dismay received letters from all declining the proposal. This put us in the horse business. We bought 150 horses and went into the market to buy hay and sell manure, running a regular monthly loss of $3500 to $4500. This went on for almost a year, when one day the phone rang and a rather uncertain voice announced that he was Mr. E. J. Noble. Knowing by reputation that he was the owner of the American Broadcasting Company, I promptly told him that I had never heard of him. He said, "Some time ago you suggested that we buy your barn for a TV station. Perhaps we'd better have a look at it."

To make a long story short, we leased the academy to him and subsequently sold it to him at a profit of $600,000. He converted it into the most modern TV station in the United States. Some months later when we were lunching together at "21" he said he was going to invite me to become a director of ABC. He asked me if I knew why, and when I replied that I did not he said, "Because you're the first man to make money out of TV."

We had a much longer struggle in the transaction which we recently consummated in the 34th Street midtown shopping center of Manhattan. There we found an unusual situation in that Macy's, which is the largest department store in the world, doing an annual business of up to $200,000,000, is separated from its chief competitor, Gimbel Brothers, by a single block running from the south side of 34th Street to the north side of 33rd Street. It seemed to us that if a large assemblage of smaller properties within this block could be engineered we could redevelop the property in the form of an arcade or through-street merchandising so that the customers of both great merchants, as they passed back and forth from 33rd to 34th Street, could do window shopping or comparative shopping on their way.

Such assemblage, however, held many obstacles because of the existing leases. There were a variety of buildings, including a firehouse, a hotel, and a theater, all of which would have to be removed. In order to acquire the firehouse, Webb & Knapp had to persuade the city that it was in the interest of efficiency and that it would ease traffic if the patrol at 29th Street was combined with the one at 33rd Street in a new station at 31st Street. We offered to build a new firehouse 75 feet wide in accordance with the specification of the city and exchange it on an even basis for the fifty-year-old, 50-foot firehouse standing on 33rd Street. The city agreed.

We have just signed leases with the F. W. Woolworth Company for a new building that will occupy part of the site of the old firehouse, the Herald Square Hotel, and the Savoy Theater, and which will be the largest store in the Woolworth chain throughout the United States. This new Woolworth's will serve as an arcade; it will syphon off customers. Thus there will be a steady current instead of the log jam which exists between Macy's and Gimbel's; all will receive the benefit of greater customer circulation. Incidentally, it has taken us nearly ten years to clear the block.

Our most challenging project in Manhattan involved the land that is now called the United Nations zone. This area runs north from 42nd Street to approximately 48th Street, and east from First Avenue to the East River. It is a rectangular section of about 500 feet east and west, and about 2000 feet north and south—roughly a million square feet.

At the time that we first heard or thought of it, the property easterly from First Avenue from 42nd to 49th was called the slaughterhouse district of New York, and was occupied by the abattoirs of the Swift and Wilson companies. They had been there since the 1870s or '80s. Prior to that time it was a pesthole, and when it came to granting a privilege to slaughter cattle on Manhattan, it was decided that the best place for it was that pesthole area to the east. The slaughterhouses were built there then. They were the best that were built at the time, and probably for slaughterhouses they were pretty good-looking. But as time went on, the Grand Central zone came into concept, the subsurface rapid transit was developed, and the Grand Central Station was conceived. That 42nd Street zone became probably the most intensive and the most interesting new development of any urban area in the United States. It was a great tribute to the planning and the foresight of the people who recognized its possibilities. I don't know of anything more important in long-term thinking than what was done at this place in the first decade of the century.

When the old steam railroad line was submerged under Park Avenue, which was a slum area, and air rights were built over the railroad tracks, there took place one of the most magnificent pieces of urban redevelopment ever seen. And it was so important and so virile that it overcame everything in its way—except the slaughterhouses. Its zone of influence moved easterly about as far as Second Avenue. It couldn't take in any more than that because the physical stench of the slaughterhouses prevented it. But those slaughterhouses remained there while they built apartment houses that rented in the '20s for $500 and more a room, almost within niblick shot of the slaughterhouses.

But nobody did anything about the slaughterhouses. They stayed there indefinitely. I recall when I first went into the real-estate business as a broker that they said of the slaughterhouses, "They will never be sold," because nobody could ever get a franchise to build a thing like that in Manhattan again anywhere, even though from time to time the properties were offered to us for sale. They never could be delivered, and every time somebody talked of it, it became a joke.

In the early part of 1946 when a broker called up and said he wished to offer the slaughterhouses I asked him to see one of my associates. This had been going on in my own experience for over twenty years. He came and went, and a few minutes later the man to whom I had assigned him came in, and I said, "What did that fellow want?"

"Oh," he said, "the old chestnut, slaughterhouses."

"I presume you gave him the usual brushoff."

And he said, "Yes, sure, nothing to it. By the way, he said he was related to the Swifts."

"What?"

"Yes."

"Are you sure? Let's get him back here," I said.

So we got the broker back, and I said, "What makes you think you can deliver these slaughterhouses?"

"Well," he said, "my daughter is the sole heir to the Swift fortune and I think I can do it."

I said, "Sit down." Which he did. I said, "What do you want for them?"

He said, "Swift and Wilson have agreed that they want $17 a square foot, take one, take all. They have pooled their properties."

"Are you sure you can deliver?"

His reply was "Yes."

"What is the best price?" I asked.

"Seventeen dollars."

"Are you aware of the fact that the properties on the other side of First Avenue, running up and down and westerly all the way over to Second Avenue, are selling for $5 a square foot and less?"

He said, "I know it's a ridiculous price but that is what they want."

"Will you take back an offer of a lesser amount?"

"No," he said, "I've got to keep on offering it until I get a buyer."

I asked, "Have you offered it anywhere else?"

He replied, "No."

"Well," I said, "I'll talk about it with my associates if you'll wait a few minutes."

So I went inside and talked with my partners. "Here is the greatest opportunity that I have ever seen in my life," I said, "and I never expect to see one like it again. This is the situation. Regardless of whether the properties are selling for $5 per foot, $1 per foot, half a dollar a foot, $3 a foot, around this area that they want $17 per foot for, that has nothing to do with it. The only reason they are selling for $4 a foot or $5 a foot is because the slaughterhouses are here. If you can think in *pro forma* terms of X, the slaughterhouses, there is no excuse for the $5 land and there is no excuse for the $17 land. The whole thing is worth $50. Actually, by eliminating the abomination, you can pull the whole thing up by its own bootstraps."

A very simple rule of real-estate economics. It was so centrally located, so beautifully located, with the site and size and dimensions of the property such that there were limitless potentials. Regardless of whether you could see them all the way through to the end at first view, you knew that they were there. "Therefore," I said, "I advocate buying the property for $17 a foot." Which we did. We also bought the $5 land. We bought some land for less, some for as little as $1 a foot.

There was one fellow, an Italian, who had put his life savings into a purchase for $10,000 of the only outstanding property on the east side of First Avenue that did not belong to the slaughterhouses. That was the northeast corner of 42nd Street. Fifty by one hundred—$10,000. That is $2 per foot. We sent the broker over to buy that property, and his wife said she wouldn't sell it for less than $12,000. He came back and said, "Wife wants thirteen!" I said, "Buy it." This little dialogue went on between the broker and wife until finally we paid her $100,000. And that piece of real estate today would be worth a minimum of $500,000. A minimum! It would be a bargain at that price.

And it all happened the moment we said, there are no slaughterhouses. Just say it. Wipe them out with a piece of rubber. Here is the new concept of this development—this Grand Central zone at the East River point. Seventeen dollars a foot was meaningless. So was anything else. When you have a plot that size, located that way in an urban area, the values are almost infinite, limited only by your imagination, your courage, your ideas and your ability to execute them.

3

We had a concept for the development of what is now the United Nations area which was very much publicized. That concept arose after much study in which Mrs. Zeckendorf was a great aid because her thinking from a woman's viewpoint was of enormous help in projecting the residential phase of this development, which started commercial at the south and wound up residential at the north end at Beekman Place. We developed this plan, and the plan came into model form and was given a lot of publicity. On December 6, 1946, I read in the paper that the United Nations were going to Philadelphia because they were unwilling to go to the Flushing Meadows that New York offered them, they were rejected in the Westchester-Greenwich area where they wished to go, and the Russians had said that no "first class" diplomat would go to San Francisco. That morning I told Mrs. Zeckendorf that I was going to put those birds on the platform. And she said, "What birds on what platform?" And I said, "Those UN birds on the platform on the East River."

I called the Mayor that day and he said, "What's your idea?"

I said, "I hereby offer you—" I said, "Do you want to keep those fellows in New York?"

And he said, "Yes, I'd give anything to do that."

"Well," I said, "put this down. I'll offer you seventeen acres of land on the East River from 42nd Street north at any price the United Nations wish to pay. That will be their new home."

Now, the important thing about this whole thing is the value of the visualization of a concept. Thanks to *Life* magazine, a few other magazines, and a lot of newspapers, a great deal of publicity was given to the design that we had for the redevelopment of the area, so that when they brought around the Site Committee of the United Nations, no two of whom spoke the same language—and they were all ready to build a Tower of Babel—they were shown first the property and then the visualization of the plan. They saw this development along the East River and they recognized that it could look like what they had always dreamed of for the United Nations. I am sure that if they had just been shown those red brick slaughterhouses with no concept, they never could have understood what we were talking about. But they did understand it because they saw it in print. And within eight days, notwithstanding the eighteen months of previous searching, Mr. Rockefeller, who recognized its potential, offered the money to buy it for the United Nations. The United Nations approved the site, and eight days later it was a *fait accompli*.

When it came to the development of an approach to the United Nations—a monumental boulevard that was going to be grand enough, beautiful enough, functional enough, as would be warranted by such a basic conception—we proposed a minimum concept for redevelopment. We said that as a minimum the city should do the following: it should use its power of eminent domain, its right to redevelop communal area, and it should resell the surrounding zones so that the benefits of automatically increased valuation would go to the community and not to the guys who did nothing to get it. That may sound communistic or socialistic. But I cannot see any reason why the people who own those cold-water tenements in the area of the United Nations should be permitted to get a free ride or to hold up indefinitely, at their own will and whimsey, the redevelopment of an area that should be rededicated.

We presented that idea to the City Fathers. "Condemn the north side of 46th Street to the south side of 49th Street from First Avenue to Third Avenue," we said. That area would involve six square blocks: the north side of 46th to the south side of 47th, the north side of 47th to the south side of 48th, and on up to 49th; three blocks north, two blocks east and west, from First Avenue to Second, Second Avenue to Third. Those blocks are precise, gridiron blocks, 200 feet north and south each, roughly 800 feet east and west, and the intervening streets are 60 feet.

We said, "Take the two central blocks, the ones from the north side of 47th to the south side of 48th from First Avenue to Second Avenue, from Second Avenue to Third Avenue, which means a strip 200 feet long and 1600 feet wide plus the intervening street beds of 60 feet each, the street bed of 48th and the street bed of 47th. You have 120 feet of street bed, 200 feet of block, or 320 feet north and south by 1600 feet east and west. Redesign that for a great boulevard: 320 feet is 230 per cent of New York's widest street, Park Avenue, which is 140 feet. Let that be a great boulevard for pedestrians and for well-designed traffic, with subsurface traffic and subsurface parking. And then you will wind up with these four blocks which you also condemned, from the north side of 46th to the south side of 47th, and the north side of 48th to the south side of 49th. Then take those four blocks, rezone them, dictate what may and may not be built, and say that they shall now go up at auction to the highest bidder, providing they are built that way. To assure you, the city, that you will take no loss for your speculation in having bought six blocks, but that you will get the two central blocks, plus the streets that you are going to use for this great boulevard, absolutely for nothing, we will guarantee to make a bid ourselves for a minimum figure which will equal 120 per cent of the assessed valuation of all six blocks, land and buildings. That 120 per cent is what we shall pay for the four blocks, so that you get the two blocks for free."

I also proposed that the four blocks should have levied against them a land assessment which would equal the full tax assessment of all the land, of all the buildings, of all six blocks, and that any improvements on top of that should be levied at the regular rate of assessment. The *pro forma* value of those four blocks fronting on that communal way and their plottage assembly value, which has been achieved by a single condemnation, is so vast as to make it a good real-estate investment for hard money, not boondoggling money. Here is a case where two thirds is greater than three thirds. Here is a case exactly like the situation with the slaughterhouses at $17 a foot against $5 surrounding land value. It is a subtle redevelopment by a new concept, and the center of New York could have been vastly improved at no one's expense, not even at the expense of the fellows who were condemned, because they would have gotten more than they ever dreamed of getting at 120 per cent of assessed value. The City Fathers made one of the greatest mistakes of their lives when they turned us down, but we are still hopeful they will come to their senses and reverse their decision before the opportunity is wholly lost.

Again it comes back to concepts. I don't believe that cities are lost unless we are prepared to abandon them. The present tendency indicates that we are ready to abandon them. I deplore that. I think that if any great challenge exists in this country for the architects and designers, the real-estate economists and builders, the urban redevelopers and the city planners, it is the saving of a city.

I am not against decentralization. I think every new means of transportation that comes along in the progress of mechanized development causes farther and farther flung communities. I believe those communities have to go out to meet the problem that arises from the new mode of transportation. But I do not believe it is necessary to have cities die on the vine and rot at the core. I think they can be things of beauty, light, and economic functionalism; but they have got to be attacked by a combination of three kinds of thinkers: the real-estate economist, the designer and engineer, and the city planner and civic thinker.

URBAN
LAND DEVELOPMENT

PHILIP DAVID
Associate Professor of Urban Land Development
Graduate School of Business Administration
Harvard University

1970

RICHARD D. IRWIN, INC.   HOMEWOOD, ILLINOIS
IRWIN-DORSEY LIMITED, GEORGETOWN, ONTARIO

First Printing, October, 1970

Case material of the Harvard Graduate School of Business Administration is made possible by the cooperation of business firms who may wish to remain anonymous by having names, quantities, and other identifying details disguised while basic relationships are maintained. Cases are prepared as the basis for class discussion rather than to illustrate either effective or ineffective handling of administrative situations.

Library of Congress Catalog Card No. 72–91791

Printed in the United States of America

To Hilary

PREFACE

The idea for a course in Urban Land Development at the Harvard University Graduate School of Business Administration was originated by former Dean George F. Baker whose strong and enthusiastic support converted the idea into a reality. Dean Baker, along with Senior Associate Dean George F. F. Lombard, provided me with the freedom and encouragement to develop the Urban Land Development course.

In the process of developing the course, this casebook was written. The course and casebook endeavor to provide material useful for the training of administrators in the field of land development and real estate. The field is a broad one, covering many types of development—from a single-family house to an entire "New Town." The case studies approach the subject from many different points of view—investor, developer, mortgage lender, interim lender on construction loans, government policy makers, and citizens interested in knowing more about ways of changing the condition of their cities.

In structuring the course, Dean Lombard was most helpful in isolating the unique inputs of real estate development. Of special importance are: the strong interrelationship between the government and the developer; the impact of federal taxation; the management and control of risk; and the economics of real estate development.

Many have assisted in creating, writing, and editing this casebook, and I am deeply indebted to them for their contribution. William Poorvu, the first Research Associate for this course, gratuitously contributed his time and his extensive knowledge about this field to help develop the course and the cases in this book. We worked together through many nights in order to have case material available for the next class. Gary Welch, Research Assistant, made an important contribution by writing some of the cases sponsored by the Program of Business Leadership and Urban Problems. His contribution extended to putting the material together and filling in the gaps where they existed. Mark Goldweitz, Research Assistant, made an important contribution by writing many of the cases dealing with government programs and problems of low-income housing. Ryan Galli, Research Assistant, revised many of the cases to conform with the new tax laws and assisted in finally getting the material into casebook form. I consider all the above my coauthors.

I owe a special debt of gratitude to Eli Shapiro, who is responsible for the cases being in a casebook. He not only assisted me in developing an outline for the casebook, but also arranged for its publication. He gave unselfishly of his time and concern.

Other colleagues assisted, through encouragement or suggestions, in the development of the course and the cases: Dan Throop Smith, for whose course the original Tax Note was written; John V. Linter and Lawrence E. Thompson, who gave much time and encouragement; Henry A. Lambert, Senior Vice President of Canal Randolph, Inc., who was especially helpful in providing materials for several of the cases and in reviewing and giving me the benefit of his advice on the overall casebook.

I owe special thanks to Mrs. Rachael K. Daitch who has successfully directed the entire production of this book. Her combination of efficiency and good humor is most appreciated. This book could never have been completed without her assistance.

Finally, I am grateful to my wife Hilary for her encouragement and forbearance during its preparation.

September, 1970   Philip David

CONTENTS